S0-AML-386

SHELTON STATE COMMUNITY
COLLEGE
JUNIOR COLLEGE DIVISION
LIBRARY

Articles on American Slavery

An eighteen–volume set collecting nearly four hundred of the most important articles on slavery in the United States

Edited with Introductions by
Paul Finkelman
State University of New York,
Binghamton

DISCARD

A Garland Series

Contents of the Series

1. Slavery and Historiography
2. Slave Trade and Migration: Domestic and Foreign
3. Colonial Southern Slavery
4. Slavery, Revolutionary America, and the New Nation
5. Slavery in the North and the West
6. Fugitive Slaves
7. Southern Slavery at the State and Local Level
8. The Culture and Community of Slavery
9. Women and the Family in a Slave Society
10. Economics, Industrialization, Urbanization, and Slavery
11. Law, the Constitution, and Slavery
12. Proslavery Thought, Ideology, and Politics
13. Rebellion, Resistance, and Runaways Within the Slave South
14. Antislavery
15. Medicine, Nutrition, Demography, and Slavery
16. Religion and Slavery
17. Free Blacks in a Slave Society
18. Comparative Issues in Slavery

8600
30055
Garland

VOL. 9

Women and the Family in a Slave Society

Edited with an Introduction
by Paul Finkelman

Garland Publishing, Inc.
New York & London
1989

Introduction copyright © 1989 by Paul Finkelman
All Rights Reserved

Library of Congress Cataloging-in-Publication Data
Women and the family in a slave society/ edited with an introduction by Paul Finkelman.
p. cm.—(Articles on American slavery; vol. 9)
Includes bibliographical references.
ISBN 0–8240–6789–4 (alk. paper)
1. Slaves—United States—Social conditions. 2. Slaves—United States—Family conditions. 3. Afro-Americans—Families. 4. Women slaves—United States—Social conditions. 5. Afro-American women—Social conditions. 6. Slaves—Southern States—Social conditions. 7. Slaves—Southern States—Family relationships. 8. Afro-Americans—Southern States—Families. 9. Women slaves—Southern States—Social conditions. 10, Afro-American women—Southern States—Social conditions. I. Finkelman, Paul. II. Series.
E443.W66 1989
305.8'96073—dc20 89–23506

Printed on acid-free, 250-year-life paper
Manufactured in the United States of America
Design by Julie Threlkeld

General Introduction

Few subjects in American history have been as compelling as slavery. This should not surprise us. Slavery affected millions of Americans, north and south. Afro-Americans, Euro-Americans, and Native Americans were involved in the system. All antebellum Americans were affected, directly or indirectly, by slavery. Slavery especially affected Americans from 1861 until well after Reconstruction. As Lincoln noted in his famous second inaugural address: "The slaves constituted a peculiar and powerful interest. All knew that this interest was somehow the cause of the war."

The goal of this series is to reprint the key articles that have influenced our understanding of slavery. This series includes pioneering articles in the history of slavery, important breakthroughs in research and methodology, and articles that offer major historiographical interpretations. I have attempted to cover all major subtopics of slavery, to offer wide geographic representation and methodological diversity. At the same time, I have resisted the temptation to reprint highly technical articles that will make sense only to specialists in certain fields. For example, I have not included a number of important slavery related articles on economics, law, theology, and literary criticism (to offer just a few examples) because they appeared to be beyond the interest of most generalists.

I have used articles from a wide variety of scholarly journals. I have also used essays and articles in edited volumes, as long as the main focus of those volumes was not slavery, abolition, or black studies. It is my hope that such books are readily available to scholars and students and will show up through card catalogues or on-line catalogue searches. For the same reason I have not reprinted chapters from books about slavery, which are often found in anthologies. With a few exceptions, I have not reprinted articles that later became chapters of books on the same subject. In a few cases I have strayed from this general rule of thumb. I have also generally avoided essay reviews of books, unless the essays go well beyond the common book review or even essay review format. I have also tried to avoid certain famous historiographical controversies that resulted in large numbers of essays being collected and published. With some exceptions, therefore, I have not included the many articles attacking the "Elkins" thesis or Fogel and Engerman's Time on the Cross. Students and scholars interested in these two enormously important scholarly works, and the criticism of them, will find a great deal on both in their card catalogues. Finally, I have also excluded articles from Encyclopedias and dictionaries. These editorial decisions mean that many famous essays and articles will not be found in these volumes. Indeed, a few very important scholars are not represented because all of their work has been in books that are directly on the subject of slavery. Finally, some important articles were left out because we were unable to secure permission from the copyright holders to reprint them in this series.

This project was made easier by the hard work and dedication of Carole Puccino and Leo Balk at Garland Publishing, Inc. A project of this magnitude would not be possible without the help of a number of other scholars, who read lists of proposed articles and discussed the whole problem of slavery with me. I am especially grateful for the help and suggestions of Catherine Clinton, Robert Cottrol, Jill DuPont, Seymour Drescher, Linda Evans, Ronald Formasano, John Hope Franklin, Kermit L. Hall, Robert Hall, Graham Hodges, Michael P. Johnson, Charles Joyner, Alan Kulikoff, Greg Lind, David McBride, Randall Miller, Alfred Moss, James Oakes, Albert J. Raboteau, Judith Schafer, Robert Sikorski, John David Smith, Jean Soderlund, Margaret Washington, William M. Wiecek, Julie Winch, Betty Wood, and Bertram Wyatt-Brown. Two SUNY-Binghamton students, Marci Silverman and Beth Borchers, helped me with much of the bibliographic work on this project. Carol A. Clemente and the inter-library loan staff at SUNY-Binghamton were absolutely wonderful. Without their patience, skills, and resourcefulness, I would have been unable to complete these volumes.

—Paul Finkelman

Contents

Volume Introduction xi

Dorothy Burnham. "Children of the Slave Community in the United States," *Freedomways* 19 (1979) 75–81. 1

Catherine Clinton. "Caught in the Web of the Big House: Women and Slavery," in Walter J. Raser, Jr., R. Frank Saunders, Jr., and John L. Wakelyn, *The Web of Southern Social Relations: Women, Family & Education* (Athens: University of Georgia Press, 1985) 19–34. 9

Catherine Clinton. "Fanny Kemble's Journal: A Woman Confronts Slavery on a Georgia Plantation," *Frontiers* 9 (1987) 74–9. 26

Maria Diedrich. "'My Love is Black as Yours is Fair': Premarital Love and Sexuality in the Antebellum Slave Narrative," *Phylon* 47 (1987) 238–47. 32

E. Franklin Frazier. "The Negro Slave Family," *Journal of Negro History* 15 (1930) 198–259. 42

Robert W. Fogel and Stanley L. Engerman. "Recent Findings in the Study of Slave Demography and Family Structure," *Sociology and Social Research* 63 (1979) 566–89. 104

Joan Rezner Gundersen. "The Double Bonds of Race and Sex: Black and White Women in a Colonial Virginia Parish," *Journal of Southern History* 52 (1986) 351–72. 129

Herbert G. Gutman.	"Slave Culture and Slave Family and Kin Network: The Importance of Time," *South Atlantic Urban Studies* 2 (1978) 73–88.	151
Michael P. Johnson.	"Smothered Slave Infants: Were Slave Mothers at Fault?" *Journal of Southern History* 47 (1981) 493–520.	167
Jacqueline Jones.	"'My Mother Was Much of a Woman': Black Women, Work, and the Family Under Slavery," *Feminist Studies* 8 (1982) 235–69.	195
Charles W. Joyner.	"The Creolization of Slave Folklife: All Saints Parish, South Carolina, As a Test Case," *Historical Reflections/Réflexions Hitoriques* 6 (1979) 435–53.	231
Allan Kulikoff.	"The Beginnings of the Afro-American Family in Maryland," in Aubrey Land, ed., *Law, Society and Politics in Early Maryland* (Baltimore: Johns Hopkins, 1977) 171–96	251
Suzanne Lebsock.	"Free Black Women and the Question of Matriarchy: Petersburg, Virginia, 1784–1820." *Feminist Studies* 8 (1982) 271–92.	277
Ronald L. Lewis.	"Slave Families at Early Chesapeake Ironworks," *Virginia Magazine of History and Biography* 86 (1978) 169–79.	299
Ann Patton Malone.	"Searching for the Family and Household Structure of Rural Louisiana Slaves, 1810–1864," *Louisiana History* 28 (1987) 357–79.	311
Todd L. Savitt.	"Smothering and Overlaying of Virginia Slave Children: A Suggested Explanation," *Bulletin of the History of Medicine* 49 (1975) 400–04.	334

Judith K. Schafer.	"'Open and Notorious Concubinage': The Emancipation of Slave Mistresses by Will and the Supreme Court in Antebellum Louisiana," *Louisiana History* 28 (1987) 165–82.	339
Loren Schweninger.	"A Slave Family in the Ante Bellum South," *Journal of Negro History* 60 (1975) 29–44.	357
Orville W. Taylor.	"'Jumping the Broomstick': Slave Marriage and Morality in Arkansas," *Arkansas Historical Quarterly* 17 (1958) 217–231.	373
Deborah G. White.	"Female Slaves: Sex Roles and Status in the Antebellum Plantation South," *Journal of Family History* 8 (1983) 248–61.	388
David K. Wiggins.	"The Play of Slave Children in the Plantation Communities of the Old South, 1820–1860," *Journal of Sport History* 7 (1980) 21–39.	403
Betty Wood.	"Some Aspects of Female Resistance to Chattel Slavery in Low Country Georgia, 1763–1815," *The Historical Journal* 30 (1987) 603–22.	423
Acknowledgments		443

Introduction

In the past two decades women's history and family history have been among the most vibrant subfields of American history. The growth of scholarship in these fields has had an enormous effect on the study of slavery. Scholars are only beginning to understand the nature of life in the slave community and especially family and gender relations within that community.

Under the law of every southern state slaves could not legally be married. Nor did slaves have a legal right to control their own children. Nevertheless, slave families did exist, slave marriages took place, and slaves raised their children. All this took place at the sufferance of masters.

Marriage ceremonies varied, and historians have conflicting views of them. For example, Eugene Genovese argues that "Planters themselves often performed wedding services, and many took impressive pains with the festivities." However, John Blassingame asserts that "The marriage ceremony in most cases consisted of the slaves' simply getting the master's permission and moving into a cabin together."[1] One former slave remembered that "My fader and mudder ain't marry; slave do't marry—dey just lib togedder."[2] Devout masters often provided a religious ceremony according church rules, with either a white or black minister presiding. Most white ministers urged their flock to treat slave marriages as they would the marriages of free people, and make sure that slaves were united under the laws of God, even if their marriages were not recognized by the laws of man. Such preaching affected some masters. For example, between 1841 and 1860 half the marriages in South Carolina's Episcopal churches were slave marriages.[3] The figures were not as great in evangelical churches, but nevertheless, ministers of all Christian denominations in the South performed church weddings for slaves.

One aspect of slave marriage that is particularly confusing is the "broomstick ceremony." According to some scholars, slave marriages were often followed by a ceremony called "jumping the broomstick." This ceremony followed the wedding, and was used to determine "which one gwine be boss of your household," as one slave remembered. John Blassingame believes that this ceremony has "confused" both the descendants of slaves and "later historians." Blassingame argues that the ceremony was not the marriage, but something that occurred after the marriage.[4] However, other scholars assert that "the most frequent method of marrying two slaves was the custom of jumping the broomstick."[5] It is, of course, possible that in some places the "broomstick" ceremony was actually a marriage ceremony, and in others it was, as Blassingame notes, "A humorous test to determine who would exercise the most authority in a union."[6] As Herbert Gutman notes, "Jumping the broomstick served as the most common irregular slave marriage ritual. Sometimes sanctioned and even participated in by owners, it transformed a 'free' slave union into a legitimate slave marriage."[7]

Slave marriages and slave families were vulnerable to the whims of owners and the exigencies of the economy. Probably most slave couples lived together in the same place, but this was not always the case. Substantial numbers of slave couples lived apart because they were owned by different masters. Couples that were once together were also separated by sales. Some slaves took vows "until death or distance do you part." While adultery was frowned upon within a plantation community, remarriage after separation by sale or migration was common and invariably accepted.

During and after the Civil War the United States Army and the Freedman's Bureau registered tens of thousands of slave marriages, indicating the vitality of these unions, despite the lack of legal sanction and often of religious ceremony. Records for Mississippi and Louisiana reveal that in those two southwestern states more than twenty percent of the partners had previously been married to another slave in the upper South, but that this marriage was destroyed by sale or migration.[8] This figure suggests the magnitude of the hardship caused to slaves by the interstate slave trade and interstate migration.

Most slave children were raised by one or both of their parents, but this was not always the rule. Frederick Douglass, for example, was raised by his grandmother. He saw his mother only a few times in his early childhood and then never again. Other children were separated from their parents because of sales or other acts of their owners. It was not uncommon to give slave children as gifts for such occasions as communion or marriage.

The slave family, and all relationships within that family, were ultimately vulnerable to the realities of slave life. As property, slaves could be bought, sold, rented out, or shipped away whenever a master wished to do so, or because of economics or other hardship, had to do so. The constant migration of slave owners from the upper South to the lower South disrupted slaves and their family life, far more than it did whites. Slave children or slave wives might be left behind; slave men might be sold south. Slave families were always vulnerable.

Migration patterns also affected slave women, and their opportunity for freedom, differently than slave men. More males than females were sent to the Southwest during the cotton booms of the antebellum period. Thus, in the upper South there were more women than men; while in the lower South the opposite was true. Because manumission was easier in the upper South, and the manumission rates were much higher, slave women stood a somewhat better chance of gaining freedom than did slave men.

Women under the peculiar institution also faced hardships unknown to their white counterparts. Slave women were often required to work at the same agricultural jobs as were slave men; yet, they also had domestic and child-rearing chores and tasks that men were not expected to perform. At the same time, slave women were also more likely than men to have nonagricultural jobs, as servants, cooks, maids, and wet nurses. Working as a house servant , however, may not always have been a benefit. Some scholars have argued that house servants faced enormous psychological pressures from their proximity to their owners, who had such enormous power over them.

Just as the law helped define and limit the marriage and family relations of slaves, so too the legal status of slave women helped shape their world. Some slave women had meaningful and loving relations with their owners. Women in these relationships, and the children they had, were more likely to be manumitted than any other slaves in the South. For this reason slave women, as a group, probably had a better chance of gaining freedom than slave men.

Such women, however, were the lucky few. Most slave women had an entirely different experience with the white men that owned them. The crime of rape of a slave was unknown to the legal codes of the South. Thus, the sexual exploitation of slave women by masters and other whites was common. Throughout the South masters were free to treat their slaves—male and female—as they wished. This made slave women especially vulnerable to exploitation, abuse, and rape. "The sexual dynamic of slavery," as Catherine Catherine Clinton states, "continues to lie just beneath the surface of southern history as a tightly coiled tangle of issues we must unravel."[9] The same might be said for all family and gender relationships under slavery. The essays in this volume explore some of these problems.

—*Paul Finkelman*

Notes

1. Eugene D. Genovese, *Roll, Jordon, Roll: The World the Slaves Made* (New York: Pantheon Books, 1974) 475; John Blassingame, *The Slave Community* (2nd ed., New York: Oxford University, 1979) 165.
2. Quoted in Herbert Gutman, *The Black Family in Slavery and Freedom* (New York: Random House, 1976) 273.
3. Blassingame, *The Slave Community*, 169.
4. Quoted in Eugene D. Genovese, *Roll, Jordon, Roll*, 478. For an important discussion of this practice see Blassingame, *The Slave Community*, 166–67.
5. Albert J. Raboteau, *Slave Religion: The "Invisible Institution" in the Antebellum South* (New York: Oxford University Press, 1980) 228.
6. Blassingame, *The Slave Community*, 166.
7. Gutman, *The Black Family*, 275.
8. Herbert Gutman, *Slavery and the Numbers Game* (Urbana: University of Illinois Press, 1975) 126–30.
9. Catherine Clinton, *The Plantation Mistress* (New York: Pantheon Books, 1982) 199.

Further Reading*

Allen, Walter.	"Black Family Research in the United States: A Review, Assessment and Extension," *Journal of Comparative Family Studies* 9 (1978) 167–90.
Blassingame, John.	*The Slave Community* (New York: Oxford University Press, 1972).

* Publisher's Note: We were unable to obtain permission from the copyright holders to reprint some of the articles on this list.

Burton, Orville. *In My Father's House Are Many Mansions: Family and Community in Edgefield, South Carolina*. Chapel Hill: University of North Carolina Press, 1985.

Cassity, Michael J. "Slaves, Families, and 'Living Space': A Note on Evidence and Historical Context," *Southern Studies* 17 (1978) 209–15.

Clinton, Catherine. *The Plantation Mistress: Woman's World in the Old South* (New York: Pantheon Books, 1982).

DuBois, W.E.B., ed. *The Negro American Family* (Atlanta: Atlanta University Publications, 1908).

Fogel, Robert, and Stanely Engerman. *Time on the Cross*, 2 Vols. (Boston: Little Brown, 1974).

Fox-Genovese, Elizabeth. *Within the Plantation Household* (Chapel Hill: University of North Carolina Press, 1988).

Frazier, E. Franklin. *The Free Negro Family: A Study of Family Origins Before the Civil War* (Nashville: Fisk University Press, 1932).

Frazier, E. Franklin. *The Negro Family in the United States* (Chicago: University of Chicago Press, 1939).

Genovese, Eugene D. *Roll, Jordan, Roll: The World the Slaves Made* (New York: Pantheon Books, 1974).

Gutman, Herbert. *The Black Family in Slavery and Freedom* (New York: Pantheon Books, 1976).

Gutman, Herbert. "Slave Family and Its Legacies," *Historical Reflections* 6 (1979) 183–99.

Gutman, Herbert. *Slavery and the Numbers Game* (Urbana: University of Illinois Press, 1975).

Hine, Darlene Clark. "Female Slave Resistance: The Economics of Sex," *Western Journal of Black Studies* 3 (1979) 123–27.

Jones, Jacqueline. *Labor of Love, Labor of Sorrow: Black Women from Slavery to the Present* (New York: Basic Books, 1985).

Mathias, Arthur. "Contrasting Approaches to the Study of Black Families," *Journal of Marriage and Family* 40 (1978) 667–76.

Mullin, Michael. "Women and the Comparative Study of American Negro Slavery," *Slavery and Abolition* 6 (1985) 25–40.

Owens, Leslie Howard. *This Species of Property: Slave Life and Culture in the Old South*. (New York: Oxford University Press, 1976).

Scott, Anne F. "Women in a Plantation Culture: Or What I Wish I Knew About Southern Women," in Jack Censer, ed., *South Atlantic Urban Studies, Volume 2* (Columbia: University of South Carolina Press, 1978) 24–33.

Stowe, Stephen M. *Intimacy and Power in the Old South: Ritual Lives of the Planters*. (Baltimore: John Hopkins University Press, 1987).

Steckel, Richard H. "Slave Marriage and the Family," *Journal of Family History* 5 (1980) 406–21.

Webber, Thomas L. *Deep Like the Rivers: Education in the Slave Quarter Community, 1831–1865* (New York: W.W. Norton, 1978).

White, Deborah Gray. *Ar'n't I a Woman?: Female Slaves in the Plantation South* (New York: W.W. Norton, 1985).

Women and the Family in a Slave Society

CHILDREN OF THE SLAVE COMMUNITY IN THE UNITED STATES

DOROTHY BURNHAM

CHILDREN OF THE SLAVE COMMUNITY in the United States were victimized as no other group of children in our history has ever been. The quality of their lives was determined in every respect by those who profited from their enslavement.

The children were descendants of slaves who had come from diverse African cultures. Research into that period of African history demonstrates that all of the cultures were marked by systems of child rearing in which the control of the children was in the hands of both loving parents and elders of an extended tribal community. The slaves did their best to continue this treatment of their children under the conditions of slavery. However, during the entire period of slavery, colonial and state laws gave control of the lives, behavior and upbringing of the slave children to the enslavers.

The 1836 Annual Report of the Boston Female Anti-Slavery Society summarized the situation this way, "All rights reside in the master. Punishment for misbehavior and determination of what that misbehavior is. . . . Anything he does is moderate correction. *Neither evidence of mother or any other person shall be received against him.*"[1]

The slave owner made all decisions in regard to what the child would consume, what teaching, religious and otherwise, would be given, and when and where the child would start working.

Among the African peoples as among parents everywhere, the hope for children, for their health and happiness and for their development into

---

Dorothy Burnham, a member of the Board of Freedomways Associates, has contributed articles and book reviews to the magazine since 1961. She is a teacher and advisor in the Science Department of Empire State College, New York City.

intelligent, courageous and creative members of the community was an overriding concern. In contrast to these aspirations, and although there were differences in the ways in which slave masters treated children, the purpose of slave child rearing was that of achieving maximum profit from the property. The concern of the slaveholder was only that of raising a docile slave, obedient to master and overseer, one who was able to produce the most work for the least input of food, clothing and housing.

The slaveholders were a small minority of the American population in the 18th and 19th centuries, but through their wealth and position they were able to gain control of the colonial and state legislatures and pass bills guaranteeing their property rights in their slaves. In this period, laws were passed which designated slave children as chattel property and established that the infants of slave mothers would follow the conditions of the mother and would be the property of the mother's master. These laws and other colonial and state laws pretty much proscribed the arena of activity of the child. The establishment of the masters' property rights in the child abrogated the rights of the parents to make any decisions in regard to the welfare of their children.

The master proceeded to use these rights over his property in every aspect of life and always in his own interest as he saw it. The rearing of slave children was strictly delineated on most of the large plantations. The overseers were given written and oral instructions for the care of the children as if they were cattle or pigs. One South Carolina planter's instructions to his overseer are typical. It noted that a separate building was to be provided for the small children. "The unweaned," he directed, "are to be brought to it at sunrise after suckling and left in charge of the nurse. . . . Sucklers [nursing mothers] are not required to leave their houses until sunrise. . . ."[2] Explicit directions then follow for feedings for the infant during the day with the note that the nursing mother is expected to do *only* 3/5 of a day's work in the fields.

The cruel overworking of the new mother of course caused grave health problems for the Afro-American woman and accounted for many early deaths among the women. By means of this deliberate breaking of the bond between mother and child, the master tried to establish that the infant was not primarily a part of a family or tribal group but an item on a property list.

Other instructions quoted from the overseers' manuals give detailed directions for the food and clothing allotments for the children and infants. The weighing and measuring of the food portions and the description of the clothing provided emphasize that the outlay was to be as small as possible. Testimony of the ex-slaves corroborates these documents. The deprivation of the slave children of food, clothing and shelter is well described in the narratives of the ex-slaves interviewed by the Works Progress Administration[3] workers in the 1930's and by John B. Cade[4] and others. It is clearly evident that the instructions for provisions have nothing to do with the comfort or happiness of the child, but had everything to do with raising a productive slave.

In all cultures, childhood is a time of preparation for children to assume their role in the adult community. Parents and elders take pride in helping children to learn and treasure the history, culture, religion and occupations of their people. The customs of slavery shortcircuited this childhood right. Tribes and relatives from Africa were separated usually before the slave passage was begun so that the African tribal cultures, customs and history could not be shared and passed down through the generations except in a fragmentary manner. Secondly, the slaveholder assumed the right to determine the training and education of the slave child.

Since the slave child was destined for slave work, the learning fostered by the slave master was only that which would train the child to become a good and obedient servant. Law and custom dictated that formal education and book learning would be denied the children. One law passed in Virginia in 1831 banned all meetings of free Negroes in schools, churches, meeting houses or any other place by day or night in which they (the slaves) shall be taught under whatsoever pretext.[5] This was typical of slave codes in the southern states.

It is interesting to note that the opposition to education for Blacks also included poor whites. Conway observes that a campaign for a free school in Virginia for white farm and working children was defeated. "The poor whites, it was plainly declared, must be ignorant; for if they were educated, they would revolutionize Southern society."[6]

The opposition to training and education Black children extended into the non-slaveholding states. In the North there was sharp and bitter opposition to schooling for Afro-Americans. In Ohio in the 1830s, black schools were wrecked and teachers beaten. In Connecticut, when anti-slavery leaders attempted to establish a manual training school for Negroes, a New Haven town meeting voted 700 to 4 against it. And in 1831 when Prudence Crandall opened a school for black girls in Canterbury, Connecticut, she was jailed. Young white boys incited by their elders threw manure in her well, wrecked and burned the school and drove away the pupils. It is interesting to note that Ms. Crandall's inspiration to establish the school for black girls came about as a result of an unsuccessful attempt to integrate her previous all-white, exclusive academy by inviting a young black girl to become a student.

Christian religious teaching was permitted in some cases but the message to the slave child was that the attainment of humility and obedience was the greatest blessing. The other learning that was drilled into the heads of the slave children as well as the rest of the community was the belief in the innate inferiority of the African and his descendants. Both white and Black were taught to believe that the forebears of slaves had no history or culture worth recording. Up until the present century, both groups were taught that Africa was a primitive and savage land. They were taught in every way possible that white skin and straight hair were beautiful and black skin and tight curly hair were ugly and to be despised. Everything was done to strip the slave child of self-confidence and pride. One senses that it was only through the greatest perseverance that the parents and older men and women were able to reach out and teach their children how to survive the attacks on their egos.

In his new book on the Dred Scott decision, Fehrenbacher writes of the development of the slave laws and codes in the United States. He notes that it was some time after the beginning of the slave trade in the United States that the defense of slavery became biological in character. "In short first came the Negro. Then the institution of slavery and finally racism of the kind that asserts the genetic inferiority of the Negro."[7]

In a perversion that exists down to the present day, the acculturation of black children in a white society includes teaching them of their innate racial inferiority. Those interested in perpetuating slavery, after depriving the black child of access to his own or any other culture and learning then proceeded to compare them to white children. The "fact" of the innate intellectual inferiority of the black child became a part of the established folklore of American science.

The training of the children for work became a part of the economic system having to do with increasing the wealth of the master. Frequently young boys were hired out to work with skilled workers. Skills taught to the young slave boys included masonry, plastering, painting, shoemaking, milling, blacksmithing. The master gained by pocketing all the wages paid the young slave. Secondly, he gained a slave who had a skill, who could then work on the plantation or be hired out for higher wages.

This training of young slave boys in skilled work caused some conflicts among the white mechanics who saw the black labor as unfair competition. Typically, instead of demanding freedom and fair wages for the slaves, they demanded that the training of Blacks in skilled trades be terminated.

Further, they demanded the restriction that the skilled Blacks not be allowed to take apprentices other than their own sons.[8,9]

Young girls as well as boys were hired out to the cotton mills and shoe factories, with their pay going to the owners. The same miserable conditions obtained for child labor in these factories as in those where the white children worked in New England. The difference was that the pay went to the slave owner and not to the family of the child laborer. Sydnor says that "Some slaveholding families in Mississippi did not own an acre of land and were supported in whole or in part by the income from hiring out slaves."[10] There is some evidence that the hiring out of women slaves rather than selling them was done to insure that the owner would retain rights to own their children.

The owner looked upon everything the non-working child consumed as a loss. Therefore, the pressure was to get the child out and working as soon as possible. It was but a short step from childhood to work. Sojourner Truth, who was born a slave in New York, remembers that all the children of her parents were sold at young ages for work. And she, herself, was taken and sold at auction at the age of 10 or 11 to a farmer who put her to work immediately in his kitchen. It was common for girls of 6 and 7 to be taken into the plantation big house to help with the cooking, cleaning and care of the children. Their day's work began at sunrise and ended only when the evening chores were done. In many cases, the ex-slaves describe how they worked in the kitchens until they were 12 or 13 years old and then were sent to the fields to work. Plantation records list the children of 10, 11 and 12 as one-half or one-third hands, indicating the amount of work they were expected to perform. Sydnor talks of seeing the children of 6 years old picking cotton, carrying water, scattering cotton seed, knocking down old cotton stalks, helping to put up fences and being generally useful on the farms.

The custom of putting the children to work at an early age not only shortened their childhood growing and learning years but the imposition of work that was uncommonly hard led to ill health and the shortening of the life span. In addition using the children for work frequently caused their early separation from their parents. The testimonies of the ex-slaves and the slave narratives bear witness to this wretched practice. One Kentucky free Black married a slave woman and took care of her children. But as soon as the children were able to work, they were taken from the couple who had raised them by the mother's master.[11] Letters from the slave traders indicate this separation of children who were ready to go into the working force from their mothers. Conway, for example, notes that one trader wrote, "You ask about little girls and boys. All I can say is that they are always ready for sale, but they must be purchased right or they do not pay much profit."[12]

Frederick Douglass was taken from his mother when he was an infant. Moses Roper was sold at the age of 6. The black slave John Brown was 10 when he was separated from his mother. Moses Grandy's earliest memories are of hiding in the woods with his mother who had lost so many children to the slave traders that she was desperately trying to keep the remaining one with her. Josiah Henson remembers the separation at the age of 5 or 6. "Young as I was then—the iron entered my soul. . . I seem to hear my poor mother weeping now. This was one of my earliest observations of men. An experience which I only share with thousands of my race. The bitterness to the individual who suffers it cannot be diminished by the frequency of its recurrence, while it is dark enough to overshadow the whole afterlife with something blacker than a funeral pall."[13]

In addition to this testimony, the evidence both from the slave traders' lists of children for sale and from the newspapers of the day refutes the claims both of the slaveholders and some latter-day historians that separations were rare and not in the economic interest of the slaveholder. There is no doubt that the sale of surplus slave children and the deliberate breeding of slave children for market resulted in the separation of thousands of children from their parents and communities.

Bills were introduced in a number of states to prevent the separation of families by sale but failed of passage. The planters were powerful and they were able to convince the legislators that their property rights would be violated if they could not dispose of the children they owned as business profits dictated.

Slavery was a period in which a few people working entirely in their own interests to build enormous private fortunes persuaded a nation that the barbarity of enslavement was a normal part of the human condition. Colonial governments, state legislatures, the national government all joined in perpetuating a system in which slaves and the children of slaves were denied all human rights. The right of the child to health, education, respect, understanding and security was violated in the extreme.

Fortunately, there were those men and women, slaves and free Blacks, and white abolitionists who carried on an unrelenting struggle for the freedom of the slaves. In the community, the slaves themselves, the mothers and fathers and the elders did what little they could to shield and save the children from the worst of the violence and brutality. They saved the scraps of food and clothing for the children; they passed on the knowledge and traditions when they could and they invented substitutions for book learning. And most importantly of all, in the face of intolerable conditions, they were able to maintain the bonds of friendship and community which helped the children to survive and develop.

REFERENCES

1. *Boston Female Anti-Slavery Society*. Annual Report, 1836.

2. Willie Lee Rose, ed., *A Documentary History of Slavery in North America* (Oxford Press, 1976), pp. 349, 350.

3. Federal Writers' Project, *Slave Narratives—A Folk History of Slavery in the United States* (Washington, D.C. Library of Congress Project, 1936).

4. John B. Cade, "Out of the Mouths of Ex-Slaves—Oral History 1929," *Journal of Negro History*, 20,3 (1935).

5. Theodore Whitfield, *Slavery Agitation in Virginia, 1829-1832* (Baltimore: Johns Hopkins Press, 1830), p. 52.

6. M.D. Conway, *Testimonies Concerning Slavery* (London: Chapman and Hall, 1864).

7. Don E. Fehrenbacher, *The Dred Scott Case* (New York: Oxford Press, 1978), p. 12.

8. Charles Sydnor, *Slavery in Mississippi* (Baton Rouge: Louisiana State University Press, 1966), p. 180.

9. Whitfield, p. 122.

10. Sydnor, p. 173.

11. E.S. Abdy, *Journal of Residence and Tour in the United States*, p. 353.

12. Conway, p. 23.

13. Josiah Henson, "Memories of Childhood" in *Black Slave Narratives*, John F. Bayliss, ed. (London: Collier-Macmillan Ltd., 1970), pp. 106, 107.

Caught in the Web of the Big House: Women and Slavery

Catherine Clinton

In Pauli Murray's absorbing account of her family's history, *Proud Shoes,* she provides a rare and compelling perspective on slavery and its human consequences. Weaving together oral accounts and traditional historical records, she introduces an intriguing cast of characters. Murray's moving recollections of her grandmother, Cornelia Smith, especially illuminate the complexity of antebellum southern race relations.

Born in North Carolina in 1844, the child of a slave mother and a white father, Cornelia Smith was obsessed with her ancestors. Her granddaughter recalls that tales of illustrious forefathers bolstered Cornelia's self-image during her later years. Murray recalled her grandmother's admonition: "Hold your head high and don't take a back seat to nobody. You got good blood in you—folks that counted for somebody—doctors, lawyers, judges, legislators. Aristocrats, that's what they were, going back seven generations right in this state."[1] It was not until she was older that Murray was able to decode the contempt with which her aunts and grandfather treated these accounts of white ancestors. For as she matured, Pauli Murray discovered that this aristocratic pedigree carried a price.

When her grandmother dissolved into sorrow recounting the experiences of her own mother, Harriet, Pauli Murray's appreciation of the ambivalence of these emotions increased. Harriet was a fifteen-year-old mulatto slave of indeterminate racial mixture when she was bought in 1834 by the prestigious Smith family of Orange County, North Carolina.

Dr. Francis Smith owned a home in Hillsboro, a family plantation, Price's Creek (a fourteen-hundred-acre spread within three miles of Chapel Hill), and two dozen slaves. Smith, a member of the state legislature, was one of the most influential men in the county and also served as a trustee of the nearby University of North Carolina. Dr. Smith bought Harriet as a maid for his daughter, Mary Ruffin Smith, the eldest of his three children. The two younger siblings, sons Frank and Sidney, were attending college.

Harriet proved a model servant for her mistress. Only after her marriage in 1839 to a local free-born mulatto, Reuben Day, did she relinquish her sleeping pallet outside Mary Smith's door. When Harriet chose a mate, the doctor gave his permission for the couple to marry. Day was given rights to visit Harriet in the cabin the Smiths assigned her on their Hillsboro lot. In 1842 their son Julian was born.

Day was a thrifty and energetic artisan who might have been able to purchase freedom for his wife and child if events had not intervened. When the Smith boys returned home after completing their educations, harmony within the household disintegrated. Mary Smith watched with alarm as her two brothers competed for the attention of her maid. One day, when Sidney lunged for Harriet and the ensuing fracas was heard by the entire household, Francis warned his brother to keep his hands off her. The Smith parents, embarrassed by their sons' rivalry, ignored the matter, and Mary was unable to influence her brothers' behavior.

Shortly thereafter, Sidney threatened Harriet's husband, ordering him not to return to her cabin. In 1843, after a severe beating and a death threat from both brothers, Day fled the county, leaving behind his wife and child. By now the Smith brothers' pursuit was the subject of town gossip. Abandoned by her husband, unprotected by both her mistress and the household patriarch, Harriet was at the mercy of not one but two malicious predators. Each evening, she nailed her door shut, barricading herself in her cabin. Unfortunately, these precautions failed to protect her.

One night Sidney broke into Harriet's cabin and raped her. This practice became a nightly ritual—the smashing of the door, the sound of a woman screaming, the cries for mercy, the beating, the moans, and finally silence. Members of the slave community turned a deaf ear to Harriet's shrieks, and the Smiths ignored the nocturnal disturbances. Then one evening, as Sidney left Harriet's cabin, Frank attacked his brother. The next morning a slave found Sidney unconscious in the yard, soaked in his own blood. Sidney was slow to recover from the head injury he had suffered and took to drink. After this fraternal battle, however, Sidney never again molested Harriet.

Within months Harriet gave birth to a daughter whom she named Cornelia. Although Dr. Smith and his wife were ashamed and Mary Smith was "mortified," Sidney became boastful about his slave progeny. As if this scandal were not enough, Frank soon began to visit Harriet's cabin. The slave woman did not put up a struggle; she apparently was resigned to the situation. Harriet gave birth to three more daughters within the next eight years, all fathered by Frank Smith.

The births of these mulatto babies threw the Smith family into a serious crisis. If they sold Harriet and her children, the Smiths would rightly be accused of selling their own blood. Yet these illegitimate offspring were a stain upon the honor of the Smith name. Indeed, after the second daughter was born, the family moved out of town onto the plantation to escape neighborhood gossip. Not surprisingly, Mary Smith was the most guilt-ridden of the owner family, caught between morality and her pride. The entire white household suffered the consequences. Pauli Murray effectively conveys the contradictions: "Conscience is a ruthless master and the Smiths were driven into an enslavement no less wasteful than Harriet's. They were doomed to live with blunted emotions and unnatural restraints, to keep up appearances by acting out a farce which fooled nobody and brought them little comfort."[2]

Murray finishes the saga by describing the white family's increasing isolation from society. Frank, Sidney, and Mary never married, spending their lives involved in polite "charade." The mulatto daughters were not raised in the slave quarters but within the white household. As Murray comments, "The Smiths were as incapable of treating the little girls wholly as servants as they were of recognizing them openly as kin."[3] Indeed, Cornelia and her sisters looked to Mary Smith rather than to Harriet for guidance and approval. Their aunt increasingly took control of their supervision, becoming a surrogate mother. Yet these Smith daughters remained inferiors, required to sit in the "negro balcony" of the University of North Carolina Chapel of the Cross when their aunt took them to church. Even though she took great pains with their upbringing, having them trained in the Episcopal faith before their baptism in the campus chapel (indeed, confirmed alongside the daughter of the university president), Mary Smith clearly had mixed emotions about raising these girls. A legacy of pain and ambivalence accompanied advantages of birth and rearing.[4]

The various strands of intimacies and blood which wove together black and white in the Old South created a tangle of issues that is enormously difficult to unravel. Even the passage of time does not give us enough distance from these explosive topics. Nevertheless, it is essential for our understanding of women's lives and especially for exploring sexuality in the Old South that we address these important topics.

Many complexities and myriad contradictions were apparent at the time. A survey of antebellum southern travel literature reveals references to relationships between masters and their female slaves.[5] Not only did observers mention these illicit liaisons, but several commented on the hypocrisy such connections reveal. Fanny Kemble, the famed English actress, who married a wealthy Georgia slaveowner, provides sharp commentary about her months on her husband's sea island plantation:

> Nobody pretends to deny that, throughout the South, a large proportion of the population is the offspring of white men and colored women. . . . Mr —— (and many others) speaks as if there were a natural repugnance in all whites to any alliance with the black race; and yet it is notorious, that almost every Southern planter has a family more or less numerous of illegitimate colored children. . . . If we are to admit the theory that the mixing of the races is a monstrosity, it seems almost as curious that laws should be enacted to prevent men marrying women toward whom they have an invincible natural repugnance.[6]

Kemble criticizes southerners who make racist claims about the inferiority and repulsiveness of blacks, observing tartly that despite owners' complaints that their slaves were foul-smelling, many still managed to share the beds of female chattel. She does not imagine slaves would smell any worse if they were freed.[7] Kemble, like other British critics of slavery, harps on the theme of hypocrisy.[8]

Members of the southern planter class who recorded their critiques of slavery did not often attack the immorality of owners. Most bemoaned the immorality of slaves.[9] The few who acknowledged that male planters could and did fall from grace treat the matter casually, offering a variety of lame excuses ranging from black female promiscuity to protection of white women from sexual licentiousness.

Few scholars have bothered to explore this question systematically, and, as I have argued elsewhere, their efforts have been feeble.[10] New records are available, however, and black voices—from slave narratives, from Works Progress Administration (WPA) interviews, and from documents collected by the Freedmen's Bureau—testify to the inaccuracy of "whitewashing" the slave experience. Even a cursory survey of the published nineteenth-century narratives and the WPA interviews of the twentieth century reveals scores of black descriptions of sexual connections between white masters and slave women. The passion and bitterness of this black testimony ring true.

Lewis Clarke, a former slave during the antebellum era, lectured a northern audience on behalf of abolitionism: "How you would like to have *your* sisters, and *your* wives, and *your* daughters, completely, tee-totally, and altogether, in the power of a master.—You can picture to yourselves a little, how you would feel; but oh, if I could *tell* you!" He then confessed the cruel dilemma of his sister: "She was whiter than I am, for she took more after her father. When she was sixteen years old, her master sent for her. When he sent for her again, she cried, and didn't want to go. She told mother her troubles, and she tried to encourage her to be decent, and hold up her head above such things, if she could. Her master was so mad, to think she complained to her mother, that he sold her right off to Louisiana; and we heard afterward that she died there of hard usage."[11]

Her sad fate was not uncommon. Madison Jefferson, another emancipated slave, told a similar tale: "Women who refuse to submit themselves to the brutal desires of their owners, are repeatedly whipt to subdue their virtuous repugnance, and in most instances this hellish practice is but too successful—when it fails, the women are frequently sold off to the south."[12] Jefferson went on to describe his own abusive owner, a member of the Methodist church, who beat one of his slaves senseless: "At length [he] accomplished his purpose, while she was in a state of insensibility from the effects of a felon blow inflicted by this monster."[13]

Sexual abuse of young slave girls, especially those who worked within the big house, was a crime of which many slaves complained.[14] Herbert Gutman's research indicates that these patterns of exploitation persisted past slavery. The records of the Freedmen's Bureau reveal that white men were slow to break the habit of abusing black women.[15]

Sexual abuse manifested itself in various ways. "Slave breeding" was an indignity of which many slaves complained. Slaves bitterly resented masters' attempt to control mating by matching up couples. In addition to manipulating pair bonding, some masters might rent or borrow men for stud service, subjecting their female slaves to forced breeding or rape. These inseminators appear in the slave narratives in the guise of "stockmen," "travelin' niggers," or "breedin' niggers." Casual references and the slang terms used to describe these men give credence to the commonality of such practices. One former slave recalled that stockmen were "weighed and tested." On the other extreme, a former slave recalled castrations and that "runty niggers" were operated on like hogs, "so dat dey can't have no little runty chilluns." Although Paul Escott, discussing his research on the slave narratives, warns that evidence of such incidents was rare, he argues that "mere numbers cannot suggest the suffering and degradation they caused, and it is likely that reticence caused some underreporting."[16]

Masters attempted to control reproduction in other ways. Slave women were expected to bear children as frequently as possible. If they failed to give birth, they might be sold. Barren women were shunned by their communities and punished by their owners. All of these factors impaired slave sexuality and crippled the stability of traditional family structure.

Evidence from both blacks and whites indicates that forced interracial sex was more common than slave breeding.[17] Blacks often were coaxed before they would reveal sexual exploitation. One exchange with a former slave from Alabama reflects this syndrome: " 'Granny,' I said, 'did your master harm you in another way?' She did not understand at once, then as she gained my meaning, she leaned over and answered, 'did you see dat girl in de house below here? Dat's my chile by him. I had five, but dat de only one livin' now. I didn't want him, but I couldn't do nothin'. I uster say "What do yer want of a woman all cut ter pieces like I is?" But 'twant no use.' "[18]

It is also important to note that blacks were reluctant to discuss such matters, especially with racial and sexual factors inhibiting responses. In fact, evidence from the appendixes of Escott's survey of the WPA interviews indicates that the sex and race of the interviewer influenced the frequency of former slaves' revelations concerning interracial sex. For example, more than 13 percent of the WPA interviewees confessed to having a white father when interviewed by a black female, although only 5.3 percent of those interviewed by white males responded yes to the question and only 4.4 percent of those questioned by a white woman. Concerning queries about forced sex, these ratios are even more dramatic: white female interviewers reported that only 6.1 percent of their respondents claimed slaves were sexually exploited and only 8.6 percent of those interviewed by white males. But 13 percent of those questioned by 65 black male interviewers reported forced sex and 18 percent of the former slaves interviewed by black females. If we assume that former slaves were more honest with interviewers of their own race—and indeed black women might have been more comfortable to reveal such practices to a woman than to a man—we might conclude that forced sex was a problem on roughly one out of five plantations.

An interview with former slave Harry McMillan was equally revealing.

When asked about the morality of slave women, he confessed that although most were church members, girls were more likely to succumb to sexual temptation than were boys. McMillan reported, "Sometimes the Masters, where the Mistress was a pious woman, punished the girls for having children before they were married. As a general thing the Masters did not care, they like the colored women to have children." When an interviewer directly asked McMillan, "Suppose a son of the Master wanted to have intercourse with the colored women, was he at liberty?" the former slave demurred that white owners were "not at liberty" because it was considered a stain "on the family." But he admitted that "there was a good deal of it." McMillan remembered masters who kept "one girl steady," others who maintained "sometimes two on different places," regardless of whether they were married or unencumbered by white wives. His vivid recollection—"if they could get it on their own place it was easier, but they would go wherever they could get it"—demonstrates that, as a rule, white males in slave society were at liberty to exploit slave women, despite family or Christian obligations to the contrary.[19]

McMillan was not depicting his own or his family's encounters with sexual exploitation. Many blacks discussed the abuse of other slaves on the plantation, perhaps unwilling to recount the indignities to which their own kin were subjected.[20] Their revelations reflect genuine horror when they describe the practice of masters who auctioned off their own offspring.[21]

Another category of cruelty was reported as "miscegenation." In other words, slaves perceived the coercive forces at work within plantation society as exploitive as well. This exploitation is more subtle and, as a result, more difficult to extract from historical records. But nonetheless, not only must the glaring contradictions of slavery be brought to light, but the shadowy and elusive inconsistencies that continue to confound us. There are clues to these closeted practices as well.

As we saw with the complex tale of Pauli Murray's ancestry, white men and enslaved women could and did form long-term liaisons, which may not have been founded on mutual feeling but often grew into relationships that demonstrated fidelity and devotion. The records show that not all black female–white male liaisons were maintained or even initiated by brute force.

Perhaps most remarkable within the spectrum of interracial connection was the system of *plaçage,* which developed in New Orleans. This port city was renowned for its unique Franco-American culture, particularly the European influence on sexual and social mores. In addition, with the excessive ratio of free women of color to free men of color within this southern city (one hundred women to fifty-seven men in 1850),[22] contractual concubinage flourished. The system that developed guaranteed these women both male protectors and financial support for illegitimate children. The city was famous for its "quadroon" or "fancy girl" balls at which the refined, cultivated daughters of the *gens de couleur libres* were put on display for the dandies of Louisiana society. The balls, attended only by free mulatto women and white men, provided the means for matching up *placées* with protectors. After brief courtship, a formal contract between the girl's family and her protector was signed. *Plaçage* guaranteed financial security for these women of color and perpetuated concubinage. A quadroon *placée* often groomed her octoroon daughter to follow her example; sons were encouraged to pursue artisanal trades. This elaborate system of codification was peculiar to New Orleans, although evidence of legal protection of concubines and their children appears in Charleston and Mobile as well, and owner-slave liaisons developed throughout the South.

The offspring of these interracial unions, slave or free, were referred to as "natural children." They appear in the wills of planters, often along with their mothers, as beneficiaries of their fathers' generosity.[23] The fate of slave concubines and their natural children following an owner's death most often depended upon whether white relatives honored the will. A white widow or legitimate children were likely to ignore the wishes of the testator for their own financial advantage.[24]

Many slave concubines improved the status of themselves and their offspring through their involvements with wealthy owner-lovers. In his *Yazoo, or on the Picket Line of Freedom in the South,* A. T. Morgan, a northern planter who married a black woman and settled in Mississippi after the Civil War, described the phenomenon. Morgan argued that because colored concubines achieved prestige "according to the rank of their white 'sweethearts,'" the kept women of color reigned within "black society" in Yazoo City, Mississippi. A daughter often followed in her mother's footsteps, and upon extreme occasion, "*in her very tracks.*" Ironically, if a woman of color was freed and married a black, her status was lowered within "colored society."[25]

As in many other instances, slavery reinforced the rule of white supremacy. Slave women involved in illicit relationships with white men were accorded more privilege than those who contracted regular unions with black men. Because both sets of relations were outside the law, the woman's status depended solely upon the rank of the man with whom she shared her bed and had no relation to any attempts to replicate traditional patterns of virtue and legitimacy. Evidence indicates that mulatto concubines might wield more influence than free women of color because of the complex perversities fostered by slavery.

So slave women, given the limited options they faced within severely circumscribed spheres, might improve their lots by liaisons with owners, as Lewis Clarke, in his lecture to a white audience, acknowledged: "A woman's being a slave, don't stop her having genteel ideas; that is, according to their way, and as far as they can. They know they must submit to their masters; besides, their masters, maybe, dress 'em up, and make 'em little presents, and give 'em more privileges, while the whim lasts."[26] The divorce records and wills of slaveowners provide testimony of the power and influence many black concubines possessed.[27]

Despite the abundant evidence of warmth and even affection between concubines and owners, these liaisons also provoked instability and conflict. Harriet Jacobs recalled in her autobiography, *Incidents in the Life of a Slave Girl* (1861), that at the age of sixteen she deliberately contracted a relationship with a "Mr. Sands" and became pregnant by him. She confessed, "It seems less degrading to give one's self, than to submit to compulsion."[28] Jacobs's affair was part of a complicated chain of circumstances. After being harassed by her own master for more than a year and persecuted by her watchful mistress, she succumbed to the attentions of a white gentleman who expressed sympathy about her dilemma. Jacobs confided: "I knew the impassable gulf between us but to be an object of interest to a man who is not married and not her master is agreeable to the pride and feelings of a slave." When her owner began to build a cottage outside of town where he intended to keep her as his sexual companion, Jacobs became pregnant by her lover and hoped her master would sell her to him.

This plan collapsed when her mistress accused Jacobs of sleeping with her master and her white lover failed to buy her (although he eventually purchased their two children after his marriage). This case demonstrates the utter powerlessness of these women, who more often were pawns than agents in the complex network of interracial affairs.

Former slave Sella Martin described an even more perverse scheme. Her white father was manipulated into a liaison with a quadroon slave by his aunt:

> Mr. Martin, her brother's only child, and her only heir, was destined by the old folks in both families to marry a young lady of wealth and position, who was some eight years his junior; and that this purpose might not be thwarted by her nephew forming attachments elsewhere while the girl was a minor,

> Mrs. Henderson, by methods known only to the system of slavery, encouraged, and finally secured a relationship between Mr. Martin and my mother, of which my sister Caroline and myself were the fruits. She had a separate establishment set up for her on the estate; that is, she had a cabin all to herself, which is very rare, except in such cases. Her duties about the house were merely nominal, and her fare was from the table of her mistress.[29]

Although exceptional, this case is another example of the way slavery could distort sexual relations.

Many examples can be found of white women on plantations attempting to prevent interracial liaisons. The burdens of humiliation and responsibility seem to have fallen more heavily on women than men. One black woman described the rude awakening of her grandmother, Mathilda:

> She were near thirteen-year old, behind the house tee-teein when young marster came up behind her. She didn't see him, but he put his hand up her dress and said, "Lay down, Tildy." . . . And so this thing happened, and her stomach began to get big. One day, grandma and old mistress, they was putting up clean clothes. Old mistress had a pair of socks in her hand. She said, "Tildy, who been messin wit you down there?" Grandma say, "Young marster." Old mistress run to her and crammed these socks in her mouth and say, "don't you ever tell nobody. If you do, I'll skin you alive."[30]

The violent reaction of the mistress and her attempt to silence any testimony of a sexual connection are the most common responses within the records of plantation slavery. Wives as often as mothers agonized over illicit interracial affairs.

Owner-slave liaisons not only wreaked havoc within black families, they created violence and resentment among members of white families as well. Lacking the power to prevent sexual activities between male owners and slaves, white women on plantations struggled to discourage sons, shame brothers, and conceal marital infidelities. The jealousy and hatred many white women harbored for the slave women to whom their husbands were attached was legend within the Old South.

White southern women uniformly scorned black women's physical attributes. Mary Chesnut's diary illuminates her prejudices: "There will never be an interesting book with a negro heroine down here. We know them too well. In fact they are not picturesque—only in fiction do they shine. Those beastly negress beauties. Animals—tout et simple." In a later entry she describes a "beautiful mulatress" but qualifies her judgment: "that is, as good-looking as they ever are to me. I have never seen a mule as handsome as a horse—and I know I never will."[31] Complaining about the "unattractiveness" of black women was perhaps an unconscious defense mechanism against the "attraction" many white men acted upon within southern society. An undertone of hysteria appears in many diaries of plantation mistresses when black women are discussed. Some women pathetically clung to the notion that owners slept with their slaves, as one woman claimed, "by no other desire or motive but that of adding to the number of their slaves," neglecting the reality that there was no shortage of black men available for this purpose.[32]

Travelers, observers, court records, and slave narratives all testify to the hostility many white women felt toward black concubines. In these situations they may have felt equally at the mercy of white men. Harriet Jacobs's mistress, the slave confessed, "watched her husband with unceasing vigilance; but he was well practised in means to evade it."[33] Southern masters, used to ruling unchallenged in sexual matters as single men, were loath to bridle their licentiousness after marriage, even to please their wives.[34]

Plantation matrons had few options when confronted with their husbands' infidelities with a slave. Some might beg their husbands' fathers for assistance, and others might look to their own parents for comfort, but generally women were expected to turn a blind eye toward these dalliances.[35] Under extreme circumstances, if a husband abused his privilege by flaunting an affair, a wife might demand that the slave be sold. If her husband refused, she could retaliate by petitioning for divorce, citing infidelity as legal grounds for dissolution. Although the very wealthiest of slaveowners were not often sued for divorce (the upper ranks of society rarely allowed their names to be soiled by scandal), many divorce petitions filed during the antebellum era demonstrate the humiliations to which white wives might be subjected.

Evidence from the county records of Virginia reveals the scope of the problem. An Augusta woman complained in 1814 that her husband took her slave Milly "in his own wife's bed." Milly gave birth to a mulatto shortly thereafter. A Henry County wife reported in 1820 that her husband took to bed with him, night after night for three months, a female slave—in the same bedroom with his wife. In an 1837 petition from King William County an abused wife revealed that not only was her spouse smitten with a hired female slave but he "suffered and even encouraged the said negro woman, Grace, to use not only the most insolent language, but even to inflict blows upon the said Elizabeth, his wife."[36]

And in a detailed 1848 petition from Henry County, a wife provided testimony from friends to verify her husband's extreme cruelty. One witness confided that the husband "frequently slept with her, the said negro servant girl—sometimes on a pallet in his wife's room and other times in an adjoining chamber. He often embraced and kissed her in my presence." Another visitor to the household testified: "He directed the said servant girl to seat herself at the table from which I had just risen—to which Mrs. N. objected, saying to the girl, if she seated herself at that table that she would have her severely punished. To this Mr. N. declared that in that event he would visit her [Mrs. N] with a like punishment. Mrs. N then burst into tears and asked if it was not too much for her to stand."[37]

Perhaps some of these situations led to the explosive violence that sometimes occurred within the big house. Certainly the sexual liaisons between black women and white men stirred up anger and resentment within the slave cabins and provoked equal disharmony among members of the white family, most notably injuring women within the planter household. In an interview, J. W. Lindsay described such discord: "Sometimes white mistresses will surmise that there is an intimacy between a slave woman & the master, and perhaps she will make a great fuss & have her whipped, & perhaps there will be no peace until she is sold."[38]

The presence of a slave concubine and, secondarily, her bastard children promoted conflict within the plantation household. Such women's mere existence would cause pain for most wives, but their constant presence was a burden few women could tolerate. Most responded by lashing out at the helpless victims—the slave women. Evidence suggests that mistresses were free with the whip when dealing with women and children. It is futile to advance any single causal factor, but women's need to attack their rivals and their husbands' illegitimate offspring surely inspired some violence. Fears and suspicion played as large a role as fact in motivating many white women.[39]

In the vast records of slavery, not just the papers of slaveowners and white institutions but also slave narratives, both whites and blacks confirm that mistresses attempted to enforce Christian principles and to deal morally with a very brutal and dehumanizing system. Yet how are we to explain the barbarity of white women torturing and even killing slaves? Former slave James Curry reported to his abolitionist audience: "I could relate many instances of extreme cruelty practised upon plantations in our neighborhood, instances of *woman* laying heavy stripes upon the back of *woman,* even under circumstances which should have removed every feeling but that of sympathy from the heart of *woman,* and, which was sometimes attended with effects most shocking."[40] Curry might have been referring to the fact that the whipping of pregnant women could and did result in miscarriages. Murderous assaults might have been provoked by jealous rage. Appreciation of the dynamics at play can broaden our understanding of antebellum households.

Mary Armstrong of Houston, Texas, at the age of ninety-one, still remembered her first mistress:

> Old Polly, she was a Polly devil if there ever was one, and she whipped my little sister what was only nine months old, and just a baby, to death. She come and took the diaper offen my little sister and whipped till the blood just ran—just cause she cry like all babies do, and it kilt my sister. I never forgot that, but I got some even with that Old Polly devil and it's this-a-way.
>
> You see, I'se 'bout ten year old and I belongs to Miss Olivia, what was that old Polly's daughter, and one day Old Polly devil comes to where Miss Olivia lives after she marries, and tries to give me a lick out in the yard, and I picks up a rock about as big as half your fist and hits her right in the eye and busted the eyeball, and tells her that's for whippin' my baby sister to death. You could hear her holler for five miles, but Miss Olivia, when I tells her, says, 'Well, I guess Mama has learnt her lesson at last.' "[41]

This story is remarkable not only for the barbarity it describes but for the vengeance Mary Armstrong wreaked and the response of her second mistress, Polly's daughter. One can only wonder what emotional conflicts influenced this strange series of events.

Historical records abound with senseless acts of cruelty. Elizabeth Sparks recounted that her mistress's mother beat her with a broom or a leather strap and that severe whippings were inflicted for such trifles as burning bread. Susan Merrit described being knocked in the head for trying to learn to read and being forced to walk barefoot through a bed of coals after being accused of carelessness. Several slaves reported that abusive mistresses administered daily whippings as morning rituals.[42] Therefore, despite the general goodwill she supposedly maintained toward her charges and despite the positive impact the majority of slaves claimed she had on their lives,[43] the plantation mistress could and did succumb to the cruelties fostered by southern slavery.

Although many cruelties may have been motivated by the existence of concubines and illegitimate mulattoes, it is also possible that white women, like white men, sometimes perpetrated violence without any rational cause. Scholars sensitive to the complexities of human motives realize that there are many events that can never be fully reconstructed and many facets of a given circumstance that may never be fathomed. Yet we must attempt to explore below the surface of historical records, to reveal the deeper meanings of people's experiences.

Perhaps we will never be able to determine causal factors for either individual or even group behavior within slave society. By looking at the "darker side" of the system of slavery, however, at the dynamics that have been obscured by modesty or distorted for numerous motives, we may discover some lost insights into this complex chapter of the southern past. It may be essential to place gender and sexuality in the foreground of our portrait of the Old South in order to sharpen our focus on some important areas of exploitation and suffering. The prolonged emphasis on slavery as an economic system has blurred our ability to understand the critical dynamics of slavery as a social system.

Women, both black and white, were ensnared within the confines of southern slave society. Color and class gave white women the privilege to exercise control over their lives, but evidence demonstrates that many were nevertheless victimized by a system that subjected them to prolonged humiliation and severe psychological stress. The problems of white women pale in comparison to those that plagued slave women in white households and black women within southern society. In some cases the anguish and frustration of white women compounded black women's difficulties, resulting in the physical and emotional abuse of slave mothers and children. Even though they were pitted against one another by a racist sexual ideology, black and white women were often trapped in similar situations: both were at the mercy of male will. Southern women have rarely been able to identify their common interests, to recognize that they were "sisters under the skin," until the modern era.

We need to investigate the complex past attuned to many of the issues that emerge from my opening vignette: Cornelia Smith's divided loyalties and mixed heritage. Scholars are quick to chronicle the tales of whips and chains but less eager to tackle more subtle forms of exploitation. Pauli Murray encourages us to see that both sexes and both races were trapped, struggling in vain against barely visible restraints. We must illuminate the web that entangled black and white, men and women, to reconstruct the bonds of blood and emotion that drew white and black together as well as bringing them into competitive conflict. Only by examining these critical aspects of sex and race will we be able to gauge the impact of slavery and its continuing legacy.

Notes

The author wishes to thank the members of the Harvard History Dinner Group for their comments.

1. Pauli Murray, *Proud Shoes* (New York: Harper & Row, 1978), p. 33.

2. Ibid., p. 47.

3. Ibid., p. 49.

4. It was doubtless a great triumph for Pauli Murray when she was first ordained as an Episcopal minister in 1977. Becoming an official of the church as a woman and indeed a woman of color was a private victory as well as a public accomplishment; one month after her ordination, she conducted the service in the same church where her grandmother Cornelia had been baptized in 1854.

5. Marquis de Chastellux, *Travels in North America,* 2 vols. (Chapel Hill: University of North Carolina Press, 1961), 2:241; Ferdinand Bayard, *Travels of a Frenchman in Maryland and Virginia* (Ann Arbor: University of Michigan Press, 1950), p. 20; William N. Blane, *An Excursion through the United States and Canada* (1824; rpt. New York: Negro University Press, 1969), p. 204.

6. Fanny Kemble, *Journal of a Residence on a Georgian Plantation in 1838–1839* (1964; rpt. Chicago: Afro-Am Press, 1969), pp. 14–15.

7. Ibid., p. 23.

8. J. S. Buckingham, *The Slave States of America,* 2 vols. (London: Fisher, Son & Co., 1842), 2:241.

9. Susan Nye Hutchinson Diary, July 29, 1815, and September 6, 1829, Southern Historical Collection, University of North Carolina, Chapel Hill; letter in Bumpas Papers, August 15, 1844, ibid.

10. See Catherine Clinton, *The Plantation Mistress: Woman's World in the Old South* (New York: Pantheon, 1982), pp. 212–13, 220–21.

11. John Blassingame, ed., *Slave Testimony: Two Centuries of Lectures, Speeches, Interviews and Autobiographies* (Baton Rouge: Louisiana State University Press, 1977), p. 156.

12. Ibid., p. 221. See also Dorothy Sterling, ed., *We Are Your Sisters: Black Women in the Nineteenth Century* (New York: Norton, 1984), pp. 26–27.

13. Blassingame, *Slave Testimony,* p. 221.

14. Ibid., pp. 128, 279–80, 347, 382.

15. Herbert Gutman, *The Black Family in Slavery and Freedom* (New York: Pantheon, 1976), pp. 83–84, 395–99.

16. Paul Escott, *Slavery Remembered: A Record of Twentieth Century Slave Narratives* (Chapel Hill: University of North Carolina Press, 1980), p. 45.

17. Ibid., p. 43.

18. Blassingame, *Slave Testimony,* p. 540.

19. Ibid., p. 382.

20. Escott, *Slavery Remembered,* p. 44.

21. See "Testimony of Tabb Gross," in Blassingame, *Slave Testimony,* p. 347.

22. Sterling, ed., *We Are Your Sisters,* p. 27. Although one might be tempted to argue that an imbalanced sex ratio of white men to white women contributed significantly to the institution of *plaçage,* evidence indicates that the codification of these interracial liaisons rarely appears outside of a few urban ports—New Orleans and to a lesser extent Mobile and Charleston. The cultural climate of

these cities fostered a distinctly European cosmopolitanism, which must be seen as a more crucial factor shaping race relations than mere demographics. The higher ratio of men to women was more acute in the Mississippi and Alabama interior, an area in which there is no evidence that *plaçage* was common or recognized, although illicit liaisons were frequently and informally established.

23. Ibid., pp. 29–31; Clinton, *Plantation Mistress,* pp. 213–14.

24. See James Hugo Johnston, *Race Relations in Virginia and Miscegenation in the South, 1776–1860* (1937; rpt. Amherst: University of Massachusetts Press, 1970), p. 232; Clinton, *Plantation Mistress,* pp. 214, 217.

25. Gutman, *Black Family,* pp. 392–93.

26. Blassingame, *Slave Testimony,* p. 157.

27. Sterling, ed., *We Are Your Sisters,* pp. 26, 30–31; Johnston, *Race Relations,* pp. 232, 239, 247.

28. Sterling, ed., *We Are Your Sisters,* p. 23.

29. Blassingame, *Slave Testimony,* p. 702.

30. Sterling, ed., *We Are Your Sisters,* p. 25.

31. C. Vann Woodward, ed., *Mary Chestnut's Civil War* (New Haven: Yale University Press, 1982), p. 243.

32. See Clinton, *Plantation Mistress,* pp. 91, 190, 211.

33. Sterling, ed., *We Are Your Sisters,* p. 21.

34. Kemble, *Journal,* p. 228; Edward Abdy, *Journal of a Residence and Tour of North America,* 3 vols. (London: John Murray, 1835), 2:93; Charles Elliot, *The Sinfulness of Slavery in the United States,* 2 vols. (Cincinnati, 1857), 2:69, 152.

35. See Clinton, *Plantation Mistress,* pp. 81, 211–12, 214–15.

36. Johnston, *Race Relations,* pp. 239, 241, 245–46.

37. Ibid., p. 247.

38. Blassingame, *Slave Testimony,* pp. 400–401.

39. Sterling, ed., *We Are Your Sisters,* pp. 21, 23; Solomon Northup, *Twelve Years a Slave* (Buffalo, N.Y.: Orton & Mulligan, 1854), pp. 198–99.

40. Blassingame, *Slave Testimony,* p. 138.

41. Norman Yetman, ed., *Voices from Slavery* (New York: Holt, Rinehart and Winston, 1970), pp. 18–19.

42. Ibid., pp. 297–98, 225, 252.

43. Clinton, *Plantation Mistress,* pp. 187–89.

Fanny Kemble's Journal: A Woman Confronts Slavery on a Georgia Plantation

Catherine Clinton

> In asking her [a female slave] about her husband and children, she said she had never had any husband; that she had had two children by a white man of the name of Walker, who was employed at the mill on the rice-island; she was in the hospital after the birth of the second child she bore this man, and at the same time two women, Judy and Sylla, of whose children Mr. K— [Mr. King, the overseer] was the father, were recovering from their confinements. It was not a month since any of them had been delivered when Mrs. K— came to the hospital, had them all three severely flogged, a process which *she* personally superintended, and then sent them to Five Pound . . . with farther orders to the drivers to flog them every day for a week . . . if I make you sick with these disgusting stories, I can not help it; they are the life itself here . . . Sophy went on to say that Isaac was her son by Driver Morris, who had forced her while she was in her miserable exile at Five Pound. Almost beyond my patience with this string of detestable details, I exclaimed—foolishly enough, heaven knows—"Ah, but don't you know—did nobody ever tell or teach any of you that it is a sin to live with men who are not your husbands?" Alas! . . . what could the poor creature answer but what she did, seizing me at the same time vehemently by the wrist: "Oh yes, missis, we know—we know all about dat well enough; but we do any thing to get our poor flesh some rest from de whip; when he made me follow him into de bush, what use me tell him no? he have strength to make me." I have written down the woman's words; I wish I could write down the voice and look of abject misery with which they were spoken. . . .[1]

Fanny Kemble's *Journal of Residence on a Georgian Plantation*—a record of her months on her husband's Sea Island estates during the winter of 1838-39—has become one of the most frequently cited nineteenth-century descriptions of American slavery. Like those of Frederick Law Olmsted and Harriet Martineau, Kemble's account, published in 1863, is valued for the author's eye for detail and her eyewitness authenticity. Kemble's powerful prose and her stature as a literary personage lend added consequence to this record of life on a plantation.

One facet of this valuable document seems to have been neglected in many of the scholarly discussions of it: the feminist component of Kemble's attack upon slavery. Kemble was not only a writer concerned with the inhumanity of slaveowners toward slaves, but also a woman struggling against the patriarchal prerogatives within her society.

In my forthcoming book on Kemble,[2] I look not just at this single journal, Kemble's most famous publication, but at the eleven volumes comprised in the six separate publications of her journals, including writings from her adolescent years until she was well into her sixties. This treasure trove of reflections, coupled with voluminous unpublished correspondence on deposit in archives, allows us to trace the development of Kemble's thought, her commitment to the anti-slavery movement, and her idiosyncratic views on feminism.

Kemble was born in 1809 into the first family of the English stage. She had no interest in becoming an actress, but was devoted to the theater; after finishing her schooling, she spent her time writing plays and poetry in anticipation of a career as a writer. But in 1829, when her father's major source of income, Covent Garden, was faced with foreclosure, she made her debut in London and became an overnight sensation. In 1832, after years on tour in England, her father took her to America, where she became the toast of New York, Philadelphia, Baltimore,

---

Catherine Clinton teaches southern history, women's history, and feminist theory at Harvard University. She is the author of The Plantation Mistress *(1982),* The Other Civil War *(1984), and a forthcoming study of Fanny Kemble. She is currently working on a study of plantation life during the Civil War and Reconstruction, focusing on the role of black and white women before and after Emancipation.*

FRONTIERS Vol. IX, No. 3 © 1987 FRONTIERS Editorial Collective

Washington—in short, every town in which she played. She was courted by dozens of prospective suitors. In June, 1834, after a protracted courtship, she married Pierce Butler, the son of a Philadelphia doctor and the nephew and heir of a wealthy Georgia planter. Against her parents' wishes she gave up her career and settled with Butler in Philadelphia; her father returned to England following the wedding.

This well-born daughter of an English actor was ill-prepared for her role as an American wife, especially as mistress of a plantation. A contemporary southern matron wrote in a memoir that "the three golden threads with which domestic happiness is woven" were "to repress a harsh answer, to confess a fault and to stop (right or wrong) in the midst of self-defense, in gentle submission."[3] Kemble's temperament was hardly suited to submission and obedience, and her independent life as an actress had done little to soften her natural inclinations.

The newlyweds' incompatibility became apparent in the first few months of marriage. Arguments erupted over Kemble's duties as a wife, her attitude toward her in-laws, her insistence upon publishing, over her husband's objections, the journal of her American tour. Less than six months a bride, Kemble reflected unhappily in a letter to Anna Jameson, a British author and friend, "Kindred if not absolutely similar minds do exist, but they do not often meet, I think and hardly ever unite." In an attempt to look on the brighter side, she added,

> I suppose the influence of those who differ from us is more wholesome, for in mere *unison* of thought and feeling there could be no exercise for forbearance, toleration, self-examination by comparison with another nature, or the sifting of one's own opinions and feelings, and the testing their accuracy and value, by contact with opposite feelings and opinions.[4]

Kemble and Butler tested the limits of this theory; disharmony constantly reigned. Even after Kemble had settled into her new home in Branchtown and given birth to her first child, a daughter named Sarah, melancholy prevailed. She wrote shortly after her first wedding anniversary to her husband, proposing to leave him:

> I am weary of my useless existence, my superintendence in your house is nominal; you have never allowed it to be otherwise. . . . If you procure a health nurse for the baby she will not suffer; and provided she is fed, she will not fret after me. Had I died when she was born you must have taken this measure, and my parting from her now will be to her as though she had never known me, and to me far less miserable than at any future time.[5]

To a friend, she confessed, "I was at first a little disappointed that my baby was not a man-child, for the lot of women is seldom happy."[6]

Butler traced his wife's despair to postpartum depression and encouraged her to pursue other interests. Unfortunately for him, the pursuits she chose were not only atypical for a society matron, but also wholly unsuitable for the wife of a slaveowner: writing and politics. She devoured contemporary political treatises, and was extremely moved by the work of her good friend Unitarian minister William Ellery Channing. When Channing published a tract entitled *Slavery* in 1835, Kemble was so touched by his anti-slavery views that she herself wrote a scathing political indictment of slavery. She suppressed publication of her views, for fear her house might be burned down; but she nevertheless forcefully articulated them within her own family circle and the drawing rooms of Philadelphia, where her husband's slave holdings were well known. Only later did she reflect:

> I had not the remotest suspicion of,—the amazement and dismay, the terror and disgust with which such theories as those I have expressed in it must have filled every member of the American family with which my marriage had connected me. I must have appeared to them nothing but a mischievous madwoman.[7]

Pierce Butler did not officially inherit his slave property until March, 1836, and Kemble often proclaimed that she had not known she was marrying into slaveowning when she wed Butler—an assertion that seems naive at best. (In Kemble's defense, it must be said that Butler was not, when she met him, identifiably "southern," having been born and bred in the North, and many of his attitudes undoubtedly did reflect Yankee rather than planter mentality. Once their inheritance was secured, however, the Butler brothers became quintessentially pro-slavery.) On discovering the source of her husband's wealth, Kemble felt that she would rather earn her own living, even if it meant going back on the stage (which she claimed to have loathed), then answer for "what I consider so grievous a sin against humanity." She formulated her own plan of action:

> I feel that we ought to embrace the cause of these poor people. They will be free assuredly, and that before many years; why not make friends of them instead of deadly enemies? why not give them at once the wages of their labor? . . . Oh, how I wish I were a man! How I wish I owned these slaves instead of being supported (disgracefully, as it seems to me) by their unpaid labor.[8]

It is not clear what Butler thought of such an articulate abolitionist statement from his own wife—although he had long encouraged her friendship with Channing. Whatever the two pretended, their relationship remained on disaster course, with only a few rests between battles.

In the winter of 1836, Butler was forced to travel to Georgia to attend to plantation business, and sent his wife on a visit to her family in England, joining her later. Butler's indulgence and the couple's separation eased tensions between the two. After their return to Pennsylvania, a second daughter was born in 1838 on her sister's third birthday.

This reconciliation was tenuous at best. Kemble increasingly realized her husband's shortcomings, although she did not attack Butler so much as she railed against the social confines that plagued her as a wife. She believed that she shared these problems with the majority of women:

> A woman should be her husband's best friend, his best and dearest friend, as he should be hers; but friendship

> is a relation of equality in which the same perfect respect for each other's liberty is exercised on both sides; and that sort of marriage, if it exists at all anywhere, is I suspect very uncommon everywhere. . . . A woman should I think love her husband better than anything on earth except her own soul; which I think a man should respect above everything else but his own soul; and there is a very pretty puzzle which a good many people have failed to solve. . . . It is indeed, a difficult problem.[9]

Like her deep reservations about the institution of marriage, Kemble's political opposition to slavery was not launched directly against slaveowners, but focused on the "system" that allowed one human to hold another in bondage. It is fascinating to watch the way in which her views shifted radically after her brief experiment in living on her husband's rice plantations. That winter in Georgia marked the disintegration of the Butler marriage and the flowering of Kemble's commitment to the anti-slavery movement.

Butler did not want Kemble to accompany him on his trip to the Sea Islands in the winter of 1838, but her mother had just died and he felt obliged to take his wife with him rather than leave her alone with her grief. Believing that her impassioned anti-slavery views were founded on ignorance, he further trusted that he could educate her to his own way of thinking. With a bravado all too typical among southern planters, he thought that slaves themselves demonstrated their own inferiority and contact would expose the necessity for enslavement, rather than the evils of slaveowning. Butler took his wife south with him, confident that eyewitness exposure to plantation life would alter her position.

Kemble set out for Georgia with mixed emotions:

> Assuredly, I *am* going prejudiced against slavery, for I am an Englishwoman in whom the absence of such a prejudice would be disgraceful. Nevertheless, I go prepared to find many mitigations in the practice to the general injustice and cruelty of the system—much kindness on the part of the masters, much content on that of the slaves . . . (p. 15).

Kemble had strong reasons for adopting this stance. Although her marriage remained rocky, she had just given birth to her second child and had pledged herself to a program of model matronly behavior. The couple's usual antagonism was in a period of remission. Kemble hoped that conditions on Butler Island would contradict her anti-slavery convictions, just as her husband promised. At worst, she felt her fears might be confirmed. Both Kemble's and Butler's assumptions were faulty—a terrible mistake that marked the beginning of the end of their marriage.

Despite her anti-slavery bent, Fanny Kemble's cultural baggage included the common nineteenth-century racial prejudices. Unlike many of her New England and most certainly all of her southern acquaintances, however, Kemble believed that the "racial characteristics" ascribed to slaves were environmentally induced rather than genetically transmitted. For example, she vehemently attacked the myth that blacks were by nature filthy and smelly: "A total absence of self-respect begets these hateful physical results, and in proportion as moral influences are remote, physical evils will abound" (p. 62). She used sarcasm as well as argument to undermine white mythology.

> But as this very disagreeable peculiarity does not prevent Southern women from hanging their infants at the breasts of negresses, nor almost every planter's wife and daughter from having one or more little pet blacks sleeping like puppy-dogs in their very bedchamber, nor almost every planter from admitting one or several of his female slaves to the still closer intimacy of his bed, it seems to me that this objection [foul smelling] to doing them right is not very valid. I can not imagine that they would smell much worse if they were free . . . (p. 23).

Despite her prejudices, Kemble's commentaries provide vivid insights into plantation life.

The opening sections of her journal are merciless, as Kemble pointedly scorns the hypocrisy to which she is daily witness:

> There is no law in the white man's nature which prevents him from making a colored woman the mother of his children, but there *is* a law on his statute books forbidding him to make her his wife . . . it seems almost as curious that laws should be enacted to prevent men marrying women toward whom they have an invincible natural repugnance (p. 15).

She is utterly disgusted by the greed that underlies philosophical justifications of slavery:

> The only obstacle to immediate abolition throughout the South is the immense value of human property, and, to use the words of a very distinguished Carolinian, who thus ended a long discussion we had on the subject, "I'll tell you why abolition is impossible: because every healthy negro can fetch a thousand dollars on the Charleston market at this moment" (p. 78).

Fascinating in themselves, these insights are especially remarkable as observations by the wife of a slaveowner. As a woman Kemble has a special perspective on the plantation system, one that is revealed most often in a subconscious fashion. After exchanging views with her female counterparts in residence on the Georgia Sea Islands, she reports:

> We had a long discussion on the subject of slavery, and they took, as usual, the old ground of justifying the system *where* it was administered with kindness and indulgence. It is not surprising that women should regard the question from this point of view; they are very seldom just, and are generally treated with more indulgence than justice by men (p. 286).

Her commentary is finely tuned to sexual differences:

> I know that the Southern men are apt to deny the fact that they do live under an habitual sense of danger; but a slave population, coerced into obedience, though unarmed and half fed, *is* a threatening source of constant insecurity, and every southern *woman* to whom I have spoken on the subject has admitted to me that they live in terror of their slaves (pp. 295-96).

And her writing catalogs her increasing frustrations with those "evils of slavery" that she, as a woman, finds especially repugnant.

In her first description of life on the plantation, she explains that

> tasks of course profess to be graduated according to the sex, age, and strength of the laborer; but in many instances this is not the case, as I think you will agree when I tell you that on Mr. [Butler]'s first visit to his estates he found that the men and the women who labored in the fields had the same task to perform. This was a noble admission of female equality, was it not—and thus it had been on the estate for many years past. Mr. [Butler], of course, altered the distribution of the work, diminishing the quantity done by the women (p. 28).

This passage is layered with ironies. First, Kemble plainly states that what is "professed" is not always the case on the plantation, a passing thought that multiplies into a nightmarish perspective by the journal's end, when Kemble bewails the horrors of this charade "Christianity." Kemble makes clear that plantation life and southern culture are built on deceiving appearances, fanciful exaggerations calculated to enhance the picture of slavery, which was being increasingly besmirched by the abolitionist campaign.

Second, Kemble's harsh, sarcastic comment on "female equality" when she talks about women's parallel exploitation is typical of this journal, which is one of the first methodical indictments of slavery's effects upon women. Kemble is also one of the primary critics who systematically indicts the system for its pernicious effects upon white men's morality—effects that have negative repercussions among white planter families. This charge is made with equal vehemence in the diary of Mary Chesnut, the wife of a southern slaveowner and member of the Confederate cabinet,[10] but Kemble is almost entirely alone among prominent critics in her condemnation of slavery's effects upon black women. She provides a sustained, sympathetic treatment of the plight of slave women missing in most other accounts.

Finally, Kemble makes an even bleaker comment on her husband, almost mocking him in this segment. This excerpt is even more ironic when seen in its context: the journal details Kemble's numerous and repeated pleas for her husband to relieve women of their harsh field labor. She begs for cooperation from her husband and the overseer, to no avail. Both men argue that slaves who complain to her are lazy and deceitful, and Kemble is frequently shamed by her husband's role in punishing these complainers. Only a few weeks after this entry, Kemble writes:

> Mr. [Butler] was called out this evening to listen to a complaint of overwork from a gang of pregnant women. I did not stay to listen to the details of their petition, for I am unable to command myself on such occasions, and Mr. [Butler] seemed positively degraded in my eyes as he stood enforcing upon these women the necessity of their fulfilling their appointed tasks. . . . I turned away in bitter disgust (p. 79).

It was almost more than Kemble could stand that she could do so little good on her husband's plantation. And it alarmed her that struggling for reform often had an opposite effect: her intervention might get a slave whipped—or worse. Her efforts to introduce hygiene into the slave cabins backfired when she discovered that a slave

> had been flogged for what she told me [that the women did not have time to keep their children clean], none of the whole company in the room denying it or contradicting her. I left the room because I was so disgusted and indignant that I could hardly restrain my feelings, and to express them could have produced no single good result (pp. 37-38).

Even so, Kemble persisted, despite Butler's objections, in bringing the complaints of the slaves to her husband. She repeatedly begged for more food, no separation of families, lighter work loads for pregnant and nursing mothers, longer leave from the fields for newly delivered mothers. Her crusade against many of the overseer's policies rocked plantation authority, and her husband's indifference turned to anger. In the end, Butler chose his overseer over his wife. Even the slaves recognized the bind Kemble experienced, and sympathized. The recollections of a former slave support Kemble's veracity, in emotional as well as factual terms:

> I remember Miss Fanny well. I was just a boy. I was told to wait on her, to carry messages, and do what she asked me to do. She was a good lady, but sad a lot of the time. She hadn't been there long before all of us on the place knew she wasn't happy. I heard talk. Mr. Butler, he wanted her to stay away from the quarters. But she went there and me with her. . . . The women when they was sick or in need they'd get me to tell Miss Fanny. She'd go to them. The overseer, he complained. And Mr. Butler he would get mad with her. But she went.[11]

The gulf between Butler and his wife widened during their days together in Georgia. Kemble found her husband's rigid enforcement of plantation discipline detestable and her own situation intolerable:

> And to all this I listen, I, an Englishwoman, the wife of the man who owns these wretches, and I cannot say: "That thing shall not be done again; that cruel shame and villainy shall never be known here again." I gave the woman meat and flannel, which were what she came to ask for, and remained choking with indignation and grief long after they had all left me to my most bitter thoughts (p. 241).

Her articulated abhorrence of slavery became a wall between Kemble and her husband, but the dimensions of this barrier remained a private matter until the journal was published in 1863.

Kemble might never have released the journal for publication, had it not been for the sympathetic press the Confederate states received during the Civil War. She had originally prepared her journal as a keepsake for her dear friend Elizabeth Sedgwick. When Sedgwick circulated the manuscript among New England abolitionists in 1840, Lydia Maria Child encouraged Kemble to publish her diary to let the world see the horrors of slavery. Kemble long refused, demurring that she was a "guest" on the Butler family's plantation and she could not betray them. By the middle of the war, however, nearly a quarter century had passed, and she had been divorced from her husband for over a decade. A staunch supporter of the Union—though her youngest daughter, Fanny, had declared herself a Rebel—Kemble, like other anti-slavery enthusiasts, feared that the British might trade scruples for cotton. Her conscience compelled her to bring this "underground" book to light. In 1863 the journal was published in England and, shortly thereafter, in America.

One consistently neglected aspect of Kemble's book is the feminist rage that filters through this document. It may seem foolish to label as "feminist" yet another "strong-minded" nineteenth-century woman who lived before the term was coined; who did not participate in any of the many organizations that beckoned women to feminist activism; who in fact throughout her life dissociated herself from organized feminism.[12] Nevertheless, Kemble's analysis of slavery is informed, if not awash, with feminist ideology. She assuredly considers gender a primary category for consideration of her experiences, and factors gender into most if not all of her observations on social relations. Further, she is committed to changing the status of women within society as a key to improving society generally. Both of these facts justify "deconstructing" Kemble's text as a feminist document.

Indeed, Kemble takes a classical "first wave" position in identifying the evils of society as bound up in patriarchal oppression of women. She is outraged by her husband's indifference to injustice. She details the punishing routine to which slave women are subjected on the plantation; she is vehement about the inhumanity that allows pregnant women and mothers to be treated so callously. She bitterly assaults a system that so casually fosters the separation of husbands from wives, and even of children from mothers. Both complaints are common in anti-slavery literature, but in Kemble's book, they are central, far outweighing any concerns about the effects of slavery on free labor.

Especially in documenting the sexual exploitation of women slaves, Kemble clearly articulates the sins of slavery within a feminist framework. Although, as many scholars have argued, this theme was an unconscious ploy by many abolitionists to sensationalize the attack upon slavery, Kemble had more obvious and immediate motives: she was shocked and horrified by her discoveries and committed them to paper as soon as she witnessed them. As a reviewer pointed out in the New York *Evening Post* in 1863, "Her sex brought her specially in contact with slave women. A man, unless he had been a physician, would have known nothing of most of the sorrows and sufferings which were confided to her without scruples."[13]

Confronted with the sexual double standard slavery fostered, with the sexual violence within their society and, in some cases, within their own homes, most white southern women, especially plantation mistresses, chose to blame the victims.[14] Kemble made no such compromise; she laid the blame squarely on the shoulders of white southern men. Her book is laced with references to this peculiarly male "southern dishonor":

> I felt rather uncomfortable and said no more about who was like who, but came to certain conclusions in my own mind as to a young lad who had been among our morning visitors; and whose extremely light color and straight, handsome features and striking resemblance to Mr. K.[ing] had suggested suspicions of a rather unpleasant nature to me, and whose sole acknowledged parent was a very black negress of the name of Minda. I have no doubt at all, now, that he is another son of Mr. K[ing], Mr. [Butler]'s paragon overseer (p. 162).

Her distaste for Mr. King mounts with increasing evidence of his base character:

> [Mr. K] . . . forced her, flogged her severely for having resisted him, and then sent her off, as a farther punishment to Five Pound—a horrible swamp in a remote corner of the estate, to which the slaves are sometimes banished for such offenses as are not sufficiently atoned for by the lash (p. 199).

But in Kemble's construction, King is neither an exceptional case nor the Christian gone astray on an isolated plantation. She comments on the fate of a mulatto girl condemned to a harsh life in the rice fields: "In any of the southern cities the girl would be pretty sure to be reserved for a worse fate. . . ." (p. 240). The debauchery of women is not accidental, she argues, but a calculated byproduct of slavery. This evil, Kemble charges, permeates all of southern society.

In her final weeks on her husband's estate, Fanny Kemble was asked by a young slave named Aleck to teach him to read. Kemble accepted the challenge, and her discussion of it mirrors feminist irony:

> Unrighteous laws are made to be broken—perhaps—but then, you see, I am a woman, and Mr. [Butler] stands between me and the penalty. If I were a man, I would do that and many a thing besides, and doubtless should be shot some fine day from behind a tree by some good neighbor . . . but teaching slaves to read is a finable offense, and I am *feme couverte* and my fines must be paid by my legal owner, and the first offense of the sort is heavily fined, and the second more heavily fined, and for the third, one is sent to prison (p. 230).

She finds further irony in the despotism of individual plantation owners, which allows her to teach Aleck with little fear of penalty or prison:

> Some owners have a fancy for maiming their slaves, some brand them, some pull out their teeth, some shoot them a little here and there (all details gathered from advertisements of runaway slaves in Southern papers); now they do all this on their plantations, where nobody comes to see, and I'll teach Aleck to read, for nobody is here to see, at least nobody whose seeing I mind (p. 231).

But this was a relatively weak form of protest, and Kemble left Georgia after affording Aleck only a few attempts at learning the alphabet.

Kemble's anger and resentment were not left behind in Georgia. We have evidence of a deeper, more permanent disaffection following her southern sojourn. Letters from Butler to his wife's friend Elizabeth Sedgwick indicate that

Kemble began to refuse to sleep with her husband either during or shortly after their trip to Georgia. A biographical study published by one of Kemble's descendants speculates that the bedding of slaves by masters was not an abstract issue for Kemble, but rather an unpleasant reality she was forced to face while in Georgia. Upon their return north, the couple separated while Kemble visited the Sedgwicks in the Berkshires. When Butler was called back to Georgia the following winter, he left his wife and children behind in Pennsylvania, informing them only the day before his departure that he proposed to travel unaccompanied.

Butler almost died on this visit to Georgia, and through the intervention of friends the couple were, once again, reunited. It was nevertheless painfully and publicly acknowledged that Kemble and Butler suffered irreconcilable differences. Charles Greville noted in his diary: "Among the most prominent causes of their disunion is her violent and undisguised detestation of slavery while he is a great slave proprietor."[15] We can also trace a feminist subtext within Kemble's journals during the years leading up to her divorce from Butler—an extremely messy and sensational trial in 1848-49 that led to Kemble's loss of the custody of her daughters and the publication of humiliating intimate details about her marriage. (The publicity surrounding the trial included reports that Butler had had an affair with his children's governess, and that in 1844 he had fought a duel with one of his best friends, James Schott, who had caught Butler in a compromising position with Mrs. Schott.) Kemble had known about Butler's sexual liaisons with other women for up to seven years before she left him in 1845 (after being denied access to her daughters).

The overlapping of the personal and political was an extremely painful ordeal for Kemble, revealed in meticulous detail within the *Journal of Residence on a Georgian Plantation*, and expanded on in her other writings. Seen in historical context, her anti-slavery arguments and her attacks on slavery as a form of patriarchal oppression give us a window into an even more painful intersection of the personal and political: the plight of women slaves.

If we choose to look, we can see Kemble's text as more than descriptive, as analysis of a most powerful, political variety. And we can employ her evidence to extend our own analysis of the interdependence of systems of exploitation, the ways in which gender, race, and class interacted within nineteenth-century southern society. Used in this way, feminism is not merely a product to be manufactured by scholars, but a process, a perspective, an interpretive tool that affords us a deeper appreciation of the many-tentacled grasp slavery maintained on social interactions within the Old South, and of its legacy for us today.

NOTES

1. Frances Anne Kemble, *Journal of Residence on a Georgian Plantation in 1838-1839* (New York: Harper & Brothers, 1863), pp. 227-29. Further references will be cited parenthetically in the text.
2. Catherine Clinton, *Fanny Kemble's Journals* (Cambridge, Mass.: Harvard Univ. Press, forthcoming).
3. Caroline Gilman, *Recollections of a Southern Matron* (New York: 1838), p. 257. Gilman herself was a convert to southern matronhood, having been born and reared as a Yankee.
4. Frances Anne Kemble, *Records of Later Life* (New York: Henry Holt & Co., 1882), p. 2. Hereafter cited as *RLL*.
5. *Mr. Butler's Statement* (privately published, 1850), p. 23.
6. Kemble, *RLL*, p. 25.
7. Kemble, *RLL*, p. 31.
8. Kemble, *RLL*, pp. 41-42.
9. Kemble, *RLL*, p. 70.
10. See Catherine Clinton, *The Plantation Mistress: Woman's World in the Old South* (New York: Pantheon, 1982), p. 199.
11. Ralph McGill, *The South and the Southerner* (Boston: Little Brown & Co., 1959), p. 155.
12. See Frances Anne Kemble, *Journal of Residence in America* (London: John Murray, 1835), p. 165; and Frances Anne Kemble, *Further Records* (New York: Henry Holt & Co., 1891), I, pp. 39, 106-08, 315.
13. John Anthony Scott, ed., *Journal of Residence on a Georgian Plantation* (New York: Alfred A. Knopf, 1961), p. liv.
14. See Catherine Clinton, "Caught in the Web of the Big House: Women and Slavery," in *The Web of Southern Social Relations*, ed. Walter J. Fraser, Jr., R. Frank Saunders, Jr., and Jon L. Wakelyn (Athens: Univ. of Georgia Press, 1985).
15. Charles Greville, *The Greville Diary*, ed. Philip W. Wilson (London: Heinemann, 1927), II, p. 547.

By MARIA DIEDRICH

"My Love Is Black As Yours Is Fair"*: Premarital Love and Sexuality in the Antebellum Slave Narrative

> Were I an absolute queen of these United States, my first missionary enterprise would be to send to Africa, to bring its heathen as *slaves* to this Christian land, and keep them in bondage, until compulsory labor had tamed their beastliness, and civilization had prepared them to return as missionaries of progress to their benighted black brethren.[1]

IT WAS IN THE EARLY YEARS of the Civil War that the American writer Mary H. Schoolcraft made this emphatic statement in the preface to her novel *The Black Gauntlet*. She glorified the civilizing achievements of the Southern slavemasters in their unselfish act of delivering millions of Africans from the utter darkness of a barbaric existence. And as late as 1925, the historian J. S. Bassett was still able to characterize slavery as "a hard school" in which "the Africans learned some good lessons":

> It was the force of slavery that taught him [the African] to labor with some degree of regularity, it was the authority of the master that taught him to improve his ideas of morality, it was the superior authority of the white race that induced him to change fetishism for a rude and simple kind of Christianity.[2]

Slavery as a philanthropic institution for the deliverance of black savages, who, due to their natural inferiority, were unable to free themselves from their mental darkness, slavery as an institution in which charitably disposed whites took tender care of their black children — Schoolcraft's and Bassett's interpretations of the so-called peculiar institution are highly representative for the ideological justification and idealization of slavery which dominated American literature well into the 20th century.

For a century, white historians and sociologists conveniently ignored that the history of slavery had not only been written by white masters, but also by their victims: manumitted or fugitive slaves wrote or dictated their book-length autobiographies, the slave narratives, in the decades before the Civil War. Yet, white scholars, who used diaries, letters and autobiographies written by white Southerners as source material for their studies refused to rely on the blacks' evidence as it could be traced in the slave narratives, reasoning that "there are only few reliable records of what went on in the midst of

* The title is from Countee Cullen's "A Song of Praise," *Black Voices. An Anthology of Afro-American Literature*, ed. A. Chapman (New York, 1968), p. 383.

[1] Mary H. Schoolcraft in Charles H. Nichols, Jr., "Slave Narratives and the Plantation Legend," *Phylon*, 10 (1949): 202.

[2] J.S. Bassett, *The Southern Plantation Overseer as Revealed in His Letters* (Northampton, 1925), p. 22.

slaves."[3] White texts were defined as source material, black texts were denounced as mere propaganda — a perfect example of white American "scholarly doublethink."[4]

The slave narrative represents the black Americans' première in the field of written literature as well as in a literature whose authors can be identified as individuals.[5] Their writers conceived them as tracts against slavery; not as glorifications of individual achievements only, but, as the ex-slave Henry Bibb states, as "my humble testimony on record against this man-destroying system . . . .[6] The slave narrative transformed the individualistic *I* of traditional autobiography into an *I* willing to dedicate every atom of this self to the black community; it was pluralized into an identifying *we* in the sense of Walt Whitman's "Whoever degrades another degrades me."[7]

As polemic treatises against slavery, all events and problems discussed in the slave narratives were submitted to one exclusive aim — to prove the blacks' right and capability of being integrated into American society on terms of equality. From the many motives which confront us in those texts, this paper discusses only one — that of premarital love and sexuality. In a close analysis of three representative slave narratives — those of Henry Bibb, Harriet Brent Jacobs and J. D. Green[8] — it demonstrates how the self-definition of those slave authors as propagandists against slavery and for equal rights determined the choice of subject as well as the argumentative strategy of these narratives.

When Thomas Jefferson wrote his *Notes on the State of Virginia* (1782) he excluded blacks radically from his definitions of equality. But even Jefferson had to admit that he discovered among slaves examples "of the most rigid integrity, and as many as among their better instructed masters, of benevolence, gratitude, and unshaken fidelity."[9] No doubt Jefferson evoked features which were to characterize Uncle Tom, a Negro stereotype beloved by white America. Yet, on the other hand, he could not help making allowances for the equality of blacks not only in terms of moral perception, but also in relation to what the Scottish Enlightenment, in its differentiation between head and heart, defined as a quality of the heart, stressing the heart's superiority over the head.[10] Apologists of slavery, however, changed Jefferson's reluctantly positive characterization of blacks into another argument for slavery by reinterpreting this emphasis on qualities of the heart in blacks as proof of their emotional childishness and intellectual inferiority. Still, the authors of the slave narratives adopted this acknowledgement of emotional equality

---

[3] Kenneth M. Stampp, *The Peculiar Institution. Slavery in the Ante-Bellum South* (New York, 1956), p. 88.
[4] W.W. Nichols, "Slave Narratives: Dismissed Evidence in the Writing of Southern History," *Phylon*, 32 (1971): 404.
[5] Cf. my book *Ausbruch aus der Knechtschaft. Das amerikanische Slave Narrative zwischen Unabhaengigkeitserklaerung und Buergerkrieg* (Heidelberg, 1982), p. 11.
[6] Henry Bibb, *Narrative of the Life and Adventures of Henry Bibb, an American Slave* (1849), in *Puttin' on Ole Massa. The Slave Narratives of Henry Bibb, William Wells Brown, and Solomon Northup*, ed. Gilbert Osofsky (New York, 1969).
[7] Walt Whitman, "Song of Myself," *Leaves of Grass and Selected Prose*, ed. S. Bradley (New York, 1949), p. 23.
[8] Bibb, op. cit.; H.B. Jacobs, *Incidents in the Life of a Slave Girl* (Boston, 1861); and J.D. Green, *Narrative of the Life of J.D. Green, A Runaway from Kentucky* (Huddersfield, 1864). Further references will appear in the text.
[9] Thomas Jefferson, *Notes on the State of Virginia* (Chapel Hill, 1955), p. 142.
[10] Cf. G. Wills, *Inventing America. Jefferson's Declaration of Independence* (Garden City, 1978), p. 224.

in order to integrate it in their chain of argument. Love and sexuality thus became major motives in their writings.

The characterization of Afro-Americans as creatures dominated entirely by their sexuality was always a popular apologetic argument for the oppression of blacks in the American South. Political, social and economic strategies were corroborated on the pretense of having to protect society, and especially white womanhood, from the blacks' sexual urge. Black Americans were drawn up as frightening sex symbols, a characterization which led to grudging glorification as well as cruel persecution. They were defined as sex maniacs — men as aggressive studs, women as lascivious whores.[11] White America emphatically proclaimed the blacks' insensibility for ideal love as it was defined by 19th century society, especially in its romantic transfiguration.

As they were ascribed inferior positions in nearly all domains of life, many blacks did not protest against this over-subscription of their sexual qualities, but believed in having found at least one area in which their superiority was manifest. Thus, the writers of the Harlem Renaissance interpreted Afro-Americans' unconstrained approach to sexuality as final proof of their powerful vitality. The authors of the slave narratives, however, differed radically from both positions described above: as people who were constantly denounced as brutes, they insisted on their capacity of controlling their carnal desires, of experiencing love in the same richness and complexity as any other responsible human being.

In Henry Bibb's autobiography, published in 1849, we find a description of love among slaves, in which all lines of argument characterizing the antebellum slave narrative are united. At the age of eighteen Bibb meets the light-skinned, extremely attractive slave girl Malinda. For him she becomes the incarnation of the ideal woman, in whom physical, intellectual and spiritual beauty are ideally joined:

> Malinda was a medium sized girl, graceful in her walk, of an extraordinary make, and active in business. Her skin was of a smooth texture, red cheeks, with dark and penetrating eyes. She moved in the highest circle of slaves, and free people of color. She was also one of the best singers I ever heard, and was much esteemed by all who knew her, for her benevolence, talent, and industry. In fact, I considered Malinda to be equalled by few, and surpassed by none. (p.74)

In this girl physical attractiveness, diligence, intelligence, kind-heartedness and social respectability form a harmonious whole, reminiscent of the ideal heroines in the novels of James Fenimore Cooper, Harriet Beecher Stowe, Jane Austen, Sir Walter Scott and Charles Dickens.

At first Bibb bans any thought of deepening the relationship, knowing that love and family ties will obstruct his plan of running away from slavery. But his love soon conquers his reason, and "in spite of myself, before I was aware of it, I was deeply in love". (p 75) Love is here interpreted as a natural phenomenon, and the man who fights it for rationality's sake only will sin

[11] Cf. W. Jordan, *White Over Black. American Attitudes toward the Negro, 1550-1812* Baltimore, 1969), pp 150ff.

against nature. An exclusive ratiocinativeness is thus, in accordance with Romantic belief, denounced as a perversion of nature: by accepting his love Bibb frees himself from the isolation of the very selfhood which Romanticism had tried to conquer as the true source of evil in man, and he achieves a "union of feeling" (p.75) with another human being. Following Wordsworth's

> Love, now a universal birth
> From heart to heart is stealing;
> From earth to man, from man to earth:
> — It is the hour of feeling"[12]

he surrenders to his all-consuming love experience.

In the ensuing passages of the autobiography he delineates the phase of courtship between the lovers in a way highly adapted to the representation of wooing in Romantic literature and to the Victorian ideals of propriety. The reader is reminded of David Copperfield's meeting with his beloved Agnes as well as of Milton's description of an Eve, characterized by "softness and sweet attractive grace," who "Yielded with coy submission, modest pride, And sweet, reluctant, amorous delay,"[13] when he reads in Bibb's narrative:

> That Malinda loved me above all others on earth, no one could deny. I could read it by the warm reception with which the dear girl always met me, and treated me in her mother's house. I could read it by the warm and affectionate shake of the hand, and gentle smile upon her lovely cheek. I could read it by her always giving me the preference of her company; by her pressing invitations to visit even in opposition to her mother's will. I could read it in the language of her bright and sparkling eye, penciled by the unchangable [sic] finger of nature, that spake but could not lie. (p.75)

The ex-slave draws a picture of love between blacks that characterizes abolitionist literature since Aphra Behn's idealized evocation of the Oroonoko — Imoinda relationship in her romance *Oroonoko, or, The History of the Royal Slave* (London, 1678): all memories of the pain, humiliation and misery of everyday slave life pale into insignificance at the sight of this young black gentleman paying his respect to his worthy love.

Even the problems which the lovers encounter at first do not at all differ from those the reader knows from traditional love stories, but the lovers stand all the tests of romance. The particularity of their situation only becomes visible when they decide to get married: they cannot translate their decision into action without asking the permission of their slavemasters. Considering the propriety to which the lovers submitted their wooing, Bibb here reveals the immoral irrationality of a white man's title to regulate even the most intimate relations in a slave's life.

Similar to the protagonists of the novels and romances of the 18th and 19th centuries, the lovers in Bibb's autobiography are subjected not only to tests of their integrity, which the outside world forces upon them, but they also submit to trials they impose upon themselves: Bibb loves Malinda, but he confronts this relationship with qualifications, which prove that he has preserved his rational capacities despite the depth of his love. As a Christian, he

[12] William Wordsworth, "To My Sister," *The Oxford Anthology of English Literature*, eds. Frank Kermode, and John Hollander (New York, 1973), vol. 1, p. 129.
[13] John Milton, *Paradise Lost*, IV: 310-11.

will only marry a pious girl; as a slave, he believes in his duty before God to free himself from the fetters of slavery, and only a woman willing to share his struggle for liberty can be his partner. Before Malinda he takes the solemn oath:

> I never will give my heart or hand to any girl in marriage, until I first know her sentiment upon the all-important subjects of Religion and Liberty. No matter how well I might love her, nor how great the sacrifice in carrying out these God-given principles. And here I pledge myself from this course never to be shaken while a single pulsation of my heart shall continue to throb for liberty. (p.76)

Bibb's love is thus also, but never exclusively, romantic passion. He accepts his feelings, but he never forgets the puritan warning against love as an "irrational act, and therefore not fit for a rational creature," the warning "to love anyone farther than reason will allow us."[14] Sound principles, here principles of a religious and political nature, have priority over emotional inclinations, and thus Bibb performs according to mores and patterns of social behavior which contemporary romantic and sentimental literature prescribed for their idealized heroes.[15] Only when Malinda lives up to his demands does Bibb offer her marriage, and she reacts as the ideal heroine of her days should: "She very modestly declined answering the question then, considering it to be one of a grave character, and upon which our future destiny greatly depended." (p.77)

Bibb has to wait two weeks for a positive answer, and being lovers conscious of their responsibility they enter into a contract, considered as their final challenge, stating,

> that we would marry if our minds should not change within one year; that after marriage we would change our former course and live a pious life; and that we would embrace the earliest opportunity of running away to Canada for our liberty. Clasping each other by the hand, pledging our sacred honor that we would be true, we called on high heaven to witness the rectitude of our purpose. (p.77)

The emphasis on flight as a moral obligation stresses the particularity of their situation, yet, the pathos of this scene coincides with that of any oath of allegiance in Romantic literature. Southern whites characterized blacks as brutes; the modern historian Blassingame stresses that in the slaves' everyday life "an imperfect understanding of the unnatural puritanical code of their masters freed blacks from the insuperable guilt complexes that enslaved nineteenth-century white Americans in regard to sex,"[16] but Bibb insists on a picture of slave life in which slaves experience love as a total spiritual and intellectual relationship in its sublime complexity. They are willing and able to live up to the responsibilities springing from this love.

The writings of the romantic poet Percy Bysshe Shelley demonstrate that Romanticism developed concepts of love which also included sexuality as a

---

[14] R. Baxter in Richard H. Tawney, *Religion and the Rise of Capitalism* (Harmondsworth, 1972), p. 242.
[15] Cf. H.R. Brown, *The Sentimental Novel in America, 1789-1860* (New York, 1959), p. 306.
[16] John W. Blassingame, *The Slave Community. Plantation Life in the Ante-Bellum South* (New York 1971), p. 85.

vital, positive component.[17] Bibb, however, avoids mentioning sexuality in depicting his relationship with Malinda, and he submits his delineation of his love entirely to the Victorian ideal of propriety. Thus, he not only fulfills the expectations of readers who closely adhered to the narrow 19th-century understanding of morality, but he also creates counter-evidence to the biased pictures which the South drew of its slaves. Sexuality is mentioned in one context only — as a form of menace entering a slave's life from the outside: the uneducated slave Henry Bibb never takes liberties with his bride; it is the white master who tramples down all limits of decency. When Bibb asks his permission to be married, it is granted — but "with but one condition, which I consider too vulgar to be written in this book." (p.79) By dark suggestions alone Bibb succeeds in marking his white master as the sexual aggressor, and he now turns the accusation of uncontrolled brutishness, which was originally intended as a label for blacks, against whites. It is the slaves who are capable of complex, responsible love relationships, while white men who are morally weakened by the extent of their power, succumb to their own passion. Bibb is thus not satisfied with drawing up a counter-picture against prejudice by adhering to traditional romantic ideals, but he takes the offensive by attaching to the master class those negative characteristics which were traditionally ascribed to the slaves as a stigma of their inferiority.

Yet, Bibb's is more than just a reversal of theses: in its dialectics his argumentation also reveals the potential progressiveness of the contemporary conservative concept of morality for slaves. For Samuel Richardson's 18th-century heroine Pamela, sexual integrity becomes her expression of middle-class self-esteem in view of the aristocracy's sexual aggressiveness, and like her the slave defends his right to his body. In doing so he appeals to a value system the realization of which to him in his powerlessness must necessarily be objective progress at a time when these values had long lost their original progressive meaning in a middle-class society.

No doubt Bibb creates an idealized image of love among slaves, evoking ideal white standards as depicted in contemporary sentimental literature; it is, however, an image which is strictly subjected to his political intentions. His imitation of white literary models is not a sign of this black writer's aesthetic weakness, but a vital component of his propagandistic strategy. He addresses his autobiography to white readers, whom he wants to draft as allies in the blacks' struggle against slavery, and he can only recruit those whites who are thoroughly steeped in the ideals of a white middle-class respectability by allaying their fear of and prejudice against blacks. Conscious of racist sexual biases as justifications of the enslavement of blacks as well as of their sexual violations and exploitations, he counters these arguments by portraying the black lover as a perfect counterpart to the idealized white 19th-century lover. It is a clear understanding of contemporary white psychology, not intellectual mediocrity, that induces Bibb to employ this highly effective argumentative strategy.

---

[17] Cf. Percy Bysshe Shelley, "A Discourse on the Manners of the Ancient Relative to the Subject of Love. A Fragment," *The Complete Works of Shelley. Vol. VII: Prose*, eds. R. Ingpen, W.E. Peck (London, 1961), p. 288.

In 1861 Harriet Brent Jacobs published her autobiography, *Incidents in the Life of a Slave Girl*, in which she displays a radically different approach to the love and courtship motives. Where Bibb chooses idealization, she opts for a greater realism, which no doubt shocked contemporary readers. This slave woman, who was sexually harrassed by her master, describes two love episodes within which a clear development toward an unflinching realism becomes visible. As a young girl Harriet falls in love with a free black who wants to buy her freedom. Though she senses the hopelessness of this relation, she loves the man, as she confesses, "with all the ardour of a young girl's first love." (p.58) The romantic exuberance of her love makes her repress all doubts concerning the chances of survival for this love, but it is the disillusioned woman, purged by bitter experience, who formulates the autobiography's desperate central question:

> WHY does the slave ever love? Why allow the tendrils of the heart to twine around objects which may at any moment be wretched away by the hand of violence? When separations come by the hand of death, the pious soul can bow in resignation, and say, "Not my will, but thine be done, O Lord!" But when the ruthless hand of man strikes the blow, regardless of the misery he causes, it is hard to be submissive. I did not reason thus when I was a young girl. Youth will be youth. I loved, and I indulged the hope that the dark clouds around me would turn out a bright lining. I forgot that in the land of my birth the shadows are too dense for light to penetrate. (p.58)

In their willingness to love, in their ability to lose and to find themselves in their love of another human being regardless of external circumstances the slaves prove their equality as men. They, too, are susceptible to a love against which man can fight only by denying everything natural within him.

The slave girl loves, but she also demonstrates the depth of her love by being able to renounce it. Once she realizes that her master will never free her, as he himself wants to possess her sexually, once she understands that she can hope for no womanly solidarity from her mistress, who hates her for her beauty and believes that "slaves had no right to any family ties of their own; that they were created merely to wait upon the family of the mistress" (p.59),[18] she decides "to spare my love the insults that had cut so deeply into my own soul." (p.59) She implores him to go North, where he will be truly free, while she succumbs to her fate: "With me the lamp of hope had gone out. The dream of my girlhood was over, I felt lonely and desolate." (p.66)

Like Agnes in *David Copperfield*, she proves her ability to love by renunciation for the sake of the man she loves. Here, too, love is not described in terms of an erotic experience, but as a relationship between responsible human beings, who, by living up to their ideals, accept the rules of propriety, and who can also sacrifice love for love's sake. Thus again, animal-like sexual aggressiveness does not emanate from the black lovers, but from those whites who have power over them.

---

[18] The relationship between female slaves and their mistresses is discussed in E. Smith, "Historical Relationships between Black and White Women," *The Western Journal of Black Studies*, 4 (Winter 1980): 251-55; M.B. Craw, "Diamond in Dirt Theory, Seasoning the Female Slave," *Perspectives on Afro-American Women*, eds. W.D. Johnson and Thomas L. Green (Washington, D.C., 1975), pp. 26 ff.

Still, Harriet Jacobs differs from the traditional romantic heroine. After she has lost her lover she does not isolate herself in her grief in order to weep in eternal self-abnegation. She is willing to commit herself in a new relationship when she meets an unmarried white man who knows about her master's aggressiveness and pities her:

> So much attention from a superior person was . . . flattering; for human nature is the same in all. I also felt grateful for his sympathy, and encouraged by his kind words. . . . By degrees, a more tender feeling crept into my heart. (p.84)

Love is no longer a perfect experience of harmony, but a desperate act of escapism in a girl who characterizes herself as "reckless in my despair." (p.84) The innocence of her first love cannot be repeated, for Harriet as a slave was robbed of her innocence when still a mere child. Therefore, she does not even try to excuse her acts as those of an innocent pursued, but explains them from her state of disillusionment:

> The influence of slavery has had the same effects that they had on other young girls; they had made me prematurely knowing, concerning the evil ways of the world. I knew what I did, and I did it with deliberate calculation. (p.83)

Thus she agrees to become the white man's mistress not only because she is overwhelmed by love or because she, the naive girl, is seduced against her will, but because she acquires a feeling of freedom, equality and power from giving love freely. Her love achieves a radically new quality and is transcended into a form of resistance[19] against her master:

> . . . to be an object of interest to a man who is not married, and who is not her master, is agreeable to the pride and feelings of a slave. . . . It seems less degrading to *give* one's self, than to submit to compulsion. There is something akin to freedom in having a lover who has no control over you, except that which he gains by kindness and attachment. . . . Revenge and calculation of interest, were added to flattered vanity and sincere gratitude for kindness. I knew nothing would enrage Dr. Flint so much as to know that I favored another; and it was something to triumph over my tyrant even in that small way. (p.84)

To her contemporary readers this woman's confession came as a shock. Bibb's Malinda is innocence personified during their courtship; she becomes innocence pursued as her master demands her sexual submission; and when he finally overpowers her she is transformed into a victim. As her story of suffering is told from a man's perspective, she remains a passive object throughout these three stages of development. Harriet Brent Jacobs, however, describes her ordeals from a woman's point of view, and she breaks radically with any sentimentalization of pain: she not only refuses to escape into the attitude of innocence pursued, but she even avows having consciously capitalized on her sexuality in order to assert and to revenge herself. She does not idealize her acts by evoking an overwhelming love, but speaks only of "a more tender feeling" toward a man who partly understands and tries to help her. By honestly revealing her motives she stands for a realism reminiscent of DeFoe's Moll Flanders.

---

[19] Resistance among female slaves is discussed in D.C. Hine, "Female Slave Resistance: The Economics of Sex," *The Western Journal of Black Studies*, 3 (1979): 123-27.

Common to all these love scenes is their intention to prove the blacks' ability for complex and respectable forms of love, to document their emotional and intellectual equality. The authors hardly ever break away from this functionlized pattern of arguing. In those few cases, however, in which they vary this scheme, a refreshing sense of humor and self-irony is revealed. Thus the very Henry Bibb whom we know from his sentimental eulogies to Malinda wittily describes his first attempts to win a slave girl's love by employing magic: a black two-headed doctor tells him he can win any girl by touching her skin with a bone, and consequently Bibb attacks his intended love while she takes a walk with her lover. Jumping toward her he

> . . . fetched her a tremendous rasp across her neck with this bone, which made her jump. But in place of making her love me, it only made her angry with me. (p.73)

Yet, this mishap does not deter Bibb, and when he hears that one of her locks, hidden in his shoes, will tie her to him forever, he tries to get some of her hair. Relying on the powers of magic, he once more attacks:

> I grasped hold of a lock of her hair, which caused her to screech, but I never let go before I had pulled it out. This of course made the girl mad with me, and I accomplished nothing . . . . (p.73)

The slave's version of "The Rape of the Lock"!

In his narrative, J.D. Green develops one episode from his life as a slave into a marvellous satire on Romanticism's idealized love descriptions. At the age of seventeen Green finds himself, as he says, "deeply smitten in love with a yellow girl" (p.15) named Mary. He offers a romantically brimming picture of her beauty:

> I certainly thought that she was the prettiest girl I had ever seen in my life. Her color was very fair, approaching almost to white; her countenance was frank and open, and very inviting; her voice was as sweet as the dulcimer, her smiles to me were like the May morning sunbeams in the spring, one glance of her large dark eyes broke my heart in pieces, with a stroke like that of an earthquake. O, I thought, this girl would make me a paradise, and to enjoy her love I thought would be heaven. (p.15)

Unlike Bibb in his characterization of Malinda, Green only lists physical qualities, and consequently his feelings are not described in terms of love, but passion. Thus the reader is not the least surprised when Green discovers this "almost angel in human shape" (p.16) in another man's arms. Green's despair is overwhelming:

> My teeth clenched and bit my tongue — my head grew dizzy, and I began to swim round and round, and at last I found myself getting up from the ground, having stumbled from the effect of what I had seen. I wandered towards home, and arriving there threw myself on the straw and cried all night. (p.16)

Caught in melodramatic excess, Green enjoys the role of the disappointed lover, but in the following events he depicts himself as a fool with a delightful sense of humor: already the reason he offers for not killing his rival reveals the superficiality of his feelings as well as his cunning. He will not kill him, as he himself would then be hanged, "and the devil would have us both, and some other negro will get Mary." (p.16) His attempt to win Mary back then becomes a hilarious caricature of the Werther-motif: Green pretends wanting to hang himself, but his beauty calmly smokes her pipe while he struggles in his trap. She frees him only after he has lost consciousness, for her dog "coming in contact with the stool, knocked it right away from under my feet . . . " (p.18). Green makes no attempt at moralizing, but laughs freely at his own foolery.

This episode, however, acquires a meaning transcending its function as ironic comment on romantic love when the characterization of Mary after the relationship ended is included in the interpretation. Green takes no cheap revenge by morally disqualifying Mary, but he depicts her as a woman who is as capable of deep emotional involvement as is her black lover, the slave Dan. He describes how one day Dan heard Mary's screams for help as her master was raping her, and at this "sight of the outrage on her whom . . . he loved better than his own soul" (p.19) Dan lost control over himself. He killed the white rapist. For this he is burnt at the stake, and Mary commits suicide. The comic episode thus ends tragically and links up with the slave narrative's chain of proofs for the slave's complex emotional capacities.

As all these examples show, the argumentation of the slave narratives to illustrate the slaves' concept of love and sexuality accepts romantic literature as its model: they focus on lovers whose love, though it is returned, is bound to end tragically. They live in a society unable to tolerate this love, and an antagonistic power — the slavemaster — who in the absolutism of his rights functions as fate, persecutes and destroys this love. The slave authors, however, differ from their romantic predecessors by not limiting themselves to evocations of pain and its lyrical transfiguration, but they also insist on analyzing the causes of this pain and accusing its creators. By pointing at the dreary social reality which is responsible for the individual lover's suffering, the ex-slaves transcend the impression of exceptional individual suffering and transform it into the grief of an entire people. In all its individuality the slave's love experience becomes representative of that of the whole community of slaves.

THE NEGRO SLAVE FAMILY

INTRODUCTION

"But in spite of numerous exceptions, the marital and family rights of the slaves were perhaps generally recognized," says Reuter in a chapter on Negro Sex and Family Life in his recent book on the Negro problem.[1] This extremely cautious, but, on the whole, rather indefinite statement of the attitude of masters towards the family relations of their slaves, is representative of a widespread belief which has been used by apologists for slavery to support their contention that the integrity of slave families was never violated. On the other hand, the abolition literature of the antebellum crisis abounds in stereotyped descriptions of soul stirring scenes of slave families being ruthlessly torn asunder.

DuBois, who regarded the absence of legal marriage, legal family, and legal control over children as the essential features of the slave family, says, "This is not inconsistent with much teaching of the morals of modern family life to slaves; the point is that the recognition of the black family from 1619 to 1863 was purely a matter of individual judgment or caprice on the part of the master. Public opinion and custom counted for much, and the law tended to recognize some quasi family rights—forbidding, for instance, in some cases the separation of mothers and very young infants—yet on the whole it is fair to say that while to some extent European family morals were taught the small select body of house servants and artisans both by precept and example, the great body of field hands were raped of their own sex customs and provided with no binding new ones. Slavery gave the monogamic family ideal to slaves, but it compelled and desired only the imperfect practice of its most ordinary morals."[2]

At the same time, to restrict the recognition of the Negro

[1] Reuter, Edward B., *The American Race Problem.* (New York, 1927), pp. 202.

[2] DuBois, W. E. B., *The Negro American Family.* (Atlanta, 1908), pp. 21-22.

family to the individual judgment and caprice of the masters, is to overlook the influence of human relations that constantly tended to break down formal controls and legal definitions, and the force of traditions within the institution of slavery. The institution of slavery which grew up on American soil was the natural product of the exploitation of the continent. As an industrial system it responded to the labor needs of an agricultural country with "open resources."[3] Slavery thrived where the economic basis of its growth continued to exist, and died out where these conditions disappeared.[4] There were considerable differences, moreover, in the character of slavery in Virginia and North Carolina and in the lower South. The real social relations which existed between men under the institution of slavery are not to be found in legal definitions of the rights of masters and slave, nor in the romantic tradition in which antebellum life in the South has been enshrined.[5] Social interaction between masters and slaves created a moral order in which the lives of the whites and Negroes were intertwined.[6] At the same time the Negroes lived in a little society of their own which represented some degree of moral

[3] Nieboer, H. J., *Slavery as an Industrial System*, pp. 383-385. Nieboer defines "open" and "closed" resources as follows: "All the peoples of the earth, whether they subsist by hunting, fishing, cattle-breeding, agriculture, trade or manufactures, may be divided into two categories. Among the peoples of the first category the means of subsistence are open to all; everyone who is able bodied and not defective in mind can provide for himself independently of any capitalist or landlord. Among some of these peoples capital is of some use, and some valuable lands are already held as property; but those who are destitute of such advantages can perfectly well do without them, for there are still abundant natural supplies open to them. Among the peoples of the other category subsistence depends on resources of which the supply is limited and therefore people destitute of these resources are dependent on the owners. It may be convenient to suggest technical names for these two catgories. We shall speak of peoples with open resources and people with closed resources."

[4] Herrick, Cheeseman A., *White Servitude in Pennsylvania*, Introduction; *Documentary History of American Industrial Society*, Vol. I, pp. 88-89. See Phillips, Ulrich B., *American Negro Slavery*, p. 150, concerning George Washington's Apprehension concerning slave property.

[5] Gaines, Francis Pendleton, *The Southern Plantation*, Chap. VII.

[6] Phillips, *op. cit.*, p. 313.

autonomy. It is necessary, therefore, to study the character of the social life of the slaves in order to determine how forces within their own social life contributed to the organization and the stability of the Negro family.

In a study of the Negro family during slavery it is necessary to consider the transplantation of African family mores to American soil. It is often assumed that the burden of the African cultural heritage still weighs upon the Negro family. Weatherford says, "The early slaves, therefore, did not bring with them to America a very exalted idea of morals or of family life. There was no real home life, and the bond between husband and wife was very loose. Slavery did comparatively little to change this condition, though it did give a bit more privacy, and the relation of husband and wife, while still loose, had at least the example of the white people to strengthen it, and was not very frequently broken up.'"[7] The author, however, does not give facts to support this assertion.

Tillinghast, without any more authority for the statement, makes the same opinion more explicit. He says, "The West African father felt little concern in his children; the mother, while showing impulsive affection for them at times, had no idea whatever of systematically correcting and training them. Thus, at the time the Negroes came to this country there had not been developed in the race strong and enduring parental affections nor more than a very slight sense of responsibility for careful bringing up of the children.'"[8] Not many years ago, a social worker claimed that her understanding of the present loose family relationships of colored clients was aided by a knowledge of African customs, and quoted Madison Grant in support of the influence of race in behavior.[9]

[7] Weatherford, W. D., *The Negro From Africa to America*, p. 42.

[8] Tillinghast, Joseph Alexander, *The Negro in Africa and America. Publications of the American Economic Association*, p. 160.

[9] "It may seem incredible that any trace of such customs should survive in present day America, but before I learned of them I sought in vain for light on some of the conjugal habits of colored clients." Sherman, Corinne, "Racial Factors in Desertion." Family, III (October-January, 1922-23), p. 224.

These statements concerning the influence of African sex mores imply or express the popular belief that primitive peoples possess no regulated sex relations. This idea which has been associated with African tribes is probably due to the absence of definite prohibitions against premarital sexual intercourse. Summing up the situation, however, Margold, who has made a study of social control of sexual conduct among African and other primitive peoples, says "The sexual 'freedom' individuals have among these peoples is, in the first place, definitely limited and clearly restrained through taboos, wherever current, regarding exogamy and incest. These constitute fundamental and all-powerful social controls of the sex conduct of the boys and girls concerned."[10]

Indicating the institutional character of premarital sex relations the same author adds, "Among the Nandi and Masai of the Uganda Protectorate, the younger professional warriors, who live with immature girls as a regular and sanctioned practice, can do so only until the girls attain the age of puberty. After puberty the girls must either be married or sent home to their mothers."[11]

The idea of an original state of uncontrolled sex behavior or promiscuity, moreover, has been abandoned by anthropologists. According to Malinowski, "We know that even in the most licentious cultures nothing like 'promiscuity' exists or could ever have existed. In every human culture we find, first of all, systems of well-defined taboos. . . . . Next in importance to the taboo of incest is the prohibition of adultery. While the first serves to guard the family, the second serves for the protection of marriage."[12]

The question of the influence of African sex mores, good or bad, upon the Negro family in America, however, raises the more fundamental question as to what extent the African social heritage was brought to America by the slaves. In attempting to account for the persistence of the African

[10] "Racial Factors in Desertion." Family, III (October-January, 1922-23), pp. 45-46.

[11] *Ibid.*, pp. 50-51.

[12] Malinowski, Bronislaw, *Sex and Repression in Savage Society*, p. 195.

social heritage in the American environment, it is necessary to take into account the diversity of cultures in Africa. But so far it does not appear that opinions concerning the influence of African traditions amount to more than speculations. No study has been made of the Negro's culture in America, so that it could be related to specific cultural traits in Africa. Charles Ball, who was a slave, gives in the story of his life an account of practices which may have been brought from Africa. He says that there were several slaves, "Who must have been, from what I have since learned, Mohammedans; though at that time, I had never heard of the religion of Mohammed. There was one man on this plantation, who prayed five times every day, always turning his face to the east, when in performance of his devotions."[13]

There, is however, scarcely any evidence that the traditions and practices of Africa ever took root in American soil.[14] According to Dr. Park, "the amount of African tra-

[13] Ball, Charles, *Slavery in the United States. A Narrative of the life and Adventures of Charles Ball, A Black Man*, p. 127.

[14] Robert Russa Moton tracing his family back to Africa says: "About the year of 1735, a fierce battle was waged between two strong tribes on the west coast of Africa. The chief of one of these tribes was counted among the most powerful of his time. This chief overpowered his rival and slaughtered and captured a great number of his band. Some of the captives escaped, others died, others still committed suicide, till but few were left. The victorious chief delivered to his son about a dozen of this forlorn remnant, and he, with an escort, took them away to be sold into slavery. The young African pushed his way through the jungle with his bodyguard until he reached the coast. Arrived there, he sold his captives to the captain of an American slave ship and received his pay in trinkets of various kinds, common to the custom of the trade. Then he was asked to row out in a boat and inspect the wonderful ship. He went, and with the captain and the crew saw every part of the vessel. When it was all over they offered him food and he ate it heartily. After that he remembered no more till he woke to find himself in the hold of the ship chained to one of the miserable creatures whom he himself had so recently sold as a slave, and the vessel itself was far beyond the sight of land. After many days the ship arrived at the shores of America; the human cargo was brought to Richmond and this African slave merchant was sold along with his captives at public auction in the slave markets of the city. He was bought by a tobacco planter and carried to Amelia County, Virginia, where he lived to be a very old man. This man was my grandmother's great grandfather." Moton, Robert Russa, *Finding a Way Out*, pp. 3-4.

dition which the Negro brought to the United States was very small.'"[15] He adds: "In fact, there is every reason to believe, it seems to me, that the Negro, when he landed in the United States, left behind him almost everything but his dark complexion and his tropical temperament." The same thing may be said of several stocks brought from Europe to America. This is what complete Americanization means.

The manner in which Negro slaves were collected in Africa and disposed of after their arrival in this country would make it improbable that their African traditions were preserved.

"The great markets for slaves in Africa," says Dr. R. E. Park, further, "were on the West Coast, but the old slave trails ran back from the coast far into the interior of the continent, and all the peoples of Central Africa contributed to the stream of enforced emigration to the New World. In the West Indies a good deal was known among slave-traders and plantation owners about the character and relative value of slaves from different parts of Africa, but in the United States there was less knowledge and less discrimination. Coming from all parts of Africa, and having no common language and common tradition, the memories of Africa which they brought with them were soon lost.

"There was less opportunity in the United States also than in the West Indies for a slave to meet one of his own people, because the plantations were considerably smaller, more widely scattered, and especially, because as soon as they were landed in this country,

[15] "It is very difficult to find in the South today anything that can be traced directly back to Africa. This does not mean that there is not a great deal of superstition, conjuring, "root doctoring" and magic generally among the Negroes of the United States. What it does mean is that the superstitions we do find are those which we might expect to grow up anywhere among an imaginative people, living in an intellectual twilight such as exists on the isolated plantations of the Southern States. Furthermore, this superstition is in no way associated, as it is in some of the countries of Europe, southern Italy for example, with religious beliefs and practices. It is not part of Negro Christianity. It is with him as it is with us, folklore pure and simple. It is said that there are but two African words that have been retained in the English language. One of these is the word Buckra, from which comes Buckroe Beach in Virginia. This seems remarkable when we consider that slaves were still brought into the United States clandestinely up to 1862."—Park, Robert E., "The Conflict and Fusion of Cultures," *Journal of Negro History*, Vol. IV, p. 117.

slaves were immediately divided and shipped in small numbers, frequently no more than one or two at a time, to different plantations. This was the procedure with the very first Negroes brought to this country. It was found easier to deal with the slaves, if they were separated from their kinsmen. On the plantation they were thrown together with slaves who had already forgotten or only dimly remembered their life in Africa. English was the only language of the plantation. The attitude of the slave plantation to each fresh arrival seems to have been much like that of the older immigrant towards the greenhorn. Everything that marked him as an alien was regarded as ridiculous and barbaric.''[16]

Data on the Negro family during slavery for this study, however, have been taken not from works of opinion but to a large extent from biographies and autobiographies of slaves. The authenticity of many published slave biographies has been questioned by historians on the ground that they represent the propaganda literature of abolitionists. But although some of these published accounts, which range in length from short pamphlets of less than fifty pages to bound volumes of five hundred pages, reflect the zeal and arguments of the abolitionists, many of them are the naïve stories of the slaves, themselves. The prefaces to some of these books inform the reader that they were taken down in the language of the slaves; while some of those written by ex-slaves who have acquired education and culture, exhibit a detachment towards their experiences which makes them valuable documents. In the case of two documents which have been used in this study we have the story of the careers of the families over a long period. The Plummer family history tells the story of the family from the period of the American Revolution to the present century. It contains many letters relating to the family and furnishes a narrative of the struggles and achievements of the family in relation to the affairs of the Negro communities in which they have worked.

Biographical and autobiographical documents on the Negro family, printed in the *Journal of Negro History,* have

[16] Park, Robert E., *op. cit.*, p. 117.

been carefully examined. In addition to these printed documents the writer made an independent collection of family histories and utilized the collection of ex-slave biographies in the Department of Social Science at Fisk University. Published plantation records, the observations of those who have come into contact with slavery, and other historical documents have also been studied for events relating to the Negro family.

In the records of everyday events of the plantation one finds unquestionable historical information on the Negro family. Likewise in the use of autobiographies and biographies, reliance has been placed upon the events in lives of the slaves, rather than upon their reflections upon slavery and their masters. Often the behavior of both slaves and masters, as well as the naïve statements of slaves are at variance with the more conscious and conventional remarks upon slavery as an institution.

The selection and use of materials in our study of the Negro family have been restricted mainly to an attempt to determine to what extent the Negro family functioned as a cultural group free from external control. On the one hand, this has led to a study of the social life of the slave on the ground that the character and permanence of the slave family were affected considerably by the support given the family by the social milieu in which the slave acquired a conception of himself as a person. Our investigation, on the other hand, has led us to the study of influence of the masters on the integrity of the slave family; the extent to which a family consciousness was developed; the status of the individual members of the family; the discipline of children; and finally the beginnings of a real family tradition.

I. SOCIAL LIFE OF THE SLAVES

Although theoretically and legally, except for some humane restrictions, the slaves were not persons but utilities with no will of their own, social interaction within their own world on the plantation created a social life among them with nearly all of the features of any society. In some cases, the regard of the master for the personality of his slaves was such as to prevent the employment of an overseer.[17] This was probably characteristic of those masters who stood in a paternal relation to their slaves and were sometimes bound to them by the tie of blood. Writing, concerning his master who was also his father, Langston says: "His views with regard to slavery and the management of slaves upon a plantation by overseers, were peculiar and unusual. He believed that slavery ought to be abolished. But he maintained that the mode of its abolition should be by the voluntary individual action of the owner. He held that slaves should be dealt with in such manner, as to their superintendence and management, as to prevent cruelty, always, and to inspire in them, so far as practicable, feelings of confidence in their masters. Hence, he would employ no overseer, but, dividing the slaves into groups, convenient for ordinary direction and employment, made one of their own number the chief director of the force.'"[18]

The social life of the slaves, moreover, was safeguarded from much arbitrary outside interference by the sentiment on the part of masters against the molestation of their slaves, so long as their behavior was not a flagrant menace to social order. Sometimes the strong attachment which masters had for their slaves made them rise in their defense against the community. When the slaves on one plantation had killed patrollers who had attacked them during a dance, according to Steward, his master "was filled with sorrow for the loss of his slaves, but not alone, as is generally the case in such instances, because he had lost so much property. He truly regretted the death of his faithful servants, and boldly rebuked the occasion of their sudden decease. When

[17] Thompson, John, *The Life of John Thompson, a Fugitive Slave; containing His History of 25 Years in Bondage, and His Providential Escape,* pp. 64-65.

[18] Langston, John M., *From the Virginia Plantation to the National Capital,* p. 12.

beset and harassed by his neighbors to give up his slaves to be tried for insurrection and murder, he boldly resisted, contending for the natural right of the slaves, to act in their own defense, and especially when on his own plantation and in their own quarters. They contended, however, that as his slaves had got up a dance, and had invited those of the adjoining plantations, the patrol was only discharging their duty in looking after them; but the gallant old Colonel defended his slaves, and told them plainly that he should continue to do so to the extent of his ability and means.' "[19]

The masters in placing slaves in positions of authority created some distinction in status among them.[20] More significant for our study are those characteristic features of social life, which arose as the result of social interaction within the circle of the life of the slaves. In Ball's account of the behavior of his grandfather, who was brought from Africa, the conception which he had of himself seemed to be related to his status in Africa. "Indeed, old Ben, as my grandfather was called," said he, "had always expressed great contempt for his fellow slaves, they being, as he said, a mean and vulgar race, quite beneath his rank and the dignity of his former station. He had, during all the time that I knew him, a small cabin of his own, with about half an acre of ground attached to it, which he cultivated on his own account, and from which he drew a large portion of his subsistence."[21]

Douglass' grandmother also enjoyed the distinction of living in a cabin separate from the quarters. "Whether because she was too old for field service, or because she had so faithfully discharged the duties of her station in early life," said Douglass, "I know not, but she enjoyed the high

[19] Steward, Austin, *Twenty-two years a Slave, and Forty years a Freeman; Embracing a correspondence of Several Years, While President of Wilberforce Colony, London Canada West*, p. 38.

[20] Pickard, Mrs. Kate E. R., *The Kidnapped and The Ransomed. Being the Personal Recollections of Peter Still and His Wife "Vina" After Forty Years of Slavery*, p. 155.

[21] Ball, Charles, *op. cit.*, pp. 11-12.

privilege of living in a cabin separate from the quarters, having only the charge of the young children and the burden of her own support imposed upon her. She esteemed it great good fortune to live so, and took much comfort in having the children.''[22] Bishop Coppin says: "Our people, both slave and free, were not all a common lot, on one level. There were divisions, classes and distinctions among them.''[23] In his autobiography, Bibb, who escaped from slavery, wrote of a mulatto slave with a fine voice as "moving in the highest circle of slaves and free people of color.''[24] This higher status was probably due to her mixed blood, as well as her talent for singing.

Aside from any speculation as to the biological influence of white blood in creating a more energetic type of person, the mulatto slaves generally had a conception themselves that raised them above the level of the common slaves. They often petitioned for less arduous tasks on the grounds that field work was exceedingly difficult on account of their white blood.

Frances Kemble writes on this point:

"The mulatto woman, Sally, accosted me again today, and begged that she might be put to some other than field labor. Supposing she felt herself unequal to it, I asked her some questions, but the principal reason she urged for her promotion to some less laborious kind of work was, that hoeing in the field was so hard to her on *"account of her color,"* and she therefore petitions to be allowed to learn a trade. I was much puzzled at this reason for her petition, but was presently made to understand that, being a mulatto, she considered field labor a degradation; her white bastardy appearing to her a title to consideration in my eyes. The degradation of these people is very complete, for they have accepted the contempt of their masters to that degree that they profess, and really seem to feel it for themselves, and the faintest admixture

[22] Douglass, Frederick, *Life and Times of Frederick Douglass, His Escape from Bondage, and his Complete History to the Present*, p. 14.

[23] Coppin, Bishop L. J., *Unwritten History*, p. 80.

[24] Bibb, Henry, *The Narrative of the Life and Adventures of Henry Bibb, an American Slave*, pp. 33-34.

of white blood in their black veins appears at once, by common consent of their own race, to raise them in the scale of humanity.''[25]

Nevertheless, these distinctions among the slaves, even when founded upon color, furnished the basis of a social order and control arising not externally but within the conceptions of the slaves themselves. The slave, moreover, was not only giving expression to the valuation which he placed upon color, but he was reflecting the social values which the white master class exemplified in their behavior. Mulatto slaves were usually taken into the house as servants.[26] "It is a custom as to the mulatto children, that the males born on an estate should never be employed as field Negroes, but as tradesmen: the females are brought up as domestics about the house. . . . ."[27]

The distinction between the house slaves and the field slaves was one that not only had significance for the slaves, but persisted into freedom. An ex-slave wrote recently concerning this distinction, that "there was a social distinction with the slaves. The house and personal servants were on a higher social plane than the field slaves, while the colored person, who would associate with the 'po' white trash' were practically outcasts, and held in very great contempt. The slaves belonging to the lower class of white folks, were not considered on the same level as those belonging to the 'quality folks,' and the slaves of these families were always proud of, and bragged of their connection with the better families. Thus we had our own social distinctions, which were based largely on the social standing of the masters, and within the inner circle, on the position occupied in the plantation or home affairs. That same little indefinable difference that existed between the social levels of the white

[25] Kemble, Frances A. (Mrs. Butler), *Journal of a Residence on a Georgian Plantation*, pp. 193-194.

[26] *Plantation and Frontier*, p. 46.

[27] Extracts from M. G. Lewis' *Journal of a West India Proprietor*, Observations in January and March, 1815. *Doc. Hist. Amer. Ind. Soc.*, Vol. II, *Plantation and Frontier*, p. 134.

folks, existed between Colored people, and even at present that same little distinction still exists. It is from the plantations and homes of the 'quality folks,' that the better class of Colored people of the present day south, have been recruited. These same people as a rule, own their homes, or still hold good positions with the old families. They are clean, many of them well educated, and enjoy the confidence and respect of the white people today just as they did in the days before the war. On the other hand, the shiftless, improvident and irresolute class of today came largely from the families of a lower social order before the war. There are, of course, exceptions to this general order of affairs.''[28]

Likewise in the observations of travelers we find testimony to the superior status of the domestic slaves. ''The colored domestic servants,'' says Lyell, ''are treated with great indulgence at Tuscaloosa. One day some of them gave a supper to a large party of their friends in the house of a family which we visited, and they feasted their guests on roast turkeys, ice-creams, jellies and cakes.''[29]

One slave referring to the advantage that he had over the field hands, writes: ''I was now made a house slave. My duties were to wait on the table and help in the kitchen. I was extremely glad of this promotion as it afforded me a better chance of obtaining good food. . . . . At this period I had a tolerably good time of it, being employed in the kitchen helping to cook, or waiting at the table, and listening to the conversation going on, I learned many things of which the field hands were entirely ignorant.''[30]

Another slave acquires a superior status by becoming the body servant of the master's son. ''Then my business,'' said he, ''was to wait upon him, attend to his horse, and go

[28] Anderson, Robert, *From Slavery to Affluence: Memoirs of Robert Anderson, Ex-slave*, pp. 29-30.

[29] Lyell, Charles, *Second Visit to the United States*, Vol. II, p. 72, in *Doc. Hist. Amer. Ind. Soc.*, Vol. II, *Plantation and Frontier*, p. 46.

[30] Frederick, Francis, *Autobiography of Rev. Francis Frederick of Virginia*, pp. 9, 15.

with him to and from school; for neglect of which, as he fancied, I often got severe floggings from him. Still, I did not wish my situation changed, for I considered my station a very high one; preferring an occasional licking, to being thrown out of office. Being a gentleman's body servant, I had nothing more to do with plantation affairs, and, consequently, thought myself much superior to those children who had to sweep the yard. I was about twelve years old when given to John Wagar.'"[31]

It was this improvement in status and contact with a larger world that not only gave the house servant a higher conception of himself as a slave but made slavery more irksome. Lewis Clarke, a mulatto slave, while admitting the advantages over the field hands, complained of being subject to the arbitrary will of the master class. He said, "There were four house-slaves in this family, including myself, and though we had not, in all respects, so hard work as the field hands, yet in many things our condition was much worse. We were constantly exposed to the whims and passions of every member of the family; from the least to the greatest, their anger was wreaked upon us."[32]

Contact with the master class, too, sometimes created restlessness in those of the improved status. His biographer wrote, "No doubt he began to swell somewhat with that feeling of superiority that the house-servant always felt over the field-hand. Unconsciously he partook more or less of the forms of life, language, traits and habits of the 'white folks,' even to the extent that suddenly his mistress discovered that he was adopting their language entirely which she solemnly forbade. While giving ready promise to resume the plantation patois, he found it impossible. His tongue as well as his very nature would drift to the more refined manners and rhythmic language of the 'big house.' Even an occasional cuff from his mistress

[31] Thompson, John, *op. cit.*, pp. 24-25.

[32] Clarke, Lewis Garrard, *Narrative of the Sufferings of Lewis and Milton Clarke, Sons of a Soldier of more than Twenty Years Among the Slave-holders of Kentucky, One of the So-called Christian States of North America*, pp. 15-16.

failed to restrain him. But this incidental change of relations could not make him forget the humiliations of bondage, but rather sharpened his appreciation of its unreasonableness and unrighteousness.''[33]

This same advantage of being a house servant and distinction which went with it is thus described by Bishop Coppin, ''In cases where the housemaid was daily with the members of the family and the guests who mingled with them, a difference could be seen in appearance and general deportment. Often the house girl at the Big House was the lady at the quarters. She wore the cast-off clothing of her mistress. In many cases, where the mistress was kindly disposed, she took especial pride in dressing her maid in such finery as to place her above the common lot; or, to make her outshine all the neighborhood house girls.''[34]

Lunsford Lane who was a slave and later established himself as freedman, enjoyed the advantage of the house-slaves. ''I had endured what a freeman would indeed call hard fare,'' said he, ''but my lot, on the whole, had been a favored one for a slave. It is known that there is a wide difference in the situations of what are termed house servants, and plantation hands. I, though sometimes employed upon the plantation, belonged to the former which is the favored class.''[35]

In the social affairs of the slaves the superior status of the house servants was generally recognized. In the account of a dance, Steward says, ''It was about ten o'clock when the aristocratic slaves began to assemble, dressed in the cast-off finery of their master and mistress, swelling out and putting on airs in imitation of those they were forced to obey from day to day.''[36] ''House servants,'' said he further, ''were, of course, 'the stars' of the party; all eyes were

[33] Davis, D. Webster, *The Life and Public Services of Rev. William Washington Browne*, pp. 13-14.

[34] Coppin, Bishop L. J., *op. cit.*, p. 37.

[35] Lane, Lunsford, *The Narrative of Lunsford Lane*, pp. 18-19.

[36] Steward, Austin, *Twenty-two Years a Slave and Forty Years a Freeman*, p. 30.

turned to them to see how they conducted, for they, among slaves, are what a military man would call 'fugle-men.' The field hands, and such of them as have generally been excluded from the dwelling of their owners, look to the house servant as a pattern of politeness and gentility. And indeed, it is often the only method of obtaining any knowledge of the manners of what is called 'genteel society'; and are sometimes greatly envied, while others are bitterly hated.''[37]

The division of labor on the plantation which gave opportunity for the expression of individual talent carried with it certain social distinctions. As Coppin relates, ''Those who had musical talent often became 'fiddlers,' and some of them were considered quite expert with the bow.''[38] These fiddlers often appeared at the dinner parties in the masters' homes; and sometimes their owners profited as well as the slaves from their talent.[39] Giving an account of the status of the different occupations, Frederick Douglass said:

'' 'Uncle' Tobey was the blacksmith, 'Uncle' Harry the cartwright, and 'Uncle' Abel was the shoemaker, and these had assistants in their several departments. These mechanics were called 'Uncles' by all the younger slaves, not because they really sustained that relationship to any, but according to plantation etiquette as a mark of respect, due from the younger to the older slaves. Strange and even ridiculous as it may seem, among a people so uncultivated and with so many stern trials to look in the face, there is not to be found among any people a more rigid enforcement of the law of respect to elders than is maintained among them. I set this down as partly constitutional with the colored race and partly conventional.''[40]

''Among other slave notabilities, I found here one called by everybody, white and colored, 'Uncle' Isaac Copper. Once in a while a negro had a surname fastened to him by common consent. This was the case with 'Uncle' Isaac Copper. When the 'Uncle' was dropped, he was called Doctor Copper. He was both our Doctor of Medicine and our Doctor of Divinity. Where he took his degree I am unable to say, but he was too well established in his profession to permit question as to his native skill, or attainments.

[37] Steward, Austin, *Twenty-two Years a Slave and Forty Years a Freeman*, pp. 31-32.

[38] Coppin, Bishop L. J., *op. cit.*, p. 48.

[39] Ball, Charles, *op. cit.*, pp. 218-219.

[40] Douglass, Frederick, *op. cit.*, p. 30.

One qualification he certainly had. He was a confirmed cripple, wholly unable to work, and was worth nothing for sale in the market. Though lame he was no sluggard. He made his crutches do him good service, and was always on the alert looking up the sick, and such as were supposed to need his aid and counsel. His remedial prescriptions embraced four articles. For diseases of the body, epsom salts, and castor oil; for those of the soul, the 'Lord's prayer,' and a few stout hickory switches.''[41]

The most influential personalities among the slaves were the preachers. These preachers became the interpreters of a religion which the slaves had developed on American soil. This religion was not a heritage, as many assume, from Africa.[42] It was other worldly because the world of everyday life was the world of the white man. In the heaven beyond this world, the Negro found a fulfillment of all his wishes. ''The world, as the African understood it, was full of malignant spirits, diseases and forces with which he was in constant mortal struggle. His religious practices were intended to gain for him immunity in this world, rather than assurance of the next. But the Negro in America was in a different situation. He was not living in his own world. He was a slave and that, aside from the physical inconvenience, implied a vast deal of inhibition. He was, moreover, a constant spectator of life in which he could not participate; excited to actions and enterprises that were forbidden to him because he was a slave. The restlessness which this situation provoked found expression, not in insurrection and rebellion—although of course there were Negro insurrections—but in his religion and his dreams of another and freer world. I assume, therefore, that the reason the Negro so readily and eagerly took over from the white man his heaven and apocalyptic visions was because these materials met the demands of his peculiar racial temperament and furnished relief to the emotional strains that were provoked in him by the conditions of slavery.''[43]

[41] Douglass, Frederick, *op. cit.*, p. 31.

[42] Wilson, G. R., ''The Religion of the American Negro Slave: His Attitude Toward Life and Death,'' *Journal of Negro History*, Vol. VIII, pp. 41-71.

[43] Park, Robert E., *op. cit.*, p. 128.

Although the house-servants because of their favored position in relation to the master class were early admitted to the churches, it was only with the coming of the Methodists and Baptists that the masses of the slaves "found a form of Christianity that they could make their own."[44] The white ministers were never as close to the people as the black preachers. Anderson emphasizes the difference in services conducted by the white ministers and those under the leadership of their own ministers in their own way. "We people on the plantation," said he, "had our church services the same as the white folks. We did not always have a church to hold our services in, but we usually had a preacher, and sometimes white preachers would hold services for us, to which special services all the colored folks were invited. Our preachers were usually plantation folks just like the rest of us. Some man who had a little education and had been taught something about the Bible, would be our preacher. The colored folks had their own code of religion, not nearly so complicated as the white man's religion, but more closely observed. . . . . When we had meetings of this kind, we held them in our own way and were not interfered with by the white folks."[45]

John Jasper was one of the most distinguished of the Negro preachers near the end of slavery. Hatcher, describing him as "an aristocrat," said, "His mode of dress, his manner of walking, his lofty dignity, all told a story. He received an aristocratic education, and he never lost it. Besides this, he had a most varied experience as a slave. He grew up on the farm, and knew what it was to be a plantation hand. He learned to work in the tobacco factory. He worked also in the foundries, and also served around the houses of the families with whom he lived; for it must be understood that after the breaking up of the Peachy family he changed owners and lived in different places. These things enlarged his scope, and with that keen desire to know

[44] Park, Robert E., *op. cit.*, pp. 118-119.

[45] Anderson, Robert, *op. cit.*, pp. 22-23.

things he learned at every turn of life.'"[46] "From his own account of himself," says Hatcher further, "he was fond of display, a gay-coxcomb among the women of his race, a fun-maker by nature, with a self-assertion that made him a leader within the circles of his freedom.'"[47]

The appearance of Jasper at the funeral of a slave which was always an occasion among the slaves for ceremony and pageantry is described in the following account:

"There was one thing which the Negro greatly insisted upon, and which not even the most hard-hearted masters were ever quite willing to deny them. They could never bear that their dead should be put away without a funeral. Not that they expected, at the time of burial, to have the funeral service. Indeed, they did not desire it, and it was never according to their notions. A funeral to them was a pageant. It was a thing to be arranged for a long time ahead. It was to be marked by the gathering of the kindred and friends from far and wide. It was not satisfactory unless there was a vast and excitable crowd. It usually meant an all-day meeting, and often a meeting in a grove, and it drew white and black alike, sometimes almost in equal numbers. Another demand in the case—for the slaves knew how to make their demands—was that the Negro preacher 'should preach the funeral' as they called it. In things like this, the wishes of the slaves generally prevailed. 'The funeral' loomed up weeks in advance, and although marked by sable garments, mournful manners and sorrowful outcries it had about it hints of an elaborate social function with festive accompaniments. There was much staked on the fame of the officiating brother. He must be one of their own color, and a man of reputation. They must have a man to plough up their emotional depths, and they must have freedom to indulge in the extravagancies of their sorrow. These demonstrations were their tribute to their dead and were expected to be fully adequate to do honour to the family.

It was in this way that Jasper's fame began. At first, his tempestuous, ungrammatical eloquence was restricted to Richmond, and there it was hedged in with many humbling limitations. But gradually the news concerning this fiery and thrilling orator sifted itself into the country, and many invitations came for him to officiate at country funerals.'"[48]

Concerning the funerals among the slaves Coppin writes:

[46] Hatcher, William E., *John Jasper, The Unmatched Negro Philosopher and Preacher*, pp. 30-35.

[47] *Ibid.*, p. 16.

[48] *Ibid.*, pp. 36-38.

"One of the big days among our people was, when a funeral was held. A person from New Jersey who was not acquainted with our customs, heard it announced that: 'next Sunday two weeks the funeral of Jenet Anderson will be preached.' 'Well,' said the stranger, 'how do they know that she will be dead.' The fact was, she was already dead, and had been for some time. But, according to our custom, a custom growing out of necessity, we did not hold the funeral when the person was buried. The relatives—and friends—could not leave their work to attend funerals. Often persons would be buried at night after working hours. If the deceased was a free person, and the immediate family could attend a week day funeral, there might be others, both friends and relatives who could not attend, hence, the custom became general."[49]

Besides the funerals there were holiday occasions among the slaves when they were given an opportunity to enjoy social intercourse. Usually these holidays followed the laying by of the crop. The Christmas holidays were always the occasion for festivities.

" 'We, on the plantation,' said Anderson, 'had our social gatherings and social functions just as our white masters had. Oftimes when the white folks had a social gathering, a party or ball, there was a provision for a similar gathering for the colored folks, or sometimes they were permitted to come and look on at the parties and balls. We had occasional dances and parties in the evening, to which the colored people from several of the adjoining plantations were often asked. We danced some of the dances the white folks danced, the minuette, the reels, and other dances common in those days, but we liked better the dances of our own particular race, in which we tried to express in motion the particular feelings within our own selves. These dances were individual dances, consisting of shuffling of the feet, and swinging of the arms and shoulders in a peculiar rhythm of time developed into what is known today as the Double Shuffle, Heel and Toe, Buck and Wing, Juba, etc.' "[50]

Austin Steward thus describes a "grand dance" which was authorized by his master for Easter night.

"When they were all assembled, the dance commenced; the old fiddler struck up some favorite tune, and over the floor they went; the flying feet of the dancers were heard, pat, pat, over the apartment till the clock warned them it was twelve at midnight, or what

[49] Coppin, Bishop L. J., *op. cit.*, p. 55.

[50] Anderson, Robert, *op. cit.*, pp. 30-31.

some call 'low twelve,' to distinguish it from twelve o'clock at noon; then the violin ceased its discordant sounds, and the merry dancers paused to take breath. Supper was then announced, and all began to prepare for the sumptuous feast. It being the pride of slaves to imitate the manners of their master and mistress, especially in the ceremonies of the table, all was conducted with great propriety and good order. The food was well cooked and in a very plentiful supply. They had also managed in some way to get a good quantity of excellent wine, which was sipped in the most approved and modern style. Every dusky face was lighted up, and every eye sparkled with joy. However ill fed they might have been, here, for once, there was plenty. Suffering and toil was forgotten, and they all seemed with one accord to give themselves up to the intoxication of pleasurable amusement.''[51]

It was during these festivities especially at Christmas time that there was much match making. Northup says:

"They seat themselves at the rustic-table, the males on one side, the females on the other. The two between whom there may have been an exchange of tenderness, invariably manage to sit opposite; . . . . The ivory teeth, contrasting with their black complexions exhibit two long, white streaks the whole extent of the table. All around the bountiful board a multitude of eyes roll in ecstacy. Giggling and laughter and the clattering of cutlery and crockery succeed. Cuffee's elbow hunches his neighbor's side, impelled by an involuntary impulse of delight; Nelly shakes her finger at Sambo and laughs, she knows not why and so the fun and merriment flows on.''[52]

II. CHARACTER OF THE NEGRO FAMILY IN SLAVERY

A. *Influence of Masters on Family Relations*

Undoubtedly the masters had an interest not only in the propagation of their slave property; but they were concerned about the connection which the sexual union of slaves on the plantations established. Usually, it appears, slaves secured permission to marry. An overseer in a letter to his employer said, "I have given Chesley Permission to marry Molly, Sarah's daughter. I would like to Noe if you object to it. I have put up a New house for Chesley.''[53] Re-

[51] Steward, Austin, *op. cit.*, pp. 30-31.

[52] Northrup, Solomon, *op. cit.*, pp. 215-216.

[53] *Florida Plantation Records. Missouri Hist. Society*, pp. 92-93.

ferring to another such instance, he said, "Esaw and biner has asked permission to Marry. I think it a good Match. What say you to it?"[54]

A slave owner wrote another saying, "As my boy Reuben has formed an attachment to one of your girls and wants her for a wife this is to let you know that I am perfectly willing that he should, and with your consent marry her. His character is good, he is honest, faithful and industrious."[55] Davis, a slave who enjoyed considerable freedom of movement, wrote concerning consumating his courtship that "we were both slaves, and of course had to get the consent of our owners, before we went further."[56]

The master's control over the mating of his slaves went further than merely giving permission to the slave to marry the person of his choice. It was often, it appears, a command to marry according to the wishes of the master. A slave, who had been purchased and compelled to leave his wife and family, according to one narrative, was "compelled to take a young woman named Hannah, as a wife, and to abandon his former one. By Hannah he had a good many children, but after he had been with her about eight years he was sold away from her and their children to one Robert Ware, of Decatur Town, in DeKalb County, Georgia, about ten miles from Stevens' place."[57] A young mulatto girl, whose fiancée had escaped to the North through Harriet Tubman, also fled to the North "in fear and desperation" when she learned that her master had determined to give her to one of his Negro slaves as a wife.[58] With the instructions to the slaves as to the amount of tobacco they were expected to cultivate, according to a slave, "was the order for us to 'get married,'

[54] *Florida Plantation Records. Missouri Hist. Society*, p. 140.

[55] *Doc. Hist. Amer. Ind. Soc.*, Vol. II, *Plantation and Frontier*, p. 45.

[56] Davis, Noah, *The Narrative of the Life of Rev. Noah Davis, A colored man written by himself, at the age of fifty-four*, pp. 26-27.

[57] Brown, John, *Slave Life in Georgia*, p. 63.

[58] Tubman, Harriet, *Harriet, the Moses of her people*, by Mrs. Sarah H. Bradford, p. 57.

according to Slavery, or in other words, to enrich his plantation by a family of young slaves.''[59]

A Negro sailor on an English ship, after having been deserted in an American port, was sold into slavery. The narrative of a slave who was on the same plantation to which he was sent says:

''When he had been some three or four years on the plantation, his master bade him take a wife. John told him he had one in England, and two dear children. Then his master flogged him for saying so, and for insisting upon it that he was free and a British subject. At last, to save his poor body from the torture of the cowhide and the paddle, he promised his master never to say as much again, and to look out for a wife. In Jones County, and about five miles from Stevens' plantation, there lived another planter named John Ward. John Glasgow, having to go backwards and forwards on errands, saw and at length selected a young, bright, colored girl named Nancy, and they were married, in the way that slaves are; that is, nominally. This did not please Stevens, because Nancy being Ward's property, her children would be Ward's also; so John was flogged for marrying Nancy, instead of one of Stevens' 'likely gals,' and was forbidden to visit her. Still he contrived to do so without his master's discovering it. The young woman was of a very sweet disposition, it seems, and knew all about John's misfortunes, and his having a wife and children in England. She was very kind to him, and would weep over him, as she dressed his sore and bleeding back when he crept to her log cabin at dead of night, so it was no wonder he came to love her and the three children she bore him, whilst all the time talking of his English wife and children, whom he should never see more; never, never.''[60]

Aside from the economic motive that might prompt slave holders to have their slaves marry, it appears in the following excerpt that mistresses sought this means of controlling the master's sex relations with the female slaves:

''Mistress told sister that she had best get married, and that if she would, she would give her a wedding. Soon after a very respectable young man, belonging to Mr. Bowman, a wealthy planter, and reputed to be a good master, began to court my sister. This very much pleased Mistress, who wished to hasten the marriage. She

[59] Jackson, Andrew, *Narrative and Writings of Andrew Jackson of Kentucky*, p. 8.

[60] Brown, John, *op. cit.*, pp. 37-38.

determined that her maid should be married, not as slaves usually are, but that with the usual matrimonial ceremonies should be tied the knot to be broken only by death. The Sabbath was appointed for the marriage, which was to take place at the Episcopal Church. I must here state that no slave can be married lawfully, without a fine from his or her owner. Mistress and all the family, except the old man, went to church, to witness the marriage ceremony, which was to be performed by their minister, Parson Reynolds. The master of Josiah, my sister's destined husband, was also at the wedding, for he thought a great deal of his man. Mistress returned delighted from the wedding, for she thought she had accomplished a great piece of work. But the whole affair only enraged her unfeeling husband, who, to be revenged upon the maid, proposed to sell her. To this his wife refused consent. Although Mrs. T. had never told him her suspicions or what my sister had said, yet he suspected the truth, and determined to be revenged. Accordingly, during another absence of Mistress, he again cruelly whipped my sister. A continued repetition of these things finally killed our Mistress, who the doctor said, died of a broken heart. After the death of this friend, sister ran away leaving her husband and one child and finally found her way to the North. None of our family ever heard from her afterwards, until I accidentally met her in the streets in Philadelphia. My readers can imagine what a meeting ours must have been. She is again married and in prosperity."[61]

To the same extent that the slave in forming a conjugal relation was subject to the wishes of his master he was under the will of the latter in continuing that relationship. Beyond the will of the master were the contingencies of family fortunes such as changes in the economic status and deaths which affected the stability of the slave family. Washington Irving who recognized as a peculiar evil of slavery the fact that slaves are "parted from their children" reflected philosophically in his journals, "but are not white people so, by schooling, marriage, business, etc." [62] Bruce who writes with detachment concerning slavery tells how the division of the property upon the death of his master broke up his family. "My parents belonged," he said, "to Lemuel Bruce, who died about the year 1836, leaving two children, William Bruce and Rebecca Bruce, who went to live with their aunt,

[61] Thompson, John, *op. cit.*, pp. 33-34.

[62] Irving, Washington, *op. cit.*, Vol. 3, p. 115.

Mrs. Prudence Perkinson; he also left two families of slaves, and they were divided between his two children; my mother's family fell to Miss Rebecca, and the other family, the head of which was known as Bristo was left to William H. Bruce. Then it was that family ties were broken, the slaves were all hired out, my mother to one man and my father to another. I was too young then to know anything about it, and have to rely entirely on what I have heard my mother and others older than myself say.''[63]

Josiah Henson, like Bishop L. H. Holsey,[64] records the same misfortune on the death of his master. "In consequence of his decease," said Henson, "it became necessary to sell the estate and the slaves, in order to divide the property among the heirs; and we were all put up at auction and sold to the highest bidder, and scattered over various parts of the country. My brothers and sisters were bid off one by one, while my mother, holding my hand, looked on in an agony of grief, the cause of which I but ill understood at first, but which dawned on my mind with dreadful clearness, as the sale proceeded. My mother was then separated from me, and put up in her turn. She was bought by a man named Isaac R. residing in Montgomery county, and then I was offered to the assembled purchasers. My mother, half distracted with the parting forever from all her children, pushed through the crowd while the bidding for me was going on, to the spot where R. was standing. She fell at his feet, and clung to his knees, entreating him in tones that a mother only could command to buy her Baby as well as herself, and spare to her one of her little ones at least. Will it, can it be believed that this man, thus appealed to, was capable not merely of turning a deaf ear to her supplication, but of disengaging himself from her with such violent blows and kicks, as to reduce her to the necessity of creeping out of his reach,

[63] Bruce, Henry Clay, *The New Man, Twenty-nine Years a Slave, Twenty-nine Years a Free Man*, p. 13.

[64] Bishop Holsey's master was his father, but at his death things changed—Holsey, L. H., *Autobiography*, p. 9.

and mingling the groan of bodily suffering with the sob of a breaking heart?"[65]

The following vivid description of the method of dividing property in slaves upon the death of the owner also shows the effects of the settlement of estates upon the integrity of the slave family.

> "It was a bright, sunshiny morning, in the autumn season, at about the commencement of tobacco cutting time. At the appointed hour, nearly the whole of us had congregated in the great yard, under the sycamore tree. A fourth part of the Negroes on the estate, had been kept back by Betty Moore, as her share, her husband's will giving her the right of making a selection. Besides these, she had taken my brother, Silas, and my sister, Lucy, whom she reserved on behalf of her eldest daughter, the wife of Burrell Williams. They were fine, strong children, and it was arranged they should remain with Betty till she died, and then revert to Burrell Williams. All who were there stood together, facing the Executors, or Committee as they were called, who sat on chairs under the same sycamore tree I have spoken of. Burrell Williams, James Davis, and Billy Bell, held themselves aloof, and did not in any manner interfere with the proceedings of the Committee who sold us off into three lots, each lot consisting of about twenty-five or thirty, as near as I can recollect. As there was a good deal of difference in the value of the slaves, individually, some being stronger than others, or more likely, the allotments were regulated so as to equalize the value of each division. For instance, my brother Silas and my sister Lucy, who belonged rightly to the gang of which I and my mother and other members of the family formed a part, were replaced by two of my cousins Annikie's children, a boy and a girl; the first called Henry, the other Mason, who were weak and sickly. When the lots had been sold off, the names of the men, women and children composing them were written on three slips of paper, and these were put into a hat. Burrell Williams then came forward and drew, James Davis followed, and Billy Bell came last. The lot in which I and my mother were was drawn by James Davis. Each slip was then signed by the Committee, and the lot turned over to the new owner."[66]

It appears, however, that consideration for the family ties of the slaves prevented the breaking of families at times when the estate had to be divided. In one instance in dividing up an estate among the mother and her four children, the

[65] Henson, Josiah, *The Life of Josiah Henson*, pp. 3-4.
[66] Brown, John, *op. cit.*, pp. 6-8.

slaves "were placed in five lots, and these were so arranged as to keep the families together."[67] Since these lots were of unequal value the difference in the distribution was made up from other property. John Thompson, who writes in his autobiography that the first act of slavery recorded in his memory was the sale of his sister,[68] says in referring to the division of the estate upon the death of his mistress that his "father's family" went to the same master.

There is, however, plenty of testimony to show that the family bonds of the slaves were ignored when economic considerations were involved. The demand for slaves on the plantations of the lower South always increased their economic value. One slave says that he was sold for three hundred and ten dollars when ten years of age because of the rise in the price of cotton.[69] Harriet Tubman tells how the dilapidated state of things about the "Great House" was the occasion for the disappearance of slaves—either sold or hired out.[70] It was in the slave trade where men were dealing with slaves as commodities that the least sentiment was shown towards the family ties of the slaves. The *Alexandria Gazette* commenting on the slave trade in the National capital, said, "Here you may behold fathers and mothers leaving behind them the dearest objects of affection, and moving slowly along in the mute agony of despair; there, the young mother, sobbing over the infant whose innocent smile seems but to increase her misery. From some you will hear the burst of bitter lamentation, while from others the loud hysteric laugh breaks forth, denoting still deeper agony. Such is but a faint picture of the American slave-trade."[71]

In an autobiography of a slave we are furnished with a transaction in St. Louis where the marital relations between

[67] Pickard, Mrs. Kate E. R., *op. cit.*, p. 151.

[68] Thompson, John, *op. cit.*, pp. 13-14.

[69] Brown, John, *op. cit.*, p. 15.

[70] Tubman, Harriet, *op. cit.*, p. 17.

[71] Quoted in Brown, William Wells. *Narrative of William W. Brown*, pp. 113-114.

a slave, who lost his wife, was decided by the bidding of the speculators in slaves.

"A man and his wife, both slaves, were brought from the country to the city, for sale. They were taken to the room of Austin & Salvage, auctioneers. Several slave-speculators, who are always to be found at auctions where slaves are to be sold, were present. The man was first put up and sold to the highest bidder. The wife was next ordered to ascend the platform. I was present. She slowly obeyed the order. The auctioneer commenced, and soon several hundred dollars were bid. My eyes were intensely fixed on the face of the woman, whose cheeks were wet with tears. But a conversation between the slave and his new master attracted my attention. I drew near them to listen. The slave was begging his new master to purchase his wife. Said he, 'Master, if you will only buy Fanny, I know you will get the worth of your money. She is a good cook, a good washer, and her last mistress liked her very much. If you will only buy her now how happy I shall be.' The new master replied that he did not want her, but if she sold cheap he would purchase her. I watched the countenance of the man while the different persons were bidding on his wife. When his new master bid on his wife you could see the smile upon his countenance, and the tears stop; but as soon as another would bid, you could see the countenance change and the tears start afresh."[72]

The same writer gives us a description of the callous attitude of a slave trader who complained of a child's crying "and told the mother to stop the child's d—d noises, or he would." He continues:

"The woman tried to keep the child from crying but could not. We put up at night with an acquaintance of Mr. Walker, and in the morning, just as we were about to start, the child again commenced crying. Walker stepped up to her and told her to give the child to him. The mother tremblingly obeyed. He took the child by one arm, as you would a cat by the leg, walked into the house and said to the lady, 'Madam, I will make you a present of this little nigger; it keeps such a noise that I can't bear it.' 'Thank you, sir,' said the lady. The mother as soon as she saw that her child was to be left, ran up to Mr. Walker and falling upon her knees, begged him to let her have her child; she clung around his legs, and cried, 'Oh, my child! my child! master, do let me have it again! Oh, do, do, do! I will stop its crying if you will only let me have it again.' When I saw this woman crying for her child so piteously,

[72] Quoted in Brown, William Wells, *Narrative of William W. Brown*, pp. 110-112.

a shudder—a feeling akin to horror—shot through my frame. I have often since in imagination heard her crying for her child.—'"[73]

Even slave traders seemed to be affected at times by the parental affection shown children. It is recorded that a slave trader at one such transaction, "hung down his head and wiped the tears from his eyes; and to relieve himself from a scene so affecting, he said, 'Mary you can go some way with your mother, and return soon.' Turning to mother, he said, 'old woman, I will do the best I can for your daughter; I will sell her to a good master.' "[74]

J. W. C. Pennington's family which was broken up by the sale of his mother and children in Maryland was restored through the purchase of his father. "When I was about four years of age," said he, "my mother, an older brother and myself, were given to a son of my master, who had studied for the medical profession, but who had not married wealthy, and was about to settle as a wheat-planter in Washington County, on the western shore. This began the first of our family troubles that I knew anything about, as it occasioned a separation between my mother and the only two children she then had, and my father, did not continue long; my father being a valuable slave, my master was glad to purchase him.'"[75]

Among the restraining influences upon the selling of slaves without regard for their family ties should be mentioned the blood relationships to the masters. Loguen speaks of being the pet of his white father[76] who sought to save his mother from being sold[77] A mulatto who relates how his white grandfather objected to the breaking up of a family, tells how his grandfather's wishes were disregarded in the case of his own family when it came to dividing up the estate.

[73] Brown, William Wells, *op. cit.*, pp. 47-48.

[74] Thompson, John, *op. cit.*, p. 15.

[75] Pennington, James W. C. *The Fugitive Blacksmith*, pp. 1-2. See also Douglass, Frederick, *op. cit.* p. 19. Loguen, Jermain Wesley, *The Rev. J. W. Loguen, as a Slave and as a Freeman*. pp. 119-120.

[76] Loguen, Jermain Wesley, *op. cit.*, p. 23.

[77] *Ibid.*, p. 79.

"When I was about six years of age, the estate of Samuel Campbell, my grandfather, was sold at auction. His sons and daughters were all present at the sale, except Mrs. Banton. Among the articles and animals put upon the catalogue, and placed in the hands of the auctioneer, were a large number of slaves. When everything else had been disposed of, the question arose among the heirs, 'What shall be done with Letty (my mother) and her children?' John and William Campbell, came to mother, and told her they would divide her family among the heirs, but none of them should go out of the family. One of the daughters—to her everlasting honor be it spoken—remonstrated against any such proceeding. Judith, the wife of Joseph Logan, told her brothers and sisters, 'Letty is our own half sister, and you know it; father never intended they should be sold.' Her protest was disregarded, and the auctioneer was ordered to proceed. My mother, and her infant son, Cyrus, about one year old, were put up together and sold for $500. Sisters and brothers selling their own sister and her children.'"[78]

B. *The Family Group*

We have considered so far the influence of the masters in general on the integrity of the slave family. We now propose to inquire into the nature of the slave family as a group of persons having social relations.[79] It is our purpose to determine to what extent there was developed in slavery a family consciousness and a family organization in which the rôles of the different members of the family were defined and recognized. Moreover, we are especially interested in determining the extent of control, the building up of a family tradition, and how the personality of the Negro was formed in the matrix of the family. Of course, in such an investigation we must take into the account the relation to the masters who figured more or less in the world of the Negro slave.

Let us consider first the extent to which the slave was acquainted with his ancestry. From the biographies and autobiographies of slaves it appears that the knowledge which slaves had of their ancestry varied considerably. Bishop

[78] Clarke, Milton, *op. cit.*, p. 69. See also Brown, William Wells, *op. cit.*, pp. 62-64.

[79] Burgess, E. W., *The Family as a Unity of Interacting Personalities, The Family* Vol. VII., pp. 3-9.

Lane, who was born in 1834 in Madison County, Tennessee, says that he was "reared almost motherless and fatherless, having no parental care and guidance given" him.[80] Another slave who remained with his parents until nine years of age knew his parents and the names of his five brothers and sisters.[81] Booker Washington, who was born in slavery about 1858 or 1859, knew nothing of his ancestry except his mother and the reports that his father was a white man living on a nearby plantation.[82] Although Frederick Douglass possessed no knowledge of his father and knew his mother only through "little glimpses" of her at night when she came to see him, he was well acquainted with his mother's parents who had some standing in the neighborhood.[83] Josiah Henson, who was born, June 15, 1789, in Charles County, Maryland, says that his knowledge of his father was restricted to his appearance "one day with his head bloody and his back lacerated. He was in a state of great excitement, and though it was all a mystery to me at the age of three or four years, it was explained at a later period, and I understood that he had been suffering the cruel penalty of the Maryland law for beating a white man. His right ear had been cut off close to his head, and he had received a hundred lashes on his back. He had beaten the overseer for a brutal assault on my mother, and this was his punishment. Furious at such treatment, my father became a different man, and was so morose, disobedient, and intractable that Mr. N— determined to sell him. He accordingly parted with him, not long after, to his son, who lived in Alabama; and neither my mother nor I ever heard of him again."[84]

Concerning another slave, who was left an orphan, his biographer said, "Anderson cannot remember his father, but has heard him described as a person of light mulatto

[80] Lane, Bishop Isaac, *Autobiography*, p. 47.

[81] Jones, Thomas H., *Experience and Personal Narrative of Uncle Tom Jones*, p. 7.

[82] Washington, Booker T., *Up From Slavery*, p. 2.

[83] Douglass, Frederick, *op. cit.*, pp. 14-15.

[84] Henson, Josiah, *op. cit.*, pp. 1-2.

complexion who pursued the occupation of a servant on board the steam boats employed on the Mississippi. While Anderson was yet an infant, his father made his escape from slavery, and, it was believed, went to South America. When seven years of age, his mother, having given offence to her master, was sold to a negro trader for transportation to the slave market of New Orleans, and he was left an orphan.''[85]

In a large number of stories of the lives of slaves we find a knowledge not only of the mother but also the name of the father as well.[86] In some cases the slaves as set forth in the excerpt below were able to trace their descent to an ancestor who was brought to America from Africa.

''My name is John Brown. How I came to take it, I will explain in due time. When in slavery I was called Fed. Why I was so named, I cannot tell. I never knew myself to have any other name, nor always by that; for it is common for slaves to answer to any name as it suits the humour of the master. I do not know how old I am, but think I may be any age between thirty-five and forty. I fancy I must be about thirty-seven or eight as nearly as I can guess. I was raised on Betty Moore's estate, in Southampton County, Virginia, about three miles from Jerusalem Court House and the little Nottoway river. My mother belonged to Betty Moore. Her name was Nancy; but she was called Nanny. My father's name was Joe. He was owned by a planter named Benford, who lived at Northampton, in the same state. I believe my father and his family were bred on Benford's plantation. His father had been stolen from Africa. He was of the Eboe tribe. I remember seeing him once, when he came to visit my mother. He was very black. I never saw him but that one time, and though I was quite small, I have a distinct recollection of him. He and my mother were separated, in consequence of his master going further off, and then my mother was forced to take another husband. She had three children by my father; myself, and my brother and sister, twins. My brother's

[85] Anderson, John, *The Story of the Life of John Anderson*, the Fugitive Slave. London 1863, p. 9.

[86] See Lane, Lunsford, *The Narrative of Lunsford Lane*, p. 5; Davis, N., *The Narrative of the Life of Rev. Noah Davis, A Colored Man*, p. 59; Thompson, John, *op. cit.*, p. 13; Browne, W. W. *op. cit.*, p. 11; Floyd, Silas Xavier, *Life of Charles T. Walker, The Black Spurgeon*, pp. 19-20; Adams, John Quincy, *Narrative of the Life of John Quincy Adams, when in Slavery and now as a Freeman*, p. 5; Steward, Austin, *op. cit.*, p. 13. Frederick, Francis, *Autobiography of Rev. Francis Frederick of Va.*, p. 5; Pennington, James W. C., *op. cit.*, passim; Bruce, H. C., *op. cit.*, p. 16; Langston, John M., *op. cit.*, p. 13.

name was Silas, and my sister's Lucy. My mother's second husband's name was Lamb. He was the property of a neighboring planter and miller named Collier. By him she had three children; two boys, Curtis and Cain, and a girl between them called Irene.''[87]

Charles Ball says that "his grandfather was brought from Africa, and sold as a slave in Calvert County, in Maryland, about the year 1730.''[88] He continues:

"I never understood the name of the ship in which he was imported nor the name of the planter, who bought him on his arrival, but at the time I knew him he was a slave in a family called Mauel, who resided near Leonardtown. My father was a slave in a family named Hantz, living near the same place. My mother was the slave of a tobacco planter, an old man, who died, according to the best of my recollection, when I was about four years old, leaving his property in such a situation that it became necessary, as I suppose, to sell a part of it to pay his debts. Soon after his death, several of his slaves, and with others myself, were sold at publick vendue. My mother had several children, my brothers and sisters, and we were all sold on the same day to different purchasers. Our new masters took us away, and I never saw my mother, nor any of my brothers or sisters afterwards. This was, I presume, about the year 1785. I learned subsequently from my father, that my mother was sold to a Georgia trader, who soon after that carried her away from Maryland. Her other children were sold to slave-dealers from Carolina, and were also taken away, so that I was left alone in Calvert County, with my father, whose owner lived only a few miles from my new master's residence.''[89]

In the biographies and autobiographies of Negroes we find frequent references to white ancestry. Bishop L. H. Holsey writes, "I was born in Georgia, near Columbus, in 1842, and at that time was the slave of James Holsey, who was also my father. He was a gentleman of classical education, dignified in appearance and manner of life, and represented that old antebellum class of Southern aristocracy who did not know enough of manual labor to black their own shoes or saddle their own horses. Like many others of his day and time he never married, but mingled to some extent,

[87] Brown, John, *op. cit.*, pp. 1-2.

[88] Ball, Charles, *op. cit.*, p. 7; See also Holsey, L. H. *op. cit.*, p. 9; Asher, Jeremiah, *An Autobiography with Details of a Visit to England*, pp. 1-2.

[89] Ball, Charles, *op. cit.*, p. 7.

with those families of the African race that were his slaves—his personal property.''[90]

William Grimes, born in King George County, Virginia, in 1784, gives his white ancestry. ''My father, —,'' said he, ''was one of the most wealthy planters in Virginia. He had four sons; two by his wife, one, myself, by a slave of Doct. Steward, and another by his own servant maid. In all the Slave States, the children follow the condition of their mother; so that although in fact, the son of ——, I was in law a bastard and slave, and owned by Doct. Steward.''[91]

Another account gives white ancestry on both sides.

''My father was from 'beyond the flood'—from Scotland, and by trade a weaver. He had been married in his own country, and lost his wife, who left to him, as I have been told, two sons. He came to this country in time to be in the earliest scenes of the American Revolution. He was at the battle of Bunker Hill, and continued in the army to the close of the war. About the year 1800, or before, he came to Kentucky, and married Miss Letitia Campbell, then held as a slave by her dear and affectionate father. My father died, as near as I can recollect, when I was about ten or twelve years of age. He had received a wound in the war, which made him lame as long as he lived. I have often heard him tell of Scotland, sing the merry songs of his native land, and long to see its hills once more.'' . . . . ''I was born in March, as near as I can ascertain, in the year 1815, in Madison County, Kentucky, about seven miles from Richmond, upon the plantation of my grandfather, Samuel Campbell. He was considered a very respectable man, among his fellow robbers, the slave-holders. It did not render him less honorable in their eyes, that he took to his bed Mary, his slave, perhaps half white, by whom he had one daughter, Letitia Campbell. This was before his marriage.''[92]

The white ancestry of Negroes, including the well-known cases of Douglass and Washington, who played a prominent part in the history of the Negro, has frequently been emphasized by those who have made a study of Negro life.[93]

[90] Holsey, *op. cit.*, p. 9.

[91] Grimes, William, *Life of William Grimes*, p. 5.

[92] Clarke, Lewis Garrard., *op. cit.*, pp. 7-8.

[93] Reuter, E. B., ''The Superiority of the Mulatto,'' *American Journal of Sociology*. Vol. XXIII. pp. 83-106; *The Mulatto in the United States;* Herskovits, Melville J., *The American Negro.*

At the same time this fact has been regarded as a cause of demoralization of the sex life of the Negroes.[94] White ancestry is significant in the study of Negro family not only because it became the basis of social distinctions among the slaves and formed the group which was most often emancipated, but because the numerous instances of white fathers enhanced the dominating rôle of the Negro mother in the slave family. Douglass, whose father was reputed to be white, says succinctly: "Of my father I know nothing."[95] Washington did not even know the name of the white man who was said to have been his father.[96] In many cases, of course, the white father was not only known but his paternal interest in the family was such as to create fond attachment between his slave children and himself.

On the other hand, the relationship took another form. "My grandfather was a mulatto," said another Negro, "His father was his owner. I have often heard him say that the only person in the world he was ever afraid of was his father until he was grown. His father had a lot of property and owned a large number of slaves. One member of the family was congressman for a long time and owned nearly half of —— County, Georgia. My grandfather was unlike most colored people with white relations in that he didn't like them. He said his father was especially mean. My grandfather often told how his father would punish him. His father let him marry a mulatto on another plantation but whenever he was angry with my grandfather he would prevent him from going to see his wife and threaten him that he would make him marry a wife on the plantation."[97]

In the family relationships of the slaves, individuals developed personalities that became part of the family consciousness. Douglass says that his grandmother and grandfather were considered "old settlers" in the neighborhood

[94] DuBois, W. T. B., *op. cit.*

[95] Douglass. *op. cit.*, p. 15.

[96] Washington, Booker, T. *op. cit.*, p. 2.

[97] *Family History Manuscript*, Writer's Collection.

and that his "grandmother, especially, was held in high esteem, far higher than was the lot of most colored people in that region." "She was a good nurse, and a capable hand in making nets used for catching shad and herring, and was, withal, somewhat famous as a fisherwoman. I have known her to be in the water waist deep, for hours, seine-hauling. She was a gardner as well as fisherwoman, and remarkable for her success in keeping her seedling sweet potatoes through the months of winter, and easily got the reputation of being born to 'good luck.' In planting time Grandmother Betsey was sent for in all directions, simply to place the seedling potatoes in the hills or drills; for superstition had it that her touch was needed to make them grow. This reputation was full of advantage to her and her grandchildren, for a good crop, after her planting for the neighbors, brought her a share of the harvest."[102]

Other instances may be added. Northup writes of his father as "a man respected for his industry and integrity" though he was born a slave.[103] Moton's grandmother, a woman of remarkable physical and mental vigor, who carried the keys on her master's plantation, was supposed to possess the characteristics of her great grandfather, an exceptionally fine specimen of physical manhood directly from Africa.[104] In such instances we find the beginnings of a family tradition.

In some slave families we find a high degree of organization and a deep sense of family solidarity. When Pennington's father was given a whipping, says he, "This act created an open rupture with our family—each member felt the deep insult that had been inflicted upon our head; the spirit of the whole family was roused; we talked of it in our nightly gatherings, and showed it in our daily melancholy aspect."[105]

Moreover, in his family there was such solidarity that

[102] Douglass, *op. cit.* p. 14.

[103] Northup, Solomon, *Twelve Years a Slave*, p. 19.

[104] Moton, Robert Russa, *op. cit.* pp. 4-6.

[105] Pennington, J. W. C., *The Fugitive Blacksmith; or Events in the History of James W. C. Pennington*, p. 7.

the offence against the family affected his conception of himself which he found in his rôle as a skilled mechanic. "I had always aimed to be trustworthy," said he, "and feeling a high degree of mechanical pride, I had aimed to do my work with dispatch and skill; my blacksmith's pride and taste was one thing that had reconciled me so long to remain a slave. I sought to distinguish myself in the finer branches of the business by invention and finish; I frequently tried my hand at making guns and pistols, putting blades in pen knives, making fancy hammers, hatchets, sword-canes, &c., &c. Besides I used to assist my father at night in making straw hats and willow-baskets, by which means we supplied our family with little articles of food, clothing and luxury, which slaves in the mildest form of the system never get from the master; but after this, I found that my mechanic's pleasure and pride were gone. I thought of nothing but the family disgrace under which we were smarting, and how to get out of it."[106]

The organization and the solidarity of the slave family too, was based upon the economy of the slave household and the organization of the family group within the cabin. Although some writers have laid great stress upon the indiscriminate mixing of the sexes and kindred in the slave huts, there is much evidence to show that it was equally true that the family groups were often treated as units and rationed as such.[107] Moreover, it should not be forgotten that there was greater regard for the integrity of the slave family in Maryland, Virginia, and North Carolina, where slavery was disintegrating, than on the large plantations of the lower South. Because of the dependence of the children upon the mother it appears that the mother and smaller children were sold together. We find advertisements like the following:

> "A Wench, complete cook, washer and ironer, and her four children—a Boy 12, another 9, a Girl 5, that sews; and a Girl about 4 years old. Another family—a Wench, complete washer and ironer, and her Daughter, 14 years old, accustomed to the house."[108]

[106] Pennington, J. W. C., *The Fugitive Blacksmith; or Events in the History of James W. C. Pennington*, p. 8-9.

[107] *Florida Plantation Records*, pp. 513-514.

[108] *Doc. Hist. Amer. Ind. Soc.*, Vol. II, *Plantation and Frontier*, p. 58.

Although the father is absent in many transactions involving the slave family, in the following description we have a type of family organization in which the father's position is supreme.

"Lydia, the woman whom I have mentioned heretofore, was one of the women whose husbands procured little or nothing for the sustenance of their families, and I often gave her a quarter of a rackoon or a small opossum, for which she appeared very thankful. Her health was not good—she had a bad cough, and often told me, she was feverish and restless at night. It appeared clear to me that this woman's constitution was broken by hardships, and sufferings, and that she could not live long in her present mode of existence. Her husband, a native of a country far in the interior of Africa, said he had been a priest in his own nation and had never been taught to do any kind of labor being supported by the contributions of the publick; and he now maintained as far as he could, the same kind of lazy dignity, that he had enjoyed at home. He was compelled by the overseer to work, with the other hands, in the field, but as soon as he had come into his cabin, he took his seat and refused to give his wife the least assistance in doing anything. She was consequently obliged to do the little work, that it was necessary to perform in the cabin; and also to bear all the labour of weeding and cultivating the family patch or garden. The husband was a morose, sullen man, and said he formerly had ten wives in his own country, who all had to work for, and wait upon him; and he thought himself badly off here, in having but one woman to do anything for him. This man was very irritable, and often beat and otherwise maltreated his wife, on the slightest provocation, and the overseer refused to protect her, on the ground that he never interfered in the family quarrels of the black people. I pitied this woman greatly, but as it was not in my power to remove her from the presence and authority of her husband, I thought it prudent not to say or do anything to provoke him further against her."[109]

Another slave born in Tennessee in 1844 recalls in her autobiography as given recently to an investigator that her master, "had four families of slaves, i. e., Aunt Caroline's family, Uncle Tom's family, Uncle Dave's family and the family of which I was a member. None of these others were related by blood to us. My father had several brothers who lived on other places..... Each family had a cabin and there were but four cabins on the place."[110]

[109] Ball, Charles, *op. cit.*, pp. 203-205.

[110] "*Autobiography of an Ex-Slave,*" Manuscript, Author's Collection.

The designation of these families seems to point to the head or dominant figures in the family. Two of the families are designated according to the male head and one by a female head. The status of the male heads in these families is related to the fact that they were on a small plantation and had a status more nearly that of tenants rather than field hands on the large plantations. The high status of these slave families is also evidenced by the fact that each family had its own cabin. While the name of the fourth family is not given we learn further in the document that the mother was the dominant person in the family. The father was "made after the timid kind" and "would never fuss back" at his wife. She was constantly warning her husband:

"Bob, I don't want no sorry nigger around me. I can't tolerate you if you ain't got no backbone."[111]

Although many of the slave documents are not as explicit as the above in assigning to the mother the dominant rôle in the family group the frequency with which one meets the statement that the father escaped from slavery or was seen seldom or not at all is sufficient evidence of the mother's place. The father was the visitor often to the home presided over by the mother. One slave writes that he did not see his father sufficient to "become familiar with him as a father," and "A few years later he married another woman from another plantation. They never had a family, but the wife had a daughter by the master."[112] Another slave says concerning his paternity, "All that I know about it (male parentage) is, that my mother informed me that my father's name was James Bibb."[113]

It was the mother who ultimately provided the child's needs and at the cost often of great suffering defied the masters. "I remember well my mother often hid us all in the woods, to prevent master selling us," said a former

[111] "*Autobiography of an Ex-Slave,*" Manuscript, Author's Collection.

[112] Anderson, Robert, *op. cit.*, p. 5.

[113] Bibb, *op. cit.*, p. 14.

slave. "When we wanted water, she sought for it in any hole or puddle, formed by falling trees or otherwise: it was often full of tadpoles and insects: she strained it, and gave it round to each of us in the hollow of her hand. For food, she gathered berries in the woods, got potatoes, raw corn, &c. After a time the master would send word to her to come in, promising he would not sell us. But, at length, persons came, who agreed to give the prices he set on us. His wife, with much to be done, prevailed on him not to sell me; but he sold my brother, who was a little boy. My mother, frantic with grief, resisted their taking her child away; she was beaten and held down: she fainted, and when she came to herself, her boy was gone. She made much outcry, for which the master tied her up to a peach tree in the yard, and flogged her."[114]

"Sister asked me to speak to mother," said another. "I ran and called her; she hesitated a good deal, but the shrieks of her child at length overcame every fear, and she rushed into the presence of, and began to remonstrate with, this brute. He was only the more enraged. He turned around with all the vengeance of a fury, and knocked poor mother down, and injured her severely. When I saw the blood streaming from the shoulders of my sister, and my mother knocked down, I became completely frantic, and ran and caught an axe, and intended to cut him down at a blow. My mother had recovered her feet just in time to meet me at the door. She persuaded me not to go into the spinning room, where this whipping took place. Sister soon came out, covered with blood. Mother washed her wounds as well as she could. In six days after this, sister was chained to a gang of a hundred and sixty slaves, and sent down to New Orleans. Mother begged for her daughter; said she would get some one to buy her; a gentleman offered to do this, after she was sold to the slave driver."[115]

[114] Grandy, *op. cit.*, pp. 5-6.
[115] Clarke, Milton, *op. cit.*, p. 74.

In the independent efforts to maintain the slave households we find collective activities which centered about the family groups as an independent economy carried on in the neighborhood of the quarters on the plantations. "A large field," said Pickard, "was divided into as many little patches as there were field hands on the plantation; and every slave could here work nights and Sundays to cultivate his crop. Some raised cotton, others corn; and many planted their patches entirely to water-melons. If the overseer chanced to be "far'ard" with his work, and there was not much grass among the corn and cotton, they could sometimes have a half holiday on Saturday to work for themselves. But chiefly they depended on their Sundays. Early in the morning they were out with mules and ploughs, and till late at night, they toiled to raise their little crops. When the moon shone brightly, if they were getting "in the grass", they often remained at work all night."[116]

"On every plantation, with which I ever had any acquaintance," said Charles Ball, "the people are allowed to make patches, as they are called—that is, gardens, in some remote and unprofitable part of the estate, generally in the woods, in which they plant corn, potatoes, pumpkins, melon &c., for themselves. These patches they must cultivate on Sunday, or let them go uncultivated. I think, that on this estate, there were about thirty of these patches, cleared in the woods; and fenced—some with rails and others with brush—the property of the various families. The vegetables

[116] Pickard, Mrs. Kate E. R., *op. cit.*, p. 124. The following item appears in a plantation journal. "Saterday 5. Pleasant today. 2 to stock. 1 sick, Sariah, 1 Minding Children. As I am on planting and is Ready (y) to go to worken the crop on Monday, I have give the Negros today to plant ther little crops for themsevels. A. R. McCall, Overseer. Give the Negros one weeks lowan of Meat and surup." Florida Plantation-Chemonie. p. 471. Although we have in the following description of the fare of the slaves what was the usual practice on the larger plantation it appears that individual efforts on the part of families could improve the diet. "The slaves go to the field in the morning; they carry with them meal, wet with water, and at *noon* build a fire on the ground, and bake it in the ashes. After the labors of the day are over, they take their *second* meal of ashcake. (Philemon Bliss, Esq., Elyria, Ohio; resident in Florida, 1834-5)."—Goodell, *op. cit.*, p. 143.

that grew in these patches, were always consumed in the families of the owners; and the money that was earned by hiring out, was spent in various ways; sometimes for clothes —sometimes for better food than was allowed by the overseer, and sometimes for rum; but those who drank rum, had to do it by stealth. By the time the sun was up an hour, this morning, our quarter was nearly as quiet and clear of inhabitants, as it had been at the same period on the previous day.''[117]

The father however, does appear also in the rôle of the provider of the slave household. ''But Vina and her children, thanks to Peter's industry and self-denial had always decent clothing, and their cabin boasted many convenient articles of furniture, such as slaves seldom possess. They had also better food than most of their companions, for to the scant allowance of bacon and corn meal which was doled out to Vina on Sunday mornings, Peter often found means to add a little coffee and sugar, or a few pounds of flour.''[118]

When the slave family was broken up we have other members of the family assuming the rôle of the provider and maintaining the family unity.

''When my mother was sold, I had one brother, William, and three sisters, Silva, Agga, and Emma. My father and mother were both pure blooded African Negroes and there is not a drop of white blood in my veins, nor in those of my brother and sisters. When mother was taken from us, Emma was then a baby three years old. Silva, the oldest of the children, was fourteen, and she was a mother to the rest of us children. She took my mother's place in the kitchen as cook for my boss. Working under the direction of the boss' wife, or 'Missus' as we called her, my sister bought provisions, cooked the meals, knitted and served for the plantation. She also made my boss' clothes.''[119]

The family communism however is described more fully by another.

''These apples served us for a relish with our bread, both for breakfast and dinner, and when I returned to the quarter in the eve-

[117] Ball, Charles, *op. cit.*, p. 128.

[118] Pickard, Mrs. Kate E. R., *op. cit.*, pp. 141-142.

[119] Anderson, Robert, *op. cit.*, p. 5.

ning, Dinah (the name of the woman who was at the head of our family) produced at supper, a black jug, containing molasses, and gave me some of the molasses for my supper. I felt grateful to Dinah for this act of kindness, as I well knew that her children regarded molasses as the greatest of human luxuries, and that she was depriving them of their highest enjoyment, to afford me the means of making a goard full of molasses and water. I therefore proposed to her and her husband, whose name was Nero, that whilst I should remain a member of the family, I would contribute as much toward its support as Nero himself; or, at least, that I would bring all my earnings into the family stock, provided I might be treated as one of its members, and be allowed a portion of the proceeds of their patch or garden. This offer was very readily accepted, and from this time, we constituted one community, as long as I remained among the field hands on this plantation."[120]

"Before Christmas I had sold more than thirty dollars worth of my manufactures; but the merchant with whom I traded, charged such high prices for his goods, that I was poorly compensated for my Sunday toils and nightly labours; nevertheless, by these means I was able to keep our family supplied with molasses, and some other luxuries, and at the approach of winter I purchased three coarse blankets, to which Nero added as many, and we had all these made up into blanket-coats, for Dinah, ourselves and the children."[121]

C. *Care of Children*

The control of the children by parents on the plantation was not of long duration. On some plantations the care of the children was assigned to an old woman. When there was no woman to serve in this capacity the children were left alone.[122] Booker T. Washington says, "The early years of my life, which were spent in the little cabin, were not very different from those of thousands of other slaves. My mother, of course, had little time in which to give attention to the training of her children during the day. She snatched a few moments for our care in the early morning before her work began, and at night after the day's work was done. One of my earliest recollections is that of my mother cooking a chicken late at night, and awakening her children for the purpose of feeding them."[123]

[120] Ball, Charles, *op. cit.*, p. 148.

[121] Ball, Charles, *op. cit.*, pp. 149-150.

[122] Pickard, Mrs. Kate E. R., *op. cit.*, pp. 163-164.

[123] Washington, Booker T., *Up From Slavery*, p. 4.

If the cabins were far from the field, it seemed that the mothers took their children to the field to suckle.[124] Generally the mothers were permitted to return to the cabins to nurse their children during the day.[125] Bibb says that his wife's "business was to labor out in the field the greater part of her time, and there was no one to take care of poor little Frances, while her mother was toiling in the field. She was left at the house, to creep under the feet of an unmerciful old mistress, whom I have known to slap with her hand the face of little Frances, for crying after her mother, until her little face was left black and blue."[126]

Another slave's mother who was "one of the ordinary field laborers, often left the infant with the younger children all day; returning at night she frequently found him playing with lizards, scorpions, &c. Both he and they seemed to be pained when his excited mother took him in charge. Throughout all his life he was a lover and student of Nature in general."[127]

At a certain age the children were assigned to labor on the plantation. Steward says, "When eight years of age, I was taken to the 'great house' or the family mansion of my sister, to serve as an errand boy, where I had to stand in the presence of my master's family all the day, and a part of the night, ready to do anything which they commanded me to perform."[128]

Booker T. Washington recalls his initiation into service at the "big house". "When I had grown to sufficient size," said he, "I was required to go the 'big house' at mealtimes, to fan the flies from the table by means of a large set of paper fans operated by a pulley. Naturally much of the conversation of the white people turned upon the subject of freedom and the war, and I absorbed a good deal of it. I remember that at one time I saw two of my young mis-

[124] Clarke, Lewis, *op. cit.*, p.127.
[125] Ball, Charles, *op. cit.*, p. 116.
[126] Bibb, Henry, *op. cit.*, pp. 42-43.
[127] Browne, W. Wash., *op. cit.*, pp. 11-12.
[128] Steward, Austin, *op. cit.*, p. 20.

tresses and some lady visitors eating ginger cakes in the yard. At that time those cakes seemed to me to be absolutely the most tempting and desirable things that I had ever seen; and I then and there resolved that, if I ever got free, the height of my ambition would be reached if I could get to the point where I could secure and eat ginger cakes in the way that I saw those ladies doing.''[129]

A slave born in Maryland described his childhood saying, "Accordingly, when between five and six years of age, I was assigned to the duties of housework, to wait on my mistress and to run errands. When she went out driving I had to accompany her in the capacity of a page, to open the gates and to take down guard fences for her to drive through. That I might be found at night as well as by day my sleeping apartment was in her chamber on a truckbed, which was during the day time snugly concealed under her bedstead and drawn out at night for the reposing place of Isaac's weary body while he dreamed of days yet to come. I remained in this distinguished position until I was about fifteen years old, when a change in common with all slave life had to be made either for the better or for the worse.''[130]

In other cases the children were given work in the fields with the other slaves. Josiah Henson referred to his earliest employments as to carry buckets of water to the men at work, and to hold a horseplough, used for weeding between the rows of corn, and as he grew older and taller to take care of master's saddle-horse. "Then," said he, "a hoe was put into my hands, and I was soon required to do the day's work of a man; and it was not long before I could do it, at least as well as my associates in misery.''[131]

Often the slave child's early years were spent with the white children on the plantation. Lunsford Lane spent his early boyhood in playing with the other boys and girls, colored and white, in the yard, and occasionally doing such

[129] Washington, Booker T., *op. cit.*, pp. 9-10.
[130] Mason, Isaac, *Life of Isaac Mason as a Slave*, p. 11.
[131] Henson, Josiah, *op. cit.*, p. 6. See also Brown, John, *op. cit.*, p. 12.

little matters of labor as one of so young years could. "I knew no difference between myself and the white children," said he, "nor did they seem to know any in turn. Sometimes my master would come out and give a biscuit to me, and another to one of his own white boys; but I did not perceive the difference between us. I had no brothers or sisters, but there were other colored families living in the same kitchen, and the children playing in the same yard, with me and my mother."[132]

The older brothers and sisters were often charged with the care and discipline of the young children. "At this period," said a slave, "my principal occupation was to nurse my little brother whilst my mother worked in the field. Almost all slave children have to do the nursing, the big taking care of the small, who often came poorly off in consequence. I know this was my little brother's case. I used to lay him in the shade, under a tree, sometimes, and go to play, or curl myself up under a hedge, and take a sleep."[133]

Anderson, an ex-slave, writing recently of his discipline under his sister, said:

"It was part of sister's work to run the spinning wheel and the loom to prepare the cloth, and to cut and sew the cloth into clothes for the plantation and for the boss' family. My other sisters had to help with this work, but Silva, being the oldest, was forced to shoulder all the responsibility. 'Silva would sit up until late hours of the night working, and then would have to be up early in the morning to do the cooking for the family. Not only did she work, herself, but she made me work too. Although I was six years old when mother was taken away, she had taught me a number of things. My sister continued this education. She taught me how to patch my own clothes (such as I had), to piece quilts, to braid foot mats out of corn shucks, and to make horse collars with corn shucks.'[134] . . . . 'Part of my duty as a child, working under the direction of my sister was to carry the food from the kitchen to the table. As our fare was always meager, and I was always hungry, I would sometimes shake the biscuit plate or stump my toe and let a biscuit fall on the ground or floor. After it had fallen on the floor, of course, no one would eat it, and I would get it. I would carry them back to the kitchen and tell my sister what hap-

[132] Lane, Lunsford, *op. cit.*, pp. 5-6.

[133] Brown, John, *op. cit.*, pp. 3-4.

[134] Anderson, Robert, *op. cit.*, p. 6.

pened. I usually got my ears boxed, or got spanked, but I always got the biscuits.' "[135]

Douglass received his religious training under one of the slaves who had acquired status as a religious teacher. Douglass said, "I was early sent to Doctor Isaac Copper, with twenty or thirty other children, to learn the Lord's prayer. The old man was seated on a huge three-legged oaken stool, armed with several large hickory switches, and from the point where he sat, lame as he was, he could reach every boy in the room. After standing a while to learn what was expected of us, he commanded us to kneel down. This done, he told us to say everything he said. "Our Father"—this we repeated after him with promptness and uniformity—"who art in Heaven" was less promptly and uniformly repeated, and the old gentleman paused in the prayer to give us a short lecture, and to use his switches on our backs."[136]

Davis, says that both his mother and father "were pious members of the Baptist church." He adds that "because of their godly example, I formed a determination, before I had reached my 12th year, that if I was spared to become a man, I would try to be as good as my parents. My father could read a little, and make figures, but could scarcely write at all. His custom, on those Sabbaths when we remained at home, was to spend his time in instructing his children or the neighboring servants out of a New Testament, sent him from Fredericksburg by one of his older sons. I fancy I can see him now, sitting under his bush arbor, reading that precious book to many attentive hearers around him. Such was the esteem I had for my pious father, that I have kept that blessed book ever since his death, for his sake; and it was the first New Testament I read, after I felt the pardoning love of God in my soul."[136a]

It was in regard to the religious life that we find most of

[135] Anderson, Robert, *op. cit.*, p. 9.

[136] Douglass, Frederick, *op. cit.*, p. 31.

[136a] Davis, Noah., *op. cit.*, pp. 9-10.

tradition regarding the ancestors in the slave families. "My grandmother was an exceedingly pious woman," says Frederick.[136b] Holsey describes his mother as "an intensely religious woman.[136c] Another slave, whose autobiography is bombastic and full of episodes designed to show that the author possessed occult powers, says he was like his mother who "had a presentiment that she was not designed by Providence to rear me."[136d]

The religious instruction of the slaves was intended as a means of control and teaching morality. It affected considerably the strength of the marital bond between slaves as well as the relations with the children.

". . . . The benefits may be seen by the most superficial observer. They have so improved that they seem to be almost another set of beings. Their improvement has been in proportion to their instruction. They are orderly, well-behaved and seem to strive to fulfil the relative duties of life. They are faithful in their marriage relations. Immorality is discountenanced. They generally attend the house of God on the Sabbath."[137] . . . .

". . . . Parents love their children, and in most cases, the children obey their parents. The duties of husband and wife are faithfully performed. I have heard of few instances of want of chastity amongst them, and but one case, in several years, has occurred of an unmarried woman having a child, on a plantation comprising, perhaps, 10 or 15 such."[138]

The most important aspect of the religious instruction of the slaves was the fact that, as can be seen from the following report, there developed controls within their own society which restrained transgressors.

". . . . It has been remarked that Negroes are very fond of their children, though very indifferent to their other relations. The improvement I have been struck with, is in the character and

[136b] Frederick, Francis, *op. cit.*, p. 7.

[136c] Holsey, L. H., *op. cit.*, p. 9.

[136d] Hayden, W., *Narrative of William Hayden*, Cincinnati 1846. p. 17.

[137] Charleston, S. C., *Proceedings of the Meeting, May 13-15, 1845. On the Religious Instruction of the Negroes, Together with the Report of the Committee, and the address to the Public*, p. 38.

[138] *Ibid.*, p. 54.

manifestation of this affection shown in the care they take of their children, the provision they make for them, and their willingness to have them controlled and instructed. I perceive, also, improvement in their tempers and intercourse as husbands and wives. The last point in which improvement is to be looked for respects their morality. In this a change for the better is seen in the greater frequency of marriage, the greater permanency of the relation, and the rebuke which a growing sense of virtue administers to transgressors. If in the church, they are expelled—if out of it, they lose, in some degree, the standing which they held before among their fellow servants.''[139]

D. *Marriage*

Consistent with the slave code, the slave, as a rule, could not enter into a marriage contract.[140] "A slave cannot even contract matrimony, the association which takes place among slaves, and is called marriage, being properly designated by the word *contubernium,* a relation which has no sanctity, and to which no civil rights are attached.''[141]

An opinion[142] handed down by Judge Matthews in Louisiana in 1819 held that while slaves with the consent of their master may marry and had the *moral* power to agree to marry, such an act did not produce any civil effects. Moreover, it was also stated in the judicial opinion that the contractual and legal character of such unions were dormant during slavery but became actual from the moment of freedom.

Although slaves were not legally married the act of marrying is mentioned repeatedly in the slave narratives. One slave writes, "I was married to Lucilla Smith, the slave of Mrs. Moore. We called it and we considered it a true marriage, although we knew well that marriage was not permitted to the slaves, as a sacred right of the loving heart. Lucilla was seventeen years old when we were married. I

[139] Charleston, S. C., *Proceedings of the Meeting, op. cit.*, p. 57.

[140] Goodell, William, *American Slave Code,* p. 105.

[141] Stroud's *Sketch of the Slave Laws,* p. 61, quoted by Goodell, *op. cit.*, p. 106.

[142] Goodell, *op. cit.*, p. 107.

loved her with all my heart and she gave me a return for my affections, with which I was contented.'"[143]

Lunsford Lane tells of his marriage in slavery. "Perceiving that I was getting along so well, I began, slave as I was, to think about taking a wife. So I fixed my mind upon Miss Lucy Williams, a slave of Thomas Devereau, Esq., an eminent lawyer in the place; but failed in my undertaking. Then I thought I never would marry; but at the end of two or three years my resolution began to slide away, till finding, I could not keep it longer I set out once more in pursuit of a wife. So I fell in with her to whom I am now united, Miss Martha Curtis, and the bargain, between us was completed. I next went to her master, Mr. Boylan, and asked him, according to custom, if I might 'marry this woman?' His reply, was 'Yes, if you will behave yourself?' I told him I would. 'And make her behave herself?' To this I also assented; and then proceeded to ask the approbation of my master, which was granted. So in May 1828, I was bound as fast in wedlock as a slave can be.'"[144]

It has been shown above that the slave was compelled to obtain permission from his master in order to enter into marital relations with other slaves. The reality and influence of the family in the life of the slaves is evidenced by the fact that in the act of marrying the authority of the parents is also often recognized. One slave must win the consent of one Aunt Lucy who stands in relation of a guardian.[145]

Another slave thus describes the difficulties which stood in the way of his marriage.

> "My mother-in-law opposed me, because she wanted her daughter to marry a slave who belonged to a very rich man living nearby, and who was well known to be the son of his master. She thought no doubt that his master or father might chance to set him free before he died, which would enable him to do a better part by her

[143] Jones, Thomas, *op. cit.*, p. 24.
[144] Lane, Lunsford, *op. cit.*, pp. 10-11.
[145] Pickard, *op. cit.*, p. 112.

daughter than I could! And there was no prospect then of my ever being free. But his master has neither died nor yet set his son free, who is now about forty years of age, toiling under the lash, waiting and hoping that his master may die and will him to be free.''[146]

The influence of the family mores of the whites is seen in the case of a slave woman "who was spoken to by her friends about going with a man so soon after the death of her husband.''[147] Although there is evidence of the lack of ceremony in many cases when the slaves entered into the marital relation, this does not seem to have been the case generally with the house servant. In a letter of an overseer to the owner of a plantation in Florida, we find what approaches to a divorce process.

"You directed Me to send you all of the Names of the Negroes on Chemoonie in Famleys which I will doe in My Next Letter which will be on the 15th of this inst. Jim asked Me to let him have Martha for a wife so I have gave them Leaf to Marry. both of them is very smart and I think they are well Matched also Lafayette Renty asked for Leaf to Marry Lear I also gave them Leaf. Rose, Rentys other wife, ses that she dont want to Live with Renty on the account of his having so Many Children and they weare always quarling so I let them sepperate. Lear ses she is willing to Help Renty take care of his Children.''[148]

In the case of the house servants especially there was some sort of ceremony connected with the marriage.[149] One slave remembers attending a marriage in Richmond in the house of the master.[150] Another ex-slave telling the story of her life, says her

"Mother was sixteen when she was married and her father eighteen, and both belonged to the same people. She said her father used to come up from the quarters to see her mother. They married in the white folks dining-room, and everything was fixed up lovely for them.''[151]

[146] Bibb, Henry, *op. cit.*, pp. 39-40.
[147] Anderson, John, *op. cit.*, p. 45.
[148] *Florida Plantation Records, John Evans to George Noble Jones*, p. 63.
[149] Calhoun, A. W., *A Social History of the American Family*, Vol. II, p. 249.
[150] "Life History of an Ex-Slave," manuscript.
[151] "Autobiography of an Ex-slave, 84 years old," manuscript.

Francis Frederick gives more details in the following description of a slave wedding:

"The man's name was Jerry, that of his intended was Fanny. In the first place Jerry had to get the consent of Fanny's mistress and master, whether or not he could have Fanny. On presenting himself he was asked if he really loved Fanny, to which he replied, 'Yes, indeed marm.' 'How do you know you love her, Jerry?' asked the lady. 'Because since me lub Fanny me lub everything on de plantation, de hosses and all de tings, dey all seem better den anybody elses since me lub me Fanny.' After a few more words Mr. and Mrs. Ord consented to let Jerry have Fanny, 'But,' said Fanny's mistress, 'we don't whip Fanny, Jerry, and you must not whip her either.' Jerry, bowing low, said, 'No, missus, if Fanny nebber get a whipping until I gib her one she'll nebber git one.' 'Well, Jerry,' said Fanny's mistress, 'you must get January's Tom or Morton's Gilbert (these were two black men who were authorized to marry the slaves) to marry you two weeks from this night, and tell your master and mistress we will give Fanny a supper, and shall be very glad to see them, since we are going to have a great many white ladies and gentlemen here. Tom made his appearance at Fanny's mistress. He had on a pair of black trousers, a little too large in the leg, a coat fitting very well all to the tails, which were long; some one had given him a white waistcoat and a white cravat, which was only a little less stiff than its wearer; a pair of white gloves completed his attire. Fanny's mistress had dressed her in white muslin, she had on a pair of light shoes, her head decked with white and red artificials. Her bridesmaid was attired somewhat similar. The happy pair were seated in the middle of a large kitchen; Fanny had a very pleasant countenance, and was admired very much by her friends, but most of all by Jerry. After a while the parson was called for, at the sound of that dignified title, up jumped Tom. 'It is time,' said Fanny's mistress, 'for you to begin the ceremony.' 'Yes Marm,' said Tom. 'Now Tom could not read a word, but he had learned the marriage service by heart, from his master's grandson, and as luck or mischief would have it, the book was laid upside down. He now commenced with the book in his hand, inverted as he had picked it up, as though he were actually reading the service. The ladies were infinitely amused at this, but Tom thought the laughter was caused by the couple he was joining in the holy bonds of matrimony. After the happy pair were pronounced man and wife, Jerry was told to salute his bride, but being a field hand he was totally ignorant of the meaning of the word salute, but, on being told it meant kiss his wife, he seized her round the neck and made the room resound with the smacks he gave her."[152]

[152] Frederick, Francis, *op. cit.*, pp. 28-31.

A ceremony connected with the marriage of slaves which appears frequently in the documents is "jumping over the broom." The grandson of a slave whose family had acquired considerable stability which persisted into freedom describes his grandparents' marriage as follows:

"According to the customs of slavery Miles got the consent of Doctor Ridley to marry Charlotte. His acquiescence was equivalent to license and ceremony. True enough, such a union was not a creation of law, but it served its purpose in those days better than wedding-bells and statutory enactments do in most cases today. However, Miles believed in ceremony, so he and Charlotte 'jumped' several times back and forth over a broom repeating, 'I marry you.' "[153]

The marriage ceremony aside from the consent of the masters to form the union and the obligations imposed by the slave marriage, however, were apparently regarded as having nothing to do with the slave status and as amusing incidents of slave life. In the following ceremony which was used in a northern colony the contradiction between the slave status and the contractual nature of marriage was clearly recognized and the marriage of slaves was given a specified limited status.

"You, Bob, do now, in ye Presence of God and these Witnesses, Take Sally to be your wife;

"Promising, that so far as shall be consistent with ye Relation which you now sustain as a servant, you will Perform ye Part of an Husband towards her: And in particular, as you shall have ye Opportunity & Ability, you will take proper Care of her in Sickness and Health, in Prosperity & Adversity;

"And that you will be True & Faithful to her, and will Cleve to her only, so long as God, in his Providence, shall continue your and her abode in Such Place (or places) as that you can conveniently come together,—Do You thus Promise?

"You Sally, do now, in ye Presence of God, and these Witnesses, Take Bob to be your Husband;

"Promising, that so far as your present Relation as a Servant shall admit, you will perform the Part of a Wife towards him: and in particular,

"You promise that you will Love him; And that as you shall

[153] Fisher, Miles M., *The Master's Slave, Elijah John Fisher*, p. 5.

have the Opportunity & Ability, you will take a proper Care of him in Sickness and Health; in Prosperity and Adversity:

"And you will cleave to him only, so long as God, in his Providence, shall continue his & your Abode in such Place (or places) as that you can come together. . . . . Do you thus Promise? I then, agreeable to your Request, and with ye Consent of your Masters & Mistresses, do Declare that you have License given you to be conversant and familiar together as Husband and Wife, so long as God shall continue your Places of Abode as aforesaid; And so long as you Shall behave yourselves as it becometh servants to doe:

"For you must both of you bear in mind that you remain still, as really and truly as ever, your Master's Property, and therefore it will be justly expected, both by God and Man, that you behave and conduct yourselves as Obedient and faithful Servants towards your respective Masters & Mistresses for the Time being:

"And finally, I exhort and Charge you to beware lest you give place to the Devel, so as to take occasion from the license now given you, to be lifted up with Pride, and thereby fall under the Displeasure, not of Man only, but of God also; for it is written, that God resisteth the Proud but giveth Grace to the humble.

"I shall now conclude with Prayer for you, that you may become good Christians, and that you may be enabled to conduct as such; and in particular, that you have Grace to behave suitably towards each Other, as also dutifully towards your Masters & Mistresses, Not with Eye Service as Men pleasers, ye Servants of Christ doing ye Will of God from ye hearts."

"(Endorsed)

"Negro Marriage."[154]

E. *Stability of Family Ties*

In this account of the slave family it may appear that slavery in its most favorable aspects has been portrayed, although data which we have used have been drawn from all of the slave states. The object has not been to show up slavery either favorably or unfavorably but to discover those beginnings of the Negro family under the institution of slavery which gave stability to the family and built up a tradition that was handed down. All slaves could not boast

[154] Brown, William Wells, *The Rising Sun;* Chap. XXXI. Concerning the ceremony he writes: "This was prepared and used by the Rev. Samuel Phillips, of Andover, whose ministry there, beginning in 1710, and ending with his death, in 1771, was a prolonged and eminently distinguished service of more than half the eighteenth century."

with Josiah Henson that "when I was about twenty-two years of age, I married a very efficient, and, for a slave, a very well-taught girl belonging to a neighboring family, reputed to be pious and kind, whom I first met at the chapel I attended; and during nearly forty years that have since elapsed, I have had no reason to regret the connection, but many, to rejoice in it, and be grateful for it. She has borne me twelve children, eight of whom survive, and promise to be the comfort of my declining years."[155]

The marital tie to many slaves was no more than what is given expression to by the slave in the following incident.

"For what service particular did you want to buy?" inquired the trader of my friend. "A coachman." "There is one I think may suit you, Sir," said he; "George step out here." Forthwith a light-coloured Negro, with a fine figure and good face, bating an enormous pair of lips, advanced a step from the line, and looked with some degree of intelligence, though with an air of indifference upon his intended purchaser. "How old are you, George?" he inquired. "I don't recollect, Sir 'xactly—b'lieve I'm somewhere 'bout twenty-dree." "Where were you raised?" "On master R—'s farm in Wirginny." "Then you are a Virginian Negro?" "Yes, massa, me full blood Wirginny." Did you drive your master's carriage?" "Yes, massa I drove ole missus' carriage more dan four years." "Have you a wife?" "Yes, massa, I lef' young wife in Richmond, but I got a new wife here in de lot. I wish you buy her massa, if you gwing to buy me."[156]

But there is no question that the present Negro family took root under the institution of slavery. Bishop Gaines writing of his family says "the colored people generally held their marriage (if such unauthorized union may be called marriage) sacred, even while they were yet slaves. Many instances will be recalled by the older people of the South of the life-long fidelity and affection which existed between the slave and his concubine—the mother of his children. My own father and mother lived together for over sixty years. I am the fourteenth child of that union, and I can truthfully

[155] Henson, Josiah, *op. cit.*, pp. 19-20.

[156] *Slavery in America. With Notices of the Present State of Slavery and the Slave Trade Throughout the World*, p. 128.

affirm that no marriage, however made sacred by the sanction of law, was ever more congenial and beautiful. Thousands of like instances might be cited to the same effect.'"[157]

That there developed within the circle of the slave family enduring sentiments that held the members of the family together is attested by numerous cases. Between children whose parents were dead or had been sold the natural bond of sympathy and affection appears in their devotion and sacrifices for their relatives. A slave says concerning his early life,[158] "My brother Jeff was the only kin I had that I knew anything about while I was coming up." Jeff ran off to the Yankees when the war started. "Jeff was gone and I sometimes cried because he was my only brother and I felt lonesome all the time." Finally Jeff came back for his brother but after leading him within the Union lines lost him during an engagement.

Booker Washington recalls his older brother's generosity in regard to a shirt. "In connection with the flax shirt," said he, "my brother John, who is several years older than I, performed one of the most generous acts that I ever heard of one slave relative doing for another. On several occasions when I was being forced to wear a new flax shirt, he generally agreed to put it on in my stead and wear it for several days, till it was "broken in". Until I had grown to be quite a youth this single garment was all that I wore.'"[159]

Runaway slaves were tracked because of their known devotion to the members of their family. The following is quoted from Savannah, Georgia, July 8, 1837.

"Ran away from the subscriber, his man Joe. He visits the city occasionally, where he has been *harbored by his mother and sister.* I will give one hundred dollars for proof sufficient to *convict his harborers.*"

"R. P. T. Mongin"[161]

[157] Gaines, Wesley J., *The Negro and The White Man*, p. 144.

[158] *Fisk University Collection of Ex-slave Biographies.*

[159] Washington, Booker T., *op. cit.*, p. 12.

[161] Goodell, *op. cit.*, p. 119.

The regard of wives and husbands for each other is apparent according to the following advertisement which appeared in the Richmond *Enquirer*, Feb. 20, 1838.

"$50 REWARD.—Ran away from the subscriber his Negro man Pauladore, commonly called Paul. I understand GEN. R. Y. HAYNE* *has purchased his wife and children* from H. L. PINCKNEY, Esq., * * and has them now on his plantation at Goose-creek, where, no doubt, the fellow is frequently *lurking*."

"T. Davis."

"$10 REWARD for a negro woman named Sally, 40 years old. We have reason to believe said Negro to be lurking on the James River Canal, or the Green Spring neighborhood, where, we are informed, *her husband*, resides."

POLLY C. SHIELDS

"Mount Elba, Feb. 19, 1838."[162]

Ball who escaped from slavery in Georgia and found his way to his wife's cabin in Maryland,[163] gives a picture of a native African's devotion for his dead child

"Cruel as this man was to his wife, I could not but respect the sentiments which inspired his affection for his child; though it was the affection of a barbarian. He cut a lock of hair from his head, threw it upon the dead infant, and closed the grave with his own hands. He then told us the God of his country was looking at him, and was pleased with what he had done. Thus ended the funeral service."[164]

In the following account of the refuges who followed the Union armies we have in the midst of the disorder the devotion of a man and his wife to their children.

"The hardships they underwent to march with the army are fearful, and the children often gave out and were left by their mothers exhausted and dying by the roadside and in the fields. Some even put their children to death, they were such a drag upon them, till our soldiers, becoming furious at their barbarious cruelty, hung two women on the spot. In contrast to such selfishness, she told us of one woman who had twelve small children—she carried one and her husband another and for fear she should lose the others she tied them all together by the hands and brought them all off safely, a march of hundreds of miles. The men have all been put

[162] Goodell, *op. cit.*, p. 119.

[163] Ball, *op. cit.*, p. 361.

[164] *Ibid.*, p. 205.

to work in the quartermaster's department or have gone into the army, and the families are being distributed where they can find places for them.''[165]

In the literature on the Negro family during slavery there is constant reference to the regular visits of the father or husband to his family when they resided on different plantations. Probably one evidence of the strength of the family was the fact that the threat to sell the children, or the mother or the father away from the family was always a potent form of control. One slave recalled that his mistress wanted him to get married in order that he might become reconciled to slavery.[166] The strength of the affectional bond between the father and his wife and children is clearly illustrated in the case of Ball's father who lost his family.

> ''My father never recovered from the effects of the shock, which this sudden and overwhelming ruin of his family gave him. He had formerly been of a gay social temper, and when he came to see us on Saturday night, he always brought us some little present such as the means of a poor slave would allow—apples, melons, sweet potatoes, or, if he could procure nothing else, a little parched corn, which tasted better in our cabin, because he had brought it. He spent the greater part of the time, which his master permitted him to pass with us, in relating such stories as he had learned from his companions, or in singing the rude songs common amongst the slaves of Maryland and Virginia. After this time, I never heard him laugh heartily, or sing a song. He became gloomy and morose in his temper, to all but me; and spent nearly all his leisure time with my grandfather, who claimed kindred with some royal family in Africa, and had been a great warrior in his native country.''[167]

The character of the slave family was affected to a large extent by the different aspects of the slave system. Where the slave trade was in full force there was no regard for the personality of the slave and no one has appeared a more hated figure than the slave trader. Negroes became mere utilities and all the ties that bind men to other human beings were ignored. Cases of the treatment of the family re-

[165] Pearson, Elizabeth, *War Letters From Port Royal*, pp. 293-294.

[166] Brown, William Wells, *op. cit.*, pp. 87-88.

[167] Ball, Charles, *op. cit.*, p. 9.

lations of the slaves where business transactions were involved have been given.[168] Occasionally an account indicates the little regard that was shown for slaves who were rooted up and placed on the market. "When I joined the coffle," said Charles Ball, "there was in it a Negro woman named Critty, who has belonged to one Hugh Benford. She was married, in the way that slaves are, but as she had no children, she was compelled to take a second husband. Still she did not have an offspring. This displeased her master, who sold her to Finney. Her anguish was intense, and within about four days from the time I saw her first, she died of grief. It happened in the night, whilst we were encamped in the woods."[169]

The same disregard for the family relations of the slaves, which has been noted in the case of the large plantation,[170] is found on the frontier of the plantation system. Lyell observed during his second visit to the United States that "the condition of the Negroes is least enviable in such out-of-the-way and half-civilized districts, where there are many adventurers and uneducated settlers, who have little control over their passions, and who, when they oppress their slaves, are not checked by public opinion as in more advanced communities."[171]

Labor demands on the larger plantations which showed no consideration for the personalities of the slaves often created an inequality between numbers of the two sexes that led to complete demoralization. Said one observer, "Those who cannot obtain women (for there is a great disproportion between the numbers of the two sexes) traverse the woods in search of adventures, and often encounter those of an un-

[168] See pages 224-227.

[169] Brown, John, *op. cit.*, p. 17.

[170] Ball, *op. cit.*, p. 107. "In these thirty-eight cabins, were lodged two hundred and fifty people, of all ages, sexes, and sizes. Ten or twelve were generally employed in the garden and about the house."

[171] Lyell, Charles, *Second Visit to the United States* Vol. II, 181 describing conditions in Missouri. In *Documentary History of American Industrial Society*, Vol. II., p. 45.

pleasant nature. They frequently meet a patrole of the whites, who tie them up and flog them, and then send them home.''[172]

In the case of those slaves on the plantation where a patriarchial relationship had grown up we often find a stable family life that compares favorably with the family life in peasant communities.[173]

"It was a rare thing, indeed, for slave girls to reach majority before being married or becoming mothers. Be it said to the credit of Sarah O. Hilleary that she taught those girls the value of a good name, and personally watched over them so carefully that it was known far and near. She allowed them to be married in her dining-room instead of in the cabin, and, with ceremony. She always had to see and pass upon the man who was to marry one of her maids. She did all she could to impress them with the importance of being clean, honest, truthful, industrious, and religious."

"So loving, kind, faithful and obedient was Emily that her mother really overtaxed her with the care of her younger brothers and sisters, whenever she was not waiting upon 'Miss Sallie.' So happy and content was Emily that she did not marry until she was 26 years old."

The marriage of the couple who founded the Plummer family is described in the book in which we have the record of the family.

"While visiting her Aunt Lucy at Riverdale, in 1839, Emily said to her Aunt, while passing one of the servants, 'I wonder what is that brown-skin, colored gentleman looking at me so hard for?' Little did she then dream that he was to be her husband. In due time, Adam was permitted to visit Emily at 'Three Sisters,'' having passed Miss Sallie's inspection. However, later, when she found Adam had taught Wm. Arnold how to read and write, she said that had she known Adam was a "lettered" man she would never have let him come on her place. At any rate fate so arranged that on Sunday, May 30, 1841, Adam and Emily, with Miss Fannie Carrick as bridesmaid, journeyed to Washington, D.C., to the pastor of the New York Avenue and Fourteenth Street Presbyterian Church, the Reverend Richardson, to be married. They were informed that a license must first be bought. So Adam went to Wm. B. Brant, and obtained the same. Returned to the minis-

[172] *Travels in Louisiana and the Floridas, in the year 1802*, by *Berquin Duvallon*. pp. 79-94. in the *Journal of Negro History*, Vol. II, p. 172.

[173] Plummer, Nellie Arnold. *Out of the Depths or The Triumph of the Cross.*

ter and they were married. He took her home to "Three Sisters." He returned to Riverdale. For the next ten years they lived thus, being permitted to visit her every Saturday evening, when he could stay until time for work early Monday morning. He walked all that distance, carrying heavy loads—almost too heavy for a horse. And yet they thought they were happy!"[174]

CONCLUSION

The examination of printed documents as well as those collected from ex-slaves gives evidence of a wide range of differences in the status of the Negro family under the institution of slavery. These differences are related to the character of slavery as it developed as an industrial and social system. Where slavery assumed a patriarchal character the favored position of the house servants, many of whom were mulattoes, facilitated the process by which the family mores of the whites were taken over. Thus close association of master class and the slaves often entailed such moral instruction and supervision of the behavior of the slave children that they early acquired high standards of conduct which seemed natural to them. Sexual relations between the white masters and the slave women did not mean simply a demoralization of African sex mores but tended to produce a class of mulattoes, who acquired a conception of themselves that raised them above the black field hands. In many cases these mulattoes either through emancipation or the purchase of their freedom became a part of the free class where an institutional form of the Negro family first took root.

On the other hand, the sexual relations between the masters and the slave women tended to give the mother in the slave family even a more dominant rôle than was the case ordinarily where the paternity of the father and his place in the family circle received recognition. Even where the Negro father was recognized and played a conspicuous part with the family he often had the status of a mere visitor when he was on another plantation. When he was on the

[174] Plummer, *op. cit.*, pp. 28-29.

same plantation his authority was always limited, and in a crisis the mother stood out as the more secure symbol of parental authority and affection.

Of fundamental importance for the stabilization of the slave family and the development within the family circle of enduring sentiments was the social life of the slaves themselves. Within their relatively autonomous social world there were distinctions of status and social functions. They had their own religious and moral leaders and in some communities a public opinion was powerful enough to restrain unapproved conduct.

Where the plantation system was breaking down and Negro artisans achieved a semi-free status and acquired property the slave family tended to become stabilized. In such cases the slave family was held together by more than the affectional bonds that developed naturally among its members through the association in the same household and the affection of parents for their offspring. However, even under the most favorable conditions of slavery the exigencies of the slave system made the family insecure in spite of the internal character of the family. In the case of field hands who were cut off from contacts with the whites and those slaves who were carried along as mere utilities in the advance of the plantation system family relations became completely demoralized.

E. FRANKLIN FRAZIER

RECENT FINDINGS IN THE STUDY OF SLAVE DEMOGRAPHY AND FAMILY STRUCTURE

Robert W. Fogel and Stanley L. Engerman*

*Recent works on the demographic patterns of slave and white populations in the U.S. and the slave population of the British West Indies are examined in order to summarize the principal new findings and to highlight several still unresolved issues. Studies presenting new data on fertility, mortality, and family structure are analyzed to determine the relative contributions of different factors to the differing demographic performance of U.S. slave and British West Indian slaves, and to point to certain similarities in patterns between U.S. slaves and southern whites.

Issues relating to the demographic performance and family patterns of New World slaves have long formed a central part of the examination of slave societies. Often discussed by contemporaries, and used as aspects both of the antislavery critique and the proslavery defense, many of the earlier contentions have been carried forward into the historical literature. In the past decade, however, there has been a significant shift in the study of these issues, due mainly to the more systematic utilization of primary data sources. For differing reasons, scholars in a wide variety of areas have mined these data sources to provide new information and to define behavioral patterns with increased detail and accuracy. On many questions we now have a clearer view of what the demographic patterns and family structures were and know better what needs to be explained.

This paper attempts to summarize the principal new findings, as well as to highlight several still unresolved issues. We concentrate on work relating to the slave populations of mainland North America and the British West Indies, but similar work has been undertaken for other New World slave societies.

Population Trends

1. The basic demographic comparison relating to New World slavery was forcibly presented in Philip Curtin's *The Atlantic Slave Trade* (1969). Although contemporaries had been aware of the wide differences in the growth rates of the U.S. and other slave populations, it was

Curtin's quantitative estimates that highlighted the magnitude of these differences and brought the question to the attention of modern scholars. While some of his estimates have been modified, his basic comparison remains intact. The United States received about 6 percent of all Africans arriving in the New World during the period of the slave trade (1500-1870), but had about one-quarter of the New World black population in 1825, and about 31 percent in 1950. The British West Indies received 17 percent of all slave imports, but had only about 10 percent of the black population in 1825, and about 5 percent in 1950. The other Caribbean islands had patterns similar to the British, with a large excess of the accumulated total of slave imports over the black population living at the end of the slave era.[1]

These numbers imply that the rate of natural increase of slaves was much more rapid in the United States than elsewhere. This, as figure 1 shows, was the case. It is clear that the United States slave population throughout the eighteenth and nineteenth centuries was growing at rates in excess of not only slaves in Jamaica but of the population in Europe as well, a rate of increase similar to that of United States whites. There was a marked acceleration in the rate of natural increase during the first half of the eighteenth century (indeed, the first decade or two of the century may have been a period of natural decrease). The rate of natural increase probably continued to accelerate into the early nineteenth century after which it began to decelerate, not only for blacks but also for whites as well. Jamaican rates, which are based on estimates prepared by Michael Craton (1971, 1975), indicate that while there was a fairly steady reduction in the rate of natural decrease in the eighteenth and early nineteenth centuries, natural decrease persisted in Jamaica down to the end of the slave era. There were some differences among the West Indian islands. Barbados, for example, achieved a positive rate of natural increase between 1800 and the abolition of British slavery in 1834 (Higman, 1976b; Roberts, 1977).

2. It is difficult to disentangle the relative contributions of fertility and mortality to the gap between the U.S. and West Indian rates of natural increase because of the direct and indirect impacts of the slave trade. As many as one-third of the imported slaves died during their first few years in the New World (a process euphemistically referred to as "seasoning"), and the slave trade left a significant imprint on the distribution of ages (most slaves imported were in the mid or late teens and twenties) and the sex ratio (over three-fifths were male) (see Craton, 1974: 194-97; Klein, 1978). Since imported slaves were always more numerous in the West Indies than in the United States, unstandardized comparisons of vital rates are apt to be somewhat misleading.

With this caveat in mind, it is useful to compare the crude birth and death rates of slaves in the U.S. and Jamaica at roughly the second quarter of the nineteenth century, after the closing of the international slave trade. For the United States in about 1830, prevailing estimates indicate a crude birth rate of about 55 per thousand and a crude death rate of about 30 per thousand. For Jamaica, based upon adjustments to estimates made by Barry Higman (1976a), the crude birth rate during the period 1817-1834 was about 33 and the crude death rate for the same period was about 36 (Fogel, 1977b; Engerman, 1976). Thus the largest part of the explanation for the difference between the United States and Jamaican rates of natural increase c. 1830 was the difference in fertility, not mortality. While there was a higher mortality rate for slaves in the West Indies than in the United States South, the differential in death rates was just one-quarter as large as the differential in birth rates. Moreover, for the white (and possibly the black) population the mortality differential between the United States North and the United States South was quite marked (see, e.g., Walsh and Menard, 1974; D. B. Smith, 1978; Dunn, 1972: 300-34). And, while United States slave fertility rates were exceptionally high by any standard, the crude birth rates of West Indian slaves (frequently called low by contemporaries) were at levels similar to those prevailing in Europe at the time. The similarity in Jamaican and European crude birth rates covers over significant differences in the underlying demographic determinants. We shall return to this question in the next section. Here we wish to emphasize that what was unusual was not that the crude birth rates of West Indian slaves were so low, but that those of United States slaves were so high.

It is difficult to extrapolate the Jamaican estimates back to the eighteenth century. Craton's data indicate that death rates were higher in the eighteenth than in the nineteenth century, and explain more of the United States-Jamaican differences in rates of natural increase. But even if the Jamaican crude death rate was as high as 50 per thousand in the mid-eighteenth century, it is probable that fertility was still the major factor in the differential between the two rates of natural increase. The United States had achieved a high fertility regimen before 1750, and it is probably that the Jamaican fertility rates were at least as low in 1750 as in 1830. Indeed, given the relative differences in fertility between Creoles and Africans, pointed to by Higman (1973) for the early nineteenth century, the increased proportion of creoles among Jamaican slave women, by itself, would have led to a rise in the Jamaican crude birth rates during the eighteenth century. The increase of the proportion of females aged 15-45 to the total Jamaican slave population had a similar effect on the crude birth rate.

Fertility Patterns

3. Recent data for Chesapeake slaves, presented by Russell Menard (1974) and by Allan Kulikoff (1977), indicate that measured fertility increased over the first two-thirds of the eighteenth century.[2] Both point to an early period of relatively low birth rates (and of natural decrease) during the late seventeenth and early eighteenth centuries, but beginning about the second quarter of the eighteenth century fertility became high enough to sustain natural increase (cf. Craven, 1971). Factors that changed rates of natural increase from negative to positive included the rise in the ratio of native-born to African females in the childbearing ages, an early age at first birth (estimated by Kulikoff at between 18 and 19), and a relatively short birth interval. This combination of factors was different from the combinations which prevailed in both Europe and Africa. The age at first birth was considerably lower than in England at this time (probably by about 8 years), while the child-spacing interval was apparently shorter than it had been in Africa (perhaps by as much as a year).[3] Thus the notion that there might have been a distinct Afro-American demographic pattern cannot be dismissed. But it is possible that a similar demographic pattern existed among white southerners at this time, so that what is being observed is a regional phenomenon rather than a uniquely black phenomenon.

Data bearing on the fertility of U.S. slaves for the period from 1770 to 1820 are not readily available at present. After 1820 the census permits detailed estimates of child-women ratios, and table 1 presents the estimates of Richard Steckel (1977) for the years 1820-1860. While the 1820 level is roughly comparable with Kulikoff's eighteenth century estimates, there was a decline in slave fertility during the last three decades of the antebellum era (see figure 2). This decline occurred in both the older areas of the Upper South and more newly-settled areas of the Lower South. The child-women ratios for slaves, unlike those of whites, were higher in the Upper South than in the Lower South, but overall, down to 1840, southern white fertility exceeded that of slaves, and there were only minor differences in the levels of the child-women ratios of the two populations in 1850 and 1860.[4] The fertility decline in the antebellum period for blacks started somewhat later than that of whites and was not as rapid as for whites, but a marked acceleration in the black fertility decline occurred after 1880 (see, among others, Okun, 1958; Farley, 1970; Engerman, 1977).

4. Less is known about the British West Indian fertility pattern. As already noted, the data presented by Craton and by Higman suggest some fertility increase in the eighteenth and early nineteenth century.

with a change in the relative importance of creole females in the population. Fertility rates among the West Indian islands did vary in the nineteenth century. The crude birth rate in Barbados, for example, was over 40 in the 1820's while in the newer areas of Trinidad and British Guiana, which were receiving imports from the older West Indian colonies, the crude birth rate was at most, 30 (see Higman, 1976b). The first Jamaican population censuses point to a crude birth rate between 1844 and 1861 of about 40 (Roberts, 1957:43, 269). This might indicate that there was a small upward shift in the fertility schedule after emancipation, but the changing composition of the population with respect to age and sex makes such a conclusion hazardous. The fertility rates of Creoles in Jamaica were higher than those of the African-forn, but this gap was probably not as great as the creole-African gap in the United States. This is a critical point, since it has much to do with the persistence of a negative rate of natural increase in Jamaica for more than a century after the United States rate became positive. Thus the basic difference in fertility between the United States and Jamaica relected the differing fertility rates of United States and Jamaican Creoles, and not just differences in the relative importance of Creole and African-born women in the two societies.

5. No simple economic explanation cast in terms of slave prices, price-hire ratios, and the availability of slave imports can explain the secular trends of fertility in either the United States or the West Indies. Among contemporaries, the fertility patterns were frequently explained as the consequence of decisions dictated by masters, who were presumed to have manipulated slave fertility in response to changes in import availability and price patterns. Such arguments cannot account for the United States-West Indian fertility differences since it is clear that these differences existed both while the international slave trade was open and after it closed. High fertility was achieved by United States slaves nearly a century before the slave trade closed. Moreover, the fertility rate of U.S. slaves declined, instead of rising, during the last three decades of the antebellum era, including the decade and a half after 1845 when slave prices rose quite rapidly. Indeed, over the 40 years from 1820 to 1860 the movement in the child-women ratios of slaves is not correlated with either the prices or the price-hire ratios of slaves (see Fogel, 1977b).

This does not mean that economic factors were not at work, but rather that if they were at work their route of impact was complex. It also suggests that other factors, usually thought of as cultural and moral rather than economic, were also highly influential. In general, it is likely that arguments which presume either that the master had complete power over slave sexual behavior and family mores or that he had none are misleading simplifications.

6. The close correspondence between slave and southern white fertility trends and patterns in the United States is noteworthy. Both slaves and southern whites, in the Chesapeake, experienced an initial natural decrease, reversed after approximately two or three generations. For whites after c. 1700, and for slaves after c. 1720, rates of natural increase were positive and accelerating, and quickly achieved levels unique by world standards. The explanation for the temporal gap between the onset of white and black positive rates of natural increase has not yet been investigated. One likely factor is that slave imports did not become substantial until several decades after the onset of substantial white immigration into the Chesapeake region.

More detailed comparisons are possible for years between 1820 and 1860, based upon measures derived by Steckel (1977) from census data. The slave child-women ratio was about 90 percent that of southern whites in 1820, but by 1850 the two ratios were roughly equal. The primary reason for this relative change was the sharper decline in the ratio among whites than slaves after 1840, at about 0.9 percent per annum from 1840 to 1860 for whites as against 0.3 percent for slaves. White fertility in the North Central states was comparable to that in the South. In other words, the mid-nineteenth century slave fertility rate was not markedly higher than the rates of whites, except for the rates in the older New England and Middle Atlantic states. Nor was this gap of long standing. It arose because of the rapid decline in the New England and the Middle Atlantic fertility rates from levels that had prevailed into the first quarter of the nineteenth century.

It is at the interregional level of analysis that differences in the child-women ratios of southern whites and slaves are most marked. Table 1 shows that for slaves, child-women ratios in the West were in the range of 2 to 7 percent lower than in the East. But for whites, the western ratios are 14 to 25 percent higher. What these data suggest is not that the "frontier" effect was in the opposite direction for slaves than for whites but that, for reasons still to be identified, the "frontier" effect on fertility was absent among slaves. The small East-West differences in the slave child-women ratios do not, as has often been assumed, necessarily imply differences in the slave fertility schedules of the two regions but are probably due in whole or in part to differences in the mortality schedules. Interregional differences of 2.5 to 5 years in life expectation would result in a 3 to 6 percent spread in the child-women ratios, even if both regions had identical fertility schedules.[5] Currently available information on mortality is too fragmentary to permit the measurement of the interregional difference in life expectation for either slaves or whites in the South, but those data which are available suggest that the intra-South mortality rate differences are higher in the West and could be of the indicated order of magnitude. Slaves in the East and the West thus appear to have had about the same gross reproduction rates. This finding suggests that certain features of the slave system either insulated slaves from, or generated influences counter to, those factors that caused upward shifts in the fertility schedules of whites residing in the less densely settled regions of the nation (see, e.g., Yasuba, 1962; Easterlin, 1976; Leet, 1976).[6]

7. One of the more fruitful debates relating to the determinants of U.S. slave fertility rates concerns the estimation of the age at which childbearing began and the gap between this age and the age of menarche. Touched off by the presentation in *Time on the Cross*, the early phases of the debate posed two key questions: how to measure properly the age of slave mothers at the birth of their first child from imperfect data in a population growing as rapidly as that of United States slaves; and how to determine the "age of fecundity."[7] A recent paper by Trussell and Steckel (1978) has dealt with both of these questions. Using a statistic proposed by Hajnal, the singulate mean, they place the mean age of the first-birth schedule of female slaves in the mid-nineteenth century at 20.6 to 21.0 years. This is roughly 5 to 6 years earlier than the age at first birth in Europe (cf. D. S. Smith, 1977) and about two years earlier than that for southern whites. Kulikoff (1977), computing the same statistic for slaves on two Chesapeake plantations in the 1770's, found that the mean age of the first-birth schedule was 19.1, which suggests that the first-birth schedule may have shifted toward higher ages between the American Revolution and the Civil War.[8]

Trussell and Steckel also utilized a hitherto neglected body of data to estimate the age of menarche. This is the height-by-age-and-sex data contained in the manifests of vessels involved in the coastwise shipping of slaves after 1808. From these data they computed annual growth velocities and found that during the late antebellum era the peak of the adolescent growth spurt came at age 13, which, as they point out, implies that menarche came between ages 14 and 15. After allowing for the "waiting time until the first birth," a gap of several years remained between the "age of fecundity" and the age of first childbearing.

The height-by-age-and-sex data of the type utilized by Trussell and Steckel have a number of important uses in addition to the determination of the age of menarche. Several environmental and genetic factors affect rates of physical maturation and achieved heights, and such physiological data have implications for nutritional and other health-related issues. Various bodies of data on height and weight have been examined or are now being processed (see Fogel, et al., 1978). Figure 3 presents a comparison of female heights by age, from 8 to 18, for four different populations. The heights of Trinidad slaves born in the Caribbean have been calculated from slave registration reports for the early nineteenth century; those of American and British females pertain to the 1870s and are from samples published by Bowditch (1877) and by the Anthropometric Committee of the British Association for the Advancement of Science (1884).[9]

Perhaps the most outstanding feature of figure 3 is that Trinidad creoles were substantially shorter than the other three populations at every age. On the other hand, the U.S. slave, Massachusetts, and British populations have quite similar height-by-age profiles. Another important feature is that the Trinidad creole women continued to grow into their twenties while the women in the other three populations achieved their adult height by age 18. The mean terminal heights of the four populations (in inches) were as follows: Trinidad creoles, 61.5; U.S. slaves, 62.7; girls of American parentage in Massachusetts, 62.0; and Britain, 62.8.[10] The U.S. slave figure is not significantly different from that of the British but it is significantly greater (at the 0.001 level) than both the Massachusetts average and the Trinidad creole average. The mean terminal height of African-born slaves in Trinidad was just 60.5 inches or 1.0 inches shorter than the Trinidad creoles, who in turn were 1.2 inches shorter than the U.S. slaves.[11] Both differences are statistically significant.

Several conjectures are suggested by these data. One is that much of the difference between the height of U.S. slaves and African-born slaves was closed with the first generation of slaves born in North America. Another is that the Trinidad diet was probably superior to the African diet but not as good as the U.S. slave diet. That Trinidad creoles attained close to the same terminal height as the three relatively tall populations shown in figure 3, but took several years longer to achieve their full growth, suggests that Trinidad slaves experienced moderate but not severe relative malnutrition. That the average adult heights of U.S. slaves c. 1840 was equal to, or in excess of, the average attained by Boston and British females a full generation later suggests that U.S. slaves had experienced a diet that was nutritionally, if not gastronomically, superior to that available to the urban working class of these regions during the mid-nineteenth century.[12] The conjectural nature of these comments should be reemphasized, since we are at quite an early stage in the analysis of the data bearing on the points at issue.

8. Recent work has both indicated the patterns to be explained and methods for determining the relative importance of particular factors in accounting for differences in fertility among United States slaves and West Indian slaves (see, for example, Steckel, 1977; Dunn, 1977; Craton, 1978b; Fogel, 1977b; Klein and Engerman, 1978). The explanation of these differences is proceeding both at the socio-economic and at the purely demographic level. At the demographic level the research has been aimed at factoring the fertility differentials among four variables: the ages of mothers at their first and last births, the proportion of women ever bearing a child, and the length of the interval between births. The findings to date suggest that child-spacing, as well as the proportion of women bearing children, explain a large part of these fertility differences. The child-spacing differences, in turn, may be related to diet, disease, environment, work routine, or cultural practices. The chief cultural factor singled out thus far is the period of lactation. The West Indies not only had longer child-spacing intervals than the U.S. but also may have retained the African practice of continuing lactation for 2 to 3 years (combined with taboos against sexual intercourse during lactation). Among U.S. slaves the period of lactation appears to have been usually limited to one year. Of course, better comparative data on lactation are required before the demographic impact of the variations in lactational practices can be determined (see Klein and Engerman, 1978).[13]

The importance of the major crop produced and of the size of units has been examined by Higman (1976a) for Jamaica and by Steckel (1977) for the United States. On Jamaica, where most slaves lived on relatively large (by United States standards) units and sugar was usually the major crop, crude birth rates do not differ very much by size of unit or crop produced. Birth rates on sugar units were about 10 percent below those on units producing other crops, and there was a positive, but non-significant, correlation between size and birth rates (Higman, 1976a: 115-38, 248-49). In the United States, fertility was relatively high in counties specializing in tobacco, and was inversely related to plantation size (Steckel, 1977: 104, 219-24).[14] Childbearing began at earlier ages on the smaller units, and smaller units had fewer childless females than did the larger units.

9. Steckel (1977: 103, 233-45) has examined the relationship between the fertility rates of U.S. slaves and southern whites in 1860, both of which were quite high. Those who commented during antebellum times on the slave fertility pattern often overlooked the possibility that the relatively high fertility rates, compared with those of the northeast and Europe, were a southern and not just a slave phenomenon during the mid-nineteenth century. It now appears that the factors affecting

age at first birth are more complicated than was implied by the simple slave-white dichotomy. Steckel has found that slaves began childbearing at about age 21, or about one-and-three-quarter years before southern whites. The early age of slave marriage and childbearing may have been related to the absence of those financial and property constraints that served to delay marriage among free workers. But other factors were also involved since both southern slaves and southern whites commenced childbearing several years earlier than did women in New England or in Britain.[15]

In contradistinction to the apparent differences in child-spacing intervals between slaves in the United States and in the West Indies, the child-spacing intervals for southern whites and U.S. slaves were basically similar (Steckel, 1977: 103, 112-14).

Both southern whites and slaves had, by northern rural and postbellum black standards, what appears to have been a relatively high degree of childlessness among females who had completed the childbearing period (15 to 20 percent) (Steckel, 1977: 103).[16] While this figure is similar to that of the percentage never-married in Western europe at this time, (Easterlin, 1978:39) it is above the rates of childlessness estimated for rural northern wives (ages 40-49), 3.8 percent , and for ever-married nonwhites who passed through their childbearing years between 1865 and 1910, just below 9 percent (see Hajnal, 1965; Easterlin, et al., 1978:39 Taeuber and Taeuber, 1971: 378). While the rates of childlessness of both the slaves and the southern whites were not unusual by European standards, they are sufficiently different from experience elsewhere in North America to require an explanation. In the case of slaves Steckel points out that the rate of childlessness increased significantly with plantation size.

10. Antebellum commentators frequently posited a relationship between family structure and fertility. Slaveholders throughout the New World argued that stable, two-parent households would lead to higher fertility rates (and greater work effort) than one-parent households. Similar views were expressed by travelers to North America who attributed the high fertility rate of U.S. slaves partly to the prevalence of two-parent households. Recent analyses of data for Jamaica by Higman (1976a: 173-75) and of the W.P.A. narratives by Stephen Crawford (1979; cf. Fogel 1977a) indicate that these observations were correct. Higman points to a higher fertility rate among those co-resident with a mate in Jamaica, and Crawford's analysis points to the same result for the United States. Recent work has established that slaves in both areas lived in two-parent households more frequently, and that such households were more frequently maintained for prolonged periods of time, than previously believed (see, e.g., Genovese,

1974; Gutman, 1975; Higman, 1975; Craton, 1979). The proportion of two-parent households was greater among U.S. slaves than among West Indian slaves. The differences between the fertility rates of one-parent and two-parent households within each society, however, were not of a sufficiently large magnitude for the proportion of two-parent h9useholds, by itself, to explain much of the overall fertility differential between the U.S. and the West Indies.

11. Although some progress has been made, many issues are still unresolved in the work on fertility. It now seems well-established that the nutritional content of the United States slave diet was relatively good by the standards of the time, but less has been established about the relative adequacy of the West Indian diet and its possible effects on the ages of menarche and menopause, and, thus, on the childbearing span. Similarly, the impact of differences in work routines associated with different crops, and the manner in which they might have influenced reproductive capacity, is not known. Little has been established regarding the extent to which rates of childlessness of slaves represented factors relating to planter restrictions on marital opportunities, slave cultural patterns, or to some form of relatively widespread sterility among slave females due to disease or diet. While differences in child-spacing may be related to differences in lactation periods and to various social beliefs, environmental factors (including the diet) might also be involved. Moreover, the explanation for the apparent differences in lactational practices between the United States and the West Indies remains uncertain.

Mortality

12. The work on mortality patterns has lagged behind that of fertility. This lag is to a considerable degree due to the difficulty in obtaining the data needed to compute death rates, to determine the immediate causes of death, and to identify underlying explanatory factors. Census data, probate lists, and birth lists on plantations can be used to provide relevant measures of fertility, but the first two of these sources can be of only limited usefulness in measuring mortality. Even in those sources which list death by age as well as by cause, such as the United States census schedules of mortality for 1850 and 1860 and some of the sets of plantation records, the extent of under-reporting is so large that the usefulness of these sources for many issues is quite limited.

13. The data which are available for the nineteenth century indicate that the United States slaves had a lower mortality rate than slaves in the West Indies, but a higher mortality rate than that experienced by U.S. whites. There appears, moreover, to have been wide cyclical

variations in the crude death rates of U.S. slaves and southern whites during the last four decades of the antebellum era, but such cycles are not evident in the death rates of northern whites (Fogel, et al., 1978). It is probable that, in the United States, the crude death rates of blacks were higher in 1880 than in 1860, and that it was not until 1910 that they returned to antebellum levels (Meeker, 1976).

14. Barry Higman (1976a: 105-38, 248-49) has investigated the determinants of mortality in Jamaica in 1832. He found that crude death rates on sugar plantations were nearly 40 percent higher than those on units producing other crops, reflecting in part the strong positive relationship between crude death rates and plantation size.

15. There is as yet no study of death rates for U.S. slaves comparable to that of Higman's, although Steckel's (1980) analysis of infant mortality indicates higher death rates on plantations producing rice than other crops, and a weak positive relationship between death rates and plantation size. Steckel also suggests some downward trend in the rate of infant mortality during the nineteenth century, but if so, the available data indicate that it was of limited magnitude.

16. There has been more work on the patterns and trends of mortality in the Atlantic slave trade. Curtin (1969: 275-86) and Klein (1978) have pointed to the sharp decline in transoceanic mortality rates during the eighteenth century (see also Chandler, 1972). They have indicated the effect of sailing time on mortality, with Klein pointing to the importance of the difference between actual and expected sailing time in accounting for the occurrence of atypically high mortality voyages (cf. Klein and Engerman, 1975). While slave ships were more crowded than other vessels, there is, within the observed range, no statistically significant relationship between mortality rates and the number of slaves carried per registered or measured ton of each vessel. Even allowing for differences in sailing time and the extent of crowding, large differences remain based upon port of departure in Africa, suggesting the possible importance of African factors in explaining the patterns of mortality during the ocean crossing. In general the levels of white mortality on specific slave vessels were similar to those of the slaves, and the white and slave mortality schedules seem to have shifted at roughly the same rate over time.

17. Clearly there are many unresolved issues and possibilities for progress in the study of slave mortality. Better estimates of life expectation and age-specific mortality rates are possible, based upon systematic analysis of the usable set of plantation records, and of registration and census manuscripts. More detailed analyses of physiological data can cast light on the possible role of the diet, while more systematic studies of observations by physicians and planters, such as those by

the Kiples (1976) and by Savitt (1978), will help to define disease-specific distributions of morbidity and mortality (see also Craton, 1978a). More attention also needs to be given to the impact of movements into new regions and the way that different disease environments may have affected patterns of mortality. At issue here is both the initial movement of slaves to the New World and their geographic redistribution after arrival.

Family and Household Structure

18. Much recent work has led to a substantial revision of earlier views on the slave family. Earlier writings presumed a relative absence of stable mating patterns among slaves, and implied that long-lasting two-parent households were relatively rare under slavery, thus linking the slave experience to issues relating to the twentieth-century black family. The validity of this depiction of the slave family and household has been questioned, particularly for the United States. In general, works in several different slaveowning areas have revealed that two-parent households of long duration were widespread among slave populations. While such households appear with considerably greater frequency in the United States than in Jamaica or Brazil, the two-parent household was a significant institution in all New World societies so far studied quantitatively.[17]

Recent work has concentrated on structural patterns of family organization, and many issues of origin and significance remain to be resolved.[18] While little is known about the family patterns most frequent in the parts of Africa from which U.S. slaves came, the role of family in kin and lineage groupings could bear only limited resemblance under slavery to their importance within Africa. Rules about preferential and prohibited marriages, and the incidence of polygyny, differed between the United States and parts of Africa, as did attitudes towards premarital sexual activity. There were obvious difficulties in slave attempts to re-establish African patterns in the United States, and little is yet known about the relative importance of internal and external influences upon the development of Afro-American family pattern.

Work by Higman (1975, 1978) and by Craton (1978b, 1979) for Jamaica, Trinidad, Barbados, and the Bahamas present generally similar findings and questions about evolving family patterns in the West Indies. While the two-parent household was generally less dominant than among United States slaves, it occurred with greater frequency than earlier believed, and may even have been slightly higher for the African-born than for the Creoles. The family-unit household was least common in Trinidad. About one-half of Trinidad slaves were recorded as living outside family units, and about one-half of those residing in family units were in two-parent households. For the Bahamas, Craton (1979) estimates that about 85 percent of slaves resided in family units, and, of these, about three-quarters lived in two-parent households. Less data are currently available for Jamaica, but those which have been published indicate a higher frequency of residence in family units than in Trinidad but less than in the Bahamas. Female-headed households were more frequently recorded in towns than in rural areas, although the extent to which this may have reflected different ownership is not yet established. In none of these areas was there any evidence of polygyny as a widespread practice, and there is no evidence to suggest that serial monogamy was a frequent pattern.

The importance of internal and external influences upon the West Indian slave family patterns, and the explanation for the differences in the inter-island patterns are not yet established. However, the striking differences in the distributions of household types between the Bahamas, Jamaica, and Trinidad suggest that external factors were quite powerful. The sharp differences in the proportion living in family units cannot be explained by variations in the African ethnic origins of the slaves in the three colonies, although African origins may have influenced other behavior. After the middle of the eighteenth century it appears that the prevalence of the two-parent household was inversely related to the rate of settlement of an area, which probably explains, in part, the high frequency with which Trinidad slaves were listed as living outside of family units. There also appears to have been a relationship between the mortality rate and household structure, although the direction of causation is not entirely clear.

Of importance also is the explanation for the seeming difference between the U.S. and West Indian post-emancipation patterns. Work by Gutman (1975) and others investigating the United States case argue persistence of two-parent black households at rates comparable to those of whites until the 1930s, after which there is an increase in the importance of female-headed households. But the West Indian pattern apparently involved relatively high rates of illegitimacy and relatively low rates of marital stability throughout the post-emancipation period (see Roberts, 1957: 263-306).

19. Ongoing research is concerned with a more careful description of the frequency distribution of various categories of family organization and behavior, including categories of sexual and family mores and their demographic and cultural consequences. While data bearing on mores are quite fragmentary, there are substantial bodies of data

bearing on the distribution of household structures and kinship patterns that existed among slaves in both the United States and the British West Indies. Results to date indicated that the distribution of kinship and household structures not only differed between slaves and whites but also among and within the various slave societies. It is interesting to note that the new work has tended to focus upon different questions than those raised by earlier scholars. Previous discussions of the "absent father" were often concerned less with the issue of whether the father was actually living with his children than with the limits on his role in childraising due to the status of enslavement. Similar questions were also raised by earlier scholars about the mother's role in childraising among slaves.

One important advance is the new light shed on the frequency of marriages across farms in the United States. In such cases slave mothers and fathers were usually owned by different individuals and often resided on different units, with a variety of visitation arrangements. Crawford (1979) estimates that on units with 15 or fewer slaves, roughly 60 percent of the households were headed by two parents. On 30 percent of these two-parent households, the parents resided on different units. As shown by both Crawford and Steckel (1977: 227), the relative frequency of divided-residence "marriages" declined with plantation size (cf. Fogel, 1977a; Gutman, 1975: 141). While it is an important corrective to observe that divided-residence households need not imply an unstable "marriage," it remains to be determined whether this household type had a different impact on the development of children than households in which both parents resided together. In general, both in the United States and the West Indies, residence and childraising patterns varied more among slave than among free families, even within a general acceptance of the two-parent-household norm.

Footnotes

*Harvard University and University of Rochester, respectively. Research underlying parts of this paper was supported by National Science Foundation grants GS-3262, GS-27262, and SOC 76-002. We have been aided by helpful comments made on an earlier draft by Claudia Goldin, Edward Meeker, Richard Sheridan, Richard Steckel, and James Trussell.

[1] The slave trade estimates in this paragraph are derived from Curtin (1969: 88-89), with the data for the United States revised as discussed by Fogel and Engerman (1974: II, 27-32; I, 14). The distribution of the 1825 black population is from Fogel and Engerman (1974: I, 28). The 1950 black population shares are based on the Rosenblat estimates as adjusted by Klein (1971).

While parts of Curtin's estimates have been revised by Anstey, Inikori, Postma, Eltis, and others, the patterns he depicted remain basically unaltered. Brazil received by far the largest number of slave imports in the New World, 38 percent of the overall total. In absolute magnitude the United States had received only about 600,000 slaves, but had over four and one-half million blacks at the time of emancipation. In the British West Indies total slave imports were at least 1,700,000 but the black population at the time of emancipation in 1834 was below three-quarters of a million.

[2] In these studies fertility is measured by child-women ratios. Their conclusions are based on small samples, but are consistent with demographic data for larger populations.

[3] Wrigley's (1966) estimated mean age at first marriage for women in Colyton, England during the years 1720-1799 is between 26 and 27. Menard (1977) estimates the mean age at marriage for female whites born in the Chesapeake in the seventeenth century at below 19. For suggestive discussions of the difference between child-spacing intervals in Africa and the United States, see Menard (1974) and Klein and Engerman (1978).

[4] It is important to keep in mind that child-women ratios are affected by mortality. This fact must be taken into account when child-women ratios are used for the comparative analysis of fertility, especially when the differences in child-women ratios are small. Cf. the discussion in section 6.

[5] This result can be obtained from Coale and Demeny (1966) using GRR = 3.5 for West mortality levels 5-7.

[6] Mortality differentials also affect the interpretation of child-women ratios as indices of differential fertility between slaves and whites. Since slave mortality rates appear to have been higher than those of southern whites, the child-women ratios tend to underestimate slave fertility relative to southern white fertility. For the same reason, the child-women ratios tend to underestimate southern white fertility relative to that of northern whites. Declining mortality in the North probably served to retard the rate of decline in the child-women ratios, so that the rate of decline in the northern fertility schedule is probably understated by the movement in these ratios. The effect of mortality on the temporal movement in southern child-women ratios is more ambiguous because of the apparent cycles in southern mortality rates (see Fogel, 1977b).

[7] See Fogel and Engerman (1974: I, 137-39) and Herbert Gutman and Richard Sutch (1976: 134-62). As used here, the "age of fecundity" is the average age at which slave women would have conceived their first live birth if they had been having sexual intercourse regularly from the time they first became ovulatory.

[8] The European averages are not strictly comparable to those produced by Trussell and Steckel and by Kulikoff since they are not singulate means. Moreover the European studies generally give age at marriage rather than at first birth.

[9] Data on the average heights of Cuban slaves in the 1850's are presented in Fraginals (1977).

[10] The Massachusetts data were collected from public schools in the Boston area (Bowditch, 1877). Care must be exercised in any comparisons because of the mixing of generations and of occupational classes in the various data sources, and the numbers are presented here for suggestive purpose without these necessary refinements.

[11] Heights of Trinidad slaves born in Africa are not available for the years of most rapid growth because relatively few slaves were under age 13 when imported and because Britain prohibited the further importation of slaves into her colonies in 1807.

[12] Well-fed Britains, U.S. whites, and U.S. blacks today have approximately the same adult height, which suggests that their genetic potential for growth was roughly equivalent. Cf. Eveleth and Tanner, 1976: 222.

[13] The age of menarche in the West Indies in the early nineteenth century was discussed by John Roberton (1841-2; 1848) and E. J. Tilt (1850), and can be calculated from the Trinidad height-by-age data to be compared with that in the United States.

[14] The fertility rates in areas producing rice and sugar were below the southern slave average. See also Klein and Engerman, 1978.

[15] Wrigley (1966) estimates a mean age at first marriage in Colyton, England of 24.9 in the years 1800-1824, and 23.3 in the years 1825-1837.

[16] It should be noted that these estimates are sensitive to, among other factors, ages of leaving households, so it is not yet clear whether these are a real phenomenon or a statistical artifact.

[17] For the slave family in Brazil, see Graham (1976), Slenes (1975), and Ramos (1978), and for a recent study of Mexico, see Duke (1977). Most studies of the slave family to date have focused on the presence (or absence) of the two parents. The extent to which these families are best described as nuclear or extended is often difficult to establish on the basis of currently-available sources.

[18] For a useful comparison of the household structure of slaves on some large U.S. plantations with English patterns, see Laslett (1977).

Table 1

Number of Children Under Ten per Thousand Women Ages 15-49 Among Southern Whites and Slaves, 1820-1860

Census Year	Whites			Slaves		
	Eastern	Western	Total	Eastern	Western	Total
1820	1,518	1,859	1,635	1,490	1,457	1,482
1830	1,430	1,785	1,571	1,499	1,460	1,486
1840	1,421	1,704	1,556	1,434	1,370	1,406
1850	1,257	1,435	1,353	1,396	1,314	1,354
1860	1,203	1,374	1,303	1,369	1,278	1,318

Source: Steckel (1977:3), based on census data. States in the eastern section are: Delaware, District of Columbia, Georgia, Maryland, North Carolina, South Carolina, and Virginia; those in the western section are: Kentucky, Mississippi, Tennessee, Louisiana, Missouri, Alabama, Arkansas, Florida (from 1830), and Texas (from 1850).

Figure 1

Approximate Average Annual Rates of Natural Increase for Various Populations, 1700 - 1900

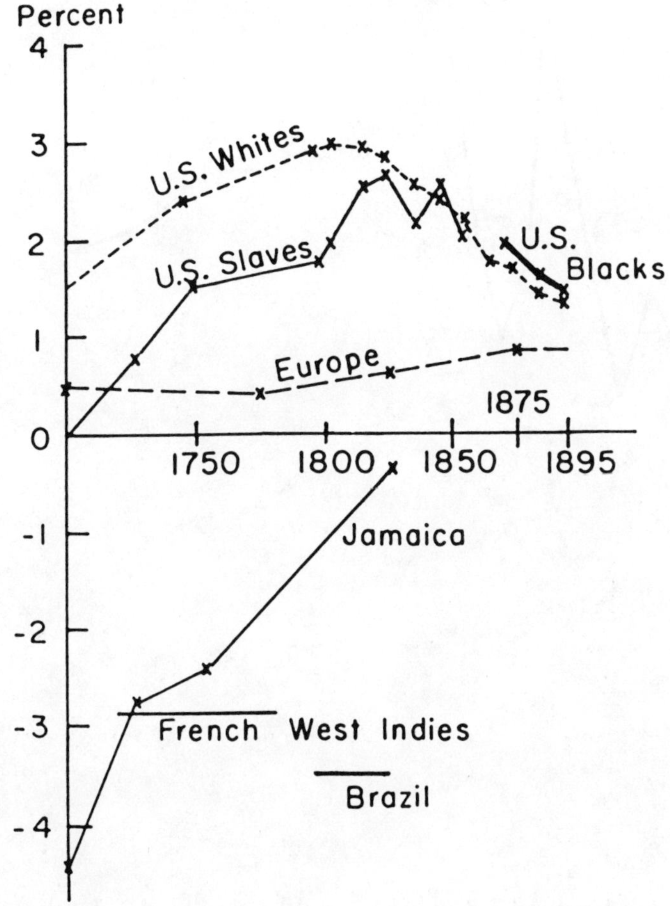

Sources:

to Figure 1: See Fogel (1977a) for a discussion of sources and methods.

Figure 2

Trends in the Number of Slave Children under 5 per 1,000 Women Ages 15-49, Prince George's County, Maryland, 1725-1779 and U.S. South, 1820-1860.

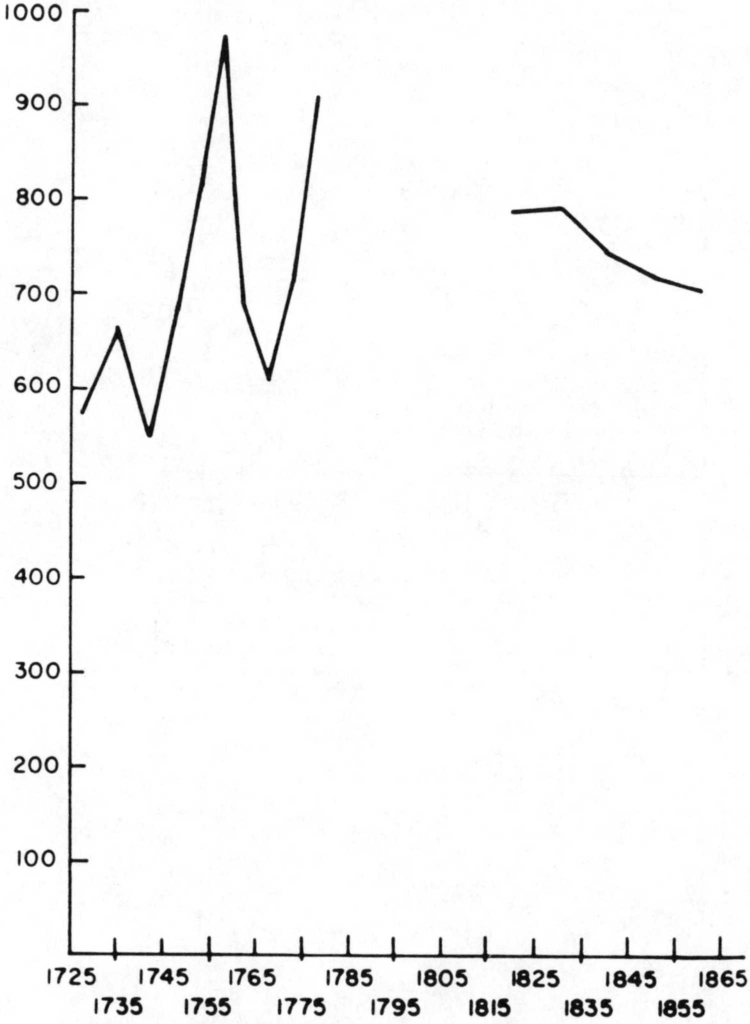

Sources:
Figure 2: Derived from Kulikoff (1977:411) and Steckel (1977:3).

Figure 3

Estimates of Heights of Females Ages 8–18
U.S. Slaves, Trinidad Slaves, Massachusetts Whites and British Whites, Nineteenth Century

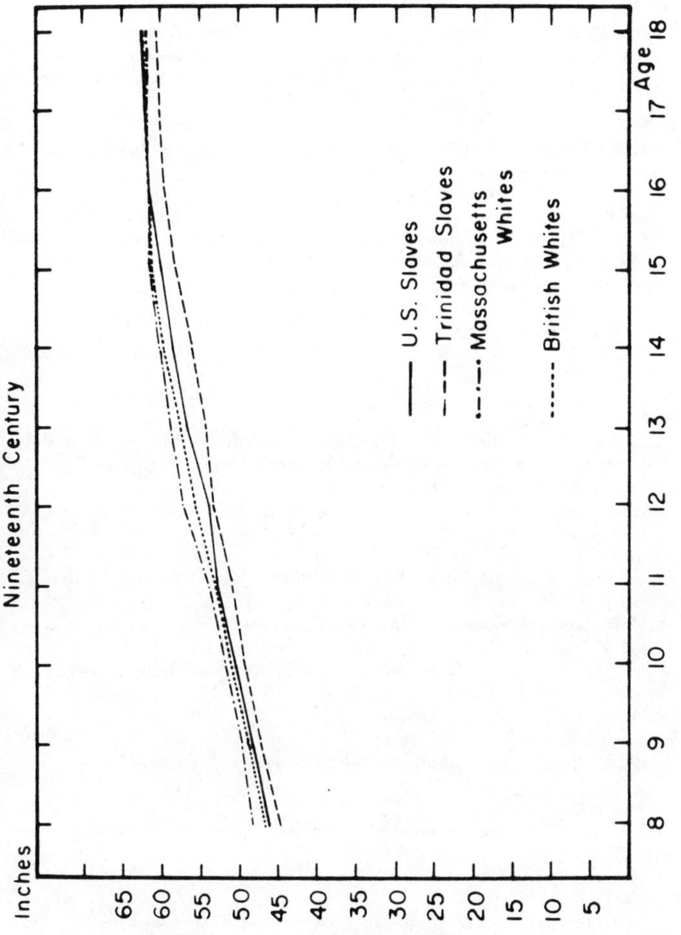

Sources:

Figure 3:

U.S. Slaves: **Trussell and Steckel** (1978:502); Trinidad slaves born in the **Caribbean**: **Trinidad** slave registrations for 1814, T71/501 (Public Record Office, **London**); Massachusetts school girls of **American** parentage: Bowditch (1877:44); British females, all classes: **Anthropometric** Committee (1884:291).

REFERENCES

Anthropometric Committee, British Association for the Advancement of Science
1884 "Final Report." Pp. 253-306 in Report of the Fifty-Third Meeting of the British Association for the Advancement of Science (1883). London: John Murray.

Bowditch, H. P.
1877 "The Growth of Children" in Eighth Annual Report of State Board of Health of Massachusetts. Boston: Wright.

Chandler, David L.
1972 A Study of Health Conditions Among Negro Slaves in the Viceroyalty of New Granada and Its Associated Slave Trade, 1600-1810. Unpublished Ph.D. thesis, Tulane University.

Coale, Ansley J. and Paul Demeny
1966 Regional Model Life Tables and Stable Populations. Princeton: Princeton University Press.

Craton, Michael
1971 "Jamaican Slave Mortality: Fresh Light from Worthy Park, Longville and the Tharp Estates." Journal of Caribbean History 3 (November): 1-27.
1974 Sinews of Empire. New York: Anchor.
1975 "Jamaican Slavery." Pp. 249-84 in Stanley L. Engerman and Eugene D. Genovese (eds.), Race and Slavery in the Western Hemisphere. Princeton: Princeton University Press.
1978a Searching for the Invisible Man. Cambridge, Mass.: Harvard University Press.
1978b "Hobbesian or Panglossian? The Two Extremes of Slave Conditions in the British Caribbean." William and Mary Quarterly 35 (April): 324-56.
1979 "Changing Patterns of Slave Family in the British West Indies." Journal of Interdisciplinary History.

Craven, Wesley Frank
1971 White, Red, and Black. Charlottesville: University of Virginia Press.

Crawford, Stephen C.
1979 The Autobiography of an Oppressed Class. Forthcoming Ph.D. thesis, University of Chicago.

Curtin, Philip D.
1969 The Atlantic Slave Trade. Madison: University of Wisconsin Press.

Duke, C.
1977 "The Family in Eighteenth-Century Plantation Society in Mexico." Pp. 226-46 in Vera Rubin and Arthur Tuden (eds.), Comparative Perspectives on Slavery in New World Plantation Societies. New York: New York Academy of Sciences.

Dunn, Richard S.
1972 Sugar and Slaves. Chapel Hill: University of North Carolina Press.
1977 "A Tale of Two Plantations: Slave Life at Mesopotamia in Jamaica and at Mount Airy in Virginia." William and Mary Quarterly 34 (January): 32-65.

Easterlin, R. A.
1976 "Population Change and Farm Settlement in the Northern United States." Journal of Economic History 36 (March): 45-75.

Easterlin, R. A., et al.
1978 "Farms and Farm Families in Old and New Areas: The Northern States in 1860." Pp. 22-84 in Tamara K. Haveven and Maris A. Vinovskis (eds.), Family and Population in Nineteenth-Century America. Princeton: Princeton University Press.

Engerman, S. L.
1976 "Some Economic and Demographic Comparisons of Slavery in the United States and the British West Indies." Economic History Review 29 (April): 258-75.
1977 "Black Fertility and Family Structure in the United States, 1880-1940." Journal of Family History 2 (Summer): 117-38.

Eveleth, Phyllis B. and J. M. Tanner
1976 Worldwide Variation in Human Growth. Cambridge: Cambridge University Press.

Farley, Reynolds
1970 Growth of the Black Population. Chicago: Markham.

Fogel, R. W.
1977a "Cliometrics and Culture: Some Recent Developments in the Historiography of Slavery. Journal of Social History 11 (Fall): 34-51.
1977b "Recent Developments in the Demography of Slavery." Unpublished.

Fogel, Robert William and Stanley L. Engerman
1974 Time on the Cross (2 vols.). Boston: Little, Brown.

Fogel, R. W., et al.
1978 "The Economics of Mortality in North America, 1650-1910: A Description of a Research Project." Historical Methods Newsletter 11 (Spring): 75-108.

Fraginals, M. Moreno
1977 "Africans in Cuba: A Quantitative Analysis of the African Population in the Island of Cuba." Pp. 187-201 in Vera Rubin and Arthur Tuden (eds.), Comparative Perspectives on Slavery in New World Plantation Societies. New York: New York Academy of Sciences.

Genovese, Eugene D.
1974 Roll, Jordan, Roll. New York: Pantheon.

Graham, R.
1976 "Slave Families on a Rural Estate in Colonial Brazil." Journal of Social History 9 (Spring): 382-402.

Gutman, Herbert G.
1975 The Black Family in Slavery and Freedom, 1750-1925. New York: Pantheon.

Gutman, H. and R. Sutch
1976 "Victorians All? The Sexual Mores and Conduct of Slaves and Their Masters." Pp. 134-62 in Paul A. David, et al., Reckoning with Slavery. New York: Oxford University Press.

Hajnal, J.
1965 "European Marriage Patterns in Perspective." Pp. 101-43 in D. V. Glass and D. E. C. Eversley (eds.), Population in History. London: Edward Arnold.

Higman, Barry W.

1973 "Household Structure and Fertility on Jamaican Slave Plantations: A Nineteenth-Century Example." Population Studies 27 (November): 527-50.

1975 "The Slave Family and Household in the British West Indies, 1800-1834." Journal of Interdisciplinary History 6 (Autumn): 261-87.

1976a Slave Population and Economy in Jamaica, 1807-1834. Cambridge: Cambridge University Press.

1976b "The Slave Populations of the British Caribbean: Some Nineteenth Century Variations." Pp. 60-70 in Samuel Proctor (ed.), Eighteenth-Century Florida and the Caribbean. Gainesville: University of Florida Press.

1978 "African and Creole Slave Family Patterns in Trinidad." Journal of Family History 3 (Summer): 163-80.

Kiple, K. and V. Kiple

1976 "Slave Child Mortality: Some Nutritional Answers to a Perennial Puzzle." Journal of Social History 10 (Spring): 284-309.

Klein, Herbert S.

1971 "Patterns of Settlement of the Afro-American Population in the New World." Pp. 99-115 in vol. I of Nathan I. Huggins, et al. (eds.), Key Issues in the Afro-American Experience. New York: Harcourt Brace Jovanovich.

1978 The Middle Passage. Princeton: Princeton University Press.

Klein, H. S. and S. L. Engerman

1975 "Shipping Patterns and Mortality in the African Slave Trade to Rio de Janeiro, 1825-1830." Cahiers d'Etudes Africaines 15 (no. 59): 381-98.

1978 "Fertility Differentials Between Slaves in the United States and the British West Indies: A Note on Lactation Practices and Their Possible Implications." William and Mary Quarterly 35 (April): 357-74.

Kulikoff, A.

1977 "A 'Prolifick' People: Black Population Growth in the Chesapeake Colonies, 1700-1790." Southern Studies 16 (Winter): 391-428.

Laslett, Peter

1977 Family Life and Illicit Love in Earlier Generations. Cambridge: Cambridge University Press.

Leet, D. R.

1976 "The Determinants of the Fertility Transition in Antebellum Ohio." Journal of Economic History 36 (June): 359-78.

Meeker, E.

1976 "Mortality Trends of Southern Blacks, 1850-1910: Some Preliminary Findings." Explorations in Economic History 13 (January): 13-42.

Menard, R. R.

1974 "The Maryland Slave Population, 1658 to 1730: A Demographic Profile of Blacks in Four Counties." William and Mary Quarterly 32 (January): 30-54.

1977 "Immigrants and Their Increase: The Process of Settlement in Early Colonial Maryland." Pp. 88-110 in Aubrey C. Land, et al. (eds.), Law, Society, and Politics in Early Maryland. Baltimore: John Hopkins University Press.

Okun, Bernard

1958 Trends in Birth Rates in the United States Since 1870. Baltimore: Johns Hopkins University Press.

Ramos, Donald
1978 "The Black Family in Brazil, 1760-1840." Unpublished.

Roberton, J.
1841-2 "On the Period of Puberty in Negro Women." London Medical Gazette 30: 677-82.
1848 "On the Period of Puberty in the Negro." Edinburgh Medical and Surgical Journal 69: 69-77.

Roberts, G. W.
1957 The Population of Jamaica. Cambridge: Cambridge University Press.
1977 "Movements in Slave Population of the Caribbean During the Period of Slave Registration." Pp. 145-60 in Vera Rubin and Arthur Tuden (eds.), Comparative Perspectives on Slavery in New World Plantation Societies. New York: New York Academy of Sciences.Savitt, Todd L.
1978 Medicine and Slavery. Urbana: University of Illinois Press.

Slenes, Robert
1975 The Demography and Economics of Brazilian Slavery, 1850-1880. Unpublished Ph.D. Thesis, Stanford University.

Smith, D. B.
1978 "Mortality and Family in the Colonial Chesapeake." Journal of Interdisciplinary History 8 (Winter): 403-27.

Smith, D. S.
1977 "A Homeostatic Demographic Regime: Patterns in Western European Reconstitution Studies." Pp. 19-52 in Ronald Demos Lee (ed.), Population Patterns in the Past. New York: Academic.

Steckel, Richard
1977 The Economics of U.S. Slave and Southern White Fertility. Unpublished Ph.D. Thesis, University of Chicago.
1980 "Slave Mortality: Analysis of Evidence from Plantation Records." Social Science History.

Taeuber, Irene B. and Conrad Taeuber
1971 People of the United States in the 20th Century. Washington: Government Printing Office.

Tilt, E. J.
1850 "Reflections on the Causes Which Advance or Retard the Appearance of First Menstruation in Women . . ." Monthly Journal of Medical Science 11: 289-96.

Trussell, J. and R. Steckel
1978 "The Age of Slaves at Menarche and Their First Birth." Journal of Interdisciplinary History 8 (Winter): 477-505.

Walsh, L. S. and R. R. Menard
1974 "Death in the Chesapeake: Two Life Tables for Men in Early Colonial Maryland." Maryland Historical Magazine 69 (Summer): 211-27.

Wrigley, E. A.
1966 "Family Limitation in Preindustrial England." Economic History Review 19 (April): 82-109.

Yasuba, Yasukichi
1962 Birth Rates of the White Population in the United States, 1800-1860. Baltimore: Johns Hopkins University Press.

The Double Bonds of Race and Sex: Black and White Women in a Colonial Virginia Parish

By JOAN REZNER GUNDERSEN

PHILLIS, A BLACK SLAVE, AND ELIZABETH CHASTAIN LESUEUR, HER mistress, worked and raised families together for over thirty-two years in King William Parish, Virginia. In their small world, about thirty miles west of Richmond, shared ties of gender created a community of women but not a community of equals. The bonds of race and slavery provided constraints that divided the experience of Phillis from that of Elizabeth. Like most women of their day, they left but a faint trail through the records. Elizabeth Chastain LeSueur was probably the older, born about 1707, while all that is certain about Phillis is that she was born before 1728. Both women died sometime after David LeSueur's estate went through probate in early 1773. Both bore and raised children, worked at the many domestic tasks assigned to women in the colonies, and experienced the growth of slavery in their region. The similarities and differences between their lives (and the lives of the other women of the parish) reveal much about the ways gender and race interacted in the lives of colonial women.[1]

[1] Elizabeth was the daughter of Pierre and Anne Soblet Chastain. I approximated her birth date from the known birth years of male siblings and the order of children as listed in Pierre's will. In other words, the only clues to her age come from records about males. Phillis had to be sixteen or older in 1744 when she appears on the King William Parish Tithe List. "June, 1744 – A List of King William Parish," in R. A. Brock, ed., *Documents Chiefly Unpublished, Relating to the Huguenot Emigration to Virginia and to the Settlement at Manakin-Town* . . . . (Richmond, 1886), 113; hereinafter cited as 1744 Tithe List; will of Pierre Chastain, November 20, 1728, Deeds and Wills, Goochland County (Virginia State Library, Richmond), microfilm; the Virginia State Library has microfilm and photostatic copies of all extant colonial records from the state, hence all subsequent references to county records will refer to the holdings in the Virginia State Library; will of David LeSueur, February 24, 1772, Wills, Cumberland County; inventory of David LeSueur, April 26, 1773, Wills, Cumberland County.

MS. GUNDERSEN is an associate professor of history and director of women's studies at St. Olaf College.

THE JOURNAL OF SOUTHERN HISTORY
Vol. LII, No. 3, August 1986

The lives of black women such as Phillis have yet to be explored in depth by the new social historians. We have, however, learned something about the lives of women like her mistress, Elizabeth Chastain LeSueur.[2] In recent years historians have examined the life expectancy of seventeenth-century blacks, the effects of demographics and demand upon the introduction of slavery in the Chesapeake, the impact of a black majority upon South Carolina development, the patterns of slave resistance in eighteenth-century Virginia, and the structure of eighteenth-century slave families.[3] In all of this the black woman appears as a cipher, notable in the seventeenth century and first part of the eighteenth by her absence and by her lack of overt resistance to slavery; she seems essential only to the study of fertility. But just as the experience of white women such as Elizabeth Chastain LeSueur differed from that of white males in the colonies, the black female's experience in slavery differed from the male's, and to ignore that difference would be to misunderstand the nature of slavery. Gender not only separated female slaves from males, it also forged bonds with white women. After all, black women lived among whites, and in order fully to understand their lives, it is necessary to compare their experiences with those of white women. Only then can we begin to understand what it meant to be black and female in colonial Virginia.

[2] For a general discussion of the experiences of antebellum black women see Jacqueline Jones, *Labor of Love, Labor of Sorrow: Black Women, Work, and the Family from Slavery to the Present* (New York, 1985), and Deborah Gray White, *Ar'n't I A Woman?: Female Slaves in the Plantation South* (New York and London, 1985). The work on the colonial plantation mistress begins with the classic study by Julia Cherry Spruill, *Women's Life and Work in the Southern Colonies* (Chapel Hill, 1938). Recent studies include Lois Green Carr and Lorena S. Walsh, "The Planter's Wife: The Experience of White Women in Seventeenth-Century Maryland," *William and Mary Quarterly*, 3d Ser., XXXIV (October 1977), 542–71; Joan R. Gundersen and Gwen Victor Gampel, "Married Women's Legal Status in Eighteenth-Century New York and Virginia," *William and Mary Quarterly*, 3d Ser., XXXIX (January 1982), 114–34; Daniel Blake Smith, *Inside the Great House: Planter Family Life in Eighteenth-Century Chesapeake Society* (Ithaca, N. Y., and London, 1980); Darrett B. and Anita H. Rutman, "'Now-Wives and Sons-in-Law': Parental Death in a Seventeenth-Century Virginia County," in Thad W. Tate and David L. Ammerman, eds., *The Chesapeake in the Seventeenth Century: Essays on Anglo-American Society* (Chapel Hill, 1979).

[3] For a discussion of the origins of the black family in the Chesapeake that includes information on women, although not written from their perspective, see Allan Kulikoff, "The Beginnings of the Afro-American Family in Maryland," in Aubrey C. Land, Lois Green Carr, and Edward C. Papenfuse, eds., *Law, Society, and Politics in Early Maryland* (Baltimore and London, 1977). Russell R. Menard, "The Maryland Slave Population, 1658 to 1730: A Demographic Profile of Blacks in Four Counties," *William and Mary Quarterly*, 3d Ser., XXXII (January 1975), 29–54; Edmund S. Morgan, *American Slavery, American Freedom: The Ordeal of Colonial Virginia* (New York, 1975), 295–315; Peter H. Wood, *Black Majority: Negroes in Colonial South Carolina from 1670 through the Stono Rebellion* (New York, 1974); Gerald W. Mullin, *Flight and Rebellion: Slave Resistance in Eighteenth-Century Virginia* (New York and London, 1972), 103–105; Herbert G. Gutman, *The Black Family in Slavery and Freedom, 1750–1925* (New York, 1976), 1–230. Gutman uses material from 1750 to 1860 as though it were part of one general period.

This essay looks at slavery from a comparative female perspective in King William Parish during the eighteenth century. The findings suggest that the bonds of a female slave were twofold, linking her both to an interracial community of women and setting her apart as a slave in ways that make evident the special burden of being black and female in a white, patriarchal society.[4] The local parish records, including tithe records for nearly every year between 1710 and 1744, provide a unique opportunity to illuminate the role of the black woman in a small plantation setting and to document the development of slavery within a new community just as it became the major labor source for the colony.[5]

The slave women who arrived at King William Parish in the early eighteenth century did not make a simple transfer from an African past to an English colonial present (even with intermediary stops). Rather, they came to a community itself in transformation from a French Protestant refugee culture to an English colonial one. The Virginia House of Burgesses created King William Parish for Huguenot refugees who settled at Manakin Town in 1700. Changing county boundaries placed the settlement at various times in Henrico, Goochland, Cumberland, and Chesterfield counties before 1777. The tiny handful of slaves present before 1720 belonged to a community in which French was the dominant language.[6] The decade of the 1720s, during which the first expansion of the slave population occurred, is also the period in which the Huguenot community leadership and property passed into the hands of those who, like Elizabeth Chastain

[4] See Gutman, *The Black Family*, 335–39, and T. H. Breen and Stephen Innes, *"Myne Owne Ground": Race and Freedom on Virginia's Eastern Shore, 1640–1676* (New York, 1980), 22–23, for other historians who note that blacks and whites might be part of a community together.

[5] This essay is part of a larger community study that includes use of family reconstitution techniques. King William Parish was an Anglican parish created especially for the Huguenot settlers at Manakin. The parish always received special treatment, including exemption from paying the salary for clergy set by law, but its vestry and clergy were under Anglican discipline. The basic records available include the King William Parish Vestry Book (with tithe lists), 1707–1750, the King William Parish Register (births), 1724–1750, and profiles of black and white members of the community drawn from the county records of Henrico, Goochland, Cumberland, Chesterfield, and Powhatan counties. These records include estate inventories, wills, deeds, guardian accounts, estate administrations, and white family records. I have traced the blacks in the community after 1744 by identifying the white families in the area and then using their estate records to find blacks. Miscellaneous records from other counties and parishes have filled specific gaps. The study ends in 1776, but in order to complete profiles of the people I have used materials after that date. The King William Parish Vestry Book is a single volume, in French, housed at the Virginia Historical Society in Richmond. The King William Parish Register is printed in Brock, ed., *Documents*, 77–111.

[6] Vestry records and church services were in French. The parish used a French translation of the Anglican prayerbook while continuing Huguenot traditions of limited admission to communion. Beginning in 1719, at the request of Robert Jones, one service in six was given in English. The wills of Manakin settlers filed before 1720 were all in French. King William Parish Vestry Book, December 26, 1718. The vestry book has been translated and published, but because of errors in the published version's tithe lists I have used the original manuscript.

LeSueur, either had arrived in Virginia as infants or had been born there.[7] An epidemic in 1717–1718 greatly disrupted the community and its institutions, speeding the transfer of leadership to a new generation.[8]

The economy of King William Parish, based on wheat and other grains, was also in transition, and the adoption of slavery was a reflection of this change. The first black women thus had to adapt to both a culture and an economy in transition. In the 1720s some land passed into English hands, and tobacco became a secondary crop. Slavery and tobacco together grew in importance in the parish over time. English interlopers did not introduce either slavery or tobacco, but they did provide a bridge to the agricultural patterns of the rest of the colony. The first slaveholding families in the community, including Elizabeth LeSueur's family, were French, and the purchase of slaves signified their claim to be members of the gentry.[9]

When Abraham and Magdalene Salle purchased Agar, an adult black female, in 1714, she joined a handful of other blacks at Manakin. The only other black woman, Bety, had arrived in the parish the year before. Agar began and ended her three decades of service in Manakin as part of a black female population outnumbered by black men, but for a decade in the middle (1720–1730), she was among the majority or was part of an evenly divided black population. Since black and white women in the Chesapeake were also outnumbered by men, Agar was part of a double minority. In King William Parish the circumstances of immigration had created nearly even sex ratios for both races. By 1714, for example, the white community had only slightly more adult men than women.[10] Recent studies throughout the

[7] David LeSueur was a second-generation Huguenot refugee, but he was born in London in 1703. He came to Virginia about 1724. William and Susan Minet, eds., *Livre des Tessmoignages de L'Eglise de Threadneedle Street, 1669–1789* (London 1909), 175. There was a major changeover in the vestry at this time. Eight new vestrymen were elected August 25, 1718. King William Parish Vestry Book, August 25, 1718.

[8] The church records are very thin for this period, and there is also a gap in the county records. Later evidence indicates that most of those who disappeared from the records in this period died. For example, a dispute over land revealed that the husband and all four sons of the Mattoon family died in quick succession, leaving sole ownership with the wife Susannah. Petition of Susannah Carner, June 17, 1730, and June 12, 1734, in H. R. McIlwaine, Wilmer L. Hall, and Benjamin J. Hillman, eds., *Executive Journals of the Council of Colonial Virginia* (6 vols., Richmond, 1925–66), IV, 222, 326.

[9] For example, the Salle family was the first to own slaves in the community, and Abraham Salle served as a justice of the peace appointed specially for the French community. Elizabeth Chastain LeSueur's father, Pierre Chastain, was the other special magistrate. He bought his first slave in 1713.

[10] A census of white inhabitants in 1714 included 71 men, 62 women, 85 boys, and 70 girls, for a total of 288. The lower number of girls may reflect early ages of marriage (some out of the community) for women. I have corrected the totals of boys and girls to include the orphans. The census listed them by name but counted them only in the grand total. "List

TABLE 1

NUMBER AND SEX RATIO OF ADULT BLACKS IN MANAKIN
1711–1744

Year	Males	Females	Unknown	Sex Ratio
1711	2	0	0	2:0
1712	5	0	0	5:0
1713	3	1	0	3:1
1714	4	2	0	2:1
1715	4	3	0	4:3
1717	6	3	0	2:1
1719	6	3	0	2:1
1720	3	4	0	3:4
1723	11	11	0	1:1
1724	11	11	0	1:1
1725	8	9	0	8:9
1726	8	7	0	8:7
1730	31	21	6	3:2
1731	28	19	10	7:5
1732	30	21	0	11:9
1733	33	24	3	4:3
1735	45	22	0	2:1
1744	66	51	0	11:8.5

SOURCE: Tithe lists, King William Parish Vestry Book; 1744 Tithe List in Brock, ed., *Documents*, 112–16.

Chesapeake have documented the shortage of black women in slave communities, and while the sex ratio at King William Parish favored men, it was seldom as severe as that reported for other areas. Thus the sense of being part of a female minority was less obvious than elsewhere in the colony.[11]

The King William Parish slave population grew slowly. The originally unbalanced black population achieved a better balance between the sexes, then became more one-sided, and finally returned to a nearly balanced state (see Table 1). By 1720 Agar was one of four black women out of a total of seven slaves in the community. Throughout the 1730s the adult sex ratio became more skewed, leaving women outnumbered 2:1, but well before the Revolution it had balanced.[12] Overall, from 1710 to 1776, the parish's adult sex ratio

Generalle de tous les François Protestants Refuges, Establys dans la Paroisse du Roy Guillaume, Comte d'Henrico en Virginia, y Compris les Femmes, Enfans, Veuses, et Orphelins," in Brock, ed., *Documents*, 74–76.

[11] Menard, "The Maryland Slave Population," 32–34.

[12] There are no tithe lists for 1716, 1721–22, 1727–28, and 1740–43. The lists for 1729, 1734, and 1736–40 record only the number of tithes charged to each head of a family rather than list individual names. Part of the 1744 list also was returned this way, but by using other records I could determine the slaves involved for most of those families.

for blacks was 6:5, or nearly even.[13] This is very close to the ratio that the whites of the parish had achieved by 1714. Thus only early in the settlement's history did the majority-minority experience of black and white women diverge.[14]

Interplay between patterns of importation and natural increase explain the shifting sex ratios. The more balanced sex ratios of the early years were an unintentional outgrowth of purchase patterns for imported slaves. Upriver slave purchasers received the leftovers from importation. Since adult males were the most desirable, and also available in greater numbers, the Tidewater planters purchased nearly all males in the early part of the eighteenth century.[15] Conversely, the slaves who reached the Piedmont in these earlier years included proportionately more women and children. By mid-century the majority of imports went to the Piedmont, providing an expansion of male field labor and unbalancing the sex ratios.[16] As a native-born slave population came of age beginning in the 1750s, the ratio was once more evenly balanced.[17]

Throughout Agar's life at Manakin (1714–*c.* 1748) she was constantly part of a racial minority, for whites outnumbered blacks until after 1750. By the late 1730s black men and women comprised half of the tithables of King William Parish. Since white women were excluded from the count of tithables, and since there were many more white children than black, Agar and other blacks were still part of a minority in the community, but among a majority of those who worked the fields. Agar probably died in the late 1740s, a few years after the LeSueurs purchased Phillis. Phillis lived in a community almost evenly divided between whites and blacks and between men

[13] Tithe Lists, King William Parish Vestry Book; 1744 Tithe List, in Brock, ed., *Documents*, 112–15. In 1730 the tithe lists showed fifty-two slaves with a ratio of about three men for every two women. In the next several decades the ratio rose so that men outnumbered women 2:1. The parish tithe lists are not available after 1750, but evidence from estate inventories and wills suggests that the numbers of men and women had again become more equal by 1776.

[14] The numbers are approximate because it was not possible to be sure that I had made all record linkages for a particular slave. Thus the figures inevitably include a bias enlarging the total. On the other hand, since the birth and tithe records are incomplete, the study also has missed a random number of slaves drawn from both sexes. The major sources for the profiles of slaves are the tithe lists 1710–44, wills and inventories of people associated with Manakin, and the King William Parish Register in Brock, ed., *Documents*, 77–111.

[15] Allan Kulikoff, "The Origins of Afro-American Society in Tidewater Maryland and Virginia, 1700 to 1790," *William and Mary Quarterly*, 3d Ser., XXXV (April 1978), 233–34.

[16] Allan Kulikoff, "A 'Prolifick' People: Black Population Growth in the Chesapeake Colonies, 1700–1790," *Southern Studies*, XVI (Winter 1977), 391–94. Kulikoff notes that the period 1710–40 was a transitional one, moving from importation of West Indian slaves to direct importation from Africa. This shift skewed sex ratios to produce a heavier male bias.

[17] The evidence suggests that despite slower growth of the total slave population, Manakin went through the initial patterns of growth and importation at about the same time and with less trauma than the Tidewater counties studied by Allan Kulikoff. Kulikoff, "The Origins of Afro-American Society," 226–59.

and women, but belonging to a numerical majority did not loosen either the bonds of slavery or gender.

Ironically, black women had an opportunity for a more normal family life than did black men because they were less desirable purchases. Because black women were outnumbered by men in King William Parish, it was easier for women to form families. Even so, the evidence suggests that black women took their time.[18] Several factors complicated a black woman's search for a partner. The dispersed patterns of ownership meant few black women lived in a slave quarter or with other blacks. Initially blacks, and especially black women, were scattered singly or in small groups among those families who owned slaves. Over one-third of the families owned some slaves or rented them.[19] No family before 1744 paid taxes on more than six blacks over age sixteen. Before 1744 only two or three families owned enough slaves to have both adult males and females. Thus black women had to search for mates on nearby farms. Furthermore, many black women lived relatively short times in Manakin, disappearing from the tithe records after only a few years. Bety, the first female slave in the parish, for example, appears on only four tithe returns. Such transience delayed the process of forming a family. In the early years this experience did not necessarily set black women apart from whites; immigrants of whatever race tended to marry later. As the community aged, however, the black woman's delay in starting a family did set her apart, for native-born white women began families earlier than their immigrant sisters, black or white.

There is only fragmentary evidence to suggest whether the slaves of Manakin were imported directly from Africa, or the West Indies, or if they were purchased from other colonial owners. Almost all slaves bore Anglicized names. The names of the slaves do suggest that the same kinds of compromises between African and English cultures that Peter H. Wood found in South Carolina also existed in colonial Virginia.[20] The process of having the county courts decide the age of young immigrant slaves has identified a small percentage of the black population in King William Parish as imports. Importers usually registered newly arrived Africans at a county in the Tidewater and then brought them upriver for sale. Thus the records in the King William Parish area do not normally distinguish between slaves imported from abroad and those born elsewhere in Virginia.[21]

[18] Russell R. Menard has argued that a predominately male population inhibited family formation among blacks in early Maryland. This is true only if one views the matter from the perspective of a male slave or defines a family as headed by a male. Menard, "The Maryland Slave Population," 34–35.

[19] The tithe list for 1730 includes seventy-three white family units. Of these, twenty-six included blacks. 1730 Tithe List, King William Parish Vestry Book.

[20] Wood, *Black Majority*, 181–86.

[21] The problems encountered by Stephen Chastain over the payment of duties for a boy he

Whatever these names may reveal about the origins of Manakin's black residents, black and white women were subjected to the same gender-imposed cultural restraints in naming. Of course, only white males had the security of a stable surname, but putting that issue aside, naming patterns reveal a subtle power structure in which gender played as important a role as did race. It is fitting that the first black woman resident in King William Parish was called Bety, because Bett (Beti, Bety, Betty) would prove to be one of the most common names for slave women in the parish. Of the 737 blacks studied, the 336 women bore only 71 names. Nine of these names were used seventeen times or more and account for over half of all the women. Conversely, the 401 men bore 117 names, only 5 of which were used seventeen times or more, representing only one-quarter of all male names. Thus the men bore more individualistic names. The men's names included those with more recognizable African roots such as Ebo, Manoc, and Morocco. The women's names were more Anglicized. The most common female names among slaves were western names that closely resembled African ones, such as Betty and Jude. Hence the names represent a compromise of cultures. It is possible that the lack of recognizable African roots reflected the insistence by owners that black women fit the cultural norms for women while accepting the idea that black men might be "outlandish."[22]

Slave naming patterns may have been affected by the French community. Manakin whites bear frustratingly few names, especially among women. Nine women's names account for over 90 percent of the more than 600 white women associated with the Manakin community before 1776. While both black and white women drew their names from a much smaller pool than did men, the pool of black names had a diversity to begin with only eventually matched by white families who added new names through intermarriage. That black women shared the same names more frequently than black men parallels the pattern of the white community. But there was a further commonality among women's names that cut across racial lines. Slave names were often the diminutives of white names, for example, Betty

purchased in 1714 support this hypothesis. Chastain thought that the duty had been paid by the ship captain and tried to collect compensation from the captain after a court ruled Chastain liable. Order Book, July 6, 1714, August 1714, and October 1714, Henrico County.

[22] The most common women's names were Betty, Hannah, Jenny, Sarah, Jude, Lucy, Moll, Nann, and Jane or Janne. The most common men's names were Will, Tom, Dick, Frank, and Jack. These are not the same names that Herbert G. Gutman found most common among nineteenth-century blacks, despite naming patterns that should have reproduced family names in the next generation. Gutman did find that women's naming patterns were different from men's. Gutman, *The Black Family*, 187. Darrett and Anita Rutman found very similar naming patterns among the slaves of Middlesex County, Virginia, from 1650 to 1750. Darrett B. and Anita H. Rutman, *A Place in Time: Explicatus* (New York and London, 1984), 98–99.

for Elizabeth and Will for William. White women also were known by diminutives such as Sally, Patsy, and Nancy. They appear this way even in formal documents such as wills. Nicknames and diminutives are not used for adult white males. Hence diminutives were shared by women, both black and white, but not by all groups of men. White women shared in unaltered form several common names with black women, including Sarah, Hannah, and Janne. Male slaves did not bear the same names as white males, although a white youth might be called by a nickname such as Tom, which was also a common slave name. On legal documents and at adulthood, however, white men claimed the distinction granted by the formal versions of their names. Slaveowners apparently found it more necessary to distinguish between white and black males than to distinguish between white and black females by changing the form of their names or choosing names for slaves not used by whites. Such distinctions in naming patterns helped to reinforce the status and power of white men.

The records unfortunately do not reveal who did the naming of black women, whether immigrant blacks influenced the choice of names assigned them or whether owners or mothers chose the names of black children. Control over the power of naming was an important indicator of the power relationship that existed between owner and slave, but general cultural constraints also shaped the choices made by whoever exercised that power. Tradition greatly limited the naming patterns of whites. The oldest children bore grandparents' names, the next oldest were their parents' namesakes, and younger children were named for siblings of their parents. Occasionally a family would use the mother's family name as a first name for a younger child.[23] However, the important point is that general cultural constraints determined naming patterns, not individuals, and the gender constraints of Virginia meant that women of both races shared a naming experience that offered them fewer choices, accorded them less individuality, and reinforced a dependent status.

Childbirth is an experience shared by women of all races, but in King William Parish the patterns of childbearing reveal another way in which black women lived within a community of women and yet encountered a separate experience. Next to the ordinary rhythms of work, childbirth may have been the most common experience for women. Pregnancy, childbirth, and nursing provided a steady background beat to the lives of women in the colonies. Recent research

[23] For example, the names of the children of David and Elizabeth Chastain LeSueur included David and Elizabeth (each used twice due to the death of a child), Chastain, Peter (her father's name), Catherine (his mother's), John (her brother's), James (her uncle's), Samuel, Tell, and Martell. The last three names may have been new to the family or were a part of David's background.

has shown that colonial white women made childbirth a community event, infused with rituals of support by other women, and that these rituals of lying-in were shared with black women.[24] The evidence from Manakin, however, suggests that the risks of childbirth were greater for black women than for white. Although they may have participated in the rituals surrounding childbirth, black women were the center of attention less frequently because they had fewer children; moreover, participation in this women's culture required them to abandon some of their African traditions. Truly, childbirth was a bittersweet experience for black women.

The fragmentary King William Parish Register includes the records of births of slaves among forty-eight owners for the years from 1724 to 1744.[25] The parish register reveals only the owner's name, not the mother's, but since most white families claimed only one or two black women it is possible to trace the childbearing history of individual women.[26] The average birth interval was about 28 months, but was often less than two years. The experience of Marie, a slave of Jean Levillain, illustrates the point. Marie's first two children were born 19 months apart, followed by intervals of 24, 25, 11, 14, and 30 months.[27] In general, for the black women of Manakin, the most frequent interval was 20 months. Fifty-six percent of the birth intervals were between 15 and 34 months. However, another quarter of the intervals fell into a block running 36 to 47 months. The interval between births, however, was much more ragged than these figures suggest. Many women had long gaps in their childbearing histories. Other women had few or no children. For example, Pegg, the slave of Barbara Dutoy, had only one child in twelve years.

[24] Mary Beth Norton, *Liberty's Daughters: The Revolutionary Experience of American Women, 1750-1800* (Boston and Toronto, 1980), 78; Richard W. Wertz and Dorothy C. Wertz, *Lying-In: A History of Childbirth in America* (New York, 1977), 4-6; Catherine M. Scholten, "'On the Importance of the Obstetrick Art': Changing Customs of Childbirth in America, 1760 to 1825," *William and Mary Quarterly*, 3d Ser., XXXIV (July 1977), 426-45. Norton's work specifically mentions southern birthing experiences; the others look at childbirth as a general social custom brought from England.

[25] By comparing the tithe lists and parish register it was possible to determine that sixty-four black women over age sixteen lived in the parish during at least part of the years covered by the register. There were 151 births registered, 113 during the period 1724-44.

[26] Nothing illustrates the patriarchal nature of society better than a birth registration system that has infants born to males. The church records record only births, not baptisms, making clear that the owners registered these births so that there would be proof of age, an important factor when the slave would become taxable at sixteen.

[27] King William Parish Register, in Brock, ed., *Documents*, 80-100. Marie was Levillain's only adult female slave until 1735, when Nan was added to the tithes. Marie's last two childbirths overlap with the first of Nan's, but it is possible to sort out which births belong to each mother. The information on black births is taken from the parish register, with what support is available elsewhere. The information for white births includes wills, family records, and records of other parishes. The birth intervals for blacks are thus limited to the period covered by the King William Parish Register, but white births covered the whole eighteenth century.

TABLE 2

BIRTH INTERVALS FOR WOMEN ASSOCIATED WITH MANAKIN

Interval in months	*Black Births 1724–1744* *number*	*percent*	*White Births 1701–1783* *number*	*percent*
0–8	0	0	2	1
9–14	6	9	5	3
15–19	10	14	23	11
20–24	12	17	58	29
25–29	15	21	44	22
30–34	3	4	25	12
35–39	8	12	22	10
40–44	7	10	4	2
45–49	3	4	5	3
50–54	1	2	6	3
55–59	0	0	2	1
60+	5	7	6	3
Total	70	100	202	100

SOURCES: King William Parish Register in Brock, ed., *Documents*; William Macfarlane Jones, ed., *The Douglas Register* (Richmond, Va., 1928).

While the average and median for childbirth intervals were similar for black and white women in the parish, there were also major differences. The black woman was much more likely to have an intermittent history of childbirth with long gaps, ending much sooner than it did for the whites of Manakin. Birth intervals for whites were more tightly clustered around 24 months than black births. Seventy-four percent of the white births fell in the interval between 15 and 34 months (see Table 2). Elizabeth Chastain LeSueur, for example, bore children every two to three years with almost clockwork regularity from 1728 to 1753, while her slave Phillis had two children 30 months apart and then had no more children for at least seven years.[28]

The child-spacing patterns for black and white women of King William Parish provide important clues to the adaptation of black women to American slavery and their participation in a community culture surrounding childbirth. African customs of nursing were different from those of Europeans. In Africa women often nursed children for more than three years, abstaining from sexual relations during that period. Black women continued these patterns in the Caribbean slave communities, as did seventeenth-century blacks in the Chesapeake.

[28] The LeSueurs registered births in King William Parish in 1728, 1733, 1735, 1738, 1740, 1744, 1747, and 1750. David LeSueur's will included three children not in this listing, twins born in 1753 and a daughter who must have been born in 1742, given her own date of marriage and history of childbirth. The LeSueurs were out of the parish in 1730 and may have had a child then too. As for Phillis, the last seven years of the parish register include no slave births for the LeSueur family.

The secondary cluster of birth intervals of three to four years suggests that a number of immigrant black women, including Phillis, continued that tradition in the Manakin area. European women, however, nursed for a shorter time and had resultingly closer birth intervals of about two years.[29] Marie and a number of other black women in the parish adopted the shorter European traditions of nursing. Whether this adoption of European custom came at the urging of owners or as part of a cultural accommodation by black women, the result was that Marie and others like her had one more bond with white women.

In another way, however, the birth intervals explain how childbirth set black and white women apart, for black women had many fewer children per mother than the white women did. Childbearing histories for twenty-eight black women and fifty-five white women appear in Table 2. Twice as many white women provided almost three times the number of birth intervals as did black women. The difference may be a result of fewer black births, owners more frequently forgetting to register black births, or a combination of the two. All of the possibilities suggest a different experience for black women. Other evidence, such as estate inventories, suggests that fewer births account for most of the difference. Because many black women lived in King William Parish for fewer than their total childbearing years, it was necessary to transform the raw figures into data for a stable community in order to make comparisons with the experience of whites. A stable population would have been represented by just under nineteen black women living in the parish continuously throughout the twenty-year period. They would have averaged 6.01 children to produce the births actually registered. While this compares favorably with figures for the total children born to the French immigrant generation at King William Parish, it is considerably lower than the average number of children born by the later generations of white settlers at Manakin. Some white women also ended their childbearing after only a few children, or had long gaps due to the death of a spouse or physical problems, but most produced a steady stream of children spaced two years apart.[30] If black women had borne children spaced at the average interval without interrup-

[29] Menard, "The Maryland Slave Population," 38–41; Herbert S. Klein and Stanley L. Engerman, "Fertility Differentials between Slaves in the United States and the British West Indies: A Note on Lactation Practices and Their Possible Implications," *William and Mary Quarterly*, 3d Ser., XXXV (April 1978), 368–72.

[30] It is difficult to get complete information on the childbearing histories of women from King William Parish, but I have compiled secure evidence on 101. The 28 immigrant women on whom I have information bore 138 children, or an average of 4.9. The 45 native-born women bore 484 children, or an average of 10.75. I deliberately have not used completed family size since that figure is based on intact marriages. I have chosen instead to compile the complete childbearing histories of women, even if they were cut short by death or continued through several marriages, because this views the topic through the eyes of the woman.

tion, it would have taken only 14.2 years to reach the family size indicated by the stable population calculations.

That most black women were immigrants and most whites were native-born accounts for some of the difference in numbers of children, for immigrant women often delayed starting families while searching for mates or found their marriages disrupted. Others reached menopause before they had been in the Manakin area twenty years. The gaps in the middle of black women's childbearing years, however, are at least as significant as any shortening of the years at risk by late starts. Those mid-life gaps in childbearing were due in part to black life expectancy. Africans and other immigrants to the South had high death rates, even in the more healthful eighteenth century. Disruptions caused by the death of a partner could inhibit the total number of children a woman bore, especially while the black community was small, for finding a new partner might take years. Although white women also lost partners, by 1730 the population of King William Parish was colonial-born and more resistant to the endemic fevers. Thus their marriages were more stable. The slave population, however, continued to be heavily immigrant and thus continued to have a higher rate of marriage disruption. Transfers of ownership and removal to other areas increased the possibility of separation from partners and hence lowered the number of children born.

Childbearing was a part of the rhythm of a woman's life, but that rhythm had a different beat for black women. All twelve of Elizabeth LeSueur's children were born in October, November, or December. Phillis's known childbirths, however, were in April and October. Two-thirds of King William Parish's black births, however, occurred between February and July. The months of August through January saw relatively few black births. Black women, then, usually conceived during the months of May through October. The white women of Manakin show a much different pattern of births. Births were heavy in the fall and early spring and lowest in June, July, and August (see Figure 1). White conceptions were lowest in the fall; blacks were lowest in the deep winter.[31] Black women thus were in the later stages of pregnancy during the heavy labor season of spring planting. Surely this affected their health.

[31] A similar pattern was reported by the Rutmans and Charles Wetherell for Middlesex County, Virginia. Darrett B. Rutman, Charles Wetherell, and Anita H. Rutman, "Rhythms of Life: Black and White Seasonality in the Early Chesapeake," *Journal of Interdisciplinary History*, XI (Summer 1980), 29–53. I have chosen to chart the actual births rather than the cosine measure of variance from the expected average because the actual births provide a clearer picture for those who are not demographers. The cosine pattern for King William Parish, however, is a reasonable fit with the Rutman data.

FIGURE 1
BIRTH MONTHS FOR MANAKIN CHILDREN
1724–1750

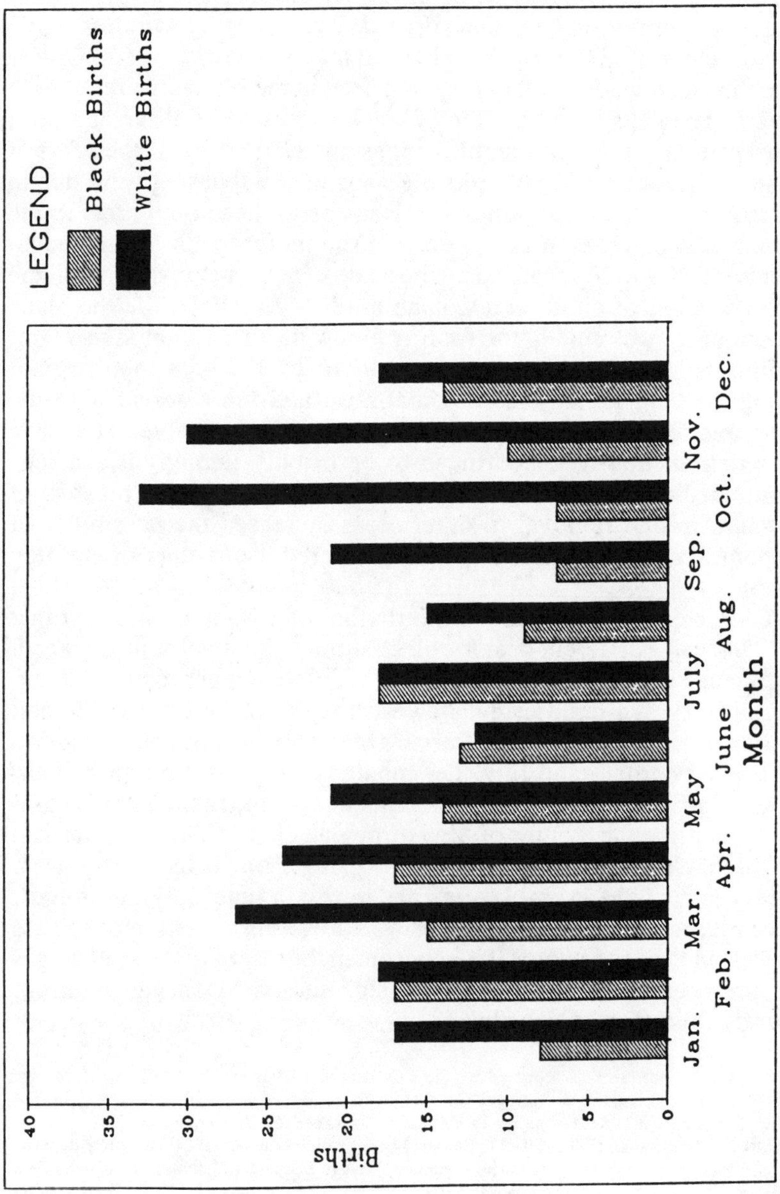

The puzzling question of why black women had their children on a different cycle from white women has no ready solution. Black women were certainly not planning their pregnancies in order to receive reduced work loads during the spring, because there is evidence that the loads were not reduced. It is possible that black men and women had more contact with each other during the summer and fall while they were tending and harvesting crops. In the cold months black women may have been kept close to the plantation house working on domestic projects such as spinning, and thus were not free to meet with their partners. White women had no such constraints. Opportunity for conception increased when the cold months brought white men closer to the hearth fires.

The white women of Manakin expected their children to survive to adulthood.[32] A black woman could not. King William Parish death records are fragmentary, so slave deaths appear only in a few cases where the record of birth includes a note of the infant's death.[33] Circumstantial evidence, however, suggests high infant and child mortality. Only 44 out of 151 of the slave children whose births were recorded in the parish register appear in any other legal and church record, and for some that second appearance was as a child. Death explains many of the disappearances.[34] For example, Beti, slave of Gideon Chambon, bore children Jean (John) in 1727 and Marye in 1733. When Chambon's estate inventory was filed in 1739 neither child appeared on the list. Given Chambon's age and economic condition, the most likely explanation is that the children died, not that he

[32] The infant mortality rate for Manakin families is low. Many families saw all of their children reach adulthood. Infant mortality seems restricted to a few families and probably reflected conditions specific to those families.

[33] Examples of infant deaths are the births of Moll, born December 31, 1740, and died January 11, 1740/1, slave of Martha Chastain; and Judith, born April 9, 1740, and died June 19, 1740, slave of John Villain, Jr., King William Parish Register, in Brock, ed., *Documents*, 99–100. In this area Elizabeth LeSueur and Phillis reversed the common patterns. The two children of Phillis whose births were recorded in the parish register both were still with the family thirty years later. Elizabeth LeSueur's first two children died before age twenty-one. A third died unmarried at age thirty-one. *Ibid.*, 81–104; will of David LeSueur III, June 26, 1769, Wills, Cumberland County, and will of David LeSueur I, February 24, 1772, *ibid.* Because of the repeated use of first names within a family I have adopted a system of identifying those with the same first and last names by Roman numerals assigned by order of birth.

[34] Gutman found a similar mortality level among nineteenth-century blacks. Gutman, *The Black Family*, 124. The county records of the counties for the years Manakin was included in each of their bounds include only one deed of gift of a King William Parish slave and no outright sales of blacks living in Manakin. In fact, there are few transfers of blacks other than by will in these records for anyone. It is possible that such sales were not normally recorded, but the lack of evidence for slave sales in the region from the *Virginia Gazette*, the fact that slaves do not appear as property to be sold in estate sales reported to the courts, that so many slaves can be traced through transfers by will and estate records, the existence of a few recorded deeds, and the curious provision of Virginia law that slaves were real estate, not personal property, all add weight to the conclusion that few slave children disappeared from these records because of sales.

sold or gave them away. Similarly, Magdalene, born in 1744, does not appear in any records after the filing of John Harris's will when she was seven. Owners registered two and three children by the same name over the years. John Chastain, for example, registered the births of black newborns named Fillis on March 24, 1745/6 and June 12, 1753. Only one slave of that name appears on his estate inventory. Likewise, Bartholomew Dupuy's slave Sara bore sons named Jack in both 1727 and 1730. Apparently they were doing what many families also did following the death of a white child, that is, replacing it by another of the same name.[35]

The work patterns of black women fostered the high death rate among their children by exhausting mothers and making infant care difficult. The experiences of Aggy, a slave of the Levillain family, provide some clues to the relationship between work, childbearing, and infant mortality. Aggy (Agar) had been born in Manakin on August 7, 1733, as the slave of Jean Levillain; she passed by will to Jean's son Anthony Lavillain in 1746.[36] Four years later, when Aggy was seventeen, Anthony died intestate, leaving Aggy the property of Anthony's newborn daughter Mary and the subject of an administered estate for the next fifteen years. Aggy's first child was born when she was eighteen. Two years later she had another. Throughout those years she worked in the fields, while the administratrix of the estate, Elizabeth Lavillain Young Starkey, recorded expenses for "nursing" both small children. The youngest, a girl, died by age three. In 1763 Aggy, by then thirty, again became pregnant. The pregnancy was not easy, however, for the records show payments to Mrs. Chastain for treating Aggy "when sick" and attending Aggy's lying-in.[37]

Aggy's life illustrates the black pattern of work and childbearing in King William Parish. Beginning in her teens Aggy had two children spaced two years apart, but then there was a ten-year gap before she had another child. From 1754 to 1756 Aggy was hired out. Then she returned to work with the other slaves growing tobacco, wheat, and corn for the estate. John Levillain, Anthony's brother and, after

[35] Chambon was illiterate. His name appears in the records with several different spellings. I am using the form that appears most often. King William Parish Register, in Brock, ed., *Documents*, 80, 88, 105–106, 110, 79, 84; inventory of Gideon Chambon II, August 21, 1739, Wills, Goochland County; inventory of John Harris, March 26, 1753, Wills, Cumberland County.

[36] The father and son spelled their last names differently. I have used the spelling each man preferred. King William Parish Register, in Brock, ed., *Documents*, 89. Will of John Levillain, June 17, 1746, Deeds and Wills, Goochland County.

[37] Anthony Lavillain's widow, Elizabeth Jones Lavillain, remarried twice while administering the estate. Her name changed on different sections of the records filed with the court. Anthony Lavillain estate management records, August 21, 1754, August 25, 1755, September 1757, and August 24, 1764, Will Book, Orphans Court, Cumberland County.

1754, Mary's guardian, did see that Aggy got medical treatment during her difficult later pregnancy, but the records Levillain filed with the court for income to the estate credit her with the same share of work on the crops as other slaves, so he had not reduced her work. Such practices would increase the risk of infant mortality.[38]

The records for the Manakin area do not reveal much about the birth customs for black women, but Charlotte Chastain's appearance during Aggy's lying-in was not the only time a white midwife was paid for the delivery of a black woman's baby in the Manakin area.[39] Thus while the Manakin families might not have been rich enough to provide the elaborate lying-ins for black women that Mary Beth Norton has described, the birth experience was not left entirely to the black community.[40] Since we also know that black women helped at the births of white children, the physical act of giving birth may have been one of the most significant ways in which black and white women served each other in a single community.

As with the other aspects of their lives, work both separated and brought black women together with whites. Virginia's tithe laws made clear the distinctions. White women such as Elizabeth Chastain LeSueur were not counted in figuring the tithe. In fact, they only appeared on the tithe lists when widowed with slaves or male children sixteen years or over. On the other hand, black women like Phillis were counted. Ironically, it is easier to trace black women from year to year in the community since they are listed on the tithes than it is to trace white women. Eventually, in 1769, free black women received the same exemption as white women, but slave women remained a part of the tithe. In other words, black women were considered a basic part of the agricultural labor force in a way that white women were not.[41] Undoubtedly, Phillis had spent part of her time working in the LeSueur fields. When the LeSueurs purchased her they had no children old enough to help with farm work, and David and Elizabeth LeSueur were planting without any regular help. Phillis's arrival assured Elizabeth that she could withdraw from occasional help in the fields to her many household duties and garden.

[38] Anthony Lavillain estate management records, August 24, 1764, Will Book, Orphans Court, Cumberland County.

[39] There were several adult Chastain women in the area, but Charlotte Judith Chastain, wife of the clerk of the vestry and local surgeon (and sister-in-law to Elizabeth Chastain LeSueur), was the most likely to have been a midwife. The records for management of the Frances Bernard estate include payments to Mrs. Robertson for "Delivering her [Mary Bernard's] Negro Woman" and to Mrs. Burnett for the same. Frances Bernard estate management records, August 1755 and August 1760, Will Book, Orphans Court, Cumberland County.

[40] Norton, *Liberty's Daughters*, 66–67.

[41] William Waller Hening, [ed.], *The Statutes at Large: Being A Collection Of All The Laws of Virginia, From The First Session Of The Legislature In The Year 1619* (13 vols., Richmond, New York, and Philadelphia, 1819–23), VIII, 393.

While white women seldom worked away from home, black women sometimes did. Slave rentals kept the labor supply flexible, cut costs for care by owners, and provided an income for widows and orphans. Two major sources for rental slaves were estates managed to provide an income for widows and orphans, and wealthy farmers who hired out their surplus women and children slaves. Women slaves were hired out more frequently than men.[42] Thus black women might be separated from family and friends in order to secure the income that allowed a white woman to remain on the family farm. Agar, who had arrived at Manakin in 1714, spent the 1730s hired out by the widow Magdalene Salle, while the family's other adult slave, Bob, stayed on the plantation. Only when Magdalene's son came of age and assumed management of the plantation did Agar return to the plantation. Widow Barbara Dutoy also rented her slaves to other residents of Manakin from 1726 to 1733. In both cases rental gave the widow an income without the worry of planting. It allowed minimum disruption to the widow's life, but at the expense of disrupting the slave woman's life.[43]

Surviving orphans court records and wills document other hiring out of slaves in the Manakin area. Jean Levillain hired out Aggy from 1754 to 1756 for a charge of about £4 each year. Some hiring was short-term. James Holman hired out a black woman for two weeks time while managing Peter Martin's estate. In addition, nine children's births appear in the parish register without their owners paying tithes on an adult woman. The mothers were probably rented out and appeared under the renter's name on the tithe list.[44] A hired slave could move frequently; for example, Lucy seems to have been hired by Abraham Salle in 1724, Jack Griffin in 1732 and 1733, and Pierre

[42] The Manakin evidence is very similar to that reported by Sarah S. Hughes for the late eighteenth century. Hughes, "Slaves for Hire: The Allocation of Black Labor in Elizabeth City County, Virginia, 1782 to 1810," *William and Mary Quarterly*, 3d Ser., XXXV (April 1978), 268–72.

[43] Several of the tithe lists from the 1730s do not list dependents by name, so it is hard to trace slaves. Magdalene Salle inherited Bob and Agar in 1730/1. In 1733 Agar appears as a tithe of John Martin, whereas Bob appears under Magdalene Salle's name. In 1744 Magdalene Salle is credited with two tithes, presumably Bob and Agar. Joseph and Pegg were slaves of Pierre Dutoy. His widow Barbara inherited them, but only once do they appear under her name. They are listed with several different families until 1733, when they appear under Barbara's new son-in-law, Thomas Porter. King William Parish Vestry Book, 1723–36; will of Abraham Salle II, March 1, 1730/1, Miscellaneous Papers, Henrico County; will of Pierre Dutoy, October 3, 1726, Deeds and Wills, Henrico County.

[44] Anthony Lavillain estate management records, August 25, 1755, August 24, 1764, Wills, Orphans Court, Cumberland County; Peter Martin estate management records, March 19, 1754, Deeds and Wills, Orphans Court, Goochland County. The slave births were to Joseph Bingley, James Brian, David LeSueur, Daniel Perault, Thomas Porter, Nicholas Soulie, Jacob Trabue, and Giles Allegre. King William Parish Register, in Brock, ed., *Documents, passim*. The births were not to mothers under sixteen. Nicholas Soulie registered his first slave birth in 1728 but had no slave tithes until 1732. It is unlikely that one of his slaves gave birth at age twelve.

Louis Soblet in 1734 and 1735.[45] The rental of female slaves thus seems to have been an integral part of the Manakin labor system, allowing aspiring farmers to add to their small labor forces while providing income for widows and orphans. Once again the community's perception of black women primarily as field hands set black and white women apart.

Phillis might have spent much of her time in the fields, but she also worked with Elizabeth LeSueur on the many tasks associated with women's work. Domestic work was not a single occupation but a variety of highly skilled tasks shared by women on the plantation.[46] For example, clothmaking occupied both white and black women in the Manakin area. When David LeSueur died in 1772, the family owned working farms in both Buckingham and Cumberland counties. Only the home plantation in Cumberland, however, had cotton, wool and cotton cards, a wool wheel, two spindles, four flax wheels, and parts for two looms. Elizabeth obviously oversaw and worked with Phillis and Phillis's two grown daughters in the making of a variety of cloth.[47] The LeSueurs were not unusual, for inventories throughout the Manakin region mention several crops including flax, the tools necessary to produce linen thread, and, somewhat less frequently, looms for weaving.[48] The Lavillain estate, for example, purchased two spinning wheels. These wheels were for the use of Aggy and Nan, slaves of the estate who continued to be credited with a share of the crops of tobacco and grains. John Levillain simply added cloth production to the women's field duties.[49] The usefulness of women in the tasks of cloth production may have encouraged owners to purchase women slaves. From its beginning the colony at Manakin provided Virginia cloth, used to clothe slaves and the poor. Black women worked with white women in this production on the small farm, thus providing another way in which a community of women cut across racial lines.

[45] Tithe lists, 1724, 1732–35, King William Parish Vestry Book.

[46] Menard, "The Maryland Slave Population," 53. Menard argues that while male slaves had a variety of skilled occupations to draw them away from the fields, women had only domestic work and cloth production. Domestic work, however, in the eighteenth century was made up of quite diverse, highly skilled activities. For a good description of the many skills of colonial domestic work see Laurel Thatcher Ulrich, *Good Wives: Image and Reality in the Lives of Women in Northern New England, 1650–1750* (New York, 1982), 11–86.

[47] Despite David LeSueur's status as a vestry member, his seventeen slaves, and landholdings of more than a thousand acres, his inventory is that of a simple farming family with only a few luxury items. There is little doubt that Elizabeth Chastain worked at household tasks and did not just supervise them. Inventories of David LeSueur, April 26, 1773, Wills, Cumberland County.

[48] See for example the inventory of Peter Faure, April 16, 1745, Deeds and Wills, Goochland County.

[49] The two black women were the only women for whom the estate might have purchased the wheels. The heiress, Mary, was away at school. Anthony Lavillain estate management records, August 24, 1764, Will Book, Orphans Court, Cumberland County.

The smallness of slaveholdings and the relatively short life expectancies of owners created major instabilities in the lives of black women that exceeded the uncertainties of life for their white mistresses. Although owners recognized that black families existed, and while there is convincing evidence that kinship ties were strong among blacks, the value of slaves as property meant that black family stability was tied to the life cycle of their owners.[50] Short life expectancies and parental willingness to establish adult children on farms of their own as soon as possible accelerated the cycle in the Manakin area. Life patterns in the late seventeenth and early eighteenth centuries were such that most Chesapeake parents expected to die before all their children came of age.[51] One result of this expectation was the willingness of parents to give adult children their shares of the estate when they came of age or married. For example, Elizabeth Chastain's brother John and sister Judith were already living on their shares of land when their father Peter wrote his will.[52] Thus even a long-lived owner was no guarantee of stability in a slave family.

Most blacks in the Manakin area changed hands upon the death of an owner or the coming of age of a child of the owner. Because slaves were valuable legacies to children, they were often divided among several heirs. Daughters, especially, received slaves as their share of the estate, either as dowries or legacies. With slaveholdings small, black families were divided at each period of change within the white family. Most bequests in the Manakin area (except for life interests to widows) were of one or two slaves. David LeSueur, for example, granted each of his eight surviving children one slave. Phillis, her two oldest children, and another male (probably husband to her daughter) stayed with their mistress, Elizabeth Chastain LeSueur, but all of Phillis's younger children and grandchildren were scattered.[53] Owners when possible left very small children with slave mothers or bequeathed the slave mother to a married son or daughter and the slave's children to the children of the son or daughter. Thus black women received some recognition of bonds with children not accorded to men. In fact, the estate appraisers often perceived infants and mothers as one, giving a single value to a mother and her small child. Frequently they did not even bother to list the infant's name.[54]

[50] Herbert G. Gutman develops this insight extensively in his book, *The Black Family*, 154–55, 138.

[51] Rutman and Rutman, "'Now-Wives and Sons-in-Law'," 153–82.

[52] Will of Peter Chastain, November 20, 1728, Deeds and Wills, Goochland County. Joan R. Gundersen, "Parental Control and Coming of Age in Virginia," paper read at the Winona Conference on Changing Images of the American Family, Winona, Minn., November 1979.

[53] LeSueur owned seventeen slaves, mostly members of two black families. Will of David LeSueur I, February 24, 1772, Wills, Cumberland County; and inventories of David LeSueur, April 26, 1773, *ibid.*

[54] See the inventories of Isaac Salle, August 17, 1731, Deeds and Wills, Goochland County;

Black women might wait for years before the pain of such divisions became real. While the marriage of older children of the owners caused some separation among black families, the major estate divisions came when the owner died. Many estates remained intact for years awaiting the coming of age of minor children or the remarriage or death of a widow. Thus the fate of black women (and men) depended on the fate of their white mistresses.[55] For example, Kate was a slave of Anthony Rapine when he died in 1737. Rapine gave his wife, Margaret, a life interest in half the estate with all eventually to go to his daughter, Maryanne Martin. Since Maryanne and her husband lived with the Rapines, Kate's life went on unchanged. In 1740 she bore a daughter, Hannah. Three years later Maryanne Martin was widowed and soon after she remarried. She deeded Kate and Hannah to her year-old son, Peter Martin, shortly before remarrying. In 1747, ten years after Anthony Rapine died, the estate was finally divided between Margaret Rapine and Thomas Smith, who had married the now-deceased Maryanne. Kate and Hannah (by then age seven) were listed together on the inventory and passed into Smith's possession. He then turned Kate and Hannah over to Peter's new guardian in 1749. At last, after twelve years, Kate and Hannah were forced to move.[56] The black woman on a larger estate had a better chance of remaining with kin following the death of an owner. The few large estates included in the study divided slaves on the basis of where they lived, often giving a particular farm and its slaves to an heir.[57]

The slave woman lived and worked in a very small community at Manakin. Since each family owned only a few slaves, a black community could not exist on a single plantation. The farms at Manakin were small enough (the original allotments were 133 acres each) that visiting between farms would be possible, and thus a wider community might have existed. The birth patterns, however, suggest that

David LeSueur, April 26, 1773, Wills, Cumberland County; Peter Harris, February 26, 1776, *ibid.*; Peter Guerrant, September 1750, *ibid.*; and John Harris, April 26, 1753, *ibid.* See the wills of Peter Harris, August 28, 1775, *ibid.*; James Holman, September 24, 1753, *ibid.*; Stephen Watkins, *c.* 1759, Wills, Chesterfield County; John Martin, May 3, 1736, Deeds and Wills, Henrico County; Jacob Trabue, *c.* 1772, Wills, Chesterfield County; and Abraham Salle, March 1, 1730/1, Miscellaneous, Henrico County.

[55] See the wills of Stephen Chastain, August 21, 1739, Deeds and Wills, Goochland County; Francis Flournoy, *c.* 1770, Wills, Chesterfield County; and Peter Anthony Lookado, Wills, July 25, 1768, Cumberland County.

[56] Deed of Gift, Maryanne Martin to Peter Martin, September 20, 1743, Deeds, Goochland County; division of Rapine estate, September 17, 1747, Wills, *ibid.*; Order Book, September 16, 1747, *ibid.*; Order Book, November 27, 1749, Cumberland County. Anthony Rapine died in 1737. Will of Anthony Rapine, November 15, 1737, Deeds and Wills, Goochland County.

[57] See for example the wills of Jacob Michaux, June 27, 1774, Wills, and John James Dupuy, February 27, 1775, Wills, both of Cumberland County.

such visiting was limited. Although the dispersed black population might have hindered the formation of a black community, the tasks of the black woman put her in constant contact with whites. Family members on a small farm labored in the fields alongside the slaves, and women's chores such as spinning might be done with the wife and daughters of the owner. Historians have speculated that slaves who lived on small plantations or in areas isolated from a black community probably adopted white values and customs more readily than those who could fashion a creole life-style with other blacks.[58] For the black woman this meant partial acceptance into the special world of women's society. Such acceptance made more poignant the contrast in birth rates, child mortality, and family stability between blacks and whites.

Life for black women in the Manakin area was filled with insecurity. Some risks, such as childbirth, were shared with white women, but others were not. As part of a double minority black women enjoyed a favorable marriage market, but dispersion of holdings threatened the families formed by black women with separation. Some slaves on large plantations could begin to develop distinct creole societies near Manakin, but that was possible only after 1750 and only for a small proportion of slaves. Slave rentals, which affected women more than men, added another dimension of instability to that ensured by the short life spans of spouses and owners. The decisions made by widows to remarry, farm, or hire out slaves for income not only determined whether white families would remain intact, but whether black ones would too. Most black women in the Manakin area lived on small farms or quarters where their field work was supplemented by sharing in the household tasks of the white women on the farm. The "bonds of womanhood" surrounded her life as much as the bonds of slavery, beginning with the very choice of a name. Childbearing was especially frustrating for the black woman, filled with the pain of frequent infant death, heavy workloads when pregnant, and separation from children. But childbirth also meant sharing in a woman's network that stretched across racial lines. The life of a black woman was thus constantly subjected to the cross-pressures of belonging to a woman's subculture without full membership.

[58] Kulikoff, "The Origins of Afro-American Society," 229, 245.

SLAVE CULTURE AND SLAVE FAMILY AND KIN NETWORK: The Importance of Time.*

Herbert G. Gutman

More than half a century has passed since W. E. B. DuBois published his pioneering study of the Afro-American family in which he complained of being "faced by a lamentable dearth of material." DuBois found conventional historical sources quite limited:

> It is difficult to get a clear picture of the family relations of slaves, between the Southern apologist and his picture of cabin life, with idyllic devotion and careless toil, and that of the abolitionist with his tale of family disruption and cruelty, adultery and illegitimate mulatoes. Between these pictures the student must steer carefuly to find a reasonable statement of the average truth.[1]

DuBois's words were written in 1909, but despite the vast literature on Afro-American slavery published since that time the same complaint could have been made in 1950 or 1974. Study of the slave family has been greatly handicapped by much more than a dearth of sources.

* From a paper presented at a conference on "Society and Culture in South Carolina," College of Charleston, March 27, 1976. For a fuller exposition of themes described therein, see Herbert G. Gutman, *The Black Family in Slavery and Freedom, 1750–1925* (New York, 1976).

Reductionist "sociological" models, an explicit or implicit assumption that slave culture was only "imitative" in origin, and the absence of general comparative work on the history of the family greatly misshaped the study of the slave family and kinship system. Even E. Franklin Frazier, the foremost student Afro-American family in this century, revealed these handicaps in his many substantial works. Frazier, for example, found no evidence of slave kinship beyond the immediate family (except, that is, for the greatly exaggerated "three-generation" male-absent household). According to Frazier, the so-called "maternal family" was the most common among enslaved Afro-Americans. Frazier viewed that type of family as a legitimate adaptation by Africans and their Afro-American descendants to the harshness of Anglo-American enslavement. Only elite slaves—the house servants and the artisans—managed to sustain the conventional two-parent family, and that resulted from their relatively secure economic status and their accessibility to conventional "white or owner-class models."[2] The use of a new sort of evidence—plantation birth registers which recorded for more than two generations the date of birth of slave children and usually listed the names of both parents—allows us to begin a fundamental revision of the traditional description of the Afro-American slave family. It is possible to describe a developing slave kinship system and to show its roots in the adaptive capacities of enslaved Africans and their several generations of enslaved Afro-American descendants. It is also possible to put aside decisively for the first time the simple "imitative" models of slave culture and to begin instead to deal with culture-change under slavery in quite sophisticated ways. "The slave trade and slavery," the anthropologist Sidney W. Mintz has written, "gave rise to special conditions of culture change under which the slaves were compelled to fashion new life-styles in the face of tremendous repression."[3]

These new documents allow us to examine some of the ways in which this happened and to see how a common Afro-American slave family and kinship system developed in quite different slave settings in the hundred years preceding general emancipation. "A system of kinship and marriage," the British anthropologist A. R. Radcliffe-Brown has written, "can be looked at as an arrangement which enables persons to live together and co-operate with one another in an orderly social life." Enslavement made the possibilities of "an orderly social life" unusually difficult for Africans and their Afro-American descendants, but historians have focused too narrowly on just those difficulties and therefore given inadequate attention to the ways in which adaptive family and kinship arrangements coped with those difficulties. Such an arrangement, Radcliffe-Brown continues, "links persons together by convergence of interest and sentiment and . . . controls and limits those conflicts that are always possible."[4]

Much that deserves and is given detailed attention in a larger manuscript on the Afro-American family now completed is neglected in the pages that follow. Little is said, for example, about slave sexual behavior, slave marriage rituals, slave surnames, and slave child-rearing practices. Instead, the focus is on the slave kinship system, what that system tells us about the sources of a precarious but present slave family stability, the relationship between the immediate family and the enlarged kinship group, slave marriage rules, and slave given name practices.

This paper focuses on one South Carolina cotton plantation and its slave community—the Good Hope plantation (owned, incidentally, by the direct forbears of John Foster and Allen Dulles, men who figured prominently in the reshaping of mid-twentieth-century corporate American society). But the familial and kinship arrangements found among the Good Hope slaves were not unique to this small group of enslaved Afro-Americans. Strikingly similar patterns are found among plantation slaves living in Virginia, North Carolina, Alabama, and Louisiana. The Good Hope slave men, women, and children are important because they shared common beliefs and behavioral patterns with other enslaved Afro-Americans. The Good Hope plantation birth register recorded only four demographic items about each newborn slave child; its date of birth, its given name, and the given names, when known, of both parents. The first birth listed took place in Africa in 1760 (sixteen years before the signing of the Declaration of Independence) and the last ninety-seven years later (three years before Abraham Lincoln's election as president). Recording the names of at least six blacks born in eighteenth-century Africa and twelve others not yet ten years old when the Civil War started, the full register combined lives which encapsule nearly the entire early Afro-American historical experience: birth in Africa, enslavement, cotton plantation slavery, emancipation, and, finally, life as quasi-free men and women. The register also revealed the consanguinal and marital ties connecting four generations of enslaved Afro-Americans with a total historical experience stretching well over a century. The register is an unusual historical document. Its usefulness rests on its relative completeness, the length of time it covers, and especially on the listing of the names of fathers as well as slave mothers. This information allows us to examine in new ways such vital matters as the length of slave unions, naming practices among the enslaved, the presence of exogamous taboos in selecting marital partners, and the emergence of significant intergenerational slave kinship networks which bound together the immediate families of slaves with their families of origin and made possible the transmission over time of an adaptive slave culture. A summary of what the register reveals follows.

1. The last birth recorded in the Good Hope register was dated 1857. That year, 175 slaves lived on the plantation. Between 1820 and 1857, 154 children had been born. In 1857, 110 of them lived with one or both parents. Eleven others had taken slave spouses, and the rest—nearly one in four—had died. Nearly all (94 percent) of the 175 resident slaves lived in familes either as husband or wife or as children with one or both parents. The few single persons were nearly all elderly persons who had known earlier settled marriages. The oldest, Patty, had been born in 1774. The register reveals even more. Good Hope slave women bore a first child at an early age, 18 or 19, far below the age reported by Robert Fogel and Stanley Engerman in *Time on the Cross*. The size of families in 1857, not surprisingly, varied according to the age of parents, but most children born into families that started between 1800 and 1849 grew up in large families. More than half (54 percent) lived in households where a mother had eight or more children.

2. The register also told how long slave couples had lived together in settled unions. Most men older than 30 had known such unions for many years. All between the ages of 35 and 44 had lived in settled

unions for between 10 and 17 years. All but three of the nine men 45 and older had known the same slave wife for at least 20 years. (These data, incidentally, are reinforced by slave marriages recorded in 1866 by thousands of former Virginia and North Carolina slaves in civil and military marriage registers.) These lengthy slave unions cast considerable doubt on the conventional wisdom which argues that the absence of legal marriage and "any generally accepted mode of establishing mating relationships outside of legally recognized marriage, among themselves" meant that the "mating of slaves was typically unstable."[5]

3. Only analysis of the *full* Good Hope birth register tells why these marriages held together and reveals something of their interior meaning to the enslaved themselves. By reorganizing the register into separate family groupings arranged in time by the date of first child's birth in each family (prior to 1800, 1800 to 1819, 1820 to 1839, and 1840 to 1857), the full register unfolds some of the significant ways in which Africans, their children, and their grandchildren adapted in a coherent way to enslavement. A few men and more women had children by two or more mates, but nearly all Good Hope slave parents fit a large pattern of settled unions. Forty-two separate families started between 1800 and 1857, and 94 different slaves were listed as parents. Seventy-seven (83 percent) had children by a single mate. Only three fathers had children by more than one woman. That more women had children by different mates did not mean that "licentious" or "indiscrimate" mating commonly occurred among the Good Hope slave women. Most women settled permanently with a single spouse. About one-third of the 44 mothers had children by two or more men, most of these by only two. The common practice among these women was to have a first child by one male and then settle into a permanent union with a second mate. A handful of women had children by unnamed fathers, but they, too, settled into permanent unions. This evidence—and much other evidence not detailed in this brief paper—indicates a sexual pattern that was neither promiscuous nor "prudish." Prenuptial intercourse was quite common among these and other enslaved Afro-Americans but in no way contradictory to settled slave unions. Slaves and observant Northern and Southern whites (few in

number, to be sure) noticed just this pattern. The plantation white Mary Chestnut put it well. Slave women, she said, "can redeem themselves—the 'impropers' can. They can marry decently, and nothing is remembered against these colored ladies."[6] In their mating and sexual behavior, the Good Hope slaves did not differ from many other premodern cultural groups, dissociating, as Bronislaw Malinowski put it, "the two sides or procreation, that is sex and parenthood."[7] But for most slave women, prenuptial pregnancy resulted in subsequent marriage. That, too, was a part of their belief system. Asked in 1863 if some slave women had children prior to marriage, the Georgia slave Harry McMillan told the American Freedman's Inquiry Commission: "Yes, sir, but they are thought low of among their companions unless they get a husband before the child is born and if they cannot the shame grows until they do get a husband."[8]

4. The absence of legal restraints meant to uphold marital and moral norms among the enslaved did not mean that sanctions legitimizing settled slave unions and a code of moral and social behavior failed to develop among the enslaved themselves. Such sanctions, however, had their primary roots within a cumulative slave experience, did not have to be regularly imposed upon different generations of slaves by benevolent or harsh owners, and depended upon much more than the willingness of owners to allow slaves to remain together. That much is clear if we examine the Good Hope register by linking together the separate generations (1800–1819, 1820–1839, 1840–1857) of slave families and then studying the varied relationships based on affinal and consanguinal slave ties that *developed among them over time.* An examination of all slave unions formed between 1800 and 1857 and all the children born to these individual slave unions shows that, over time, these settled unions became linked together in an enlarged and integrated slave kinship structure. Such ties which connected generations of slaves separated by "time" but also connected particular families of slaves at fixed moments in time formed the underpinning of an adaptive slave culture which regularly helped to define the identity of particular slave men, women, and children. It was in such settings that slave children absorbed values from parents, grandparents, and even more distant blood kin. The child was not socialized simply

by its owner. A "near family" and a "far family" existed and such families had their roots in historical time. That is why E. Franklin Frazier was so profoundly wrong in arguing that "when one undertakes the study of the Negro he discovers a great poverty of traditions and patterns of behavior that exercise any real influence on the formation of the Negro's personality and conduct."[9] Among the Good Hope slaves—and all other plantation communities studied—the values and adaptive experiences of eighteenth-century and early nineteenth-century blacks, native Africans among them, could be passed directly to slave children through an emerging family and kin network. Such values included slave mating, sexual, and marital practices. Enslavement profoundly disadvantaged the Good Hope plantation blacks, but did not deny to them the opportunity to know parents and grandparents and to learn from them and from other older kin.

5. The Good Hope birth register contains vital information revealing a *consciousness* among the enslaved of the importance of kin ties outside the immediate family. Good Hope slaves probably had limited choices in selecting mates, and most took as spouses members of the twelve families that had come together between 1800 and 1819. But the constrictions imposed by the powerful social fact of ownership did not cause indiscriminate mating or a loose selection of marital partners. It has been seen how the Good Hope kin group expanded over time so that by the 1840s and the 1850s younger slaves in large numbers had many blood relatives on the plantation. Despite this fact, only one of the settled slave unions that took place between 1800 and 1857 involved a slave man and a slave woman with close blood ties. Fanny and Lewis had the same grandmother (Fanny) but different grandfathers (Chance R. and Billy). Not a single other union formed among the Good Hope slaves involved a man and woman as close to one another as first cousins. The presence of an exogamous ban among the Good Hope slaves—that is, a restraint upon marriage fixed by the boundaries of the kinship group—suggests strongly that such a taboo had its roots in their belief system or culture. Where rules of exogamy exist, Malinowski insisted, "it is clear that repression acts with at least as great force as with us."[10] More than this, as A. R. Radcliffe-Brown points out in discussing exogamous practices in diverse

African societies, "the rule of exogamy . . . is a way of giving institutional recognition" to the "bond of kinship" and serves as "part of the machinery for establishing and maintaining a wide-ranging kinship system."[11] The strength of the exogamous taboo among the Good Hope slaves is indicated by its persistence over time and by its presence on a large Virginia and an even still larger Louisiana plantation. The sources of this taboo remain obscure. But if the largest South Carolina planters were typical of Southern planters, it is clear that these exogamous slave beliefs and practices were not "copied" from the beliefs and practices of the owners of slaves. Drawing from the 1860 federal manuscript census, Chalmers Gaston Davidson has sketched a collective portrait of the 440 South Carolina men and women who owned at least one hundred slaves. (All but forty of these persons were born in South Carolina.) Davidson concludes:

> . . . [T]hey were most amazingly interwed, the marriages of cousins being almost the rule rather than the exception. Whether this occurred for reasons of propinquity or property was questionable (and as questioned) then as now. Nor was this a sectional phenomenon. The Gists of up-country Union, the Mobleys of Fairfield, the Ellerbes of Chesterfield, and the Westons and Adamses of Lower Richland were altogether as inbred by 1860 as were the Fripps of St. Helena's Parish, the Jenkins-Townsend-Seabrook clan of Edisto Island, or the Maners, Roberts, and Lawtons of St. Peter's. Before the Confederate defeat brought their world to a crashing end, the separate septs of Allston, Heyward, and Porcher apparently expected and were expected to marry only within their circle of blood or bond, in spite of European tours and summers at the springs. And these three, incidentally, were the largest planting connections in the State.[12]

Slave exogamy as contrasted to planter endogamy among these South Carolinians tell us convincingly that mimetic theories of slave culture—even the most sophisticated—are gravely flawed. But the patterns of marriage and kinship among eighteenth-century and early nineteenth-century Southern whites in all social classes need much more careful study before it can be argued that exogamous slave marital beliefs and practices had their primary roots within slave culture itself or in an adaptation of antecedent West African beliefs and practices. It is known, however, that the diverse West African tribes from which these slaves had descended all had as a clan function the regulation of marriage. Among them, "mating between sib (clan) mates or other relatives of legally established affiliation" was "forbidden as incestuous." Descent lines, furthermore, were traced in part to "ensure that no common affiliation" stood "in the way" of marriage. A study of diverse contemporary African patterns furthermore concludes that "individual choice is limited by prohibitions against marriage with related persons, the extent of which varies from tribe to tribe but is nearly always much wider than in the western world, often including all members of a lineage." The sources of a nearly similar taboo among the Good Hope slaves cannot be inferred from just such evidence. Much additional study of sexual and marital taboos among slaves and free whites is needed before the origins of such taboos among these and other Afro-American slaves are understood. But their origin counts for much less than the fact that a social principle existed among the Good Hope slaves which limited the selection of mates, that this principle was as powerful in the 1850s as in earlier decades. Other sources than plantation birth registers, furthermore, indicate the presence of an exogamous taboo among enslaved Afro-Americans. A song remembered by the former slave Allen Parker made explicit reference to the prohibition of cousin marriages:

> Sally's in de garden siftin' sand,
> And all she want is a honey man.
> De reason why I wouldn't marry,
> Because she was my cousin.
>
> O, row de boat ashore, hey, hey,
> Sallys in de garden siftin' sand.[13]

Parker was not a Good Hope plantation slave, and that is what makes this evidence so important. In the 1930s, the elderly former slave Phillis Thomas reported to federal interviewers yet another song that emphasized the exogamous beliefs of the slaves:

Herodias go down to de river one day,
Want to know what John Baptist have to say.
John spoke de words at de risk of he life,
Not lawful to mary yous brudder's wife.[14]

Phillis Thomas had been a Texas slave child. Taboos rooted in exogamous beliefs apparently had traveled with the slaves in the great forced migration of blacks from the Upper to the Lower South.

6. Yet another kind of evidence drawn from the Good Hope birth register—the names given to newborn slave children—indicates the presence of powerful kin ties to the immediate family and to the larger kin grouping among these South Carolina slaves. Such naming practices—and what happened on the Good Hope plantation happened even more commonly on the other plantations studied—are significant evidence that the kin ties went far beyond the "formal" connection hinted at by mere diagrammatic lines. Within particular families, children in significant numbers carried the given names of either a parent, a grandparent, or another blood relative. The parents of three adults belonging to the families that started between 1800 and 1819 are known, that is, those Good Hope slaves closest in time to actual enslavement. In each of these families, a child had the name of a slave father or a slave grandfather. Enslavement radically altered the lives of the South Carolina blacks and made it impossible for them to recreate the kinship structures known among West African blacks but had not destroyed a functional and purposive familial and social memory. In adapting domestic arrangements to enslavement in a distant land, these and other blacks had not forgotten their immediate forebears. They had not surrendered attachments to and identification with immediate and even "distant" kin. Naming practices linked generations of blood kin. In two of three Good Hope slave families that started between 1820 and 1849, at least one newborn child carried the name of a slave father or a slave grandparent. The influential historian of American slave society Ulrich B. Phillips misjudged Afro-Americans profoundly in his pioneering works. He summed up one of his most glaring errors in a single sentence. "With 'hazy pasts and reckless futures,' " said Phillips of the enslaved Afro-Americans, "they lived in each moment as it flew."[15] It was as if Africans and their de-

scendants had to be taught to "remember." In their lengthy slave unions, the exogamous nature of these unions, and the names given to some children born to these unions, the Good Hope slaves revealed in their behavior how little about them was understood by contemporaries and later by nearly all historians. And so did the former South Carolina slave Pen Eubanks who told an interviewer in 1937, "I is got memory, but I ain't got no larning; dat I is proud of, kaise I is seed folks wid larning dat never knowed nothing worth speaking about." Eubanks was born in 1854, the same year that the Good Hope slaves Fanny and Lewis named their newborn daughter for her paternal grandmother Bridget![16]

7. There is yet another point to be made, and it relates to the larger question of how one examines the behavior of enslaved and other exploited classes. The Good Hope slave birth register in its entirety demonstrates much of importance about the family life and kin networks that developed among these enslaved South Carolinians. Most significantly, the register reveals the essential need for *an enlarged time perspective* in examining and understanding the familial beliefs and behavior of enslaved Afro-Americans just prior to their emancipation and in grasping the varied adaptive capacities of such men and women so essential to an understanding of the developing Afro-American slave culture. This is not a trivial point. Analysis of the birth register showed that when allowed plantation slaves sustained monogamous marriages for many years, had exogamous mating practices, and named many children for close and distant kin. The register, moreover, suggests the powerful role played by the slaves themselves in shaping these developments. Despite their deepening contact with enslavement and their further detachment in time from their West African origins, kin ties among these and other slaves grew more powerful within each generation and between generations after 1820. These generations, incidentally but hardly insignificantly, were not "equal" to one another in significance. "It is obvious," the historian Marc Bloch insisted, "that the periodicity of the generations is by no means regular. As the rhythm of social change is more or less rigid, the limits contract or expand. There are, in history, some generations which are long and some which are short. Only observation enables us to per-

ceive the points at which the curve changes its direction." Bloch's wise strictures apply to the study of enslaved Afro-Americans as well as to all other historical groupings sharing a common experience. But it is first important to realize that enslaved Afro-Americans themselves experienced generational ties particular to the circumstances of the enslaved. The Good Hope slaves knew such ties as social facts.

We know of them more than a century later *only* because a nearly complete birth register lasting for almost a century had survived to allow us to examine a small community of enslaved Afro-Americans in a time perspective nearly always denied to the social historian concerned with lower-class population, slave or free and black or white. "If we stop history at a given point," the British historian E. P. Thompson has written in yet another connection, "then there are no classes but simply a multitude of individuals with a multitude of experiences. But if we watch these men over an adequate period of social change, we observe patterns in their relationships, their ideas, and their institutions." "Class," Thompson observed, "is defined by men as they live their own history, and, in the end, that is its only definition."[17] Concepts such as culture and adaptation so essential to the study of all lower-class populations require precisely the same enlarged time perspective stressed by Thompson. Little of genuine *social* importance about the Good Hope slaves and especially about their familial life and kinship networks can be learned by studying them at a "given moment" in time. We thereby deny *them* (not us) a functional (or usable) "past." We can see why and how this is so by assuming that nothing in their history differed but that the Good Hope plantation owners began recording slave births *in 1830, not in 1760*, and listed for the years 1830 to 1857 precisely the same information for these newborn slaves as appeared in the complete register. The data of such a *partial* register would reveal to the student of the Afro-American slave family and of Afro-American slave culture that there were thirty different families, fourteen of them composed of parents and their unmarried children. In seven other families, children had taken spouses and started "second-generation" families of their own. The partial register reinforced what the complete register revealed in important ways: at least five children had been born into each of thirteen families; the percentage of slaves bearing children by just a single spouse (81 percent) hardly differed; a few women had children by unnamed fathers; most slave couples had lived together for many years. So far the partial register had not distorted the actual familial and communal experiences of the Good Hope blacks. But it was nevertheless flawed in fundamental ways. Fixed by so narrow a boundary of time—just about *thirty years*—even so detailed and rich an historical document as this one could not reveal a single familial and marital connection rooted in consanguinal and affinal ties that had started *prior to 1830*. As a result, the partial register hid much of what the slaves living between 1830 and 1857—and even later in time—*had, in fact, experienced and felt*. All that the partial register obscured about these blacks was *their prior history*, a period of time in which separate families had meshed together into a tightly knit slave community. The full register, as we have seen, revealed the development *over time* of complex kin networks within a particular generation and, more significantly perhaps, between generations. *The partial register told an opposite story*—a false tale. One could only infer from it that most Good Hope slaves lived in isolated "nuclear" households, unconnected by blood or marriage to other slave households. It cannot be learned from the partial document that slave first cousins did not marry. The partial document did not tell more than that three slave sons had their father's names. It did not even hint that a slave child carried the name of a slave grandparent. And much else remained hidden. It did not tell, for example, that Duck was the daughter of Gadsey and Cuffee, that Patty and Molly were sisters, that Sophy's grandmother lived on the plantation, and that Rachel had two aunts and two uncles among the plantation's slaves. Marriage as recorded in the partial register failed to connect any two families, and most children listed only had kin ties to their family of origin. Nothing, of course, was further from the actual experiences of the Good Hope blacks. The partial register entirely obscured from historical vision the integrative slave kin ties formed before 1830 and sustained after that date. These important ties are known to us from a distance of about 150 years only because the entire slave birth register started in the mid-eighteenth century thereby allowing us to examine the development of a slave family structure and kinship network over time.

The inadequacies of the partial register direct attention to yet another point, a historiographic point of some importance. Almost without exception, historians of the slave family and of slave culture have followed the scheme sketched by the pioneering student of the slave family E. Franklin Frazier. In his major works, Frazier entirely ignored the slave family prior to 1840. That theoretical error rested, in part, upon a factual error. Frazier believed that "it was not until 1840 that the number of Negro women equaled that of men."[18] Frazier and others therefore gave scant attention to slave kinship ties beyond the immediate family. That, however, had more to do with a flawed sociology than with the realities of everyday slave life. To commence with a body of evidence that cannot reveal kin networks is to guarantee that kin networks will not emerge from even the most serious study. The examination of slave behavior, including family life, which begins in 1830 (or even in 1815) starts by ignoring the historical roots (the developing and changing slave culture) that shaped slave behavior after 1830. That has, in fact, been one of the gravest shortcomings in the vast literature on the enslaved Afro-American. Historical time has been held constant. Almost without exception, static, or synchronic, "models"—implicitly or explicitly held—have dominated the study of the enslaved. E. Franklin Frazier and Kenneth M. Stampp started their studies of the enslaved too late in time. Ulrich B. Phillips held the racial factor constant over time. Eugene D. Genovese's "dialectics" remain frozen in time. The sociological model of Stanley M. Elkins and the cliometric models of Robert Fogel and Stanley Engerman (except when dealing with such matters as the price of slaves and the price of cotton) give no attention to historical time. It turns out, of course, that neither slaves nor free men and women can accumulate historical experiences and thereby adapt to changing circumstances when dealt with in so static a fashion. The near-total absence of diachronic studies tell us why no historical work yet written begins to explain how and why a slave living in the 1850s on the eve of his or her emancipation differed from or shared values with his or her grandparents who had lived in the 1790s in the aftermath of their enslavement. Such a time perspective is not emphasized to accumulate points in the frequently arid disputes over methodological matters that keep historians busy and inflate reputations. It is stressed because it is an essential clue toward understanding the enslaved themselves.

The full Good Hope plantation birth register uncovers for us some of the powerful sensibilities that existed among enslaved Afro-Americans and which had their roots in the ways in which adaptive familial arrangements and kin networks developed among them in the eighteenth and early nineteenth centuries. The Good Hope slaves were not unique. Examination of other plantations birth registers is not possible in this short paper. But these registers do no more than compliment the process of adaptation suggested among the Good Hope slaves. A Virginia plantation register, which also includes data on slave purchase and slave sale and gift, shows that over two generations a fragmented body of slaves purchased separately from their families of origin and later sold or given away as gifts to an owner's sons behaved no differently from the more settled Good Hope slaves. Their transfer to other owners did no more than spread the kinship grouping over a wider geographical space. A Louisiana sugar plantation register reveals patterns of naming for aunts and uncles (as well as necronymic naming) that suggest concepts of kin obligation rooted in the relationship between an immediate family and a family of origin. The registers everywhere hint at the powerful importance of adult siblings in the enlarged slave kinship structure. That is most clearly revealed in a North Carolina plantation register where the first recorded birth is June 1776. These registers confirm in powerful ways what the Good Hope register revealed. It is ironic that all of this is known to us because an ancestor of John Foster Dulles, then living in Philadelphia, ordered that careful records be kept of slave births and deaths. Not in a Bible, to be sure, but in a business ledger. The historian David Hackett Fischer is right. "The stuff of history," he observes, "is things that happen—not things that are."

NOTES

[1] W. E. B. DuBois (1909). *See* Herbert G. Gutman, *The Black Family in Slavery and Freedom, 1750–1925* (New York, 1976).

[2] E. Franklin Frazier, *The Negro Family in the United States* (Chicago, 1939).

[3] Sidney W. Mintz, "Creating Culture in the Americas," *Columbia Forum*, XIII (Spring 1970), 4–11; and "Toward an Afro-American History," *Journal of World History*, XIII (1971), 317–32.

[4] A. R. Radcliffe-Brown, "Introduction," in A. R. Radcliffe-Brown and Daryll Forde, eds., *African Systems of Kinship and Marriage* (New York, 1950), pp. 3, 66–67.

[5] M. G. Smith, "Social Structure in the British Caribbean about 1820," *Social and Economic Studies*, I (1953), 71–72.

[6] Mary B. Chesnut, *A Diary from Dixie* (New York, 1949), pp. 121–23.

[7] Bronislaw Malinowski, "Parenthood—The Basis of Social Structure," in V.F. Calverton and Samuel D. Schmalhausen, eds., *New Generation: The Intimate Problems of Modern Parents and Children* (New York, 1930), pp. 129–43.

[8] Testimony of Henry Judd and Harry McMillan, American Freedmen's Inquiry Commission, 1863, file 3, Letters Received, Office of the Adjutant General Main Series, Reel 20, National Archives.

[9] Frazier, *The Negro Family in the United States. See* Gutman, *The Black Family*, Tables 11 and 12, pp. 48–58.

[10] *See* Gutman, *The Black Family*, p. 88.

[11] Radcliffe-Brown, *African Systems of Kinship and Marriage.*

[12] Chalmers Gaston Davidson, *The Last Foray, The South Carolina Planters of 1860: A Sociological Study* (Columbia, S.C., 1971), pp. 5–6.

[13] Allen Parker, *Recollections of Slavery Times* (1885), pp. 66–67.

[14] Phillis Thomas in *American Slaves, Texas Narratives*, V, pp. iv, 92–94.

[15] Ulrich B. Phillips, *Life and Labour in the Old South* (Boston, 1929), p. 196.

[16] Pen Eubanks in *American Slave, South Carolina Narratives*, II, pp. ii, 27–29.

[17] E. P. Thompson, *The Making of the English Working Class* (New York, 1963), p. 11.

[18] Frazier, *The Negro Family in the United States*, pp. 23–24.

Smothered Slave Infants: Were Slave Mothers at Fault?

By Michael P. Johnson

In the South Carolina upcountry district of Abbeville in 1850 a one-month-old slave girl named Harriet was reported to the census marshal Charles M. Pelot as having died in December 1849 because she was "Smothered by carelessness of [her] mother." Similar reports are scattered throughout the mortality schedules of the United States census for the southern states. Allice Burrow, a six-month-old slave girl in Henrico County, Virginia, "was Smouthered by her Mother Lying on her while asleep"; in Tippah County, Mississippi, the two-month-old slave girl Biddy was "Accidentally overlaid by [her] mother in her Sleep"; in Cobb County, Georgia, an eight-month-old slave boy was "Overlaid by [his] Mother"; in Spartanburg District, South Carolina, a five-month-old slave girl was said to have been "Overlaid by [her] mother and smothered."[1] The grim record goes on and on.

In 1860 the slave states accounted for 94 percent of the nation's 2,129 reported deaths by suffocation. Most of these victims "were probably the children of slaves," the published mortality census

[1] All citations are from Manuscript Census Returns, Seventh Census of the United States, 1850, South Carolina, Schedule 3, Mortality, South Carolina Microcopy Number 2, roll 1; and Manuscript Census Returns, Eighth Census of the United States, 1860, Georgia, Schedule 3, Mortality, National Archives Microfilm Series T-655, roll 8; Virginia, Schedule 3, Mortality, National Archives Microfilm Series T-1132, roll 5; Mississippi, Schedule 3, Mortality, Mississippi Department of Archives and History Microfilm, roll 2730; South Carolina, Schedule 3, Mortality, South Carolina Microcopy No. 2, roll 1. These are cited hereafter by state, year, and county or district. Quotations in the text are, in order of their appearance, from South Carolina Mortality Schedules, 1850, Abbeville District, frame 3; Virginia Mortality Schedules, 1860, Henrico County, 309; Mississippi Mortality Schedules, 1860, Tippah County, 2 (second paged series); Georgia Mortality Schedules, 1860, Cobb County, 162; and South Carolina Mortality Schedules, 1860, Spartanburg District, frame 378. I am indebted to the late Andrew B. Appleby, Joyce O. Appleby, Carl N. Degler, Jonathan S. Dewald, Stanley L. Engerman, Karl G. Hufbauer, and Jonathan M. Wiener for their critical reading of an earlier version of this article.

Mr. Johnson is associate professor of history at the University of California at Irvine.

The Journal of Southern History
Vol. XLVII, No. 4, November 1981

TABLE 1

SMOTHERING DEATHS IN 1860

State	*Whites*	*Slaves*	*White Death Rate*	*Slave Death Rate*	*Slave Death Rate/White Death Rate*
Georgia	10	259	0.5	18.5	37
Mississippi	6	213	0.6	17.5	29
South Carolina	2	122	0.2	10.8	54
Virginia	5	230	0.2	16.6	83
Totals	23	824	0.3	16.0	53

speculated.[2] In 1850, when the published census made a separate calculation of slave and white deaths, 82 percent of the victims of suffocation were slaves.[3] According to a calculation in the 1860 published census slaves were nine times more likely than whites to die of suffocation, a larger interracial gap than for any other cause of death.[4] However, all these figures drastically understate the difference between slaves and whites in the reported incidence of smothering. The appropriate comparison is between death rates. The number of smothered slaves per 1,000 living slave infants should be compared with the number of smothered whites per 1,000 white infants. In 1850 the death rate for smothered slaves was 28 times larger than that for whites.[5] In 1860, according to data from the manuscript mortality schedules of Georgia, Mississippi, South Carolina, and Virginia summarized in Table 1, slave infants were 53

[2] The 1860 published mortality census did not separate slave deaths from white deaths. U. S. Census Office, *Statistics of the United States (Including Mortality, Property, &c.,) in 1860* . . . (Washington, 1866), 252.

[3] There were 934 reported suffocation deaths in 1850, of which 764 were slaves. J. D. B. De Bow, *Mortality Statistics of the Seventh Census of the United States, 1850* (Washington, 1855), 28.

[4] The calculation was based on the 1850 federal mortality data and mortality statistics from Kentucky, New York City, South Carolina, and New Orleans. U. S. Census Office, *Statistics of the United States . . . in 1860,* 281–83.

[5] The 1850 death rate for slave infants who died by smothering was 8.4; that for whites was 0.3. Of course, many deaths from all causes were not reported. Several census marshals made notes similar to that of B. F. Buckner, the marshal in Beaufort District, South Carolina, in 1860, who wrote, "Difficult to obtain correct returns of mortality—few Records of same being kept—and in many instances changes of Overseers & Agents the first of the year—Consequently many deaths unreturned." South Carolina Mortality Schedules, 1860, Beaufort District (St. Peter's Parish), frame 246. The result, as the published 1860 census made clear, was that many deaths were unreported. The exact extent of underenumeration varied widely from place to place, depending both on the reports made to the census marshals and the diligence and expertise of the marshals themselves. Given this underenumeration, any calculation of a death rate is at best an approximation of the actual rate. For the best estimates of death rates for the black population see Jack E. Eblen, "New Estimates of the Vital Rates of the United States Black Population During the Nineteenth Century," *Demography,* XI (May 1974), 301–19.

times more likely to die of smothering than were southern white infants.[6] Between 1790 and 1860 smothering was responsible for the deaths of over 60,000 slave infants.[7]

The reason so many slave children were smothered was quite clear to contemporaries. Slave mothers were careless. As they slept with their infants, they accidentally overlaid and smothered them. The fault clearly lay with the mothers. ". . . I wish it to be distinctly understood that nearly all the accidents occur in the negro population," wrote Pelot, adding, "which goes clearly to prove their great carelessness & total inability to take care of themselves."[8] Although many southerners would have considered Pelot's statement an exaggeration, virtually all would have agreed that the smothering deaths were accidental. Again and again census marshals noted "smothered accidentally" or "overlaid by accident." None of the smothering deaths in Georgia, Mississippi, South Carolina, and Virginia in 1860 produced even a hint of infanticide. There was simply no motive. An observer "will see how very prolific the female slaves are," Pelot noted, "which shows conclusively that their minds are at ease & that they are reconciled and satisfied with the station which God has pleased to place them in."[9] A content, sleepy

[6] The data in Table 1 and in all the other tables and figures in this article, with the exception of Table 6, were collected from the manuscript mortality schedules of the 1860 federal census of Georgia, Mississippi, South Carolina, and Virginia. The data include every person in each of these states whose cause of death was listed in the 1860 mortality schedules as smothered, overlaid, or suffocated. Most of the victims were reported as having been smothered (77 percent); those reported as having been overlaid or suffocated accounted for 18 and 5 percent respectively. The death rates in Table 1 were obtained by dividing the total number of smothering deaths in each state and in the four states together by the total number of living white and slave infants in each state and in the four states together. (Infants are defined as children who are less than one year old.) Today, smothering death rates would be expressed as the number of smothering deaths per thousand live births. But since the number of live births in 1860 is unknown, the number of living infants has been used for the denominator of the death-rate calculation. This method of calculating the death rate has been used throughout this article.

[7] This is a conservative estimate based on the assumption that the 1860 smothering death rate of sixteen deaths per thousand living slave infants was constant from 1790 to 1860. The number of slave infants (again, defined as those under one year of age) was estimated for the census years from 1790 to 1840 by assuming that 7.9 percent of the slaves under ten were infants (which was the case in 1850) and by assuming that the population under ten was 34 percent of the total population in the years from 1790 to 1810. The number of slave infants in each year was estimated by a simple linear regression of the decadal infant estimates. With this procedure, the estimated number of smothering deaths between 1790 and 1860 was 62,191. Of course, a nonlinear regression procedure, different annual slave infant population estimates, and shifts in the death rate would all affect the exact numerical result. But since it is unlikely that the smothering death rate declined during this period and since the actual slave infant population was probably larger than that estimated by the linear-regression procedure, the total number of smothered slave infants was probably well over 60,000.

[8] South Carolina Mortality Schedules, 1850, Abbeville District, frames 11-12.

[9] *Ibid.*, frames 16-17.

slave mother carelessly rolled over her infant and smothered it.

Of course, carelessness could be compounded by exhaustion. Thomas Affleck, a planter in the hill country of Mississippi, reported in a southern medical journal that "not a few [slave infants] are over-laid by the wearied mother, who sleeps so dead a sleep as not to be aware of the injury to her infant . . . ."[10] Other medical writers concurred about the dangers of hard work for slave women.[11] But none of the census marshals in the states surveyed in this article recorded any remarks that suggested masters contributed to the smothering deaths by working slave women too hard. Yet the census data suggest very strongly that the heavy physical labor masters assigned to slave women—not the carelessness of the slave mothers—was the major reason so many slave infants were "smothered."

In fact, it is extremely unlikely that these slave infants were victims of smothering. Several historians have recently argued that suffocation deaths were caused by Sudden Infant Death Syndrome (SIDS). Todd L. Savitt's pioneering study of the smothered slaves listed in the death registers of twenty-four Virginia counties and two towns between 1853 and 1860 identified "a remarkable epidemiological correspondence [between smothered slaves and modern victims of SIDS], both in age and in seasonal variation." Savitt pointed out that medical scientists do not fully understand the etiology of SIDS, but he suggested that an "important factor" in the large difference between the smothering death rates of slaves and whites was "the marked underreporting of white suffocation deaths . . . , probably due in part to the social stigma associated with child smothering."[12] Robert William Fogel and Stanley L.

[10] Affleck, "On the Hygiene of Cotton Plantations and the Management of Negro Slaves," *Southern Medical Reports,* II (1851), 435. Of course, masters could blame overseers for overworking slave women, as did Thomas Jefferson: ". . . the loss of 5 little ones in 4 years induces me to fear that the overseers do not permit the [slave] women to devote as much time as is necessary to the care of their children: that they view their labor as the 1st object and the raising of their child but as secondary. I consider the labor of a breeding woman as no object, and that a child raised every 2 years is of more profit than the crop of the best laboring man. in this, as in all other cases, providence has made our interests and our duties coincide perfectly. . . . I must pray you to inculcate upon the overseers that it is not their labor, but their increase which is the first consideration with us." Jefferson to Joel Yancey, January 17, 1819, Edwin M. Betts, ed., *Thomas Jefferson's Farm Book: With Commentary and Relevant Extracts from Other Writings* (Princeton, 1953), 43.

[11] See for example John H. Morgan, "An Essay on the Causes of the Production of Abortion Among Our Negro Population," *Nashville Journal of Medicine and Surgery,* XIX (August 1860), 117, 120–21; [Edmund M. Pendleton], "On the Susceptibility of the Caucasian and African Races to the Different Classes of Disease," *Southern Medical Reports,* I (1850), 338.

[12] Savitt, *Medicine and Slavery: The Diseases and Health Care of Blacks in Antebellum*

Engerman offered a similar interpretation, arguing that deaths actually caused by "undisclosed infections" were probably more likely to be "reported as suffocation for slaves than for free men" because of "the jaundiced view of the overseers who reported the death statistics to the census takers."[13]

Although neither Savitt nor Fogel and Engerman estimated how much of the difference between white and slave smothering rates could be accounted for by white underreporting and slave overreporting, both studies emphasized that the mothers of the children were not responsible for the deaths.[14] Modern research has demonstrated, as Savitt said, "that children cannot be smothered as long as there is any circulating air available, even when the infant is beneath the covers or wedged against the sleeping mother."[15] Instead of accidental suffocation, specific mineral deficiencies may have been responsible for these deaths, Kenneth F. Kiple and Virginia H. Kiple have argued.[16] Although the Kiples acknowledged that scientists have not uncovered any compelling evidence of the role of calcium and magnesium deficiencies in SIDS, they nonetheless asserted that the similarities between SIDS and the "nutritional tetany" sometimes caused by these mineral deficiencies "strongly indicate a nutritional etiology" for SIDS and smothered slaves.[17] "Black children were victims of a conspiracy of nutrition, African environmental heritage, and North American climatic circumstances rather than planter mistreatment," they concluded.[18]

Richard Sutch suggested just the opposite conclusion in his searching critique of Fogel and Engerman's analysis of slave nutrition. "The staggering difference between slave and white infant suffocation rates . . . would appear as reflections of extreme pov-

---

Virginia (Urbana, Chicago, and London, 1978), 124 (first quotation), 126 (second and third quotations). See also Savitt, "Smothering and Overlaying of Virginia Slave Children: A Suggested Explanation," *Bulletin of the History of Medicine*, XLIX (Fall 1975), 400–404.

[13] Fogel and Engerman, *Time on the Cross: The Economics of American Negro Slavery* (Boston and Toronto, 1974), 126; cited hereinafter as *Time on the Cross*, I.

[14] However, in a note Fogel and Engerman make the confusing statement that "Virtually all of the difference between the free and slave suffocation rates might be explained by what has recently been identified as the 'sudden infant death' syndrome." *Time on the Cross: Evidence and Methods—A Supplement* (Boston and Toronto, 1974), 101, note 4.5.4; cited hereinafter as *Time on the Cross*, II.

[15] Savitt, *Medicine and Slavery*, 124.

[16] Kiple and Kiple, "Slave Child Mortality: Some Nutritional Answers to a Perennial Puzzle," *Journal of Social History*, X (Spring 1977), 284–309.

[17] *Ibid.*, 296. Although one SIDS researcher, Joan L. Caddell, has argued that magnesium deprivation is related to SIDS, other scientists have failed to confirm her findings and are skeptical about the significance of mineral deficiencies. See Marie Valdes-Dapena, "Sudden Unexplained Infant Death, 1970 Through 1975: An Evolution in Understanding," *Pathology Annual*, XII, Pt. 1 (1977), 139–40.

[18] Kiple and Kiple, "Slave Child Mortality," 299.

erty, low birth weights, and poor postnatal care," Sutch argued.[19] Although the close association of these factors with SIDS is undisputed, Sutch did not develop further his implication that the planters were responsible for their lethal impact on slave children.[20] All these scholars agreed that smothered slaves were actually victims of SIDS but differed sharply over the significance and explanation of the high incidence of smothering among slaves. The conflicting interpretations and their rather narrow empirical base warrant a step-by-step reconsideration of the evidence that smothered slaves were SIDS victims, of the difference between slave and white smothering rates, and of the implications of recent medical research for understanding why so many slaves were "smothered."

First, consider the evidence of smothering. The remarks of the census marshals suggest that infants whose deaths were attributed to smothering were in fact found dead in bed. Usually census marshals simply recorded the cause of death as "smothered" or "overlaid." But in Fauquier County, Virginia, the marshal reported two slave infants who were "Supposed to have been smothered in bed . . . ."[21] In Carroll County, Georgia, a slave girl three months old was reported "Smothered probably."[22] The tentative nature of these remarks suggests that smothering was not observed or certain but inferred from the circumstances in which the dead child was found. James Kincannon, the census marshal in Noxubee County, Mississippi, listed "Found dead" as the cause of death of a nine-month-old slave girl and noted: "Supposed to have been Smothered."[23] Even more detailed notes were made by Thomas R. Nisbet, the marshal in Lancaster District, South Carolina. Alongside the report of a slave infant whose cause of death he listed as "Sudden," Nisbet noted, "found Dead in the Bed." Another slave infant who was "overlaid" was, Nisbet wrote, "found Dead in the morning."[24] Indeed, according to D. W. Johnson, the marshal in Union District, South Carolina, in 1850, the actual number of

[19] Sutch, "The Care and Feeding of Slaves," in Paul A. David *et al.*, *Reckoning with Slavery: A Critical Study in the Quantitative History of American Negro Slavery* (New York, 1976), 292.

[20] The best overviews of recent SIDS research are Richard L. Naeye, "Sudden Infant Death," *Scientific American*, CCXLII (April 1980), 56–62; Marie A. Valdes-Dapena, "Sudden Infant Death Syndrome: A Review of the Medical Literature, 1974-1979," *Pediatrics*, LXVI (October 1980), 597–614; Valdes-Dapena, "Sudden Unexplained Infant Death," 117–45; and J. Bruce Beckwith, *The Sudden Infant Death Syndrome* (Rockville, Md., 1975). The history of SIDS research is analyzed in Karl G. Hufbauer and Michael P. Johnson, "The Social History of SIDS Research in the United States, 1945–1974," unpublished manuscript in possession of the author. A version of the paper was presented at the October 1979 meeting of the Society for the Social Studies of Science.

[21] Virginia Mortality Schedules, 1860, Fauquier County, 214.

[22] Georgia Mortality Schedules, 1860, Carroll County, 75.

[23] Mississippi Mortality Schedules, 1860, Noxubee County, 1 (seventh paged series).

[24] South Carolina Mortality Schedules, 1860, Lancaster District, frames 237, 235.

smothered slave infants was much larger than that reported: "A very large proportion of the Deaths of Infant Slaves [whose cause of death was] reported as Unknown Sudden were supposed to have been caused by their mothers' overlying them during Sleep. The presumptive evidence of this fact was of the strongest character."[25]

Taken together, these fragmentary notes of the census marshals suggest that slave infants who were reported to have been smothered, suffocated, or overlain by their mothers were actually found dead in bed. Since a mother slept with her infant, she was presumed to be responsible for smothering it. The death was presumed to be accidental because there was no evidence that the child was sick—in which case death would have been attributed to another cause. The slave mother's grief probably persuaded her master that the death was indeed accidental and that she was responsible.[26] And in fact, the slave mother probably felt responsible for the tragedy.

Ex-slave Tabby Abbey's testimony is compelling. Born in Virginia in 1833, Tabby Abbey was sold at the age of sixteen and taken to Mississippi, near Tunica. "I never did work 'round de white folks' house but always done field work, mostly clarin' new groun'," she told her interviewer in 1936. "I had one baby in my life, a long time ago; but I went to sleep one day when I wuz nussin' him and rolled over on him and smothered him to death. I like to went crazy for a long time atter dat."[27] How many other slave mothers "like to went crazy" after their babies were discovered dead in their beds cannot be known. But it is possible to establish that it is extremely unlikely that the slave infants were actually smothered by their mothers.

The mortality data provide three important kinds of evidence that most of the smothered slaves were actually SIDS victims: the circumstances in which the dead child was discovered, the child's age, and the month of death. It is well established that SIDS victims die during sleep and are typically discovered dead in their bed, their parents having had no warning that they were seriously ill or distressed.[28] The same circumstances that led masters and slave

[25] South Carolina Mortality Schedules, 1850, Union District, frame 199.

[26] Savitt quotes a master's letter to his brother: "Last week Tilla overlaid /when asleep/ and killed her youngest child—a boy 6 or 7 months old. This was no doubt caused by her own want of care and attention." *Medicine and Slavery,* 124.

[27] George P. Rawick, Jan Hellegas, and Ken Lawrence, eds., *The American Slave: A Composite Autobiography, Supplement,* Series I (12 vols., Westport, Conn., and London, Eng., 1977), VI: *Mississippi Narratives,* Pt. 1, pp. 3-4. Volumes in this series are cited hereinafter as Rawick *et al.*, eds., *American Slave.*

[28] Indeed, "sleep apnea," or the cessation of breathing during sleep, is currently thought to be the final episode before death. See Naeye, "Sudden Infant Death," 56; and Naeye, "The Sudden Infant Death Syndrome: A Review of Recent Advances," *Archives of Pathology and Laboratory Medicine,* CI (April 1977), 165-67; Valdes-Dapena, "Sudden Unexplained Infant Death," 133; and Beckwith, *Sudden Infant Death Syndrome,* 27.

FIGURE 1. AGE AT DEATH: SMOTHERED SLAVES

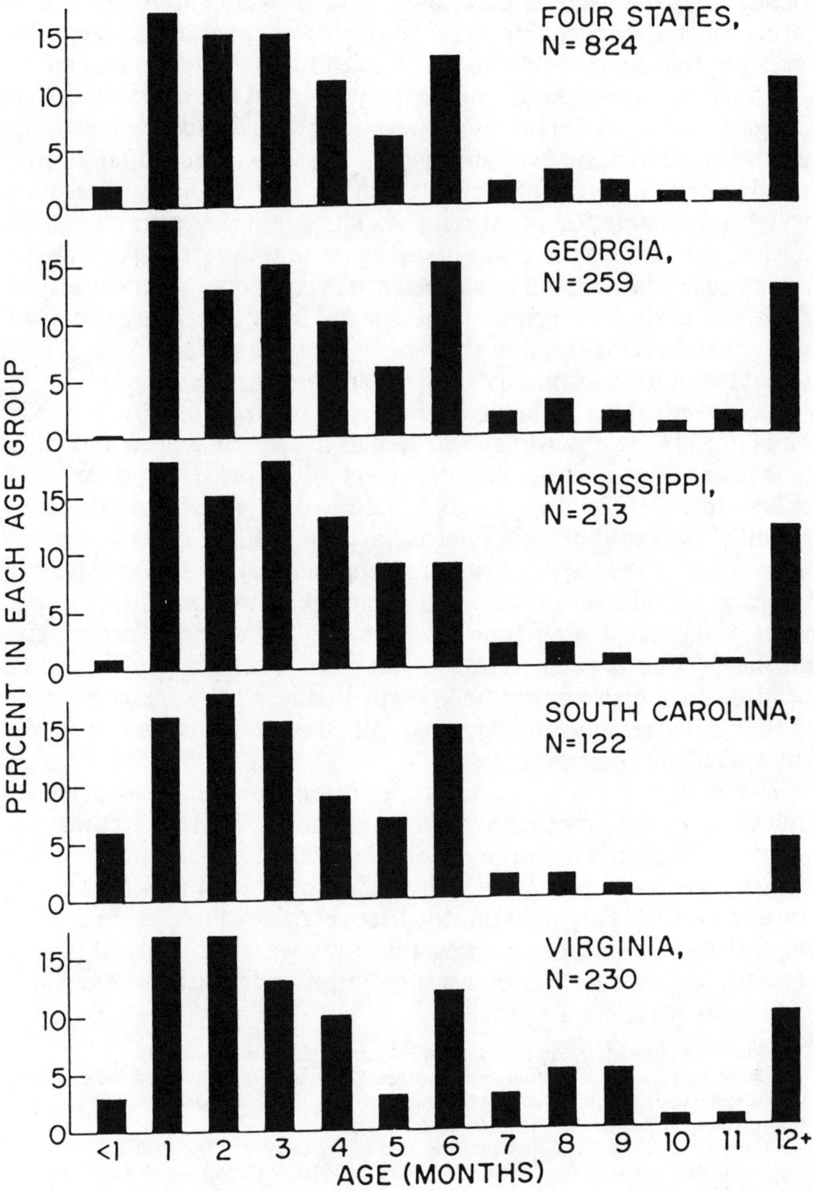

mothers to conclude that the slave infants had been smothered strongly suggest, in light of modern medical knowledge, that the infants succumbed to SIDS. But the most conclusive evidence comes from the age distribution of "smothered" slaves.

According to Dr. J. Bruce Beckwith, an authority on SIDS, "The sparing of very young infants, peak incidence between 2 and 4 months, and rapid decline before the age of 6 months are common to virtually all studies [of SIDS]. We are aware of no other condition with this unique age distribution."[29] As Figure 1 demonstrates, the age distribution of smothered slaves in all four states was quite close to the unique SIDS pattern. Overall, only 2 percent of the smothered slaves were less than one month old, over three-quarters were between one and six months old, and nearly 90 percent were less than one year old.

The discrepancies between the smothered slaves' age distribution and the SIDS pattern are relatively easy to explain. The ages of smothered slaves were not reported as accurately as the ages of SIDS victims. When an infant dies of SIDS today, its age is reported at the time of death. In contrast, the smothered slave infants' deaths were reported by either the master or an overseer up to a year after the slave infant had died. Even if the precise age of the infant had been known to the master or overseer at the time of death, it is likely that it was remembered less accurately when it was reported to the census marshal. For example, the large proportion of six-month-old smothered slaves is almost certainly an artifact of inaccurate age reporting. Many masters apparently responded to a census marshal's question about the age of a slave infant with, "Oh, about six months." This sort of imprecision in the age reports makes the conformity of the age distribution of the smothered slaves to the unique pattern of SIDS all the more remarkable. Of course, the death of some of the smothered slave infants was probably caused by something other than SIDS. As Beckwith explains, "Any sizeable series of sudden, unexpected infant deaths will include a number of cases in which generally acceptable causes for death will be uncovered by postmortem study."[30] A careful study of five hundred such infants in the state of Washington found that 15 percent of the deaths could be explained by causes other than SIDS.[31] Since none of the slave infants was autopsied, there is every reason to

[29] Beckwith, *Sudden Infant Death Syndrome*, 9.

[30] *Ibid.*, 2. An analysis of 59,379 pregnancies which resulted in 125 SIDS deaths is reported in Richard L. Naeye, Bertha Ladis, and Joseph S. Drage, "Sudden Infant Death Syndrome: A Prospective Study," *American Journal of Diseases of Children*, CXXX (November 1976), 1207–10. See also Naeye, "Sudden Infant Death," 56–62.

[31] Beckwith, *Sudden Infant Death Syndrome*, 2–3.

FIGURE 2. AGE AT DEATH: ALL SLAVE INFANTS and SMOTHERED SLAVE INFANTS

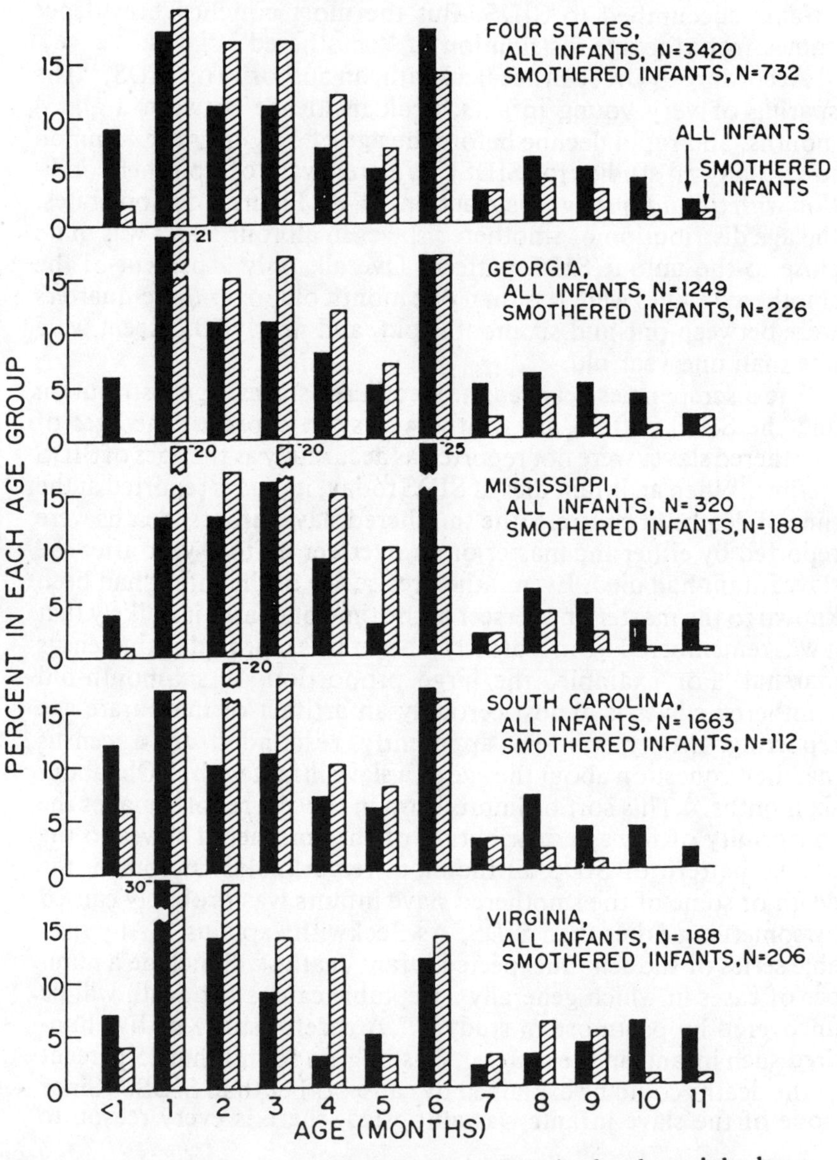

expect that at least a similar fraction of their deaths might have causes other than SIDS. That would probably account for many of the smothered slaves who were over one year old.[32]

[32] However, the age of SIDS victims in the Naeye, Ladis, and Drage study ranged from two weeks to eighteen months.

But before the age distribution of the smothered slaves can be used as evidence that the infants were actually victims of SIDS, we must make certain that the age distribution is not simply an artifact of the mortality reports. Perhaps, for example, the ages of all slave infants whose deaths were reported to the census marshals show the same pattern as the smothered slave infants. If this were true, then the smothered slave infants' age distribution was not evidence of a unique disease syndrome but simply part of a larger pattern of unreliable age reporting. Figure 2 demonstrates that the age distribution of smothered slave infants was in fact different from that of all slave infants whose deaths were reported in 1860.[33] In the four states together the proportion of deaths below one month of age among all slave infants was more than four times that among smothered infants; between one and four months of age—the peak months of SIDS incidence—smothered infant deaths exceeded all infant deaths 66 percent to 47 percent; and from six months on the pattern reversed, the proportion of all infant deaths being greater than that of smothered infants. Chi-square tests comparing the age distribution of smothered slave infants and all slave infant deaths in the four states together and in each state individually had p values of less than 0.001.

The similarity of the age distribution of smothered slaves to the unique SIDS age pattern makes it extremely likely that the slave infants were victims of SIDS. If the age distribution does nothing else, it virtually disproves the notion that these deaths were caused by smothering or suffocation. If that was indeed the cause, as is often assumed by laymen even today in SIDS cases, then, as Beckwith notes, "Why is the very young infant spared, at a time when he seems most vulnerable, yet by the time of peak incidence, between 2 and 3 months, good head control has been achieved?"[34] The same

[33] The age distribution of all slave infant deaths reported in Figure 2 was determined by analyzing all reported slave infant deaths in the 1860 federal mortality schedules of fifty-nine Georgia counties, thirteen Mississippi counties, six Virginia counties, and all South Carolina districts. In each state, the victims of smothering in the sample counties (that is, those counties for which all infant deaths were analyzed) were included among all infant deaths. Therefore, the difference between the age distribution of smothered infants and all *other* infants was more pronounced than that shown in Figure 2, which makes the strongest test for the difference. Since the number of sample counties was relatively small in Mississippi and Virginia, the number of smothering deaths included in the sample of all infant deaths in these states was also small; most of the smothering deaths in these states were not included in the sample of all infant deaths. The chi-square test employed below is a measure of the likelihood that the pattern observed with the smothered slave infants could have arisen by chance from the larger population of all slave infant deaths, even though in actuality the age distribution pattern of smothered slaves was not different from the larger pattern. The probability that the observed difference occurred by chance is expressed by p. For example, if p is equal to 0.001, then there is one chance in a thousand that the observed difference arose by chance.

[34] Beckwith, *Sudden Infant Death Syndrome*, 25. Important early studies that challenged the suffocation interpretation include Paul V. Woolley, Jr., "Mechanical Suffocation

FIGURE 3. DEATH MONTH: SMOTHERED SLAVES

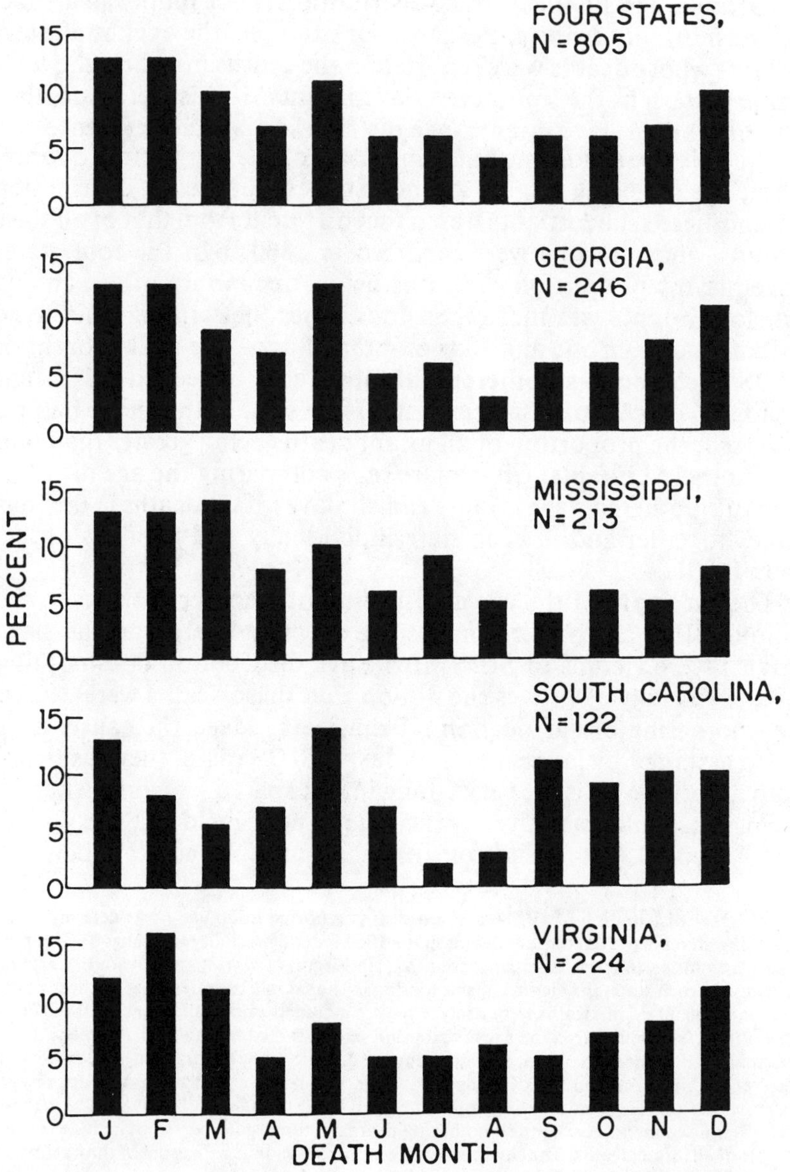

During Infancy: A Comment on Its Relation to the Total Problem of Sudden Death," *Journal of Pediatrics,* XXVI (June 1945), 572–75; and Jacob Werne and Irene Garrow, "Sudden Deaths of Infants Allegedly Due to Mechanical Suffocation," *American Journal of Public Health,* XXXVII (April 1947), 675–87.

FIGURE 4. DEATH MONTH: ALL SLAVE INFANTS and SMOTHERED SLAVES, FOUR STATES

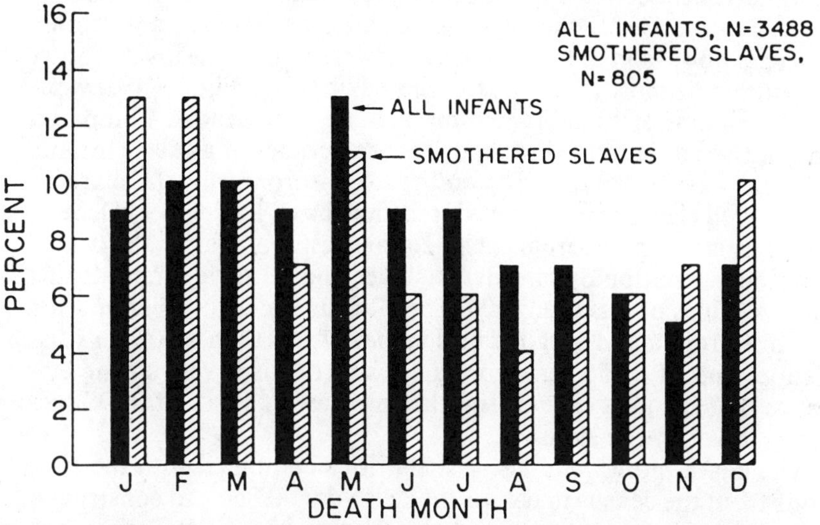

question applies to the infanticide interpretation of these deaths.[35] If slave mothers were bent on infanticide, why did they wait so long? In short, whatever caused the deaths of these slave infants, they were not smothered intentionally or accidentally by their mothers.

Additional evidence that these slave infant deaths were caused by SIDS comes from the death-month distribution. "Nearly all workers have observed seasonal variations in SIDS incidence, with fewer cases occurring in the summer months," Beckwith reports.[36] Figure 3 shows that the same pattern characterized the smothered slaves. In each state the summer months had a lower incidence of smothering deaths.

Since the census was taken during the summer of 1860 it is possible that the dip in incidence during the summer was an artifact of memory. If a slave had suffocated in August 1859 his master would have had to remember the death for a year to report it the following June. For example, the high incidence of smothering reported for the month of May was almost certainly the result of masters' fresh memory of the recent past. Perhaps masters' faulty memories accounted for the low summertime incidence of smothering.

[35] For a refutation of the infanticide interpretation of SIDS proposed by S. S. Asch, "Crib Deaths: Their Possible Relation to Postpartum Depression and Infanticide," *Mt. Sinai Journal of Medicine*, XXXV (May–June 1968), 214–20, see Walter A. Kukull and Donald R. Peterson, "Sudden Infant Death and Infanticide," *American Journal of Epidemiology*, CVI (December 1977), 485–86.

[36] Beckwith, *Sudden Infant Death Syndrome*, 11.

This possibility is ruled out by the monthly distribution of deaths of all slave infants. If memory were the only explanation for the summertime decline in smothering incidence, then the decline should also exist for the incidence of all other slave infant deaths. There is no reason to suppose that masters would selectively forget the summertime deaths of smothered infants. Figure 4 demonstrates that masters did remember summertime deaths. Compared to smothered slaves, a disproportionate number of all slave infants died between April and September. A disproportionate share of smothered slaves died in the winter months of November, December, January, and February. Chi-square tests comparing the death-month distribution of smothered slaves and all slave infant deaths gave *p* values of less than 0.001 for all four states together and for South Carolina and Virginia and values of less than 0.002 for Mississippi and of 0.056 for Georgia. In short, this is very strong evidence that the incidence of smothering was, like that of SIDS, actually lower in the summer.

The death-month and age distributions combined with the citations from the census marshals make it very difficult to construct a persuasive case that smothered slaves were not SIDS victims. Instead, the mortality data strongly support the conclusion of Savitt and others that the slaves died of SIDS. Although slave mothers did not literally smother these infants, as contemporaries believed, perhaps they did or neglected to do something else that was responsible for the deaths. How else can one account for the large difference between the death rates of smothered slave and white infants?

One of the possibilities mentioned earlier is that more white infants were "smothered" than the census manuscripts indicate. The twenty-three white smothering deaths reported to the census marshals in Georgia, Mississippi, South Carolina, and Virginia in 1860 conformed closely to the age and death-month distributions of the smothered slaves, as Figure 5 shows. Although the number of deaths is too small to conclude with certainty that these white infants died of SIDS, the peak incidence at two months of age and the disproportionate number of wintertime deaths suggest very strongly that they did. Additional evidence comes from Calhoun County, Mississippi, where census marshal W. R. Sykes recorded the death of the two-month-old white infant James W. Smith, whose cause of death was "Smothered by mother," Sykes adding "overlayed by whilst asleep."[37] Other white parents may have refused to admit

[37] Mississippi Mortality Schedules, 1860, Calhoun County, 5.

FIGURE 5. SMOTHERED WHITES, N=23

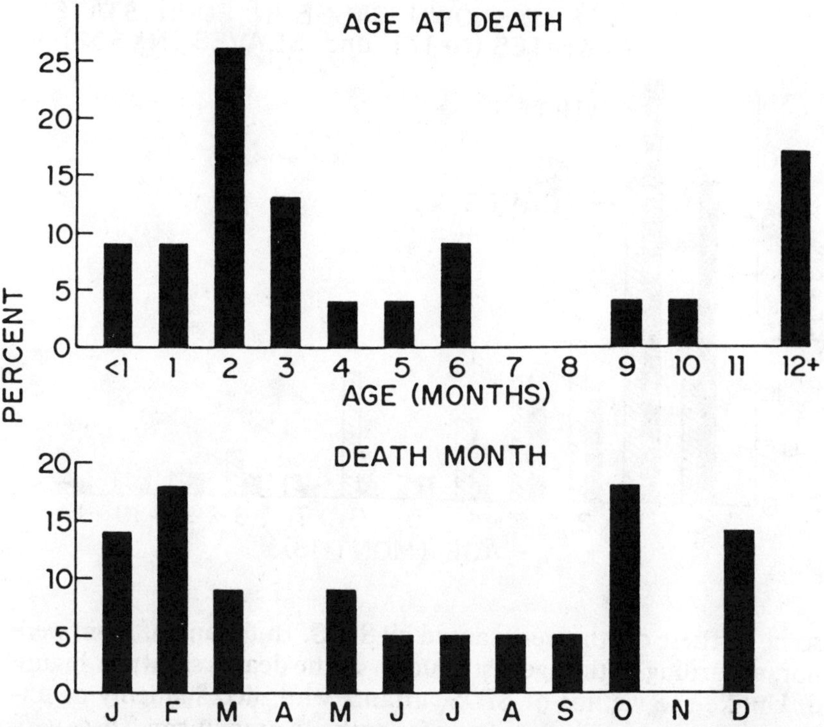

such deaths to the census marshals, or smothering may have been suspected as a cause of death less often because fewer white mothers slept with their infants. Or maybe white parents attributed the death of a "smothered" infant to another cause. If we pursue the hint of census marshal D. W. Johnson that many infants whose deaths were probably caused by "overlaying" were reported as having died suddenly of unknown cause, then it appears that whites were indeed more subject to "overlaying" than is suggested by the data on smothered infants alone.

The 1860 manuscript mortality schedules of the four states studied in this article contain reports of 171 white infants who died suddenly of unknown cause.[38] Predictably, many more such deaths were reported for slave infants, 652 in all. It is quite possible that

[38] That is, these infants are all those in the 1860 federal mortality schedules of these states who were listed by the census marshal with a cause of death of either "unknown" or "sudden" and with zero or "sudden" listed in the length of illness. Of course, older children also died suddenly of no known cause, but they were not included in these calculations.

FIGURE 6. AGE AT DEATH: SUDDEN INFANT DEATHS, OF UNKNOWN CAUSE IN FOUR STATES, WHITES (N=171) and SLAVES (N=652)

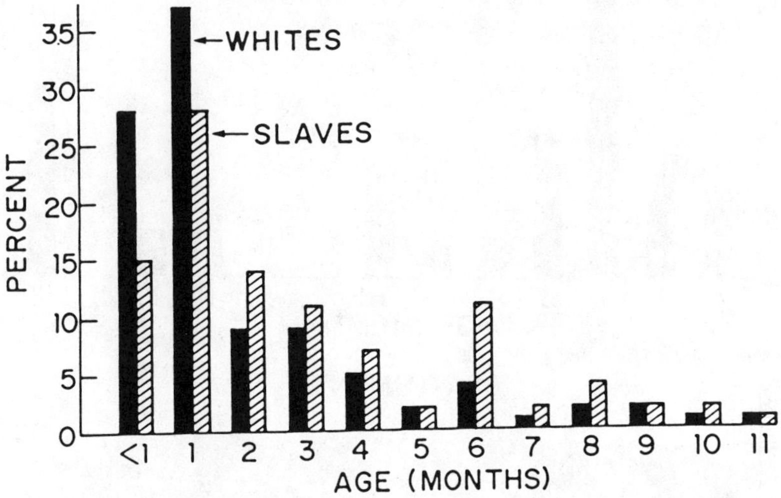

some of these deaths were caused by SIDS. But many of them were not, according to the age distribution of the deaths shown in Figure 6. Unlike the victims of SIDS, infants who died suddenly of unknown cause were likely to be one month old or younger. These very young infants probably did not die of SIDS. Many of the older infants may have died of SIDS, but it is impossible to be certain from this evidence alone. At least these data prove that white infants were indeed subject to dying suddenly and unexpectedly for no known reason. That syndrome was not confined as exclusively to slave infants as suggested by the data on smothering deaths alone.

Nonetheless, slave infants were much more subject than white infants to sudden, unexpected death, whether or not it was called smothering. The death rate for sudden death of unknown cause for white infants was 2.5; the rate for slave infants was five times greater, 12.7. Although this is much smaller than the fifty-three-fold difference between white and slave death rates for smothering, it is clear that slave infants were much more subject to sudden, unexpected death than whites. It is very unlikely that there were enough unreported white deaths to equalize these differences. Instead, being a slave somehow increased an infant's risk of dying suddenly and unexpectedly because it was "smothered" by its mother. But why?

Modern studies have consistently found that "SIDS victims have a greater proportion of young mothers of low socioeconomic and educational level, who live in crowded housing and have little prenatal care."[39] The most recent research also indicates that the SIDS victims are not normal, healthy infants. Instead, SIDS victims exhibit a variety of "neurologic abnormalities" which constitute "multiple evidences of probable neonatal brain dysfunction . . . ."[40] The exact relationship between the SIDS infant's neurological abnormalities and the mother and her environment is not clear. In a report on the most recent research Dr. Richard L. Naeye points out that four of the six factors that have been identified as contributing to SIDS "have been shown to either damage the fetus or place it at increased risk of damage"; in particular, "(1) a bacterial infection of the amniotic fluid, (2) anemia in the mother and (3) the use by the mother of cigarettes or (4) barbiturates."[41] Although these factors will only account for about a third of all sudden infant deaths, Naeye believes that, "Their greatest significance may be their indication that fetal life is a fruitful area in which to continue the search for the origins of the syndrome." The respiratory control centers in the brain are located in the brain stem which, according to Naeye, "is a particularly vulnerable target for

[39] Naeye, Ladis, and Drage, "Sudden Infant Death Syndrome," 1210. Of course, this statement should not be misconstrued to mean that all SIDS victims come from poor families. As Beckwith notes, "Despite its greater attack rate among the underprivileged, SIDS is in fact no respecter of class or social position." *Sudden Infant Death Syndrome,* 11. See also Valdes-Dapena, "Sudden Unexplained Infant Death," 124–27; P. Froggatt, Margaret A. Lynas, and G. MacKenzie, "Epidemiology of Sudden Unexpected Death in Infants ('Cot Death') in Northern Ireland," *British Journal of Preventive and Social Medicine,* XXV (August 1971), 119–34; Robert Strimer, Lester Adelson, and Robert Oseasohn, "Epidemiologic Features of 1,134 Sudden, Unexpected Infant Deaths: A Study in the Greater Cleveland Area from 1956 to 1965," *Journal of the American Medical Association,* CCIX (September 8, 1969), 1493–97; and Marie Valdes-Dapena *et al.*, "Sudden Unexpected Death in Infancy: A Statistical Analysis of Certain Socioeconomic Factors," *Journal of Pediatrics,* LXXIII (September 1968), 387–94.

[40] Naeye, Ladis, and Drage, "Sudden Infant Death Syndrome," 1209; quotations in text and this note. In particular, the infants who became SIDS victims exhibited "abnormalities in respiration, feeding, temperature regulation, and specific neurologic tests." However, none of these abnormalities was great enough to allow physicians to identify the infants who were likely to die of SIDS. Several research teams are currently working on methods of identifying high-risk infants; see for example R. G. Carpenter *et al.*, "Multistage Scoring System for Identifying Infants at Risk of Unexpected Death," *Archives of Disease in Childhood,* LII (August 1977), 606–12.

[41] The other two factors, not specifically related to pregnancy, are infant blood type *B* and crowded housing. The latter has been shown to contribute to mild respiratory infections which "increase the frequency and duration of apneic spells in infants who are prone to apnea." Naeye, "Sudden Infant Death," 60–61; includes quotations both in text and this note. The environmental and demographic characteristics of mothers of SIDS victims are also "associated with excessive fetal injury and perinatal mortality" in general. Naeye, Ladis, and Drage, "Sudden Infant Death Syndrome," 1210. See also Naeye and William A. Blanc, "Influences of Pregnancy Risk Factors on Fetal and Newborn Disorders," *Clinics in Perinatology,* I (September 1974), 187–95.

damage during fetal life because it has a higher metabolic rate than other areas of the brain have. Specifically, the brain stem is vulnerable to damage by low levels of both oxygen and glucose in the blood."[42] This modern knowledge of the general significance of fetal neurological development and the specific risks associated with amniotic fluid infections, maternal anemia, and poor nutrition suggests why so many slave infants were "smothered."

The hard physical labor required of pregnant slave women is the most promising explanation for the high incidence of SIDS among slave infants. Recent research has demonstrated that hard work can have serious consequences for pregnant women. Naeye's study of fetal amniotic fluid infections in Ethiopia, for example, found that the frequency of infections "was greater in the poorest gravid women, in those engaged in hard physical labor, and in twins." "Poverty restricts the quantity and quality of food intake in Ethiopian pregnant women while hard physical labor has a caloric cost," Naeye explains, adding that "The nutritional requirements of pregnancy are greater with twins than with single born infants."[43] A similar relationship between hard work and nutrition probably prevailed among pregnant slave women in the antebellum South.

The nutritional value of the slave diet has been the subject of intense controversy.[44] The best recent evidence indicates that the typical slave diet may have been adequate in caloric quantity but deficient in nutritional quality.[45] The nutritional requirements of a pregnant slave woman were obviously greater both in calories and in specific nutrients. In particular, a pregnant woman required about 65 percent more dietary protein, two and one-half times as much calcium, and three hundred more calories per day than a nonpregnant, nonlactating woman.[46] Sutch has pointed out that a slave "could subsist" on a typical slave ration if the assigned work in-

[42] Naeye, "Sudden Infant Death," 61.

[43] Naeye *et al.*, "Amniotic Fluid Infections in an African City," *Journal of Pediatrics*, XC (June 1977), 969. "Many other factors associated with the [sudden infant death] syndrome appear to lose their high risk in the absence of an infection of the amniotic fluid," Naeye reports. "Sudden Infant Death," 61. For a comparison of SIDS death rates in countries throughout the world see Valdes-Dapena, "Sudden Unexplained Infant Death," 123–24.

[44] See Savitt, *Medicine and Slavery*, 90–103; Fogel and Engerman, *Time on the Cross*, I, 109–15; II, 87–98; Sutch, "Care and Feeding of Slaves," 231–301; Leslie H. Owens, *This Species of Property: Slave Life and Culture in the Old South* (New York, 1976), 50–69; Eugene D. Genovese, *Roll, Jordan, Roll: The World the Slaves Made* (New York, 1974), 62–63, 540–49, 603–604, 638–39; John W. Blassingame, *The Slave Community: Plantation Life in the Antebellum South* (New York and other cities, 1972), 158–59; Kenneth M. Stampp, *The Peculiar Institution: Slavery in the Ante-Bellum South* (New York, 1956), 282–89.

[45] Savitt, *Medicine and Slavery*, 92; Sutch, "Care and Feeding of Slaves," 233–82; Kiple and Kiple, "Slave Child Mortality," 294–99.

[46] Savitt, *Medicine and Slavery*, 92.

cluded such "'light' to 'moderate'" tasks as cooking, house cleaning, hoeing, plowing, or clearing brush. "Heavy" work, including "such plantation-type activities as dragging logs, felling trees, and digging ditches," greatly increased a slave's caloric needs.[47] Although direct evidence of the rations for pregnant slave women is lacking, the high caloric cost of hard work had to have an adverse effect unless the diet was adjusted accordingly. Even if one assumes the very best about the diet of pregnant slave women—namely that they had the same diet as pregnant white women—it is clear that pregnant slave women had to do more hard physical labor than pregnant white women. That was probably why the incidence of SIDS was higher among slave infants.[48]

Several antebellum medical writers commented on the dangers of hard work for pregnant slave women. A Tennessee physician, John H. Morgan, wrote that "the exposure to which negro women are subjected as field hands during menstruation and pregnancy," along with "The promiscuous and excessive intercourse of the sexes" were "among the principal causes of sterility and abortion." "And many diseases to which they are incident arise from the same cause," he added. In particular, he argued that "The functions of menstruation and pregnancy being so peculiarly delicate, negroes suffer seriously during those periods from hard labor and exposure in bad weather, frequently being badly fed and badly clothed . . . ."[49] A Georgia physician, Edmund Monroe Pendleton, wrote that the much greater incidence of abortion and miscarriage among slaves "either teaches that slave labor is inimical to the procreation of the species from exposure, violent exercise, &c., or, as the planters believe, the blacks are possessed of a secret by which they destroy the foetus at an early stage of gestation." Pendleton did not doubt the existence of abortifacients, but he considered it a "question for the philosopher and the philanthropist" whether slave

[47] Sutch, "Care and Feeding of Slaves," 267–68.

[48] Modern studies have uniformly reported a higher incidence of SIDS among blacks. For example, a recent study of SIDS in North Carolina found that the SIDS death rate for whites was 1.23 per thousand live births, while that for blacks was 3.75. Other studies have reported similar differences. However, there is no evidence to suggest that this is the result of a specific genetic heritage. Jack H. Blok, "The Incidence of Sudden Infant Death Syndrome in North Carolina's Cities and Counties: 1972–1974," *American Journal of Public Health,* LXVIII (April 1978), 367–72; Thaddeus J. Bell, Joel S. Sexton, and Sandra E. Conradi, "The Status of Sudden Infant Death Syndrome (1974), and SIDS in Charleston County, South Carolina," *Journal of the South Carolina Medical Association,* LXXI (October 1975), 312–15; Valdes-Dapena, "Sudden Unexplained Infant Death," 124–26; Naeye, Ladis, and Drage, "Sudden Infant Death Syndrome," 1207–1208, 1210; Sutch, "Care and Feeding of Slaves," 287–92; Naeye, "Sudden Infant Death," 60.

[49] Morgan, "An Essay on the Causes of the Production of Abortion Among Our Negro Population," 117 (first three quotations), 121 (last two quotations).

women were "acquainted with them . . . and whether the natural instinct of the mother to love and protect her offspring should be overruled so frequently by the moral obtundity of this class of people . . . ."[50] To the question, "Are negro women, under the ordinary regime of plantations, as prolific as white?", a Mississippi observer answered: "Yes: more so, when not overworked."[51] These experienced and informed observers clearly recognized the dangers of hard work for pregnant slave women.

Some masters were equally aware of the risks of hard work. James R. Sparkman wrote that on the South Carolina rice plantation he managed "Allowance is invariably made for the women so soon as they report themselves *pregnant* they being appointed to such light work as will insure a proper consideration for the offspring."[52] Ex-slave Polly Turner Cancer reported that on the Mississippi cotton plantation where she worked around the house "Ole Marster wudn't let de wimmen do no heavy liftin' coz he wanted dem de have big fine babies; he always sed, 'I don't want no runts.' When we picked cotton he always made de men tote de sacks."[53] Lula Flannigan remembered that her Georgia master "wuz watchful ter see dat 'omans had good keer when dey chilluns wuz bawned. Dey let dese 'omans do easy, light wuk towuds de last fo' de chilluns is bawned, en den atter wuds dey doan do nuffin' much twel dey is well en strong ergin."[54] Although slaveowners clearly benefited from the birth of healthy slave children this testimony suggests that those who took steps to limit the work of pregnant slave women did so late in pregnancy, usually in the last trimester and often in the last few weeks. Such practices may have forestalled premature delivery, but they were too late to have had a significant effect on the influence of hard work on fetal development. And according to slaves many masters did not even observe these precautions.

Harry McMillan, a forty-year-old South Carolina field hand, was asked by the American Freedmen's Inquiry Commission in 1863, "The women had the same day's work as the men; but suppose a woman was in a family way was her task less?" "No, sir," McMillan replied; "most of times she had to do the same work. Sometimes the wife of the planter learned of the condition of the woman and

[50] [Pendleton], "On the Susceptibility of the Caucasian and African Races to the Different Classes of Disease," 338.

[51] Affleck, "On the Hygiene of Cotton Plantations and the Management of Negro Slaves," 434.

[52] Sparkman to Benjamin Allston, March 10, 1858, J. Harold Easterby, ed., *The South Carolina Rice Plantation as Revealed in the Papers of Robert F. W. Allston* (Chicago, 1945), 346. Italics in the original.

[53] Rawick *et al.*, eds., *American Slave,* VII: *Mississippi Narratives,* Pt. 2, p. 350.

[54] *Ibid.,* III: *Georgia Narratives,* Pt. 1, p. 248.

said to her husband you must cut down her day's work. Sometimes the women had their children in the field.''[55] Madison Jefferson, a slave from a large Virginia estate, reported to the British and Foreign Antislavery Society in 1841 that ''He has known women who were *enceinte,* employed in plantation labour until within a few hours of their delivery; and in some cases the children have been actually brought forth in the field.''[56] James Lucas told an interviewer in 1936 of his birth 103 years earlier on a big cotton plantation along the Mississippi River, ''Trufe is I wuz bawn in a cotton field during cotton pickin time. De wimmin fixed my mammy up so she didn't lose no time.''[57] Jennie Webb, another former slave on a Mississippi cotton plantation, recalled, ''My ma wuked in de fiel's up to de day I was born. I wuz born 'twix de fiel's an' de cabins. Ma wuz tooken to de house on a ho'se.''[58]

Additional evidence of the common practice of working slave women until late in pregnancy comes from slave testimony about whipping. Former Virginia slave Jordan Johnson told an interviewer about Charlie Jones and his wife who were working in a tobacco field together. ''Was plantin' tobacco—he was settin' out an' she was hillin'. Annie was big wid chile an' gittin' near her time, so one day she made a slip an' chopped a young shoot down. Ole man Diggs, de overseer, come runnin' up screamin' at her an' it made her mo' nervous, an she chopped off 'nother one. Ole overseer lif' up dat rawhide an' beat Annie 'cross de back an shoulders 'till she fell to de groun'.''[59] Lizzie Williams remembered that on the Mississippi cotton plantation where she worked ''I[']s seen nigger women dat was fixin' to be confined do somethin' de white folks didn't like. Dey [the white folks] would dig a hole in de ground just big 'nuff fo' her stomach, make her lie face down an whip her on de back to keep from hurtin' de child.''[60] South Carolina slave Solomon Bradley told the American Freedmen's Inquiry Commission, ''I have seen a woman in the family way punished by making a hole in the ground for her stomach when she was stretched out for whipping.''[61] Clara Young, a former field hand on a plantation near

[55] John W. Blassingame, ed., *Slave Testimony: Two Centuries of Letters, Speeches, Interviews, and Autobiographies* (Baton Rouge, 1977), 380.

[56] *Ibid.,* 221. Italics in the original.

[57] Rawick *et al.,* eds., *American Slave,* VIII: *Mississippi Narratives,* Pt. 3, p. 1337.

[58] *Ibid.,* X: *Mississippi Narratives,* Pt. 5, p. 2250.

[59] Charles L. Perdue, Jr., Thomas E. Barden, and Robert K. Phillips, eds., *Weevils in the Wheat: Interviews with Virginia Ex-Slaves* (Charlottesville, 1976), 160.

[60] She also reported that ''Lots o' times de women in dat condition [pregnant] would be plowin', hit a stump, de plow jump an' hurt de child to where dey would loose it an law me, such a whippin as dey would get!'' Rawick *et al.,* eds., *American Slave,* X: *Mississippi Narratives,* Pt. 5, p. 2337.

[61] Blassingame, ed., *Slave Testimony,* 372. For other instances see *ibid.,* 220, 380.

Aberdeen, Mississippi, recalled that her cousin had been whipped so severely by the overseer that she died the next morning. ". . . she was jest sebenteen years ol' and was in de fambly way for de fust time, and could't work as hard as de rest."[62] Although many overseers and masters may not have been so cruel, far too many were. Yet the most significant disclosure in the slaves' testimony is that it was not at all uncommon for pregnant slave women to do the same tasks as other slaves and to be expected to perform them as efficiently.

Annie Coley's mother was a field hand whose master rewarded her for having twelve children by taking her out of the fields and assigning her to weaving. But Annie Coley remembered an incident which proved that slave women did not simply depend on the self-interest of the master for their protection:

> But ole Boss Jones had a mean overseer who tuk 'vantage of the womens in the fiel's. One time he slammed a niggah woman down that was heavy, en cause her to hev her baby—dead. The niggah womens in the Quarters jumped on 'im and say they gwine take him to a brushpile and burn him up. But their men hollered for 'em to turn him loose. Then Big Boss Jones came en made the womens go back to the Quarters. He said, "I ain' whipped these wretches fer a long time, en I low to whip 'em dis evenin'." But all de womens hid in the woods dat evenin', en Boss never say no more about it. He sent the over seer away en never did hev no more overseers.[63]

The slave women on Annie Coley's plantation courageously and successfully resisted the overseer's cruelty. Yet it is significant that what aroused their hostility was not that a pregnant slave woman was working in the fields but that she was horribly abused. Even a "reasonable" master like Boss Jones expected pregnant slave women to work hard; the women in his quarters must have realized the futility of protesting that. Many other masters apparently did not lighten the work routine of pregnant slave women soon enough to diminish the effects of hard work on the developing fetus. "All my child hood life I can never remember seeing my pa or ma gwine to wuk or coming in from wuk in de day light as dey went to de fiel's fo' day an' wuked 'til after dark," Jennie Webb recalled. "It wuz wuk, wuk, all de time."[64]

Evidence that "smothered" slave infants were among the consequences of hard work for pregnant slave women comes from the different death rates in the rice, cotton, tobacco, and upcountry

[62] Rawick *et al.*, eds., *American Slave,* X: *Mississippi Narratives,* Pt. 5, p. 2402. For another similar incident see *ibid.*, 1927.

[63] *Ibid.*, VII: *Mississippi Narratives,* Pt. 2, pp. 441–42.

[64] *Ibid.*, X: *Mississippi Narratives,* Pt. 5, p. 2250. See also *ibid.*, 2199.

TABLE 2

GEORGIA, 1860: DEATH RATES OF SMOTHERED SLAVES AND ALL SLAVE INFANTS

	Cotton Counties	*Piedmont and Pine Barrens Counties*	*Coastal Rice Counties*	*State*
Death Rate of Smothered Slaves	21.0	10.7	4.6	18.5
(N)	(233)	(22)	(4)	(259)
Death Rate of All Slave Infants	158	128	203	156
(N)	(1,068)	(86)	(96)	(1,250)

NOTE: The death rates for all slave infants were derived from the deaths of all slave infants in fifty-nine sample counties. The rate for the entire state was calculated by weighting the death rate for each region by the relative share of the state's slave infants.

TABLE 3

SOUTH CAROLINA, 1860: DEATH RATES OF SMOTHERED SLAVES AND ALL SLAVE INFANTS

	Low Country	*Middle Districts*	*Upcountry*	*State*
Death Rate of Smothered Slaves	7.6	13.2	11.1	10.8
(N)	(21)	(40)	(61)	(122)
Death Rate of All Slave Infants	150	147	146	147
(N)	(414)	(443)	(808)	(1,665)

NOTE: The death rates for all slave infants were computed from the deaths of all slave infants in the state.

regions of the South. In general, where the production of staple crops for market was primary and where gang labor prevailed, the death rates for smothered slave infants were highest. Georgia is an excellent example, as Table 2 demonstrates. In the cotton counties of central and southwest Georgia—which contained 78 percent of the state's slaves and produced 94 percent of the state's cotton—the smothering death rate was almost twice that in the less market-oriented Piedmont and Pine Barrens counties—which produced only 6 percent of the state's cotton although they contained nearly a third of the state's population. This contrast between regions of maximum and minimum staple-crop production was not simply the result of a higher overall death rate for slave infants in the cotton counties. The death rate for all slave infants in the cotton counties

TABLE 4

MISSISSIPPI, 1860: DEATH RATES OF SMOTHERED SLAVES AND ALL SLAVE INFANTS

	River and Black-Belt Counties	*Pine-Hills Counties*	*State*
Death Rate of Smothered Slaves	16.6	20.2	17.5
(N)	(153)	(60)	(213)
Death Rate of All Slave Infants	120	94	114
(N)	(287)	(33)	(320)

NOTE: The death rates for all slave infants were derived from the deaths of all slave infants in thirteen sample counties. The rate for the entire state was calculated by weighting the death rate for each region by the relative share of the state's slave infants.

was only 20 percent higher than that in the Piedmont and Pine Barrens. An even sharper contrast existed between Georgia's cotton and rice counties. In the coastal counties that produced 99 percent of the state's rice, the smothering death rate was less than one-fourth that in the cotton counties.[65] But the coastal counties were not a healthier environment for slave infants; the death rate for all slave infants in the coastal counties was nearly a third higher than that in the cotton counties. Although slaves in both regions were producing staple crops for market, in the rice region their work was organized largely by the task system, while gang labor prevailed in cotton areas.

A similar pattern existed in South Carolina as Table 3 illustrates. In the cotton-producing middle districts and upcountry—which respectively accounted for 33 percent and 56 percent of the cotton produced in the state and which contained 25 percent and 45 percent of the state's slaves—the smothering death rate was significantly higher than in the rice-growing low country. The smothering death rate in the middle districts was 74 percent higher than in the low country; the upcountry rate was 46 percent higher. Yet the death

[65] The obvious climatic difference between the regions does not appear to be a likely explanation for the different smothering death rates. Modern studies have discounted the effect of climate on SIDS. For example, the death rate from SIDS in Stockholm, Sweden, in 1974 was 0.06, while the rate in Memphis, Tennessee, between 1965 and 1974 ranged between 3.10 and 0.9. See Valdes-Dapena, "Sudden Unexplained Infant Death," 123–24; Beckwith, *Sudden Infant Death Syndrome,* 11; Philip S. Spiers, James J. Schlesselman, and Stephen G. Wright, "Sudden Infant Death Syndrome in the United States: A Study of Geographic and Other Variables," *American Journal of Epidemiology,* C (November 1974), 380–89; and Donald R. Peterson, Donovan J. Thompson, and Nina M. Chinn, "A Method for Assessing the Geographic Distribution and Temporal Trends of the Sudden Infant Death Syndrome in the United States from Vital Statistics Data," *ibid.,* 373–79.

TABLE 5

VIRGINIA, 1860: DEATH RATES OF SMOTHERED SLAVES AND ALL SLAVE INFANTS

	Tidewater Counties	Piedmont Counties	Western Counties	State
Death Rate of Smothered Slaves	12.9	22.6	4.1	16.6
(N)	(61)	(161)	(8)	(230)
Death Rate of All Slave Infants	227	222	338	228
(N)	(35)	(131)	(65)	(231)

NOTE: The death rates for all slave infants were derived from the deaths of all slave infants in six sample counties. The rate for the entire state was calculated by weighting the death rate for each region by the relative share of the state's slave infants.

rate for all slave infants in the low country was virtually identical to the rates in the state's cotton regions.

In Mississippi, as Table 4 shows, the pattern was similar to that in the cotton regions of South Carolina. The cotton counties along the Mississippi River and in the black belt adjoining Alabama actually had a slightly lower smothering death rate than the pine hills. Yet, what is striking about the death rates for these two regions is not their difference but their similarity, like that between the South Carolina middle districts and upcountry. The similarity probably arose from a common commitment to cotton cultivation for market. The ratio of slaves to cotton production in the two regions was identical; the river and black-belt counties contained 78 percent of the state's slaves and produced 78 percent of the state's cotton, while the pine-hills counties produced 22 percent of the state's cotton with the same proportion of the state's slaves.

In Virginia, where the staple crop was tobacco and where there was considerable regional variation in the devotion to its production for market, the pattern of smothering death rates resembled that in Georgia. Although the Tidewater counties contained 36 percent of the state's slaves, they produced only 15 percent of the state's tobacco and, as Table 5 shows, the death rate of smothered slaves in the Tidewater was much less than that in the Piedmont. In fact, the smothering death rate in the market-oriented Piedmont counties—which contained 51 percent of the state's slaves and produced 84 percent of the state's tobacco—was 75 percent higher than that in the Tidewater. In the less market-oriented western counties—which contained 13 percent of the state's slaves but produced only 1 percent of the state's tobacco—the smothering death rate was less than one-fifth of that in the Piedmont. Yet the death rate for all slave infants in the western counties was over 50 percent higher than that in the Piedmont.

Overall, the highest regional smothering death rates were in areas devoted to staple-crop production with gang labor. In rice areas, where the task system was employed, or in regions less intensely devoted to staple-crop production, the smothering death rates were lower. This is a pattern one would expect to find if the hard work that masters assigned to pregnant slave women were the major cause of slave smothering deaths. But whether market-oriented production, cotton or tobacco cultivation, gang labor, and close white supervision conspired to make heavier demands on pregnant slave women than a more diversified and less intensely market-oriented production or than rice cultivation and the task system cannot be irrefutably proved. However, the different smothering death rates in the South's agricultural regions make this possibility plausible and worth accepting as somewhat more than a tentative hypothesis.

If the labor that masters assigned to pregnant slave women was the major explanation for the high incidence of SIDS among slave infants, then the smothering death rates should have dropped dramatically after emancipation. Freedmen and freedwomen successfully resisted the planters' efforts to reestablish gang labor. Black women withdrew from the heavy, closely supervised field work they had done as slaves.[66] The family sharecropping system still required black women to work in the fields. But precisely because the sharecroppers' labor was organized by black family members rather than by masters, pregnant black women could be sheltered from the heaviest, most exhausting tasks. And indeed, after emancipation the smothering death rates plummeted.

According to mortality data collected in the 1880 federal census the death rate for smothered black infants in the South was only one-fifth of that in 1860. As Table 6 shows, the smothering rates along the South Atlantic and Gulf coasts remained lower than those of the interior, but all the rates had fallen precipitously compared to 1860. In fact, they had fallen to a level indistinguishable from rates for blacks in the northern regions, although they remained over four times greater than the white rates. Perhaps part of the decline was caused by black parents' reticence about admitting to a census

[66] See Jonathan M. Wiener, "Class Structure and Economic Development in the American South, 1865–1955," *American Historical Review*, LXXXIV (October 1979), 973–76; Wiener, *Social Origins of the New South: Alabama, 1860–1885* (Baton Rouge and London, 1978), 36–38, 42–47, 66–69; Herbert G. Gutman, *The Black Family in Slavery and Freedom, 1750–1925* (New York, 1976), 167–68; Roger L. Ransom and Richard Sutch, *One Kind of Freedom: The Economic Consequences of Emancipation* (Cambridge and other cities, 1977), 44–47.

TABLE 6

DEATH RATES OF SMOTHERED INFANTS IN 1880

Region	*Smothered White Infants*	*Smothered Black Infants*	*All Black Infants*
South Atlantic[1]	0.4	1.7	144
Gulf Coast[2]	0.4	1.1	119
Piedmont[3]	1.0	3.4	157
Black Belt[4]	0.7	3.0	143
South Appalachian[5]	0.5	3.9	111
The South[6]	0.7	3.2	127
Northern Mississippi River Belt[7]	0.6	3.4	112
Missouri River Belt[8]	0.9	3.9	152

NOTE: These regional subdivisions are the only ones for which the mortality data are reported in categories appropriate for the calculation of death rates of smothered black and white infants. For a map of these regions see John S. Billings, *Report on the Mortality and Vital Statistics of the United States as Returned at the Tenth Census (June 1, 1880)* (2 parts in 3 vols., Washington, 1885–1886), Pt. II, between pages x and xi. For the exact counties included in each region see *ibid.*, Pt. I, xiv–xvi.

[1] Includes coastal and Tidewater counties from Virginia to Georgia.
[2] Includes all of Florida and Gulf Coast counties of Alabama, Louisiana, Mississippi, and Texas.
[3] Includes the Piedmont region of Virginia and North Carolina.
[4] Includes the Black Belt and cotton counties of South Carolina, Georgia, Alabama, and Mississippi.
[5] Includes the hill regions of Virginia, West Virginia, Kentucky, North Carolina, Tennessee, Georgia, and Alabama.
[6] Includes the five regions listed above.
[7] Includes the counties along the northern Mississippi from its confluence with the Ohio River north to Minnesota.
[8] Includes counties along the Missouri River from just west of St. Louis north and west to North Dakota.

official that one of their children had been smothered. That possibility cannot be ruled out, but it seems unlikely that reticence alone would account for such a dramatic decrease in the smothering death rate.

Of course, neither slave women nor their masters could have known about the connection between hard work, pregnancy, and smothering. Medical writers agreed, and masters were well aware, that hard work was not good for pregnant slave women. But the large number of smothered slave infants and the testimony of the slaves themselves are powerful evidence that many masters found it easier to ignore the risks of hard work for pregnant slave women than the promise of a cash crop safely harvested. Masters may not have acted any differently had they known better. Not knowing, they easily blamed slave mothers for smothering their infants. Slave women had to do the master's work and to bear the shame and guilt for one of its tragic consequences. At least, Tabby Abbey did.

"MY MOTHER WAS MUCH OF A WOMAN": BLACK WOMEN, WORK, AND THE FAMILY UNDER SLAVERY

JACQUELINE JONES

"Ah was born back due in slavery," says Nanny to her granddaughter in Zora Neale Hurston's novel, *Their Eyes Were Watching God,* "so it wasn't for me to fulfill my dreams of whut a woman oughta be and to do." Nanny had never confused the degrading regimen of slavery with her own desires as they related to work, love, and motherhood: "Ah didn't want to be used for a work-ox and a brood-sow and Ah didn't want mah daughter used dat way neither. It sho wasn't mah will for things to happen lak they did." Throughout her life, she had sustained a silent faith in herself and her sisters that was permitted no expression within the spiritual void of bondage. "Ah wanted to preach a great sermon about colored women sittin' on high, but they wasn't no pulpit for me," she grieved.[1]

Nanny's lament offers a challenge to the historian who seeks to understand American slave women — their unfulfilled dreams as well as their day-in, day-out experiences. Despite recent scholarly interest in the relationship between women's work and family life on the one hand and Afro-American culture on the other, a systematic analysis of the roles of slave women is lacking. In her pioneering article entitled "Reflections on the Black Woman's Role in the Community of Slaves" (published over a decade ago), Angela Davis made a crucial distinction between the work that women were forced to perform for a master and the domestic labor that they provided for their own families. But her emphasis on the political implications of nurturing under slavery has not received the in-depth consideration it deserves.[2]

For example, a few scholars have explored the roles of the bondwoman as devoted wife and mother, physically powerful

Feminist Studies 8, no. 2 (Summer 1982). © 1982 by Feminist Studies, Inc.

fieldworker, and rebellious servant. Herbert G. Gutman has illuminated the strength of kin ties within the slave community, and Eugene D. Genovese has furthered our understanding of black-white, male-female relations on the antebellum plantation. However, most historians continue to rely on the gender-neutral term "slave" — which invariably connotes "male" — and race supersedes sex as the focal point of their discussions. Consequently, questions related to the sexual division of labor under slavery and the way in which task assignments in the fields, the "Big House," and the slave quarters shaped the experiences of black women have largely gone unanswered — and unasked.[3]

Moreover, historians primarily concerned with the status of American women have examined the effects of patriarchy on various classes and ethnic groups over time; in the process they have highlighted variations on the theme of women's distinctive work patterns as determined by changing economic conditions, combined with traditional cultural assumptions about women's domestic responsibilities. Yet within the context of current feminist scholarship, slave women as a group remain for the most part neglected, perhaps because they existed outside the mainstream of the industrial revolution and (together with their menfolk) had few opportunities to put into practice their own ideas about appropriate work for women and men. According to this view, slave women were something of a historical aberration, a "special case" that has little relevance to current theoretical and methodological perspectives on women's work.[4]

The purpose of this article is to suggest that the burdens shouldered by slave women actually represented in extreme form the dual nature of all women's labor within a patriarchal, capitalist society: the production of goods and services and the reproduction and care of members of a future work force. The antebellum plantation brought into focus the interaction between notions of women *qua* "equal" workers and women *qua* unequal reproducers; hence a slaveowner just as "naturally" put his bondwomen to work chopping cotton as washing, ironing, or cooking. Furthermore, in seeking to maximize the productivity of his entire labor force while reserving certain domestic tasks for women exclusively, the master demonstrated how patriarchal and capitalist assumptions concerning women's work could reinforce one another. The "peculiar institution" thus involved forms of oppression against women that were unique manifestations of a more universal condition. The following discussion focuses on female slaves in the American rural South between 1830 and 1860 — cotton boom years that laid bare the economic and social underpinnings of slavery and indeed all of American society.[5]

Under slavery, blacks' attempts to maintain the integrity of family life amounted to a political act of protest, and herein lies a central irony in the history of slave women. In defiance of their owners' tendencies to ignore gender differences in making work assignments in the fields, the slaves whenever possible adhered to a strict division of labor within their own households and communities. This impulse was exhibited most dramatically in patterns of black family and economic life after emancipation. Consequently, the family, often considered by feminists to be a source (or at least a vehicle) of women's subservience, played a key role in the freed people's struggle to resist racial and gender oppression, for black women's full attention to the duties of motherhood deprived whites of their power over these women as field laborers and domestic servants.[6]

Interviewed by a Federal Writers Project (FWP) worker in 1937, Hannah Davidson spoke reluctantly of her experiences as a slave in Kentucky: "The things that my sister May and I suffered were so terrible . . . . It is best not to have such things in our memory." During the course of the interview, she stressed that unremitting toil had been the hallmark of her life under bondage. "Work, work, work," she said; it had consumed all her days (from dawn until midnight) and all her years (she was only eight when she began minding her master's children and helping the older women with their spinning). "I been so exhausted working, I was like an inchworm crawling along a roof. I worked till I thought another lick would kill me." On Sundays, "the only time they had to themselves," women washed clothes, and some of the men tended their small tobacco patches. As a child she loved to play in the haystack, but that was possible only on "Sunday evening, after work."[7]

American slavery was an economic and political system by which a group of whites extracted as much labor as possible from blacks through the use or threat of force. A slaveowner thus replaced any traditional division of labor that might have existed among blacks before enslavement with a work structure of his own choosing. All slaves were barred by law from owning property or acquiring literacy skills, and although the system played favorites with a few, black females and males were equal in the sense that neither sex wielded economic power over the other. Hence property relations — "the basic determinant of the sexual division of labor and of the sexual order" within most societies[8] — did not affect male-female interaction among the slaves themselves. To a considerable extent, the types of jobs slaves did, and the amount and regularity of labor they were forced to devote to such jobs, were all dictated by the master.

For these reasons the definition of slave women's work is problematical. If work is any activity that leads either directly or indirectly to the production of marketable goods, then slave women did nothing *but* work.[9] Even their efforts to care for themselves and their families helped to maintain the owner's work force, and to enhance its overall productivity. Tasks performed within the family context — childcare, cooking, and washing clothes, for example — were distinct from labor carried out under the lash in the field or under the mistress's watchful eye in the Big House. Still, these forms of nurture contributed to the health and welfare of the slave population, thereby increasing the actual value of the master's property (that is, slaves as both strong workers and "marketable commodities"). White men warned prospective mothers that they wanted neither "runts" nor girls born on their plantations, and slave women understood that their owner's economic self-interest affected even the most intimate family ties. Of the pregnant bondwomen on her husband's expansive Butlers Island (Georgia) rice plantation, Fanny Kemble observed, "they have all of them a most distinct and perfect knowledge of their value to their owners as property," and she recoiled at their obsequious profession obviously intended to delight her: "Missus, tho' we no able to work, we make little niggers for Massa." One North Carolina slave woman, the mother of fifteen children, used to carry her youngest with her to the field each day, and "when it get hungry she just slip it around in front and feed it and go right on picking or hoeing. . . ," symbolizing in one deft motion the equal significance of the productive and reproductive functions to her owner.[10]

It is possible to divide the daily work routine of slave women into three discrete types of activity. These involved the production of goods and services for different groups and individuals, and included women's labor that directly benefited first, their families, second, other members of the slave community, and third, their owners. Although the master served as the ultimate regulator of all three types of work, he did not subject certain duties related to personal sustenance (that is, those carried out in the slave quarters) to the same scrutiny that characterized fieldwork or domestic service.

The rhythm of the planting-weeding-harvesting cycle shaped the lives of almost all American slaves, 95 percent of whom lived in rural areas. This cycle dictated a common work routine for slaves throughout the South, though the staple crop varied from tobacco in the Upper South to rice on the Georgia and South Carolina Sea Islands, sugar in Louisiana, and the "king" of all agricultural products, cotton, in the broad swath of "Black Belt" that dominated the whole region. Of almost four million slaves, about one-half labored on farms with holdings of twenty slaves or more; one-quarter endured bondage with at least fifty other people on the same plantation. In its most basic form, a life of slavery meant working the soil with other blacks at a pace calculated to reap the largest harvest for a white master.[11]

In his efforts to wrench as much field labor as possible from female slaves without injuring their capacity to bear children, the master made "a noble admission of female equality," observed one abolitionist sympathizer with bitter irony. Slaveholders had little use for sentimental platitudes about the delicacy of the female constitution when it came to grading their "hands" according to physical strength and endurance. Judged on the basis of a standard set by a healthy adult man, most women probably ranked as three-quarter hands; yet there were enough women like Susan Mabry of Virginia, who could pick four or five hundred pounds of cotton a day (one hundred and fifty to two hundred pounds was considered respectable for an average worker), to remove from a master's mind all doubts about the ability of a strong, healthy, woman fieldworker. As a result, he conveniently discarded his time-honored Anglo-Saxon notions about the types of work best suited for women, thereby producing many "dreary scenes" like the one described by northern journalist Frederick Law Olmsted: during winter preparation of rice fields on a Sea Island plantation, a group of black women, "armed with axes, shovels and hoes . . . all slopping about in the black, unctuous mire at the bottom of the ditches." Although pregnant and nursing women suffered from temporary lapses in productivity, most slaveholders apparently agreed with the (in Olmsted's words) "well-known, intelligent, and benevolent" Mississippi planter who declared that "labor is conducive to health; a healthy woman will rear most children." In essence, the quest for an "efficient" agricultural work force led slaveowners to downplay gender differences in assigning adults to field labor.[12]

Dressed in coarse osnaburg gowns; their skirts "reefed up with a cord drawn tightly around the body, a little above the hips" (the traditional "second belt"); long sleeves pushed above the elbows and kerchiefs on their heads, female field hands were a common sight throughout the antebellum South. Together with their fathers, husbands, brothers, and sons, black women were roused at four A.M. and spent up to fourteen hours a day toiling out of doors, often under a blazing sun. In the cotton belt they plowed fields; dropped seed; and hoed, picked, ginned, and sorted cotton. On farms in Virginia, North Carolina, Kentucky, and Tennessee, women hoed tobacco; laid worm fences; and threshed, raked, and bound wheat. For those on the Sea Islands and in coastal areas, rice culture included raking and burning the stubble from the previous year's crop; ditching; sowing seed; plowing, listing, and hoeing fields; and harvesting, stacking, and threshing the rice. In the bayou region of Louisiana, women planted sugarcane cuttings, plowed, and helped to harvest and gin the cane. During the winter, they performed a myriad of tasks necessary on nineteenth-century farms of all kinds: repairing roads, pitching hay, burning brush, and setting up post and rail fences. Like Sara Colquitt of Alabama, most adult females "worked in de fields every day from 'fore daylight to almost plumb dark." During the busy harvest season, everyone was forced to labor up to sixteen hours at a time — after sunset by the light of candles or burning pine knots. Miscellaneous chores occupied women and men around outbuildings regularly and indoors on rainy days. Slaves of both sexes watered the horses, fed the chickens, and slopped the hogs. Together they ginned cotton, ground hominy, shelled corn and peas, and milled flour.[13]

Work assignments for women and men differed according to the size of a plantation and its degree of specialization. For example, on one Virginia wheat farm, the men scythed and cradled the grain, women raked and bound it into sheaves which children then gathered and stacked. Thomas Couper, a wealthy Sea Island planter, divided his slaves according to sex and employed men exclusively in ditching and women in moting and sorting cotton. Within the two gender groups, he further classified hands according to individual strength so that during the sugarcane harvest three "gangs" of women stripped blades (medium-level task), cut them (hardest), and bound and carried them (easiest). However, because cotton served as the basis of the southern agricultural system, distinct patterns of female work usually transcended local and regional differences in labor-force management. Stated simply, most women spent a good deal of their lives plowing, hoeing, and picking cotton. In the fields, the notion of a distinctive "women's work" vanished as slaveholders realized that "women can do plowing very well and full well with the hoes and equal to men at picking."[14]

To harness a double team of mules or oxen and steer a heavy wooden plow was no mean feat for any person, and yet a "substantial minority" of slave women mastered these rigorous activities. White women and men from the North and South marvelled at the skill and strength of female plow hands. Emily Burke of eastern Georgia saw women and men "promiscuously run their ploughs side by side, and day after day. . . and as far as I was able to learn, the part the women sustained in this masculine employment, was quite as efficient as that of the more athletic sex." In his travels through Mississippi, Olmsted watched as women "twitched their plows around on the headland, jerking their reins, and yelling to their mules, with apparent ease, energy, and rapidity." He saw no indication that "their sex unfitted them for the occupation."[15]

On another estate in the Mississippi Valley, Olmsted observed forty of the "largest and strongest" women he had ever seen; they "carried themselves loftily, each having a hoe over the shoulder, and walking with a free, powerful swing, like *chasseurs* on the march." In preparing fields for planting, and in keeping grass from strangling the crop, women as well as men blistered their hands with the clumsy hoe characteristic of southern agriculture. "Hammered out of pig iron, broad like a shovel," these "slave-time hoes" withstood most forms of abuse (destruction of farm implements constituted an integral part of resistance to forced labor). Recalled one former slave of the tool that also served as pick, spade, and gravedigger: "Dey make 'em heavy so dey fall hard, but de bigges' trouble was liftin' dem up." Hoeing was backbreaking labor, but the versatility of the tool and its importance to cotton cultivation meant that the majority of female hands used it a good part of the year.[16]

The cotton-picking season usually began in late July or early August and continued without interruption until the end of

December. Thus for up to five months annually, every available man, woman, and child was engaged in a type of work that was strenuous and "tedious from its sameness." Each picker carried a bag fastened by a strap around her neck and deposited the cotton in it as she made her way down the row, at the end of which she emptied the bag's contents into a basket. Picking cotton required endurance and agility as much as physical strength, and women frequently won regional and interfarm competitions conducted during the year. Pregnant and nursing women usually ranked as half-hands and were required to pick an amount less than the "average" one hundred and fifty or so pounds per day.[17]

Slaveholders often reserved the tasks that demanded sheer muscle power for men exclusively. These included clearing the land of trees, rolling logs, and chopping and hauling wood. However, plantation exigencies sometimes mandated women's labor in this area, too; in general, the smaller the farm, the more arduous and varied was women's fieldwork. Lizzie Atkins, who lived on a twenty-five-acre Texas plantation with only three other slaves, remembered working "until slam dark every day"; she helped to clear land, cut wood, and tend the livestock in addition to her other duties of hoeing corn, spinning thread, sewing clothes, cooking, washing dishes, and grinding corn. One Texas farmer, who had his female slaves haul logs and plow with oxen, even made them wear breeches, thus minimizing outward differences between the sexes. Still, FWP interviews with former slaves indicate that blacks considered certain jobs uncharacteristic of bondwomen. Recalled Louise Terrell of her days on a farm near Jackson, Mississippi: "The women had to split rails all day long, just like the men." Nancy Boudry of Georgia said she used to "split wood jus' like a man." Elderly women reminisced about their mothers and grandmothers with a mixture of pride and wonder. Mary Frances Webb declared of her slave grandmother, "in the winter she sawed and cut cord wood just like a man. She said it didn't hurt her as she was strong as an ox." Janie Scott's description of her mother implied the extent of the older woman's emotional as well as physical strength: she was "strong and could roll and cut logs like a man, and was much of a woman."[18]

Very few women served as skilled artisans or mechanics; on large estates, men invariably filled the positions of carpenter, cooper, wheelwright, tanner, blacksmith, and shoemaker. At first it seems ironic that masters would utilize women fully as field laborers, but reserve most of the skilled occupations that required manual dexterity for men. Here the high cost of specialized and extensive training proved crucial in determining the division of labor; although women were capable of learning these skills, their work lives were frequently interrupted by childbearing and nursing; a female blacksmith might not be able to provide the regular service required on a plantation. Too, masters frequently "hired out" mechanics and artisans to work for other employers during the winter, and women's domestic responsibilities were deemed too important to permit protracted absences from the quarters. However, many young girls learned to spin thread and weave cloth because these tasks could occupy them during confinement.[19]

The drive for cotton profits induced slaveowners to squeeze every bit of strength from black women as a group. According to the estimates of Roger L. Ransom and Richard Sutch, in the 1850s at least 90 percent of all female slaves over sixteen years of age labored more than 261 days per year, eleven to thirteen hours each day. Few overseers or masters had any patience with women whose movements in the field were persistently "clumsy, awkward, gross, [and] elephantine" for whatever reasons — malnutrition, exhaustion, recalcitrance. As Hannah Davidson said: "If you had something to do, you did it or got whipped." The enforced pace of work more nearly resembled that of a factory than a farm; Kemble referred to female field hands as "human hoeing machines." The bitter memories of former slaves merely suggest the extent to which the physical strength of women was exploited. Eliza Scantling of South Carolina, only sixteen years old at the end of the Civil War, plowed with a mule during the coldest months of the year: "Sometimes me hands get so cold I jes' cry." Matilda Perry of Virginia "Use to wuk fum sun to sun in dat ole terbaccy field. Wuk till my back felt lak it ready to pop in two."[20]

At times a woman would rebel in a manner commensurate with the work demands imposed upon her. "She'd git stubborn like a mule and quit." Or she took her hoe and knocked the overseer "plum down" and "chopped him right across his head." When masters and drivers "got rough on her, she got rough on them, and ran away in the woods." She cursed the man who insisted he "owned" her so that he beat her "till she fell" and left her broken body to serve as a warning to the others: "Dat's what you git effen you sass me." Indeed, in the severity of punishment meted out to slaves, little distinction was made between the sexes: "Beat women! Why sure he [master] beat women. Beat women jes' lak men." A systematic survey of the FWP slave narrative collection reveals that women were more likely than men to engage in "verbal confrontations and striking the master but not running away," probably because of their family and childcare responsibilities.[21]

Family members who perceived their mothers or sisters as particularly weak and vulnerable in the fields conspired to lessen their work load. Frank Bell and his four brothers, slaves on a Virginia wheat farm, followed his parents down the long rows of grain during the harvest season. "In dat way one could help de other when dey got behind. All of us would pitch in and help Momma who warn't very strong." The overseer discouraged families from working together because he believed "dey ain't gonna work as fast as when dey all mixed up," but the black driver, Bell's uncle, "always looked out for his kinfolk, especially my mother." James Taliaferro told of his father, who counted the corn rows marked out for Aunt Rebecca ("a short-talking woman that ole Marsa didn't like") and told her that her assignment was almost double that given to the other women. Rebecca indignantly confronted the master, who relented by reducing her task, but not before he threatened to sell James's father for his meddling. On another plantation, the hands surreptitiously added handfuls of cotton to the basket of a young woman who "was small and just couldn't get her proper amount."[22]

No slave women exercised authority over slave men as part of their work routine, but it is uncertain whether this practice reflected the sensibilities of the slaveowners or of the slaves themselves. Women were assigned to teach children simple tasks in the house and field and to supervise other women in various facets of household industry. A master might "let [a woman] off fo' de buryings 'cause she know how to manage de other niggahs and keep dem quiet at de funerls," but he would not install her as a driver over people in the field. Many strong-willed women demonstrated that they commanded respect among males as well as females, but more often than not masters perceived this as a negative quality to be suppressed. One Louisiana slaveholder complained bitterly about a particularly "rascally set of old negroes" — "the better you treat them the worst they are." He had no difficulty pinpointing the cause of the trouble, for "Big Lucy, the leader, corrupts every young negro in her power." On other plantations, women were held responsible for instigating all sorts of undesirable behavior among their husbands and brothers and sisters. On Charles Colcock Jones's Georgia plantation, the slave Cash gave up going to prayer meeting and started swearing as soon as he married Phoebe, well-known for her truculence. Apparently few masters attempted to co-opt high-spirited women by offering them positions of formal power over black men.[23]

In terms of labor-force management, southern slaveowners walked a fine line between making use of the physical strength of women as productive workers and protecting their investment in women as childbearers. These two objectives — one focused on immediate profit returns and the other on long-term economic considerations — at times clashed, because women who spent long hours picking cotton, toiling in the fields with heavy iron hoes, and walking several miles a day sustained damage to their reproductive systems immediately before and after giving birth. For financial reasons, slaveholders might have "regarded pregnancy as almost holy," in the words of one medical historian. But they frequently suspected their bondwomen (like "the most insufferable liar" Nora) of shamming illness — "play [ing] the lady at your expense," as one Virginia planter put it. These fears help to account for the reckless brutality with which owners forced women to work in the fields during and after pregnancy.[24]

Work in the soil thus represented the chief lot of all slaves, female and male. In the Big House, a division of labor based on both gender and age became more apparent, reflecting slaveowners' assumptions about the nature of domestic service. Although women predominated as household workers, few devoted their energies full time to this kind of labor; the size of the plantation determined the degree to which the tasks of cleaning, laundering, caring for the master's children, cooking, and ironing were specialized. According to Eugene Genovese, as few as 5 percent of all antebellum adult slaves served in the elite corps of house servants trained for specific duties. Of course, during the harvest season all slaves, including those in the house, went to the fields to make obeisance to King Cotton. Thus the lines between domestic service and fieldwork blurred during the day and during the lives of slave women. Many continued to live in the slave quarters, but rose early in the morning to perform various chores for the mistress — "up wid de fust light to draw water and help as a house girl" — before heading for the field. James Claiborne's mother "wuked in de fiel' some, an' aroun' de house sometimes .

. . ." Young girls tended babies and waited on tables until they were sent outside — "mos' soon's" they could work — and returned to the house years later, too frail to hoe weeds, but still able to cook and sew. The circle of women's domestic work went unbroken from day to day and from generation to generation.[25]

Just as southern white men scorned manual labor as the proper sphere of slaves, so their wives strove (often unsuccessfully) to lead a life of leisure within their own homes. Those duties necessary to maintain the health, comfort, and daily welfare of white slaveholders were considered less women's work than black women's and black children's work. Slave mistresses supervised the whole operation, but the sheer magnitude of labor involved in keeping all slaves and whites fed and clothed (with different standards set according to race, of course) meant that black women had to supply the elbow grease. For most slaves, housework involved hard, steady, often strenuous labor as they juggled the demands made by the mistress and other members of the master's family. Mingo White of Alabama never forgot that his slave mother had shouldered a work load "too heavy for any one person." She served as personal maid to the master's daughter, cooked for all the hands on the plantation, carded cotton, spun a daily quota of thread, wove and dyed cloth. Every Wednesday she carried the white family's laundry three-quarters of a mile to a creek, where she beat each garment with a wooden paddle. Ironing consumed the rest of her day. Like the lowliest field hand, she felt the lash if any tasks went undone.[26]

Although mistresses found that their husbands commandeered most bondwomen for fieldwork during the better part of the day, they discovered in black children an acceptable alternative source of labor. Girls were favored for domestic service, but a child's sex played only a secondary role in determining household assignments. On smaller holdings especially, the demands of housework, like cotton cultivation, admitted of no finely honed division of labor. Indeed, until puberty, girls and boys shared a great deal in terms of dress and work. All children wore a "split-tail shirt," a knee-length smock slit up the sides: "Boys and gals all dress jes' alike . . . . They call it a shirt iffen a boy wear it and call it a dress iffen the gal wear it." At the age of six or so, many received assignments around the barnyard or in the Big House from one or more members of the master's family. Mr. and Mrs. Alex Smith, who grew up together, remembered performing different tasks. As a girl she helped to spin thread and pick seeds from cotton and cockle burrs from wool. He chopped wood, carried water, hoed weeds, tended the cows, and picked bugs from tobacco plants. However, slave narratives contain descriptions of both girls and boys elsewhere doing each of these things.[27]

Between the ages of six and twelve, black girls and boys followed the mistress's directions in filling woodboxes with kindling, lighting fires in chilly bedrooms in the morning and evening, making beds, washing and ironing clothes, parching coffee, polishing shoes, and stoking fires while the white family slept at night. They fetched water and milk from the springhouse and meat from the smokehouse. Three times a day they set the table, helped to prepare and serve meals, "minded flies" with peacock feather brushes, passed the salt and pepper on command and washed the dishes. They swept, polished, and dusted, served drinks and fanned overheated visitors. Mistresses entrusted to the care of those who were little more than babies themselves the bathing, diapering, dressing, grooming, and entertaining of white infants. In the barnyard black children gathered eggs, plucked chickens, drove cows to and from the stable and "tended the gaps" (opened and closed gates). (In the fields they acted as human scarecrows, toted water to the hands, and hauled shocks of corn together.) It was no wonder that Mary Ella Grandberry, a slave child grown old, "disremember[ed] ever playin' lack chilluns do today."[28]

In only a few tasks did a sexual division of labor exist among children. Masters always chose boys to accompany them on hunting trips and to serve as their personal valets. Little girls learned how to sew, to milk cows and churn butter, and to attend to the personal needs of their mistresses. As tiny ladies-in-waiting, they did the bidding of fastidious white women and of girls not much older than they. Cicely Cawthon, age six when the Civil War began, called herself the mistress's "little keeper"; "I stayed around, and waited on her, handed her water, fanned her, kept the flies off her, pulled up her pillow, and done anything she'd tell me to do." Martha Showvely recounted a nightly ritual with her Virginia mistress. After she finished her regular work around the house, the young girl would go to the woman's bedroom, bow to her, wait for acknowledgment, and then scurry around as ordered, lowering the shades, filling the water pitcher, arranging towels on the washstand, or "anything else" that struck the woman's fancy. Mary Woodward, only eleven in 1865, was taught to comb her mistress's hair, lace her corset, and arrange her hoop skirts. At the end of the toilet Mary was supposed to say, "You is served, mistress!" Recalled the former slave, "Her lak them little words at de last."[29]

Sexual exploitation of female servants of all ages (described in graphic detail by Harriet Jacobs in Lydia Maria Child's *Incidents in the Life of a Slave Girl*) predictably antagonized white women. Jealousy over their husbands' real or suspected infidelities resulted in a propensity for spontaneous violence among many. Husbands who flaunted their adventures in the slave quarters increased the chance that their wives would attack a specific woman or her offspring. Sarah Wilson remembered being "picked on" by the mistress, who chafed under her husband's taunts; he would say, "'Let her alone, she got big, big blood in her,' and then laugh."[30]

A divorce petition filed with the Virginia legislature in 1848 included a witness's testimony that the master in question one morning told his slave favorite to sit down at the breakfast table "to which Mrs. N [his wife] objected, saying. . . that she (Mrs. N.) would have her severely punished." Her husband replied "that in that event he would visit her (Mrs. N.) with a like punishment. Mrs. N. then burst into tears and asked if it was not too much for her to stand." This husband went to extreme lengths to remind his spouse of slave-mistress Mary Chesnut's observation that "there is no slave, after all, like a wife." In the black woman the mistress saw not only the source of her own degradation, she saw herself — a woman without rights, subject to the impulses of an arrogant husband-master.[31]

To punish black women for minor offenses, mistresses were likely to attack with any weapon available — a fork, butcher knife, knitting needle, pan of boiling water. Some of the most barbaric forms of punishment resulting in the mutilation and permanent scarring of female servants were devised by white mistresses in the heat of passion. As a group they received well-deserved notoriety for the "veritable terror" they unleashed upon black women in the Big House.[32]

Interviews with former slaves suggest that the advantages of domestic service (over fieldwork) for women have been exaggerated in accounts written by whites. Carrying wood and water, preparing three full meals a day over a smoky fireplace or pressing damp clothes with a hot iron rivaled cotton picking as backbreaking labor. Always "on call," women servants often had to snatch a bite to eat whenever they could, remain standing in the presence of whites, and sleep on the floor at the foot of their mistress's bed (increasing the chances that they would sooner or later be bribed, seduced, or forced into sexual relations with the master). To peel potatoes with a sharp knife, build a fire, or carry a heavy load of laundry down a steep flight of stairs required skills and dexterity not always possessed by little girls and boys, and injuries were common. Chastisement for minor infractions came with swift severity; cooks who burned the bread and children who stole cookies or fell asleep while singing to the baby suffered every conceivable form of physical abuse, from jabs with pins to beatings that left them disfigured for life. The master's house offered no shelter from the most brutal manifestations of slavery.[33]

For any one or all of these reasons, black women might prefer fieldwork to housework. During his visit to a rice plantation in 1853, Olmsted noted that hands "accustomed to the comparatively unconstrained life of the negro-settlement detest the close control and careful movements required of the house servants." Marriage could be both a means and an incentive to escape a willful mistress. Jessie Sparrow's mother wed at age thirteen in order "to go outer de big house. Dat how come she to marry so soon. . . ." Claude Wilson recalled many years later that "his mother was very rebellious toward her duties and constantly harassed the 'Missus' about letting her work in the fields with her husband until finally she was permitted to make the change from the house to the fields to be near her man." Other women, denied an alternative, explored the range of their own emotional resources in attempting to resist petty tyranny; their "sassiness" rubbed raw the nerves of mistresses already harried and highstrung. A few servants simply withdrew into a shell of "melancholy and timidity."[34]

The dual status of a bondwoman — a slave and a female — afforded her master a certain degree of flexibility in formulating her work assignments. When he needed a field hand, her status as an able-bodied slave took precedence over gender considerations, and she was forced to toil alongside her menfolk. At the same time, the master's belief that most forms of domestic service required the attentions of a female reinforced among slave women the traditional role of woman as household worker.

The authority of the master in enforcing a sexual division of labor was absolute, but at times individual women could influence his decisions to some extent. In certain cases, a woman's preferences for either fieldwork or domestic service worked to her advantage. For example, the rebelliousness of Claude Wilson's mother prompted her removal from the Big House to the field, a change she desired. Similarly, masters might promise a woman an opportunity to do a kind of work she preferred as a reward for her cooperation and diligence. On the other hand, a slave's misbehavior might cause her to lose a position she had come to value; more than one prized cook or maid was exiled to the fields for "sassing" the mistress or stealing. A system of rewards and punishments thus depended on the preferences of individual slaves, and a servant determined to make life miserable for the family in the Big House might get her way in any case.[35]

In the field and Big House, black women worked under the close supervision of whites (the master, overseer, or mistress) at a forced pace. The slaves derived few, if any, tangible benefits from their labor to increase staple-crop profits and to render the white family comfortable (at least in physical terms). However, their efforts to provide for their own health and welfare often took place apart from whites, with a rhythm more in tune with community and family life. For slave women, these responsibilities, although physically arduous, offered a degree of personal fulfillment. As Martha Colquitt remarked of her slave grandmother and mother who stayed up late to knit and sew clothes "for us chillun": "Dey done it 'cause dey wanted to. Dey wuz workin' for deyselves den." Slave women deprived of the ability to cook for their own kinfolk or discipline their own children felt a keen sense of loss; family responsibilities revealed the limited extent to which black women (and men) could control their own lives. Furthermore, a strict sexual division of labor in the quarters openly challenged the master's opportunistic approach to slave women's work.[36]

A number of activities were carried out either communally or centrally for the whole plantation by older women. On smaller farms, for example, a cook and her assistants might prepare one or all of the meals for the other slaves each day except Sunday. Similarly, an elderly woman, with the help of children too young to work in the fields, often was assigned charge of a nursery in the quarters, where mothers left their babies during the day. To keep any number of little ones happy and out of trouble for up to twelve to fourteen hours at a time taxed the patience of the most kindly souls. Slave children grew up with a mixture of affection and fear for the "grandmothers" who had dished out the licks along with the cornbread and clabber. Other grannies usurped the position of the white physician (he rarely appeared in any case); they "brewed medicines for every ailment," gave cloves and whiskey to ease the pain of childbirth, and prescribed potions for the lovesick. Even a child forced to partake of "Stinkin' Jacob tea" or a concoction of "turpentine an' castor oil an' Jerusalem oak" (for worms) would assert years later that "Gran'mammy was a great doctor," surely a testimony to her respected position within the slave community, if not to the delectability of her remedies.[37]

On many plantations, it was the custom to release adult women from fieldwork early on Saturday so that they could do their week's washing. Whether laundering was done in old wooden tubs, iron pots, or a nearby creek with batten sticks, wooden paddles, or washboards, it was a time-consuming and difficult chore. Yet this ancient form of women's work provided opportunities for socializing "whilst de 'omans leaned over de tubs washin' and a-singin' dem old songs." Mary Frances Webb remembered wash day — "a regular picnic" — with some fondness; it was a time for women "to spend the day together," out of the sight and earshot of whites.[38]

Much of the work black women did for the slave community resembled the colonial system of household industry. Well into the nineteenth century throughout the South, slave women continued to spin thread, weave and dye cloth, sew clothes, make soap and candles, prepare and preserve foods, churn butter, and grow food for the family table. Slave women mastered all these tasks with the aid of primitive equipment and skills passed on from grandmothers. Many years later, blacks of both sexes exclaimed over their slave mothers' ability to prepare clothing dye from various combinations of tree bark and leaves, soil and berries; make soap out of ashes and animal skins; and fashion bottle lamps from string and tallow. Because of their lack of time and materials, black women only rarely found in these activities an outlet for creative expression, but they did take pride in their resourcefulness and produced articles of value to the community as a whole.[39]

Black women's work in home textile production illustrates the ironies of community labor under slavery, for the threads of cotton and wool bound them together in both bondage and sisterhood. Masters (or mistresses) imposed rigid spinning and weaving quotas on women who worked in the fields all day. For example, many were forced to spin one "cut" (about three hundred yards) of thread nightly, or four to five cuts during rainy days or in the winter. Women of all ages worked together and children of both sexes helped to tease and card wool, pick up the loom shuttles, and knit. In the flickering candlelight, the whirr of the spinning wheel and the clackety-clack of the loom played a seductive lullabye, drawing those who were already "mighty tired" away from their assigned tasks.[40]

As the "head spinner" on a Virginia plantation, Bob Ellis's mother was often sent home from fieldwork early to prepare materials for the night's work; "She had to portion out de cotton dey was gonna spin an' see dat each got a fair share." Later that evening, after supper, as she moved around the dusty loom room to check on the progress of the other women, she would sing:

> Keep yo' eye on de sun,
> See how she run
> Don't let her catch you with you work undone,
> I'm a trouble, I'm a trouble,
> Trouble don' las' always.

With her song of urgency and promise she coaxed her sisters to finish their work so they could return home by sundown: "Dat made de women all speed up so dey could finish fo' dark catch 'em, 'cause it mighty hard handlin' dat cotton thread by fire-light."[41]

In the quarters, group work melded into family responsibilities, for the communal spirit was but a manifestation of primary kin relationships. Here it is possible only to outline the social dynamics of the slave household. The significance of the family in relation to the sexual division of labor under slavery cannot be overestimated; out of the mother-father, wife-husband nexus sprang the slaves' beliefs about what women and men should be and do. Ultimately, the practical application of those beliefs (in the words of Genovese) "provided a weapon for joint resistance to dehumanization."[42]

The two-parent, nuclear family was the typical form of slave cohabitation regardless of the location, size, or economy of a plantation; the nature of its ownership; or the age of its slave community. Because of the omnipresent threat of forced separation by sale, gift, or bequest, this family was not "stable." Yet, in the absence of such separations, unions between husbands and wives and parents and children often endured for many years. Marital customs, particularly exogamy, and the practice of naming children after the mother's or father's relatives (the most common pattern was to name a boy after a male relative) revealed the strong sense of kinship among slaves. Households tended to be large; Herbert G. Gutman found families with eight living children to be quite common. Out of economic considerations, a master would encourage his work force to reproduce itself, but the slaves welcomed each new birth primarily as "a social and familial fact." A web of human emotions spun by close family ties — affection, dignity, love — brought slaves together in a world apart from whites.[43]

In their own cabins, the blacks maintained a traditional division of labor between the sexes. Like women in almost all cultures, slave women had both a biological and a social "destiny." As part of their childbearing role, they assumed primary responsibility for childcare (when a husband and wife lived on separate plantations, the children remained with their mother and belonged to her master). Women also performed operations related to daily household maintenance — cooking, cleaning, tending fires, sewing and patching clothes.[44]

Fathers shared the obligations of family life with their wives. In denying slaves the right to own property, make a living for themselves, participate in public life, or protect their children, the institution of bondage deprived black men of access to the patriarchy in the larger economic and political sense. But at home women and men worked together to support the father's role as provider and protector. In the evenings and on Sundays, men collected firewood; made shoes; wove baskets; constructed beds, tables, and chairs; and carved butter paddles, ax handles, and animal traps. Other family members appreciated a father's skills; recalled Molly Ammonds, "My pappy make all de funiture dat went in our house an' it were might' good funiture too," and Pauline Johnson echoed, "De furn'chure was ho-mek, but my daddy mek it good an' stout." Husbands provided necessary supplements to the family diet by hunting and trapping quails, possums, turkeys, rabbits, squirrels, and raccoons, and by fishing. They often assumed responsibility for cultivating the tiny household garden plots allotted to families by the master. Some craftsmen, like Bill Austin's father, received goods or small sums of money in return for their work on nearby estates; Jack Austin, "regarded as a fairly good carpenter, mason, and bricklayer," was paid in " hams, bits of cornmeal, cloth for dresses for his wife and children, and other small gifts; these he either used for his small family or bartered with other slaves."[45]

These familial duties also applied to men who lived apart from their wives and children even though they were usually allowed to visit only on Saturday night and Sunday. Lucinda Miller's family "never had any sugar, and only got coffee when her father would bring it to her mother" during his visits. The father of Hannah Chapman was sold to a nearby planter when she was very small. Because "he missed us and us longed for him," she said many years later, he tried to visit his family under the cover of darkness whenever possible. She noted, "Us would gather 'round him an' crawl up in his lap, tickled slap to death, but he give us dese pleasures at painful risk." If the master should happen to discover him, "Us could track him de nex' day by de blood stains," she remembered.[46]

Hannah McFarland of South Carolina well remembered the time when the local slave patrol attempted to whip her mother, "but my papa sho' stopped dat," she said proudly. Whether or not he was made to suffer for his courage is unknown; however, the primary literature of slavery is replete with accounts of slave husbands who intervened, at the risk of their own lives, to save wives and children from violence at the hands of white men. More often, however, fathers had to show their compassion in less dramatic (though no less revealing) ways. On a Florida plantation, the Minus children often rose in the morning to find still warm in the fireplace the potatoes "which their father had thoughtfully roasted and which [they] readily consumed." Margrett Nickerson recalled how her father would tenderly bind up the wounds inflicted on her by a maniacal overseer; in later years, her crippled legs preserved the memory of a father's sorrow intermingled with her own suffering.[47]

The more freedom the slaves had in determining their own activities the more clearly emerged a distinct division of labor between the sexes. During community festivities like log rollings, rail splittings, wood choppings, and corn shuckings, men performed the prescribed labor while women cooked the meals. At times, male participants willingly "worked all night," for, in the words of one former slave, "we had the 'Heavenly Banners' (women and whiskey) by us." A limited amount of primary evidence indicates that men actively scorned women's work, especially cooking, housecleaning, sewing, washing clothes, and intimate forms of childcare (like bathing children and picking lice out of their hair). Some slaveholders devised forms of public humiliation that capitalized on men's attempts to avoid these tasks. One Louisiana cotton planter punished slave men by forcing them to wash clothes (he also made chronic offenders wear women's dresses). In *This Species of Property*, Leslie Howard Owens remarks of men so treated, "So great was their shame before their fellows that many ran off and suffered the lash on their backs rather than submit to the discipline. Men clearly viewed certain chores as women's tasks, and female slaves largely respected the distinction."[48]

The values and customs of the slave community played a predominant role in structuring work patterns among women and men within the quarters in general and the family in particular. Yet slaveholders affected the division of labor in the quarters in several ways; for example, they took women and girls out of the fields early on Saturdays to wash the clothes, and they enforced certain task assignments related to the production of household goods. An understanding of the social significance of the sexual division of labor requires at least brief mention of West African cultural preferences and the ways in which the American system of slavery disrupted or sustained traditional (African) patterns of women's work. Here it is important to keep in mind two points. First, cotton did not emerge as the South's primary staple crop until the late eighteenth century (the first slaves on the North American continent toiled in tobacco, rice, indigo, and corn fields); and second, regardless of the system of task assignments imposed upon antebellum blacks, the grueling pace of forced labor represented a cruel break from the past for people who had followed age-old customs related to subsistence agriculture.[49]

Though dimmed by time and necessity, the outlines of African work patterns endured among the slaves. As members of traditional agricultural societies, African women played a major role in producing the family's food as well as in providing basic household services. The sexual division of labor was more often determined by a woman's childcare and domestic reponsibilities than by any presumed physical weakness. She might engage in heavy, monotonous fieldwork (in some tribes) as long as she could make provisions for nursing her baby; that often meant keeping an infant with her in the field. She cultivated a kitchen garden that yielded a variety of vegetables consumed by the family or sold at market, and she usually milked the cows and churned butter.[50]

West Africans in general brought with them competencies and

knowledge that slaveowners readily exploited. Certain tribes were familiar with rice, cotton, and indigo cultivation. Many black women had had experience spinning thread, weaving cloth, and sewing clothes. Moreover, slaves often used techniques and tools handed down from their ancestors — in the method of planting, hoeing, and pounding rice, for example. Whites frequently commented on the ability of slave women to balance heavy and unwieldy loads on their heads, an African trait.[51]

The primary difficulty in generalizing about African women's part in agriculture stems from the fact that members of West African tribes captured for the North American slave trade came from different hoe-culture economies. Within the geographically limited Niger Delta region, for example, women and men of the Ibo tribe worked together in planting, weeding, and harvesting, but female members of another prominent group, the Yoruba, helped only with harvest. In general, throughout most of sub-Saharan Africa (and particularly on the west coast) women had primary responsibility for tilling (though not clearing) the soil and cultivating the crops; perhaps this tradition, combined with work patterns established by white masters in this country, reinforced the blacks' beliefs that cutting trees and rolling logs was "men's work." In any case it is clear that African women often did fieldwork. But because the sexual division of labor varied according to tribe, it is impossible to state with any precision the effect of the African heritage on the slaves' perceptions of women's agricultural work.[52]

The West African tradition of respect for one's elders found new meaning among American slaves; for most women, old age brought increased influence within the slave community even as their economic value to the master declined. Owners, fearful lest women escape from "earning their salt" once they became too infirm to go to the field, set them to work at other tasks — knitting, cooking, spinning, weaving, dairying, washing, ironing, caring for the children. (Elderly men worked as gardeners, wagoners, carters, and stocktenders.) But the imperatives of the southern economic system sometimes compelled slaveowners to extract from feeble women what field labor they could. In other cases they reduced the material provisions of the elderly — housing and allowances of food and clothing — in proportion to their decreased productivity.[53]

The overwhelming youth of the general slave population between 1830 and 1860 (more than one-half of all slaves were under twenty years of age) meant that most plantations had only a few old persons — the 10 percent over fifty years of age considered elderly. These slaves served as a repository of history and folklore for the others. Harriet Ware, a northern teacher assigned to the South Carolina Sea Islands, reported in 1862, "'Learning' with these people I find means a knowledge of medicine, and a person is valued accordingly." Many older women practiced "medicine" in the broadest sense in their combined role of midwife, root doctor, healer, and conjurer. They guarded ancient secrets about herbs and other forms of plant life. In their interpretation of dreams and strange occurrences, they brought the real world closer to the supernatural realm and offered spiritual guidance to the ill, the troubled, and the lovelorn.[54]

For slaves in the late antebellum period, these revered (and sometimes feared) women served as a tangible link with the African past. Interviewed by an FWP worker in 1937, a Mississippi-born former slave, James Brittian, recalled his own "grandma Aunt Mary" who had lived for 110 years. A "Molly Gasca [Madagascar?] negro," she was plagued by a jealous mistress because of her striking physical appearance; "Her hair it was fine as silk and hung down below her waist." Ned Chaney's African-born Granny Silla (she was the oldest person anyone knew, he thought) commanded respect among the other slaves by virtue of her advanced age and her remarkable healing powers: "Ever'body set a heap of sto' by her. I reckon, because she done 'cumullated so much knowledge an' because her head were so white." When Granny Silla died, her "little bags" of mysterious substances were buried with her because no one else knew how to use them. Yet Chaney's description of his own mother, a midwife and herb doctor, indicates that she too eventually assumed a position of at least informal authority within the community.[55]

As a little girl in Georgia, Mary Colbert adored her grandmother, a strong field hand, "smart as a whip." "I used to tell my mother that I wished I was named Hannah for her, and so Mother called me Mary Hannah," she recalled. Amanda Harris, interviewed in Virginia when she was ninety years old, looked back to the decade before the war when her grandmother was still alive: "Used to see her puffin' on dat ole pipe o' her'n, an' one day I ast her what fun she got outen it. 'Tain't no fun, chile,' she tole me. 'But it's a pow'ful lot o' easment. Smoke away trouble, darter. Blow ole trouble an' worry 'way in smoke.'" Amanda started smoking a pipe shortly before her grandmother died, and in 1937 she declared, "Now dat I'm ole as she was I know what she mean." In the quiet dignity of their own lives, these grandmothers preserved the past for future generations of Afro-American women.[56]

Within well-defined limits, the slaves created — or preserved — an explicit sexual division of labor based on their own preferences. Wives and husbands and mothers and fathers had reciprocal obligations toward one another. Together they worked to preserve the integrity of the family. Having laid to rest once and for all the myth of the slave matriarchy, some historians suggest that relations between the sexes approximated "a healthy sexual equality."[57] Without private property, slave men lacked the means to achieve economic superiority over their wives, one of the major sources of inequality in the ("free") sexual order. But if female and male slaves shared duties related to household maintenance and community survival, they were nonetheless reduced to a state of powerlessness that rendered virtually meaningless the concept of equality as it applies to marital relations.

Developments during the turbulent postwar years, when the chains of bondage were loosened but not destroyed, made clear the significance of black women's work in supporting the southern staple-crop economy. They also revealed the connection between patterns of women's work and black family life — a connection that had, at least to some degree, remained latent under slavery. Black women did their part in helping to provide for their families after the war. Female household heads had a particularly difficult time, for under the "free labor" system, a mother working alone rarely earned enough to support small children who were themselves too little to make any money. Relatives in a better financial situation often "adopted" these children, or took the whole family under their care.[58]

After the war, black women continued to serve as domestic servants, but large numbers stopped going to the fields altogether, or agreed to work only in harvest time. Indeed, from all over the South came reports that "the negro women are now almost wholly withdrawn from field labor." Ransom and Sutch, in their study of the economic consequences of emancipation, estimate that between one-third and one-half of all the women who worked in the fields under slavery provided proportionately less agricultural labor in the 1870s. This decline in overall female productivity was the result of two factors: many wives stayed home, and the ones who did continue to labor in the fields (like black men) put in shorter hours and fewer days each year than they had as slaves.

Crop output in many locales dropped accordingly, and white landowners lamented their loss, "for women were as efficient as men in working and picking cotton."[59]

In their speculation about the sources of this "evil of female loaferism," whites offered a number of theories, from the pernicious influence of northern schoolteachers to the inherent laziness of the black race. Actually, black women and men responded to freedom in a manner consistent with preferences that had been thwarted during slavery. Husbands sought to protect their wives from the sexual abuse and physical punishment that continued to prevail under the wage system of agricultural labor. Wives wanted to remain at home with their children, as befitted free and freed women; many continued to contribute to the family welfare by taking in washing or raising chickens.[60]

By 1867, freed people who wanted to assert control over their own productive energies had reached what some historians term a "compromise" with white landowners anxious to duplicate antebellum crop levels. This "compromise" came in the form of the sharecropping system, a family organization of labor that represented both a radical departure from collective or "gang" work characteristic of slavery and a rejection of the wage economy so integral to the (North's) fledgling industrial revolution. Freed families moved out of the old slave quarters into cabins scattered around a white man's plantation; they received "furnishings" (tools and seed) and agreed to pay the landlord a share of the crop — usually one-half of all the cotton they produced — in return for the use of the land and modest dwelling. Under this arrangement, black husbands assumed primary responsibility for crop management, and their wives devoted as much attention as possible to their roles as mothers and homemakers. During the particularly busy planting or harvesting seasons, a woman would join her husband and children at work in the field. In this way she could keep an eye on her offspring and still put to use her considerable strength and skills unmolested by white men.[61]

The Reconstruction South was not the best of all worlds in which to foster a new order between the races — or the sexes. Faced with persistent economic exploitation and political subservience within white-dominated society, black men sought to assert their authority as protectors of their communities and families. Outwardly, they placed a premium on closing ranks at home. This impulse was institutionalized in the freed people's churches ("Wives submit yourselves to your husbands" was the text of more than one postbellum sermon) and political organizations. One searches in vain for evidence of female participants in the many black conventions and meetings during this period, although this was perhaps in part attributable to the fact that women did not have the right to vote. Black women remained militantly outspoken in defense of their families and property rights, but they lacked a formal power base within their own communities. And in an atmosphere fraught with sexual violence, where freedwomen remained at the mercy of white men and where "the mere suggestion" that a black man was attracted to a white woman was "enough to hang him," a black husband's resentment might continue to manifest itself in his relations with those closest to him. A Sea Island slave folktale offered the lesson that "God had nebber made a woman for the head of a man." In the struggle against white racism this often meant that black women were denied the equality with their men to which their labor — not to mention justice — entitled them.[62]

The sexual division of labor under slavery actually assumed two forms — one system of work forced upon slaves by masters who valued women only as work-oxen and brood-sows, and the other initiated by the slaves themselves in the quarters. Only the profit motive accorded a measure of consistency to the slaveholder's decisions concerning female work assignments; he sought to exploit his "hands" efficiently, and either invoked or repudiated traditional notions of women's work to suit his own purposes. In this respect, his decision-making process represented in microcosm the shifting priorities of the larger society, wherein different groups of women were alternately defined primarily as producers or as reproducers according to the fluctuating labor demands of the capitalist economy.[63]

Within their own communities, the slaves attempted to make work choices based on their African heritage as it applied to the American experience. Their well-defined sexual division of labor contrasted with the calculated self-interest of slaveowners. Slave women were allowed to fulfill their duties as wives and mothers only insofar as these responsibilities did not conflict with their masters' demands for field or domestic labor. As sharecroppers, freed people sought to institutionalize their resistance to the whites' conviction that black women should be servants or cotton pickers first, and family members only incidentally. In working together as a unit, black parents and children made an explicit political statement to the effect that their own priorities were inimical to those of white landowners.

To a considerable extent, the freed family's own patriarchal tendencies — fathers took care of "public" negotiations with the white landlord while mothers assumed primary responsibility for childcare — resulted from the black man's desire to protect his household in the midst of a violently racist society. The postbellum black nuclear family never duplicated exactly the functions of the white middle-class model, which (beginning in the late eighteenth century) drew an increasingly rigid distinction between masculine and feminine spheres of activity characteristic of commercial-industrial capitalism. Clearly, the peculiar southern way of life suggests that an analysis of black women's oppression should focus not so much on the family as on the dynamics of racial prejudice. However, black women and men in the long run paid a high price for their allegiance to a patriarchal family structure, and it is important not to romanticize this arrangement as it affected the status and opportunities of women, even within the confines of black community life. Women continued to wield informal influence in their roles as herb doctors and "grannies," but men held all positions of formal political and religious authority. Ultimately, black people's "preferences" in the postwar period took shape within two overlapping caste systems — one based on race, the other on gender. Former slaves were "free" only in the sense that they created their own forms of masculine authority as a counter to poverty and racism.

The story of slave women's work encapsulates an important part of American history. For here in naked form, stripped free of the pieties often used in describing white women and free workers at the time, were the forces that shaped patriarchal capitalism — exploitation of the most vulnerable members of society, and a contempt for women that knew no ethical or physical bounds. And yet, slave women demonstrated "true womanhood" in its truest sense. Like Janie Scott's mother who was "much of a woman," they revealed a physical and emotional strength that transcended gender and preached a great sermon about the human spirit.

NOTES

The author would like to acknowledge the helpful suggestions and comments provided by Rosalind Petchesky and other members of the *Feminist Studies* editorial board and by Michael P. Johnson. Research for this project (part of a full-length study of black women, work, and the family in America, 1830-1980) was funded by a grant from the National Endowment for the Humanities.

[1]Zora N. Hurston, *Their Eyes Were Watching God* (London: J.M. Dent and Sons, 1938), pp. 31-32. Novelist, folklorist, and anthropologist, Hurston (born 1901, died 1960) had collected a massive amount of primary data on the culture and folklore of Afro-Americans before she began work on*Their Eyes Were Watching God.* In 1938 she served as supervisor of the Negro Unit of the Florida Federal Writers Project which compiled interviews with former slaves. Her various writings are finally receiving long-overdue literary attention and critical acclaim. See Robert E. Hemenway, *Zora Neale Hurston: A Literary Biography* (Urbana: University of Illinois Press, 1977); and a recent anthology: Zora N. Hurston, *I Love Myself When I Am Laughing. . . And Then Again When I Am Looking Mean And Impressive*, ed. Alice Walker (Old Westbury, N.Y.: Feminist Press, 1980).

[2]Angela Davis, "Reflections on the Black Woman's Role in the Community of Slaves," *The Black Scholar* 3 (December 1971): 3-15. For other works that focus on slave women, see Mary Ellen Obitko, "'Custodians of a House of Resistance': Black Women Respond to Slavery," in *Women and Men: The Consequences of Power*, ed. Dana V. Hiller and Robin Ann Sheets (Cincinnati: Office of Women's Studies, University of Cincinnati, 1977), pp. 256-59; Deborah G. White, "Ain't I A Woman? Female Slaves in the Antebellum South" (Ph.D. dissertation, University of Illinois-Chicago Circle, 1979). White's work examines several important themes related to slave women's work and family life, but her study lacks a coherent theoretical framework. She asserts that slave women gained considerable "self-confidence" because they achieved "equality" with men of their race, and even suggests that emancipation resulted in a "loss" of women's "equality"; freedom amounted to "a decline in the status of black women" (p. 51). When used in this context, the concepts of equality and status lose all meaning and relevance to the complex issues involved; White's argument obscures the subtleties of black female-male relations under bondage and after emancipation.

The volume edited by Gerda Lerner, *Black Women in White America: A Documentary History* (New York: Randam House, 1972), includes material on the history of slave women.

[3]Herbert G. Gutman, *The Black Family in Slavery and Freedom, 1750-1925* (New York: Pantheon Books, 1976); Eugene D. Genovese, *Roll, Jordan, Roll: The World the Slaves Made* (New York: Randam House, 1974); Leslie Howard Owens, *This Species of Property: Slave Life and Culture in the Old South* (New York: Oxford University Press, 1976); John D. Blassingame, *The Slave Community: Plantation Life in the Old South* (New York: Oxford University Press, 1972); Paul A. David et al., *Reckoning With Slavery: A Critical Study in the Quantitative History of American Negro Slavery* (New York: Oxford University Press, 1976); Paul D. Escott, *Slavery Remembered: A Record of Twentieth-Century Slave Narratives* (Chapel Hill: University of North Carolina Press, 1978).

In some specialized studies, women are largely excluded from the general analysis and discussed only in brief sections under the heading "Women and Children." See, for example, Robert S. Starobin, *Industrial Slavery in the Old South* (New York: Oxford University Press, 1970); and Todd L. Savitt, *Medicine and Slavery: The Diseases and*

Health Care of Blacks in Antebellum Virginia (Urbana: University of Illinois Press, 1978).

[4]For examples of studies of specific groups of women and the relationship between their work and family life, see Nancy F. Cott, *The Bonds of Womanhood: 'Woman's Sphere' in New England, 1780-1835* (New Haven: Yale University Press, 1977); Thomas Dublin, *Women at Work: The Transformation of Work and Community in Lowell, Massachusetts, 1826-1860* (New York: Columbia University Press, 1979); Milton Cantor and Bruce Laurie, eds., *Class, Sex, and the Woman Worker* (Westport, Conn.: Greenwood Press, 1977); Virginia Yans McLaughlin, "Patterns of Work and Family Organization: Buffalo's Italians," *Journal of Interdisciplinary History* 2 (Autumn 1971): 297-314; Leslie Woodcock Tentler, *Wage-Earning Women: Industrial Work and Family Life in the United States, 1900-1930* (New York: Oxford University Press, 1979).

General overviews and theoretical formulations that fail to take into account the experiences of slave women include Patricia Branca, "A New Perspective on Women's Work: A Comparative Typology," *Journal of Social History* 9 (Winter 1975): 129-53; W. Elliot Brownlee, "Household Values, Women's Work, and Economic Growth, 1800-1930," *Journal of Economic History* 39 (March 1979): 199-209; Maurine Weiner Greenwald, "Historians and the Working-Class Woman in America," *International Labor and Working-Class History*, no. 14/15 (Spring 1979): 23-32; Alice Kessler-Harris, "Women, Work, and the Social Order," in *Liberating Women's History: Theoretical and Critical Essays*, ed. Berenice A. Carroll (Urbana: University of Illinois Press, 1976), pp. 330-43.

[5]On women's "productive-reproductive" functions and the relationship between patriarchy and capitalism, see Joan Kelly, "The Doubled Vision of Feminist Theory: A Postcript to the 'Women and Power' Conference," *Feminist Studies* 5 (Spring 1979): 216-27; Heidi Hartmann, "Capitalism, Patriarchy, and Job Segregation by Sex," and Zillah Eisenstein, "Developing a Theory of Capitalist Patriarchy and Socialist Feminism," and "Some Notes on the Relations of Capitalist Patriarchy," in *Capitalist Patriarchy and the Case for Socialist Feminism*, ed. Zillah R. Eisenstein (New York: Monthly Review Press, 1979); Annette Kuhn and AnnMarie Wolpe, "Feminism and Materialism" and Veronica Beechey, "Women and Production: A Critical Analysis of Some Sociological Theories of Women's Work," both in *Feminism and Materialism: Women and Modes of Production*, ed. Annette Kuhn and AnnMarie Wolpe (London: Routledge and Kegan Paul, 1978).

Several scholars argue that the last three decades of the antebellum period constituted a distinct phase in the history of slavery. Improved textile machinery and a rise in world demand for cotton led to a tremendous growth in the American slave economy, especially in the Lower South. A marked increase in slave mortality rates and family breakups (a consequence of forced migration from Upper to Lower South), and a slight decline in female fertility rates indicate the heightened demands made upon slave labor during the years 1830-60. See David, et al., *Reckoning With Slavery*, pp. 99, 356-57; Jack Erickson Eblen, "New Estimates of the Vital Rates of the United States Black Population During the Nineteenth Century," *Demography* 11 (May 1974): 307-13.

[6]For example, see Kelly, "Doubled Vision," pp. 217-18, and Eisenstein, "Relations of Capitalist Patriarchy," pp. 48-52, on the regressive implications of family life for women. But Davis notes that the slave woman's "survival-oriented activities were themselves a form of resistance" ("Reflections on the Black Woman's Role," p.7).

[7]Interviews with former slaves have been published in various forms, including George P. Rawick, ed., *The American Slave: A Composite Autobiography*, 41 vols., Series 1 and 2, supp. Series 1 and 2 (Westport Conn.: Greenwood Press, 1972, 1978, 1979); Social Science Institute, Fisk University, *Unwritten History of Slavery:*

Autobiographical Accounts of Negro Ex-Slaves (Washington, D.C.: Microcards Editions, 1968); Charles L. Perdue, Jr., Thomas E. Borden, and Robert K. Phillips, *Weevils in the Wheat: Interviews with Virginia Ex-Slaves* (Charlottesville: University Press of Virginia, 1976); John B. Cade, "Out of the Mouths of Ex-Slaves," *Journal of Negro History* 20 (July 1935): 294-337.

The narratives as a historical source are evaluated in Escott, *Slavery Remembered,* pp. 3-18 ("the slave narratives offer the best evidence we will ever have on the feelings and attitudes of America's slaves . . ."); Martia Graham Goodson, "An Introductory Essay and Subject Index to Selected Interviews from the Slave Narrative Collection" (Ph.D. dissertation, Union Graduate School, 1977); and C. Vann Woodward. "History from Slave Sources," *American Historical Review* 79 (April 1974): 470-81.

The Davidson quotation is from Rawick, ed., *American Slave,* Ohio Narrs., Series 1, vol. 16, pp. 26-29. Hereafter, all references to this collection will include the name of the state, series number, volume, and page numbers. The other major source of slave interview material taken from the FWP collection for this paper — Perdue, et al. — will be referred to as *Weevils in the Wheat.*

[8]Joan Kelly-Gadol, "The Social Relations of the Sexes: Methodological Implications of Women's History," *Signs* 1 (Summer 1976): 809-10, 819.

[9]For discussions of women's work and the inadequacy of male-biased economic and social-scientific theory to define and analyze it, see Joan Acker, "Issues in the Sociological Study of Women's Work," in *Working Women: Theories and Facts in Perspective,* ed., Ann H. Stromberg and Shirley Harkess (Palo Alto, Calif.: Mayfield Publishing Co. 1978), pp. 134-61; and Judith K. Brown, "A Note on the Division of Labor by Sex," *American Anthropologist* 72 (October 1970): 1073-78.

[10]Miss. Narrs., supp. Series 1, pt. 2, vol. 7, p. 350; Okla. Narrs., supp. Series 1, vol. 12, p. 110; Davis, "Reflections on the Black Woman's Role," p. 8; Frances Anne Kemble, *Journal of A Residence on a Georgian Plantation in 1838-1839* (London: Longman, Green, 1863), pp. 60, 92.

[11]Owens, *This Species of Property,* pp. 8-20.

[12]Kemble, *Journal of a Residence,* p. 28; Lewis Cecil Gray, *History of Agriculture in the Southern United States,* vol. 1 (Washington, D.C.: Carnegie Institution, 1933), pp. 533-548; *Weevils in the Wheat,* p. 199; Fla. Narrs., Series 1, vol. 17, p. 305; Charles S. Sydnor, *Slavery in Mississippi* (Gloucester, Mass.: P. Smith, 1965), p. 20; Frederick Law Olmsted, *A Journey in the Seaboard Slave States* (New York: Dix and Edwards, 1856), p. 470; Frederick Law Olmsted, *A Journey in the Back Country* (New York: Mason Brothers, 1860), p.59.

[13]Olmsted, *A Journey in the Seaboard Slave States,* p. 387; Ala. Narrs., Series 1, vol. 6, p. 87. Work descriptions were gleaned from the FWP slave narrative collection (*American Slave* and *Weevils in the Wheat*) and Gray, *History of Agriculture.* Goodson ("Introductory Essay") has indexed a sample of the interviews with women by subject (for example, "candlemaking," "carding wool," "field work," "splitting rails.").

For pictures of early twentieth-century black women of St. Helena's Islands, South Carolina, wearing the second belt, see photographs in Edith M. Dabbs, *Face of an Island: Leigh Richmond Miner's Photographs of St. Helena's Island* (New York: Grossman, 1971). The caption of one photo entitled "Woman with Hoe" reads: "Adelaide Washington sets off for her day's work in the field. The second belt or cord tied around the hips lifted all her garments a little and protected the long skirts from both early morning dew and contact with the dirt . . . . [according to] an African superstition . . . the second cord also gave the wearer extra strength" (no pp.). Olmsted, *Slave States,* p. 387, includes a sketch of this form of dress.

[14] *Weevils in the Wheat,* p. 26; Gary, *History of Agriculture,* p. 251; planter quoted in Owens, *This Species of Property,* p. 39.

[15] Genovese, *Roll, Jordan, Roll,* p. 495; Burke quoted in Gray, *History of Agriculture,* p. 549; Olmsted, *A Journey in the Back Country,* p. 81. For former slaves' descriptions of women who plowed, see Okla. Narrs., Series 1, vol. 7, p. 314; Fla. Narrs., Series 1, vol. 17, p. 33.

[16] Olmsted quoted in Sydnor, *Slavery in Mississippi,* p. 68; *Weevils in the Wheat,* p. 77. Of the women who worked in the South Carolina Sea Islands cotton fields, Harriet Ware (a northern teacher) wrote, "they walk off with their heavy hoes on their shoulders, as free, strong, and graceful as possible." Elizabeth Ware Pearson, ed., *Letters from Port Royal Written at the Time of the Civil War* (Boston: W.B. Clarke, 1906), p. 52.

[17] Stuart Bruchey, ed., *Cotton and the Growth of the American Economy: 1790-1860* (New York: Harcourt, Brace & World, 1967), p. 174. See the documents under the heading "Making Cotton" and "The Routine of the Cotton Year," pp. 171-80. For examples of outstanding female pickers see Ala. Narrs., Series 1, vol 6, p. 275 ("Oncet I won a contest wid a man an' made 480 pounds."); *Weevils in the Wheat,* p. 199.

[18] Texas Narrs., supp. Series 2, pt. 1, vol. 2, pp. 93-94; Miss. Narrs., supp. Series 1, pt. 1, vol. 6, pp. 235-36, and pt. 2, vol. 7, p. 404; Tex. Narrs., Series 1, pt. 3, vol. 5, p. 231; Ind. Narrs., Series 1, vol. 6, p. 25; Ga. Narrs., Series 1, pt. 1, vol. 12, p. 113; Okla. Narrs., Series 1, vol. 7, p. 314; Ala. Narrs., Series 1, vol. 6, p. 338.

[19] For a general discussion of slave artisans in the South see Gray, *History of Agriculture,* pp. 548, 565-67; Sydnor, *Slavery in Mississippi,* p. 9. Roger L. Ransom and Richard Sutch, in *One Kind of Freedom: The Economic Consequences of Emancipation* (Cambridge: Cambridge University Press, 1977), discuss "Occupational Distribution of Southern Blacks: 1860, 1870, 1890" in app. B, pp. 220-31. The works of Starobin *(Industrial Slavery),* and James H. Brewer, *The Confederate Negro: Virginia's Craftsmen and Military Laborers, 1861-1865* (Durham: Duke University Press, 1969), focus almost exclusively on male slaves. See also Herbert Gutman and Richard Sutch, "Victorians All? The Sexual Mores and Conduct of Slaves and their Masters," in David, et al., *Reckoning With Slavery,* p. 160; Gutman, *Black Family,* pp. 599-600. The "hiring out" of men and children frequently disrupted family life.

[20] Ransom and Sutch, *One Kind of Freedom,* p. 233; Olmsted, *Slave States,* p. 388; Ohio Narrs., Series 1, vol. 16, p. 28; Kemble, *Journal,* p. 121; S.C. Narrs., Series 1, pt. 4, vol. 3, p. 78; *Weevils in the Wheat,* pp. 223-24. Genovese describes the plantation system as a "halfway house between peasant and factory cultures" *(Roll, Jordan, Roll,* p. 286). For further discussion of the grueling pace of fieldwork see Herbert G. Gutman and Richard Sutch, "Sambo Makes Good, or Were Slaves Imbued with the Protestant Work Ethic?" in David, et al., *Reckoning With Slavery,* pp. 55-93.

[21] Ala. Narrs., Series 1, vol. 6, p. 46; Fla. Narrs., Series 1, vol. 17, p. 185; *Weevils in the Wheat,* pp. 259, 216; Va. Narrs., Series 1, vol. 16, p. 51; Escott, *Slavery Remembered,* pp. 86-93. Escott includes an extensive discussion of resistance as revealed in the FWP slave narrative collection and provides data on the age, sex, and marital status of resisters and the purposes and forms of resistance. Gutman argues that the "typical runaway" was a male, aged sixteen to thirty-five years (*Black Family,* pp. 264-65). See also Obitko, "Custodians of a House of Resistance,"; Owens, *This Species of Property,* pp. 38, 88, 95.

[22] *Weevils in the Wheat,* pp. 26, 282, 157. According to Gutman, plantation work patterns "apparently failed to take into account enlarged slave kin groups, and further study may show that a central tension between slaves and their owners had its origins

in the separation of work and kinship obligations" *(Black Family,* p. 209.).

[23]Fla. Narrs., Series 1, vol. 17, p. 191; Bennet H. Barrow quoted in Gutman, *Black Family,* p.263; Robert S. Starobin, ed., *Blacks in Bondage: Letters of American Slaves* (New York: New Viewpoints, 1974), p. 54.

In his recent study, *The Slave Drivers: Black Agricultural Labor Supervisors in the Antebellum South* (Westport, Conn.: Greenwood Press, 1979), William L. Van DeBurg examines the anomalous position of black (male) drivers in relation to the rest of the slave community.

[24]Savitt, *Medicine and Slavery,* pp. 115-20; planter quoted in Owens, *This Species of Property,* pp. 38-40; planter quoted in Olmsted, *A Journey in the Seaboard Slave States,* p. 190; Kemble, *Journal of a Residence,* p. 121. Cf. White, "Ain't I A Woman?" pp. 77-86, 101, 155-60.

[25]Genovese, *Roll, Jordan, Roll,* pp. 328, 340; Ala, Narrs., Series 1, vol. 6, p. 273; Miss. Narrs., supp. Series 1, pt. 2, vol. 7, p. 400; Tex. Narrs., Series 1, pt. 3, vol. 5, p. 45. Recent historians have emphasized that the distinction between housework and fieldwork was not always meaningful in terms of shaping a slave's personality and self-perception or defining her or his status. See Owens, *This Species of Property,* p. 113; Escott, *Slavery Remembered,* pp. 59-60.

[26]Ala. Narrs., Series 1, vol. 6, pp. 416-17. In her study of slave mistresses, Anne Firor Scott gives an accurate description of their numerous supervisory duties, but she ignores that most of the actual manual labor was performed by slave women. See *The Southern Lady: From Pedestal to Politics, 1830-1930* (Chicago: University of Chicago Press, 1970), p.31.

[27]Tex. Narrs., Series 1, pt. 4, vol. 5, p. 11; Ind. Narrs., Series 1, vol. 6, p. 83. See also Miss. Narrs., supp. Series 1, pt. 1, vol. 6, pp. 54-55, 216, 257, 365, 380-81.

[28]The FWP slave narrative collection provides these examples of children's work, and many more. Ala. Narrs., Series 1, vol. 6, p. 157; Genovese, *Roll, Jordan, Roll,* pp. 502-19; Owens, *This Species of Property,* p. 202.

In early adolescence (ages ten to fourteen), a child would normally join the regular work force as a half-hand. At that time (or perhaps before), she or he received adult clothing. This *rite de passage* apparently made more of an impression on boys than girls, probably because pants offered more of a contrast to the infant's smock than did a dress. Willis Cofer attested to the significance of the change: "Boys jes' wore shirts what looked lak dresses 'til dey wuz 12 years old and big enough to wuk in de field . . . and all de boys wuz mighty proud when dey got big enough to wear pants and go to wuk in de fields wid grown folkses. When a boy got to be man enough to wear pants, he drawed rations and quit eatin' out of de trough [in the nursery]." Ga. Narrs., Series 1, pt. 1, vol. 12, p. 203. For other examples of the significance of change from adults' to children's clothing, see Tex. Narrs., Series 1, pt. 3, vol. 5, pp. 211, 275; p. 4, pp. 109-110; Ga. Narrs., Series 1, pt. 1, vol. 12, p. 277; Genovese, *Roll, Jordan, Roll,* p. 505.

[29]Ga. Narrs., supp. Series 1, pt. 1, vol. 3, p. 185; *Weevils in the Wheat,* pp. 264-65; S.C. Narrs., Series 1, pt. 4, vol. 3, p. 257.

[30]Okla. Narrs., Series 1, vol. 7, p. 347; White "Ain't I A Woman?" pp. 210-15; L. Maria Child, ed., *Incidents in the Life of a Slave Girl, Written By Herself* (Boston: L. Maria Child, 1861).

[31]James Hugo Johnston, *Race Relations in Virginia and Miscegenation in the South, 1776-1860* (Amherst: University of Massachusetts Press, 1970), p. 247; Mary Boykin Chesnut, *A Diary From Dixie,* ed. Ben Ames Williams (Cambridge, Mass.: Harvard University Press, 1980), p. 49.

[32]Fla. Narrs., Series 1, vol. 17, p. 35. For specific incidents illustrating these points, see *Weevils in the Wheat*, pp. 63, 199; Okla. Narrs., Series 1, vol. 7, pp. 135, 165-66; Tenn. Narrs., Series 1, vol. 16, p. 14. Slave punishment in general is discussed in Escott, *Slavery Remembered*, pp. 42-46; Owens, *This Species of Property*, p. 88; Savitt, *Slavery and Medicine*, pp. 65-69; Gutman and Sutch, "Sambo Makes Good," pp. 55-93; Frederick Douglass, *Narrative of the Life of Frederick Douglass, An American Slave* (Cambridge: Harvard University Press, 1960), pp. 60-61. These examples indicate that Anne Firor Scott is a bit sanguine in suggesting that although southern women were sensitive to the "depravity" of their husbands, "It may be significant that they did not blame black women, who might have provided convenient scapegoats. The blame was squarely placed on men." See Anne Firor Scott, "Women's Perspectives on the Patriarchy in the 1850s," *Journal of American History* 61 (June 1974): 52-64.

[33]Genovese, *Roll, Jordan, Roll*, pp. 333-38. See, for example, the document entitled "A Seamstress is Punished" in Lerner, ed., *Black Women in White America*, pp. 18-19.

[34]Olmsted, *A Journey in the Seaboard Slave States*, p. 421; S.C. Narrs., Series 1, pt. 4, vol. 3, p. 126; Fla. Narrs., Series 1, vol. 14, p. 356; Escott, *Slavery Remembered*, p. 64; Kemble, *Journal of a Residence*, p. 98; Genovese, *Roll, Jordan, Roll*, pp. 346-47.

[35]Fla. Narrs., Series 1, vol. 17, p. 356; Gutman and Sutch, "Sambo Makes Good," p. 74; Kemble, *Journal of a Residence*, p. 153; Gray, *History of Agriculture*, p. 553; Owens, *This Species of Property*, p. 113.

[36]Ga. Narrs., Series 1, pt. 1, vol. 12, p. 243; Davis, "Reflections on the Black Woman's Role," pp. 4-7. For general discussions of women's work as it related to slave communal life see also Owens, *This Species of Property*, pp. 23, 225; and White, "Ain't I A Woman?." Polly Cancer recalled that, when she was growing up on a Mississippi plantation, the master "wudn't let de mammies whip dey own chillun [or "do dey own cookin"] . . . , ef he cum 'cross a 'ooman whuppin' her chile he'd say, 'Git 'way 'ooman; dats my bizness . . . ." Miss. Narrs., supp. Series 1, pt. 2, vol. 7, pp. 340-41.

[37]Gray, *History of Agriculture*, p. 563; Olmsted, *A Journey in the Seaboard Slave States*, pp. 424-25, 697-98; Owens, *This Species of Property*, p. 47; Fla. Narrs., Series 1, vol. 17, p. 175; Ala. Narrs., Series 1, vol. 6, p. 216; Miss. Narrs., supp. Series 1, pt. 1, vol. 6, pp. 10, 23, 25, 123; Ga. Narrs., supp. Series 1, pt. 1, vol. 3, p. 27. Savitt *(Slavery and Medicine)* includes a section on "Black Medicine" (pp. 171-84) and confirms Rebecca Hook's recollection that "on the plantation, the doctor was not nearly as popular as the 'granny' or midwife." Fla. Narrs., Series 1, vol. 17, p. 175.

[38]Ga. Narrs., Series 1, pt. 1, vol. 12, p. 70; Okla. Narrs., Series 1, vol. 7, pp. 314-15; White, "Ain't I A Woman?" pp. 22-23; Tex. Narrs., Series 2, pt. 1, vol. 2, p. 98.

[39]The FWP slave narrative collection contains many descriptions of slaves engaged in household industry. Alice Morse Earle details comparable techniques used by white women in colonial New England in *Home Life in Colonial Days* (New York: MacMillan Co., 1935).

[40]See, for example, S.C. Narrs., Series 1, pt. 3, vol. 3, pp. 15, 218, 236; Tex. Narrs., Series 1, pt. 3, vol. 5, pp. 20, 89, 108, 114, 171, 188, 220; Miss. Narrs., supp. Series 1, pt. 1, vol. 6, p. 36.

[41]*Weevils in the Wheat*, pp. 88-89. George White of Lynchburg reported that his mother sang a similar version of this song to women while they were spinning (p. 309).

[42]Genovese, *Roll, Jordan, Roll*, p. 319.

[43]Gutman, *Black Family*, p. 75. Escott points out that masters and slaves lived in "different worlds" *(Slavery Remembered*, p. 20). This paragraph briefly summarizes Gutman's pioneering work.

[44]Davis, "Reflections on the Black Woman's Role," p. 7.

[45]Ala. Narrs., Series 1, vol. 6, p. 9; Tex. Narrs., supp. Series 2, pt. 5, vol. 6, pp. 2036-37; Fla. Narrs., Series 1, vol. 17, pp. 22-23; White, "Ain't I A Woman?," pp. 30-31, 65.

[46]Gutman, *Black Family,* pp. 142, 67-68, 267-78; Genovese, *Roll, Jordan, Roll,* pp. 318, 482-94; S.C. Narrs., Series 1, pt. 3, vol. 3, p. 192; Miss. Nars., supp. Series 1, pt. 2, vol. 7, pp. 380-81.

[47]Okla. Narrs., Series 1, vol. 7, p. 210; Escott, *Slavery Remembered,* pp. 49-57, 87; Owens, *This Species of Property,* p. 201.

[48]Gutman and Sutch, "Sambo Makes Good," p. 63; Owens, *This Species of Property,* p. 195; Miss. Narrs., supp. Series 1, pt. 1, vol. 6, pp. 59-60. For mention of corn shuckings in particular, see Genovese, *Roll, Jordan, Roll,* p. 318; Miss. Narrs., Series 1, vol. 7, p. 6; Okla. Narrs., Series 1, vol. 7, p. 230. In the context of traditional female-male roles, what Genovese calls the "curious sexual division of labor" that marked these festivities was not "curious" at all (p. 318).

[49]Unfortunately, much of the data about pre colonial African work patterns must be extrapolated from recent findings of anthropologists. The author benefited from conversations with Dr. M. Jean Hay of the Boston University African Studies Center concerning women's work in precolonial Africa and methodological problems in studying this subject.

[50]For a theoretical formulation of the sexual division of labor in preindustrial societies, see Brown, "A Note on the Division of Labor By Sex."

[51]Peter Wood, *Black Majority: Negroes in Colonial South Carolina From 1670 Through the Stono Rebellion* (New York: Alfred A. Knopf, 1974), pp. 59-62; P.C. Lloyd, "Osi fakunde of Ijebu," in *Africa Remembered: Narratives by West Africans from the Era of the Slave Trade,* ed. Philip D. Curtin (Madison: University of Wisconsin Press, 1967), p. 263; Marguerite Dupire, "The Position of Women in a Pastoral Society," in *Women of Tropical Africa,* ed. Denise Paulme (Berkeley: University of California Press, 1963), pp. 76-80; Olaudah Equiano, "The Life of Olaudah Equiano or Gustavus Vassa the African Written By Himself," in *Great Slave Narratives,* ed. Arna Bontemps (Boston: Beacon Press, 1969), pp. 7-10; Kemble, *Journal of a Residence,* p. 42; Pearson, ed., *Letters from Port Royal,* pp. 58, 106.

[52]Melville J. Herskovits, *The Myth of the Negro Past* (New York: Harper & Bros., 1941), pp. 33-85; Wood, *Black Majority,* pp. 179, 250; Hermann Baumann, "The Division of Work According to Sex in African Hoe Culture," *Africa* 1 (July 1928): 289-319.

On the role of women in hoe agriculture, see also Leith Mullings, "Women and Economic Change in Africa," in *Women in Africa: Studies in Social and Economic Change,* ed. Nancy J. Hafkin and Edna G. Bay (Stanford: Stanford University Press, 1976), pp. 239-64; Sylvia Leith-Ross, *African Women: A Study of the Ibo of Nigeria* (New York: Frederick A. Praeger, 1965), pp. 84-91; Ester Boserup, *Woman's Role in Economic Development* (New York: St. Martin's Press, 1970), pp. 156-36; Jack Goody and Joan Buckley, "Inheritance and Women's Labour in Africa," *Africa* 63 (April 1973): 108-21. No tribes in precolonial Africa used the plow.

[53]Olmsted, *A Journey in the Seaboard Slave States,* p. 433; Gray, *History of Agriculture,* p. 548; Kemble, *Journal of a Residence,* pp. 164, 247; Douglass, *Narrative,* pp. 76-78. According to Genovese, the ability of these elderly slaves "to live decently and with self-respect depended primarily on the support of their younger fellow slaves" *(Roll, Jordan, Roll,* p. 523); White "Ain't I A Woman?" p. 49; Miss. Narrs., supp. Series 1, pt. 1, vol. 6, p. 242.

[54]Eblen, "New Estimates," p. 306; Pearson, ed. *Letters from Port Royal,* p. 25;

Genovese, *Roll, Jordan, Roll,* pp. 522-23; Eliza F. Andrews, *The War-Time Journal of a Georgia Girl, 1864-1865* (New York: D. Appleton & Co., 1908), p. 101; Escott, *Slavery Remembered,* pp., 108-09; Owens, *This Species of Property,* p. 140; Gutman, *Black Family,* p. 218. For specific examples, see Ala. Narrs., supp. Series 1, pt. 1, vol. 6, p. 217; pt. 2, vol. 7, pp. 369-73. See also White, "Ain't I A Woman?" pp. 107-112.

[55]Miss. Narrs., Supp. Series 1, pt. 1, Vol. 6, p. 217; pt. 2, Vol. 7, pp. 369-73. See also White, "Ain't I A Woman?" pp. 107-112.

[56]Ga. Narrs., Series 1, pt. 1, vol. 12, p. 214; *Weevils in the Wheat,* p. 128

[57]Genovese, *Roll, Jordan, Roll,* p. 500. See also White, "Ain't I A Woman?" pp. 3-20, 51-54; and Davis, "Reflections on the Black Woman's Role," p. 7.

[58]This section summarizes material in an essay by the author entitled "Freed Women?: Black Women, Work, and the Family During the Civil War and Reconstruction," Wellesley Center for Research on Women Working Paper No. 61 (Wellesley, Mass., 1980). "'My Mother'" and "Freed Women" constitute the first two chapters of a book on Afro-American women, work, and the family, 1830-1980 (forthcoming).

[59]Robert Somers, *The Southern States Since the War, 1870-1* (London: MacMillan & Co., 1871), p. 59; Ransom and Sutch, *One Kind of Freedom,* p. 233; Francis W. Loring and C.F. Atkinson, *Cotton Culture and the South Considered with Reference to Emigration* (Boston: A. Williams, 1869), pp. 4-23. Other primary works that include relevant information are Frances Butler Leigh, *Ten Years on a Georgia Plantation Since the War* (London: R. Bentley, 1883); Charles Nordhoff, *The Cotton States in the Spring and Summer of 1875* (New York: D. Appleton & Co., 1876); George Campbell, *White and Black: The Outcome of a Visit to the United States* (London: Chatto and Windus, 1879).

[60]Freedmen's Bureau official quoted in Gutman, *Black Family,* p. 167.

[61]The transition from wage labor to the sharecropping system is examined in Ralph Shlomowitz, "The Origins of Southern Sharecropping," *Agricultural History* 53 (July 1979): 557-75, and his "The Transition From Slave to Freedman Labor Arrangements in Southern Agriculture, 1865-1870," *Journal of Economic History* 39 (March 1979): 333-36; Jay R. Mandle, *The Roots of Black Poverty: The Southern Plantation Economy After the Civil War* (Durham, N.C.,: Duke University Press, 1978); Joseph D. Reid, Jr., "White Land, Black Labor, and Agricultural Stagnation: The Causes and Effects of Sharecropping in the Postbellum South," *Explorations in Economic History* 16 (January 1979): 31-55; Ransom and Sutch, *One Kind of Freedom.*

Jonathan Wiener suggests that blacks' rejection of gang labor and preference for family share units "represented a move away from classic capitalist organizations." See "Class Structure and Economic Development in the American South, 1865-1955," *American Historical Review* 84 (October 1979): 984.

[62]Elizabeth Hyde Botume, *First Days Amongst the Contrabands* (Boston: Lee & Shepard, 1893), p. 166; Campbell, *White and Black,* pp. 172, 344, 364; tale entitled "De Tiger an' de Nyung Lady" quoted in Owens, *This Species of Property,* p. 144. See Leon Litwack, *Been in the Storm So Long: The Aftermath of Slavery* (New York: Alfred A. Knopf, 1979), pp. 502-56, for a detailed discussion of various freedmen's conventions held throughout the South.

[63]For an analysis of the ways in which the household responsibilities of women are defined and redefined to alter the supply of available wage-earners, see Louise A. Tilly and Joan Scott, *Women, Work, and Family* (New York: Holt, Rinehart & Winston, 1978).

The Creolization of Slave Folklife: All Saints Parish, South Carolina, As a Test Case

Charles W. Joyner

Recent historians of slavery offer a refreshing, if still somewhat less than satisfactory vision of the nature and development of Afro-American culture.[1] I believe we have finally reached the limits of the controversy framed a generation ago by the opposing conceptions of E. Franklin Frazier and Melville J. Herskovits. Frazier's assimilation model, emphasizing discontinuity with African origins and assuming acculturation to be the accommodation of Afro-Americans to Euro-American culture, was the dominant influence on a whole generation of sociologists as well as upon the mainstream of students of Negro history.[2] In contrast, Herskovits emphasized the extent of Afro-American continuity with the African past, based upon his conception of the unity of West African culture. Herskovits has been influential upon a number of anthropologists and folklorists, and (at least indirectly) upon more recent historians of slavery who have posited African roots for Afro-American culture.[3]

Charles W. Joyner is Professor of Anthropology and History at St. Andrews College, Laurinburg, N.C. During 1979-80 he is Visiting Professor in the Departments of History and Anthroplogy at the University of South Carolina.

1. John Blassingame, *The Slave Community* (New York, 1972); Gerald W. Mullin, *Flight and Rebellion* (New York, 1972); George P. Rawick, *From Sundown to Sunup* (Westport, Conn., 1972); Ira Berlin, *Slaves Without Masters* (New York, 1974); Eugene D. Genovese, *Roll, Jordan, Roll: The World the Slaves Made* (New York, 1974); Peter S. Wood, *Black Majority* (New York, 1974); Herbert S. Gutman, *The Black Family in Slavery and Freedom* (New York, 1976); Lawrence W. Levine, *Black Culture and Black Consciousness* (New York, 1977).

2. E. Franklin Frazier, *The Negro Family in the United States* (Chicago, 1939); E. Franklin Frazier, *The Negro in the United States* (New York, 1949); Gunnar Myrdal, *An American Dilemma* (New York, 1944); Nathan Glazer and Daniel Patrick Moynihan, *Beyond the Melting Pot* (New York, 1963); Kenneth M. Stampp, *The Peculiar Institution* (New York, 1956); Stanley Elkins, *Slavery: A Problem in American Institutional and Intellectual Life* (Chicago, 1959); George B. Tindall, *South Carolina Negroes, 1877-1900* (Columbia, 1952); Joel Williamson, *After Slavery: The Negro in South Carolina During Reconstruction* (Chapel Hill, 1965).

3. Melville J. Herskovits, *The Myth of the Negro Past* (Boston, 1958); Roger

The refutation of Frazier's assimilation model would seem by now to be as redundant an endeavour as yet another refutation of Sambo. Still the formulations of Herskovits and his disciples are not entirely satisfactory, either. Despite his recognition of such cultural transformations as syncretism, Herskovits' focus on the concept of "retention" is overly static and underestimates the dynamism of culture change. No group can transfer its culture intact from one environment to another. Both the natural and social context of the new environment will affect the nature and degree of cultural continuity, as will the circumstances of the migration.[4] Moreover, Herskovits' concept of "Africanisms" is at once both overly abstract and overly concrete—abstract because it depends on a notion of West African cultural homogeneity which is not supported by recent scholarship,[5] and concrete because it fails to distinguish adequately between the concepts of "culture" and "society." Clifford Geertz's distinction between culture and society is helpful in this regard. He defines culture as the mental rules governing behaviour, while society is the field of action in which behaviour takes place.[6] For example, the concept of royalty is cultural, but the embodiment of that concept in monarchies and courts is social. Societies are even less transferable than cultures from one environment to another.[7] Because of their failure to distinguish adequately between culture and society, some historians and social scientists have searched out vestigial concrete entities and ignored basic perceptions and underlying principles.

Bastide, *African Civilisations in the New World* (New York, 1971); Sidney Mintz and Richard Price, *An Anthropological Approach to the Afro-American Past: A Caribbean Perspective* (Philadelphia, 1976); Daniel J. Crowley, "The Creolization of Africanisms," paper presented at annual meeting of American Anthropological Association, 1967; Norman Whitten and John F. Szwed, eds., *Afro-American Anthropology: Contemporary Perspectives* (New York, 1970).

4. Herskovits, *Myth of the Negro Past*, pp. xxii, 167-86; Melville J. Herskovits, *Man and His Works* (New York, 1958), pp. 14, 615; Melville J. Herskovits, "Problem, Method, and Theory in Afro-American Studies," *Phylon* 7 (1945): 337-54; Mintz and Price, *Anthropological Approach to the Afro-American Past*, pp. 1-7.

5. Dan Ben-Amos, *Sweet Words: Storytelling Events in Benin* (Philadelphia, 1975); Ruth Finnegan, *Limba Stories and Storytelling* (Oxford, 1966); S.A. Babalola, *The Content and Form of Yoruba Ijala* (Oxford, 1967); P.C. Lloyd, *Africa in Social Change* (Baltimore, 1972); M.G. Smith, "The African Heritage in the Caribbean," in *Caribbean Studies: A Symposium*, ed. Vera Rubin (Seattle, 1957), pp. 34-46; Judith Irvine, "Caste and Communication in a Woloj Village," unpublished Ph.D. dissertation, University of Pennsylvania, 1973.

6. Clifford Geertz, *The Interpretation of Cultures: Selected Essays* (New York, 1973), pp. 3-30.

7. Mintz and Price, *An Anthropological Approach to the Afro-American Past*, p. 16. Thus when John Blassingame charges historians with being simplistic for describing slave social structure as imposed from without he fails to distinguish between culture and society. He is certainly correct in emphasizing the importance of understanding the slaves' value system in terms of what was considered important by the slaves themselves, but value systems are cultural, not social. See his "Status and Social Structure in the Slave Community: Evidence from New Sources," in *Perspectives and Irony in American Slavery*, ed. Harry P. Owens (Jackson, Miss., 1976), pp. 137-51.

They have looked for Africanisms in the wrong places.[8] Cultural continuities between Africa and Afro-Americans are strongest, as David Dalby points out, "at the much deeper and more fundamental level of interpersonal relationship and expressive behavior."[9]

While recent historians of slavery, writing in the tradition of Herskovits, certainly offer a more realistic view than that of their predecessors in the Frazier-Stampp-Elkins school, their interpretation of the nature and development of Afro-American culture remains unsatisfactory. Their interpretation of its nature is dubious because they stop short of conceptualizing the culture of the slaves in holistic terms.[10] Their interpretation of its development is dubious because their concept of culture change is too monistic. In their hands resistance becomes the prime shaper of cultural patterns and complex processes of culture change are reduced to a strategy for survival.[11] The challenge to historians is to transcend such fragmentized and reductionistic interpretations of culture and of culture change to come to a more accurate comprehension of the nature and development of slave culture.

A more accurate conception of the nature of slave culture is the folklife model pioneered in this country by Don Yoder. Folklife, according to Yoder, designates "the total range of folk-cultural phenomena, material as well as oral and spiritual."

> Not only does the researcher study the verbal arts of folksong, folktale, riddle, etc.—which the folklorist has long ago made his province—but

8. The unity of West African culture at the level of shared cognitive orientations is emphasized in Joseph H. Greenberg, "Africa as a Linguistic Area," in *Continuity and Change in African Cultures*, eds. William R. Bascom and Melville J. Herskovits (Chicago, 1959), pp. 15-27; Meyer Fortes, ed. *African Systems of Thought* (London, 1965); and Darryl Forde, "The Cultural Map of West Africa: Successive Adaptations to Tropical Forest and Grasslands," in *Cultures and Societies of Africa* (New York, 1960); Robin Horton, "African Traditional Thought and Western Science," *Africa* 37:1 and 2 (June and September, 1967).

9. David Dalby, "The African Element in American English," in *Rappin and Stylin' Out: Communication in Urban Black America*, ed. Thomas R. Kochman (Urbana, 1972), p. 173. Recent scholarship has begun to analyze similarities among the song styles, motor behaviour, and graphic arts of West Africans and Afro-Americans. See Roger D. Abrahams, "The Shaping of Folklore Traditions in the British West Indies," *Journal of Inter-American Studies* 9 (1967): 456-80; Robert Farris Thompson, "An Aesthetic of the Cool: West African Dance," *African Forum* 2 (1966): 85-102; Robert P. Armstrong, *The Affecting Presence* (Urbana, 1971); and several other works by Alan Lomax. See especially "The Homogeneity of African-Afro-American Musical Syle," in *Afro-American Anthropology: Contemporary Perspectives*, eds. Norman Whitten and John F. Szwed (New York, 1970); and *Folk Song Style and Culture* (Washington, D.C., 1968).

10. For instance, Blassingame ignores the development of the creole language of the slaves, Genovese and Wood the slaves' songs and tales, Levine their material culture. Gutman focusses on a single cultural institution—the family.

11. I am not contending here that slaves were docile and happy. I am simply trying to make a distinction between *necessary* causal factors and *sufficient* causal factors in historical explanation.

> also agricultural and agrarian history, settlement patterns, dialectology or folk speech, folk architecture, folk cookery, folk costume, the folk year, arts and crafts. It is this exciting totality of the verbal, spiritual, and material aspects of a culture that we mean by the term "folklife."[12]

A more accurate interpretation of the development of Afro-American culture in slavery draws upon the concept of creolization. Creolization is a concept used in linguistic scholarship to explain the convergence of two or more languages into an essentially new native tongue.[13] The earliest African slaves in any given New World area did not constitute a speech community, as the term is used by linguists. Their various African languages were often mutually unintelligible.[14] The common language which they acquired was a pidginized form of English. Pidgins are developed as a means of communication among speakers of diverse languages. A pidgin is by definition a second language. It has no native speakers. When the pidgin was passed on to the next generation, it was their native tongue. While the parents remained bilingual, the principal language of the second generation was the pidgin, which, by definition, became a creole language once it acquired native speakers. The creole continued to develop in a situation of language contact, with reciprocal influence of English and African features upon both the creole and regional standard. The English contribution was principally lexical; the African contribution was principally grammatical.[15]

The concept of creolization, applied to culture, focuses on the

12. Don Yoder, "Folklife," in *Our Living Traditions*, ed. Tristram P. Coffin (New York, 1968), pp. 47-48. See also Don Yoder, *American Folklife* (Austin, Texas, 1977), pp. 3-18; Sigurd Erixon, "Regional European Ethnology," *Folkliv*, 1937: 2/3, pp. 89-108; 1938: 3, pp. 263-94; Sigurd Erixon, "European Ethnology in Our Time," *Ethnologia Europaea*, 1 (1967): 3-11; Ronald H. Buchanan, "A Decade of Folklife Study," *Ulster Folklife* 11 (1965): 63-75; Ronald H. Buchanan, "Geography and Folk Life," *Folk Life* 1 (1963): 5-15; and J. Geraint Jenkins, "Folklife Studies and the Museum," *Museums Journal* 61 (December, 1961): 3-7.

13. Dell Hymes, ed., *Pidginization and Creolization of Languages* (London, 1971). Systematic study of pidgin and creole languages is a relatively recent phenomenon. Hugo Schuchardt, who published an article on Lingua Franca early in this century ("Die Lingua Franca," *Zeitschrift für Romanische Philologie* 33 [1909]: 441-61), is generally considered the father of pidgin scholarship. Creole scholarship did not commence until the 1930s, with the work of John Reinecke on Hawaiian Creole (*Language and Dialect in Hawaii: A Sociolinguistic History to 1835* [Honolulu, 1969]) and that of Lorenzo Dow Turner on Gullah (*Africanisms in the Gullah Dialect* [Chicago, 1949]). Since the 1960s creole scholarship has expanded annually. Reinecke and Stanley Tsuzaki now edit a quarterly newsletter, *The Carrier Pidgin*, and *A Bibliography of Pidgin and Creole Languages* has been comprehensively edited by Tsuzaki et al (Honolulu, 1975).

14. Dell Hymes, *Foundations in Sociolinguistics: An Ethnographic Approach* (Philadelphia, 1974), pp. 47-51; John Gumperz, "The Speech Community," in *Language and Social Context*, ed. Pier Paolo Giglioli (Harmondsworth, 1972), pp. 219-31.

15. Dell Hymes, introduction to part iii, *Pidginization and Creolization of Languages*, ed. Del Hymes (London, 1971), pp. 65-90; Robert A. Hall, *Pidgin and Creole Languages (Ithaca, 1965), p. 15; William A. Stewart,* "Sociolinguistic Factors in

unconscious "grammatical" principles underlying human behaviour. It was such "grammatical" principles which survived the Middle Passage and mixed in the New World with elements of the masters' culture in the crucible of a new society to create a new creolized culture. It should be noted that the creolized culture was not static, either, but continued to develop in vigorous mutual interaction with that of the masters.[16]

Not only have recent scholars of slavery been overly fragmented in their understanding of the nature of Afro-American culture and overly reductionist in their understanding of its development, they have been overly diffuse in time and space, painting on too broad a canvas for their evidence to be either conclusive or convincing. A bit of this from Mississippi, a little of that from Georgia, seasoned with a pinch of something else from Virginia, do not add up to an analysis of slavery in the South. "All events and experiences are local, somewhere," notes the poet William Stafford. How obvious, once baldly stated and explicitly perceived, and yet how little reflected in the writings of most historians. Too many historians attempt to describe and analyze wholes without having investigated concrete parts; too few construct wholes from empirically researched parts.[17]

This study attempts to apply the concept of creolization to the study of slave folklife in a geographic area and in a time-frame limited enough for the varying kinds of sources to be mutually relevant and mutually revealing. Specifically, this is a study of slave folklife on the rice plantations of the Waccamaw Neck, All Saints Parish, Georgetown District, in the South Carolina lowcountry in the 1850s and 1860s. While I have made use of plantation records, visitors' accounts, census records, probate records, etc., the slaves' "grammar of culture" can never be comprehended using only sources emanating from their masters or their masters' guests. Despite the blatant assertion of George Frederickson and Christopher Lasch that "slavery was an unrecorded experience, except from the master's point of view," there are numerous sources emanating from slaves which facilitate the study of their history "from the bottom up," including relatively untapped resources in oral tradition and material culture.[18] This study is heavily based on oral traditions of three distinct types: 1) testimonies of ex-slaves who had experienced slavery on the Waccamaw Neck; 2) testimonies of the children

the History of American Negro Dialects," *Florida FL Reporter* 5 (1967): 12-13; Sidney Mintz, "The Socio-historical Background of Pidginization and Creolization," in *Pidginization and Creolization of Languages*, pp. 153-68; Mervyn C. Alleyne, "Acculturation and the Cultural Matrix of Creolization," in *Pidginization and Creolization of Languages*, pp.169-86; David DeCamp, "Introduction: The Study of Pidgin and Creole Languages," in *Pidginization and Creolization of Languages*, pp. 13-39.

16. Herskovits apparently anticipated some such approach when he used the metaphor "the grammar of culture" in *Myth of the Negro Past*, p. 81.

17. William Stafford, *Tennessee Poetry Journal* 1 (1967): 4; Robert E. Berkhofer, Jr., *A Behavioral Approach to Historical Analysis* (New York, 1969), p. 208; Clyde Kluckhohn, "Parts and Wholes in Cultural Analysis," in *Parts and Wholes*, ed. Daniel Lerner (New York, 1953), p. 121.

18. George Frederickson and Christopher Lasch, "Resistance to Slavery," *Civil War History* 13 (1967): 318. "History from the bottom up" was used by Benjamin A.

and grandchildren of slaves on the Waccamaw Neck as to what information and attitudes were deemed important enough by the slaves to be passed on to their descendants regarding life in bondage; and 3) the testimony of folktales and legends, proverbs and songs from the Waccamaw Neck, which were not explicitly concerned with slavery but which, in conjunction with other evidence, yield crucial insights into the "grammar of culture."[19]

Slaves on the Waccamaw Neck rice plantations lived and forged their culture within a distinctive economic, ecological, and demographic environment. They lived on larger plantations than slaves elsewhere. The smallest plantation in All Saints parish in 1860 had ninety slaves; the largest 1,121. The average number of slaves was 292. They lived in an environment virtually devoid of free blacks and of mulattoes, with a higher median age, a lower ratio of males to females, and smaller proportion of youth and aged than was true of the South as a whole. Perhaps most importantly, they constituted nearly ninety percent of the population throughout the mid-

Botkin in his *Lay My Burden Down* (Chicago, 1945), p. ix. It has been popularized in recent years, without attribution to Botkin, by Jesse Lemisch, in "The American Revolution Seen from the Bottom Up," *Towards a New Past: Dissenting Essays in American History*, ed. Barton J. Bernstein (New York, 1968), pp. 3-45.

19. The first type of oral tradition is embodied in the interviews with ex-slaves during 1937-38 by Genevieve Willcox Chandler for the Federal Writers Project. The second type of oral tradition consists of my own interviews with the children and grandchildren of Genevieve Chandler's informants. The third type of oral tradition is embodied in my own folklore field collections on the Waccamaw Neck in the 1960s and 1970s, Genevieve Chandler's folklore field collections in the 1930s (housed in the W.P.A. mss. at South Caroliniana Library, University of South Carolina), and John A. Lomax's disc recordings of folksongs on the Waccamaw Neck, made in Genevieve Chandler's yard in the summers of 1936, 1937, and 1938 (housed in the Library of Congress).

There are numerous problems in the use of the slave narratives—the length of time between emancipation and the interviews, the age of the informants at the time of the interview, the age of the informants in slavery, the condition of the informants at the time of the interview (in the depth of the Great Depression), the manner of the interviewer and the conduct of the interview, the nature of the interviewer's transcription process, among others. I discuss these problems at some length in my "Slave Folklife on the Waccamaw Neck: Antebellum Black Culture in the South Carolina Lowcountry," unpublished Ph.D. dissertation, University of Pennsylvania, 1977, pp. lvi-lxix. See also John Blassingame, "Using the Testimonies of Ex-Slaves: Approaches and Problems," *Journal of Southern History* 41 (1975): 473-92, and C. Vann Woodward, "History from Slave Sources," *American Historical Review* 79 (1974). Jan Vansina's structural and comparative tests of reliability have been invaluable. See his *Oral Tradition: A Study in Historical Methodology* (Chicago, 1965). Historians have not, by and large, used slave narratives well. Blassingame largely avoids them in *The Slave Community* to concentrate on the autobiographies of runaways; Rawick uses them less than one might suppose in *From Sundown to Sunup*, since it serves as the first volume of a facsimile edition of the W.P.A. Slave Narratives. Genovese uses them as a gloss to add anecdotal material rather than as a basic source of evidence. There is good handling, and testing, of slave narratives in two folklore dissertations: Gladys-Marie Fry, "The Night Riders: A Study in Techniques of the Social Control of the Negro," unpublished Ph.D. dissertation, Indiana University, 1967 (published as *Night Riders in*

nineteenth century. In this regard the South Carolina lowcountry appears to be more nearly Caribbean in character than like other parts of the United States. The impact of the lopsided racial imbalance of culture change was momentous. It is true, as far as it goes, that the slaves were socialized into the ways their masters would have them behave, but it is also true that the heavy demographic dominance of blacks promoted the convergence of diverse African cultures. The slaves both renewed and transmuted African cultural patterns while adopting and adapting European ones, all the while sloughing off patterns from either tradition which were no longer meaningful. Nor were blacks the only participants in the creolization process on the Waccamaw Neck. Initiation of the whites into the ways of the blacks was as inevitable as the other way around.[20]

Language is the one indispensable ingredient in all human thought. One who would understand the folklife of Waccamaw Neck slaves must first

Black Folk History [Knoxville, 1975], and Kathryn Lawson Morgan, "The Ex-Slave Narratives as a Source for Folk History," unpublished Ph.D. dissertation, University of Pennsylvania, 1970.

The vitality, variety, and significance of slave folk culture has been vastly underestimated by the historical mainstream. Stampp acknowledges only its vestigial existence (*The Peculiar Institution*, pp. 362-63). Sterling Stuckey ("Through the Prism of Folklore: The Black Ethos in Slavery," *The Massachusetts Review* 9 ([1968]: 417-37) and Gilbert Osofsky ("A Note on the Usefulness of Folklore," in *Puttin' On Ole Massa*, ed. Gilbert Osofsky [New York, 1969], pp. 45-58) both assert the importance of *Leone* folklore, but never rise above the level of promise and pronouncement. Blassingame emphasizes the "therapeutic value" of slave folklore, but his treatment of folklore itself is far from satisfactory. Like other historians, he studiously ignores folkloristic theory and scholarship. For example, he emphasizes Afro-American folktale motifs as overwhelmingly African, a point on which the bulk of the evidence is against him. I agree with him that there are strong continuities between African and Afro-American folktales, but they lie at deeper and more fundamental levels than static motifs. (See *The Slave Community*, p. 26). Genovese's anachronistic approach, roaming freely over time and space, gives *Roll, Jordan, Roll* a curious static quality which accords well with his acceptance of a rather extreme African retention position (see p. 210). Both Blassingame and Genovese treat folklore too exclusively as a means of keeping Sambo at bay. Levine's *Black Culture and Black Consciousness*, the most satisfactory monographic analysis to date, emphasizes folktales, music, and humor as clues to the black mind.

20. U.S. Census Bureau, Mss. Census Returns for 1850 and 1860. Population Schedules and Slave Schedules, National Archives, Washington, D.C. Agriculture Schedules, South Carolina Archives, Columbia; Sherman L. Richards and George M. Blackburn, "A Demographic History of Slavery: Georgetown County, South Carolina," *South Carolina Historical Magazine* 76 (1975): 215-24; George C. Rogers, Jr., *The History of Georgetown County, South Carolina* (Columbia, 1970), p. 343; Philip D. Curtin, *The Atlantic Slave Trade: A Census* (Madison, 1969), p. 145; Peter Wood, *Black Majority*, pp. 13-35, 179; Winthrop D. Jordan, *White Over Black* (Chapel Hill, 1968), 84-85, 142-47; M. Eugene Sirmans, "The Legal Status of the Slave in South Carolina, 1670-1740," Journal of Southern History 28 (1962), 462-66; Richard S. Dunn, "The English Sugar Islands and the Founding of South Carolina," *South Carolina Historical Magazine* 72 (1971): 81-93; Richard S. Dunn, *Sugar and Slaves* (Chapel Hill, 1974), pp. 111-16.

attempt to understand their creole language, Gullah, for it was through Gullah that the slaves gave shape to their culture, communicated with and entertained one another, proclaimed their sense of community, and created for themselves a symbolic identity. The development of Gullah demonstrates the paradigm of creolization, first in the pidginization stage in which a number of African languages converged to form a grammar into which a largely but not exclusively English lexicon was poured,[21] and secondly in the creole stage in which the new pidgin language became the native tongue of succeeding generations of rice plantation slaves (and thus a creole).[22] Since

21. William A. Stewart,"Sociolinguistic Factors in the History of American Negro Dialects," *Florida FL Reporter* 5 (1967): 11-29; Patricia Causey Nichols, "Linguistic Change in Gullah: Sex, Age, and Mobility," unpublished Ph.D. dissertation, Stanford University, 1976, p. 1; Irma Cunnigham, "A Syntactic Analysis of Sea Island Creole ('Gullah')," unpublished Ph.D. dissertation, University of Michigan, 1970, p. 1; Dell Hymes, ed., *Pidginization and Creolization of Languages* (London, 1971), pp. 65-90; Charles A. Ferguson, "Aspects of Copula and the Notion of Simplicity: A Study of Normal Speech, Baby Talk, and Pidgins," in *Pidginization and Creolization of Languages*, pp. 141-50; Robert A. Hall, Jr., *Pidgin and Creole Languages* (Ithaca, 1965), p. 15; Basil Davidson, *Black Mother: The Years of the African Slave Trade* (Boston, 1961), p. 218; Beryl Bailey, "Towards a New Perspective on American Negro Dialectology," *American Speech* 40 (1965): 171-77; Samuel G. Stoney and Gertrude M. Shelby, *Black Genesis* (New York, 1930), p. xi; J.L. Dillard, *Black English: Its History and Usage in the United States* (New York, 1972), p. 83; David Dalby, "Americanisms that May Once Have Been Africanisms," *The Times* (London), June 19, 1969, p. 9; P.E.H. Hair, "Sierra Leone Items in the Gullah Dialect of American English," *Sierra Leone Language Review* 4 (1965): 79-84; Joseph H. Greenberg, "Africa as a Linguistic Area," in *Continuity and Change in African Cultures*, pp. 15-27; David Dwyer, *An Introduction to West African Pidgin English* (East Lansing, 1967), p. 98; Frederic C. Cassidy, *Jamaica Talk: Three Hundred Years of the English Language in Jamaica* (London, 1961), p. 17; Ivan Vansertima, "African Linguistic and Mythological Structures in the New World," in *Black Life and Culture in the United States*, ed. Rhoda Goldstein (New York, 1971), pp. 12-35; Elizabeth C. Traugott, "Principles in the History of American English—A Reply," *Florida FL Reporter* 10 (1972): 5-6, 56; William A. Stewart, "Non-Standard Speech Patterns," *Baltimore Bulletin of Education* 43 (1966): 52-65; William A. Stewart, "Patterns of Grammatical Change in Gullah," paper read in symposium, Society and Culture in South Carolina, Charleston, S.C., March 27, 1976; J.L. Dillard, "Non-Standard Negro Dialects: Convergence or Divergence?" *Florida FL Reporter* 6 (1968): 9-12; Herskovits, *Myth of the Negro Past*, pp. 278-91; Wood, *Black Majority*, pp. 168-70; Childs, *Rice Planter and Sportsman*, pp. 55-56; George C. Rogers, Jr., *Charleston in the Age of the Pinckneys* (Norman, 1969), pp. 76-77.

22. Primary sources for my analysis of the Gullah creole on the Waccamaw Neck are the Genevieve Chandler folklore collection in the W.P.A. Mss., South Caroliniana Library; the Slave Narratives from the Waccamaw Neck; *South Carolina Folk Tales*, compiled by Workers of the Writers' Program of the Work Projects Administration (Columbia, 1941); Collins, *Memories of the Southern States*, passim; and Pringle, *Chronicles of Chicora Wood*, passim. See also Nichols,"Linguistic Change in Gullah"; Cunningham, "A Syntactic Analysis of Sea Island Creole"; Patricia C. Nichols, "American Creoles," *Language in the U.S.A.*, eds. Charles A. Ferguson and Shirley Brice Heath, forthcoming; Elizabeth Closs Traugott, "Pidgins, Creoles, and the

the creole developed in a situation of language contact, it had by 1860 moved in various ways in the direction of the regional standard speech.[23] Initiation of white Carolinians into Gullah linguistic patterns was as inevitable as into other aspects of Afro-American culture, given the preponderance of the black population. By 1860 the South Carolina lowcountry was linguistically more Caribbean than American, featuring a full-blown creole language alongside a regional variety which departed from the national standard in part because of the strong Gullah influence upon it.[24]

Work patterns illustrate a particularly interesting example of cultural creolization on the Waccamaw Neck. On one level there was strong continuity with African patterns. Rice was introduced into South Carolina from Africa, and the early technological expertise was suppled by Africans, not Europeans.[25] By the mid-nineteenth century, however, the economic networks and management techniques of the rice planters, including the

Origins of Vernacular Black English," in *Black English: A Seminar*, eds. D.S. Harrison and T. Trabasso (Hillsdale, N.J., 1976), pp. 84-85; Stewart, "Continuity and Change in American Negro Dialects," *Florida FL Reporter* 6 (1968): 3-14. Useful articles on both sides of the bitter linguistic debate between dialectologists and creolists may be found in Walt Wolfram and Nona H. Clarke, *Black-White Speech Relationships* (Washington, 1971). It should be supplemented with Raven I. McDavid, Jr., "Historical, Regional, and Social Variation," *Journal of English Linguistics* 1(1967): 24-40; Raven I. McDavid, Jr., "Needed Research in Southern Dialects," in *Perspectives on the South: Agenda for Research*, ed. Edgar T. Thompson (Durham, N.C., 1967); and Herskovits, *Myth of the Negro Past*, pp. 167-86.

23. Ralph W. Fasold, "Decreolization and Autonomous Language Change,"*Florida FL Reporter* 11 (1973): 9; Stewart, "Sociolinguistic Factors in the History of American Negro Dialects," pp. 12-13; Nichols, "Linguistic Change in Gullah," pp. 3-4, and passim; Stewart, "Patterns of Grammatical Change in Gullah"; William A. Stewart, "Historical and Structural Bases for the Recognition of Negro Dialects," *Monograph Series on Languages and Linguistics*, No. 22 (Washington, 1969); David DeCamp, "Toward a Generative Analysis of a Post-Creole Speech Continuum," in *Pidginization and Creolization of Languages*, pp. 349-70; John J. Gumperz, "Linguistic Anthropology in Society," *American Anthropologist* 76 (1974): 791; J.L. Dillard, "The Historian's History and the Reconstructionist's History in the Tracing of Linguistic Variants," *Florida FL Reporter* 11 (1973): 41; Dillard, *Black English*, p. 102; Hall, *Pidgin and Creole Languages*, p. 15.

24. Julia Peterkin, *Roll, Jordan, Roll*, p. 19; John Bennett, "Gullah: A Negro Patois," *South Atlantic Quarterly* 7 (1908): 339; Rogers, *Charleston in the Age of the Pinckneys*, p. 79; William A. Stewart, "More on Black-White Speech Relationships," *Florida FL Reporter* 11 (1973): 38; Dillard, *Black English*, pp. 186-228; Raven I. McDavid and Virginia Glenn McDavid, "The Relationship of the Speech of American Negroes to the Speech of Whites," *American Speech* 26 (1951): 3-17.

25. Robert F.W. Allston, *Essays on Sea Coast Crops* (Charleston, 1854), p. 29, also printed in *DeBow's Review* 16 (1854): 589-615; A.S. Salley, Jr., *The Introduction of Rice Culture into South Carolina*, Bulletin of the Historical Commission of South Carolina, No. 6 (Columbia, 1919), pp. 10-13; Duncan Clinch Heyward, *Seed from Madagascar* (Chapel Hill, 1937), p. 4; Converse D. Clowse, *Economic Beginnings in Colonial South Carolina, 1670-1730* (Columbia, 1971), p. 124; Wood, *Black Majority*, pp. 35-62; Elliott P. Skinner, "West African Economic Systems," in *Peoples and Cultures of Africa*, ed. Elliott P. Skinner (Garden City, 1973), p. 207.

"task system," had been superimposed onto the basic system of rice culture.[26] The highly individualistic task system, in which each person was assigned a separate task to be completed without regard to the work of others, contrasted with African traditions of communal labour. Nevertheless, a tradition of quasi-communal labour underlay the task system, with slaves hoeing side-by-side, hoeing in tempo to singing, helping slower slaves keep up, all of which reflect an African communal orientation toward work.[27] In addition, some technological features, such as the widespread use of hoes as all-purpose implements and the continuing use of hand-coiled "fanner baskets" after African models, reflected the continuing influence of African "grammars" upon the work patterns of field workers.[28]

26. Gabe Lance, in Slave Narratives: A Folk History of Slavery in the United States from interviews with former slaves. Typewritten records prepared by the Federal Writers Project, 1936-1938, Work Projects Administration for the District of Columbia, sponsored by the Library of Congress. Rare Book Division, Library of Congress. Vol. 14, part iii, p. 52. Hagar Brown, Slave Narratives, 14, i, 110-11; Albert Carolina, Slave Narratives, 14, i, 197-98; Ben Horry, Slave Narratives, 14, ii, 304, 310-11; Margaret Bryant, Slave Narratives, 14, i, 147. A facsimile edition, edited by George P. Rawick under the title, *The American Slave: A Composite Autobiography* (Westport, 1972), includes parts i and ii of the South Carolina interviews in vol. 2 and parts iii and iv of the South Carolina interviews in vol. 3. Pagination is the same. Personal interviews with John Beese, Pawleys Island, S.C., January 1972, and with A.L. Lachicotte, Jr., Pawley's Island, July 28, 1975; Winyah and All Saints Agricultural Society Minutes, 1842-1861, South Carolina Historical Society, Charleston, S.C.; Plowden C.J. Weston, "Rules and Management for the Plantation,"quoted in Elizabeth Collins, *Memories of the Southern States* (Taunton, England, 1865), p. 111. An earlier and somewhat shorter version was published as "Rules of the Rice Estate of P.C. Weston, S.C.," in *DeBow's Review* 21 (1857): 38-44. Letter, James R. Sparkman to Benjamin Allston, March 10, 1858, in Robert F.W. Allston Papers, South Carolina Historical Society, Charleston, S.C., printed in J. Harold Easterby, ed., *The South Carolina Rice Plantation as Revealed in the Papers of Robert F. W. Allston* (Chicago, 1945), pp. 346-50; Letter, Almira Coffin to Mrs. J.G. Osgood, May 10, 1851, in "South Carolina through New England Eyes: Almira Coffin's Visit to the Low-country in 1851," ed. J. Harold Easterby, *South Carolina Historical and Genealogical Magazine* 45 (1944): 127-36; *Rice Planter and Sportsman: The Recollections of J. Motte Allston*, ed. Arney R. Childs (Columbia, 1953), p. 42; W. Wyndham Malet, *An Errand to the South in the Summer of 1862* (London, 1863), p. 57; Allston, *Essay on Sea Coast Crops*, pp. 36-37; Dennis T. Lawson, *No Heir to Take Its Place: The Story of Rice in Georgetown County, South Carolina* (Georgetown, 1972), pp. 10-12; Rogers, *History of Georgetown County*, pp. 324-41; Dale E. Swan, "The Structure and Profitability of the Antebellum Rice Industry: 1859," unpublished Ph.D. dissertation, University of North Carolina, 1972.

27. Hagar Brown, Slave Narratives, 14, i, 110; John Beese interview; personal interviews with Mary Small, Free Woods, S.C., August 2, 1975, and with Henry Small, Burgess, S.C., August 2, 1975; Sparkman letter, in Easterby, p. 346; William R. Bascom, "Acculturation among the Gullah Negroes," *American Anthropologist* 43 (1941): 44-45; Skinner, "West African Economic Systems," p. 209.

28. I have photographs taken on the Waccamaw Neck in the 1930s by Bayard Wooten showing fanner baskets in operation as well as the practice of hoeing side-by-side. Alice R. Huger Smith's watercolours for *A Carolina Rice Plantation of the Fifties,*

The earliest slaves had brought with them from various parts of West Africa highly developed technologies in metalwork, woodwork, leatherwork, pottery, and weaving. The contribution of skilled slave craftsmen and mechanics to the economic development of the plantations has yet to be adequately credited. Not only were these skills retained and handed down to children and grandchildren, but slaves responded eagerly to incentives to acquire new skills. As a general rule, young slaves aiming for plantation "professions" were apprenticed to senior craftsmen or craftswomen to be taught and trained. In some cases slaves were sent to Charleston or even to England to be taught particular skills, such as cabinetry. The skilled workers, especially the carpenters and mechanics, enjoyed considerable status, deference, and independence in their work patterns on the plantations, reflected in the esteem in which such skilled workers were held by black and white alike.[29]

Planters also regarded house servants to be of a higher status than that of field hands. Slaves on the Waccamaw Neck generally seemed to have shared a sense of status identification ranging from house servants at the top through drivers and artisans on down to field hands. A wide variety of work patterns are subsumed under the general label house servant: butlers, cooks, valets, maids, waiters and waitresses, laundresses, and children's nurses, among other occupations. House servants generally had lighter work than field hands on the rice plantations, but their closer contact with the master and mistress had both advantages and disadvantages. House servants were sometimes regarded as traitors by other slaves because of their more amiable relationships with the whites. In fact, however, house servants seem to have

eds. Alice R. Huger Smith and Herbert Ravenel Sass (New York, 1930), depict similar scenes. Examples of fanner baskets are exhibited in the Rice Museum in Georgetown, S.C., and the Old Slave Mart Museum in Charleston, S.C., as well as in the illustration facing p. 128 in *Key Issues in the Afro-American Experience*, eds. Nathan I. Huggins, Martin Kilson, and Danielle H. Fox (New York, 1971). I have extensive interviews with coil basketmakers Edna Rouse and Evelina Foreman, of Mt. Pleasant, S.C. See also Lawson, *No Heir to Take Its Place*, pp. 10-12; Wood, *Black Majority*, p. 61; David Doar, *Rice and Rice-Planting in the South Carolina Low Country* (Charleston, 1936), p. 33; Bascom, "Acculturation among the Gullah Negroes," pp. 45, 49; Gregory Day, "Afro-Carolinian Art: Towards the History of a Southern Expressive Tradition," *Contemporary Art/Southeast* 1 (January-February, 1978): 10-21; Gerald L. Davis, "Afro-American Coil Basketry in Charleston County, South Carolina," in *American Folklife*, ed Don Yoder (Austin, 1976), pp. 151-84; Robert Farris Thompson, "African Influence on the Art of the United States," in *Black Studies in the University: A Symposium*, eds. Armstead L. Robinson, et al (New Haven, 1969); Betty Myers, "Gullah Basketry," *Craft Horizons* 36 (June, 1976): 30-31, 81; James A. Porter, "Four Problems in the History of Negro Art," *Journal of Negro History* 37 (1942): 9-36; Elsie Clews Parsons, *Folk-Lore of the Sea Islands, South Carolina* (New York, 1923), p. 208; Melville J. Herskovits, *Myth of the Negro Past*, p. 147; Justine M. Cordwell, "African Art," in *Continuity and Change in African Cultures*, eds. William R. Bascom and Melville J. Herskovits (Chicago, 1959), p. 38.

29. Welcome Beese, Slave Narratives, 14, i, 49; Sabe Rutledge, Slave Narratives, 14, iii, 60; Margaret Bryant, Slave Narratives, 14, i, 146-47; Manuscript diary of Emily Weston (Mrs. Plowden C.J. Weston), January 1-December 31, 1859, in private

provided more runaways in All Saints Parish than field hands, perhaps because of their greater opportunities. The highly ambiguous situation of the house servants made it possible for them to occupy a special position between the "Street" and the "Big House" and to play an intermediary role in the creolization of each. They took African cultural patterns into the culinary, religious, and folkloristic patterns of the "Big House" and took European cultural patterns to the "Street." It was through the house servants that black Carolinians derived their European heritage, and white Carolinians their African heritage.[30] The influence of the house servant was perhaps especially marked in the children's nurses—surrogate mothers, in many cases—whose role in the socialization process of white children was immense.[31]

Among the rights sucessfully asserted by Waccamaw Neck slaves, "off

possession, passim; Sparkman Family Papers, Book five, Southern Historical Collection, University of North Carolina; Ben Sparkman, Plantation Record, Southern Historical Collection, University of North Carolina; James R. Sparkman Books, vol. 2, Southern Historical Collection, University of North Carolina; Robert F.W. Allston Papers, South Carolina Historical Society, Charleston, S.C.; Elizabeth W. Allston Pringle, *Chronicles of Chicora Wood* (NewYork, 1922), pp. 13-14, 168; Malet, *An Errand to the South*, pp. 80-81; Collins, *Memories of the Southern States*, pp. 7-8, 17, 55, 61, 76, 108; All Saints Waccamaw Vestry Journal, South Carolina Historical Society, Charleston, S.C.; Easterby, *The South Carolina Rice Plantation*, pp. 32, 277, 285, 425, 431; Childs, *Rice Planter and Sportsman*, p. 45; Wood, *Black Majority*, pp. 95-131; Jordan, *White Over Black*, pp. 128-29, 172-74, 406; Eugene D. Genovese, *Roll, Jordan, Roll: The World the Slaves Made* (New York, 1974), pp. 9, 389-98; Leonard Price Stavisky, "The Negro Artisan in the South Atlantic States, 1800-1860," unpublished Ph.D. dissertation, Columbia University, 1958; Leonard P. Stavisky, "Negro Craftsmanship in Early America," *American Historical Review* 54 (1949): 315-25; W.E.B. DuBois and Augustus Granville Dill, eds., *The Negro American Artisan* (Atlanta, 1912), p. 35; John Michael Vlach, "Phillip Simmons: Afro-American Blacksmith," *Black People and their Culture*, ed. Linn Shapiro (Washington, 1976), pp. 35-55; Rene Wassing, *African Art: Its Backgrounds and Traditions* (New York, 1968), pp. 52, 117, 196-97; Cordwell, "African Art," pp. 28-45; Thompson, "African Influences on the Art of the United States," p. 156; Basil Davidson, *The Lost Cities of Africa* (Boston, 1959), pp. 139-43; Michael Leiris and Jacquelyn DeLance, *African Art* (London, 1968), pp. 99-210.

30. Mariah Heywood, Slave Narratives, 14,ii,282; Ben Horry, Slave Narratives, 14, ii, 305, 311; Sabe Rutledge, in W.P.A. Mss., South Caroliniana Library, University of South Carolina; interviews with John Beese, Henry Small, Mary Small, A.L. Lachicotte; Weston, "Rules and Management for the Plantation," pp. 105-107, 110, 113, 138; Plowden C.J. Weston, *Rules and History of the Hot and Hot Fish Club of All Saints Parish, South Carolina* (Charleston, 1860); Emily Weston Diary, passim; Pringle, *Chronicles of Chicora Wood*, pp. 61-62; Collins, *Memories of the Southern States*, pp. 6, 16; Julia Peterkin, *Roll, Jordan, Roll* (New York, 1933), pp. 20-23; Easterby, *The South Carolina Rice Plantation*, pp. 33-35; 97-99, 168-69, 194-95, 345-46; Charles W. Joyner, "Soul Food and the Sambo Stereotype: Foodlore from the Slave Narrative Collection," *Keystone Folklore Quarterly* 16 (1971): 171-78; Genovese, *Roll, Jordan, Roll*, pp. 540-49.

31. Sabe Rutledge, Slave Narratives, 14, iv, 62; Margaret Bryant, Slave Narratives, 14, i, 146; Ben Horry, Slave Narratives, 14, ii, 305; interview with John

times" and holidays became increasingly guaranteed. The temporal contexts set aside as "off times" were based on four overlapping cyclical concepts of time—the daily cycle, the weekly cycle, the annual cycle, and the life cycle. Within the task system, there was no uniform daily quitting time; slaves were not through for the day until they had completed individually-assigned "tasks." Many of them used part of their daily off-time to cultivate their own plots and raise livestock, both for their own consumption and to sell to the planters. Such purchases from slaves were contrary to South Carolina law, as the planters clearly understood; but they were part of the body of rights asserted successfully by the slaves even in the face of specific legislation to the contrary.[32] Slaves who could accomplish two tasks in a single day received a full day off. Those who did so often used the time for fishing, clamming, and oystering. Saturday afternoons and Sundays were also used extensively for fishing and hunting.[33] Sunday was a day of rest from the fields. Most slaves attended church services on Sundays, and many of them also held weekly mid-week prayer meetings and daily family devotions.[34] Saturday nights were often given over to dances and social get-togethers, with entertainment by talented slave fiddlers, banjo players, and storytellers. Slaves who could obtain passes, or "tickets," could visit friends or relatives or go courting on other plantations. Some went visiting or courting without passes, braving the danger of being caught by patrols and beaten. The weekend visiting and partying both gave expression to African cultural patterns and promoted their continuing creolization.[35] In the annual cycle, no holiday was more important than Christmas, when three days were set aside for celebration, feasting, gingerbread and sweets, extra rations, portions of rum or whiskey

Beese; Jessie W. Parkhurst, "The Role of the Black Mammy in the Plantation Household," *Journal of Negro History* 23 (1938): 349-69; Paul Bohannon and Philip Curtin, *Africa and Africans*, revised ed. (Garden City, 1971), p. 115.

32. A.L. Lachicotte interview; Emily Weston Diary, April 13, December 13, 1859; Ben Sparkman Plantation Record, Southern Historical Collection; *Statutes at Large of South Carolina*, ed. David J. McCord (Columbia, 1840), VI, 516-17; James R. Sparkman, letter to Benjamin Allston, March 10, 1858, in *The South Carolina Rice Plantation*, ed. Easterby, pp. 347-48; Malet, *An Errand to the South*, p. 57; Rogers, *History of Georgetown County*, p. 348.

33. A.L. Lachicotte interview; Plowden C.J. Weston, "Rules and Management for the Plantation," in Collins, *Memories of the Southern States*, p. 107; Childs, ed., *Rice Planter and Sportsman*, p. 46.

34. Albert Carolina, Slave Narratives, 14, i, 198; Mariah Heywood, Slave Narratives, 14, ii, 284; Mary Small interview; Henry Small interview; Emily Weston Diary, passim; "Recollections of a Visit to the Waccamaw," *Living Age*, August 1, 1857, pp. 292-93; Malet, *An Errand to the South*, pp. 49-50, 74; Childs, ed., *Rice Planter and Sportsman*, p. 47; Rogers, *History of Georgetown County*, pp. 349-58.

35. Ben Horry, Slave Narratives, 14, ii, 304, 309; Mary Small interview; Henry Small interview; Plowden C.J. Weston, "Rules and Management for the Plantation," in Collins, *Memories of the Southern States*, pp. 17, 56, 61, 104-105, 107; Malet, *An Errand to the South*, pp. 49, 57, 111; Childs, ed., *Rice Planter and Sportsman*, p. 46; Rogers, *History of Georgetown County*, pp. 343-44; Howell M. Henry, *Police Control of the Slave in South Carolina* (Emory, Va., 1914), pp. 32-37.

and tobacco, gifts, fireworks, and much singing and dancing. Life-cycle celebrations, such as weddings and funerals, were marked by special patterns of expressive behaviour which also reflected the slaves' creative adaptation of African customs and beliefs to New World conditions, under the influence of a Christian theology which the slaves subtly modified to accommodate persistent African cultural grammars.[36] Partly through their use of off-times, then, Afro-Americans even within the House of Bondage carved out sufficient emotional space to further the development of their rich folk culture.

Attempts to discover the inner cultural grammars of the slaves will remain egregious speculations until careful examination is made of the stories slaves told one another in the masters' absence. My analysis of folktales on the Waccamaw Neck concentrates on human and animal trickster tales, their explicit and implicit themes, their structures, and their functions and uses in the slave community. Trickster tales are not unique to

36. Hagar Brown, Slave Narratives, 14, i, 113-14; Louisa Brown, Slave Narratives, 14, i, 115; John Beese interview, Mary Small interview; A.L. Lachicotte interview; Emily Weston Diary, January 22, December 22-28, 1859; Plowden C.J. Weston, "Rules and Management for the Plantation," in Collins, *Memories of the Southern States*, p. 107; Easterby, *The South Carolina Rice Plantation*, pp. 33, 135-36, 171, 453-54; Malet, *An Errand to the South*, p. 68; Collins, *Memories of the Southern States*, pp. 6, 12-13; Pringle, *Chronicles of Chicora Wood*, pp. 150-52; Julia Peterkin, *Roll, Jordan, Roll*, p. 10; Genovese, *Roll, Jordan, Roll*, pp. 194-202; Stamp, *The Peculiar Institution*, pp. 318-21; Herbert Gutman, *The Black Family in Slavery and Freedom, 1750-1925* (New York, 1976), pp. 269-77, 281-84; Arnold van Gennep, *The Rites of Passage* (Chicago, 1960), pp. 116-65; Arnold van Gennep, "On the Rites of Passage," in *Theories of Society*, eds. Talcott Parsons et al (Glencoe, 1961), II, 950; Victor Turner, *The Forest of Symbols* (Ithaca, 1967), pp 151-279; Victor Turner, *The Drums of Affliction* (Oxford, 1968), pp. 15-16; Herskovits, *Myth of the Negro Past*, p. 201; Bastide, *African Civilisations in the New World*, pp. 57-58, 79-82, 161-62; Geoffrey Parrinder, *African Traditional Religion* (London, 1962), p. 99; Newbell Niles Puckett, *Folk Beliefs of the Southern Negro* (Chapel Hill, 1926), pp. 79-113; Mary A. Waring, "Mortuary Customs and Beliefs of South Carolina Negroes," *Journal of American Folk-Lore* 7 (1894): 318-19; Mary A. Waring, "Negro Superstitions in South Carolina," *Journal of American Folk-Lore* 8 (1895); Portia Smiley, "Folk-Lore from Virginia, South Carolina, Georgia, Alabama, and Florida," *Journal of American Folk-Lore* 32 (1919): 357-83; H.C. Bolton, "Decoration of Graves of Negroes in South Carolina," *Journal of American Folk-Lore* 7 (1894): 305.

37. These conclusions are based upon the analysis of twenty-two animal trickster tales collected on the Waccamaw Neck by Genevieve Willcox Chandler and published as part of *South Carolina Folk Tales*, compiled by Workers of the Writers' Program of the Work Projects Administration in the State of South Carolina (Columbia, 1941), her extensive collection of human trickster tales plus numerous variants of the animal trickster tales in the W.P.A. Mss. in the South Caroliniana Library at the University of South Carolina, and my own collection of human trickster tales on the Waccamaw Neck. The use of folktales collected after emancipation for the analysis of slave folklife requires some explanation. In fact very few Afro-American folktales were collected anywhere in the South prior to the Civil War. Since, however, such folktales as those I am examining on the Waccamaw Neck were widely diffused across the South, and since their content is not only similar to each other but to such samples of antebellum

African and African-derived cultures; on the contrary, trickster tales occur universally. But they are not universally alike. Slave trickster-tales on the Waccamaw Neck exemplify tale-types and include motifs which are widely diffused throughout Europe and elsewhere.[37] However, there are strong structural and thematic resemblances between African and Waccamaw Neck animal trickster-tales.[38]

There are numerous relationships between the animal and human trickster-tales, but we must take care not to emphasize the similarities out of proportion. To miss the identification of Buddah Rabbit as a surrogate slave (on one level) is to miss the essence of the tales' central meaning to the slaves; however, other levels of meaning can be obscured by overreliance on the identification orthodoxy.[39] Buddah Rabbit, Buddah Pa'tridge, and other animal tricksters do not serve exclusively as surrogate slaves, nor as role models to be followed in all cases. Such characters demonstrate both the advantages and the limitations of the trickster role. The trickster usually (but not always) accomplishes his ends; but to do so he often has to become as cruel and vicious as his oppressors. He also seems to become as arrogant and as stupid as they; for when he is defeated, it is usually by the wiles of smaller and frailer (but trickier) creatures than himself. Thus the trickster served the

black folk narrative as survives, clearly these folktales are part of an enduring oral tradition and not merely some sudden post-emancipation compositions. Tale types in the Waccamaw Neck reportory include 2, 15, 72, 175, 1074, 1525 and 1612. Motifs include A.2325.1, A2332.4.1, A2494.4.4, H1376.5, J2413.42, K11.1 K72, K401.1, K471, K585, K607.3.2, K611, K1021, K1055, K1840, K1860, K1951, K1956, K1961. See Antti Aarne and Stith Thompson, *The Types of the Folk-Tale* (Helsinki, 1961); Erastus Ojo Arewa, "A Classification of the Folktales of Northern East African Cattle Area by Types," unpub. Ph.D. dissertation, University of California, Berkeley, 1966; Winifred Lambrecht, "A Tale Type Index for Central Africa," unpublished Ph.D. dissertation, University of California, Berkeley, 1967; Kenneth W. Clarke, "Motif Index of Folk-Tales from Culture-Area V West Africa," unpublished Ph.D. dissertation, Indiana University, 1958. The relationship of Afro-American folktales to European tale types is strongly emphasized in Richard M. Dorson, *American Negro Folk Tales* (New York, 1967), p. 15 and passim.

38. Cf. Ruth Finnegan, *Oral Literature in Africa* (Oxford, 1970), pp. 340-47; Denise Paulme, "Litterateur Orde et Comportements Sociaux en Afrique Noire," *L'homme* 1 (1961): 37-49; Denise Paulme, "Morphologie du conte Africain," *Cahiers d'etudes africaines* 45 (1972): 131-63; Lee Haring, "A Characteristic African Folktale Pattern," in *African Folklore*, ed Richard M. Dorson (Bloomington, 1972), pp. 165-79. For an indication of a continuing African presence on the Waccamaw Neck in the mid-1850s, see Albert Carolina, Slave Narratives, 14, i, 199; Ben Horry, Slave Narratives, 14, i, 306, 311; Malet, *An Errand to the South*, p. 50; Childs, *Rice Planter and Sportsman*, pp. 55-56; Pringle, *Chronicles of Chicora Wood*, p. 351.

39. Cf. Lawrence W. Levine, *Black Culture and Black Consciousness: Afro-American Folk Thought from Slavery to Freedom* (New York, 1977), pp 102-31; Finnegan, *Oral Literature in Africa*, pp. 341-47; Janheinz Jahn, *Muntu: An Outline of the New African Culture* (New York, 1961), p. 221; A.M.H. Christensen, *Afro-American Folk-Lore* (Boston, 1892), p. ix; E.E. Evans-Pritchard, *The Zande Trickster* (Oxford, 1967), pp. 28-30; Roger D. Abrahams, "Trickster, the Outrageous Hero," in *Our Living Traditions*, ed. Tristram P. Coffin (New York, 1968), p. 170.

slave community not merely as an example to emulate, but one to avoid as well.[40]

The human trickster—usually the slave, John—is less ambiguous and complex than the animal trickster on the Waccamaw Neck, perhaps mainly because of his more clear-cut identification as one of the slave community. On the Waccamaw Neck (unlike John tales elsewhere, as Richard Dorson's large collection has shown), John does not lose any contest to the master. John does occasionally trick the weak as well as the powerful in the Waccamaw Neck tales (a realistic touch), but is never outwitted by weaker and shrewder characters. Such folktales as these were used as entertainment, but served both educational and psychological functions. They exhibited important lines of continuity with African tradition, as well as syncretic reinforcement from Euro-American culture, and the marked influence of the immediate social environment upon the creative process of creolization.[41] They are eloquent testimony that at least some minds remained free even while their bodies were enslaved.

Material culture—the underlying "deep structure" which generates tangible objects—is an important and barely tapped historical source.[42] Foodways, for example—the choice of particular foods or particular means of preparing foods—may have cultural and ideological significance beyond mere subsistence, may involve issues of crucial importance to a group's sense of identity. There are reciprocal relationships between food, culture, and

40. *South Carolina Folk Tales*, pp. 19-20, 25-33; W.P.A. Mss., South Caroliniana Library; D.J.M. Muffett, "Uncle Remus Was a Hausaman?" *Southern Folklore Quarterly* 39 (1975): 153; Evans-Pritchard, *The Zande Trickster*, pp. 28-30; Levine, *Black Culture and Black Consciousness*, pp. 90-91, 119.

41. W.P.A. Mss., South Caroliniana Library, University of South Carolina. See also Zora Neale Hurston, "High John de Conquer," *American Mercury* 57 (1943): 450-58; J. Mason Brewer, "John Tales," *Publications of the Texas Folklore Society* 21 (1946): 81-104; Harry C. Oster, "Negro Humor: John and Old Marster," *Journal of the Folklore Institute* 5 (1968): 42-57; John Q. Anderson, "Old John and the Master," *Southern Folklore Quarterly* 25 (1961): 195-97; Fred O. Weldon, "Negro Folktale Heroes," *Publications of the Texas Folklore Society* 24 (1959); Richard M. Dorson, *American Negro Folk Tales*, pp. 124-70; Richard M. Dorson, *American Folklore* (Chicago, 1956), p. 186; Abrahams, "Trickster, the Outrageous Hero," p. 175.

42. Material culture is defined by Henry Glassie as "those segments of human learning which provide a person with plans, methods, and reasons for producing things which can be seen and touched" (*Pattern in the Material Folk Culture of the Eastern United States* [Philadelphia, 1968], p. 2). Thus defined, Glassie contends, material culture may "provide us with the best means available for comprehending an authentic history" (*Folk Housing in Middle Virginia: A Structural Analysis of Historic Artifacts* [Knoxville, 1975], pp. vii, 111). See also Don Yoder, "Folklife Studies in American Scholarship," in *American Folklife*, ed. Don Yoder (Austin, 1976), pp. 3-18; Don Yoder, "The Folklife Studies Movement," *Pennsylvania Folklife* 13 (1963): 43-56; Richard M. Dorson, "Concepts of Folklore and Folklife Studies," in *Folklore and Folklife: An Introduction*, ed. Richard M. Dorson (Chicago, 1972), p. 2. Cf. John Demos, *A Little Commonwealth: Family Life in Plymouth Colony* (New York, 1970), pp. 20-58; Daniel F. McCall, *Africa in Time-Perspective: A Discussion of Historical Reconstruction from Unwritten Sources* (New York, 1969), pp. xv, 28-37.

society. Societies are shaped in part by the basic human need for food, but the activities and relationships of any social group shape their cultural concepts of hunger and appetite. The planters of All Saints Parish described their slaves as "bountifully fed," and most of the living ex-slaves interviewed for the Federal Writers Project slave narratives said their own masters were good providers. Some of them, however, indicated that not all Waccamaw Neck slaves were so fortunate as they. One ex-slave noted, "Doctor Magill people hab to steal for something to eat." My interviews with children and grandchildren of All Saints slaves indicated a rather greater degree of slave dissatisfaction with the plantation cuisine. Many a meal, I was told, consisted of nothing more than corn meal mush and molasses. Often the morning and evening meals were eaten at home in the slave houses, while the midday meal (and sometimes the morning meal) was eaten at a central eating shed or in the field. Cooking for the slaves in the public-pots was crude; and utensils for eating were as crude as implements for cooking, where they existed at all. The masters' allowances were supplemented with fruits and vegetables from the slaves' small garden plots. Hunting and fishing both supplemented the allowances and provided one of the slaves' few recreations. Weddings, Christmas and sometimes other holidays were occasions for elaborate feasts on some plantations. The use of alcohol by slaves was strictly limited to such occasions, but from time to time some slaves found both incentive and opportunity to imbibe anyway. The significance of food to the slaves is perhaps best revealed in two of their proverbs: "Hunger tame wild beast" but "a full belly makes strong arms and a willin' heart."[43]

Costume is one of the basic symbols in any community, expressing not only its structure but its innermost values as well. Planters and visitors in All Saints Parish described the slaves as "bountifully clothed." Ex-slave testimonies and oral tradition reveal that the slaves were, for the most part, adequately clothed. Some clothing was purchased ready-made, but most planters ordered woolen cloth from England and had clothing made by full-time slave seamstresses on the large plantations. Cloth was also woven on the

43. William Oliver, Slave Narratives, 14, iii, 219-20; Louisa Brown, Slave Narratives, 14, i, 115; Gabe Lance, Slave Narratives, 14, iii, 91; Hagar Brown, Slave Narratives, 14, i, 113; Ben Horry, Slave Narratives, 14, ii, 309-10, 314-17, 321; Ellen Godfrey, Slave Narratives, 14, ii, 156-59; Sabe Rutledge, Slave Narratives, 14, iv, 55; John Beese interview; Henry Small interview; Mary Small interview; A.L. Lachicotte interview; W.P.A. Mss., South Caroliniana Library; Emily Weston Diary, passim; Ben Sparkman Plantation Record, Southern Historical Collection, University of North Carolina; Sparkman Family Records, Southern Historical Collection; Almira Coffin letter, pp. 127-29; Sparkman letter in Easterby, *The South Carolina Rice Plantation*, pp. 135-36; Weston, "Rules and Management for the Plantation"; Collins, *Memories of the Southern States*, pp. 6, 12-13, 105-107, 113; Childs, *Rice Planter and Sportsman*, p. 46; Pringle, *Chronicles of Chicora Wood*, pp. 151-52; Malet, *Errand to the South*, pp. 48-49; 57, 68, 118-19, 138; Don Yoder, "Folk Cookery," in Dorson, *Folklore and Folklife*, pp. 338-46; Don Yoder, "Historical Sources for American Foodways Research and Plans for an American Foodways Archive," *Ethnologia Scandinavica* 2 (1971): 41-55; Jay Allan Anderson, "The Study of Contemporary Foodways in

plantations by full-time slave weavers. While the slaves never had unrestricted choice in clothing, *how* clothing is worn is as culturally marked as *what* clothing is worn. Clothing behaviour marks age, sex, religious, marital, and status distinctions within folk communities. Among slaves the status distinction most clearly marked by clothing was that between house servants and other slaves. The white handkerchief, or bandanna, marking the high status of children's nurse, appears to be related to a West African practice expressing a high degree of personal pride. Patterns of clothing behaviour also mark distinctions among various social contexts in slave folklife, from everyday and occupational to erotic and ceremonial. The same rythmic alternation between work and festivals that is evident in so many folk communities is symbolized in clothing. For Waccamaw Neck slaves that alternation distinguished between the workaday world of the weekdays and the festive air they gave to the weekends—a distinction between the time claimed by their masters and the time available for their own purposes. Slaves washed themselves and put on their best for Saturday night visiting or partying (or both) and for church on Sunday. Clothing behaviour is an important way of expressing group consciousness; during the week the slaves belonged to the master, but on Sundays they demonstrated their mutual respect and solidarity as members of a cultural community.[44]

Henry Glassie and others have used folk architecture successfully as a means of penetrating artifactual "grammars" of people in past time. Unfortunately, most of the material remains of the old rice plantations have long since vanished. Julia Peterkin noted as early as 1933, "Many of the

American Folklife Research," *Keystone Folklore Quarterly* 16 (1971): 156; Claude Levi-Strauss, "The Culinary Triangle," *Partisan Review* 33 (1966): 586-95; Charles W. Joyner, "Soul Food and the Sambo Stereotype: Foodlore from the Slave Narrative Collection," *Keystone Folklore Quarterly* 16 (1971): 171-77; Sam Bowers Hilliard, "Pork in the Antebellum South: The Georgraphy of Self-Sufficiency," *Annals of the Association of American Georgraphers* 57 (1969); Sam Bowers Hilliard, "Hog Meat and Cornpone," *Proceedings of the American Philosophical Society* 113 (1969): 12; Genovese, *Roll, Jordan, Roll*, pp. 507, 544, 548; John Blassingame, *The Slave Community: Plantation Life in the AnteBellum South* (New York, 1972), p. 158; Robert William Fogel and Stanley L. Engerman, *Time on the Cross: The Economics of American Negro Slavery* (Boston, 1974), p. 115.

44. Ellen Godfrey, Slave Narratives, 14, ii, 159; Ben Horry, Slave Narratives, 14, ii, 310; William Oliver, Slave Narratives, 14, iii, 218-19; Sabe Rutledge, Slave Narratives, 14, iv, 60; Margaret Bryant, Slave Narratives, 14, i, 146-47; W.P.A. Mss., South Caroliniana Library; Emily Weston Diary, February 8, May 2, 7, December 3, 1859; Sparkman Family Papers, Book Six, Southern Historical Collection; James R. Sparkman Books, Book Three, Southern Historical Collection; Pringle, *Chronicles of Chicora Wood*, pp. 153-55; Collins, *Memories of the Southern States*, pp. 4-6, 70, 76; Malet *An Errand to the South*, p. 49; Easterby, *The South Carolina Rice Plantation*, p. 92; Heyward, *Seed from Madagascar*, p. 182; Childs, *Rice Planter and Sportsman*, pp. 10, 12, 46; Almira Coffin letter, p. 127; Anon., "Recollections of a Visit to the Waccamaw," *Living Age*, August 1, 1857, pp. 292-93. Cf. Petr Grigorojevic Bogatyrov, *The Functions of Folk Costume in Moravian Slovakia*, trans. R.G. Crum (The Hague, 1971); Richard Weiss, *Volkskunde der Schweiz* (Erlenbach-Zurich, 1946), pp. 140-41; Don Yoder, "Folk Costume," in Dorson, *Folklore and Folklife*, pp. 296-305.

plantations have passed away so completely that no sign of them remains except in old graveyards whose sunken weeds and broken stones are overgrown and hidden by trees and rank weeds." Housing patterns reflected the masters' view of the slaves' social status. Behind the Big House stood the kitchen, and behind the kitchen were the cabins of the house servants. Behind them were the barns, stables, carriage houses and other plantation outbuildings. Further back was the "Street"—the homes of the field hands. The prevalence of single family dwellings would seem to have had an influence on the nature of family patterns and helped to promote a sense of community among the various residents of the "Street."[45]

Thus various cultural influences converged within the slave community of All Saints Parish. The slaves' pidginized African cultural grammars directed their selective adoption and adaptation of elements of Euro-American culture to form a new creolized culture of their own. This study, by demonstrating the value of creolization theory and the holistic folklife concept to the comprehension of that process, points toward an approach to slave studies which I believe to be essential. The time has come to move away from the purely descriptive mode toward an analytical approach which poses issues germane to the understanding of culture and of its relation to society and to change. The time has come to move from sweeping surveys of broad areas and long time spans to close, careful studies which preserve the precise integrity of historical place and time. If the study of slavery is to move forward with the same intellectual excitement which has characterized its recent development, then broader (but inevitably shallower) comparative studies must be balanced by narrower (and, one hopes, richer and deeper) micro-studies. If these micro-studies are to be indeed richer and deeper, they must combine greater methodological and theoretical sophistication with closer attention to concrete realities. Clearly the concepts of creolization and of folklife have much to contribute to that development.

45. William Oliver, in Slave Narratives, 14, iii, 217; Personal interview with Sarah Ann Goback, Murrells Inlet, S.C., August 17, 1975; John Beese interview; A.L. Lachicotte interview; An Anonymous Englishman, "Rambles at Random through the Southern States," *Blackwood's Magazine*, January, 1860; Emily Weston Diary, January 1, 3, February 7, December 13, 1859; Malet, *An Errand to the South*, pp. 49, 79; Pringle, *Chronicles of Chicora Wood*, pp. 63-64; Childs, *Rice Planter and Sportsman*, p. 46; Almira Coffin letter, p. 133; Doar, *Rice and Rice-Planting*, p. 38; Peterkin, *Roll, Jordan, Roll*, pp. 9-10; cf. Glassie, *Folk Housing in Middle Virginia*, p. 145; McCall, *African in Time-Perspective*, pp. 28-37.

The author wishes to express his appreciation to the Harvard Seminar on the Comparative Study of Slave Societies, the Social Science Research Council, the National Endowment for the Humanities, and the Newberry Library for support of the research reported in this article. An earlier version was presented at the 1978 meeting of the Organization of American Historians.

EIGHT

THE BEGINNINGS OF THE AFRO-AMERICAN FAMILY IN MARYLAND

Allan Kulikoff

Sometime in 1728, Harry, a recently imported African, escaped from his master in southern Prince George's County, Maryland, and joined a small black community among the Indians beyond the area of white settlement. The following year, Harry returned to Prince George's to urge his former shipmates, the only "kinfolk" he had, to return there with him. Over forty years later, another Harry, who belonged to John Jenkins of Prince George's, ran away. The Annapolis newspaper reported that "he has been seen about the Negro Quarters in *Patuxent,* but is supposed to have removed among his Acquaintances on Potomack; he is also well acquainted with the Negroes at Clement Wheeler's Quarter on Zekiah, and a Negro Wench of Mr. Wall's named Rachael; a few miles from that Quarter is his Aunt, and he may possibly be harboured thereabouts."[1]

These two incidents, separated by two generations, are suggestive. African Harry ran away *from* slavery to the frontier; Afro-American Harry ran *to* his friends and kinfolk spread over a wide territory. The Afro-American runaway could call on many others to hide him, but the African had few friends and seemingly, no wife. These contrasts raise many questions. How did Afro-Americans organize their families in the Chesapeake colonies during the eighteenth century? Who lived in slave households? How many Afro-American fathers lived with their wives and children? What was the impact of arbitrary sale and transfer of slaves upon family life? How did an Afro-American's household and family relationships change through the life cycle?

Note: Allan Kulikoff is a fellow of the Institute of Early American History and Culture and assistant professor of history at the College of William and Mary. He would like to thank Ira Berlin, Lois Green Carr, John P. Demos, David H. Fischer, Rhys Isaac, Aubrey C. Land, Elizabeth Pleck, and the staff of the Institute of Early American History and Culture for their perceptive comments on earlier versions of this paper and, especially, Russell R. Menard for his many useful suggestions and Herbert G. Gutman for his valuable critique. Research for this essay was supported by Brandeis University through a Rose and Irving Crown fellowship and research grant and by the National Science Foundation (GS35781).

This paper attempts to answer these questions.[2] While literary documents by or about slaves before 1800, such as runaway narratives, WPA freed-slave interviews, black autobiographies, or detailed travel accounts are very infrequently available to historians of colonial slave family life, they can gather age and family data from probate inventories, personal information from runaway advertisements, and depositions in court cases. These sources, together with several diaries and account books, kept by whites, provide a great deal of material about African and Afro-American family life in the Chesapeake region.

Almost all the blacks who lived in Maryland and Virginia before 1780 were slaves. Because his status precluded him from enjoying a legally secure family life, a slave's household often excluded important family members. Households, domestic groups, and families must therefore be clearly distinguished. A household, as used here, is a coresidence group that includes all who shared a "proximity of sleeping arrangements," or lived under the same roof. Domestic groups include kin and nonkin, living in the same or separate households, who share cooking, eating, childrearing, working, and other daily activities. Families are composed of people related by blood or marriage. Several distinctions are useful in defining the members of families. The immediate family include husband and wife or parents and children. Near kin include the immediate family and all other kin, such as adult brothers and sisters or cousins who share the same house or domestic tasks with the immediate family. Other kinfolk who do not function as family members on a regular basis are considered to be distant kin.[3]

The process of family formation can perhaps best be understood as an adaptive process. My ideas about this process owe much to a provocative essay by Sidney Mintz and Richard Price on Afro-American culture. Blacks learned to modify their environment, learned from each other how to retain family ties under very adverse conditions, and structured their expectations about family activities around what they knew the master would permit. If white masters determined the outward bounds of family activities, it was Africans, and especially their descendants, who gave meaning to the relationships between parents and children, among siblings, and with more distant kinfolk. As a result, black family structure on the eve of the Revolution differed from both African and white family systems.[4]

Africans who were forced to come to the Chesapeake region in the late seventeenth and early eighteenth centuries struggled to create viable families and households, but often failed. They suffered a great loss when they were herded into slave ships. Their family and friends, who had given meaning to their lives and structured their place in society, were left behind and they found themselves among strangers. They could never recreate their families and certainly not devise a West African kinship system in the Chesapeake. The differences between African communities were too great. Some Africans lived in clans and lineages, others did not; some traced their descent from women but others traced descent from men; mothers, fathers, and other kin played somewhat different roles in each community; initiation ceremonies and puberty rites, forbidden marriages, marriage customs, and household structures all varied from place to place.[5]

Though African immigrants did not bring a unified West African culture with them to the Chesapeake colonies, they did share important beliefs about the nature of kinship. Africans could modify these beliefs in America to legitimate the families they eventually formed. They saw kinship as the principal way of ordering relationships between individuals. Each person in the tribe was related to most others in the community. The male was father, son, and uncle; the female was mother, daughter, and aunt to many others. Because their kinship system was so extensive, Africans included kinfolk outside the immediate family in their daily activities. For example, adult brothers or sisters of the father or mother played an important role in childrearing and domestic activities in many African societies.[6]

Secondly, but far less certainly, African immigrants may have adapted some practices associated with polygyny, a common African marital custom. A few men on the Eastern Shore of Maryland in the 1740s, and perhaps others scattered elsewhere, lived with several women. However, far too few African women (in relation to the number of men) immigrated to make polygynous marriages common. Nevertheless, the close psychological relationship between mothers and children, and the great social distance between a husband and his various wives and children found in African polygynous societies might have been repeated in the Chesapeake colonies. In any event, African slave mothers played a more important role than fathers in teaching children about Africa and about how to get along in the slave system. Both African custom, and the physical separation of immigrant men and women played a role in this development.[7]

Africans faced a demographic environment hostile to most forms of family life. If African men were to start families, they had to find wives, and that task was difficult. Most blacks lived on small farms of less than 11 slaves; and the small black population was spread thinly over a vast territory. Roads were rudimentary. Even where concentrations of larger plantations were located, African men did not automatically find wives. Sex ratios in southern Maryland rose from 125 to 130 (men per 100 women) in the mid-seventeenth century to about 150 in the 1710s and 1720s, and to around 180 in the 1730s. In Surry County, Virginia, the slave sex ratio was about 145 in the 1670s and 1680s, but over 200 in the 1690s and 1700s. Wealthy slaveowners did not provide most of their African men with wives; the larger the plantation, the higher the sex ratio tended to be.[8]

Africans had competition for the available black women. By the 1690s, some black women were natives, and they may have preferred Afro-

American men. White men were also competitors. Indeed, during the seventeenth and early eighteenth centuries, white adult sex ratios were as high (or higher) than black adult sex ratios. At any period whites possessed a monopoly of power and some of them probably took slave women as their common-law wives. African men competed for the remaining black women, and probably some died before they could find a wife. In 1739 African men planned an uprising in Prince George's County partly because they could not find wives.[9]

Foreign-born male slaves in Maryland and Virginia probably lived in a succession of different kinds of households. Newly imported Africans had no blood kin in the Chesapeake. Since sex ratios were high, most of these men probably lived with other, unrelated men. African men may have substituted friends for kin. Newly enslaved Africans made friends with their nearest shipmates during the middle passage, and after their arrival in Maryland, some of them lived near these men. New Negroes could live with other recent African immigrants because migration from Africa occurred in short spurts from the 1670s to the late 1730s. The high sex ratios of large plantations indicate that wealthy men bought many of these Africans. Even if his shipmates lived miles away, the new immigrant could share the experiences of others who had recently endured the middle passage.[10]

Despite the difficulties, the majority of Africans who survived for a few years eventually found a wife. In societies with high sex ratios, women tend to marry young, but men have to postpone marriage. This increases the opportunity of older men to marry by reducing the sexual imbalance. (That is, there are as many younger women as older men.) By the 1690s, large numbers of Afro-American women entered their midteens and married Afro-American and African men.[11] Because the plantations were small, and individual farm sex ratios likely to be uneven, the wives and children of married African men very often lived on other plantations. These men still lived mainly with other unrelated men, but at least they had begun to develop kin ties.[12] A few African men lived with their wives and children, and some limited evidence suggests that the longer an African lived in the Chesapeake, the more likely he was to live with his immediate family.[13]

Unlike most African men, African women commonly lived with their children. Some African women may have been so alienated that they refused to have children, but the rest bore and raised several offspring, protected by the master's reluctance to separate very young children from their mothers. Since the children were reared by their mothers, and eventually joined them in the tobacco fields, these households were domestic groups, although incomplete as families.[14]

A greater proportion of African women than African men lived with both spouses and children. These opportunities usually arose on large plantations. There was such a surplus of men on large plantations that African women who lived on them could choose husbands from several African or Afro-American men. The sex ratio on large plantations in Prince George's during the 1730s, a period of heavy immigration, was 249. This shortage of women prevented most recently arrived African men from finding a wife on the plantation. For them the opportunity to live with a wife and children was rare. More Africans probably lived with their immediate families in the 1740s; immigration declined, large planters bought more African women, and the sex ratio on big plantations fell to 142.[15]

Because African spouses were usually separated, African mothers reared their Afro-American children with little help from their husbands. Even when the father was present, the extended kin so important in the lives of African children was missing. Mothers probably taught them the broad values they brought from Africa and related the family's history in Africa and the Chesapeake. When the children began working in the fields, they learned from their mothers how to survive a day's work and how to get along with master and overseer.

Each group of Africans repeated the experiences of previous immigrants. Eventually, more and more Afro-American children matured and began families of their own. The first large generation of Afro-Americans in Maryland probably came of age in the 1690s; by the 1720s, when the second large generation had matured, the black population finally began increasing naturally.[16]

The changing composition of the black population combined with other changes to restructure Afro-American households and families. Alterations in the adult sex ratio, the size of plantations, and black population density provided black people with opportunities to enjoy a more satisfying family life. The way masters transferred slaves from place to place limited the size and composition of black households, but Afro-American family members separated by masters managed to establish complex kinship networks over many plantations. Afro-Americans used these opportunities to create a kind of family life that differed from African and Anglo-American practices.

Demographic changes led to more complex households and families. As the number of adult Africans in the population decreased, the sex ratio in Maryland declined to between 100 and 110 by the 1750s. This decline gave most men an opportunity to marry by about age 30. The number of slaves who lived on plantations with more than 20 blacks increased; the density of the black population in tidewater Maryland and Virginia rose; the proportion of blacks in the total population of Prince George's County, in nearby areas of Maryland, and throughout tidewater Virginia rose to half or more by the end of the century; and many new roads were built. The number of friends and kinfolk whom typical Afro-Americans saw every day or visited with regularity increased, while their contact with whites declined because large areas of the Chesapeake became nearly black counties.[17]

How frequently masters transfered their Afro-American slaves, and where they sent them, affected black household composition. Surviving documents do not allow a systematic analysis of this point, but several conclusions seem clear. First, planters kept women and their small children together but did not keep husbands and teenage children with their immediate family. Slaveowner after slaveowner bequeathed women and their "increase" to sons or daughters. However, children of slaveowners tended to live near their parents; thus, even when members of slave families were so separated, they remained in the same neighborhood.[18] Secondly, Afro-Americans who lived on small farms were transferred more frequently than those on large plantations. At their deaths small slaveowners typically willed a slave or two to their widows and to each child. They also frequently mortgaged or sold slaves to gain capital. If a slaveowner died with many unpaid debts, his slaves had to be sold.[19] Finally, relatively few blacks were forced to move long distances. Far more blacks were affected by migrations of slaves from the Chesapeake region to the new Southwest in the nineteenth century than by long-distance movement in the region before the Revolution.[20] These points should not be misunderstood. Most Afro-Americans who lived in Maryland or Virginia during the eighteenth century experienced separations from members of their immediate families sometime in their lives. Most, however, were able to visit these family members occasionally.

These changes led to a new social reality for most slaves born in the 1750s, 1760s, and 1770s. If unrelated people and their progeny stay in a limited geographic area for several generations, the descendants of the original settlers must develop kin ties with many other people who live nearby. Once the proportion of adult Africans declined, this process began. African women married and had children; the children matured and married. If most of them remained near their first homes, each was bound to have siblings, children, spouses, uncles, aunts, and cousins living in the neighborhood. How these various kinspeople were organized into households, families, and domestic groups depended not only upon the whims of masters but also upon the meaning placed on kinship by the slaves themselves.

The process of household and family formation and dissolution was begun by each immigrant woman who lived long enough to have children. The story of Ann Joice, a black woman who was born in Barbados, taken to England as a servant, and then falsely sold into slavery in Maryland in the 1670s, may have been similar to that of other immigrant women once she became a slave. The Darnall family of Prince George's owned Ann Joice. She had seven children with several white men in the 1670s and 1680s; all remained slaves the rest of their lives. Three of her children stayed on the Darnall home plantation until their deaths. One was sold as a child to a planter who lived a few miles away; another was eventually sold to William Digges, who lived about five miles from the Darnall farm. Both the spatial spread and the local concentration of kinfolk continued in the next generation. Peter Harbard, born between 1715 and 1720, was the son of Francis Harbard, who was Ann Joice's child. Peter grew up on the Darnall farm, but in 1737 he was sold to George Gordon, who lived across the road from Darnall. As a child, Peter lived with or very near his grandmother Ann Joice, his father, and several paternal uncles and aunts. He probably knew his seven cousins (father's sister's children), children of his aunt Susan Harbard, who lived on William Digges's plantation. Other kinfolk lived in Annapolis but were too far away to visit easily.[21]

As Afro-American slaves were born and died, and as masters sold or bequeathed their slaves, black households were formed and reformed, broken and created. Several detailed examples can illustrate this process. For example, Daphne, the daughter of Nan, was born about 1736 on a large plantation in Prince George's owned by Robert Tyler, Sr. Until she was two, she lived with her mother, two brothers, and two sisters. In 1738, Tyler died and left his slaves to his wife, children, and grandchildren. All lived on or near Tyler's farms. Three of Daphne's siblings were bequeathed to grand-daughter Ruth Tyler, who later married Mordecai Jacob, her grandfather's next-door neighbor. Daphne continued to live on the Tyler plantation. From 1736 to 1787, she had six different masters, but she still lived where she was born. Daphne lived with her mother until her mother died, and with her ten children until 1779. Children were eventually born to Daphne's daughters; these infants lived with their mothers and near their maternal grandmother. When Robert Tyler III, Robert senior's grandson and Daphne's fifth master, died in 1779, his will divided Daphne's children and grandchildren between his son and daughter. Daphne was thus separated from younger children, born between 1760 and 1772. They were given to Millicent Beanes, Robert III's daughter, who lived several miles away. Daphne continued to live on the same plantation as her four older children and several grandchildren. An intricate extended family of grandmother, sons, daughters, grandchildren, aunts, uncles, nieces, nephews, and cousins resided in several households on the Tyler plantation in 1778, and other more remote kinfolk could be found on the neighboring Jacob farm.[22]

Family separations might be more frequent on smaller plantations. Rachael was born in the late 1730s and bore ten children between 1758 and 1784. As a child she lived on the plantation of Alexander Magruder, a large slaveowner in Prince George's; before 1746, Alexander gave her to his son Hezekiah, who lived on an adjoining plantation. Hezekiah never owned more than ten slaves, and when he died in 1769, he owned only two—including one willed to his wife by her brother. Between 1755 and 1757, he mortgaged nine slaves, including Rachael, to two merchants. In 1757, Samuel Roundall (who lived about five miles from the Magruders) seized Rachael and six other slaves mortgaged to him. This and subsequent transfers can be seen

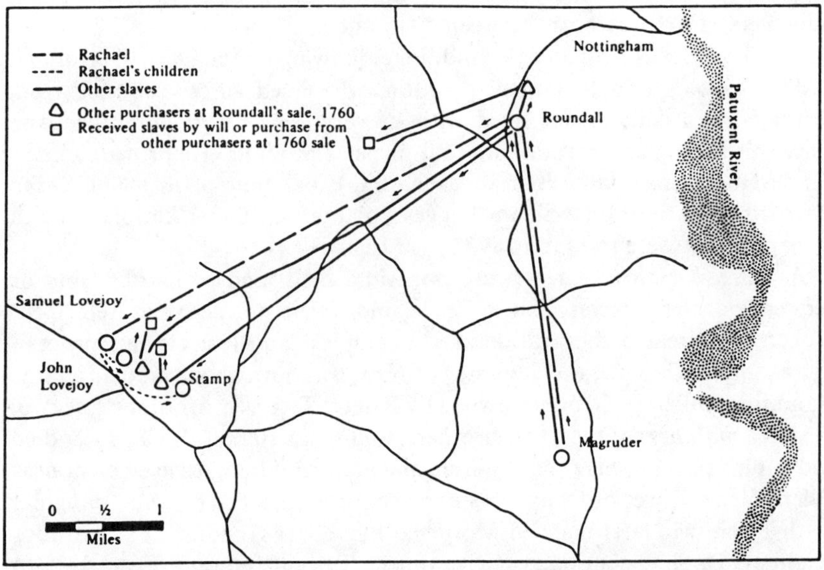

FIGURE 8.1. Sale and Later Transfer of Hezekiah Magruder's Slaves, 1755–1780

on figure 8.1. In 1760 Roundall sold Rachael and her eldest daughter to Samuel Lovejoy, who lived about nine miles from Roundall. At the same time, four other former Magruder slaves were sold: two to planters in Lovejoy's neighborhood, one to a Roundall neighbor, and one to a planter living at least fifteen miles away in Charles County. Rachael's separation from friends and family members continued. In 1761, her eldest child was sold at age three to George Stamp, a neighbor of Lovejoy. By the time Samuel Lovejoy died in 1762, she had two other children. She and her youngest child went to live with John Lovejoy, Samuel's nephew and near-neighbor, but her second child, about age two, stayed with Lovejoy's widow. Her third child was sold at age six, but Rachael and her next seven children lived with John Lovejoy until at least 1787.[23]

These three examples suggest how Afro-American households and families developed in the eighteenth century. Husbands and wives and parents and children were frequently separated by the master's transfers of family members. At the same time, as generation followed generation, households, or adjacent huts, became increasingly complex, and sometimes included grandparents, uncles, aunts, or cousins, as well as the immediate family. Since other kin lived on nearby or distant plantations, geographically concentrated (and dispersed) kinship networks that connected numbers of quarters emerged during the pre-Revolutionary era.

How typical were the experiences suggested by the examples? How were families organized into households and domestic groups on large and small

TABLE 8.1
Afro-American Household Structures on Three Large Plantations in Prince George's and Anne Arundel Counties, Maryland, 1759–1775

	Percentage in Household Type				*Percentage of Total in Household Types*
Household Type	*Males 15+*	*Females 15+*	*Children 0–9*	*Children 10–14*	
Husband-wife-children	40	43	55	44	47
Mother-children	2	17	22	10	14
Mother-children-other kin	4	14	8	13	9
Siblings	7	4	6	12	7
Husband-wife-children-other kin	2	2	2	2	2
Father-children	5	0	3	5	3
Husband-wife	2	2	0	0	1
Three generation	1	2	2	3	2
Unknown or mixed	36	16	3	12	15
Total percentage	99	100	101	101	100
Number people	142	129	178	77	526

Sources: PG Inventories, GS No. 1, f. 73 (1759; James Wardrop's, 32 slaves); and GS No. 2, ff. 334–36 (1775; Addison's 3 plantations, 109 slaves) and Charles Carroll Account Book, Maryland Historical Society (rest of slaves). The three-generation households include grandparents and grandchildren, but not the generation in between. The unknown or mixed category includes all those apparently living away from all kinfolk, but perhaps living near them. Some of the slaves in this category probably belong in the others, but the sources (especially the Addison and Wardrop documents) do not permit location of them.

quarters? Data from three large planters' inventories taken in 1759, 1773–74, and 1775, and from a Prince George's census of 1776 permit a test of the hypotheses concerning changes in household structure, differences between large and small units, and the spread of kinfolk across space. Table 8.1 details household structure on large quarters of over twenty and table 8.2 shows the kinds of households on small farms. About half of all slaves probably lived on each plantation type.[24] This evidence provides a good test, because by the 1770s most Afro-Americans could trace a Chesapeake genealogy back to immigrant grandparents or great-grandparents.[25]

Kinfolk (immediate families and near kin) on large plantations were organized into three kinds of residence groups. Most of the slaves of some quarters were interrelated by blood or marriage. Domestic groups included kinfolk who lived on opposite sides of duplex slave huts and who shared a common yard and eating and cooking arrangements. Finally, most households included members of an immediate family.

The kinship structure of large plantations is illustrated by a household inventory taken in 1773–74 of 385 slaves owned by Charles Carroll of Carrollton on thirteen different quarters in Anne Arundel County. Because Carroll insisted that the inventory be "taken in Familys with their Ages," the document permits a detailed reconstruction of kinship networks.[26] Though the complexity and size of kinship groups on Carroll's quarters were

TABLE 8.2
Afro-American Household Structures on Small Plantations (1-8 Slaves), Prince George's County, Maryland, 1776

Household Type	Percentage in Household Type: Males 15+	Females 15+	Children 0-9	Children 10-14	Percentage of Total in Household Types
Husband-wife-children	17	18	22	10	18
Mother-children	2	35	56	29	32
Father-children	2	*	4	1	2
Siblings	7	5	6	17	8
Mixed	72	42	12	43	41
Total percentage	100	100	100	100	101
Number of people	275	276	325	162	1038

Source: 1776 Census. The household types were assumed from black age structures on individual farms. Children and mothers were matched if a woman in the household could have been a mother to children in the same household. (E.g., a woman 25 years old was assumed to be the mother of children aged 4, 2, and 1 years on the same plantation). Men and women were linked as husband and wife if a man and woman in the same household were close in age (e.g., a man of 35 linked with a woman of 25). Children and young adults (to c. 25) were assumed to be siblings if no parents were in the household, and the ages of the children were close. (Children aged 8, 10, 13 were linked as siblings when no adult in household could be their parent.) A man was assumed to be father to children who lived on the same farm if no other person who could be a parent was present (man aged 35 was father to children aged 12, 10, 8 when no woman was present in household to be wife). The mixed category included all others who could not be placed: these could include kinfolk like older siblings, or brothers or parents to women with children in the same household, or they could be unrelated. If more than one type was found on a farm, it was counted as two households despite the probability that the people lived in the same hut. The statistics must be treated as educated guesses. Since slave mothers and their children were usually kept together in slave sales and in wills of masters, it is fairly certain that all the children in the first two categories lived with their mothers. The other linkages must include many errors.

* = less than ½%.

probably greater than on other large plantations, the general pattern could easily have been repeated elsewhere.[27]

The ten men and three women who headed each list were probably leaders of their quarters. Five of the quarters were named for these individuals.[28] They tended to be old slaves who had been with the Carroll family for many years. While the mean age of all adults was 37 years, the mean age of the leaders was 49, and six of the thirteen were over 55.[29] The leader often lived with many kinfolk; he or she was closely related to about 36 to 38 percent of all the other slaves on the quarter. For example, Fanny, 69 years of age, was surrounded by at least forty near kinfolk on the main plantation at Doohoregan, and Mayara James, 65 years of age, lived with 23 relatives on his quarter.[30]

The two slaves genealogies presented in figures 8.2 and 8.3 provide detailed examples of the kinds of kinship networks that could develop on quarters after several generations of relative geographic stability. Because most slave

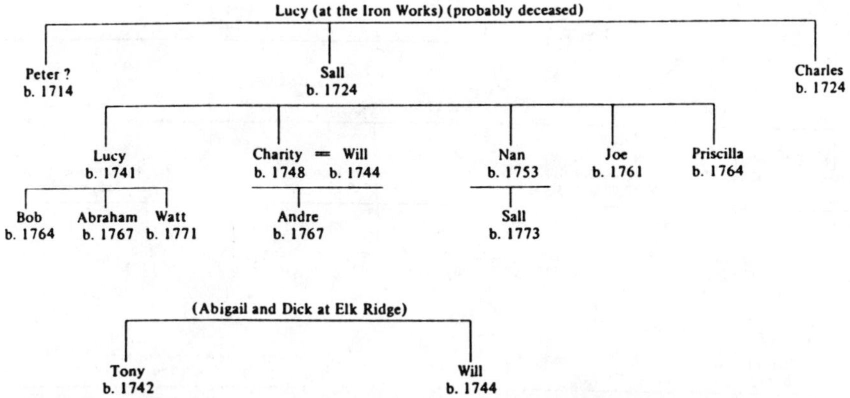

FIGURE 8.2. Kinship Ties Among Charles Carroll's Slaves at Annapolis Quarter, 1774
Source: Charles Carroll Account Book, Maryland Historical Society.
Note: Will, son of Abigail and Dick and Charity's husband, appears twice. Peter may not be Lucy's son, but it seems probable. Mark (b. 1758) and Jem (b. 1754) apparently were not related to others on the quarter, but had relatives elsewhere on Carroll's plantations.

quarters had between fifteen and thirty slaves, the network included just two or three households. The kin group shown in figure 8.2 may have been typical. Thirteen of the seventeen slaves who lived at Annapolis Quarter in 1774 were descendants of Iron Works Lucy. Ten were children and grandchildren of Sall. One of Sall's sons-in-law and his brother also lived there. Peter and Charles, other descendants of Lucy, lived on the quarter but had families elsewhere.

Nearly half the slaves who resided on Riggs Quarter, Carroll's main plantation, were kinfolk (63/130). A network of this size could develop only on the home plantation of the largest Chesapeake planters.[31] Each of the members of the group was either a direct descendant or an affine (inlaw) of old Fanny. She was surrounded on her quarter by five children, nineteen grandchildren, nine great-grandchildren, four children-in-law, and three grandchildren's spouses. The network grew through the marriage of Fanny's children and grandchildren to children of other residents of the quarter. For example, Cooper Joe, his wife, and thirteen children and grandchildren were closely related to Fanny's family. By the early 1750s Cooper Joe had married Nanny of Kate, and about 1761 Fanny's son Bob married Frances Mitchell of Kate. Joe and Nanny's children were first cousins of the children of Bob and Frances, and thereby more remotely connected to all the rest of Fanny's descendants. The alliance of the two families was cemented in 1772, when Dinah, the daughter of Kate of Fanny married Joe, the son of Cooper Joe.[32]

The intraquarter kinship network was also a work group. Fanny's and Lucy's adult and teenage kinfolk worked together in the fields. Masters separated their slaves by sex, age, and strength, and determined what each

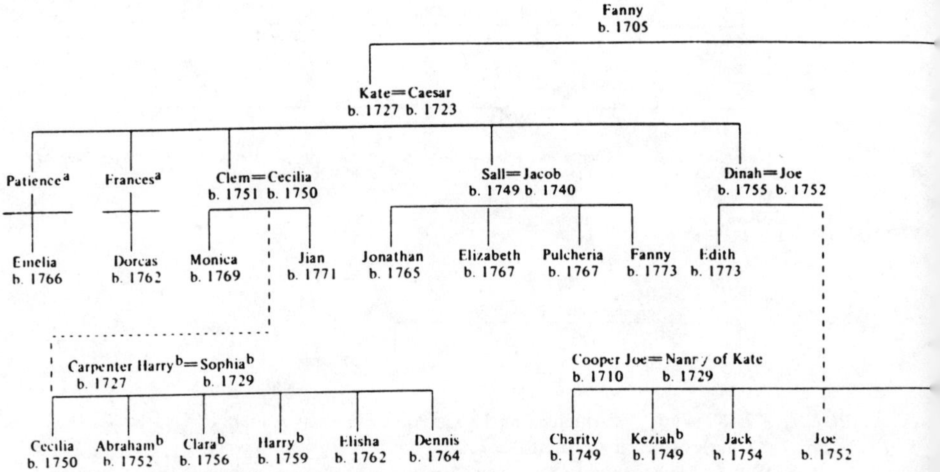

FIGURE 8.3. Fanny and Some of Her Kinfolk on Doohoregan Manor, 1773

[a]Those without a birthdate not resident on any Carroll farm. [b]Did not live at Rigg's Quarter (Fanny's Quarter). [c]This family lived at the sawmill at the main quarter of Doohoregan Manor. Frances Mitchell was a sister of Nanny, who was the wife of Cooper Joe.

Source: Charles Carroll Account Book, Maryland Historical Society.

would do, but blacks judged each other in part by the reciprocal kinship obligation that bound them together. Afro-Americans worked at their own pace and frequently thwarted their master's desires for increased productivity. Part of this conflict can be explained by the Afro-American's preindustrial work discipline, but part may have been due to the desires of kinfolk to help and protect each other from the master's lash, the humid climate, and the malarial environment.[33]

Landon Carter's lament upon the death of his trusted old slave Jack Lubbar suggests the dimensions of kinship solidarity in the fields. Lubbar had been a foreman over many groups of slaves. In his old age, he worked at the Fork quarter "with 5 hands and myself; in which service he so gratefully discharged his duty as to make me by his care alone larger crops of Corn, tobacco and Pease twice over than ever I have had made by anyone. . . ." Other blacks did not share Lubbar's desire to produce a large crop for Carter. "At this plantation," Carter writes, "he continued till his age almost deprived him of eyesight which made him desire to be removed because those under him, mostly his great grandchildren, by the baseness of their Parents abused him much." Lubbar's grandchildren and great-grandchildren, who worked together, were related in intricate ways: parents and children, maternal and paternal cousins, uncles and aunts, and brothers and sisters. They united against Lubbar to slow the work pace and conserve their energy.[34]

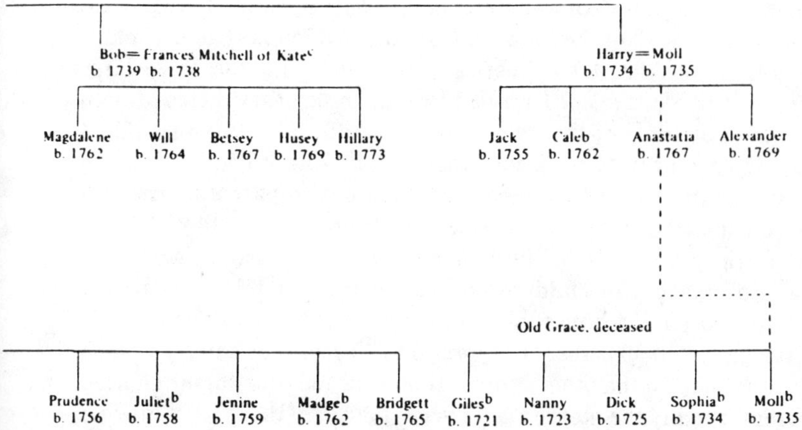

When Afro-Americans came home each night from the fields, they broke into smaller domestic groups. Their habitat set the scene for social intercourse. On large plantations "a Negro quarter is a Number of Huts or Hovels, built at some distance from the Mansion House; where the Negroes reside with their wives and Families, and cultivate at vacant times the little spots allow'd them."[35] Four early-nineteenth-century slave houses still standing in Southern Maryland suggest that slave families living on the same quarter were very close. Each house included two rooms of about sixteen-by-sixteen feet, separated by a thin wall. In three of the homes, the two huts shared the same roof but had separate doorways. Two had separate fireplaces, the residents of one duplex shared a fireplace, and one quarter (which was over a kitchen) did not have a fireplace.[36] Neither family had much privacy, and communication between them must have been commonplace. No activity could occur on one side of the hut without those on the other knowing about it. And the two halves of the hut shared a common yard, where residents could talk, eat, or celebrate.

On the quarters the smallest local residence unit to contain kinfolk was the household. Household members were not isolated from other kinfolk; they worked with their relatives in the fields, associated with neighbors in the common yard, and cooked meals or slept near those who lived on the other side of their duplex. Nevertheless, kinfolk who lived in the same household were spatially closer when at home than any other group of kin. Who lived in typical households on slave quarters? How many husbands lived with their wives and children? How many children were separated from their parents? Did kin other than the immediate family live in many households?

Nearly half of all the Afro-Americans who lived on the three large plantations described in table 8.1 resided in households that included both parents and at least some of their children. Over half of the young children on all three plantations lived with both parents, but a far higher proportion of adults and children 10 to 14 years of age lived in two-parent households on the Carroll quarters than on the three Addison farms and Wardrop's plantation in Prince George's. While 49 percent of the women, 51 percent of the men, and 52 percent of children between ages 10 and 14 on Carroll's farms lived in two-parent households, only 28 percent of the women, 24 percent of the men, and 30 percent of those 10 to 14 year olds could be found in two-parent homes on the other farms. Almost all the other children lived with one parent, usually the mother; but over a quarter of those 10 to 14 years of age lived with siblings or with apparently unrelated people.

The differences between Carroll and the other two large slaveowners is striking. Carroll, unlike all but a few other Chesapeake gentlemen, was able to provide his people with spouses from his own plantations and chose to keep adolescent children with their parents. Over six-tenths of the men (62 percent) and 28 percent of the women on Addison's and Wardrop's plantations lived with siblings, were unmarried, or lived away from spouses and children. On Carroll's quarters only 27 percent of the men and 12 percent of the women were similarly separated from wives and children.

Many blacks on these three large farms lived with or near kin other than their parents or children. About 7 percent were in the household of a brother or sister, and over a tenth (13 percent) of parents and children shared their homes with another kinsperson. There were several types of these extended households: seven included parent(s), children, and sibling(s) of the mother; two included grandmother living with her children and grandchildren; in one household grandparents took care of two young grandchildren; and in one hut, an adult brother and sister lived with her children and one grandchild.

Far less can be learned about families on small plantations. On these farms, the slave quarter could be in an outbuilding or in a small hut.[37] All the slaves, whether kin or not, lived together, cooked together, reared children together, and slept in the same hut. Table 8.2 very roughly suggests the differences in household composition of large plantations and small farms. Only 18 percent of the blacks on small units lived in two-parent households. About a third resided in mother-child households, and that included over half the young children and three-tenths of those 10 to 14 years of age. Nearly three-quarters of the men and two-fifths of the women—some unmarried—lived with neither spouse nor children. Over two-fifths of the youths 10 to 14 years of age lived away from parents and siblings.

By the 1750s, a peculiar Afro-American life cycle had developed. Afro-Americans lived in a succession of different kinds of households. Children under 10 years almost always lived with their mothers, and over half on large plantations lived with both parents. Between 10 and 14 years of age, large numbers of children left their parents' home. Some stayed with siblings and their families, others were sold, the rest lived with other kin or unrelated people. Women married in their late teens, had children, and established households with their own children. Over four-tenths of the women on large plantations and a fifth on small farms lived with husbands as well as children. The same proportion of men as women lived with spouses and children, but because children of separated spouses usually lived with their mothers, large numbers of men, even on big plantations, lived with other men.

These life cycle changes can perhaps best be approached through a study of the critical events in the lives of Afro-Americans. Those events probably included the following: infancy, leaving the matricentral cell, beginning to work in the tobacco fields, leaving home, courtship and marriage, childrearing, and old age.[38]

For the first few months of life, a newborn infant stayed in the matricentral cell, that is, received his identity and subsistence from his mother.[39] A mother would take her new infant to the fields with her "and lay it uncovered on the ground . . . while she hoed her corn-row down and up. She would then suckle it a few minutes, and return to her labor, leaving the child in the same exposure." Eventually, the child left its mother's lap and explored the world of the hut and quarter. In the evenings, he ate with his family and learned to love his parents, siblings, and other kinfolk. During the day the young child lived in an age segregated world. While parents, other adults, and older siblings worked, children were "left, during a great portion of the day, on the ground at the doors of their huts, to their own struggles and efforts."[40] They played with age-mates or were left at home with other children and perhaps an aged grandparent. Siblings or age-mates commonly lived together or in nearby houses. On the Potomac side of Prince George's County in 1776, 86 percent of those 0 to 4 years of age, and 82 percent of those 5 to 9 years of age lived on plantations with at least one other child near their own age. Many children lived in little communities of five or more children their own age. Children 5 to 9 years old, too young to work full time, may have cared for younger siblings; in Prince George's in 1776, 83 percent of all children 0 to 4 years of age lived on a plantation with at least one child 5 to 9 years of age.[41]

Black children began to work in the tobacco fields between 7 and 10 years of age. For the first time they joined fully in the daytime activities of adults.[42] Those still living at home labored beside parents, brothers and sisters, cousins, uncles, aunts and other kinfolk. Most were trained to be field hands by white masters or overseers and by their parents. Though these young hands were forced to work for the master, they quickly learned from their kinfolk to work at the pace that black adults set and to practice the skills necessary to "put massa on."

At about the same age, some privileged boys began to learn a craft from whites or (on the larger plantations) from their skilled kinfolk. Charles Carroll's plantations provide an example of how skills were passed from one generation of Afro Americans to another. Six of the eighteen (33 percent) artisans on his plantations under 25 years of age in 1773 probably learned their trade from fathers and another four (22 percent) from other kinfolk skilled in that occupation. For example, Joe, 21, and Jack, 19, were both coopers and both sons of Cooper Joe, 63. Joe also learned tc be a wheelwright, and in turn probably helped train his brothers-in-law, Elisha, 11, and Dennis, 9, as wheelwrights.[43]

Beginning to work coincided with the departure of many children from their parents, siblings, and friends. The ages of slaves in single slave households in Prince George's in 1776 (table 8.3) suggest that children were typically forced to leave home between 7 and 15 years of age, and this included many between 7 and 10. Young blacks were most frequently forced from large plantations to smaller farms.[44] The parents' authority was eliminated, and the child left the only community he had known. Tension and unhappiness often resulted. For example, Hagar, age 14, ran from her master in Baltimore in 1766. "She is supposed to be harbor'd in some Negro Quarter," he claimed, "as her Father and Mother Encourages her in Elopements, under a Pretense she is ill used at home."[45]

TABLE 8.3
Age of Slaves in One-Slave Households, 1776

Age Group	*Slaves in One-Slave Households* — *Number*	*Percentage*	*Number in Age Group*	*Percentage of Age Group in One-Slave Households*
0–4	1	1	657	*
5–9	15	19	526	3
10–14	21	27	473	4
15–19	12	15	329	4
20–29	10	13	533	2
30–39	7	9	353	2
40+	12	15	431	3
Totals	78	99	3,302	2

Source: Prince George's County Census of 1776. All but two of the fifteen slaves in the 5-9 category were ages 7, 8, or 9. Eight of the slaves in the 15–19 category were age 15.

* = less than ½.

Courtship and marriage were highly significant *rites de passage* for many Afro-American men and women. The process began earlier for women: while men probably married in their mid- to late twenties, women usually married in their late teens.[46] Men initiated the courtship. They typically searched for wives, visiting numbers of neighboring plantations, and often found a wife near home, though not on the same quarter. Some evidence for this custom, suggestive but hardly conclusive, can be seen in the sex and age of runaways. Only 9 percent (22/233) of all Southern Maryland runaways, 1745–79, were women. Few men (in terms of the total population) ran away in their late teens, but the numbers rose in the early twenties when the search for wives began, and crested between twenty-five and thirty-four when most men married and began families. Courtship on occasion ended in a marriage ceremony, sometimes performed by a Roman Catholic or Anglican clergyman, sometimes celebrated by the slaves themselves.[47] (See table 8.4.)

Marriage was more important for women than men. After the relationship was consummated, the woman probably stayed with her family (parents and siblings) until a child was born, unless she could form a household with her husband.[48] Once she had a child, she moved from her parents' home into her own hut. Though almost all women were field laborers, their role as wives and mothers gave them a few privileges. Masters sometimes treated

TABLE 8.4
Ages of Runaway Men, 1770–1779, Southern Maryland

Age Group	*Number in Group*	*Percentage in Group*	*Percentage, 1776 Census*	*Percentage in in Group/ Percentage in 1776*
15-19	4	6	19	.30
20-24	22	31	19	1.65
25-29	22	31	15	2.01
30-34	17	24	11	2.13
35-39	3	4	8	.50
40-49	4	6	13	.43
50+	0	0	15	.00
Totals	72	102	100	1.00

Source: All runaway slave ads published in the *Maryland Gazette*, 1745–79, the *Maryland Journal*, 1773–79, and *Dunlap's Maryland Gazette*, 1775–79, from Prince George's, Charles, Calvert, Frederick (south of Monocacy River), and Anne Arundel (south of Severn River, excluding Annapolis) counties, and any slave born in or traveling to those areas. Each slave runaway equals a single observation, but when the same slave ran away twice during the same time period, he was counted only once. The fourth column is from Prince George's County Census, 1776, and is included to provide a rough test of the likelihood that slaves of particular ages will run away. The index in the last column is a more precise measure of the same thing: an index of 2.01 means that about twice as many slaves in that age group ran away as one would expect from the age structures in 1776.

pregnant women—and their children after birth—with greater than usual solicitude. For example, Richard Corbin, a Virginia planter, insisted in 1759 that his steward be "Kind and Indulgent to pregnant women, and not force them then with Child upon any service or hardship that will be injurious to them." Children were "to be well looked after."[49]

There was less change in the life of most new husbands. Many continued to live with other adult men. Able to visit his family only at night or on holidays, the nonresident husband could play only a small role in childrearing. If husband and wife lived together, however, they established a household. The resident father helped raise his children, taught them skills, and tried to protect them from the master. Landon Carter reacted violently when Manuel tried to help his daughter. "Manuel's Sarah, who pretended to be sick a week ago, and because I found nothing ailed her and would not let her lie up she ran away above a week and was catched the night before last and locked up; but somebody broke open the door for her. It could be none but her father Manuel, and he I had whipped."[50]

On large plantations, mothers could call upon a wide variety of kin to help them raise their children: husbands, siblings, cousins, and uncles or aunts might be living in nearby huts. Peter Harbard learned from his grandmother, father, and paternal uncles how his grandmother's indentures were burned by Henry Darnall and how she was forced into bondage. He "frequently heard his grandmother Ann Joice say that if she had her just right that she ought to be free and all her children. He hath also heard his Uncles David Jones, John Wood, Thomas Crane, and also his father Francis Harbard declare as much." Peter's desire for freedom, learned from his kinfolk, never left him. In 1748, he ran away twice toward Philadelphia and freedom. He was recaptured, but later purchased his freedom.[51]

As Afro-Americans grew older, illness and lack of stamina cut into their productivity, and their kinfolk or masters were forced to provide for them. On rare occasions, masters granted special privileges to favored slaves. When Thomas Clark died in 1766, he gave his son Charles "my faithful old Negro man Jack whom I desire may be used tenderly in his old age." Charles Ball's grandfather lived as an old man by himself away from the other slaves he disliked. Similarly, John Wood, Peter Harbard's uncle, was given his own cabin in his old age.[52]

Many old slaves progressed through several stages of downward mobility. Artisans and other skilled workers became common field hands. While 10 percent of men between 40 and 59 years of age were craftsmen, only 3 percent of men above 60 years of age held similar positions.[53] Mulatto Ned, owned by Gabriel Parker of Calvert County, was a carpenter and cooper most of his life, but he had lost that job by 1750 when he was 65. Abraham's status at Snowden's Iron Works in Anne Arundel County changed from master founder to laborer when he could not work full time. As slaves became feeble, some masters refused to maintain them adequately, or sold them to unwary buyers. An act passed by the Maryland Assembly in 1752 complained that "sundry Persons in this Province have set disabled and superannuated Slaves free who have either perished through want or otherwise become a Burthen to others." The legislators uncovered a problem: in 1755, 20 percent of all the free Negroes in Maryland (153/895) were "past labour or cripples," while only 2 percent (637/29,141) of white men were in this category. To remedy the abuse, the assembly forbade manumission of slaves by will, and insisted that masters feed and clothe their old and ill slaves. If slaveholders failed to comply, they could be fined £4 for each offense.[54]

As Afro-American slaves moved from plantation to plantation through the life cycle, they left behind many friends and kinfolk, and established relationships with slaves on other plantations. And when young blacks married off their quarter, they gained kinfolk on other plantations. Both of these patterns can be illustrated from the Carroll plantations. Sam and Sue, who lived on Sam's quarter at Doohoregan Manor, had seven children between 1729 and 1751. In 1774, six of them were spread over four different quarters at Doohoregan: one son lived with his father (his mother had died); a daughter lived with her family in a hut near her father's; a son and daughter lived at Frost's; one son headed Moses' quarter; and a son lived at Riggs. Figure 8.3 shows how marriages increased the size and geographic spread of Fanny's relations. A third of the slaves (85/255) who lived away from Riggs Quarter (the main plantation) were kin to Fanny or her descendants. Two of Kate's children married into Fanny's family; Kate and one son lived at Frost's and another son lived at Jacob's. Cecilia, the daughter of Carpenter Harry and Sophia married one of Fanny's grandchildren. Harry and Sophia lived with three of their children at Frost's, and two of their sons lived at Riggs, where they were learning to be wheelwrights with kinsperson Joe, son of Cooper Joe.[55]

Since husbands and wives, fathers and children, and friends and kinfolk were often physically separated, they had to devise ways of maintaining their close ties. At night and on Sundays and holidays, fathers and other kinfolk visited those family members who lived on other plantations. Fathers had regular visiting rights. Landon Carter's Guy, for instance, visited his wife (who live on another quarter) every Monday evening.[56] Kinfolk, friends, and neighbors gathered in the yard around the slave cabins and talked, danced, sang, told stories, and drank rum through many an evening and special days on larger plantations.[57] These visits symbolized the solidarity of slave families and permitted kinfolk to renew their friendships, but did not allow nonresident fathers to participate in the daily rearing of their children.

The forced separation of Afro-American kinfolk by masters was not entirely destructive. Slave society was characterized by hundreds of interconnected and interlocking kinship and friendship networks that stretched from plantation to plantation and from county to county. A slave who wanted to run away would find kinfolk, friends of kinfolk, or kinfolk of friends along his route who willingly would harbor him for a while.[58] As Afro-American kinship and friendship networks grew ever larger, the proportion of runaways who were harbored for significant periods of time on slave quarters seemed to have increased in both Maryland and Virginia.[59]

There were three different reasons for slaves to use this underground. Some blacks, like Harry—who left his master in 1779, stayed in the neighborhood for a few weeks and then took off for Philadelphia—used their friends, and kinfolk's hospitality to reach freedom.[60] Others wanted to visit. About 27 percent of all runaways from Southern Maryland mentioned in newspaper advertisements from 1745 to 1779 (and 54 percent of all those whose destinations were described by masters) ran away to visit. For example, Page traveled back and forth between Piscataway and South River in 1749, a distance of about forty miles, and was not caught. He must have received help at many quarters along his route. And in 1756, Kate, 30 years old, ran away from her master, who lived near Georgetown on the Potomac. She went to South River about thirty miles distant, where she had formerly lived. Friends

TABLE 8.5
Profile of Runaways Who Visited Other Slaves, 1745–1779, Southern Maryland

	Motive of Runaway Slave				
Years	*To Visit Spouse*	*To Visit Other Kinfolk*	*To Visit Friends*	*Number of Runaways*	*Number of Visitors/ Number of Runaways*
1745–54	2	2	4	30	.267
1755–59	3	0	4	25	.280
1760–64	0	0	1	29	.035
1765–69	1	1	3	23	.217
1770–74	7	3	11	57	.368
1775–79	7	3	11	69	.304
Totals	20	9	34	233	—
% All Runaways	9	4	15	27	
% All Visitors	32	14	54	100	

Source: See table 8.4. Each slave runaway equals a single observation, but when the same slave ran away twice during the same time period, he was counted only once. The "to visit spouse" column includes husbands and wives who ran off together; the "to visit friends" column includes all slaves who visited friends, were harbored on slave quarters, or who returned to the neighborhood of a former home. (The listing of former homes is insufficient; the master must have asserted that the slave went there.) The categories are exclusive and should be read from left to right: an ad that mentions both visiting a spouse and visiting a friend is placed in the "to visit spouse" column. There were 203 ads in total. New Negroes were counted; 15 slaves could be identified as new Negroes, and if excluded from the table, the pattern would not change.

concealed her there. Her master feared that since "she had been a great Rambler, and is well known in *Calvert* and *Anne Arundel* Counties, besides other parts of the Country," Kate would "indulge herself a little in visiting her old Acquaintances," but spend most of her time with her husband at West River.[61]

Indeed, 20 of 233 Maryland runaways (9 percent) left masters to join their spouses. Sue and her child Jem, 18 months old, went from Allen's Freshes to Port Tobacco, Charles County, a distance of about ten miles, "to go and see her husband." Sam, age 30, lived about thirty miles from his wife in Bryantown, Charles County, when he visited her in 1755. Will had to go over a hundred miles, from Charles to Frederick County, to visit his wife, because her master had taken her from Will's neighborhood to a distant quarter.[62]

This essay has pointed to the basic cultural and demographic cleavage between African and Afro-American families. African immigrants, like free and servant immigrants from Britain, remembered their native land but had to adjust to the new conditions of the Chesapeake. As free Africans they had lived among many kinfolk; in the Chesapeake, kin ties were established with difficulty. Because most immigrants were young adult males and because plantations were small, two-parent households were rare. Mothers, by default became the major black influence upon Afro-American children.

After immigration from Africa slowed, the sex ratio declined, and plantation sizes increased. As generation followed generation, Afro-Americans in Maryland and Virginia created an extensive kinship system. More households, especially on large plantations, included two parents and their children. Although most households did not include kinfolk other than the immediate family, other relations lived in adjacent huts. Mothers and children worked in the tobacco fields with kinfolk, ate and celebrated with many relations, and invited kin who lived elsewhere to share in the festivities. Afro-Americans forcibly separated from relatives managed to maintain contact with them. And finally, slave resistance—whether expressed in the fields or by running away—was fostered and encouraged by kinfolk.

This article has attempted to portray African and Afro-American family life among slaves in the eighteenth-century Chesapeake. It is based upon all the available evidence and upon speculations from that evidence. Many important questions about black family life in the colonial period remain to be answered. In the first place, we need to know more about household and family structure. Could the same structures be found in other parts of the region? In South Carolina? In the northern and middle colonies? Was the pattern of change described here repeated in other areas? Secondly, we must go beyond this essay and describe in greater detail the nature of the Afro-American developmental cycle and the emotional content of relationships among kinfolk in various places at different times. When this work is completed, a clearer picture of changes in slave family life from the 1670s to the 1850s, and of regional differences in black family structure, ought to emerge.

NOTES

1. Prince George's County Court Record O, f. 414, ms., Hall of Records, Annapolis, Md., hereafter cited as PG Ct. Rec.; *Maryland Gazette* (Annapolis), 12 March 1772. All manuscripts, unless otherwise noted, can be found at the Hall of Records.

2. Pioneering essays by Russell Menard, "The Maryland Slave Populaticn, 1658-1730: A Demographic Profile of Blacks in Four Counties," *William and Mary Quarterly*, 3d ser. 32 (1975):29-54, and Peter Wood, *Black Majority: Negroes in Colonial South Carolina through the Stono Rebellion* (New York, 1974), ch. 5, suggest some characteristics of colonial black families. Much more is known about slave families in the nineteenth century. Herbert G. Gutman, *The Black Family in Slavery and Freedom, 1750-1925* (New York, 1976) is the standard reference. Other studies include Eugene D. Genovese, *Roll, Jordan, Roll: The World the Slaves Made* (New York, 1974), pp. 443-524; E. Frank Frazier, "The Negro Slave Family," *Journal of Negro History* 15 (1930):198-266; John Blassingame, *The Slave Community: Plantation Life in the Ante-Bellum South* (New York, 1972), ch. 3; George P. Rawick, *From Sundown to Sunup: The Making of the Black Community* (New York, 1972), ch. 5.

3. There are no standard definitions of household, domestic group, and family. I have borrowed my definitions of household and domestic group from Donald R. Bender, "A Refinement of the Concept of Household: Families, Co-residence, and Domestic Functions," *American Antropologist* 69 (1967):493-504, quote on p. 498. The use of "immediate family," "near kin," and "distant kin" were suggested to me by Herbert Gutman, and would be rejected by Bender.

4. Sidney W. Mintz and Richard Price, "The Study of Afro-American Culture History: Some Suggestions" (working paper presented to the Schouler Lecture Symposium, Creole Societies in the Americas and Africa, John Hopkins University, April 1973) cited with the permission of Mr. Mintz. This paper will be published in fall, 1976 by Ishi Publications, Philadelphia, as *An Anthropological Approach to the Afro-American Past: A Caribbean Perspective*, Occasional Papers in Social Change. A more systematic application of these hypotheses to the colonial Chesapeake will be found in Allan Kulikoff, "Tobacco and Slaves: Population, Economy, and Society in Eighteenth-Century Prince George's County, Maryland" (Ph.D. diss., Brandeis University, 1976), ch. 6.

5. It is difficult to be more precise because most data on African kinship systems comes from twentieth-century anthropological works. The following works suggest variations in African kinship patterns: A. R. Radcliffe-Brown, "Introduction" to *African Systems of Kinship and Marriage*, ed. Radcliffe-Brown and Daryll Ford (London, 1950), pp. 1-85; Meyer Fortes, "Kinship and Marriage among the Ashanti," ibid., pp. 252-84; Jack Goody, *Comparative Studies in Kinship* (Stanford, 1969), ch. 3; Robert Bain, *Bangwa Kinship and Marriage* (Cambridge, England, 1972); William J. Goode, *World Revolutions and Family Patterns* (New York, 1963), pp. 167-200.

6. Mintz and Price, "Afro-American Culture History," pp. 56-78 but esp. pp. 61-62; John S. Mbiti, *African Religions and Philosophy* (New York, 1969), pp. 104-9.

7. Goode, *World Revolutions*, pp. 167-68, 196; Mbiti, *African Religions*, pp. 142-45. Women in polygynous societies also nursed infants for three to four years and abstained from intercourse during part of that period. If this pattern was repeated in the Chesapeake, it was partially responsible for the low gross birth rate among blacks in seventeenth-century Maryland; see Kulikoff, "Tobacco and Slaves," ch. 4; Menard, "Maryland Slave Population," p. 41; Mbiti, *African Religions*, p. 111. For polygyny on the Eastern Shore, see "Eighteenth-Century Maryland as Portrayed in the 'Itinerant Observations' of Edward Kimber," *Maryland Historical Magazine* 51 (1956):327.

8. For Maryland, see Kulikoff, "Tobacco and Slaves," ch. 4, table 4-3; Menard, "Maryland Slave Population," p. 32, for sex ratios; Kulikoff, "Tobacco and Slaves," ch. 6, for density. For Virginia, see Robert A. Wheeler, "Mobility of Laborers in Surry County, Virginia, 1674-1703;; (paper presented at the Stony Brook, N.Y. Conference on Early Social History, June 1975), p. 6.

9. For the uprising of 1739 and some evidence concerning the competition of whites and Afro-Americans for African and Afro-American women, see Kulikoff, "Tobacco and Slaves," ch. 6.

10. Mintz and Price, "Afro-American Culture History," pp. 35-37, 61-62; Kulikoff, "Tobacco and Slaves," ch. 4, tables 4-2 and 4-3; PG Inventories, 1730-69, mss. Large plantations were those with ten or more adult slaves.

11. Menard, "Maryland Slave Population," pp. 42-47; Kulikoff, "Tobacco and Slaves," ch. 4, table 4-1 shows mean age at conception of first child of slave women born 1710-39 to be about 17.6.

12. These statements are based upon PG Wills, mss., for the 1730s and 1740s.

13. See the inventory of the plantation of Daniel Carroll of Duddington found in the Charles Carroll of Annapolis Account Book, ms 220, Maryland Historical Society, Baltimore (the inventory was never probated). The inventory was taken in 1735, a time of high slave imports, but Carroll sold rather than bought slaves. There were only two men between 15 and 29 years of age (but twelve women) on his plantations, and seven above 60; two of the four men in their 40s, two of the three in their 50s, and six of seven in their 60s or older lived with wives and children.

14. White common-law husbands found open cohabitation with black women socially undesirable. When William Hardie of Prince George's accused Daniel Carroll of Upper Marlborough, a wealthy merchant of the same county, of buggery and of keeping mulattoes, since "he . . . could use them as he pleased," Carroll sued him for slander, finding both charges equally harmful; see Clinton Ashley Ellefson, "The County Courts and the Provincial Courts of Maryland, 1733-1764" (Ph.D. diss., University of Maryland, 1963), pp. 544-46.

15. PG Inventories, 1730-44.

16. Menard, "Maryland Slave Population," pp. 42-46; Kulikoff, "Tobacco and Slaves," ch. 4.

17. These points are fully developed in Kulikoff, "Tobacco and Slaves," ch. 6.

18. These statements are based upon PG Wills, 1730-69 and court cases discussed below.

19. PG Wills, 1730-69; mortgages in PG Land Records, libers T, Y, and PP, mss. Estate sales were sometimes advertised in the *Maryland Gazette*. Slaves could not be sold from an estate until all other moveable property had been used to pay debts. Elie Valette, *The Deputy Commissary's Guide within the Province of Maryland* (Annapolis, 1774), pp. 91, 134-35.

20. Eighteen-century migrations of slaves are discussed in Kulikoff, "Tobacco and Slaves," ch. 4, and slave migrations in the nineteenth century are analyzed in idem, "Black Society and the Economics of Slavery," *Maryland Historical Magazine* 70 (1975):208-10.

21. Court of Appeals of the Western Shore, BW no. 10(1800-1801), ff. 456-83, but esp. ff. 459-60, mss.

22. Chancery Papers no. 5241 (1788) mss.; PG Wills 1:280-5; PG Original Wills, box 7, folder 66, and box 13, folder 51, mss.; PG Inventories DD no. 1, ff. 22-24; DD no. 2, ff. 379-86; GS no. 1 ff. 246-48; and ST no. 1, ff. 96-100.

23. Chancery Records 16:298-304, ms.; PG Land Record PP (second part) 4; NN, f. 407; PG Original Wills, box 7, folder 3, and box 9, folder 52; PG Inventories DD no. 1, ff. 438-41, and GS no. 2, ff. 111-12.

24. About 40 percent of Prince George's slaves lived on large units from 1750 to 1779 (estimate based upon probate inventories), and 52 percent of the slaves in that county lived on big units in 1790 (federal census); see Kulikoff, "Tobacco and Slaves," table 6-1 for references.

25. Large in-migrations of Africans to the Chesapeake region occurred in the 1670s and 1690s (see Kulikoff, "Tobacco and Slaves," ch. 4, and references there). The great-grandmother of a man born in 1755 could have immigrated from Africa as a young woman in the 1690s.

26. "A List of Negroes on Dooheregan Manor taken in Familys with their Ages Decr 1 1773," and other lists of slaves at Popular Island, Annapolis Quarter, and Annapolis taken in February and July 1774, Carroll Account Book. There were ten quarters on the 10,500 acres of Doohoregan. I am greatly endebted to Edward Papenfuse for calling this list to my attention.

27. Only a handful of people in the Chesapeake colonies owned as many slaves as Carroll. He could therefore afford to keep most of his slave families together, an option not open even to the very large slaveowner with several children and 100 slaves. Nevertheless, two-thirds of Carroll's slaves lived on units with less than 40 people, and 57 percent of them on quarters with less than 30. Only the 130 slaves who lived at Riggs (the main plantation at Doohoregan) developed more extensive kinship networks on a single quarter than was possible for slaves who lived on other large Chesapeake quarters of 15 to 30 slaves.

28. See Menard, "Maryland Slave Population, pp. 35-36 for seventeenth-century examples of quarters named for slave residents.

29. There were 139 married adults (all ages) and single people 21 years and over in the group. While 46 percent of the leaders were over 55, only 11 percent (15/138) of all adults were over 55. The oldest member of a quarter kin group did not necessarily head the list. For example, Carpenter Harry, 46, headed Frost's Quarter even though his mother, Battle Creek Nanny, 78, was also living there.

30. The statistics are means: 36 percent of all slaves counted together, 38 percent with each quarter counted separately (sum of means). The number of people related to leaders on each quarter was as follows:

Quarter	*Leader*	*Age (years)*	*No. of Kin Ties*	*No. on Quarter (excluding leader)*
Riggs	Fanny	69	40	129
Sukey's	Sukey	69	9	21
Moses'	Moses	41	7	18*
Jacob's	Jacob	34	2	21*
Mayara James	Mayara James	65	23	27
Folly	Nacy	45	7	19*
Sam's	Sam	57	6	21
Frost's	Carpenter Henry	46	8	36
Sten's	Judith†	21	7	22
Capt. Field's	Phil	34	3	7*
House Servants at Annapolis	Johnny	30	4	12
Annapolis	Peter	60	13	16
Popular Island	James	73	3	25*

Note: The first ten quarters listed were all on Doohoregan. Because affines were unknown (except for Riggs, where they were eliminated for the sake of comparison), the figures are minimums.

*Only known relations were immediate family.

†Daughter of Long Grace, 47, on that quarter, who had lost the use of her feet.

31. Only a maximum of 6 percent of all the slaves in Prince George's, Anne Arundel, Charles, and St. Mary's Counties, Md., in 1790, lived on units of more than 100. (The 6 percent is a maximum number because the census taker sometimes put slaves from several of the same master's quarters in the same entry.) *Heads of Families at the First Census of the United States Taken in the Year 1790; Maryland* (Washington, 1907), pp. 9-16, 47-55, 92-98, 104-9.

32. Joe married his mother's sister's husband's mother's grandchild.

33. See Kulikoff, "Tobacco and Slaves," ch. 7.

34. Jack Greene, ed., *The Dairy of Landon Carter of Sabine Hall, 1752-1778* (Charlottesville, 1965), p. 840 (27 July 1775).

35. Kimber, "Itinerant Observations," p. 327. See Kulikoff, "Tobacco and Slaves," ch. 6, for a fuller description of slave quarters.

36. Three of the structures are in St. Mary's; the other once stood in Prince George's. I am indebted to Cary Carson, coordinator of research, St. Mary's City Commission, for sharing the data on St. Mary's with me, and to Margaret Cook (a local historian, who lives in Oxon Hill,

Md.) for her descriptions and slides of the Prince George's hut. These ideas will be expanded elsewhere.

37. On a small plantation a slave quarter located in a kitchen is described in Provincial Court Judgments, EI no. 4, ff. 110–12, ms.

38. For a similar perspective on the succession of households and on life cycles, see Lutz Berkner, "The Stem Family and the Developmental Cycle of the Peasant Household: An Eighteenth-Century Austrian Example," *American Historical Review* 77 (1972):398–418.

39. For the matricentral cell, see Meyer Fortes, "Introduction," to *The Developmental Cycle in Domestic Groups*, ed. Jack Goody, Cambridge Papers in Social Anthropology, no. 1 (Cambridge, 1958), pp. 1–14, but esp. p. 9, and Sidney W. Mintz, "A Final Note," *Social and Economic Studies* 10 (1961):528–535, but esp. pp. 532–33.

40. Samuel Stanhope Smith, *An Essay on the Causes of the Variety of Complexion and Figure in the Human Species* (Philadelphia, 1787), p. 35; ibid., ed. Winthrop D. Jordan (Cambridge, Mass., 1965 [reprint of 1810 ed.]), pp. 61–62, 156–57.

41. Prince George's County Census, 1776, found in Gaius Marcus Brumbaugh, ed., *Maryland Records, Colonial Revolutionary, County, and Church,* 2 vols. Lancaster, Pa., 1915–28), 1–88. Since most of the county's large plantations (located on the Patuxent side of the county) are not on the census, the figures overestimate the proportion of children without playmates. The distribution of children on plantations is as follows:

No. of Children	*Percentage of Children in Age Groups*		
on Plantations	*0-4 years*	*5-9 years*	*0-14 years*
1	14	18	8
2-4	45	51	33
5-9	22	19	29
10+	19	11	31
Total Percent	100	99	101
Number	657	526	1,183

42. Kulikoff, "Tobacco and Slaves," ch. 7.

43. Carroll Account Book. Elisha and Dennis were sons of Carpenter Harry and Sophia. Joe married Dinah of Kate and Ceasar; her brother married Cecilia of Harry and Sophia. Elishia and Dennis were therefore Joe's wife's brother's wife's brothers.

44. See table 8.3. Only the children of slaveowners or those who had just bought their first slave were likely to have only one slave, so this data is a useful indicator of the age children were first sold. The transfers from large to small plantations can be seen in the fact that 12 percent of all slaves 10 to 14 years of age on large plantations, but 43 percent on small farms, lived away from parents and kinfolk (see tables 8.1 and 8.2).

45. *Maryland Gazette,* 1 Oct. 1766.

46. Kulikoff, "Tobacco and Slaves," table 4–1, shows that the median age at first conception for slave women born 1710-59 was 17 years. Age at marriage cannot be determined with precision but can be approximated from the age differences of husbands and wives. On the Carroll, Addison, and Wardrop plantations, 47 husbands were 6.8 years (mean) older than their wives, Carroll Account Book; PG Inventories GS no. 1, f. 73; GS no. 2, ff. 334–36.

47. Thomas Hughes, *History of the Society of Jesus in North America Colonial and Federal,* 4 vols. (London, 1910–17), *Text, 1645–1773,* 2:560–61; William Stevens Perry, ed., *Historical Collections Relating to the American Colonial Church,* 4 vols. (Davenport, Iowa, 1870), 4:306–7; Thomas Bacon, *Four Sermons upon the Great and Indispensible Duty of All Christian Masters and Mistresses to Bring Up Their Negro Slaves in the Knowledge and Fear of God* (London, 1750), pp. v, vii.

48. Sixty percent of all marriages of slave women, 1740–59 birth cohorts, took place between 16 and 19 years of age (marriages defined as age at first conception), Kulikoff, "Tobacco and Slaves," table 4–1. Substantial numbers of these teenage girls should have been pregnant with their first children between ages 16 and 19. If they were living with husbands, then their households would include only a husband and wife. On the three large plantations analyzed in table 8.1, there were only three husband-wife households, and the women in them were 19, 27, and 56 years old. There is evidence that five of the sixteen women, 16 to 19 years old, were married—three who had children lived with sisters; one lived with her husband; one was

separated from her husband but had no children; and the other lived with her husband and children. Ten of the other eleven lived with their parents.

49. For female occupations, see Kulikoff, "Tobacco and Slaves," ch. 7; quote from William Kauffman Scarborough, *The Overseer: Plantation Management in the Old South* (Baton Rouge, 1966), pp. 183-84.

50. Greene, *Diary of Landon Carter*, p. 777 (22 Sept. 1773).

51. Court of Appeals of the Western Shore, BW no. 10 (1800-1801), ff. 459-60; *Maryland Gazette*, 2 Nov. 1748.

52. PG Original Wills, box 10, folder 35; Charles Ball, *Fifty Years in Chains* (1836; New York, 1970), pp. 21-22; Court of Appeals of the Western Shore, BW no. 10, f. 549 (1802). These were the only examples I found in all the wills and court records I examined.

53. Kulikoff, "Tobacco and Slaves," table 7-6. Ages were collected from PG Inventories, 1730-69.

54. Snowden Account Book, Private Accounts, ms.; Inventories 43:320, ms.; Chancery Records, 7:2-12, 25-34, 50-52; William Hand Browne, et al., eds. *Archives of Maryland*, 72 vols. (Baltimore, 1883-), 50:76-78; *Gentleman's Magazine* 34 (1764):261. For two examples of ill slaves sold from master to master, see *Maryland Journal*, 28 Sept. 1778, and Chancery Records 16:469-78 (1789).

55. Carroll Account Book.

56. Greene, *Diary of Landon Carter*, pp. 329, 348, 648, 845, 1109-10; *Maryland Gazette*, 11 July 1771.

57. See references cited in Kulikoff, "Tobacco and Slaves," ch. 6, note 44.

58. My work on slavery owes much to the pioneering book of Gerald Mullin, *Flight and Rebellion: Slave Resistance in Eighteenth-Century Virginia* (New York, 1972), but my perspective on runaways differs from the ones he presents in chapters 3 and 4 of his book. Mullin has, I believe, missed the significance of kin networks in helping most runaways.

59. See table 8.5; Kulikoff, "Tobacco and Slaves," table 6-4; Mullin, *Flight and Rebellion*, p. 129, shows that the proportion of visitors (as defined in table 8.5) increased from 29% before 1775 to 38% of all runaways whose destinations can be determined from 1776 to 1800. The major problem with this data and Mullin's is the large number of unknowns (52% in Maryland and 40% in Virginia).

60. *Maryland Gazette*, 6 July 1779. Other examples of slaves using the underground to escape slavery are found in ibid., 28 April 1757, and 11 July 1771.

61. Ibid., 4 Oct. 1749; 11 Nov. 1756; for other extensive visiting networks, see ibid., 11 Aug. 1751; 12 March 1772; 30 Jan. and 22 May 1777.

62. Ibid., 9 March 1758; 6 Feb. 1755, and 12 Aug. 1773; table 8.7. John Woolman claimed that husbands and wives were often separated, *The Journal of John Woolman* (Corinth ed., New York, 1961), p. 59.

FREE BLACK WOMEN AND THE QUESTION OF MATRIARCHY: PETERSBURG, VIRGINIA, 1784-1820

SUZANNE LEBSOCK

In 1853, Eliza Gallie, a middle-aged, free black woman of Petersburg, Virginia, was arrested and charged with stealing cabbages from the patch of Alexander Stevens, a white man. She was tried in Mayor's Court and sentenced to thirty-nine lashes. There was nothing unusual in this; free black women were frequently accused of petty crimes, and for free blacks, as for slaves, whipping was the punishment prescribed by law. What made the case a minor spectacle was that Eliza Gallie had resources, and she fought back. She filed an appeal immediately, and two weeks later she hired three of Petersburg's most eminent attorneys and one from Richmond as well. "If the Commonwealth, God bless her, has not met her match in Miss Liza," a local newspaper commented, "it won't be for lack of lawyers." The case came up in Hustings Court in March 1854. Gallie's lawyers argued first of all that her ancestors were of white and Indian blood and that she should therefore be tried as a white person. The court was unconvinced. On the trial's second day, her counsel argued that she was innocent of the theft. The court was again unconvinced. Gallie was pronounced guilty and sentenced to "twenty lashes on her bare back at the public whipping post . . . ." At first she set another appeal in motion, but deciding that the case was hopeless, Eliza Gallie dismissed her lawyers and took her punishment.[1]

Gallie's case was in many ways an unusual one, and yet her story cuts straight to the central contradiction in our common image of the historic black woman. Eliza Gallie was, relatively speaking, a powerful woman, propertied, autonomous (divorced, actually), and assertive. But she was helpless in the end, the victim of the kind of deliberate humiliation that for most of us is past im-

Feminist Studies 8, no. 2 (Summer 1982). © 1982 by Feminist Studies, Inc.

agining. So it is with our perception of the history of black women as a group. On the one hand, we have been told that black women, in slavery and afterward, were formidable people, "matriarchs" in fact. On the other hand, we know that all along, black women were dreadfully exploited. Rarely has so much power been attributed to so vulnerable a group.

The contradiction can be ironed out, with sufficient attention to definition and evidence. All the evidence used here comes from Petersburg, Virginia, and it comes mainly from the Petersburg of Eliza Gallie's youth, when the first generation out of slavery, the women emancipated in the wake of the American Revolution, established a pattern of female responsibility radically different from that prevailing among whites. Petersburg had fewer than seven thousand residents in 1820, but for its time and region, it was a city of some consequence. Flour milling, tobacco manufacture, and the commerce generated by the farmers of Southside Virginia sustained Petersburg's growth, while the horse races and the theater gave it touches of urban glitter. Only two cities in Virginia had larger populations, and no other Virginia town had a higher proportion of free blacks among its people. Before the statute of 1806 brought manumissions to a near standstill, Petersburg's free black population grew at a prodigious pace, its size swelled by a high rate of emancipation in the town itself and by the hundreds of migrants from the countryside who came in search of kin, work, and community. By 1810, there were over one thousand free blacks in Petersburg; nearly one-third of Petersburg's free people (31.2 percent) were black.[2]

Some definitions are called for. The term "matriarch" has been used in so many different ways that it has become almost useless as a descriptive term. But it should be understood that the word "matriarch" would never have been applied to black women in the first place were it not for our culture's touchiness over reduced male authority within the family. It is a telling fact that "matriarchy" has most often been used as a relative term. That is, women are called matriarchs when the power they exercise relative to men of their own group is in some respect greater than that defined as appropriate by the dominant culture. Given this standard, women need not be the equals of men, much less men's superiors, in order to qualify as matriarchs. The acquisition by women of just one commonly masculine prerogative will do, and hence it becomes possible to attribute matriarchal power to some of society's most disadvantaged people. The woman who had no vote, no money, and no protection under the law was nonetheless a "matriarch," so long as she also had no husband present to compete with her for authority over her children.

Concern over the reduction of male authority has also been the touchstone of scholarship on black family life (relatively little has been written on the history of black women per se). For all the disagreements among scholars on the character of the historic black family, it has been assumed on almost all sides that female-headed families are, and were, pathological. There were two key assertions in the classic thesis advanced by E. Franklin Frazier four decades ago and revived in 1965 in the Moynihan Report. First, as a result of slavery and continued discrimination, an alarming proportion of black families were "matriarchal," that is, the husband/father was either absent or (Frazier added) he was present, but of negligible influence. Second, the woman-dominant family was unstable and disorganized, at once the symptom and cause of severe social pathology among black people.[3] The Frazier-Moynihan thesis came under heavy fire in the 1970s when scholars began to check the matriarchy image for historical accuracy. And yet the historians, too, reinforced the prevailing prejudice against female-headed households. Working for the most part with census data from the second half of the nineteenth century, several historians found that female-headed households were outnumbered by two-parent households. This, along with additional evidence of the statistical insignificance of the woman-headed household, was offered in defense of the Afro-American family: Black families were not generally matriarchal/matrifocal/female-headed (the term varies), therefore they were not disorganized, unstable, or otherwise pathological after all.[4]

This is a dangerous line of defense, and its problems are highlighted when we encounter evidence like that for early Petersburg. Here was a town in which well over half of the free black households were headed by women. Shall we therefore label it a nest of social sickness? It would make better sense to disentangle our evidence from conventional, androcentric value judgments on what is healthy and what is not.

For the time being, it would seem wise to set aside the issue of the integrity of black family life (by what standard, after all, are we to judge it?) and to concentrate instead on the impact of racial oppression on the status of women and on the distribution of power between the sexes. When we do this for Petersburg, we are confronted once again with the dual image of strength and exploitation. Women were prominent among Petersburg's free blacks. They outnumbered the men three to two, they headed more than half of the town's free black households, and they constituted a large segment of the paid labor force of free blacks. Yet this was for the most part the product of wretched poverty and persistent discrimination. The "matriarch" and the victim, it turns out, were usually the same woman.

Still, the fact remains that among free blacks there was less inequality between the sexes than there was among whites; when black women of the present say they have always been liberated, they have a point. Among those free blacks who managed to accumulate property in early Petersburg, a high proportion — about 40 percent — were women. And because they were more likely than their white counterparts to refrain from legal marriage, free black women were more likely to retain legal control over whatever property they did acquire. It may well have been that free black women valued their relative equality and did their best to maintain it.

How all this came to be is not entirely clear, for census data are sketchy, measures of wealth are crude, evidence on the occupational structure is thin, and vital records do not exist. It seems likely, however, that the preponderance of women in the free black population began with the cumulative decisions of emancipators: Women slaves stood the better chance. Before the Virginia legislature tied the hands of would-be emancipators in 1806, 173 slaves were manumitted in Petersburg.[5] Ninety-four of them (54.3 percent) were female. Of the manumitted adults, meanwhile, 59.3 percent (54 of 91) were female. Sexual intimacy, antislavery principle, and economic calculation could all have been responsible for women's easier access to emancipation.

That a number of manumissions resulted from sexual unions would seem to be a good bet for a town full of well-to-do bachelors, many of whom were a long way from home. Documentable cases, however, are few. Only one white emancipator was known to have acknowledged his kinship with his former slaves, and in only two instances is there strong circumstantial evidence of a sexual connection. In 1814, Mary Moore, a "great, large, fat, bouncing-looking" Irish woman, manumitted Sylvia Jeffers, as she was authorized to do by the will of her late brother John Jeffers. Sylvia was apparently John's daughter; in any case, in 1853 she talked the local court into escorting her across the color line, claiming descent from Indians and whites only.[6] Betsy Atkinson, too, won the special affection of her owner. A week after James Gibbon freed her, he wrote his last will. To Atkinson, he left a slave and furniture already in her possession, some livestock, and three hundred dollars.[7]

Anti-slavery principle may also have accounted for the women's edge in emancipation. Under Virginia law, the child inherited the status of the mother. To free a man, therefore, was to guarantee the freedom of but one person. The emancipation of a woman in her childbearing years might secure the freedom of generations.[8]

In the short run, meanwhile, the emancipation of a woman meant a lesser loss of income for the owner. Women suffered a distinct disadvantage in earning power, a disadvantage that began in slavery and that showed in the inability of slave women to purchase themselves. Hiring oneself out was illegal, but both women and men did it, and most of them got away with it.[9] The women who hired themselves out did not, however, command wages equivalent to those of men, or so it appears from the incidence of self-purchase. Self-purchase was uncommon in this period; from 1784 to 1820, just nine of the two hundred slaves emancipated bought themselves. Amy Jackson, who paid her master $410 in 1819, was the sole woman among them.[10]

The same disparity in earning power limited the numbers of slaves whom emancipated women managed to free in turn. Altogether, free blacks themselves were responsible for thirty-three manumissions (one-sixth of the total to 1820), and although about one-half of the black emancipators were women (7 of 15), no woman was able to liberate more than one slave. Graham Bell showed what could be done with a remunerative skill (shoemaking), hard work, and business sense. In 1792, Bell set free his wife, or possibly his daughter, and five sons. From 1801 to 1805, he emancipated his brother, two women, one of whom he had purchased "for the express purpose of manumitting or emancipating her," and a child.[11] No one else came near Bell's record, but four of the other men did manumit at least two slaves. In the years after 1820, several women would join the ranks of the multiple emancipators. Meantime, one apiece was the best they could do.[12]

Emancipation was itself a step up on the economic ladder; the woman at last owned her person and her labor. In Petersburg, she was not likely to own anything else, not in the beginning anyhow. White emancipators expected their former slaves to fend for themselves. James Campbell made it explicit in 1802 when he freed forty-two-year-old Sally, "whom I have reason to believe is an honest woman, and one that will earn by her labour a proper support for herself."[13] A few emancipators may have granted their former slaves some kind of economic assistance, but in only one deed was something promised in writing. Persons manumitted by will did not fare much better. Of the twenty-seven slaves whose freedom was directed by will, only four were staked by their masters, and three of the four were men.[14]

The emancipators no doubt believed they were giving their former slaves an even chance. Given the circumstances under which many of the women were freed, however, making a living would be an uphill struggle. Some emancipators freed the children with the mother, and while this spared the women from trying to save to buy their children (and from the pain of being unable to save enough), it did mean extra mouths to be fed. Most of these women had one child or two, but three or four or five was not unusual.[15] Age was important as well. The emancipators who stipulated the ages of the persons they freed were too few to provide a reliable sample, but the ages that were recorded suggest that relative to the men, the women were disproportionately middle-aged. A large proportion of the women set free were, or would soon be, past their best wage-earning years.

TABLE 1. AGE AT EMANCIPATION

Age	Women	Men
18-30	9	4
31-40	1	4
41-50	8	2
51 and up	0	1

The most significant handicap, however, was the near absence of occupational options. The vast majority of free black women engaged in domestic employment of one kind or another. This was not a matter of choice, and it was more a matter of sex than of race. Nothing made the women's occupational bind plainer than the apprenticeship orders issued by the court for free black children. Among the masters who took on free black boys as apprentices were a carpenter, a cabinetmaker, a painter, a cooper, a barber, a blacksmith, a hatter, a boatman, and a baker. So limited were the girls' options that the clerk hardly ever wasted ink on specifying the trade. The few specific orders contained no surprises. In 1801, Lucy Cook was ordered bound "to learn the business of a Seamstress & Washer." On the same day Polly Flood was "bound to Abby Cook, to learn to Sew & Wash &c untill of lawful age — being now about 9 years of age." Polly was bound to a second master "to learn Household business" five years later. And Polly White, an orphan just five years old, was apprenticed "to Mrs. Brewer to learn the duties of a House Servant."[16]

There were some women who broke the mold and engaged, at least part time, in more specialized occupations. Betty Morris and Aggy Jackson were nurses, Judy Denby and Judy Darvels were midwives. A few engaged in legitimate commerce. Amelia Gallé ran a bath house, Lurany Butler operated a dray, Nelly White was a baker, and Elizabeth Allerque and Sarah Elliott were licensed storekeepers.[17] As with white women, just as many pursued illegitimate commerce. At least five black women were nabbed by the Petersburg Grand Jury for keeping a "tippling house" or for selling liquor without a license.[18] The fact that specific occupations can be identified for only a dozen black women is testimony to the predominance of domestics among them. Cooks, cleaning women, washerwomen, seamstresses, and child-nurturers did not advertise, nor were they likely to surface in any of the public records.[19]

If the gentlemen of the Grand Jury had been asked, they would probably have identified prostitution as a major enterprise of free black women. In 1804, the Grand Jury registered a grievance against the invasion of free black "strangers," many of whom "come only for the purpose of Prostitution . . . ."[20] There is no telling whether or how often free black women in fact resorted to prostitution, but the Grand Jury was right about the invasion. Dismal as economic opportunities were in Petersburg, they were apparently worse in the countryside, particularly for women. Black migration from the country was thus spearheaded by women. By 1820, the sex ratio among free blacks aged fourteen and above was 85.0 (males per 100 females) for eastern Virginia as a whole. In Petersburg it was 64.5.[21]

Petersburg was, relatively speaking, a land of opportunity, and a few of the women emancipated there did register gains. Betty Call was freed on Independence Day, 1786, and within four years she managed to buy her grown son, London, from an Amelia County owner. After ten years, she set him free. Betty Call never did own any real estate, but she was taxed on a female slave (evidently hired) for years, and when she died in 1815, the sale of her household goods netted just over seventy dollars.[22] Emancipated on the same day as her mother, Teresa Call saved for nine years. In 1795, she purchased a small lot and continued to live there for decades.[23] Dolly Clark acquired a female slave five years after her manumission. On the other hand, women like Nancy Hall and Sally Steward accumulated no traceable property. Emancipated in 1799 and 1805, respectively, their continued residence in Petersburg was confirmed by entries in various public record books, but neither of them owned the land or slaves or horses or carriages that would have resulted in their appearance on the tax lists.[24]

New arrivals fared worse than the natives. Only nine free black women were among the town's taxpayers in 1810, and most of them were old-timers. All but one had lived in Petersburg as free women for at least six years. Betty and Teresa Call had both been free for twenty-four years, while Sarah Vaughan held the record for longevity on the tax lists. Vaughan owned real estate when Petersburg's first land tax book was assembled in 1788, and thirty years later she still held, and presumably rented out, her "4 small tenements."[25] On the average, the nine women had been paying taxes for almost nine years, and they held on to what they had. In the decade after 1810 three of them died, but the remaining six, all landowners, were still paying real estate taxes in 1820.

By that time they had more company. In 1820, there were thirty-eight free black women among the taxpayers. However one chooses to measure it, this was an impressive relative increase. In 1810, black women constituted but 2.2 percent of (9 of 413) of the town's taxpayers. In 1820, their proportion was 5.5 percent (38 of 687). The increase is not attributable to any relative growth in the free black female population. A count of the percentage of taxpayers among heads of families does help control for possible population shifts; similarly, it indicates a doubling of property holding among free black women. In 1810, 5.1 percent (7 of 138) of the black women designated as heads of families in the census schedules were also listed in the tax books; by 1820, the proportion had risen to 10.1 percent (17 of 168). All in all, blacks were gaining on whites, women were gaining on men, and black women were gaining on black men.[26]

At least three developments accounted for the sudden economic ascent of a portion of the free black female population. With the deaths of propertied men, a few black women claimed their inheritances. More important were the hard-won savings of the women themselves. And third, it looks very much as though the Panic of 1819 forced slaveholders to put their slaves on the market at prices more women could afford.

Among the black female taxpayers of 1810, only Molly James had acquired her property by inheritance. James was the heir to the house and lot her husband had owned at his death in 1804. By 1820, two more legacies marked the passing of the first generation of prosperous black men. Graham Bell in 1817 left to his wife, Mary, a life estate in one of his town lots, while Elizabeth Graves was daughter and one of two surviving heirs of Richmond Graves, a livery stable operator.[27] Mary Ann Vizonneau and Amelia Gallé, meanwhile, were heirs of white merchants. Vizonneau's Scottish father, John Stewart, had threatened to disown her when she married Andre Thomas Vizonneau. But moments before his death in 1813, Stewart relented and directed that Mary Ann be given "all the money he then had in the Bank and the house & Lot he then lived on," on the condition "that her husband . . . might have no manner of Controul over, or right, to the same." This was a considerable bequest, worth over eighteen thousand dollars, and it made Mary Ann Vizonneau one of the wealthiest women in Petersburg.[28]

Amelia Gallé was also the heir of a white merchant. She had earned her inheritance. Amelia Gallé was still a slave when she first arrived in Petersburg, and she was known by a slave name, Milly Cassurier. In 1800, French merchant Jean Gallé bought her for eighty pounds, and he emancipated her four years later, after she had borne him a son. Jean Gallé died in 1819, and while in his will he termed Milly "my housekeeper," it was clear from the provisions of the will that she had been his wife in every sense but the legal one. He acknowledged her son Joseph as his natural son. He left to the two of them the greater part of his estate. And he enjoined Milly to act as mother to his "mulatto Girl slave" Catherine Gregory, charging her "to support the said Catherine and bring her up to lead a moral and religious life.[29]

Jean Gallé also left to Milly Cassurier his bathhouse, a business she had apparently been running for years. When she assumed sole management of the bathhouse in the spring of 1820, she became the first black businesswoman in Petersburg to exploit the full possibilities of newspaper advertising. At first she settled for a two-sentence announcement that the bathing season had arrived. By midsummer, however, her appeal was more effusive.

> The character of this bath, is so well known that it needs no comment. The subscriber is resolved if possible to improve it, by consulting the comfort and convenience of the visitants — and to enable her to do so more effectually, she humbly solicits a continuation of that patronage which has so liberally supported the institution till this time. Having had several years experience in this business, the subscriber believes she will generally succeed in pleasing — and therefore, with stronger confidence humbly solicits a portion of the public support . . . .

For several years thereafter, she opened the season with just a brief announcement. Two or three months later, as the heat of the Virginia summer grew tediously oppressive, she would follow with greater fanfare. "She has the pleasure of tendering to her patrons," came the notice of May 1823, "her most grateful thanks for their former encouragement, and begs a continuance of the same." August brought the harder sell.

> HEALTH
>
> Purchased Cheap!
>
> In consequence of *Small Change* being scarce, and wishing to contribute towards the health of the ladies and gentlemen, the subscriber has the pleasure to inform her patrons and the public, that she has reduced the price of her baths to 25 CENTS for a single one. She will make no comments on the necessity of Bathing in warm weather: — suffice it to say, that with Mr. Rambaut's FAMILY MEDICINES, and some Cold or Warm BATHS, the health of her friends will keep at a proper degree of the thermometer, without the aid of Calomel or any other mineral Medicines.[30]

These advertisements were not just a means of drumming up business. They were also the means by which a free black claimed for herself the respect due a propertied widow. In her first advertisement, she signed herself "Milly Cassurier." In the second, she was "Milly Galle." She signed the third "Amelia Galle." In the fourth, she was "Amelia Galle, widow." How far others accorded her the respect she asked for is an open question. She made some progress with the census taker, who listed her as "Milly Gallie," but to the tax collector she was still Cassurier, "col^{d} at Galle's."[31]

Amelia Gallé, Mary Ann Vizonneau, Elizabeth Graves, and Mary Bell were the only black female taxpayers of 1820 whose property was (documentably) acquired by inheritance. More significant was the economic maturation of the women themselves, and here the foremost success story belonged to Elizabeth Allerque. "Madame Betsy," she was called, "a French colored woman" who was probably a refugee from St. Dominigue She was, in any case, well connected with Petersburg's French immigrant community, and the connections in combination with her commercial talent spelled steady financial progress. Allerque first opened a store in 1801. At some point she added a partnership with French merchant André Vizonneau (Mary Ann Vizonneau's father-in-law), who in 1809 made sure that Allerque would be paid her full share of the proceeds when the firm was dissolved by his death: "I declare that the partnership which I had entered into with Elizabeth Alergues was joint and equal both as to capital and profit . . . ." Five years later, French physician L. J. Hoisnard wrote his will, charging Allerque with the care and legal guardianship of his daughter. Moreover, "in consideration of her good attention to me during the latter part of my life," Hoisnard left to Allerque and her two children a legacy of a thousand dollars.[32] Even without this bequest, Elizabeth Allerque would have done well for herself. She first invested in real estate in 1806 and improved it several times thereafter. In 1806, too, she became a slaveholder for the first time. Allerque was one of Petersburg's few black commercial slaveholders; in 1806 she advertised in the Richmond and Norfolk newspapers for the return of her runaway woman Charlotte. Madame Betsy died in 1824, free of debt and the owner of land and six slaves.[33]

Most free black women had neither the skills nor the connections of an Elizabeth Allerque, but a few had enough savings to take advantage of the Panic of 1819. While the general economic dislocation that surrounded the Panic must have caused great suffering among many black women, it also afforded the better-placed the opportunity to hire or purchase slaves for the first time. (The tax lists, unhappily, do not indicate whether the taxpayer owned or hired the slave.)[34] As more and more whites scrambled to find the money to pay their debts, more and more slaves were put up for hire or sale, and probably at bargain prices. There is no estimating just how many slaves changed hands during the Panic years. In 1819 and 1820 alone, however, Petersburg owners mortgaged over 240 slaves; these slaves would be sold at auction for whatever they would bring if the owners failed to pay their creditors on schedule.[35]

For the master class the time was unnerving, for the slaves it was potentially disastrous, but for the free black woman with some savings, here was a rare opportunity, a chance to acquire a loved one or a laborer. Three-quarters of the black women taxed in 1820 (27 of 38) made their debuts on the tax lists in 1819 or 1820. And all but two of the newcomers were taxed on one or more slaves.

It was in slaveholding that black women registered their greatest gains by 1820 and in slaveholding that they came closest to economic parity with black men. In 1820, forty-six slaves were held by black men, forty-five by the women. Women were farther from equality in other measures of the black sex ratio of wealth, but they were gaining on the men. Two-fifths (13 of 32) of the black landowners of 1820 were women, a somewhat larger fraction than in 1810.[36] Two-fifths of the black taxpayers of 1820 were women, up from one-fourth in 1810. And two-fifths of the tax collected from free blacks in 1820 was collected from women, again, up from one-fourth in 1810.

Measured against comparable figures for whites, these were stunning proportions. In 1820 women were but 12.8 percent of the white taxpayers (76 of 593), and they accounted for only 3.5 percent of the tax money collected from whites.

This glaring disparity in the status of black and white women relative to men of the same race fades somewhat when sex ratios are taken into consideration. It should also be said that free black women were more likely than were white women to maintain their legal eligibility to control property. Virginia was a common-law state, and the common law made razor-sharp distinctions between single and married women. Single women and widows had the same property rights and obligations as men. But the instant a woman married, she surrendered both her rights and her obligations to her husband; if she had owned taxable property, the surrender was manifested in her summary disappearance from the tax lists.[37]

It is impossible to estimate how many of Petersburg's free black women shunned lawful matrimony, but the qualitative evidence suggests that the proportion was high, higher than among whites. The sex ratio, the law, poverty, and preference conspired to keep a great many free black women single, and to the extent that women remained single, they remained free agents in the economic realm.

The sex ratio and the law together dictated the single life for one-third of Petersburg's free black women. Because blacks were not permitted to marry whites, and slaves were not permitted to marry anyone, the pool of marriageable men was restricted to free blacks, and there were simply not enough of them to go around.

A few black women did take up with whites, and more, apparently, were coupled with slaves. These matches yielded some interesting economic arrangements. Milly Cassurier, when she was still known by that name, acquired property in her own right while she was living with Jean Gallé, something she could not have done had the two of them been married.[38] When a free woman cohabited with a slave, meanwhile, here were the legal materials for a complete sex-role reversal, for the woman assumed all legal rights and responsibilities for the pair. In 1800, a slave named David White was jailed for going at large and trading as a free person. The fine for White's misdeeds fell on his wife, Polly Spruce, a free woman who had hired White for the year and who was therefore legally answerable for his behavior. Nearing her death years later, Jane Cook found it necessary to make special provision for her slave husband, Peter Matthews. Cook had purchased two small boats, "the Democrat and the experiment," as her husband's agent and with his money. These she bequeathed to Matthews, appointing a free black man to act as his agent and to stand guardian to her daughter, to whom she left her own property.[39]

The women whose mates were white or enslaved had no choice but to remain technically single, but it is by no means certain that all of them would have married had they been given the chance. When free black women entered into partnerships with men who were also black and free, legal wedlock was not the inevitable result. For one thing, marrying did cost money. Ministers were authorized to charge one dollar for their services, and the clerk's fee was a quarter. If a poor couple found that amount an obstacle, they likely found it well-nigh impossible to locate a third party willing to post the $150 bond required to obtain the license.[40]

Nonmarriage among free blacks, however, was evidently as much a matter of ethics as of expenses, for even the propertied showed no consistent tendency to make their conjugal ties legal ties. Christian Scott was hardly well-to-do, but he did own some animals and a goodly stock of household furniture; "having for some time past lived with Charlotte Cook by whom I have a son called Jesse Mitchell . . . ," Scott explained, "And being desirous from the friendship & Regard I bear to the said Charlotte Cook & affection to my said Son, to convey the property aforesaid to them," Scott deeded them the property, dividing it exactly as it would have been divided had Scott married Cook and then died intestate (without a will). James Vaughan was far wealthier than Scott. He was also in trouble. In 1806 Vaughan was tried for the murder of "his supposed wife," Milly Johnston. After his conviction, a contrite Vaughan was permitted to write a will to direct the distribution of an estate that included cash and bonds worth over two thousand dollars, a town lot, three horses, and four slaves. Vaughan gave half of his estate to Sarah Vaughan, his daughter by Polly Hull. The other half went to John Vaughan, his son by Ann Stephens. Whether James Vaughan's relationships with Johnston, Hull, and Stephens were simultaneous or sequential is both unclear and beside the point. The point is that he did not marry any of them.[41]

So much the better for the women's control over their property and wages. Polly Hull, for example, bought a town lot a few months before James Vaughan wrote his will and was taxed on it for more than a decade thereafter.[42] There were other free black women in roughly similar circumstances. Charlotte Rollins was part of an uneasy triangle that included a free black named Captain Billy Ash and a slave named Julius. Ash was tried for "shooting and wounding" Julius in 1802, and Rollins's sister and brother-in-law were examined in the case: "On their being asked if Charlotte was wife of the prisoner, it was answered, that they both, the prisoner & Julius, resorted where she was." It is unclear what became of Billy Ash, but Charlotte Rollins never married him or anyone else. In 1810, she was listed as the head of a three-person family, and in 1817, she disposed of her household furniture and kitchen utensils by deed of gift, a probable substitute for the writing of a will. [43] Nelly White, unhappily, was unable to enjoy the property she had acquired in her baking business. In 1811, White was examined on suspicion of knifing a free man named Tom, and a witness described their relationship. "Tom & the Prisoner had lived in the same House, in different apartments — and been considered as man & wife but lived badly together after wrangling." White was convicted in District Court and sent to the penitentiary. She left behind "some property & Estate," and the town sergeant was ordered to look after it while she served her sentence.[44]

A member of one of Petersburg's most prominent free black families, Molly Brander married once, but opted for cohabitation the second time around. The first time, she married Nathan James. After his death in 1804, Molly began a new family, taking James Butler "as her husband tho not lawfully married," and adopting her orphaned niece. Because she did not marry Butler, Molly James retained her rights to the house and lot she had inherited from her first husband, and when she died intestate in 1812, her mother and brothers inherited the property in turn. Before her death, however, Molly James had told her family that she wanted the lot to pass to James Butler and her adoptive daughter; the family complied in 1815 by means of a deed of gift.[45]

Just how commonly black women acquired some kind of property and retained legal control over it by not marrying the men in their lives is a mystery, for evidence surfaces only sporadically in trial reports (hence the prevalence of violent crime in the preceding paragraphs) and in a very occasional deed. Moreover, these few documents give no clues as to whether the women deliberately refused marriage for the sake of maintaining their property rights. The legacy and continued presence of slavery no doubt provided cause enough. Slave marriages were necessarily based on mutual consent; for a good many black couples, consent was sufficient in freedom as well, an attitude that the black churches would combat with mixed success in the decades that followed.[46] Still, it may have been that women so recently emancipated, and women accustomed to providing for themselves, did not give up their legal autonomy lightly.[47] Certainly free black women had unique incentive for staying single. For the woman who hoped to buy an enslaved relative, legal wedlock meant that her plan could be sabotaged at any time by her husband or by her husband's impatient creditors. The common-law disabilities of married women added an ironic twist to chattel slavery's strange fusion of persons and property: Matrimony could pose a threat to the integrity of the free black woman's family.

Whether by necessity, deliberation, or default, sufficient numbers of free black women avoided legal marriage to constitute a major departure from the white norm. The contrast with the experience of white women was sharper still in the extent to which black women shouldered the burden of supporting their families. If most of the women listed by the census taker as "heads of families" were primary breadwinners, then the magnitude of economic responsibility borne by free black women was truly staggering. In 1810, 56.3 percent (138 of 245) of the free black households of Petersburg were headed by women. For 1820, the figure was 58.1 percent (168 of 289). In 1820, these female-headed households sheltered over one-half (52.3 percent) of all free black persons living in black households and an even larger proportion (57.3 percent) of free black children under fourteen.

So uninformative are these early census returns, and so suspect the given numbers, that no satisfactory reconstruction of household composition is possible.[48] From the unembellished hashmarks that made up the 1820 schedules, the one safe conclusion is that there was no typical free black household structure. The most commonplace household type (87 of 289) was, it appears, the female-headed family containing one woman and her (?) children. Further guesswork suggests that the second most frequent arrangement was the male-headed household containing an adult couple and their children (51 of 289).[49] Thirty-seven households were composed of but one person, twenty-nine of them female, and there were apparently twenty-four childless couples. The remaining households, about one-third of the total, contained persons of ages and sexes that defy categorization. Worth noting, however, is the incidence of extended or augmented families. One-fifth of all free black households contained at least one "surplus" person over the age of twenty-five.[50]

It should be emphasized that there was no typical household structure among whites either.[51] The difference was that Petersburg's multiform white households were overwhelmingly male-headed. The proportion of white households headed by women was 15.7 percent in 1810 and 17.0 percent ten years after. In addition, a disproportionately small number of whites lived in these female-headed households. The census taker of 1820 found only 13.3 percent of white children under sixteen resident in female-headed households, while 12.8 percent of all white persons lived in households headed by women.[52]

Nineteenth-century census data usually raise more questions than they answer, and this is particularly true of the early returns. It is impossible to discern the precise family structure within households, much less assess the meaning of familial roles played by neighbors and nonresident kin. This last blind spot is especially troublesome given the probability that for numerous free blacks, spouses and close kin remained the slaves of white owners. Least of all does the census tell us anything about love, commitment, giving children a chance in life — those qualities that despite our disclaimers usually lurk behind our reading of the numbers.

These problems only begin the list of the source limitations that frustrate any attempts to recapture the experience of the mass of free black women. We do know that there was a flourishing free black Baptist church in Petersburg before 1820 and that in 1820 a Sunday school run by free blacks had girls as well as boys among its two hundred students.[53] But there are no records for the church in this period and none at all for the Sunday school. Newspapers reported next to no local news. The whites whose correspondence is preserved wrote of their own kind; only rarely did they discuss their slaves, and free blacks were never mentioned. While the local public records are surprisingly rich, they are decidedly slanted toward the property owners. The majority of free black women thus appear to us only as names — or worse, as numbers — on the census schedules.

The conclusion nevertheless stands. In a slave society of the early nineteenth century, there developed among free blacks a relatively high degree of equality between the sexes. There is not much material here for romanticizing. For free black women, the high rate of gainful employment and the high incidence of female-headed households were symptoms of oppression. Neither was chosen from a position of strength; both were products of a shortage of men and of chronic economic deprivation. The high incidence of female property holding, meanwhile, was largely the consequence of a system that limited the achievement of black men.

Yet there was autonomy of a kind, and the fact that its origins lay in racial subordination should not detract from its significance. The autonomy experienced by the free black women of Petersburg was relative freedom from day-to-day domination by black men. We cannot say for certain how free black people looked on this. The fact that so many couples refrained from legal marriage, however, at least suggests that the women valued their autonomy and that one way or another the men learned to live with it. The tragedy for the nineteenth century — or one of many tragedies — was that white people were unable to use the free black example to call their own gender arrangements into question, that no one outside the free black community took anything positive from the free black experience. Perhaps we can do better.

NOTES

The author wishes to thank the Colonial Williamsburg Foundation and the Woodrow Wilson National Fellowship Foundation Program in Women's Studies for their support of the research on which this article is based. She would also like to thank Sharon Harley for her comments on an earlier version of the article.

[1]*South-Side Democrat,* 29 November, 12 December 1853 (first quotation), 17 March, 18 March, 20 March 1854; Minutes, 15 December 1853, 16 March, 17 March 1854 (second quotation).

All references to minutes, deeds, wills, accounts, and marriages are to the records of the Petersburg Hustings Court, on microfilm in the Virginia State Library, Richmond, Va. References to land books, personal property books, and legislative petitions are to the original manuscripts in the Virginia State Library.

[2]Calculated from *Aggregate Amount of Persons Within the United States in the Year 1810* (Washington, 1811), p. 55a. According to this census, Petersburg contained 1,089 free blacks, 2,173 slaves, and 2,404 whites. The town's free black population grew to only 1,165 by 1820. In reading these figures, allowance shou'd be made for probable undercounting.

[3]E. Franklin Frazier, *The Negro Family in the United States* (Chicago: University of Chicago Press, 1939); U.S. Department of Labor, Office of Policy Planning and Research, *The Negro Family: The Case for National Action* by Daniel P. Moynihan (Washington, D.C.: U.S. Government Printing Office, 1965.) More detailed summaries of these works may be found in the articles by Gutman, Lammermeier, and Shifflett, cited in note 4.

[4]John W. Blassingame, *Black New Orleans 1860-1880* (Chicago and London: University of Chicago Press, 1973), pp. 79-105; Frank F. Furstenberg Jr., Theodore Hershberg, and John Modell, "The Origins of the Female-Headed Black Family: The Impact of the Urban Experience," pp. 211-33; Herbert G. Gutman, "Persistent Myths About the Afro-American Family," pp. 181-210; Crandall A. Shifflett, "The Household Composition of Rural Black Families: Louisa County, Virginia, 1880," pp. 235-60, all in *Journal of Interdisciplinary History* 6 (Autumn 1975); Herbert G. Gutman, *The Black Family in Slavery and Freedom, 1750-1925* (New York: Pantheon Books, 1976), pp. 432-60; Paul J. Lammermeier, "The Urban Black Family of the Nineteenth Century: A Study of Black Family Stucture in the Ohio Valley, 1850-1880," *Journal of Marriage and the Family* 35 (August 1973): 440-56; Elizabeth H. Pleck, "The Two-Parent Household: Black Family Structure in Late Nineteenth-Century Boston," *Journal of Social History* 5 (Fall 1971): 3-31. Pleck, however, does point out the value-laden nature of terms like "family disorganization," and in *Black Migration and Poverty: Boston 1865-1900* (New York: Academic Press, 1979), has reevaluated the significance of two-parent households.

[5]This may be a slight overcount; of the two dozen slaves directed freed by will, some may have remained in slavery due to owners' indebtedness or to litigation. The law of 1806 discouraged manumission by requiring all newly freed persons to leave the state within one year of emancipation, and for a time it was extremely effective. There were no emancipations in Petersburg from 1807 to 1810. Emancipations began again in 1811, but from 1811 to 1820 were granted at less than half their pre-1807 rate, even though a new statute of 1816 made it easier for the manumitted to obtain permission to remain in Virginia.

The female advantage in emancipation seems to have been more than a reflection of the sex ratio among slaves; calculations from the Personal Property Book for 1790 show that females constituted only a 51.5 percent majority of slave adults.

[6]Mary Cumming to Margaret Craig, December 1811, Margaret and Mary Craig Letters, Virginia Colonial Records Project, Alderman Library, University of Virginia, Charlottesville, Virginia (quotation); Wills I, 238 (1796); Deeds IV, 304 (1815); Luther P. Jackson, "Manumission in Certain Virginia Cities," *Journal of Negro History* 15 (July 1930): 310. John Jeffers's will also authorized the emancipation of Sylvia's mother.

[7]Deeds V, 324 (1818); Wills II, 163 (1819).

[8]Luther P. Jackson counted the deeds of emancipation recorded in Petersburg and Richmond from 1784 to 1806 and found more in Petersburg, even though it was the smaller city. This he attributed to the early presence in Petersburg of antislavery Methodists. See Jackson, "Manumission," pp. 281-82. By my count, six Methodists accounted for almost one-fifth of Petersburg emancipations to 1806.

[9]Six women were apprehended and jailed for hiring themselves out. The court had the choice of selling them or fining their masters; two of the six were ordered sold. Minutes, 5 April 1802, 5 September 1803, 2 January, 9 February, 4 April 1809, 6 May 1811. See William Waller Hening, *The New Virginia Justice, Comprising the Office and Authority of a Justice of the Peace in the Commonwealth of Virginia* . . . 2nd. ed. (Richmond: Johnson & Warner, 1810), p. 549.

[10]Deeds VI, 51 (1819).

[11]Deeds II, 157 (1792), III, 58 (quotation), 74 (1802), 236 (1805).

[12]Two of the women freed their sons; no relationship was stated by the others. Deeds II, 174 (1792), 581 (1799), 701 (1800), 737 (1801), Deeds III, 75 (1802), 116 (1803), Deeds V, 325 (1818).

[13]Deeds III, 78 (1802).

[14]Deeds III, 267 (1805); Wills II, 69 (1812), 114 (1815), 139 (1817), 161 (1819).

[15]At least sixteen women were manumitted with their children (this does not include those freed by husbands or other kin from whom they could expect financial assistance). Six had a single child, five had two children, and five had three or more.

[16]Minutes, 1 June 1801, 6 January 1806, 7 August 1809.

[17]Accounts I, 31, 55 (1808), 37 (1809), Accounts II, 189 (1821); Luther Porter Jackson, *Free Negro Labor and Property Holding in Virginia, 1830-1860* (New York and London: D. Appleton-Century Co., 1942), p. 221; Personal Property Books, 1801-1820.

[18]Minutes, 2 November 1790, 5 August 1799, 2 March 1812.

[19]There were probably more gainfully employed women among free blacks than among whites, but because the whites were more likely to escape (paid) domestic service, they are far more visible; specific occupations can be identified for more than 150 white women. These women, with a few exceptions, were milliners, dressmakers, midwives, teachers, and keepers of taverns, boardinghouses, and stores. Meanwhile, the only female occupations in which no free black women were found were teaching and millinery.

[20]Minutes, 4 November 1804.

[21]Calculated from the United States *Census for 1820* (Washington, D.C.: Gales and Seaton, 1821). The imbalance may also have been due to a higher rate of male migration to the free states. It does not appear to have been due to higher mortality rates among men, because the sex ratio was higher (71.3) among free blacks aged forty-five and above.

[22]Deeds I, 270 (1786), Deeds II, 116 (1800); Personal Property Books, 1795-1804; Accounts I, 75 (1817).

[23]Deeds I, 303 (1787), Deeds II, 379 (1795); Land Books, 1795-1820.

[24]Deeds II, 205 (1792), 593 (1799), Deeds III, 237 (1805); Personal Property Books, 1797-1802; Wills II, 69 (1812); Minutes, 5 October 1812, 8 August 1815, 5 March 1816, 17 July, 16 October 1818.

Few of the persons emancipated in Petersburg can be traced. Emancipators stated last names for fewer than one-third of the slaves freed (black emancipators were more prone than whites to state surnames), and because ex-slaves hardly ever took the name of the last owner, inference is of little help.

[25]Land Book, 1820.

[26]Taxable property consisted of land (taxed according to its annual rental value), slaves over twelve years of age (taxed by the head), horses, carriages, and exports from the tobacco warehouses. My calculations include all taxes paid by living individuals, except those paid on tobacco exports, there being no comparable taxes on other businesses.

It should be emphasized that all along, white men controlled the lion's share of the taxable wealth, ranging from 85 percent in 1790, when town matriarch Mary Marshall Bolling was in her heyday, to 94 percent in 1820. The best way to characterize the trend for the decade after 1810 is that more white women and blacks of both sexes were acquiring small pieces of an expanding pie. The following table shows the proportion, in percent, of the persons listed in the census schedules as heads of families who also paid taxes:

	1810	1820
White men	60.1	61.8
Black men	21.5	24.8
White women	14.8	30.3
Black women	5.1	10.1

[27]Deeds III, 300 (1806), Deeds IV, 351 (1815); Wills II, 141 (1817).

[28]Legislative Petitions, 23 December 1839; Wills II, 94 (1814).

[29]Deeds III, 156 (1804); Wills II, 161 (1819). Amelia Gallé's son Joseph later on became the husband of Eliza Gallie.

[30]Petersburg *Republican,* 18 April, 7 July 1820, 23 May, 22 August 1823.

[31]United States Manuscript Census Schedule, 1820; Personal Property Books, 1819, 1820.

[32]Accounts I, 91 (1814) (first quotation); Deeds IV, 332 (1815) (second quotation); Wills II, 40 (1809) (third quotation), 95 (1814) (fourth quotation).

[33]Accounts II, 68 (1824-1826); Deeds III, 279 (1806); Land Books, 1806-1820; Personal Property Books, 1801-1820; *Republican,* 29 October 1816.

[34]Slave sales were not usually publicly recorded, and this adds to the difficulty of determining the extent of slave ownership.

[35]The number of slaves mortgaged was calculated from the deed books. During the same two years, Petersburg newspapers advertised the sale of about eighty slaves "according to a deed of trust," in other words, for owners' indebtedness. Both figures given here are lower than the actual totals, because the advertisements and deeds of trust did not always stipulate the precise numbers of slaves involved. Anyone prone to discount the significance of the threat of forced sale would do well to sample some deed books. In 1819 and 1820 alone, at least one-tenth of Petersburg's slaves were put up as collateral for owners' debts.

[36]In 1810, eight of twenty-three black landowners were women.

[37]By using the legal loopholes provided by the equity tradition of jurisprudence, a few married women were able to exempt their property from the control of husbands and husbands' creditors. Mary Ann Vizonneau provides one example. Her father's

stipulation that her inheritance was not to be controlled by her husband set up a "separate estate," which was formalized in 1818 by a separation agreement executed by Vizonneau and her estranged husband. Deeds V, 284 (1818). In this period, however, separate estates were still very rare.

[38]In his will, Jean Gallé apprised his executors that the woman slave Faith and all but two of the beds in his house belonged to Cassurier and not to his estate. Wills II, 161 (1819).

[39]Minutes, 3 September 1800; Wills II, 192 (1822).

[40]Joseph Tate, *A Digest of the Laws of Virginia, which are of a Permanent Character and General Operation; Illustrated by Judicial Decisions: To which is Added, An Index of the Names of Cases in the Virginia Reporters* (Richmond: Shepherd and Pollard, 1823), pp. 415-18, secs. 1, 11, 13. Because the Marriage Register did not stipulate race, not even a rough estimate of black marriage rates can be made.

[41]Deeds V, 124 (1817); Minutes, 21 November 1806; Wills II, 182 (1821). Vaughan was born free and the son of the Sarah Vaughan who appeared year after year on the tax lists.

[42]Deeds III, 376 (1807); Land Books, 1809-1820.

[43]Minutes, 27 January 1802; Deeds V, 197 (1817).

[44]Minutes, 6 April 1811 (first quotation), 6 May 1812 (second quotation).

[45]Land Books, 1806-1812; Deeds IV, 330 (1815) (quotation).

[46]Records of the Gillfield Baptist Church suggest that as late as 1860, there was still ambivalence on the marriage issue. An entry of 29 January 1860, for example, reads: "It was moved & 2nd that the Past Action of the church be reconsidered of mutual concent being considered Man & Wife Carried — non considered Man & Wife But those joined together By Matrimony." Gillfield Baptist Church Record Book, Alderman Library.

[47]Two cases suggest that some free black women were aware of the law and concerned about its consequences. Two days before she married Jacob Brander, Nancy Curtis deeded her furniture and livestock to her teenaged children, a clear attempt to protect the rights of her own heirs. Lydia Thomas maintained her property rights in a slave and some furniture, despite her marriage to John Stewart, by entering into a prenuptial contract with him. This gave her a separate estate, much like that of Mary Ann Vizonneau. Deeds IV, 335 (1815), Deeds V, 288 (1818); Marriages, 1814, 1817.

[48]The 1810 census listed the names of free black heads of households, but the only further information given was the total number of free blacks (with a separate total for slaves) living in each household. The census for 1820 is somewhat more informative, supplying the number of persons of each sex in each of four age categories (under fourteen, fourteen to twenty-five, twenty-six to forty-four, and forty-five and above).

[49]The first figure is the total of all households in which one female from fourteen to twenty-five was listed along with one or more children under age fourteen, and in which one female of twenty-six or above was listed along with one or more persons under age twenty-six. The same age categories were used for the second figure.

[50]For female-headed households, surplus adult is defined as anyone over twenty-five listed in addition to the head. For male-headed households, surplus adults are those listed in addition to one man and one woman. There were twenty-one surplus women and six men in male-headed households, thirty surplus women and twenty-three men in female-headed households.

[51]Even counting resident slaves and free blacks out of the analysis, fewer than one-third of the households headed by whites can be reasonably classified as nuclear, that is, as being composed of an adult couple or an adult couple with their children with no surplus persons.

One-tenth of Petersburg's free blacks were listed as residing in households headed by whites. Three-fifths of these free blacks were males, and they outnumbered females resident in white households in every age group except the over-forty-four category.

[52]The incidence of female-headedness among poorer white households was considerably higher, as might be expected. In 1820, 27.1 percent of the households of nontaxpaying whites were female headed. Comparison of white and black households is complicated by the fact that different age categories were used for the two groups.

[53]Luther P. Jackson, *A Short History of the Gillfield Baptist Church of Petersburg, Virginia* (Petersburg: Virginia Printing Co., 1937); *Republican,* 17 October 1820.

SLAVE FAMILIES AT EARLY CHESAPEAKE IRONWORKS

by Ronald L. Lewis*

The belief is widespread among scholars and laymen alike that the black family emerged from slavery and the Civil War as a defunct institution. According to this interpretation, slavery prevented the development of a nuclear structure by fragmenting slave families through sale and emasculation of the black male. Thus it is asserted, the slave family acquired the matriarchal characteristics which were carried over into freedom. This fragmentation supposedly explained the alleged instability of the black family. Because of his powerlessness, the black male before and after emancipation could function only as a "guest in the house." Many twentiety-century scholars such as E. Franklin Frazier and Daniel P. Moynihan have endorsed this view of the slave family.[1]

If that were the case with agricultural slavery, and a growing body of literature on the subject questions this hypothesis,[2] it did not always apply to industrial slavery. Most southern ironworks were operated by slave labor and certainly the experience of many slave families who lived and worked at them suggested otherwise. Undeniably, the male's position was precarious whether he was an agricultural or an industrial slave. The black male was constantly frustrated in assuming authority over his household; he had to remain silent if his wife was whipped, he did not have ultimate control over the destiny of his children, and he was not the family provider in the usual manner for nuclear families.[3] Beyond these limitations, however, the male slave ironworker could do many things to bolster his position in the family.

When Frederick Law Olmsted, the well-known northern journalist, made his famous journeys throughout the South during the 1850s, he observed

---

* Dr. Lewis is an assistant professor of Black American Studies at the University of Delaware, Newark, Delaware.

1 See for example the influential studies of E. Franklin Frazier, "The Negro Slave Family," *The Journal of Negro History*, XV (April 1930), 198-258, and Daniel P. Moynihan, *The Negro Family: The Case for Federal Action* (Washington, D.C., 1965), pp. 1-40.

2 See for example, Robert William Fogel and Stanley L. Engerman, *Time on the Cross: The Economics of American Negro Slavery* (Boston, 1974), pp. 126-144; Eugene D. Genovese, *In Red and Black: Marxian Explorations in Southern and Afro-American History* (New York, 1971), chapter 5; John W. Blassingame, *The Slave Community* (New York, 1972), chapter 3; and George P. Rawick, *From Sundown to Sunup: The Making of the Black Community* (Westport, Connecticut, 1972), chapter 5.

3 Genovese, *In Red and Black*, pp. 114-115; James H. Dormon and Robert R. Jones, *The Afro-American Experience: A Cultural History through Emancipation* (New York, 1974), pp. 218-219.

that slave owners were sometimes reluctant to hire slaves to ironworks because

> They were worked hard, and had too much liberty, and were acquiring bad habits. They earned money, by overwork, and spent it for whisky, and got a habit of roaming about and *taking care of themselves*; because when they were not at work in the furnace, nobody looked out for them.[4]

Even though the master-class bias is evident, Olmsted touched on nearly every important aspect in the daily lives of blacks at ironworks. Slaves who stopped short of threatening either the ironworks regime or the institution of slavery itself generally were not harassed by ironmasters, because too much coercion could lead to either overt or covert retaliation against their interests. Consequently, "When they were not at work in the furnace, nobody looked out for them." Put another way, this meant that ironmasters did not strictly control free time, home life, or leisure activities in the slave quarters. This provided slave ironworkers, in the view of the planter class, with "too much liberty," and they "got a habit of roaming about" during leisure hours.

This relative freedom of movement during off-work hours was significant in preventing industrial slavery from becoming what Stanley Elkins identified as a "closed system" of "absolute power" which stripped the slave of his individual personality,[5] or which brutalized blacks as asserted by historians such as Kenneth Stampp.[6] Overwork played an equally significant role in mitigating the complete debasement of slave ironworkers by enabling them to earn cash or extra provisions for laboring beyond their normal tasks or quotas.

The overwork system attempted to make the industrial slave a disciplined and productive worker by merging his physical and economic interests with those of the ironmaster. In turn, this would reduce the need for physical coercion, which might do more harm than good to the ironmaster's production goals. Although the slaves who responded positively to the overwork system accepted the ironmaster's behest, they nonetheless made the choice themselves whether or not to take advantage of the incentive offered. In that sense they exercised at least some measure of discretion. If slaves decided

4 Frederick Law Olmsted, *A Journey in the Seaboard Slave States, with Remarks on Their Economy* (New York, 1859), p. 58.

5 Stanley M. Elkins, *Slavery: A Problem in American Institutional and Intellectual Life* (Chicago, 1959), chapter 3.

6 Kenneth M. Stampp, *The Peculiar Institution: Slavery in the Ante-Bellum South* (New York, 1956), p. 84.

to spend their extra time at work rather than leisure, the sums they earned were their own to do with as they pleased and provided them with even greater degrees of choice.[7] When an ironmaster utilized this system extensively, as most did, slaves could acquire a considerable measure of control over their daily lives under bondage—always within the limits of the institution, of course.

But overwork had a more subtle impact on the most fundamental aspects in the daily life of the slave community. As Olmsted noted, slaves earned money, and although some "spent it for whisky," many others improved their standard of living by purchasing extra articles of clothing and larger provisions of the food they liked best. The ability of male slaves to purchase small luxuries for themselves and for their wives and children greatly enhanced their self-esteem in the family and in the quarters. In the quarters, where the slave was rarely under the direct surveillance of the ironmaster, he could be a man. According to John Blassingame, the slave

> could express his true feelings and gain respect and sympathy in his family circle. Friendship, love, sexual gratification, fun, and values which differed from those of the master were all found in the quarters.[8]

Overwork provided the means by which slave men could act out the important role of family provider. Even unskilled slave hands frequently made large sums of money doing extra work, especially those who chopped wood for charcoal production. The 1820 overwork account of "Negro Enoch," for example, shows how Enoch greatly improved the daily fare for himself and his family at Northampton Furnace in Maryland. During 1820 Enoch purchased an extra 120 pounds of pork and 5 1/4 bushels of meal for a total debit of $21.20. On the other side of the ledger, Enoch earned credits amounting to $108.16, some of which he took in cash and some in goods, 74 3/4 pounds of pork and a little over 3 bushels of meal.[9] A more striking example of how an unskilled woodchopper would acquire the means to improve the standard of life for himself and his family can be seen in the 1820 account of "Negro Jem Aires," another slave hand at Northampton Furnace. Between April 10 and November 20, 1820, Jem Aires earned

[7] Also see, Charles B. Dew, "Disciplining Slave Ironworkers in the Ante-Bellum South: Coercion, Conciliation, and Accommodation," *The American Historical Review*, LXXIX (April 1974), 407.

[8] Blassingame, *The Slave Community*, pp. 206-207.

[9] Daybook B-19, 1815-1821, Box 9, Northampton Furnace, Ridgely Account Books, Maryland Historical Society. Charcoal was used as fuel in early iron furnaces.

$165.71 by chopping and hauling cord wood. At a time when free whites earned one dollar a day, this was a significant sum of money, especially for only seven months labor. In addition to the normal supplies provided by the ironmaster, Jem Aires spent part of his overwork pay on 20 3/4 bushels of meal, 247 pounds of pork, and 141 pounds of extra beef.[10]

Skilled slaves, however, were in the best position to earn overwork pay and, consequently, had the most money to spend on provisions for their families. For example, at Buffalo Forge in Virginia, skilled craftsmen such as Henry Tolles earned from $3.00 to $5.00 per ton for extra work at the forge. By 1858 Henry Tolles had accumulated a credit balance of $102.53 on the ironmaster's books, most of which he drew in cash.[11] Sam Williams, another skilled forgeman at Buffalo Forge, received $5.00 for each ton of finished bar iron that he produced. Williams also had a plot of ground the produce of which he could either use himself or sell to the company store at the ironworks.[12] By farming and overwork, Williams considerably improved the material quality of life for his family. Williams's account for the period between March 1855 to March 1856 was balanced at $92.23; by December 1856, his account stood at $55.35 after purchasing a number of items such as bed ticking, a barrel of flour, and coffee and sugar. At the end of 1857, when Williams's account was carried over to a new book, it totaled $155.87.[13]

The account books of early ironworks are replete with additional references to male slave ironworkers purchasing small luxury items for their wives. For example, one skilled hand at the Baltimore Iron Works in Maryland used his overwork pay during the 1730s to purchase a bed, 2 blankets, and a rug totaling £2.10.0 for his wife "Negro Flora & Children."[14] At John Blair's foundry in Virginia during May 1797, "Negro Phil" purchased for his wife shoe leather and "7 1/2 yards of ribbon."[15] At Cumberland Forge, in Maryland, "Negro Dick Snowden" purchased "1 pair Shoes for his wife."[16] Abraham was charged for "1 pr. shoes for Eliza on acct of Dick" at Union Forge in April 1825.[17] In 1850 Toller, a skilled hand at Buffalo Forge, drew $5.00 to send to his wife. At adjoining Etna Furnace, Bill Jones acquired

---

10 *Ibid.*

11 Negro Book, 1850-1858, Buffalo Forge, Weaver-Brady Papers, University of Virginia.

12 Daniel C. E. Brady, Home Journal, 1860-1865, State Historical Society of Wisconsin.

13 Negro Book, 1850-1858, Buffalo Forge, Weaver-Brady Papers, University of Wisconsin.

14 "Inventory of Ben Tasker at Baltimore Co. —1737," Box 3, Carroll-Maccubbin Papers, Maryland Historical Society.

15 Ledger of John Blair, Iron Founder, 1795-1797, College of William and Mary.

16 Cumberland Forge Day Book, 1802, Library of Congress.

17 Daybook, 1825-1836, Union Forge, Rinker-Lantz Papers, Duke University.

"1 pair Brogans for his wife," while "Daniel Dumb Boy" was debited several times for "cash to Louisa."[18]

Through overwork then, slaves could acquire self-esteem by purchasing small luxury items for their wives. Even more significant, however, they could provide additional necessities for their wives and children, which increased their esteem in the family and in the quarters. As ex-slave William Green wrote, in the eyes of the other slaves, "the man who does this is a great man amongst them."[19]

Other considerations influenced the family life of slaves at ironworks. Because operators of early ironworks, quite as much as their modern counterparts, craved predictability in their labor supply, they attempted to curb turnover among the hands as much as possible. Inevitably, of course, some black families were broken by circumstances beyond the ironmaster's control. Slave owner J. C. Dickinson, for example, wrote to one ironmaster in Virginia in October 1830 informing him of the death of the owner's mother and that Dickinson was making preparation for the "division of the negroes which is to take place Xmas." "I will be extremely glad," wrote Dickinson, "if you will give all & every one of my negroes a pass & send them home." The owner of the hired slaves realized, however, that the circumstances were unsettling to the ironmaster's operation and added that "I will aid you as much as possible in geting *[sic]* hands for another year."[20]

More frequently, however, owners of hired black ironworkers attempted to limit family separations by seeking guarantees that slave hands hired outside the local area would be permitted to go home at least once or twice a year to visit their wives. Owners often inserted a clause into the hiring bond or stipulated the proviso in their letters to ironmasters. One owner wrote two Virginia ironmasters during 1828 that they must let a slave hired to them "come home once in the course of the year to see his wife."[21] Another owner wrote to William Weaver, another prominent Virginia ironmaster, that he was going to Tennessee and "I will be much obliged to you if you will ascertain of my man Nelson whether he is wiling *[sic]* to go or not [.] if Nelson is willing to go with me to Tennessee I shall hire him out the next year untill *[sic]* the first day of September but if he has a wife and is not

[18] Negro Book, 1850-1858, Buffalo Forge, and Negro Book, 1857-1860, Etna Furnace, Weaver-Brady Papers, University of Virginia.

[19] William Green, *Narrative of Events in the Life of William Green* (Springfield, Massachusetts, 1853), p. 9.

[20] J. C. Dickinson to William Weaver, October 21, 1830, Weaver-Brady Papers, University of Virginia.

[21] R. Brooks to Jordan & Irvine, January 2, 1829, Jordan and Irvine Papers, State Historical Society of Wisconsin.

willing to part with her to go with me I am willing to sell him."[22] "I hope you will buy Paris as I would not like her to get into hands who would separate the children from the mother," wrote another slave owner to an ironmaster.[23] The master of a hired slave wrote to another ironmaster that he was going to "sell out this spring & Moove *[sic]*," and continued, "My Girl Evoline is anxious to be as near George as she can. I am disposed to sell her . . . to you and as she and George both wants [*sic*] you to buy her I am willing to accomadate *[sic]* them."[24] A few days later the owner wrote again, "George is here and insists on Me to Send you a few lines as he is very anxious for Me to sell you Evoline." He offered Evoline for $800. He could "do better than that but it would not please them [the Negroes]. [T]his is all I can or will do if you do not want her I can have her in this county at a place that Geo can get to as easy as this."[25] Because of the potentially disruptive factors in hiring a work force averaging about 100 hands, ironmasters generally tried to own at least half their labor force, represented by the skilled and semi-skilled craftsmen, to insure stability in the production process. Many ironmasters owned all or most of their personnel.

Like the above-mentioned George, many slave ironworkers actively participated in matters concerning their wives. The hiring agent for a Virginia ironmaster wrote in 1830 about a slave hand who was for hire. "Mr. Jones requested me to say to you," wrote the agent, that "Winston would not consent to go back to the ironworks having as I understand taken a wife."[26] Another slave being transferred to an ironworks made certain that his wife did not have to trudge all the way to the works on foot. A Virginia agent wrote to the ironmaster that he "paid a baggage wagon that Reuben had employed to take his wife & baggage to the Depot $1.50." The slave informed the agent that "there was to be some arrangement made to send his wife by Packet from Lynchburg to the ironworks and having no doubt you so intended I have advanced him $2.00 to pay fare."[27]

At Buffalo Forge several blacks such as Garland had wives who resided near the forge, and these hands regularly spent the remainder of the week-

---

22 R. Dickinson to William Weaver, November 15, 1829, William Weaver Papers, Duke University.

23 Pendleton Adams to James W. Harrison, October 31, 1850, *ibid.*

24 John Huff to F. T. Anderson, March 20, 1856, Anderson Family Papers, University of Virginia.

25 *Ibid.*, March 24, 1856.

26 Tuyman Wayt to Jordan & Irvine, January 6, 1830, Jordan and Irvine Papers, State Historical Society of Wisconsin.

27 F. Glasgow to F. T. Anderson, January 1, 1858, Anderson Family Papers, University of Virginia.

TABLE 1

SLAVES AT OXFORD IRON WORKS IN FAMILIES AND OCCUPATIONS

Family Unit	*Mother*	*Father*	*Children*	*Grand-parents*	*No. Children at jobs same or different from parents*		*Too young to work**	*Other***
					same	*different*		
1	1	1	6	0			6	
2	1	1	1	0				1
3	1	1	4	0	2		2	
4	0	1	3	0			3	
5	0	1	3	0			3	
6	1	1	4	0	2	2		
7	1	1	3	0	2		1	
8	1	1	2	0				2
9	1	1	5	0	1		4	
10	1	1	3	0	1	1	1	
11	1	1	0	0				
12	1	0	2	0			2	
13	1	1	3	0		3		
14	1	1	0	0				
15	1	1	8	0				8
16	1	1	13	0	4	3	5	1
17	1	1	3	0			2	1
18	1	0	8	0			5	3
19	1	1	5	0	2	1	2	
20	1	1	7	0		2	5	
21	1	1	8	1	1	6		1
22	0	1	6	0			6	
23	0	1	3	0			3	
24	1	1	7	0	1	1	5	
25	1	1	8	0	2		4	
26	1	1	8	1	1	1	6	
27	1	1	5	0	2	3		
28	1	1	5	0				5
29	0	1	3	0			3	
30	1	1	3	0	1	1		1

* Includes children between ages 10 and 14 who were "nurses" and took care of the children but did not work full time.

** Includes those slaves who cannot be associated with an occupation because it was not listed.

Source: "List of Slaves at the Oxford Iron Works in Families & Their Employment, taken January 15, 1811," Bolling Family Papers, Duke University. Compiled by the author.

end with them when work stopped on Saturday.[28] Difficulties sometimes arose with slave men who could not readily see their wives. For example, one manager of a Virginia ironworks described the problems he had with two hands in 1862:

You ask me about Griffen. I consider him a triffling [*sic*] hand. —he laid up here very often & for long periods—but it was only when we worked him about the Furnace he laid up so often that we had finally to take him away. . . . Tell him that you will put him in the wood chopping when he gets well & I will guarantee he will soon be out—that is his object now in laying up. I found that he laid up very seldom when he could get a chance to run to his wife.[29]

Manuscript material simply does not exist to reconstruct completely the daily lives and family patterns for slaves at early southern ironworks. Two particularly valuable sources, however, shed some light into the hidden corners of slave family life at David Ross's Oxford Iron Works, located in Virginia, around 1811. The first is a detailed 1811 slave enumeration listing the Oxford's black work force by family units, with the father, mother, children, and sometimes superannuary relatives grouped together. The listing is significant since Oxford was operated entirely by a slave force of 220 hands, and was one of the most important ironworks in the nation. The list is summarized in Table 1.

The second manuscript source which provides an exceptional glimpse into slave family life at southern ironworks is a letter in the David Ross Letterbook for 1812-1813. In 1812 an unmarried slave woman named Fanny, apparently for religious convictions, attempted to destroy her newborn sixth infant. The incident provoked Ross to vent at length his feelings concerning slave marriage, slave parenthood, and the position of the slave family in general:

Tis well known that I demand moderate labour from the servants. . . . I have never laid any restrictions on their worshipping the deity agreeably to their own minds (so far as rational) in any manner they please—as to their amorous connections (perfectly natural) I have not been merely passive, but have upon more occasions than one or two declared my sentiments, that the young people might connect themselves in marriage, to their own liking, with consent of their parents who were the best judges. 'Tis true I have discouraged connections out of the estate and particularly with free people of colour, because I was certain, 'twould be injurious to my people, but I have used no violence to prevent those connections for tis well known that

28 Daniel C. E. Brady, Home Journal, State Historical Society of Wisconsin.

29 William Rex to Daniel Brady, March 22, 1862, Weaver-Brady Papers, University of Virginia.

now they exist upon my estate and have not been expelled but no longer attend [*sic*]—tis very much my wish that my servants should connect themselves in a decent manner and behave as a religious people ou[gh]t to do [.] [30]

Taken together these two documents provide rare and valuable insights into how at least one leading ironmaster viewed family life among his slaves. Black slave parents at Oxford obviously exerted much more responsibility over the lives of their children than has been assumed. Ross insisted that children under ten remain with their parents, and older offspring normally remained within the family unit until marriage. Moreover, Ross encouraged slave parents to approve or disapprove of any prospective "amorous connections" since parents were the "best judges" concerning what was best for their children in that regard.

Several patterns with important social implications for slave families are revealed by the Oxford list. For example, the list indicates that members of family units not only lived together, slave artisans also frequently taught craft secrets to their sons. Thus, Big Abram was a collier and several of his children and a grandchild also worked in some phase of charcoal production. The same relationship existed in four other families of colliers, and throughout the skilled crafts generally.[31] No doubt Ross believed that a strong slave family structure was morally proper and humane. Beyond that, however, he recognized that a viable slave family helped insure the growth of his slave force and a continuation of the skills vital to iron production. Moreover, stable family arrangements helped maintain discipline and deterred runaways. That Ross fully appreciated the implications of marriage can be seen in the example of Solomon, who ran off to rejoin his wife after Ross acquired him. Recognizing the inevitable problems that would result from forcing Solomon to remain at Oxford, Ross sold him to a planter in the vicinity of his wife's home and commented that "My intention was to leave the man where he seemed desirous of living."[32]

Perhaps the most significant observation that can be made from the Oxford slave list is the fact that of the thirty individual family units cited,

---

[30] D. Ross to Robert Richardson, manager of Oxford Iron Works, April 30, 1812, The David Ross Letterbook, 1812-1813, Virginia Historical Society. The letterbook only recently became available to scholars when the society removed material pasted on its pages.

[31] D. Ross to Robert Richardson, April 30, 1812, Ross Letterbook, Virginia Historical Society; "List of Slaves at Oxford Iron Works in Families & Their Employment, taken January 15, 1811," Bolling Family Papers, Duke University.

[32] D. Ross to John Cole, November 28, 1812; to Edmond Sherman, August 19, September 8 and 13, 1813; and to Robert Wright, August 22, 1813, all in the Ross Letterbook, Virginia Historical Society. Also, see Charles B. Dew, "David Ross and the Oxford Iron Works: A Study of Industrial Slavery in the Early Nineteenth-Century South," *The William and Mary Quarterly*, 3rd ser., XXXI (April 1974), 213.

twenty-three had both mother and father present, and two units contained one grandparent. Most surprisingly, however, in only two families was the father absent while in five there was no mother. Thus, 77 percent of the Oxford families were headed by both parents, and among the 23 percent of the units where only one parent presided, the tendency was for the *father* to be the head of the family, not the mother.

While it would be useful to know the patterns of black family organization at other ironworks, the problems in restructuring that phase of slave existence are nearly insurmountable. This is particularly true for the colonial period; but throughout the slave era the incompleteness of description, lack of surnames, and the repeated use of some common slave names make reconstruction of family life an uncertain task. Still, Ross was hardly unique in seeing the importance of stable family structure for the operation of an ironworks. From the 1760s until the 1790s, for example, at Patuxent Iron Works in Maryland there was a consistently steady group of skilled and semiskilled workers and women, and it probably represented a stable family system. Unskilled hands at Patuxent, however, were less permanent members of the labor force at the ironworks than at Oxford where Ross owned all of the 220 blacks who resided there. This pattern seems to have had the same outward signs as the family structure at most other southern ironworks, where skilled and semiskilled blacks and their families provided the core of continuity while unskilled hands often tended to be hired and, consequently, relatively more transient. This pattern can be seen in Table 2.

TABLE 2

SLAVES AT PATUXENT IRON WORKS, 1769-1784

Number of Slaves	*Years at the Works*															
	1	*2*	*3*	*4*	*5*	*6*	*7*	*8*	*9*	*10*	*11*	*12*	*13*	*14*	*15*	*16*
Skilled/Male (45)	3	4		2	1			6	4	1	3	1	1	1	1	5
Women (30)	5	4	2		2	2	1	2	2	1	3	1	1	1		3
Unskilled/Male (58)	26	11	8	4	1	2	2	1	2							

Source: Journal A & B, 1767-94, Patuxent Iron Works, Maryland Hall of Records. Compiled by the author.

At least one slave family at Patuxent remained intact for thirty years. "Negro Forge Harry" first appeared in the company ledgers during the late 1760s. The same was true for his wife Nann. By the late 1790s, and in 1801, Forge

Harry's account was debited for giving sums of money to his wife and to his sons Joe, Jacob, Harry, and Dick.[33]

At ironworks where a skilled and semiskilled black labor force existed, there was a stable slave family structure; most ironmasters desired to preserve stability in the production process. Incentive systems, such as overwork, helped to strengthen the foundations of the slave family by enabling the male slave to play an important role in maintaining his wife and children, if not altering the status of bondage itself. That a large number of slave ironworkers took advantage of the opportunity indicated that black slave ironworkers did not live up to the lazy, shiftless, Sambo stereotype developed by whites to rationalize the most peculiar of American institutions. More significantly, the lives of slave ironworkers refuted the notion that slavery killed the vital core of the male slave's manhood, and, thus, a major component in the modern matrifocal family thesis.

[33] Ledger of the Executors of the Estate of Thomas Snowden, December 24, 1775–January 2, 1810, Patuxent Iron Works, Maryland Hall of Records.

Searching for the Family and Household Structure of Rural Louisiana Slaves, 1810-1864

By ANN PATTON MALONE

Illinois State University

A single aspect of the black experience in rural Louisiana will be explored in this article—the household structure of nineteenth-century slave laborers.[1] In order to gauge patterns in slave household composition, a search was conducted of plantation and parish records for documents showing family relationships and household designations. The result was a sample of 155 slave communities, representing twenty-six parishes, located in all of the major slaveholding regions of the state, inventoried over a period of fifty-four years. Data on the various slave communities came from a variety of

[1]The history of slave household organization is still a relatively new field for United States historians. This is not to state that American historians have not had much to say about the slave family of the nineteenth century South; it has been the focus of a lively debate for nearly three decades, much of it over the "stability" or "instability" of black family during slavery and the degree to which it was matrifocal. The literature on the debate is too lengthy to be cited in its entirety, but the following works are essential: Ulrich B. Phillips, *American Negro Slavery: A Survey of the Supply, Employment, and Control of Negro Labor as Determined by the Plantation Regime* (1918; reprint ed., Baton Rouge, 1966); E. Franklin Frazier, *The Negro Family in the United States* (Chicago, 1939); Kenneth M. Stampp, *The Peculiar Institution: Slavery in the Ante-Bellum South* (New York, 1956); Stanley M. Elkins, *Slavery: A Problem in American Institutional and Intellectual Life* (Chicago, 1959); George P. Rawick, *From Sundown to Sunup: The Making of the Black Community* (New York, 1972); John W. Blassingame, *The Slave Community: Plantation Life in the Antebellum South* (New York, 1972); Eugene D. Genovese, *Roll, Jordan, Roll: The World the Slaves Made* (New York, 1974); Robert William Fogel and Stanley L. Engerman; *Time on the Cross*, 2 vols. (Boston, 1974); Herbert G. Gutman, "Persistent Myths About the Afro-American Family," *Journal of Interdisciplinary History*, VI (1975), 181-210; Herbert G. Gutman, *The Black Family in Slavery and Freedom, 1750-1925* (New York, 1976); Paul A. David et al., *Reckoning with Slavery: A Critical Study in the Quantitative History of American Negro 'Slavery* (New York, 1976); Stanley L. Engerman, "Studying the Black Family," a review essay of Herbert G. Gutman's *The Black Family* . . . in *The Journal of Family History*, III (1978), 78-101. In addition to these general works on slavery, see Joe Gray Taylor's *Negro Slavery in Louisiana* (Baton Rouge, 1963). Peter Laslett analyzed the household composition of several Louisiana plantations in *Family Life and Illicit Love in Earlier Generations: Essays in Historical Sociology* (Cambridge, 1977), pp. 233-260. Many excellent demographic works have appeared in articles and dissertations, but most deal with states other than Louisiana or with slaves in other countries. Examples of these would be Jerome S. Handler and Robert S. Corruccini, "Plantation Slave Life in Barbados: A Physical and Anthropological Analysis," *Journal of Interdisciplinary History*, XIV (1983); Michael Craton, "Changing Patterns of Slave Families in British West Indies," *Journal of Interdisciplinary History*, X (1979), 1-35; B. W. Higman, "Household Structure and Fertility on Jamaican Slave Plantations: A Nineteenth Century Example," *Population Studies*, XXVII (1973), 527-550; B. W. Higman, "African and Creole Slave Family Patterns in Trinidad," *Journal of Family History*, III (1978), 163-180; B. W. Higman, "The Slave Family and Household in the British West Indies, 1800-

sources but primarily from probate court records such as inventories and appraisements, estate partitions, and estate sales bill; mortgage documents; conveyances of plantations with slave communities attached; plantation records of great variety; private papers; and correspondence.[2] In short, the inventories were drawn from any reliable source that yielded a *full listing* of

---

1834," *Journal of Interdisciplinary History*, VI (1975), 261-287; Richard S. Dunn, "A Tale of Two Plantations: Slave Life at Mesopotamia in Jamaica and Mount Airy in Virginia, 1799-1828," *William and Mary Quarterly*, XXIV (1977), 32-65; Allen Kulikoff, "The Beginnings of the Afro-American Family in Maryland," in Aubrey C. Land et al., eds., *Law, Society, and Politics* (Baltimore, 1976); and Russell B. Menard, "The Maryland Slave Population, 1658 to 1730: A Demographic Profile of Blacks in Four Counties," *William and Mary Quarterly*, XXXII (1975), 29-54.

[2]Estate records provided the greatest number of inventories showing familial groups or allowing their reconstitution. Parish records were drawn from Ascension, Assumption, Avoyelles, Catahoula, Concordia, De Soto, East Feliciana, Franklin, Iberville, Lafourche, Natchitoches, Pointe Coupée, Rapides, St. Bernard, St. James, St. Landry, St. Martin, St. Mary, Tensas, Terrebonne, Union, West Baton Rouge, East Baton Rouge, and West Feliciana parishes, although in some cases the records relating to those parishes were located elsewhere. Most useful were inventories and appraisements and estate divisions and bills of sale, but also important were mortgages of land and slaves, conveyances of land and slaves, and inventories associated with divorces and separations from bed and board. Many planter collections were used, with lists of slaves, ration lists, and cabin lists often collated with parish records in reconstitution procedures. Verbatim transcriptions of all inventories are in the files of the author. Various methods were used by the nineteenth-century enumerators of Louisiana slaves to designate groups of slaves belonging to a household or family. Households were sometimes separated by drawn lines or by spaces, the family or household was bracketed or indicated by a wavy line, or they were designated as a "family" or "belonging to the same family." Other times they were appraised as a unit and inventoried in a systematic sequence, with father, mother, children, being the usual order. Within household groups, familial relationships in the slave communities used in this study were generally described in words: "his wife," "their children," "their grandchildren." In some cases slaves of a family shared a surname. In a few cases households and families were reconstituted by combining information from several original documents.

An attempt was made to confine the cases of this study to those in which household structure and familial relationships were clearly discernible. A few inventories may be those of cabin occupants rather than household groups. And several inventories were located in which kinship groupings rather than households were used to identify slaves. In these, grown children were often assigned to the maternal line whether the adult offspring were married or not. And some attempts were made in these inventories to keep up with offspring of deceased members of a kinship line. For example, in Jean Ursin Jarreau's plantation in Pointe Coupée Parish, Judy, 23, was identified as the "daughter of Hanny, deceased"; Hippolite, 23 was the "son of Lucie"; Hannah, 38, the "daughter of Sarah deceased," was listed with Frederick, 19, "son of Hannah." And one multiple family household was identified in this manner:

Jenny, 53
Frank, 33, "child of Jenny"
Françoise, 16, "child of Lize, deceased" and "grandchild of Jenny"
Eugénie, 15, "sister of Françoise"
Rose, 13, "sister of Françoise"
Emm, 10, "sister of Françoise"
Baptiste, 26, "child of Jenny"
Esther, —, "child of Jenny"
Charles, 2 "Esther's child"
Rosette, 21, "child of Jenny"
Josephine, 11 months, "child of Rosette"

Inventory and Appraisement, May 8, 1855, in Estate of Jean Ursin Jarreau, Pointe Coupée Parish Probate Records, Inventory Volume 1854-1855, 445-457. If household designations were obvious in addition to kinship groupings, the cases were included in the sample, but if the listing by kin obscured all household designations, they were deleted from this particular study.

slaves belonging to a discernible unit clearly indicating familial and household relationships. If households and familial relationships could not be determined from a source, or from a combination of sources, the community was not used in the sample.

Following a typography adapted from Peter Laslett and the Cambridge Group, the sample communities were analyzed in terms of standard family household types and categories.[3] The data were rendered machine readable, and sums, means, and percentages were produced in all standard household types and categories to arrive at a general profile of slave household composition in rural Louisiana, 1810-1864.

Selected patterns of Louisiana slave family, household, and community organization are presented in the following pages. The patterns may not be representative of those of all Louisiana slave societies, but the sample is sufficiently large and inclusive to provide a reliable overview of trends in domestic arrangements on Louisiana plantations. And the sample provides a backdrop against which detailed case studies of slave communities can be viewed within a comparative perspective.

Louisiana Slave Household Composition, 1810-1864

In the 1810-1864 sample, 18 percent of the slaves were solitaires; 1 percent formed non-nuclear households; 73 percent resided in simple families; 2 percent comprised extended-family households; and 6 percent lived in multiple-family household units. These percentages, derived from the total sums in each household type, provide a composite profile of the sampled slave communities. The most important household types, in order of size, were the simple-family, solitaire, and multiple-family households. Extended and non-nuclear households were insignificant forms.

The simple-family household is generally acknowledged to be the dominant family household type among both slave and free populations of the nineteenth-century United States. And indeed it has been called the prevalent household type for the whole of western society for several centuries.[4] It is therefore not surprising that nearly three-fourths of the

[3]Peter Laslett, ed., ***Household and Family in Past Time: Comparative Studies in the Size and Structure of the Domestic Group Over the Past Three Centuries in England, France, Serbia, Japan and North America, with Further Materials from Western Europe*** (Cambridge, 1972), pp. 28-31, 86-89. His rules concerning presumption are followed when necessary, but almost without exception, household designations and some familial relationships were provided in the original documents used in this study.

[4]*Ibid.*, pp. 28-29. Laslett uses the term simple family to "cover what is variously described as the nuclear family, the elementary family or (not very logically, since spouses are not physiologically connected), the

sampled population were organized into various classifications of this household type. Simple-family households in the Louisiana study are those made up (1) of married couples without children, (2) of married couples with offspring, and (3) of single persons with offspring. The term nuclear family is often misused by laymen and historians to describe only that particular form of the simple or nuclear family consisting of both parents and their children when, in fact, all simple families are nuclear in form. To avoid further confusion, the term "standard-nuclear family" will be exclusively used in reference to full nuclear units composed of fathers, mothers, and their offspring.

Not only did the simple-family household type account for most of the sampled slaves, within that type, standard-nuclear families embraced 49 percent of the population. Although recent studies imply that the majority of slaves lived in standard-nuclear families, such was not the case—at least not in the Louisiana sample. In fact, for 50 percent of a slave community's membership to comprise part of standard-nuclear households indicates relative stability; less than 40 percent generally suggests disorganization and instability. And if more than 60 percent of a slave community's population are part of two-parent households, it is usually a sign of extreme maturity and stability in that community.

Persons living in the classification of married couples alone constituted 8 percent of the sampled individuals, and the remainder of the simple-family membership was organized into single-parent households encompassing 16 percent of the population. Most families in this group were made up of women and their children; 14 percent of the sampled slaves lived in female-headed households averaging three members. The prevalence of this form was widely exaggerated in the old literature of slavery, but it recently has been unrealistically downgraded as an insignificant form. Such households did not predominate on most holdings during any phase of community development, but the category is obviously an important one. On many individual plantations—especially in early phases of development—the percentage of matrifocal households was much higher.[5] On the other hand,

---

biological family." A conjugal link must in all cases be present. In Laslett's typography, he describes the possible forms of the simple family as (1) married couples without children, (2) married couples with offspring, and (3) widowed persons with offspring. In this writer's adaptation of his typography, the third form is inclusive of all unmarried parents with children in their household whether the parent(s) was widowed, divorced, or had never married. Slaves could not legally marry, bu they were presumed married when they were recognized as a married couple by their own community and owners.

[5] *Ibid.*, pp. 29, 61; Higman, "The Slave Family and Household in the British West Indies," 271. In his analysis, Laslett was primarily concerned with the numbers, types, and mean sizes of various households. He

male-headed, single-parent households—almost always composed of widowers with a child or children—rarely comprised more than the 2 percent indicated in the sampled population.

The next largest number of slaves in the overall sample was part of the solitaire-household type. Eighteen percent of the 1810-1865 slave population in the sample were solitaires. Thirteen percent of the salves were solitaire males, and 5 percent were female solitaires. A solitaire cannot be a family but is considered a household.

Non-nuclear households of the sample could be one of three kinds: (1) co-resident siblings, (2) co-resident relatives of other kinds, and (3) co-residents who were not related. Only one percent of the sampled slaves lived in non-nuclear households; most of these were co-resident siblings.

The remainder of the sampled slaves lived in complex forms, in either extended families or multiple-family households. Together, these residents formed about 8 percent of the sample. Extended-family households encompassed only 2 percent of the slaves sampled, with small percentages in each of several forms of extension. A more common complex form among Louisiana slaves was that of multiple-family households. Members of this classification comprised 6 percent of the sample, and extension of the secondary unit could be up, down, or lateral. The only multiple-family household category of significance was that in which the disposition was down; it involved 5 percent of the sampled slaves and was made up of units with a mean size of seven people.[6] Multiple-family households were frequently present in the latter stages of slave-community development since they usually involved three generations. Its most conspicuous form in Louisiana records was that of a nuclear-family unit plus an unmarried daughter and grandchild, the latter two forming the second conjugal unit.

The construction just described was the composite household organization found among 10,329 slaves who lived in Louisiana over the course of half a century. However, variations of this model existed among the sampled slave population according to the size of the slave community, the

---

usually also computes the percentages of household units in each type or category. This writer was more interested in th numbers and percentages of individual slaves in each household type or category. Unless otherwise noted, these are th percentages to which reference is made. Unit means, and percentages were also computed but these computations did not seem particularly useful in describing the social reality of slaves of all ages living in Louisiana slave communities.

[6]Laslett, *Household and Family in Past Time*, p. 29. Laslett said that multiple family households "comprise all forms of domestic groups which include two or more conjugal units connected by kinship or by marriage." Extension of the secondary conjugal unit could be up, down, or lateral. The other complex form, that of extended family households, was that consisting of "a conjugal family unit with the addition of one or more relatives other than offspring." Extensions could be upward, downward, and lateral, as in the multiple family households."

geographic area in which it was located, and, most importantly, the decade in which the community was inventoried.

The model just derived from the overall sample represents a large but static time span, 1810-1864; it does not show variations in household structure according to external events or internal cycles relating to specific time segments. Therefore, statistics were generated from the same sampled population by decennial intervals. These intervals will be briefly considered.

1800-1819

The population of Louisiana showed a higher rate of increase from 1810 to 1820 than in any other decade; its population at the dawn of the new decade was more than 100 percent greater than in 1810.[7] Cotton had been grown in Louisiana since the 1740s, but Eli Whitney's more efficient, cheaper, and simpler gin of 1793 provided the impetus for highly profitable cotton production. Following the Louisiana Purchase, a major agricultural and demographic expansion took place into the Lower Mississippi Valley.[8]

Despite wide fluctuations, cotton prices were generally high, and after the War of 1812 was over, cotton prices soared, peaking in 1817 at an enticing 33.9 cents per pound. Encouraged by high prices, Louisiana's population surged after 1815. Many of the new settlers were farmers who tilled small cotton acreages with the labor of their own sons and perhaps a few slaves, but the use of gang labor enhanced the margin of profits.[9] In the boom years from 1815-1819, ambitious Louisiana farmers and planters hungered for additional laborers. Upper South planters discovered the ready market for their surplus chattels, and the interstate trade greatly accelerated, with both New Orleans and Natchez serving as major markets.[10] Slave population increased by 99 percent from 1810-1820, a higher rate of increase than it, too, would ever again achieve.[11] Historian of Louisiana slavery Joe Gray

[7]The decennial increase, 1810-1820, of the whole population was 100.39 percent. J. D. B. DeBow, *Statistical View of the United States . . . : A Compendium of the Seventh Census . . .* (Washington, D. C., 1853), p. 65.

[8]*Reports of the Superintendent of the Census, Seventh Census* (Washington, D. C., 1853), p. 65.

[9]Taylor, *Negro Slavery in Louisiana*, pp. 59-91; Fogel and Engerman, *Time on the Cross*, p. 194; Stampp, *Peculiar Institution*, pp. 54-55; Charles Sackett Sydnor, *Slavery in Mississippi* (New York, 1933), p. 183.

[10]Taylor, *Negro Slavery in Louisiana*, pp. 37-38.

[11]The decennial increase was 99.26 percent, 1810-1820. Louisiana's slave population in 1810 was 34,600; in 1820, it had nearly doubled to 69,064. DeBow, *Statistical View of the United States*, pp. 82, 84; Phillips, *American Negro Slavery*, p. 371.

Taylor estimates that between 1810-1820 about 26,000 slaves entered the state with migrating owners or professional traders.[12]

Household composition of the 1810-1819 period was quite rudimentary, as one would expect for such an early period. Almost all of the slaves were either solitaires or members of simple-family households, but about 2 percent lived in non-nuclear units, and an additional 2 percent formed part of complex households. Solitaires comprised 18 percent of the slaves, the same percentage found in the large sample. Seventy-seven percent of the 1810-1819 slaves lived in simple families, and nearly 60 percent were part of standard-nuclear households (10 percent more in that important category than was the case in the overall model). Relatively few lived in female-headed, single-parent households, only 9 percent (compared to 14 percent in the model).

The simplicity of the 1810-1819 slave-household composition is not unexpected, but its cohesion is somewhat curious. Although it lacked much generational depth, the household structure appears to be remarkably balanced, stable, and well integrated. Why such stability during a period characterized by dramatic demographic change, war, inflation, and financial panic? The answer seems to be that the effects of the population increases, postwar cotton expansions, and the Panic of 1819 were more accurately reflected in the inventory records of the next decade. This supposition is borne out by close examination of the slave communities in the sample.

An examination of the original sources used for the household analysis confirms that some of the communities were indeed those of small planters who had migrated to the state between 1815 and 1819. Their inventories show that they had brought with them or had later purchased one or two slave families and several prime hands to aid them in clearing and planting.[13] But in addition to the small communities attached to newcomer farmers, the sample also reflects several slave communities which had been in Louisiana for many years, some since the 1780s and '90s. Their household compositions therefore reflect a more advanced stage of development. The high percentage in two-parent households, the low percentage in female-headed households, and the appearance of at least a token number of extended- and multiple-family households suggest a maturity found only in communities which had been in place for at least one or two decades. This was often the case. For example, one community in the sample was that belonging to John O'Connor who had been a planter in West Feliciana since

[12]Taylor, *Negro Slavery in Louisiana*, p. 37.

[13]Inventories, 1810-1819; 1820-1829, in files of the author, *passim.*

the late eighteenth century. When he died in 1814, his estate of thirty-nine slaves included ten solitaires (two of them elderly widows); the remainder were organized into standard-nuclear families.[14] In addition to old American planters such as O'Connor, the 1810-1819 sample contained slave communities belonging to French planters, descendants of Europeans who had long been in Louisiana.[15]

1820-1829

At the beginning of the new decade, the United States was in the throes of a major depression. Although the depression did not affect the Lower Mississippi Valley as gravely as it did many other parts of the nation, the rate of expansion was slowed. Louisiana's population increased by 41 percent in the decade, a smaller increase than that of the previous and following decades.[16] Settlers still flowed into the region during the early 1820s but not as eagerly as before, and Louisiana planters expanded their slave forces at a less frenzied pace. The slave population increased by 59 percent in the decade, but this, too, was a much smaller percentage of increase than that of the 1810-1819 period.[17] However, some shrewd Louisiana planters found the depression advantageous, profiting from a tendency among hard-hit Upper South planters to sell slaves at bargain prices.[18]

The Panic's effects on cotton prices was minimal. Between 1819 and 1824 cotton prices fluctuated but within a profitable range.[19] Despite lower prices in the latter part of the decade, Louisiana—along with Alabama, Georgia, and Mississippi—was caught up in a cotton obsession.[20] Most

[14]Inventory, November 17, 1814, in Estate of John O'Connor, West Feliciana Parish Probate Records, Succession File Drawer 70.

[15]For example, see Estate Sale, May 25, 1819, Estate of Marguerite Babin, Iberville Parish Notarial Records, Docket Volume G, 32/49; Inventory and Appraisement, April 15, 1818, Estate of Allain Zenon, West Baton Rouge Parish Probate Records, folio 60, n.p.

[16]DeBow, *Statistical View of the United States*, p. 105; *Reports of the Superintendent of the Census*, p. 151.

[17]The slave population's increase in the decade was 58.67 percent. Louisiana had 69,064 slaves in 1820 and 109,588 in 1830. DeBow, *Statistical View of the United States*, pp. 83, 84, 105.

[18]Taylor, *Negro Slavery in Louisiana*, p. 37.

[19]Sydnor, *Slavery in Mississippi*, p. 183.

[20]In 1827, a traveler up the Mississippi River was told by fellow passengers that "they could not get enough boats to bring the cotton down the Red." After having been subjected to constant talk about cotton for

slaves in Louisiana worked in upland cotton production during the 1820s, but the declining prices in the second half of the decade and the passage of a favorable sugar tariff in 1828 prompted some new planters to try sugar production. The number of sugar estates doubled from 1827 to 1830.[21]

Changes in slave household composition during the 1820s were minor, for the most part. The percentage of slaves who were solitaires decreased slightly, to 16 percent, reflecting a slower rate of slave importations. No extended forms were present, indicating that the old established communities strongly reflected in the previous period were now less significant (many of them had been dispersed through estate divisions). Moreover, the expansionistic tendency of both decades was apparent in the inventories.

In the 1820s, simple families absorbed 84 percent of the sampled slaves. This percentage is higher than that displayed in the model and in the previous decade, but it does not indicate greater stability. Instead, the enlargement of the simple family type resulted from a dramatic jump in the number of individuals living in female-headed, single-parent households. Twenty-eight percent of the 1820s slaves lived in such households, whereas only 9 percent of the sampled population of 1810-1819 had so resided. The unusually high percentage of households headed by female parents is the major departure from the household structure of the earlier period; it may well represent dislocations associated with the brisk sales and in-migrations of that earlier period, compounded by the economic reversals of the depression years.[22] The tracing of many Louisiana slave communities over four generations in case studies has conclusively demonstrated that a high percentage of female-headed households was a common characteristic of first- and even second-generation migration communities. Women severed from homes and families, sometimes including husbands, by migration or sale were often reluctant to marry in their new locations; many had additional children but preferred to head their own households. Some female-headed

---

two months, he complained that he "still dreamed of cotton" even when safely en route to St. Louis. Phillips, *American Negro Slavery*, p. 213, quoting Augusta, *Georgia Courier*, October 11, 1827.

[21]Phillips, *American Negro Slavery*, p. 166; Sydnor, *Slavery in Mississippi*, p. 183; J. C. Sitterson, *Sugar Country: The Cane Sugar Industry in the South, 1753-1950* (Lexington, Ky., 1953), p. 28.

[22]Another explanation may be possible. An examination of the inventories in the sample which showed pronounced percentages of female-headed households indicated that many were cotton plantations with between twenty-one and thirty-three slaves located in the Florida Parishes. Shortages of young, unattached males were also in evidence. Many of these women may have had mates on other plantations considering the density of slave populations and plantation holdings in those parishes. See Inventory, August 7, 1827, in Estate of John M. Williams, Concordia Parish Probate Records, Succession Volume #, 229-230; Inventory, October 11, 1822, in Estate of Rebecca Smith, West Feliciana Parish Probate Records, Inventory Volume C, 294-295; Inventory, July 27, 1821, in Estate of Sylvia Young, in West Feliciana Parish Probate Records, Inventory Volume C, 170-172.

households in the 1820s sample represented young women with only one or two small children; many of these women would marry and form standard-nuclear families in time.[23]

1830-1839

In comparison to the slower pace of the 1820s, the decade of the 1830s was extremely dynamic. Once more Louisiana's population impressively expanded. The rate of increase from 1830 to 1840 was over 63 percent, whereas that of the 1820s had been only 41 percent. The rate of increase among the slave population was somewhat less, 54 percent, but since so many slaves were already in the state due to the prodigious increases of the 1810-1819 period and the more moderate gains of the 1820s, the ratio of slaves to the whole population was higher than ever before.[24]

The accelerated migration included many non-slaveholding farmers although some of these would purchase a few slaves after arriving. But many of the migrants were planters escaping the ravaged soils of the eastern seaboard South. And by the 1830s, Louisiana's allure was two-fold: its lowlands beckoned potential sugar planters, and its upriver lands promised riches in cotton. Louisiana produced most of the nation's sugar by 1839. Sugar estates advanced greatly in the early years of the decade, drawing heavily on the internal slave trade for labor in the middle years, and stabilizing in the latter 1830s due to a reduction in the tariff and a rise in cotton prices. Although the number of sugar estates declined by 1839, this was due primarily to consolidation, and sugar remained profitable throughout the decade. Encouraged by good prices from 1832 to 1838, cotton holdings increased as well. The effects of the Panic of 1837 precipitated a serious decline in prices in 1839, but the worst effects on Louisiana's economy were not felt until the 1840s.[25]

In the wake of the Nat Turner Rebellion, a set of laws were passed in Louisiana (and other Southern states) restricting the importation of slaves by professional traders, although planters could obtain laborers on personal buying trips in the Southeast or across the river in Natchez. In 1834 the

[23] Case studies contained in Ann Patton Malone, "The Nineteenth Century Slave Family in Rural Louisiana: Its Household and Community Structure" (Ph. D., dissertation, Tulane University, 1985).

[24] The decennial increase among the whole population was 63.35 percent. The decennial increase among slaves was 53.7 percent. Louisiana had 109,588 slaves in 1830 and 168,452 in 1840. DeBow, *Statistical View of the United States*, pp. 82, 84, 105.

[25] *Reports of the Superintendent of the Census* (Washington, D. C., 1851-1852), p. 81; Phillips, *American Negro Slavery*, p. 167; Sitterson, *Sugar Country*, p. 30; Sydnor, *Slavery in Mississippi*, p. 183.

last of these statutes was repealed, and, according to Joe Gray Taylor, "The middle 1830's were the beginning of the heyday of the professional slave trader."[26] In the 1835-1837 boom years, slaves were imported in startling numbers to meet the growing demands of Louisiana's cotton and sugar producers.

Many of these general economic trends are reflected in the household constructions of sampled slave communities from 1830-1839. With the expansion of cotton and sugar production and an intensification of the slave trade, the percentage of solitaires in the sampled communities rose from 16 percent in the 1820s to 23 percent in the 1830s. Once more, males made up the larger portion of the solitaires, but both hardy young males and females were in great demand. Planters were willing to pay premium prices to obtain them.

Partly in consequence of the increased number of solitaires, the percentages of slaves occupying simple-family households was reduced. Female-headed households still encompassed 17 percent of the population, the same percentage exhibited in the model. On the other hand, households made up of fathers, mothers, and their offspring accounted for only 39 percent of the 1830s population, a striking decrease from the 51 percent of the previous decade. In societies in which the standard-nuclear family is considered the cultural norm, serious instability may be indicated when the percentage of inhabitants in that form falls to less than 40 percent. Therefore it appears that many slave communities of the 1830s were in an unstable state of flux, disrupted by the changing economy and the intensification of the slave trade.

In fact, serious imbalances were found about equally on cotton and sugar holdings. For example, Louis Landry's fifty-three slaves on a sugar estate in Ascension Parish displayed a radical skewing in household composition. Only 30 percent lived in standard-nuclear families, and 55 percent were solitaires. Charles Breaux's small community of twenty-six sugar-producing slaves in Iberville Parish had 42 percent of its laborers as

[26]Taylor, *Negro Slavery in Louisiana*, pp. 41-45. Also see Phillips, *American Negro Slavery*, p. 190. Phillips stated, "The heydey of the trade fell in the piping times of peace and migration from 1815 to 1837, for thereafter the flow was held somewhat in check, first by the hard times and then by an agricultural renaissance in Virginia." The volume of the interstate slave trade had been vigorously debated by historians of the South, particularly in regard to separations which the trade incurred among slave families. See especially Herbert G. Gutman and Richard Sutch, "The Slave Family: Protected Agent of Capitalistic Masters or Victim of the Slave Trade?," in Paul A. David et al., *Reckoning with Slavery*, pp. 94-133; Clement Eaton, *A History of the Old South: The Emergence of a Reluctant Nation* (New York, 1966), pp. 231-233; Stampp, *The Peculiar Institution*, p. 239; Fogel and Engerman, *Time on the Cross*, I, 44-58; Michael Tadman, "Slave Trading in the Antebellum South: An Estimate of the Inter-Regional Slave Trade," *Journal of American Studies*, XIII (1979), 195-220.

solitaires and half of its slaves in female-headed, single-parent households. Cotton plantations as well often exhibited a high incidence of workers having no apparent family affiliation. Cotton planter William Disharoone's slave community had as solitaires 32 percent of its population and only 40 percent in two-parent households. On the Grove Plantation of Bayou Vidal, 48 percent of 132 slaves were solitaires, and only one-fourth resided in two-parent households.[27]

Such examples indicate that many Louisiana slave communities of the 1830s were in a state of social disorganization, with a relatively high incidence of solitaires, and a low incidence of slaves forming part of standard nuclear families. The high profits accrued by the aggressive planters of the 1830s were paid for in a loss of internal cohesion within their slave communities.

1840-1849

The nation and even the booming Lower South were once more plunged into a depression by the Panic of 1837; its effects lingered throughout most of the decade of the 1840s. Although Louisiana's population continued to increase (in 1850 it was 47 percent larger than in 1840), the rate of increase was 16 percent less than that of the 1830s. The rate of increase among the slave population dropped from a 54 percent increase in the 1830s to a 45 percent increase in the 1840s.[28]

The decade was generally dismal for cotton producers.[29] Clement Eaton observed that cotton prices "fluctuated violently in the decade . . . dropping to below the cost of production. . . ."[30] In the cotton districts, mortgages of land and slaves proliferated.[31] And as prices plummeted, cotton production

[27]The Landry sugar plantation and slaves were sold in 1832, and the slaves were sold separately from the land. A general lack of regard for family organization was reflected in the sale. Children above ten were appraised separately from their parents and were sold apart in many cases. The separation of a married couple was openly stated: "Alexis, a negro [*sic*] man, aged twenty-eight years, and wife Victoire, aged sixteen, offered together in one lot not having attained the price they were estimated at . . . were sold separately." Inventory for Sale, July 29, 1831, in Estate of Louis Landry, Ascension Parish Probate Records, Inventory and Sales Volume, 1831-1832, 67-75; Parish Probate Records, Probate File #644; Inventory, October 27, 1837, in Estate of Rachel Grove, Concordia Parish Probate Records, Succession Volume I, 73-81. Also see Inventory, August 3, 1839, in Estate of William Disharoone, Concordia Parish Probate Records, Succession Volume I, 298-299.

[28]DeBow, *Statistical View of the United States*, pp. 82, 84, 105.

[29]Phillips, *American Negro Slavery*, p. 167.

[30]Eaton, *History of the Old South*, p. 213.

[31]Even planters not usually inclined to do so found it necessary to mortgage slaves. For example,

decreased. Planters in other states may have had no alternative except to produce more of the fleecy staple in order to compensate for low prices. But affluent Louisiana planters did have an alternative, and many expanded into the sugar parishes, since sugar prices were not so adversely affected by the depression. Stimulated by a higher tariff in 1842, sugar estates increased to 1,536 by 1849; consequently, the number of slaves in the sugar parishes doubled.[32]

The contraction of the economy in the 1840s prompted a return to a more normal slave-household construction, compared to that of the dynamic but disruptive previous decade. The percentage of slaves in the solitaire type remained high, 19 percent, but this was far less than the 23 percent of the 1830s. Simple families again comprised 73 percent of the slaves, and, within the simple family, 48 percent lived in the standard-nuclear families—both marked increases over the percentages of the decade before. Single-parent, female-headed households still comprised a sizeable proportion of the population, 17 percent. The portrait emerging from the analysis of the household structure during the 1840s is one of a still-disrupted composition which was moving toward greater equilibrium.[33]

Many of them short on cash, planters relied more on natural increases and less on the slave trade in the 1840s. Since many cotton farmers and planters cut back on production during the depression and slave importations slowed, existing communities had fewer adjustments to make for newcomers. With more stable slave populations, slaves in many communities formed

---

prominent cotton and sugar planter Thomas Butler wrote in 1842 of his intention to mortgage twelve slaves "wishing to raise some money in these hard times," and many of his fellow planters in West Feliciana Parish did the same. Letter, Thomas Butler to Hon. Leufroy Barras, May 3, 1842, in Thomas Butler Papers, Box 8, Folder 47, Department of Archives, Louisiana State University.

[32]The cotton export price in 1842 was but 6.2 cents per pound, and the highest price paid for cotton in New Orleans that year was 7.5 cents. In 1844 the price of cotton bottomed out at 5.9 cents, well below the cost of production, rising briefly in 1846, then dropping once again in 1848 to 6.5 cents. The effects of the depressed cotton market are reflected in low production reports in the census of 1850 (on the 1849 crop). Sydnor, *Slavery in Mississippi*, p. 183; *Reports of the Superintendent of the Census*, pp. 67, 91, 96; Sitterson, *Sugar Country*, pp. 27, 30; Eaton, *History of the Old South*, pp. 221-223; Phillips, *American Negro Slavery*, p. 167.

[33]For example, the numbers who were solitaires were significantly reduced. Some no doubt married and formed families while others were sold by cotton planters to sugar producers, and the hiring of cotton slaves to the sugar parishes was a very common practice in the 1840s. These hired solitaires may not have been reflected in the inventories of their home plantations. Solomon Northup was one of those hired out to a sugar parish. It is also clear from the decrease in the ratio of slave importations during the decade that planters, many of them short on cash, were relying more on natural increase and less on the trade. Since many cotton farmers cut back on production, they bought fewer slaves, and existing communities had fewer adjustments to make. With a more stable population, slaves of many communities formed standard nuclear families and contributed to kinship development, which would be well advanced by the next decade. Solomon Northup, *Twelve Years a Slave*, ed. by Sue Eakin and Joseph Logsdon (Baton Rouge, 1968), pp. 145, 147; Taylor, *Negro Slavery in Louisiana*, pp. 34-35.

standard-nuclear families and contributed to kinship development which would be well advanced by the next decade. The hard times did force some sales of slaves, usually those of solitaires rather than members of families. Most of these conveyances were in conjunction with sheriff's sales and estate sales. Sheriff's sales were quite common in the 1840s, and large planters such as Stephen Duncan picked up additional holdings through this means. And short money supply prompted many heirs to hold estate sales, preferring the money to the labor of their inherited workers.[34]

1850-1859

In the 1850s, the dual economy of Louisiana recovered from the doldrums of the 1840s with renewed alacrity, and the decade was characterized by sustained prosperity. The size and numbers of slaveholdings increased but the ratio of increase in whole and slave population slowed. The flood of migration of the previous decades was reduced to a small stream. New residents and their slaves, or slaves imported by professional traders, entered at a slower, more steady pace, and they were fewer in number as well.[35] The influx of the 1850s was, therefore, far less disruptive of the household and family composition of Louisiana slaves than was that of the 1830s, the other very prosperous decade. The slowdown—it should be reiterated—was not due to a depressed economy. Both cotton and sugar brought good prices in the decade, although the cost of slaves rose exorbitantly.[36]

By the 1850s the soils of the old cotton districts in even the Lower South were seriously depleted.[37] Exhaustion of the land in the older sections of the

[34]In Stephen Duncan's gift of L'Argent Plantation to his son, the plantation was identified as "consisting of 1700 acres acquired at Sheriff's Sale Nov 24 1849 . . . with all the Slaves." Donation of Land and Slaves, Stephen Duncan to S. P. Duncan, in Tensas Parish Probate Records, Wills and Donation Volume A, 68-70. Part of this plantation was owned by William Cochran until his death in 1851 at which time Duncan bought his deceased partner's portion.

Among the many estate sales of the 1840s was that of Daniel Orr's plantation in Avoyelles Parish. In the sale of slaves, several standard nuclear families were separated. Inventory for Probate Sale, November 21, 1843, in Estate of Daniel Orr, Avoyelles Parish Probate Records, Probate Sale Volume A, 97-100, 141-149.

[35]The ratio of increase for the whole population, 1850-1860, was 36.74 percent; that of slaves was 35.2 percent. This was no more than 12 percent higher than the percentage estimated for natural increases during the period. Taylor, *Negro Slavery in Louisiana*, p. 101; Joseph C. G. Kennedy, *Preliminary Report of the Eighth Census, 1860* (Washington, D. C., 1862), p. 131; DeBow, *Statistical View of the United States*, p. 82.

[36]Taylor, *Negro Slavery in Louisiana*, p. 102.

[37]An overseer encountered by Frederick Olmsted at Bayou Sara in West Feliciana parish in 1856 informed him that "this was once a famous cotton region. When it was first settled up by 'Mericans, used to be reckoned the garding of the world, the almightiest rich sile God ever shuck down." But, he admitted, it

Mississippi River cotton parishes did not usually result in great financial hardship for the largest planters in these regions, but it did prompt a shift of slaves and capital within the state. Many old planter families purchased additional plantations in the still-fertile cotton lands of northern and western parishes and invested in sugar estates of the coastal region.[38]

Louisiana's cotton production in the 1850s was surpassed only by Alabama and Mississippi, and in cane sugar production she had no equal or even close competitor among domestic producers.[39] Record sugar yields and profitable price levels for cotton produced a cocky confidence among Louisiana planters and led to increased purchases of slaves in the last half of the decade. Phillips suggests that a late decade speculation in slaves produced a veritable "Negro fever" which artifically increased their value.[40] Planters, intent on expanding their operations, were willing to pay the high prices. As Taylor has observed, "Planters were prosperous . . . and were convinced that more slaves would add to their prosperity."[41] Buying after the mid-fifties was risky, since the prices were already extraordinarily high, and many planters bought only laborers who were really needed. Therefore slave communities remained fairly stable in the 1850s. And except for sales associated with estate division, there was little incentive to sell slaves since they were rapidly increasing in value.

---

was "getting thinned down powerful fast now. Nothin' to what it was." As Olmsted traveled the road from Bayou Sara to Woodville, Mississippi, he was struck by the eroded land and abandoned plantations. Frederick Law Olmsted, *The Slave States*, ed. by Harvey Wish (New York, 1959), p. 75.

38For example see acquisitions of Stephen Duncan in St. Mary Parish. Conveyance Book O, 242-247; Donation Book A, 68-69, both in St. Mary Parish Records.

39Sydnor, *Slavery in Mississippi*, pp. 183-184; Kennedy, *Preliminary Report on Eight Census, 1860*, pp. 200-201; Sitterson, *Sugar Country*, pp. 20-30; Eaton, *History of the Old South*, pp. 224-225.

40Eaton, *History of the Old South*, p. 234. Joe Gray Taylor defines the "economic sin" of "Negro Fever" as a tendency among southwestern planters to "continually . . . buy more land and slaves with which to grow more sugar or cotton in order to buy more land and slaves." He believes that criticism of the planters was largely unjustified. The contractions in slave population increases and in the mean sizes of slave communities during hard times compels me to agree with Taylor. Taylor, *Negro Slavery in Louisiana*, p. 165. Stampp, *The Peculiar Institution*, p. 392. The Louisiana parish records provide evidence in abundance documenting the spectacular rise in slave prices during the latter 1850s. For example, compare the appraised values of a family of slaves inventoried in 1850 and sold in 1855. In 1850, sons was appraised as a group for $2,150. In 1855, the same couple, their newborn child, and two youngest sons were sold together for $3,200. The older three sons, ranging in ages from thirteen to sixteen, were sold separately for $4,735. Of course, the older ages of the sons and the addition of an infant made a difference, but the married couple were now fifty and would offset some of the value increase. The estate made $5,424 by holding the family for five years. By the way, the three older sons were all sold to different owners. Inventory, October 31, 1850, Estate of Martha C. Hargroves, Avoyelles Parish Probate Records, Inventory Volume C, 2-4; Probate Sale, 1855, Martha C. Hargroves, Sale of Probates Volume A, 282-294.

41Taylor, *Negro Slavery*, p. 52.

As a whole, Louisiana slave communities by the mid-1850s were probably as mature and stable as they had ever been, or would be again. Kinship lines were well advanced on many plantations. Units had increased in size so that about half of Louisiana's slaves lived in units of fifty or more, comparable to a small village. Slaves in these larger units found opportunities to marry within their own small societies, and by the 1850s, most abounded with close relations. The majority of slaves, 75 percent, lived in simple families; solitaires accounted for 17 percent, and complex households contained nearly 8 percent of the slaves. Almost none lived in non-nuclear forms. Within the simple family, over 52 percent of the sampled slaves lived in standard-nuclear families, and 12.5 percent resided in female-headed, single-parent households.

It is clear that the most significant movement which took place in slave family composition during the 1850s was toward internal cohesion, as exemplified by a decline in the proportion of the population without family connections, a rise in the percentage in simple, nuclear, and complex forms, and a decline since the 1840s is the proportion of slaves in female-headed, single-parent households. In human terms, more than half of the sampled slaves lived in families composed of a mother, father, and children. Another 8 percent were married and some of these would eventually have children or had had children in the past. All others, except for the solitaires, formed parts of households made up of close kin. And even among the solitaires, many—perhaps most—had close relatives on the plantations where they resided. While the composition described for the 1850s may not be ideal by modern standards, by free standards, or even by standards to which the slaves themselves aspired, it is the most nearly ideal organization observed among groups of actual slave communities in Louisiana. If the profile presented earlier derived from the entire sample represents the average household composition of 155 slave communities over a fifty-four year span, the profile of the 1850s represents the best that these slaves were able to achieve within their collective experience.

1860-1865

Though war clouds were already gathering in 1860, Louisiana economically was in good shape. In a total population of 708,002, slaves accounted for 331,726 individuals; free blacks were 18,647, and the remaining 357,629 were whites. As the new decade commenced, cotton and sugar production seemed boundless, rice production had increased, tobacco production had almost doubled, towns and villages were developing throughout the state, and even the health of the people seemed to have improved, with mortality rates dropping from those of the previous decade.[42] The first two years of the decade were reasonably tranquil, even after the Civil War began in 1861. A banner sugar crop was made that year, and Sitterson found that it was "harvested and manufactured into sugar without serious interference from war conditions."[43] Cotton, too, was grown and harvested with little difficulty in 1861.

But planters soon found that transporting and marketing their banner crops under war conditions presented serious obstacles. Planters sold some cotton to New Orleans factors, but western and northern buyers soon withdrew from the market. Foreign markets were effectively closed by a Union blockade. The huge sugar crop of 1861 found few buyers, and prices plummeted in 1861 to half that of the previous year. Surplus cotton was stored, but with most markets closed, little was planted in subsequent war years. Credit problems were as devastating as falling prices. Louisiana planter Kenneth Clark wrote a friend in 1861 that "all commercial interests are entirely destroyed. Cotton and sugar cannot be sold."[44] Provisions were scarce and expensive, cash in short supply, and marketing almost impossible. These problems were present before the fall of New Orleans in 1862 and the occupation of many black-belt parishes by late 1863.[45]

This is not the place to recount in detail the effects of the Civil War on Louisiana plantation society. Its social and economic effects were enormous and have been chronicled in numerous secondary works as well as documented in planters' journals, diaries, reminiscences, period newspapers, and, of course, in official records of both armies. Its effects on family and community life were grim for all Louisiana residents. Many white families as well as black families were dislocated or broken by war. A study of white family composition would probably show as much disruption and chaos during the mid war years as that of slave families. Unfortunately, records for either group are scarce. Parish records were often destroyed or sporadically kept; some estates were not probated for years after the deaths of individuals during war times. A token number of records were located from the 1860s which clearly designated family and household relationships, but most were from 1860 and therefore do not reflect the true extent to which slave communities were impacted by the war.

[42]Kennedy, *Preliminary Report*, pp. 22, 131, 200-203.

[43]Sitterson, *Sugar Country*, p. 207.

[44]Quoted in *ibid.*, p. 209.

[45]*Ibid.*

The sampled communities for the 1860-1864 period represent only a partial decade, and the set is smaller and less balanced because of poor record-keeping. Nevertheless, inventories of the sampled communities do reflect increased instability resulting from deteriorating conditions immediately prior to and during the Civil War. Solitaires declined to 15 percent, and there is a corresponding decline in the percentage of slaves belonging to simple families, reduced from 75 percent in the 1850s to 68 percent. Membership in standard two-parent family households also significantly declined. Individuals in such households comprised only 45 percent of the slave population, the lowest percentage since the volatile 1830s.

Another important departure was the much bigger percentage of slaves forming multiple-family households. Fourteen percent of the sampled slaves lived in such units, and another 2 percent resided in extended-family households. Most of these, by far, were contained in units of a parent/parents with an additional conjugal unit from a later generation, but practically all forms of complex family households were represented. In times of crisis, slave families absorbed needy relatives into established household units. Single or married mature parents brought into their households widowed or separated daughters, grandchildren, and orphans; couples took in siblings. This practice was common among families and households of all races during that and other wars. Many of these complex forms resulted from departures of young slave husbands and fathers—due to conscription, removals to Texas, hires to the Confederate authorities, or death.[46] But part of the increase in complex, multi-generational forms was a natural outgrowth, since the 1860s represented a late developmental phase for most slave communities.

It bears repeating that the sample was skewed by the fact that one-third of the sampled communities of the 1860s were inventoried in 1860; these closely resemble, in their household composition, communities of the latter 1850s—stable and family oriented. Without the presence of the pre-war inventories, statistics regarding household composition of the 1860s would no doubt have been far more distorted, imbalanced, and more representative of those difficult times. The seventy-five slaves belonging to a plantation

[46]On the D. W. Magill list of 1865, four males were noted to have "ranaway and joined the enemy in April, 1863"; one died at the Battle of Mansfield in April, 1864, one was accidentally shot; six were killed near St. Martinsville [*sic*] in an insurrection, and several others were in the service of the Confederacy in various capacities both in Texas and Louisiana. Also see William J. Minor's diary entries for September 28, 29, 1863, after fourteen slave men were taken by the Federal forces. Minor wrote: "The men taken off & their families were in deep distress. . . . Bill Clarke was the only man who asked me to take care of his family." "If the war continues twelve months longer all Negro men of value will be taken. The women and children will be left for their masters to maintain which they can not do." Weeks Family Papers, Tulane University; William J. Minor Plantation Diary 32, LSU.

of Alexandre DeClouet of St. Martin Parish in 1863 were probably more typical. Only one-third of his slaves were part of two-parent households, and 21 percent were members of female, single-parent units. A high 23 percent were encompassed in multiple-family households, all of which were examples of parents taking in grown children and grandchildren.[47]

A second example is the slave community belonging to David Weeks Magill. After his mother's death, Magill in 1856 inherited a sugar plantation in St. Martin Parish and 113 slaves. Through reconstitution methods, it was determined that these 1856 slaves lived in a stable, family-oriented community constituted very much like that of the model for the 1850s. Kinship systems were extremely well developed since most of the slaves were direct descendants of those belonging to the estate of Magill's grandfather, David Weeks, who died in 1834. And some were descendants of slaves belonging to Magill's great-grandfather, William Weeks. By 1863, David Magill had died at Vicksburg in service of the Confederacy. In a deposition to the court explaining why an inventory of Magill's estate could not take place in 1863, his grandmother and closest living relative, Mary Conrad Weeks Moore, stated that Magill's slaves had been removed "in April 8163 . . . to another part of the State more out of the way of depredation by the Enemy. . . ." They were transported to De Soto Parish, although a few house servants remained in St. Martinville. Some of the De Soto contingent were subsequently taken by Magill's uncle to Polk County, Texas; others were conscripted for work in the Confederate Iron Works in Texas; some men were killed in an insurrection in 1863; a few ran away and joined the Federal forces, and several died at the Battle of Mansfield in 1864. An accounting was finally made of Magill's estate in early 1865, by his overseer. At that time, sixteen were in St. Martinville; the remainder of those inventoried were in De Soto Parish. Of the 109 slaves left in the estate who had belonged to the 1856 community (or their descendants), 8 percent were solitaires, 13 percent were part of extended- or multiple-family households; one-half lived in two-parent households, and nearly 20 percent lived in female-headed, single-parent households.[48]

[47]List par 1854 Familles, Alexandre DeClouet Memorandum Book, 1853-1863; Liste de Negroes, November 15, 1865; Lists, 1860-1862, in *ibid.*, Alexandre DeClouet Papers, LSU.

[48]Petition of Mary Clara Conrad, late widow of David Weeks, deceased and now wife of John Moore, St. Martin, August 23, 1856, in Estate of Frances Weeks, widow of A. S. Magill, Probate Records, Folder 1540: Estate of Augustin S. Magill, December 24, 1851, St. Martin Parish Probate Records, Folder 1314: The Planter's Annual Record of His Negroes Upon the Plantation Made at the Close of the Year 1858," D. W. Magill's slaves, St. Martin Parish, in Weeks Family Papers, Tulane University; Deposition, Dr. John Smith, St. Martin Parish, February 17, 1866, In Estate of David Weeks Magill, Succession #1811, 6129B; List of Slaves Belonging to the Estate of D. W. Magill, deceased, March 26, 1865 (St. Martin and De Soto parishes), Weeks Family Papers, Tulane University.

A similar profile was present among exiled slaves belonging to the partnership of Prescott and Moore in De Soto Parish in 1864. There, 91 slaves were organized according to the following proportions: 2 percent were solitaires, 38 percent lived in two-parent households, 9 percent were in female-headed households, and a striking 41 percent lived in extended- or multiple-family households. Higher than usual numbers in female-headed, and multiple-family households in these examples are indicative of disruptions in family and community composition resulting from the war.[49]

An excellent treatment of the Louisiana slave family during the Civil War is provided by C. Peter Ripley.[50] He documents the effects of Union conscription of slave husbands and fathers, the impressment and hiring of male slaves by the Confederacy, the dislocations associated with removal, and the mixed record of the contraband movement. As well, former slaves' testimonies provide many poignant references to the effects of the war on their families, as do terse notations in planters' records. No matter how sweet the taste of freedom, the relatively stable family and community life that Louisiana slaves had collectively achieved by the 1850s was destroyed by the dislocations of war. Much of the confusion and restlessness observed among Louisiana blacks in the 1863-1865 period was an attempt to adjust to quasi-freedom without the familial and community support they had before the war. Many families were never reunited, and some slaves searched for years for loved ones who had been severed from them by the war or by earlier sale.

The foregoing analysis showed that although a norm can be established in regard to the household composition of 10,329 Louisiana slaves, variations occurred according to the time period in which the slaves were inventoried.

Slave communities of the sample reflected major economic trends in their domestic organizations, and they also displayed a long-range developmental cycle—from the simple to the complex, and from relative disorganization to relative stability, although these cycles displayed rising and falling patterns, according to external factors. But the communities appear to have resumed their developmental course once the crisis precipitated by external forces had been resolved. It was noted that a period of economic expansion did not necessarily result in greater stability and cohesion in slave communities. In fact, the less change imposed from outside the community, the more progress communities made in establishing stable households and extensive

[49]List of Slaves of Prescott and Moore, April 17, 1864, De Soto Parish, Weeks Papers, Box 61, Folder 76, LSU. Also used to identify family groups was an inventory of the same slaves, June 26, 1865, Folder 76.

[50]C. Peter Ripley, "The Black Family in Transition: Louisiana, 1860-1865," *Journal of Southern History*, LXI, XXIII (1975); C. Peter Ripley, *Slaves and Freedom in Civil War Louisiana* (Baton Rouge, 1976), pp. 146-159.

family-kinship networks.

The investigation of slave household composition among Louisiana slaves isolated certain household types and categories which consistently acted as barometers of change within slave community organizations: (1) the solitaire type, (2) two sub-categories of the simple family, those of the standard-nuclear family and the female-single-parent household, and (3) the multiple-family household type. Scholars have devoted much attention to the simple family. Several have quite accurately observed that most slave families were of this type, and that the largest number of households within the simple-family type were those composed of standard-nuclear families. Undoubtedly the two-parent family household was the ideal to which most (but not all) slaves aspired. But historians of the family have also overstated their case, implying that most slaves lived in standard-nuclear families; this was often not the case. Slaves in the typical Louisiana community formed part of a wide variety of household classifications. Usually only about half—and often considerably less—of slave inhabitants on a given plantation lived in standard-nuclear families, either as parents or offspring. It was not the only stable form, even if it was the ideal.

The Louisiana study confirms that revisionist historians of the 1970s and 1980s are correct in sweeping aside the myth of the matriarchy, or matrifocal domination of American slave families. But it also demonstrated that the female-headed, single-parent household was a consistent feature of Louisiana slave communities and an accepted family form. Up to a point, the proportion of persons living in single-parent households connoted disorganization and instability in a slave community since most slaves seemingly preferred membership in a double-headed family, and under optimum conditions they would have become part of such a household. However, from 10 to 15 percent of slaves in even the most stable and mature slave communities resided in female-headed, single-parent households. This proportion of female-headed, single-parent households was expected and considered quite normal in Louisiana slave societies. Single parenthood was clearly a visible alternative. The female-headed household has received much attention, but two groups in slave community organization have been given far less scholarly attention than they deserve. One is the solitaire household type, and the other is the multiple-family household with downward disposition.

Several historians of slavery have concentrated so exclusively on the slave "family" and the slave "community" that they omit consideration of the solitaires because they did not constitute families. Solitaires often comprised one-fifth of slave community's membership; they greatly affected its economic and social balance, and in many cases they formed the primary marriage pool. Solitaires formed an omnipresent group in Louisiana slave society which, in the early stages of community development, consisted primarily of young, unattached males—often new purchases—a common but volatile group in any work society or social group. In the latter developmental stages, many of the solitaires were widows and widowers over fifty who frequently were among the most respected members of their societies.

The final category often overlooked in the study of the slave family and community is that of the multiple-family type with downward disposition of the secondary conjugal unit. This was the great umbrella form in slave societies. Though it rarely accounted for many units in a slave community, the form often contained from seven to twelve individuals. Many slaves in Louisiana had the experience of being part of a multiple-family household at some point in their lives. An extreme example is that of Petit Anse in St. Mary Parish which in 1836 had no complex forms but in 1860 had three large multiple-family households which encompassed 55 percent of the population. And on another St. Mary Parish plantation, that of Tiger Island in 1860, 20 percent of the slaves lived in multiple-family households. On Oakland Plantation in West Feliciana Parish, 16 percent of the 1857 population formed part of such households.[51]

The quantitative analysis of the 155 slave communities representing various points in time over fifty-four years showed a cyclical development when those communities were broken into decennial intervals. Part of the development was simply progressive. Slave communities over time proceeded from very simple to more complex household construction. They also grew in mean size and generally proceeded to what is construed as more stable compositions. But even in the 1810-1864 sample, a cyclical as well as a progressive development was discernible, with the so-called "stable" features of slave communities (relative gender balance, large numbers in families, few solitaires, more two-parent than single-parent households, and generational depth) occurring in a rising and falling upward curve, generally in response to external factors. Despite the fluctuations, the patterns and progressions are apparent. And Herbert Gutman was probably right in assessing that the primary motivation behind the movement toward stabilization was grounded in the slaves' own cultural value system.[52]

These findings suggest that the rural Louisiana slave family, household, and community structure was even more diverse and adaptable than previously believed. Its forms were plastic, not fixed; household development was organic, not static. The domestic arrangements of

[51]Malone, "Nineteenth Century Slave Family," 131, 228, 354.

[52]Gutman, *The Black Family, passim.*

Louisiana's chattels molded to fit the changing requirements of their communities' membership and to the peculiar circumstances imposed upon them. But despite the adaptability required of them, the examined slave communities exhibited constants both in preferred household forms and in general developmental patterns. The high regard which Louisiana slaves placed on family and kinship is indisputable. It has been discussed in studies of Louisiana slavery, it has been demonstrated in Herbert Gutman's analysis of the slave families of Lewis Stirling's Louisiana plantation; it has been recounted by dozens who were once enslaved in Louisiana; and it has been expressed by many owners of slaves in the state. It can be seen in the messages that Louisiana slaves sent to kinsmen from whom they had been severed by sale or migration. The Louisiana slave households study provides some evidence that a driving need to bind themselves together in units of support and affection influenced Louisiana slaves to rebuild fractured families, households, and communities and to seek stable, balanced social organizations, sometimes against almost insurmountable odds.

SMOTHERING AND OVERLAYING OF VIRGINIA SLAVE CHILDREN: A SUGGESTED EXPLANATION

TODD L. SAVITT*

Infant mortality in ante-bellum Virginia was extremely high. During the decade of the 1850s between sixteen and twenty percent of all deaths in the state occured among children under the age of one year. The major causes of death included croup (diphtheria), diarrhea and dysentery, whooping cough, pneumonia, scarlet and other types of fever, and suffocation (also referred to as smothering and overlaying).[1] Since the 1850s medical science has substantially reduced the incidence of all but two of these diseases—pneumonia (which is today responsible for up to 27% of infant deaths between 1 and 11 months)[2] and suffocation. With regard to the latter there is strong evidence to indicate that many deaths which physicians and planters of the 1850s ascribed to suffocation, smothering and overlaying (almost all slaves) were actually cases of the disease presently known as Sudden Infant Death Syndrome (SIDS) or "crib death." The Second International Conference on Causes of Sudden Death in Infants (1970) defined SIDS as:

> The sudden death of any infant or young child which is unexpected by history, and in which a thorough post-mortem examination fails to demonstrate an adequate cause for death.[3]

* The author is indebted to his wife, Carole L. Savitt, for calling to his attention the article which led him to connect Sudden Infant Death Syndrome with overlaying, and to Professor Willie Lee Rose, now of Johns Hopkins University, for originally posing the problem of slave smothering. This publication was supported in part by NIH Grant 1 RO1 LM 02071 from the National Library of Medicine.

[1] Virginia, Register of Deaths (manuscript on microfilm), 1853-1860, Southampton County, Augusta County, Petersburg Town, Staunton Town, at Virginia State Library, Richmond, Virginia; United States, Bureau of the Census, *Mortality Statistics of the Seventh Census of the United States, 1850* (Washington, D.C., 1855), 290-295. The infant mortality rate for the entire country, by calculation from the 1850 Census, was 16.4%, and for the slaveholding states, 18.3%.

[2] United States, Department of Health, Education & Welfare, *Vital Statistics of the United States, 1967*, IIA, 2-31.

[3] Abraham B. Bergman, J. Bruce Beckwith, C. George Ray, eds., *Sudden Infant Death Syndrome, Proceedings of the Second International Conference of Causes of Sudden Death in Infants* (Seattle, 1970), 18.

[4] Marie Valdes-Dapena, *et. al.*, "Sudden unexpected death in infancy: A statistical analysis of certain socioeconomic factors," *Journal of Pediatrics*, 1968, *73:* 388; John W. Melton, *et. al.*, "Sudden and unexpected deaths in infancy," *Virginia Medical Monthly*, 1968, *95:* 63. The 45% figure was reported in Abraham B. Bergman, *et. al.*, "Studies of the sudden infant death syndrome in King County, Washington. III. Epidemiology," *Pediatrics*, 1972, *49:* 861.

It is, at present, responsible for between 10 and 30 percent (45% in one study) of deaths between the ages two weeks and eleven months, clearly establishing it as a leading killer of children under one year of age.[4]

Typical cases of overlaying share several of the unmistakable hallmarks of SIDS. Compare a twentieth-century physician's description of the latter with an overseer's and a planter's remarks on the former:

An apparently thriving two-month-old boy is found dead face down in his crib. Except for a brief mild rhinorrhea during the previous week, the child had been in excellent health from birth. At a routine well-baby check by the family doctor a few days prior to the event, he appeared robust and free of problems. On the night of death, he took his formula eagerly and was put down in his crib about 10 P.M. His mother looked in before retiring; he was sleeping peacefully on his abdomen with his face to the side. When found at 6:30 A.M., he had obviously been dead for several hours.[5]

I [Nathaniel Ryan, overseer] am sorry to inform you [Edmund Hubard, slaveowner] that Matilda has lost her youngest child she over laid it, it was well and hearty when she went to bed and found it dead sometime in the night.[6]

Last week [wrote Robert Hubard to his brother, Edmund] Tilla overlaid/when asleep/and killed her youngest child—a boy 6 or 7 months old. This was no doubt caused by her own want of care and attention.[7]

Most people, both today and 120 years ago, automatically assume that the fault lies with the parent and that death is preventable. These are false assumptions. Physicians now know that children cannot be smothered so long as there is any circulating air available, even when the infant is beneath the covers or wedged against the sleeping mother.[8]

In addition to this descriptive similarity between SIDS and overlaying, there is a remarkable epidemiological correspondence, both in age and seasonal variation. Crib death does not occur among children of all age groups. Those under two weeks and over one year are almost entirely spared; those between two weeks and four months are prime targets. In two recent studies, conducted in King County (Seattle), Washington, and Richmond, Virginia, 85% and 63% respectively, of the victims were between one and four months old. The majority of these deaths occurred during the colder six months of the

[5] J. Bruce Beckwith & Abraham B. Bergman, "The sudden death syndrome of infancy," *Hospital Practice*, November 1967, *2:* 44.

[6] Nathaniel Ryan, Saratoga, Buckingham County, Virginia, to Edmund W. Hubard, Washington, D.C., 15 December 1841, Hubard Papers (Southern Historical Collection, University of North Carolina, Chapel Hill, N.C.).

[7] Robert T. Hubard, Rosny, Buckingham County, Virginia to Edmund W. Hubard, Washington, D.C., 21 December 1841, Hubard Papers (Southern Historical Collection, University of North Carolina, Chapel Hill, N.C.).

[8] Beckwith & Bergman, "Sudden death syndrome," 50-51.

year (October through March).[9] The figures obtained from an analysis of the manuscript Register of Deaths for twenty-six Virginia counties, between 1853 and 1860, corroborate the King County and Richmond studies. Of the 226 children whose demise the parent or slaveowner attributed to overlaying, smothering or suffocation, 54% were between one month and four months of age. Fifty-six percent of the deaths occurred between October and March.[10]

The relative incidence of overlaying was much lower in ante-bellum Virginia (about 4% of infant deaths) than that of SIDS in present-day America (10 to 30% of infant deaths) for several reasons. Since people did not understand the cause of sudden infant death they usually classified it as "unknown" in

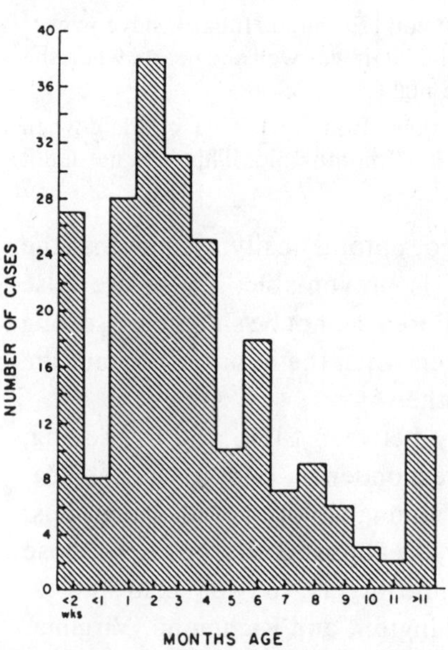

Figure 1. The age distribution of 226 cases of smothering, suffocation and overlaying in Virginia, 1853-1860.

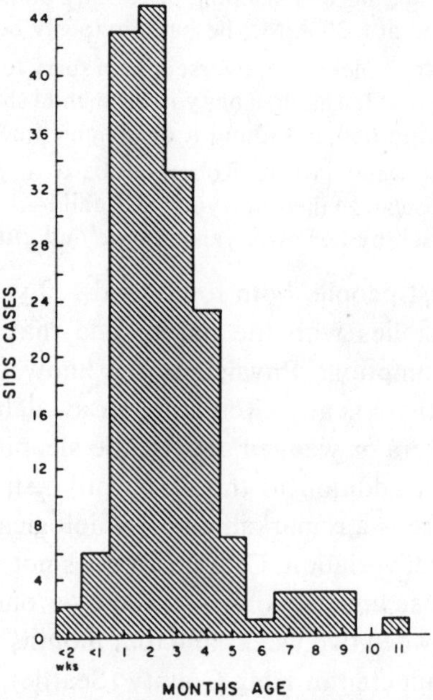

Figure 2. The age distribution of 170 SIDS cases in King County, Washington, 1965-1967. [From Bergman, *et. al.*, "Studies in the sudden infant syndrome in King County, Washington. III. Epidemiology," *Pediatrics*, 1972, *49:* 863.]

[9] Bergman, *et al.*, "Studies of sudden infant death syndrome in King County," 863; Melton, *et al.*, "Sudden and unexpected deaths in infancy," 64-65.

[10] Virginia, Register of Deaths (manuscript on microfilm), 1853-1860, Accomac, Albermarle, Amelia, Arlington, Augusta, Bedford, Botetourt, Brunswick, Cumberland, Essex, Fairfax, Fauquier, Floyd, Frederick, Greene, Greensville, Halifax, Hanover, Henrico, Henry, Isle of Wight, Lancaster, Pittsylvania and Southampton Counties; Petersburg and Staunton Towns, at Virginia State Library, Richmond, Va. The oldest child in the survey to die of suffocation was six years.

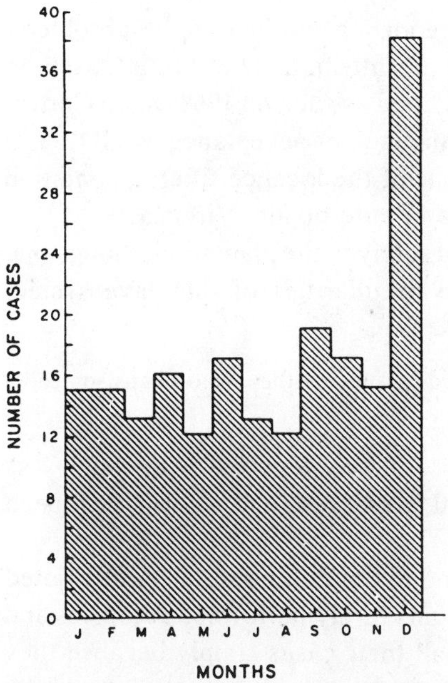

Figure 3. The months of death of 202 cases of smothering, suffocation and overlaying in Virginia, 1853-1860.

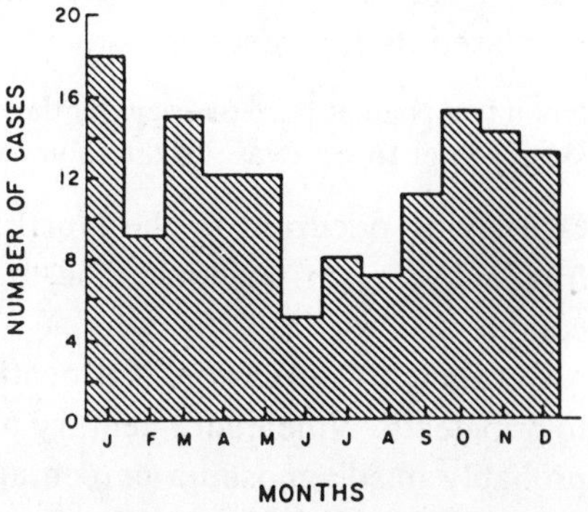

Figure 4. The months of death of 170 SIDS cases in King County, Washington, 1965-1967. [Adapted from Bergman, *et al.*, "Studies in the sudden infant death syndrome in King Country, Washington, III. Epidemiology," *Pediatrics*, 1972, *49:* 863.]

most mortality lists. We still today cannot explain this phenomenon of unexpected death in young babies, but rather than lump it with other unknown causes of death, medical scientists have provided us with the descriptive term, "Sudden Infant Death Syndrome." Another important factor was the marked under-reporting of white suffocation deaths (only about 2% of the total from this cause), probably due in part to the social stigma associated with child smothering. White parents and physicians likely attributed many sudden deaths among these children to teething, pneumonia, and, most often, to "unknown causes." Though present studies indicate that blacks do in fact have a higher incidence of SIDS than whites, and that all members of lower socio-economic groups regardless of race exhibit a similar tendency (probably due to sanitary conditions and overcrowding),[11] the 98% figure for antebellum Virginia blacks (229 of 232 smothering deaths) is much too high. It is interesting to note that in the latest available Department of Health, Educa-

[11] Valdes-Dapena, *et al.*, "Sudden unexpected death in infancy," 390-392.

tion and Welfare national survey, under-reporting continues to be a problem. Less than half of the estimated infant deaths attributable to SIDS (based on recent epidemiological studies) were classified as such on 1968 Death Certificates. Among the reasons for this were the lack of acceptance of SIDS as a disease entity, and subjectivity on the part of the local certifier, a condition remarkably similar to that which existed in ante-bellum Virginia.[12]

Smothering was not a problem confined solely to the plantation, though one early Southern writer asserted that the peculiarities of the slave system increased its incidence:

> Not a few [babies] are overlaid by the wearied [slave] mother, who sleeps so dead a sleep as not to be aware of the injury to her infant.[13]

Overlaying occurred in the North, where it was reported with much less frequency, again no doubt due to social pressures, and also in European countries.[14]

Certainly not all cases of suffocation among slave children can be attributed to crib death. Nineteenth-century physicians rarely performed autopsies and probably misdiagnosed a percentage of all their cases simply because they lacked the requisite knowledge. In addition, some slave mothers did actually commit infanticide,[15] though without their masters' knowledge. The information presented here, however, indicates that the majority of infant deaths attributed to suffocation, smothering and overlaying in ante-bellum Virginia (and the rest of the nation), were actually cases of Sudden Infant Death Syndrome.

[12] Noel S. Weiss, *et al.*, "Problems in the use of death certificates to identify sudden unexpected infant deaths," *Health Services Reports*, 1973, *88:* 555-58.

[13] Thomas Affleck, "On the hygiene of cotton plantations and the management of Negro slaves," *Southern Medical Reports*, 1851, *2:* 435.

[14] Bureau of the Census, *Mortality Statistics . . . 1850*, 28.

[15] See, for instance, the case of Opha Jane in the Powhatan County, Virginia, Order Book #29, 1851-1856, p. 501 (7 April 1856), at Virginia State Library, Richmond, Va.

"Open and Notorious Concubinage": The Emancipation of Slave Mistresses by Will and the Supreme Court in Antebellum Louisiana

By JUDITH K. SCHAFER

Murphy Institute
Tulane University

The slave in antebellum Louisiana had severely circumscribed legal rights. He could appear in court as a plaintiff only to claim his freedom; he appeared as a defendant only if accused of a crime. It was possible for him to testify for or against a fellow slave but never against a white. However, these limitations did not prevent him from being involved in thousands of lawsuits at the parish or district level and approximately 1,200 appeals to the Louisiana Supreme Court. In the overwhelming majority of these actions the bondsman was neither the plaintiff nor the defendant, but the *object*, primary or incidental, of the lawsuit.

To understand the rulings of the Louisiana Supreme Court, it is necessary to know the French civil-law system of which the court was a part. At the time Louisiana entered the Union many inhabitants of the state feared the imposition of the American common-law system, a new law in a foreign language,[1] and a threat to the power and prestige of those notaries, attorneys, and judges practicing the civil law.

Those in control of the legal system were careful to insure that Louisiana would continue to function under its traditional Civil Code after American rule began. The first constitution of the state forbade the legislature from imposing any form of common law upon the state and bound the judicial

[1]George Dargo, *Jefferson's Louisiana: Politics and the Clash of Legal Traditions* (Cambridge, Mass., 1975), p. 118. See also, Edward F. Haas's introduction to Edward F. Haas, ed., *Louisiana's Legal Heritage* (Pensacola, Fla., 1983), pp. 1-6.

structure firmly to the Civil Code. The constitution also limited the state's highest court to questions of law alone, and required it to justify every decision by citing the specific act of the legislature or article in the Civil Code that prompted each decision. Implied law and principles of equity were thus placed outside of the Louisiana system. Equity, after all, was developed to enlarge and override a scheme of law considered too rigid in scope. Louisiana judges were forbidden to bend the law or to create it in this manner and were allowed only to interpret it. Subsequent Louisiana constitutions contained the same restrictions. In the event the court might be tempted to overstep its authority, the articles limiting the power of the court were immediately followed by one that outlined the process of impeachment for the court's justices.[2]

Throughout the antebellum period the Louisiana Supreme Court heard cases involving the emancipation of slaves, and despite ever-tightening restrictions on manumission, a few bondservants continued to be legally transformed from property into free persons. In the early decades of the nineteenth century, emancipation procedures seemed relatively simple. There were two qualifications for freedom stipulated in the *Code Noir* or Black Code of 1807: that the slave be of "honest conduct" for four years before the emancipation, specifically that he had not run away or committed a criminal act, and that he had reached the age of thirty years. Both stipulations could be waived if the bondservant to be freed had saved the life of his master or his master's family.[3] The age qualification was a formidable object. Slaves under thirty were without recourse. This restriction prevented a master from freeing a family with children. It also prevented a free black man who managed to purchase his underage slave wife from freeing her until she achieved the specified age, and the children born before her emancipation were destined to be slaves for at least thirty years.

In 1827 the Louisiana legislature modified the age requirement. Slaves

[2] *Constitutions of the State of Louisiana, 1812-1898* (Baton Rouge, 1913), p. 62; *West's Louisiana Statutes Annotated: Treasties and Organic Laws, Early Constitutions, U. S. Constitution* (St. Paul, Minn., 1977), III, 35, 49, 69; *Constitutions of Louisiana of 1812, '45 & '52* (New Orleans, 1861), pp. 30, 44; *West's Louisiana Statutes Annotated*, III, 76; Albert Voorhies, *A Treatise on the Criminal Jurisprudence of Louisiana* ... (New Orleans, 1860), p. 39.

[3] *Acts Passed at the Second Session of the First Legislature of the Territory of Orleans* ... (1807) (New Orleans, 1807), p. 82; *Civil Code of the State of Louisiana* (New Orleans, 1825), Articles 185-186. The Louisiana Supreme Court stated in 1857 that if slave children could be freed, masters would be allowed "to flood the community with a class of persons who are totally incapable of supporting and taking care of themselves." *Carmouche* v. *Carmouche*, 12 La. Ann. 721 #243 (1857).

under thirty years could be freed if given permission by the judge and police jury of the parish of the owner, providing the bondservant in question was a native of the state.[4] Younger non-native slaves were probably considered more of a potential insurrection risk. An act of 1830 required newly freed bondsmen to leave the state within thirty days of their emancipation and required that the owner post $1,000 bond to insure the ex-slave's departure.[5] An amendment passed the following year excepted any slave freed for "meritorious conduct."[6]

Ten years before the United States Supreme Court's famous Dred Scott decision, the Louisiana legislature passed a law that had the same effect as the Supreme Court ruling. This act stated that no slave could claim his or her freedom on the grounds that he had been in a country or state that prohibited slavery, whether with or without consent of his master.[7]

In 1852 the Louisiana legislature added another obstacle to the manumission procedure—freed slaves were to be sent to Liberia and their masters were required to pay their passage of $150. Bondsmen not departing within twelve months following their emancipation were to be re-enslaved.[8] The state legislature was flooded with individual petitions for exceptions, and the requirement of departure for Liberia was removed in 1855. The new requirements were no less strict; to free a slave one had to sue the state in a district court. A jury decided the fate of the bondsman, and if it freed him, decided whether he could remain in the state. If so, his former master had to post $1,000 bond against his becoming a public charge.[9]

These obstacles to emancipation seem to have been less than effective, at least in New Orleans. The First District Court in that city heard eight

[4]*Acts Passed at the First Session of the Eighth Legislature of the State of Louisiana* ... (1827) (New Orleans, 1827), pp. 12-14.

[5]*Acts of the Second Session of the Ninth Legislature of the State of Louisiana* ... (1830) (Donaldsonville, La., 1830), pp. 90-94.

[6]*Acts of the First Session of the Tenth Legislature of the State of Louisiana* ... (1831) (New Orleans, 1831), pp. 98-100.

[7]*Acts Passed at the First Session of the First Legislature of the State of Louisiana* ... (1846) (New Orleans, 1846), p. 163.

[8]*Acts Passed by the Fourth Legislature of the State of Louisiana* ... (1852) (New Orleans, 1852), pp. 214-215.

[9]*Acts Passed by the Second Session of the Second Legislature* ... (1855) (New Orleans, 1855), pp. 377-391.

manumission suits in two days late in 1855. The juries granted emancipations in all eight suits, and all of the newly freed slaves were allowed to remain in the state.[10] The legislators must have been frustrated by continuing emancipations made possible by judges and juries who seemed unconcerned about increasing the free black population. In 1857 the Louisiana legislature eliminated all loopholes and totally prohibited emancipations in the state.[11]

Motives for emancipations were varied, and some are impossible to ascertain. Fear of free blacks as a class was much stronger than of individual people of color, a fear that could be overriden by bonds of love and blood relationship. A number of manumission cases heard by the antebellum Louisiana Supreme Court involved attempts by whites to free their mistresses and/or their offspring. One possible explanation for the willingness of police juries and lower courts to grant emancipaton in these circumstances was that they were only legalizing what was in some instances already in practice—some owners would no doubt treat their slave mistresses and children as though they were free.

Cases heard by the antebellum Louisiana Supreme Court that involved white masters emancipating their mulatto or black mistresses and their children usually arose from squabbles over inheritance and legacies left in the will of the master for his slave or ex-slave mistress and children. Freeing a slave mistress meant overcoming two additional legal obstacles firmly embedded in the Louisiana Civil Code. The first of these was forced heirship. It is significant that under Louisiana law freeing a slave was considered a monetary donation to that bondservant, and the state's forced heirship doctrine came into play. Forced heirship meant that legitimate children could not be disinherited unless they committed serious offenses against their parents, such as striking a parent, or failure to ransom a parent held on the high seas. If an adult died childless and was survived by one or both parents, the parent/parents must receive a portion of the estate. One's surviving parents and/or children were what the courts called "ascending and descending heirs," and Louisiana law stipulated that these were forced heirs

[10]Minute Book, 1855-1856, First District Court of New Orleans, November 22, 23, 1855. See *Murphy* v. *State* #10680 (slave Martha); *Cruzat* v. *State* #10723 (slave Victoire, alias Mamzelle); *Perret* v. *State* #10686 (Ellen); *Widow Clay* v. *State* (#10764 (Justine); *Elizabeth, f. w. c.* v. *State* #10737 (Annie alias Amelia)(; *Fortier* v. *State* #10736 (Menos alias Aimée); *Fortin* v. *State* #10734 (Adeline);*Widow Bourg* v. *State* #10735 (Gaston Delille).

[11]*Acts Passed at the Second Session of the Third Legislature of the State of Louisiana* (1857) (New Orleans, 1857), p. 55.

who must receive a portion of the deceased's estate. The exact portion varied according to how many forced heirs existed, but every possible circumstance was clearly spelled out in the law.[12] Even if a man attempting to emancipate a slave mistress had no forced heirs, he encountered the second obstacle. According to the Civil Code no one could donate more than one-tenth of one's estate to a concubine, whether male or female, black or white.[13] Therefore, if the value of the slave mistress exceeded ten percent of the estate, she could not be freed.

During the antebellum era the Louisiana Supreme Court made certain that the forced heirs received their entire inheritance, resulting in a series of decisions in which the court regarded the slaves as property rather than people. For example, William Adams, Jr., lived in what the courts called "open concubinage" with a slave named Nancy. Adams died in 1851 and left a will ordering his executor to free Nancy and give her his watch and furniture. There were also two legacies of $1,000 each for their children (it is not clear whether they were already free). Adams' legitimate white son sued to prevent the emancipation of Nancy and the legacies to her and the children on the grounds that since the entire estate was worth only $4,750, the donation to Nancy of her value and the additional legacies far exceeded the one-tenth disposable portion of the succession; Nancy alone was valued at $1,000. The Louisiana Supreme Court ruled that Nancy could not be freed and therefore could not receive a legacy, as slaves were unable to inherit anything.[14] The record is silent as to the legacies to the children, but

[12]*A Digest of the Civil Laws Now in Force in the Territory of Orleans (1808); Containing Manuscript References to Its Source and Other Civil Laws on the Same Subject. The De la Vergne Volume*. (Baton Rouge, 1971), pp. 146-158.

[13]Article 1468 of the Civil Code stipulates that "those who have lived together in open concubinage" cannot donate to each other immovable property, and are only allowed to give them one-tenth of their movable property by gift when they are alive (donation *intervivos*) or by will (donation *mortis causa*). Civil Code, Article 1468. White heirs often contested legacies to ex-slave concubines and their children by their former masters. Maurice Prévost willed property to Clarrise, f.w.c., and her daughter, Florestine, f.w.c. Both had been born in bondage and freed by Prévost before his death in 1843. The testator left the remainder of his estate to his sister, who sued to have the donations to Clarrisse and Florestine annulled because Clarrisse was Prévost's concubine and Florestine his bastard. The legacy to the ex-slaves must have been less than ten percent of the estate (no figure appears in the record) because the Louisiana Supreme Court ruled that the donations were valid. *Prévost* v. *Martel*, 10 Rob. 512 (La. 1845); see also *Bush, f.w.c.* v. *Décuir*, 11 La. Ann. 503 #4339 (1856). The Louisiana Supreme Court was more likely to allow donations exceeding ten percent to white concubines. *Lowery* v. *Kline*, 6 La. 180 #2519 (1834); *Sucession of Bousquet*, 10 Rob. 143 #5632 (La. 1845); *Carmena* v. *Blaney, 16 La. Ann. 245 #116 (1861)*.

[14]Civil Code, Article 1462.

the existence of a legitimate heir makes it doubtful that they received their inheritance.[15] In another ruling in an unsuccessful suit for freedom, the Louisiana Supreme Court stated that

> Emancipation is a donation of the value of a slave. When the donation is attacked as excessive, and evidence is given that the donor has insufficient property to justify it, it behooves the donee to show that he had.

In this case an elderly "always well-behaved" slave sued for her freedom under an 1828 will that stipulated she was to be freed upon the death of her owner. Apparently she had followed her master to New Orleans from Saint-Domingue, when she could have remained on that island and been free. Notwithstanding, the court ruled against her.[16]

Irate white heirs brought suits to the Louisiana Supreme Court on several occasions during the antebellum period to deny slave mistresses and their children their freedom and legacies left to them in the will of the master. A wealthy planter named John Anderson instructed the executors of his will to emancipate his slave Phoebe "for her long and faithful service to me" and left her 100 acres, four slaves, six cows and calves, four horses and mares, "one of my best beds and bedsteads," other assorted furniture, and "as many fowls as she may want." Anderson died possessed of upwards of 100 slaves, 2,000 arpents of land, $9,000 in debts owed him, and $4,500 cash. Despite the fact that the donations to Phoebe were less than one-tenth of the succession, Anderson's sisters and brother seized all of the estate including Pheobe, and the executors sued to have the terms of the will executed. The Louisiana Supreme Court ordered the executor to free Phoebe, and forced the

[15]*Adams* v. *Routh and Dorsey*, 8 La. Ann. 121 #3009 (1853). According to Article 226 of the Civil Code mulatto or Negro children were not allowed to sue to prove paternity unless the father was a man of color. In 1832 a free woman of color sued for a legacy left her by her white father. The Louisiana Supreme Court ruled against her because adulterous bastards were not allowed by law to inherit unless they were legally acknowledged by their fathers, and because people of color were prohibited from proving their "natural paternal descent." White children were not restricted in this manner. *Jung* v. *Doriocourt*, 4 La. 175 #2196 (1832). For other cases involving the inheritance of illegitimate children see: *Seennet* v. *Sennet's Legatees*, 3 Mart. (O.S.) 411 #13 (La. 1814); *Ripoll* v. *Morena*, 12 Rob. 552 #5376 (La. 1846). The acknowledgment of an illegitimate child in a will, if not a Negro or mulatto, entitled the child to inheritance. Civil Code, Articles, 221, 226, 227. *Jones* v. *Hunter and King*, 6 Rob. 235 #973 (La. 1843).

[16]*Prudence* v. *Bermodi*, 1 La. 234 #1888 (1830).

heirs to turn over the portion of the property that was stipulated in Anderson's will to her.[17]

Another slave woman and her child were not so fortunate. Jacob Philips, a carpenter, owned a mulatto woman, Maria, and her ten-year-old daughter, Angel. He left a will that ordered his executor to free the two bondservants and asked his white daughter to see to their emancipation "as a particular favor to her father." He also left Maria and Angel all of his movable property, stating in his will that "they have been purchased out of her own funds and by her labour. . . ." Philips' entire estate was inventoried at $1,497.25, which included the value of Maria and Angel, who were appraised at $850. After the carpenter died Maria and Angel sued Philips' executor for their freedom. The lower court ruled that since Philips had a legitimate daughter, and therefore a forced heir, she must receive her required portion of the inheritance. The Louisiana Supreme Court remanded the cases because of a procedural error, but it is unlikely they were ever freed because their value exceeded one-tenth of the estate. It is ironic that the more valuable slaves were in these circumstances, the less likely they were to be freed because of the objections of the legitimate heirs, who stood to lose the value of the slave.[18]

In some concubine-inheritance cases heard by the Louisiana Supreme Court, evidence of long-standing relationships between white men and women of color appears in the record. These liaisons were not unusual, especially in New Orleans, and were called *plaçage*. In 1809 Jean-Pierre Décuir emancipated his slave mistress, a mulatto named Josephine, who continued to live with him until his death in 1826. In 1818 Josephine purchased the bondswoman Betey and her children at a probate sale for $1,100. After Décuir's death his white heirs sued for possession of Betey and her children, claiming that Décuir had given Josephine the purchase price of the slaves as a "disguised donation"; the Louisiana Supreme Court upheld Josephine's title to the bondservants.[19]

[17]The inventory of the estate includes a slave carpenter (appraised at $900), blacksmith ($1,000), driver ($1,500), and a bricklayer and barber ($900). One of the executors, Abraham Vail, was the executor in two similar lawsuits heard by the Louisiana Supreme Court. *Anderson's Executors* v. *Anderson's Heirs*, 10 La. 29 #70 (1836). For a similar case see *Lopez's Heirs* v. *Bergel, f.w.c.*, 12 La. 197 #3031 (1838).

[18]*Maria and Angel* v. *Destréhan*, 3 La. 434 #2228 (1831).

[19]*Sandoz* v. *Gary*, 11 Rob. 529 (La. 1845). Heirs of a white man who had lived with a free woman of color from 1796 until 1845 unsuccessfully sued her, claiming that she was illegally

In a similar case the existence of a direct legal descendant and forced heir was the basis of a Louisiana Supreme Court decision to deprive Ann Sinnet, f.w.c., of a house, a lot, and a slave woman. Sinnet had lived in "open concubinage" with Joseph Uzée, who had emancipated her. During their alliance he gave her the property at issue; he had purchased the bondswoman and transferred the title to Sinnet. Later, Uzée married a white woman and fathered children by her. The Louisiana Supreme Court ruled that the house, lot, and bondswoman were the property of Uzée's legitimate children.[20]

In one concubine-emancipation case the Louisiana Supreme Court recognized the particularly helpless position of a slave woman to her master. Henry Clay Vail freed his bondswoman-mistress Jane and left her two promissory notes of $100 each. Vail's heirs alleged that emancipating Jane was a disposition of immovable property prohibited by law and sued to annul the will. In an interesting defense Vail's executor argued that Jane was not a "concubine" because she was a slave, and slaves by law were without will, meaning concubinage implied consent. Furthermore, he argued, the heirs should not benefit from the "moral turpitude" of the deceased. The executor won in the lower court but the Louisiana Supreme Court, although recognizing that female slaves were particularly vulnerable to the power of the master, ruled that the donation of freedom deprived the heirs of their rightful inheritance. The estate was worth only $1,686, of which Jane and her child Louisa were worth $900, well over one-tenth of the total value. The court based its decision on the assumption that female slaves generally participated willingly in sexual relations with their masters:

> It is true, the female slave is particuliarly exposed . . . to the seductions of an unprincipled master. That is a misfortune; but it is so rare in the case of concubinage that the seduction and

---

in possession of $155,000, which belonged to the succession of the deceased. The free woman of color was in the dry goods business, and was able to prove that the money was the result "of her industry and economy during half a century." When the Louisiana Supreme Court ruled in her favor it commented upon her relationship with the deceased: "The state in which she lived was the nearest approach to marriage which the law recognized, and in the days in which their union commenced it imposed serious moral obligations. It received the consent of her family, which was one of the most distinguished in Louisiana. . . ." *Macarty* v. *Mandeville*, 3 La. Ann. 239 #626 (1848). In a similar case a white man described his relationship with his mistress, a free woman of color, in these words, "Philonise Olivier a toujours en soin de moi, de ma maison, et de mes esclaves." (Philonise Olivier has always taken care of me, and my house, and my slaves.) *Olivier, f.w.c.* v. *Blancq*, 2 La. Ann. 517 #463 (1847).

[20] *Dupré, administrator of Sinnet* v. *Uzée*, 6 La. Ann. 280 #2101 (1851).

> temptation are not mutual that exceptions to a general rule cannot be founded upon it.[21]

While it is certainly true that some sexual liaisons between masters and slaves were voluntary on the part of the slave women, some undoubtedly were not. It may be that the court was writing for an abolitionist audience. Placing part of the blame on the slave woman helped to reinforce the pro-slavery notion that blacks had no morals and had to be kept in slavery for their own good.

Undaunted by the unfavorable decision, Vail's executor continued to work for Jane's freedom. He claimed that as Vail's heirs were not direct descendants, they had no right to a forced portion of his inheritance, and he sued for possesion of Jane and her daughter so as to free them. The irate heirs concealed the slaves and told the executor that before he "could get possession of said slaves he would be forced to find them ... or words to this effect." The heirs contended that Jane could not be legally emancipated until she was thirty (she was then twenty-five), and that they were entitled to her services until that time. The Louisiana Supreme Court again ruled for the heirs. Since the will made no mention of Jane's daughter, Louisa, she was declared the permanent property of the heirs and Jane was to serve them until she attained the age when she could be legally manumitted.[22]

Two other slave concubines were denied the freedom left to them in their masters' wills because the act of 1857 was passed between the time the will was executed and the date of the judgment by the Louisiana Supreme Court on their suit for freedom. Both lost their chance for freedom by a matter of days. In the first instance a white man named John Turnbull went before a notary and two witnesses on December 19, 1855, to formally acknowledge his five mulatto children, born of his twenty-three-year-old "griffe" slave Rachel. On the same day he made a will instructing his executor to free his

[21] *Vail* v. *Bird*, 6 La. Ann. 223 #2129 (1851).

[22] *Bird* v. *Vail, et al.*, 9 La. Ann. 176 #3454 (1854). It is not clear whether Louisa was Vail's daughter. She was born when her mother was thirteen. If so, Jane became Vail's mistress at the age of twelve.

The post-Reconstruction supreme court demonstrated a complete change in attitude toward slave concubines. In an 1878 decision the court stated:

> That mother's concubinage, the illegitimacy of her son, were the almost inevitable results of their [slaves'] condition, and ... that condition was not of their choice ... [and the] concubinage ... can not be invoked as a crime against the emancipated mother.... *Neel* v. *Hibard*, 30 La. Ann. 808 #6737 (1878).

children and their mother upon his death. He stated that if emancipation was legally impossible, his executor should take them to a country or state of their choice where slavery did not exist; the costs of transportation were to be paid by the estate. Turnbull also left one-third of his estate to Rachel and the children, to be divided equally. Turnbull died in June 1856, and his executor refused to free the slave woman or her children. Her court-appointed curator sued the executor to force him to comply with the will. The executor stated that Turnbull's acknowledgment of the children as his own was "contrary to law and good morals." The lower court ruled that Rachel and her children should receive their legacies as soon as they could be emancipated. The lower court noted in its decision that it could not blame Rachel for "her yielding obedience to his wicked desires" because this would be to punish "the weak and helpless for the sins of the strong and powerful." This recognition of the helpless position of slave women is unusual among antebellum Louisiana court decisions of this sort. Blame, when placed at all, was usually assigned to the "seductiveness" of the bondswomen.

The Act of March 6, 1857, prohibiting emancipation was passed just before the Louisiana Supreme Court rendered a decision on the executor's appeal in this case. The high court ruled that Rachel and her children could not now be legally freed, and as slaves, could neither inherit nor own property. The justices reversed the ruling favorable to Rachel, and decreed she must not only lose the appeal, but pay court costs.[23] The law of 1857 prohibiting emancipation was too strictly worded to invite any other interpretation. A similar case involving what the court called a slave "concubine and the adulterous bastards of the testator" met with the same lack of success a few months later.[24] The court denied freedom to a third petitioner two years later, stating that until the 1857 act was repealed, "slaves ... cannot stand in court for any purpose."[25]

The Louisiana Supreme Court heard a few cases that show longstanding family-like relationships among masters, female slaves, and their children. Elisha Crocker left his property to his "housekeeper" Sofa, whom he had previously freed, and his legally acknowledged children by her: Henry Hicks Crocker, Mary Bosworth, and Susan Crocker. Specifically, he allotted

[23]*Turner* v. *Smith*, 12 La. Ann. 417 #5076 (1857). A *griffe* is the offspring of a Negro and a mulatto.

[24]*Oreline* v. *Heirs of Haggerty*, 12 La. Ann. 880 (1857).

[25]*Price* v. *Ray*, 14 La. Ann. 697 #697 (1859).

$25,000 to be sent to Mary, who was married and living in California at the time of his death, and $10,000 for thirteen-year-old Susan to be put at interest for her education. Susan was also to receive all of Crocker's rental property subject to her mother's use during her lifetime, and was to remain with her mother to care for her. Sofa was to receive all the furniture in the house "as she has done more toward collecting & preserving it than I have done." He also left Sofa a slave woman and her children. Crocker designated his mulatto son as his executor and universal legatee, meaning he was to receive the remainder of the estate after the specific donations were made. The deceased planter stated in his will that he had given his white sisters and brothers one-third of his property before his death, and therefore nothing would be left to them. Far from being content with their brother's generosity while he was alive, the sisters and brothers alleged that Crocker had no right to leave more than one-fourth of his estate to his concubine and children. The reason for the figure of one-fourth, and not one-tenth, is that he had legally acknowledged his illegitimate children, and by law could leave them one-fourth of his estate.[26] Following the law as usual, the Louisiana Supreme Court reduced Sofa and her children's legacies to one-fourth of the estate.[27]

Just after the Civil War, an East Baton Rouge planter named John Kleinpeter attempted to reimburse his ex-slave mistress, Nancy Trim, for her faithfulness to him by giving her fifty acres of land for her services. In the alleged act of sale, dated December 31, 1866, he stated:

> I gave her her freedom about ten years ago, yet she holds fast, and watches and cares for me in the most tender manner, and for her good conduct, I have this day sold her fifty acres of land in the rear of my plantation.

After Kleinpeter's death in 1868 his heirs took possession of the land and began cutting timber and erecting buildings on it. Kleinpeter's executor sued to establish Trim's title to the land. The Louisiana Supreme Court ruled that since no money had changed hands "the act ... is evidence of no contract known to our law." Nancy Trim lost claim to the land.[28]

[26]Civil Code, Articles 1474, 1473.

[27]*Reed* v. *Crocker*, 12 La. Ann. 436 #4708 (1857).

[28]*Kleinpeter* v. *Harrigan*, 21 La. Ann. 196 #2088 (1869). In another case of an alliance

One Iberville Parish planter, Joseph Thompson, managed to provide adequately for his "quarteroon" mistress, Sally McBride, and his legally acknowledged son. Thompson had freed Sally in 1829 and had lived "publicly and openly" with her for twelve years. He fathered two children, one of whom survived him. In his will Thompson left his son only enough to "insure him a tolerable education and a trade" and left a $200 annuity to Sally McBride. He left the remainder of his estate to his friend Charles Henry Dickinson of Grosse Tête Bayou. Thompson died without forced heirs, but his outraged sister sued to annul the will, claiming that her brother was insane, that he was a "weak man generally in Body and Mind and that his said concubine exercised over him a powerfull and irristable [*sic*] Influence and controlled him in all his acts. . . ." Thompson's sister further alleged that Dickinson had agreed to keep the rest of the money for Thompson's illegitimate son to evade the law. However, as she could not produce proof of this accusation, the Louisiana Supreme Court ruled that the will was valid. Whether or not McBride and her son ever received any additional legacy from Dickinson is unknown.[29]

Another attempt by a wealthy man to provide for an ex-slave mistress of many years and her children failed. Leonard Compton of Alexandria died in 1841 without forced heirs. In 1825 he had freed the slave woman Fanchon and continued to live with her until his death. He fathered two illegitimate children, Scipio and Loretta, whom he legally acknowledged. A witness testified that he always showed his children "the affection of a father." In his will he left his offspring a 545-acre plantation, all of the slaves thereon, and $10,000 each in cash. To Fanchon he left the kitchen equipment, furniture, two gold watches, a horse and carriage, and other assorted livestock. He appointed V. Aaron Prescott as his executor and guardian of his children, provided funds for their support and education, and left Prescott the remainder of the estate. Compton had already sent one child to Ohio to be educated before his death. The total estate was appraised at $184,640. Compton's sister, brother, and the heirs of two deceased brothers sued to have Fanchon's legacies voided, alleging that she was a slave and as such could not inherit, and to reduce the children's share to one-fourth of the total estate. They also alleged Prescott was under secret instruction to give

---

between a white man and an ex-slave woman, an irate white woman sued her husband who had abandoned her "without cause" after six years of marriage for a woman who had once been his mother's slave. *Dorwin* v. *Wiltz*, 11 La. Ann. 514 (1856).

[29] *Hart* v. *Thompson's Executor and Legatees*, 15 La. 88 #4019 (1840).

Fanchon $20,000. Their heirs claimed that several sales to Fanchon before Compton's death were fraudulently disguised donations. The lower court found the will valid, but the Louisiana Supreme Court reversed the decision, ruling that Fanchon had to return the property sold to her by Compton because it was actually a fraudulently disguised donation, and the children's portion was lowered to one-fourth of the estate, the amount allowed to acknowledge illegitimate children. Following this decision Fanchon unsuccessfully sued in another action on a $5,000 note given to her by Compton before his death.[30]

A few cases heard by the antebellum Louisiana Supreme Court are evidence not only of long-standing alliances between white men and their slaves or former bondswomen, but also careful attempts to provide for their children. The slave Venus was born in 1787 of the slave Nancy, owned by B. Farrar of Pointe Coupée Parish. Her father, Christopher Beard, a white planter, stipulated in his will that Venus was to receive 750 arpents of land on False River at his death, instructed in the Christian religion, and "put to" a mantua maker to learn the business at the expense of the estate. Beard died in 1789. Twelve years later Farrar died, leaving a will emancipating Venus and several other slaves. Apparently, he was a humane master, as he stated in his will that he wanted his bondservants to "be used with the greatest humanity consistent with the state they are in and be made as happy as possible in their situation." After Farrar's death the land left to Venus by Beard was sold to Julien Poydras, and she sued to recover it. Since she was freed after Farrar's death and after she was left the property by Beard, the Louisiana Supreme Court ruled that as a slave at the time of Beard's death she could not inherit; Poydras's ownership was confirmed. This decision reversed that of the lower court,[31] which had awarded Venus the land and $720 in damages.

A wealthy Opelousas man, Douglas Wilkins, died possessed of an estate of $62,725.28. Wilkins emancipated his slave mistress, Leonora, and his acknowledged sons, Joseph Douglas and Charles Douglas in his will. He also left his sons $3,000 and $2,000 respectively, and stipulated that they were to be sent to a free state, educated in the three "R's," and taught a trade. He provided Leonora with an $150 annuity. Since his donations to his slave mistress and her sons did not exceed the amount legally stipulated as

[30]*Compton* v. *Prescott*, 12 Rob. 56 (La. 1845); *Morris* v. *Compton*, 12 Rob. 76 (La. 1845).

[31]*Beard* v. *Poydras*, 4 Mart. (O.S.) 348 #72 (La. 1816).

the disposable portion, the will was declared valid and the three slaves were emancipated.[32]

The Civil War interrupted several cases involving emancipation and legacies to slave or ex-slave concubines and their children and often worked to the benefit of the Negroes or mulattoes involved. Bernard Chappel freed his mistress Ida Hannah before his death, but could not free his daughter Clementine, because she was not yet thirty years old. He died in 1854; his will provided for Clementine's manumission as soon as legally possible. The will also made both mother and daughter his only heirs. Clementine was still a slave, although a *statu liber*, a legal term meaning a slave for a limited number of years. Hannah sued, claiming the whole estate, as her daughter was still a slave and could not inherit. She won in the lower court, and a court-appointed curator for Clementine, who was a minor, appealed. The war interrupted the appeal, and the case was one of the first to be decided when the Louisiana Supreme Court was re-activated in June 1865. It reversed the decision of the lower court, ruling that *statu libers* could legally inherit, and anyway the issue was moot, as Clementine was now free following the general emancipation at the end of the war.[33]

Another emancipated slave who was the child of a white man and bondswoman benefited from a post-Civil War Louisiana Supreme Court decision. In 1846 a Mr. Porter died leaving a will which instructed his executors to purchase from a Mr. Metoyer a child, the son of the slave woman Meme, and to emancipate him. He also left $1,000 to be invested for the boy for his education and support; the remainder was to be given to him when he attained the age of eighteen. Before he had reached that age, the child received his legacy in Confederate notes. After the war was over and his eighteenth birthday had passed, he sued for his inheritance, claiming that Confederate money was now worthless. The Louisiana Supreme Court ruled that since he was a minor when he first received his legacy, he could not have legally consented to the payment, and furthermore, that currency was "illicit." The court ordered the executor to pay him in legal tender.[34]

[32]*Lenora, f.w.c.* v. *Scott*, 10 La. Ann. 651 (1855). In a similar case William Weeks left $16,000 to his white son to pay boarding, clothing, and tuition for his four illegitimate children by a slave woman. The Louisiana Supreme Court ruled the donation invalid. *O'Hara* v. *Conrad*, 10 La. Ann. 638 (1855).

[33]*Hannah, f.w.c.* v. *Eggleston*, 17 La. Ann. 174 #198 (1865).

[34]*Porter* v. *Brown*, 21 La. Ann. 532 #137 (1869).

Even emancipation following the Civil War did not help two ex-slave children fathered by a white planter gain their inheritance. Abram Bird died in 1860, leaving a large estate and three legal, white heirs. After providing for them according to law, Bird provided for the emancipation of two of his slaves as soon as state law permitted (the act of 1857 had prohibited all emancipation), and left them each a legacy of $8,000. After Bird's death the legal heirs ceased to hold the two in slavery but left the bequests unpaid. After the war the ex-slaves sued for their inheritance. The legal heirs alleged that as "adulterous bastards" (Bird had a white wife as well as a slave mistress) they could not inherit. The Louisiana Supreme Court affirmed the judgment of the lower court that at the time of Bird's death they were slaves who could not have been legally emancipated, and as such, could not inherit.[35]

In one slave-concubinage case the daughters of a white man and one of his bondswomen, Adelaide, were well cared for, but not legally freed, possibly because of the enmity of a white wife. After one of the children was born, Jean-Baptiste Lagarde, an overseer, purchased Adelaide and her daughter Amelia in 1829 from his employer and treated them as free. The second daughter, Cydalize, was born after the sale; Adelaide died shortly thereafter of cholera. Lagarde paid a free woman of color, Marie Louise Audat, to raise his daughters and treat them as her own. Witnesses testified that Lagarde often stated the girls were his, and that when they were older he planned to send them to his sister in France. Lagarde subsequently married a white woman and died in 1843. The two girls were included in the inventory of his estate and auctioned off at a probate sale. Audat managed to purchase them, and immediately brought suit for their freedom. The First District Court of New Orleans declared Amelia and Cydalize free by prescription since they had lived free for more than ten years. Perhaps the reason that Lagarde did not take the legal steps to emancipate them was the resentment of his new wife, as it was obvious he intended them to be free. This may be one instance in which the court's decision ratified what was in fact reality. Obviously Audat was not going to treat the girls as her slaves.[36]

One case heard by the Louisiana Supreme Court involving an emancipated slave who was the daughter of a white master seems to have been a flagrant

[35] *Barrow* v. *Bird*, 22 La. Ann. 407 #2706 (1870).

[36] *Audat* v. *Gilly*, 12 Rob. 323 #5337 (La. 1845). For other cases that involve white fathers providing by will for their illegitimate children by slave or ex-slave woman, see *Brosnaham* v. *Turner*, 16 La. 433 (1839); *Nimmo* v. *Bonney*, 4 Rob. 179 #5138 (La. 1843).

miscarriage of justice in an instance where a father attempted to revoke the emancipation of his slave daughter. John Bazzi signed an act of emancipation in 1805 in St. Jago, Cuba, that freed the "Congo negro woman" Gertrude and her sixteen-year-old daughter Rose, who was acknowledged to be Bazzi's mulatto child. In the act Bazzi promised to comply with the legal formalities of emancipation as soon as possible. He subsequently arrived in New Orleans with Gertrude and Rose. Gertrude was stolen from him in 1819, and Bazzi never freed Rose. On the contrary, witneses testified that he beat her; one witness stated that she often complained of "assault and battery" by Bazzi who imprisoned her because he wanted to "chastize" her. In 1820 Rose sued for freedom and that of her young child.

Although no evidence can be found in the record, she must have had financial assistance from either whites or free blacks to hire an attorney and pay court costs. The record does state that Père Antonio de Sedella, the famous Père Antoine of St. Louis Cathedral in New Orleans,[37] espoused Rose's cause and had baptized her as a free person. Bazzi stated that he only executed the emancipation document to "protect" Rose and her mother on the voyage to New Orleans, because Spain and England were at war, and privateers and pirates roamed the Gulf of Mexico. Presumably Rose and her mother could be taken by pirates as cargo if it were discovered they were slaves. Bazzi claimed that he never felt bound by the act of emancipation. In his petition he expressed indignation that a lower court had freed Rose and her child from prison on a writ of *habeas corpus* and he was infuriated that Rose had since refused to serve him. Even though Rose was able to produce a certified copy of the document saying she was free, the Louisiana Supreme Court ruled that as she had arrived in Louisiana a slave, and had never been legally manumitted in the state, she and her child were slaves.[38]

[37]Antonio de Sedella (1748-1829) was a Capuchin monk sent to New Orleans during the Spanish colonial period (1779) as a representative of the Inquisition. He was deported by Governor Estevan Miró, but returned to Louisiana the next year and became the rector of St. Louis Cathedral, and one of the most beloved prelates in the history of New Orleans. The first American governor of Louisiana, William C. C. Claiborne, stated that Père Antoine "has great influence with the people of color." One author stated that he was sought out by "rich and poor, master and slave." John Smith Kendall, *History of New Orleans*, 3 vols. (Chicago and New York, 1922), I, 79-80; Albert E. Fossier, *New Orleans: The Glamour Period, 1800-1840* (New Orleans, 1957), pp. 326-335; G. William Nott, "How Louisiana Escaped the Inquisition," *Item Magazine* (May 11, 1924), 3.

[38]*Bazzi* v. *Rose and her child*, 8 Mart. (O.S.), 149 #466 (La. 1820.

In a few lawsuits heard by the Louisiana Supreme Court, irate and greedy heirs attempted to revoke legal emancipations of slave women who were mistresses of their white owners either to block donations to them by their ex-masters, or to claim the freed bondswomen as their property. Laurent Grangé legally emancipated his slave mistress, Marie Fanchonette, and their two children in 1836. After Grangé's death in 1842 the ex-bondservants were seized by the white heirs as slaves belonging to the succession. The Louisiana Supreme Court affirmed the lower court decision and declared Fanchonette and her children to be free. In the decision the justices stated: "... there is no justification or excuse for him, in aiding to reduce the plaintiff to a state of slavery, after she had been declared free by competent tribunal." Fanchonette received $100 in damages, plus a judgment of ten percent interest for frivolous appeal against the heirs.[39] In a similar lawsuit the heirs of John P. Cole attempted to claim Sarah Lee, f.w.c., as a slave belonging to his succession. Cole had freed his slave mistress ten years before his death. The Louisiana Supreme Court affirmed her emancipation, although it denied her a legacy of $3,000 left her by her former master, because it exceeded ten percent of the value of the estate.[40]

One white man attempted unsuccessfully to arrange for the freedom of the slave Marie and his son by her, both of whom belonged to another person. In his will Erasmus R. Avart ordered his executor to buy Marie and her child Gaston, and free them. Marie's master was willing to sell her and the child for a reasonable price, but Avart's heirs objected to the will, and no sale occurred. Marie sued the executor and heirs to have the terms of the will obeyed. Avart had died by his own hand; the testament had been executed between the infliction of his fatal wound and his demise. His heirs claimed that he was insane when he wrote the will and mentally incapable of making sound judgments. To prove this assertion they stated that since he was "consumed with passion" for Marie, he must have been of unsound mind! Several witnesses, including Père Antoine, testified that Avart was in full possession of his faculties. The lower court ordered Avart's executor to purchase Marie and Gaston and emancipate them. The Louisiana Supreme Court reversed the judgment and ruled that as a slave Marie could not bring suit to have the will executed as written, because slaves could only institute a legal action to prove their freedom. This case was reheard twice by the

[39]*Fanchonette* v. *Grangé*, 9 Rob. 86 (La. 1844).

[40]*Cole's Heirs* v. *Cole's Executor*, 7 Mart. (N.S.) 414 #2-1702 (La. 1829).

high court after the initial appeal. Its ruling remained unchanged.[41]

In its decisions pertaining to inheritance cases that involved slave women who had become the mistresses of their white masters, the antebellum Louisiana Supreme Court acted quite predictably, given the restrictions placed on the justices by the Civil Code and the Louisiana constitution. The law frowned upon "open and notorious concubinage," restricting *both* partners in such alliances to receiving only one-tenth of each other's estate. It is important to note here that the law was identical for all involved in these liaisons, male and female, Negro, mulatto and white. In this instance Louisiana law was oblivious to gender and color.

In cases involving slave concubines the Louisiana Supreme Court adhered to the law. Ex-slave concubines of white masters were allowed to receive one-tenth of their ex-master's estate in movable property; their illegitimate children, if formally acknowledged, were allowed their legal one-fourth. If the women and children were still slaves, they could not be freed unless their value did not exceed one-tenth or one-fourth respectively of the total estate. In ruling in this manner, the fact that slaves were valuable property overshadowed their qualities as persons under the law. White concubines were also restricted to inheriting ten percent, but at least their freedom was assured.

Louisiana's legal heritage is evident in these rulings. Obviously illicit and illegal liaisons were a threat to the institution of the family. Laws protected the legitimate family of both partners in the illegal relationship to insure that they would not be deprived of their inheritance. Of course, slaves had no legitimate families under the law, could own no property, and were in fact property themselves. These factors operated to make these laws more burdensome on them than on whites.

Concubinage and illegitimacy were not the only causes of avaricious relatives seeking to void wills freeing bondsmen and leaving them an inheritance. A number of emancipation-by-will cases that were heard by the Louisiana Supreme Court during the antebellum period did not involve concubinage or illegitimacy. Resentment over the testamentary generosity of a deceased slaveowner and simple greed inspired a series of lawsuits designed to thwart such eleemosynary donations. The Louisiana Supreme Court was more likely to agree to an emancipation of slaves that was not opposed to accepted public morality, providing all legal qualificaitons for emancipation were strictly met.

[41]*Marie* v. *Avart*, 6 Mart. (O.S.) 731 #352 (La. 1819); 8 Mart. (O.S.) 512 #488 (La. 1820); 10 Mart. (O.S.) 731 #488 (La. 1821).

A SLAVE FAMILY IN THE ANTE BELLUM SOUTH

LOREN SCHWENINGER

Twentieth century scholars of Afro-American history have offered two basically different interpretations concerning the effect of slavery on the black family. In his famous 1932 study *The Negro Family in the United States*, Negro sociologist E. Franklin Frazier asserted that slavery destroyed the black family. Fundamental economic forces and material interests, he said, shattered even the toughest bonds of black familial sentiments and parental love.[1] Supporting Frazier in the 1959 comparative analysis, *Slavery: A Problem in American Intellectual and Institutional Life*, white historian Stanley M. Elkins listed four reasons for the destruction of the black slave family: sexual exploitation, separation, miscegenation, and restrictive legal codes. "The law could permit no aspect of the slave's conjugal state to have an independent legal existence."[2] In an examination of the urban South, historian Richard C. Wade likewise concluded that "For a slave, no matter where he resided, a house was never a home. Families could scarcely exist in bondage. The law recognized no marriage."[3] And Daniel P. Moynihan, in his 1965 report, re-iterated that slavery had an extremely negative effect on the black family.[4]

Recently, three writers have put forth a far more optimistic view of the black family in bondage. Herbert Gutman, Robert Abzug and John Blassingame contend that strong family loyalties developed among slaves. Admitting the obvious institutional barriers, they argue that bondsmen used the family as a shelter against the brutalities of the Southern slave system. "Although it was weak, although it was frequently broken," Professor Blassingame writes in *The Slave Com-*

Loren Schweninger is an Assistant Professor of History at the University of North Carolina at Greensboro.

[1]E. Franklin Frazier, *The Negro Family in the United States* (Chicago: University of Chicago Press, 1939), pp. 40, 41; "The Negro Slave Family," *Journal of Negro History XV* (April, 1930), pp. 198-259.

[2]Stanley M. Elkins, *Slavery: A Problem in American Institutional and Intellectual Life* (Chicago: University of Chicago Press, 1959), pp. 53, 54.

[3]Richard C. Wade, *Slavery in the Cities: The South, 1820-1860* (New York: Oxford University Press, 1964), pp. 117-121.

[4]Lee Rainwater and William L. Yancey, *The Moynihan Report and the Politics of Controversy* (Cambridge, Massachusetts: The Massachusetts Institute of Technology Press, 1967), pp. 61, 62, 414, 415.

munity, a psychological study of Blacks in bondage, "the family provided an important buffer, a refuge from the rigors of slavery."[5] Thus, though asking the same basic question of the way in which the institution of slavery affected the black family, scholars have advanced two fundamentally different interpretations.

An investigation of one slave family will not end the controversy. In a limited sense it can only tell us about *a* family, and one that was in many respects very fortunate.[6] The members of the Thomas-Rapier slave family received an education; achieved a degree of economic independence; and eventually became free or at least "quasi-free." Moreover, they belonged to extremely permissive and beneficent masters. They lived in an urban environment (as did only 10% of the South's slave population), and hired out, though it was against the law. But, like many other Blacks in the ante bellum South, they too suffered the pains of separation (living in Alabama, Tennessee, and Canada); sexual exploitation (the slave mother bore three sons by three different white men); and the legal denial of the slave family. Yet, in spite of these institutional barriers or perhaps because of them, the members of the Thomas-Rapier family maintained their integrity. Indeed, as seen in a rare collection of slave letters, notes, and autobiographical reminiscences, they preserved a cohesive family unit for three generations. In a larger sense, then, an investigation of one slave family can perhaps shed some light on the family experiences of many slaves in the ante bellum South.

Born in Albemarle County, Virginia, about 1790, the black slave, Sally, grew up on the 1500-acre tobacco plantation of Charles S. Thomas, a friend and neighbor of Thomas Jefferson.[7] At a young age

---

[5]Herbert Gutman is working on a book length study of the black family. See: Tamara K. Hareven, editor, *Anonymous Americans: Explorations in Nineteenth-Century Social History* (Englewood Cliffs, N.J.: Prentice-Hall, Inc., 1971), p. 209; Robert H. Abzug, "The Black Family During Reconstruction," in Nathan I. Huggins, Martin Kilson and Daniel M. Fox, *Key Issues in the Afro-American Experience* (New York: Harcourt Brace Jovanovich, Inc., 1971), pp. 26-41; John W. Blassingame, *The Slave Community: Plantation Life in the Ante-Bellum South* (New York: Oxford University Press, 1971), chapter III.

[6]It is not the purpose of this paper to enter the contemporary sociological debate on the origins of the "black matriarchy." As it happened, the central figure in this slave family was a woman. All three of her slave children, however, became dominant fathers, maintaining their marriages for twenty-six, forty-two, and thirty years respectively. In addition, it is not the purpose of this essay to differentiate between the family attitudes of the mother, who remained in bondage, and her children, who eventually gained their freedom. Their family attitudes were for the most part the same.

[7]"The Autobiographical Reminiscences of James P. Thomas," Moorland-Spingarn Collection, Howard University, Washington, D.C., [1911], p. 1; hereafter "Thomas Autobiography." In the original manuscript many of the pages are out of place and

she was sent to the fields. Working from sun-up to sundown, season to season, and year to year, she (along with forty-one other slaves on the "big gang"), prepared beds, planted seeds, transplanted shoots, "wormed and topped" young plants, hung, and then stripped, sorted and bundled the final product. When she was about eighteen, Sally suffered (or accepted) the sexual advances of a white man, (probably John Thomas, the owner's eldest son); and in September 1808, she gave birth to a mulatto boy, John. Some years later she gave birth to a second mulatto child, Henry.[8] As Virginia law required that progeny take the status of the mother, both children were born in bondage, but as part of the Thomas Trust Estate, they were protected against sale or separation.[9] Consequently, when one of the heirs of the estate (again probably John) joined the westward movement of slaveholders across the Appalachians into the Cumberland river valley about 1818, Sally, John and Henry were transported to the fast growing town of Nashville, Tennessee.[10]

The city offered many opportunities. With the master's permission, Sally hired out as a cleaning lady, a practice common among urban slaves, and secured an agreement to retain a portion of her earnings. She then rented a two-story frame house on the corner of Deaderick and Cherry Streets in the central business district. Converting the front room into a laundry, and manufacturing her own soap (blending fats, oils, alkali and salt in a small vat in the front room), she established a business of cleaning clothes. She soon built up a thriving trade.[11] At the same time Sally arranged for her eldest son, John, to hire out as a waiter and poll boy to river barge Captain Richard Rapier,[12] who was

---

un-numbered. Thus the page numbers cited are only approximate; Albemarle County Probate Records, Deed Books, Book XXXII (January 2, 1835), p. 89; *ibid.*, Book VI (July 14, 1814), p. 26; *ibid.*, Book IX (November 17, 1825), p. 260; The Genealogy of a Slave Family.

[8]"Thomas Autobiography," pp. 2-7; U.S. Census Office, Sixth Census of the United States, "Population Schedules for Lauderdale County, Alabama," Vol. IV, 1840, p. 104.

[9]Winthrop Jordan, *White Over Black: American Attitudes Toward the Negro, 1550-1812* (Chapel Hill: University of North Carolina Press, 1968), p. 76; Albemarle County Probate Records, Deed Books, Book XXXII (January 2, 1835), pp. 89, 90.

[10]"Thomas Autobiography," pp. 3-6.

[11]*Ibid.*; *The Nashville Business Directory* (Nashville: Printed by John P. Campbell, 1855), *passim*; "Miscellaneous Notes of James P. Thomas," Moorland-Spingarn Collection, Howard University, Washington, D.C., n.p.

[12]Richard Rapier, described as "a large fleshy man weighing over 200 pounds," settled in Nashville about 1799. Soon he was transporting large quantities of tobacco to New Orleans and returning with sugar, teas and coffee. In 1806 he formed a "copartnership" with Lemuel T. Turner and James Jackson.

plying the Cumberland-Tennessee-Mississippi river trade, between Nashville, Florence (Alabama), and New Orleans;[13] and arranged for Henry to hire out as an errand boy to various "white gentlemen" around Nashville. Part of their earnings, along with her own, she saved in a tea cannister, which she hid in the loft, hoping someday to be able to purchase "free papers" for the children. "However, that might cost as much as $2000!" Undeterred, she conscientiously set aside part of her earnings every month, and by early 1826, she had saved over $300.[14]

Though thirty-six years old, Sally was still an attractive woman. In October 1827, in the house on Deaderick Street she gave birth to a third mulatto son, James.[15] The father was the famous ante bellum Judge John Catron, but according to the state law, which, like the law in Virginia, assigned progeny the status of the mother, James was born in bondage. "Now my own father presided over the supreme court of Tennessee [and served as a justice on the United States Supreme Court]," James later recalled, "[but] he had no time to give me a thought. He gave me 25 cents once, [and] if I [were] correctly informed, that is all he ever did for me."[16] With three children, John nineteen, Henry about sixteen, and James, Sally despaired that she might not be able to save enough to free her family.

But her despair soon turned to joy. She received word in 1829 that her eldest son had been emancipated. "I bequeath one thousand dollars to my executors for the purpose of purchasing the freedom of the mulatto boy, John, who now waits on me, and belongs to the Estate of Thomas," Richard Rapier stipulated in his will, and the Alabama General Assembly, the only legal emancipator of slaves in the state, passed a law freeing "a certain male slave by the name of John H. Rapier."[17] Then, she saw an opportunity to free Henry. With the final

---

[13]Davidson County Probate Records, Minutes, Vol. C. (July 1801), p. 405; *The Tennessee Gazette and Metro District Advertiser Repository*, March 29, 1898; *The Clarion*, September 27, 1808; *The Imperial Review and Cumberland Repository*, May 5, 1808; *The Democratic Clarion and Tennessee Gazette*, May 19, 1812, May 31, 1814.

[14]"Thomas Autobiography," chapter 1; "Miscellaneous Notes of James P. Thomas," Moorland-Spingarn Collection, Howard University, Washington, D.C., n.p. (See page 33)

[15]"Thomas Autobiography," p. 7.

[16]*Ibid.*, chapter 1; *Acts Passed at the First and Second Session of the Nineteenth General Assembly of the State of Tennessee* (Nashville: Allen Hall and A. S. Heiskel, Printers to the State, 1832), pp. 167-170.

[17]Lauderdale County Probate Records, Wills, Vol. VI (June 3, 1824), p. 117; *Acts of the Eleventh Annual Session of the General Assembly of the State of Alabama* (Tuscaloosa: McGuire, Henry and Walker, 1830), p. 36; Richard Rapier, Auburn, California, to James P. Thomas, December 14, 1877, Rapier Papers, Moorland-Spingarn Collection, Howard University, Washington, D.C., hereafter Rapier Papers.

THE GENEALOGY OF A SLAVE FAMILY

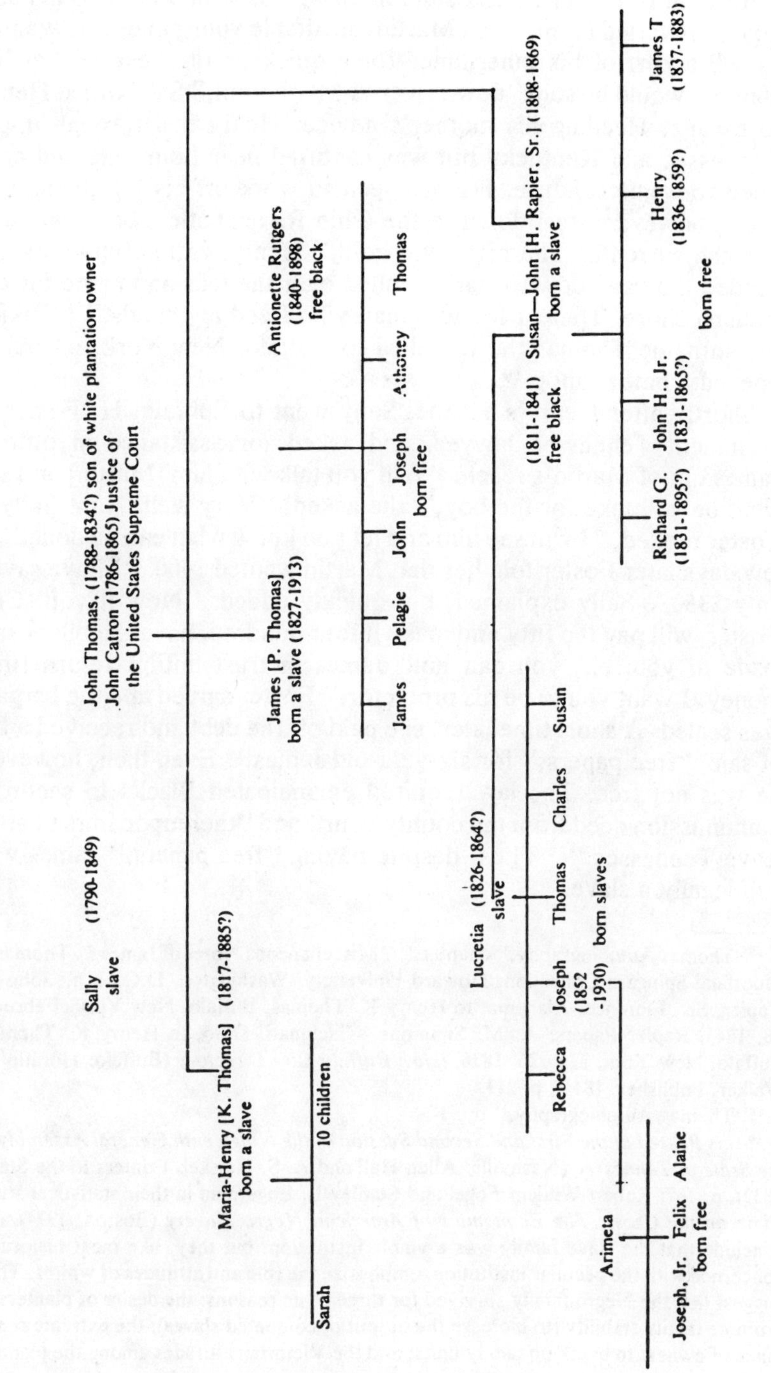

settlement of the Thomas Estate in 1834, "Sally and the two mulatto boys," reverted to one John Martin, an affable young man who wanted to sell a part of his inheritance for a quick profit. Fearing that her children would be sold "down river to Mississippi," Sally urged Henry to escape. Heeding his mother's advice, Henry fled through upper Tennessee and Kentucky but was captured near Louisville and confined to a guard house. He managed to work off his leg-chains one night, however, steal down to the Ohio River, untie a boat, and drift into the current. "The night was cold," Henry wrote afterwards. "I headed the yawl downstream, sculled over the falls and made for the Indiana shore. There I found a man who freed my hands."[18] Taking the surname Thomas, he travelled to Buffalo, New York, where he opened a barber shop.[19]

Shortly after Henry's escape, Sally went to Ephraim H. Foster, a prominent Tennessee lawyer, and asked for assistance in putting James out of Martin's reach. "Will you talk with him [Martin] and see what he will take for the boy," she asked. "Very well, Aunt Sally," Foster replied, "I will see him and let you know what can be done." A few days later Foster told her that Martin wanted $400. "I have saved only $350," Sally explained, but quickly added: "Now if you, Col. Foster, will pay the fifty and make it four hundred, have the bill of sale made to yourself, you can hold James in trust until I return [the] money. I want you to be his protector." Foster agreed and the bargain was sealed. A short time later, she paid off the debt and received a bill of sale, "free papers," for six-year-old James.[19] Even then, however, he was not free. The law required emancipated Blacks to secure a manumission deed from the county court, and "thereupon immediately leave Tennessee."[20] Thus, despite having "free papers," James was still legally a slave.

---

[18]"Thomas Autobiography," chapter 1; "Miscellaneous Notes of James P. Thomas," Moorland-Spingarn Collection, Howard University, Washington, D.C., n.p.; John H. Rapier, Sr., Florence, Alabama, to Henry K. Thomas, Buffalo, New York, February 28, 1843, Rapier Papers; A. M. Simmons, Cincinnati, Ohio, to Henry K. Thomas, Buffalo, New York, May 26, 1836, *ibid.*; *Buffalo City Directory* (Buffalo: Horatio N. Walker, Publisher, 1844), p. 213.

[19]"Thomas Autobiography," pp. 1-6.

[20]*Acts Passed at the First and Second Session of the Nineteenth General Assembly of the State of Tennessee* (Nashville: Allen Hall and A. S. Heiskel, Printers to the State, 1832), p. 167; Robert William Fogel and Stanley L. Engerman in their statistical study *Time on the Cross: The Economics of American Negro Slavery* (Boston, 1974) also conclude that the slave family was a viable institution, but they, like most historians concerned with the peculiar institution, emphasize the role and attitudes of whites. They suggest that the Negro family survived for three basic reasons: the desire of planters to promote family stability (to increase the output of contented slaves); the extreme reluctance of owners to break up family units; and the Victorian attitudes among the planting

But neither the law nor slavery seemed to curtail his activities. As a young boy, he performed a variety of chores for his mother: keeping salt in the hopper for making soap, cutting wood for the fire place, cleaning up around the house, and delivering clothes to customers. He also enrolled in the Nashville school for Blacks. Thomas recalled sitting on splintery benches, in a drafty one-room school house and listening to ill-prepared lessons on such basic subjects as "the fundamentals of reading." In addition, he remembered that the school remained open only a few months each year, the pupils, or "scholars," had to pay a very high $4 tuition fee, and that free Blacks Rufus Conrad, Daniel Watkins and Samuel Lowery taught at the school from time to time. "But often," he said, "there was no school because there was no teacher." In 1836, for instance, a black teacher, described as "a fine scholar," was taken out by whites and whipped nearly to death. "Tennesseans generally opposed educating blacks," he recalled, "they might want the same as whites." But young James had an intense desire to learn and quickly mastered the basics of mathematics, reading and writing.[21]

Having secured a rudimentary education, James hired out as an apprentice barber. Working with bondsman Frank Parrish, who had earlier established a barber shop on Public Square, he quickly learned the trade.[22] "James [is] still with Frank Parrish and has the character of a good barber, So a Gentleman told me," his brother, John Rapier, observed in 1843. "He is well thought of by the Gentlemen. James has

class, which made miscegenation extremely rare, resulting in a miniscule percent of mulattoes in the ante bellum South (7.7 in 1850 and 10.4 in 1860). Besides the impressionistic evidence used by the two cliometricians to support their contentions, the dubious relationship between the extent of sexual exploitation and the percent of mulattoes in the South in a given year (which is itself upon question), and the mis-interpretation of the quantified evidence concerning the break up of families on the New Orleans auction block between 1804-1862 (the authors suggest 84 percent of the sales involved unmarried individuals, but failed to reveal that the slave's familial status was generally not recorded), the greatest weakness of the study is the obvious inadequacy of quantification methods in evaluating the slave family. Statistical evidence does not reveal the feelings of interdependence, unity, and cohesiveness that black family members in bondage felt for one another. Robert William Fogel and Stanley L. Engerman, *Time on the Cross: The Economics of American Negro Slavery* (Boston, 1974), pp. 126-144.

[21] "Thomas Autobiography," chapters 1, 2; "Miscellaneous Notes of James P. Thomas," Moorland-Spingarn Collection, Howard University, Washington, D.C.; James P. Thomas, Nashville, Tennessee, to John H. Rapier, Jr., St. Paul, Minnesota Territory, October 3, 1856.

[22] The Nashville *Republican*, April 21, 1836; The Nashville *Daily Republican Banner*, April 9, 1841; Davidson County Probate Records, Minutes, Book E (October 4, 1853), pp. 563-564. Many times, as in this instance, probate court cases included biographical material about Blacks to illustrate their "good character." Davidson County Probate Records, Wills and Inventories, Vol. 16 (November 28, 1854), pp.429-430.

manners to please almost anyone who does not let their prejudice go far on account of color."[23] Two years later James was still with Parrish, earned $12 a month, and at the same time had begun violin lessons with one Gordan McGowan. "James will make a man of musick I think. He seems to be very fond of it."[24] Having served a five-year apprenticeship, in 1846, he opened his own barber shop. The nineteen-year-old slave established his shop in the house where he had grown up (and where his mother still operated her cleaning business), at 10 Deaderick Street. The location was ideal. Within a few steps of several banking houses, newspapers, and law firms, as well as the county court house, Market Square, and the Capitol, "the place on Deaderick," he explained, "was convenient to bankers, merchants, lawyers, politicians, and professional men." He counted among his customers six famous Tennesseans: William Carroll, one time governor; E. S. (Squire) Hall, an important businessman; General William Harding, owner of Bellemeade Estate; Ephraim Foster, a Whig political leader; and William G. (Parson) Brownlow, the Civil War governor.[25] Francis Fogg, the well-known Davidson County lawyer, visited the Thomas shop daily. "He returns to us in the evening," Mrs. Fogg noted approvingly, "with face smooth and curls nicely arranged."[26]

While attending to his duties as a barber, James listened attentively to conversations that took place among his customers. "They had time to talk in the barber shop. Nobody seemed in a great hurry. Everything was discussed—social, commercial, political and financial." He remembered conversations about the abolitionists, the advancement of cotton on the Liverpool market, the magnetism and sporting pro-

[23]John H. Rapier, Sr., Florence, Alabama, to Henry K. Thomas, Buffalo, New York, February 28, 1843, Rapier Papers.

[24]John H. Rapier, Sr., Florence, Alabama, to Richard Rapier, Buffalo, New York, April 8, 1845, Rapier Papers.

[25]"Thomas Autobiography," chapters 1, 2, 3; *The Nashville General Business Directory* (Nashville: The Daily American Book and Job Printing Office, 1853), 1-20; For the early business and financial activities of E. S. Hall in Nashville, see: John Claybrooke Papers, Manuscript Division, State Library and Archives, Nashville, Tennessee; For the activities of the other whites mentioned, see: Philip Hamer, *Tennessee: A History*, Vol. I (New York: American Historical Society, 1935), pp. 282, 370, 381, 475; "Leadership in Nashville: Biographical Sketches of 116 of the Most Prominent Citizens in Nashville," Catherine Pilcher Avery Papers, Manuscript Division, State Library and Archives, Nashville, Tennessee; "Old Days in Nashville, Tennessee: Reminiscences by Jane Thomas," (no relation to James Thomas), reprints from the Nashville *Daily American*, 1895-1896 in Jane Thomas Papers, Manuscript Division, State Library and Archives, Nashville, Tennessee; *The Official Political Manual of the State of Tennessee* (Nashville, Tennessee: Marshall and Bruce, 1890), p. 180.

[26]Ellen S. Fogg, Nashville, Tennessee, to E. H. Foster, Louisville, Kentucky, February 15, 1849, Ephraim Foster Papers, Manuscript Division, State Library and Archives, Nashville, Tennessee.

clivities of Andrew Jackson, plantation acreage along the Mississippi, and fugitive slaves. Once, he recalled being sharply questioned about runaway Blacks. "You have a brother living in Buffalo, New York, I believe," General Harding asked pointedly. "Yes," was the reply. "Well he treated me in a gruff manner. I went to ask him if he knew anything about a boy who ran off from me. I told him I only wanted to see him. I had come to Buffalo for that purpose. I received a very cold and indifferent reply." James could do little but apologize for his brother's "rudeness." Though he usually remained silent when the conversation turned to such controversial issues; at times he ventured an opinion on the slavery question. Once, for example, while shaving a young Virginia lawyer, he defended the Wilmot Proviso, a proposal to prohibit slavery in the newly acquired Mexican territories. "The set back I got caused me to be careful in the future. Among other things he told me I had no right to listen to a gentleman's conversation."[27] Despite such "set backs," James built up a flourishing business. Charging 25 cents for a haircut, 15 cents for a shave, and $1 for occasionally extracting teeth, he operated one of the most prosperous "tonsorial establishments" in Nashville. In the city's first business directory (published in 1853), he advertised in large boldface print: "JAS. THOMAS, BARBER SHOP, 10 Deaderick St."[28]

Meanwhile, Sally's other two children, freedman John H. Rapier and fugitive Henry Thomas, were also prospering as barbers. Rapier opened a shop in Florence, Alabama, soon saved over $500, purchased a white frame house on Court Street in the downtown district, and like James, converted the house into a place of business as well as a residence. In 1831, he married Susan, a free Black from Baltimore, Maryland, and in the next decade the couple had four children: Richard, John Jr., Henry and James.[29] After his wife's death in childbirth at the age of twenty-nine, he purchased a sixteen-year-old slave, Lucretia,

[27] "Thomas Autobiography," chapter 2.

[28] *Nashville Business Directory* (Nashville: Daily American Book and Job Printing Office, 1853), p. 68.

[29] Richard Rapier, Auburn, California, to James P. Thomas, December 14, 1877, Rapier Papers; In this letter Richard, John Rapier's eldest son, refers to his date and place of birth. In the "Diary and Notes of John H. Rapier, Jr.," March 10, 1857, Rapier Papers; John, Rapier's third son, likewise refers to his birth date; U.S. Census Office, Sixth Census of the United States, "Population Schedules for Lauderdale County, Alabama," Vol. IV, (1840), p. 104; James T. Rapier, Florence, Alabama to John H. Rapier, Jr., St. Paul, Minnesota Territory, September 27, 1858, Rapier Papers; "Thomas Autobiography," p. 73; *Alabama State Sentinel*, November 25, 1867; The inscription on Susan Rapier's tombstone reads: "Sacred to the memory of Susan Rapier. Born in Baltimore, Md. 25 of December 1811 departed this life at Florence Alabama 10 of March 1841—also her two infant children Jackson and Alexander—Depart my friends and dry up your tears for I must lie hear [sic] till Christ appears."

and between 1848 and 1861, they had five slave children, the youngest named Susan.[30] During the ante bellum period Rapier acquired real estate holdings in Alabama, the Minnesota Territory, and Canada, purchased valuable railroad stock, and saved $2000 in cash. By 1860, he was one of the wealthiest free Blacks in Alabama, with about $10,000.[31]

Henry Thomas also opened a barber shop. Locating in the basement of Buffalo's elegant hotel Niagara, he too built up a lucrative trade. About 1835, he married a black woman, Maria, and they had eleven children, ten boys and a girl, Sarah.[32] In 1852, to avoid apprehension by slave catchers (who were encouraged by the 1850 Fugitive Slave Law), he moved to the black community of Buxton, Canada West. With resources he had saved as a barber, he purchased one hundred acres of wilderness land, built a log house, cleared the trees, and put in a crop of corn, wheat and barley.[33] "The settlement improves slowly, but prospects are good for its success," he noted in 1856. "The lumber mill is making improvements for the neighborhood. Soon the railroad will pass through. The school is flourishing. I have six acres in wheat and 2 in barley."[34] Thus, using one of the few profitable occupations open to ante bellum Blacks, James, John and Henry were all able to achieve a degree of financial independence.

---

[30] U.S. Census Bureau, Sixth Census of the United States, Population Schedules for Lauderdale County, Alabama," Vol. IV, (1840), p. 104; United States Census Bureau, Seventh Census of the United States, Populations Schedules for Lauderdale County, Alabama," Vol. I, (1850), p. 293; United States Census Bureau, Eighth Census of the United States, Vol. VI (1860), p. 39.

[31] John H. Rapier, Sr., Florence, Alabama, to Richard Rapier, Buffalo, New York, April 8, 1845, Rapier Papers; John H. Rapier, Sr., Florence, Alabama, to John H. Rapier, Jr., St. Paul, Minnesota Territory, September 16, 1857, Rapier Papers; Lauderdale County Probate Records, Wills and Inventories, Vol. B (September 13, 1869), pp. 78-80, Land Deeds, Book II (May 3, 1844), p. 78; Book XVI (August 7, 1858), p. 324; The Florence *Gazette*, March 5, 1862; Loren Schweninger, "John H. Rapier, Sr.: A Slave and Freedman in the Antebellum South," *Civil War History*/Vol. 20, (March 1974), p. 31.

[32] A. M. Simmons, Cincinnati, Ohio, to Henry K. Thomas, Buffalo, New York, May 26, 1836, Rapier Papers; *Buffalo City Directory* (Buffalo: Horatio N. Walker, Publisher, 1844), p. 213; John H. Rapier, Sr., Florence, Alabama, to Henry K. Thomas, Buffalo, New York, February 28, 1843, Rapier Papers; "Thomas Autobiography," chapter 1; *Buffalo City Directory* (Buffalo: Jewett, Thomas and Company, Commercial Advertiser Office, 1847-48), p. 158.

[33] Henry K. Thomas, Buxton, Canada West, to John H. Rapier, Sr., Florence, Alabama, October 27, 1856, Rapier Papers; James T. Rapier, Buxton, Canada West, to John H. Rapier, Jr., St. Paul, Minnesota Territory, June 26, 1857, Rapier Papers; "Thomas Autobiography," chapter 1.

[34] Henry K. Thomas, Buxton, Canada West, to John H. Rapier, Sr., Florence, Alabama, October 27, 1856, Rapier Papers.

The members of the slave family were also successful at maintaining close family ties. Though separated by hundreds, even thousands of miles, though forbidden to travel in certain regions, and though denied postal privileges, they kept in close touch. As a slave and also when he was a free Black, John Rapier Sr. frequently visited Nashville. And between 1838 and 1846, he arranged for all four of his children to attend school in the Tennessee capital and to stay with their slave uncle and slave grandmother. "John and James are so [well] pleased with their grandmother [and school], he noted in 1843, "that they do not want to come home, so James writes."[35] A couple of years later he added: "My two sons that are with mother are well when I last hear[d] from them. I entend to go up to Nashville in the course of ten or twelve days and See them all." On that occasion Rapier confessed that he had not been to Tennessee in nearly a year. "I am extremely anxious to See the family again," he said, promising to deliver a letter from his brother, which had been smuggled into the South from the North. After a visit to the Tennessee capital, he wrote to "Brother Henry": "Mother looks as young as she did 8 years ago and works as hard and hardly takes time to talk to you." Forwarding other family news, he said that "Brother James" was doing extremely well as a barber; and of his sons, he proudly observed that Richard wrote in an excellent hand; Henry wanted to continue his education; James read extremely well "for a little boy of his age [6] and training;" and "John has wrote me two letter and writes very plain for a boy of eight, . . . and has as much taste for reading as any child I know off and is very good in arithmetic."[36] Rapier not only journeyed to Tennessee often, but about once a year, he travelled to New York or Canada.[37] After one such sojourn, he expressed concern for Brother Henry's future in the North. "I told him to buy [more] land in that country and to pay the taxes. [But] I am fearful that Brother Henry will come to want in [Canada] as I am of the opinion that [it] is poor farming country."[38] For their parts, Henry and James also expressed a deep concern for the welfare of the slave family. Henry usually concluded his letters

[35]John H. Rapier, Sr., Florence, Alabama, to Henry K. Thomas, Buffalo, New York, February 28, 1843, Rapier Papers.

[36]John H. Rapier, Sr., Florence, Alabama, to Richard Rapier, Buffalo, New York, April 8, 1845, Rapier Papers.

[37]"The Autobiography of William King," (1890), p. 255, King Papers, Public Archives of Canada, Ottawa, Ontario; King, who founded Buxton, reminisced about Rapier's frequent visits to Toronto and Buxton during the 1850's; John H. Rapier, Sr., Florence, Alabama, to John H. Rapier, Jr., Minnesota Territory, September 16, 1857, Rapier Papers.

[38]John H. Rapier, Sr., Florence, Alabama, to John H. Rapier, Jr., Minnesota Territory, September 15, 1856, Rapier Papers.

with the simple, but significant, line: "All the family is well and wishes to be remembered to you."[39] And James Thomas wrote: "A letter from your hands [John Rapier Jr.] offers me a great deal of pleasure to say nothing of the family news it imparts."[40] It seems that separation, an inherent part of the institution of slavery, had little effect on the spiritual unity of the slave family.

There was also a solidarity among the members of the Rapier family. Deeply concerned about the welfare of his children, John Rapier offered them advice on everything from economic matters to questions of morality: "Settle your debts," "Save your money," "Stay away from liquor," he admonished "The Four Boys." "Stick closer to work and Say nothing and do nothing but what is right and you will do well my sons."[41] In 1845 he wrote Richard, who was attending school in Buffalo and living with Henry Thomas: "Study your books so I can hold you up as an example to your lettle Brothers. You are blessed if you will look at your situation. You have kind relations who are anctious to see you grow up an ornament to society."[42] Perhaps the best expression of the spiritual unity of the Rapier family was written by James Thomas Rapier, James P. Thomas's namesake and one of Sally's twenty-six grandchildren. Also living with fugitive Henry Thomas, and attending school in Buxton, he wrote:

> In our boyhood . . . all four of us boys were together. We all breathed as one. [Now] we are scattered abroad on the face of the Earth. Do you ever expect to see us all together again? I do not. Just look where we are . . . John in [Minnesota]. Myself in the north. Henry and Dick in California. Father in Alabama. Did you ever think how small our family is?[43]

Among the Rapiers, as well as the Thomases, there was an almost

[39] Henry K. Thomas, Buxton, Canada West, to John H. Rapier, Sr., October 27, 1856, Rapier Papers; March 13, 1857; Henry's only daughter Sarah wrote to John Rapier, Jr.: "Through Papa and James I would like to give you some news . . . Mama and Papa are well as is the rest of the family and they sent their compliments. We shall all feel very much pleased if you make a visit to this place." Sarah Thomas, Buxton, Canada West, to John H. Rapier, Jr., Minnesota Territory, March 10, 1857, Rapier Papers.

[40] James P. Thomas, St. Louis, Missouri, to John H. Rapier, Jr., Minnesota Territory, June 17, 1858, Rapier Papers.

[41] John H. Rapier, Sr., Florence, Alabama to John H. Rapier, Jr., Minnesota Territory, September 15, 1856, Rapier Papers; John H. Rapier, Sr., Florence, Alabama to John H. Rapier, Jr., Benton County, Minnesota Territory, December 13, 1856, Rapier Papers.

[42] John H. Rapier, Sr., Florence, Alabama, to Richard Rapier, Buffalo, New York, April 8, 1845, Rapier Papers.

[43] James Rapier, Buxton, Canada West to John H. Rapier, Jr., Little Falls, Minnesota Territory, January 27, 1857, Rapier Papers.

religious devotion to the institution of the family.

The ability of the slave family to remain so close seems all the more remarkable in the face of the legal restrictions placed on Blacks. Statutes forbade a free Black from either visiting with slaves, or travelling from one state to another, both on penalty of being sold into slavery. Laws prohibited slaves from owning personal property, renting real estate, earning money, or securing an education. "No person shall hire to any slave," one Tennessee code pronounced, "the time of said slave."[44] Lawmakers prescribed a ten year prison sentence to anyone helping a slave to escape, forging a pass for a slave, harboring a runaway or inciting a Black to defy a white; and laid down the death penalty for Blacks convicted of assaulting or molesting a white woman, maliciously setting fire to a barn, preparing any poison, or conspiring to revolt. "A ring leader or Chief Instigator of any plot to rebel or murder any white," one law stated, "may be lawfully killed [on sight], if it is not practicable, otherwise, to arrest and secure him."[45] Nash-

[44]*Acts Passed at the First Session of the Fourteenth General Assembly of the State of Tennessee* (Knoxville: Heiskell and Brown, Public Printers to the State, 1821), p. 34; *Acts Passed at the Second Session of the Fourteenth General Assembly of the State of Tennessee* (Knoxville: Heiskell and Brown, Printers to the State, 1822), p. 22; *Acts Passed at the First Session of the Fifteenth General Assembly of the State of Tennessee* (Murfreesborough: J. Norvell and G. A. and A. C. Sablett, 1823), p. 76; *Acts Passed at the Extra Session of the Sixteenth General Assembly of the State of Tennessee* (Knoxville: Heiskell and Brown, 1927), 31-33; *Acts Passed at the First and Second Session of the Nineteenth General Assembly of the State of Tennessee* (Nashville: Allen A. Hall and A. S. Heiskell, Printers to the State, 1932), pp. 165-170.

[45]*Private Acts Passed at the Called Session of the Nineteenth General Assembly of the State of Tennessee* (Nashville: Allen A. Hall and F. S. Heiskell, Printers, 1832), pp. 5, 6; *Public Acts Passed at the First Session of the Twentieth General Assembly of the State of Tennessee* (Nashville: Allen A. Hall and F. S. Heiskell, Printers to the State, 1833), pp. 2, 3, 75, 76, 14, 87, 94, 99, 100, 215, 216; *Public Acts Passed at the First Session of the Twenty-first General Assembly of the State of Tennessee* (Nashville: S. Nye and Co., Printers, 1836), pp. 92, 145, 146, 167; *Acts Passed at the First Session of the Twenty-third General Assembly of the State of Tennessee* (Nashville: J. Geo. Harris, Printer to the State, 1840), pp. 82, 83; *Acts Passed by the First Session of the Twenty-fourth General Assembly of the State of Tennessee* (Murfreesborough: Cameron and Company, Printers to the State, 1842), pp. 229, 230; *Acts of the State of Tennessee Passed at the First Session of the Twenty-sixth General Assembly* (Knoxville: James C. Moses, 1846), p. 278; *Acts of the State of Tennessee Passed at the First Session of the Twenty-eighth General Assembly* (Nashville: McKennie and Watterson, Printers to the State, 1850), p. 30; *Acts of the State of Tennessee Passed at the First Session of the Twenty-eighth General Assembly* (Nashville: McKennie and Watterson, Printers to the State, 1850), p. 304; *Acts Passed at the First Session of the Twenty-ninth General Assembly* (Nashville: McKennie Printers, 1852), pp. 120, 521; *Acts of the State of Tennessee Passed at the First Session of the Thirtieth General Assembly* (Nashville: McKennie and Brown, Book and Job Printers, 1854), pp. 121, 122, 157; *Acts of the State of Tennessee Passed at the First Session of the Thirty-first General Assembly* (Nashville: Printed by G. C. Torbett and Company, 1856), pp. 71, 77; William Imes, "The Legal Status of Free Negroes and Slaves in Tennessee," *Journal of Negro History*, IV (July 1919), pp. 260, 261.

ville ordinances required free Blacks to pay a capitation (head) tax of $1 or $2, register at the court house, and "carry free papers on their person at all times." Blacks without such papers were to be treated as slaves. Moreover, Negroes were not permitted to walk the streets after dark, enter tippling houses, make weird noises, or gather within the city limits for any purpose, except public worship, and Blacks attending church were to be supervised by whites.[46]

But the slave family disregarded the elaborate code governing Blacks. Sally hired out, earned money, rented a house, and operated a business. "Mother lived so long at the corner of Deaderick and Cherry Streets," James Thomas remarked later, "that the people of Nashville thought she [was free] and owned the property." She moved about the city with little hindrance, boarded her grandchildren as they attended school, and secretly advised Henry to escape to the North.[47] In a similar manner James Thomas hired out, earned money and established a business. He eventually accumulated a large amount of personal property—furniture, mirrors, clothes, and about $1000 in cash, and while still a slave, became the manager of one of the largest barbering establishments in Nashville. He travelled to various parts of the city without a pass, entertained free Blacks in his home, and attended black church meetings. At one such gathering he recalled the black congregation, mostly slaves, singing until 12 o'clock at night. "The owners," he wrote, "seemed to care very little how much religion their servants got. They seemed to encourage it."[48] In much the same way John Rapier and Henry Thomas acquired personal property, hired out, earned as much as $50 a month, and, despite the laws against the movement of Blacks, travelled throughout the South, North, and Canada. Rapier even assisted a slave, Sam Ragland, to escape on one occasion.[49] In short, the slave family was not in the least constrained by the restrictive black codes.

Sally's dream that all of her children secure their freedom finally

[46] *Revised Laws of the City of Nashville* (Nashville: Union and American Steam Press, 1854), pp. 147, 154-58; *Revised Laws of the City of Nashville* (Nashville: Harvey M. Watterson Printers, 1850), pp. 124-26; *Acts Passed at the First Session of the Twenty-fifth General Assembly of the State of Tennessee* (Nashville: L. Gifford and E. G. Eastman, Printers, 1844), p. 18.

[47] "Thomas Autobiography," chapter 1.

[48] *Ibid.*; "Miscellaneous Notes of James P. Thomas," Moorland-Spingarn Collection, Howard University, Washington, D.C., n.d.; James P. Thomas, Louisville, Kentucky, to John H. Rapier, Jr., St. Paul, Minnesota Territory, March 1, 1856, Rapier Papers; James P. Thomas, Nashville, Tennessee, to John H. Rapier, Jr., Minnesota Territory, October 3, 1856, Rapier Papers.

[49] Loren Schweninger, "John H. Rapier, Sr.: A Slave and Freedman in the Antebellum South," Vol. 20, *Civil War History* (March 1974), *passim*.

came true in 1851, when her youngest son, James, asked Ephraim Foster to present a manumission petition to the Davidson County court. The slave and his master appeared at the courthouse in Nashville on March 6. "James has always maintained an exemplary character," Foster told the nine-judge panel hearing the case. "He has been industrious, honest, moral, humble, polite and had conducted himself as to gain the confidence and respect of whites. He is a man of great worth in his place." The testimony of such an eminent Tennessean swayed the magistrates and, after a short deliberation, they ordered "the slave James, otherwise called James [P.] Thomas, emancipated and forever set free." Thomas now addressed the court himself. He requested immunity from the 1831 law requiring manumitted Blacks to leave Tennessee. "I have deported myself in a manner requiring the confidence of whites. I have always earned a good living. I would be greatly damaged having to Start anew in some Strange Country." The judges, after receiving the required $500 good behavior bond, granted the immunity. James P. Thomas thus became the first black man in the county, perhaps the state, under the stringent emigration law of 1831, to gain legally both freedom and residency.[50]

A short time before James gained his freedom, however, Sally died of cholera.[51] A woman of great drive and dedication, she had devoted her life to freeing her children. She had hired out, started a business, and gladly put up her life savings to purchase "free papers" for James. She had also assisted Henry in his quest for freedom. Due in part to her unwavering efforts, the slaves John H. Rapier, Sr., Henry K. Thomas, and James P. Thomas, all gained free status before the Civil War. In addition, the Thomases and Rapiers all found great strength in the slave family. Members of these families were quite successful: John entered politics during Reconstruction; Henry farmed hundreds of acres in Canada; and James acquired property in St. Louis valued at $250,000;[52] while Sarah Thomas became a school teacher, James T. Rapier a Congressman, and John Rapier, Jr. a surgeon, stemmed from

---

[50] "Thomas Autobiography," pp. 1-8; Davidson County Probate Records, Minute Book E (March 6, 1851), pp. 134, 135.

[51] "Thomas Autobiography," p. 1; James Thomas said that his mother died in a cholera epidemic in 1850, but it was probably in the spring of 1849, when hundreds of Nashvillians died from the dreaded disease.

[52] The Florence *Journal*, September 18, 1869; Assessors Records, City of St. Louis, Plate 1874-1876, number B65, Blk 300, 301, 691; Assessors Records, City of St. Louis, Tax Books for 1871, Book 17 (1871), pp. 20-21; Probate Records of the City of St. Louis, Warranty Deeds, Book 452 (August 13, 1872), pp. 470, 471; "Autobiography of William King," pp. 355-360.

the security they found in the slave family.[53] It seems that for the black slave Sally, sexual exploitation, miscegenation, separation, and legal restrictions—the very forces designed, in part, to destroy the black family—gave impetus, *not* to disintegration and disunity, but to an extraordinary feeling of family loyalty, unity, and love. For Sally, her children, and her grandchildren, the slave family was indeed "a refuge from the rigors of slavery."

[53]James T. Rapier, Montgomery, Alabama, to William King, Buxton, Ontario, July 7, 1872, King Papers; Loren Schweninger, "James Rapier and Reconstruction," (PH.D. dissertation, Chicago, 1972), *passim*.

"JUMPING THE BROOMSTICK": SLAVE MARRIAGE AND MORALITY IN ARKANSAS

By Orville W. Taylor*
Baptist College, Iwo, Nigeria
West Africa

"There were no valid marriages amongst that class [the slaves], in the slave states of America before their general emancipation near the close of the civil war, nor after that did any of the States take cognizance of marriages amongst slaves, until provisions were made by statute."[1] So wrote Justice James Eakin in rendering the decision of the Arkansas Supreme Court in the case of *Gregley* v. *Jackson* in 1882. Written nearly twenty years after the end of the slave era, Justice Eakin's statement was a correct appraisal of the status of slave marriage in Arkansas. Arkansas had no laws which stated specifically that slave marriages did not exist in the legal sense, but its citizens, most of whom had come from the older slave states, merely understood that a slave, like any other piece of property, had no right to enter into any sort of legal contract. Frequently, however, slaves went through some sort of marriage ceremony before living together.

Information disclosed in an Arkansas Supreme Court case in 1950 illustrates in considerable detail various aspects of slave marriage in Arkansas.[2] "Old Joe" Edwards was a slave of the Gant Family in Union County. Before 1850 he "married" Susan, a slave belonging to the Wroten family which lived six or eight miles away, in the traditional slave marriage ceremony called "jumping the broomstick."[3] From that time until about 1865, although the requirements of the slavery system prevented them from living together constantly, Joe and Susan regarded

*Winner of the 1958 Albert L. Shader Memorial Award of the Arkansas Historical Association.

[1]*Gregley* v. *Jackson*, in *Reports of Cases Argued and Determined in the Supreme Court of the State of Arkansas in Law and Equity* (227 vols.; Little Rock, 1840-), 38, 490. Supreme Court cases will be cited hereafter in this manner: "*Gregley* v. *Jackson*, 38 Ark. 490."

[2]*Daniels* v. *Johnson*, 374 Ark. 216. No citations will be made to individual portions of the case.

[3]This ceremony evidently symbolized passage into domestic status.

each other as husband and wife, and during the years from 1850 to 1863 Susan gave birth to five children of whom Joe was the acknowledged father.

A few years after Joe married Susan he became attracted to Patsy, like himself a slave of the Gant family, who lived in an adjoining slave cabin in the Gant back yard. Patsy was the "black mammy" of the Gant children, including Nancy, who was born in 1853 and lived to be more than ninety-six years old. About 1855 Joe and Patsy were married, also by "jumping the broomstick," although Joe's marriage to Susan continued to exist and to produce children. From 1856 to 1864 Patsy bore five girls, whom Joe also recognized as his children. Thus Joe was "married" to two women and the father of two families of children simultaneously.[4]

Amid the confusion attendant upon the end of the Civil War in 1865 and the consequent freeing of all slaves, Joe terminated his two marriages and in 1866 began to live with Avaline, also a recently freed slave. The next year the union of the two was legalized by an Arkansas statute, passed by the General Assembly on February 6, 1867, entitled "An Act to declare the rights of persons of African descent." The portion pertaining to marriage decreed:

> Be it further enacted, That all negroes and mulattoes who are now cohabiting as husband and wife, and recognize each other as such, shall be deemed lawfully married from the passage of this act, and shall be subjected to all the obligations and entitled to all rights appertaining to the marriage relation; and in all cases where such persons now are, or have heretofore been so cohabiting, as husband and wife, and may have offspring recognized by them as their own, such offspring shall be deemed in all respects legitimate, as fully as if born in wedlock.

In 1868 Joe and Aveline Edwards became tre parents of J. W. (Jim), the only child born of the marriage. Both Old Joe and Aveline died by 1876, but Jim lived until 1946, leaving no descendants. During his lifetime Jim acquired property—mostly oil lands—valued variously at

[4]This was not a unique case. In 1854 S. W. Boyer offered a $100 reward for the return of his runaway slave Henry, who had "a wife near Summerville, Tennessee, and also a wife and children in St. Louis." *Arkansas True Democrat*, July 12, 1854.

from $125,000 to $3,000,000, and when he died intestate, legal actions were brought by numerous relatives to secure the estate. The claimants to the property were in three groups: the "Patsy line," composed of descendants of Old Joe, father of Jim, and the Gant slave Patsy; the "Susan line," made up of descendants of Old Joe and Susan, the Wroten slave; and the descendants of Sophronia, sister of Jim's mother Aveline.

The Union County probate judge quickly overruled the claims of the members of the Sophronia group, who had asserted that since no slave marriages had been legal, all of the children of Patsy and Susan (half-brothers and sisters of Jim) had been illegitimate, and that descent for the purpose of awarding the property should be traced from the next nearest relative, the sister of Old Joe's legal wife Aveline. The probate judge then ruled that the children of Susan and Old Joe had been legitimate and their descendants thus entitled to share the estate of Jim, but that the children of Patsy and Old Joe had been illegitimate, with their descendants deprived of a share in the estate. The judge based his decision upon the fact that Old Joe's marriage to Susan had occurred first, making, in his opinion, the second—to Patsy—bigamous and the children of it therefore illegitimate. This decision was given in spite of testimony of Mrs. Nancy Gant Britt, in whose family Patsy had been the "black mammy," that Joe and Patsy had been considered properly married by standards of the slavery period:

Mrs. Britt: Everyone in the community said that when a slave man and woman were having children they were considered married. They generally lived in the same house, or near each other.

Judge: When he took up with Patsy, he called that marrying her?

Mrs. Britt: I suppose so. That is the way they did it in those days . . .

Judge: And you say Joe and Patsy were living on the same place and were living there and had children as man and wife?

Mrs. Britt: Yes!

The descendants of Patsy appealed the decision of the Union County Probate Court, and eventually the case reached the Arkansas Supreme Court. The court agreed that the Sophronia group had no legal claim on the estate of Jim, but ruled that the descendants of Patsy were entitled to share in the property on an equal basis with those of Susan. This decision was based upon that part of the statute of 1867 which said: ". . . in all cases where such persons . . . have heretofore been so cohabiting, as husband and wife, and may have offspring recognized by them as their own, such offspring shall be deemed in all respects legitimate, as fully as if born in lawful wedlock." In other words, since Old Joe had lived with both Susan and Patsy in the marital state—even though at the same time—and had acknowledged all children born to both slave women as his own, the children had all been legitimate. It is readily apparent that the 1867 act as interpreted by the Arkansas Supreme Court had the effect of legitimatizing the children of all slave marriages in Arkansas, no matter how early they were born.

A charge persistently leveled at slaveowners through the years is that they deliberately forced their slaves—married or not—to breed and produce children as rapidly as possible, in order to reap the profits from the eventual sale of some of the children, and from the labor of others. There is no evidence to support the validity of this charge in relation to Arkansas; and even if slaveowners attempted to do so they were remarkably unsuccessful, for the slave birthrate was lower than the white.[5] Nor is there evidence in support of the contention elsewhere: Ulrich B. Phillips, the great historian of American Negro slavery, uncovered only one instance of a master forcing his slaves to cohabit regardless of their

[5] During the year 1849-1850 the slave birthrate was 24 per 1000, while the white was 35 per 1000. In 1859-1860 the rates were 30 per 1000 for slaves and 33 per 1000 for whites. *Census of* 1850 (Washington, 1853), pp. xli, 547; *Census of* 1860 (*Population*) (Washington, 1864), pp. xxxviii, xxxxix, xli. These, and other census reports which will be cited, were published by the U. S. Bureau of the Census. Historians of slavery have largely ignored the fact that slave birthrates were lower than those of white people. For example, Frederic Bancroft, the great historian of slave-trading, cited many instances of great fecundity of slave women, obviously implying that the reverse was true. Bancroft, *Slave-Trading in the Old South* (Baltimore, 1931), pp. 81-86. See also James B. Sellers, *Slavery in Alabama* (University, Alabama, 1950), p. 147, and William D. Postell, *The Health of Slaves on Southern Plantations* (Baton Rouge, 1951), pp. 151-153.

wishes, and this occurred in Massachusetts in 1636.[6] Those accusing slaveowners of enforced breeding have neglected to attempt to explain why it would have been necessary to compel slaves to satisfy one of the most basic of all human urges.

Naturally there would have been slave children whether the slaves were married or not, but many slaveowners encouraged, or even insisted upon, some sort of ceremony, and after that expected a certain degree of faithfulness of the slaves to each other. One type of informal slave marriage ceremony, "jumping the broomstick," has been mentioned; some other ceremonies were equally informal. One master near Little Rock merely wrote in the family Bible the names of his two slaves who chose to live together, admonished them to refrain from "fussin' and fightin'," and thenceforth considered them married.[7] Other slave marraige ceremonies, however, were practically as formal as those of white people. An old Negro woman who had been a slave near De Witt in Arkansas County gave this description of slave marraiges on the plantation of Colonel Jesse Chaney, who had a reputation for kindliness toward his slaves:

> When two of the slaves wanted to get married, they'd dress up as nice as they could and go up to the big house, and the master would marry them. They'd stand up before him, and he'd read out of a book called THE DISCIPLINE, and say, "Thou shalt love the Lord thy God with all thy heart, all thy strength, with all thy might, and thy neighbor as thy self." Then he'd say they were man and wife and tell them to live right and be honest and kind to each other. All the slaves would be there, too, seeing the wedding.[8]

Slaveowners usually favored marriages between their own slaves, rather than between a slave of their own and one belonging to someone else, for under such an arrangement there would be less interruption of the routine of slave life and work.[9] But of coure many slaves did marry away from home, by choice or because of the lack of an eligible partner nearby. When marriages of this sort existed, masters per-

[6]Ulrich B. Phillips, *American Neoro Slavery* (New York, 1918), p. 361. For a good refutation of the myth that slaveowners svstematically bred their slaves see Avery O. Craven, *The Coming of the Civil War* (New York, 1942), pp. 80-85.

[7]Orland K. Armstrong, *Old Massa's People* (Indianapolis, 1931), p. 165.

[8]B. A. Botkin (ed.), *Lay My Burden Down* (New York, 1946), p. 146.

[9]Armstrong, *Old Massa's People*, p. 164; *Daniels* v. *Johnson*, 374 Ark 216.

mitted the slave husband to visit his wife at stipulated times (usually on weekends), or arranged to get the couple together by buying or selling one of them. Allen Martin of the Mabelvale community near Little Rock offered in 1841 to trade 237 acres of land on Crooked Creek for his slave Dick's wife and three children, who belonged to a neighbor named Thorn.[10] Sometimes a series of sales was necessary to unite a slave couple at the home of a single owner: Robert F. Kellam, a Camden merchant, sold his slave woman Sarah and her two children to Lucius Greening in January, 1860, and two months later a Mr. Sheridan sold the slave man Sheridan to Greening, which, according to Kellam, "gett our former servant Sarah with her husband."[11]

Arkansas had no legal requirement that slave husbands and wives, or even mothers and small children, must be kept together. Any effort to keep families together was thus prompted by humanitarianism, or sometimes practical motives, since separating families often created disciplinary problems, such as running away. There were many instances of separation of families, but the records also contain indications that many owners respected the existence of the slave family as a social, if not a legal, institution, and that they attempted to preserve it whenever possible. Newspaper advertisements of slaves for sale or hire often referred to slave families. An unnamed owner offered in the Helena *Southern Shield* to hire out "two likely negroes, man and woman; the woman is a good house girl, cook, and washer: the man is an excellent field hand," and stated that "it would be preferable to hire them together, as they are man and wife."[12] B. Smith and Chester Ashley of Little Rock offered to sell a mulatto woman named Charlotte, aged forty, and her son Lewis, aged eighteen, in 1829 "to some respectable

[10]Allen Martin to Jared C. Martin, May 15, 1841, Martin Papers, in possession of Miss Blanche Martin, Little Rock. Thorn was equally solicitous of the family welfare of his slaves: before his death in October, 1850, he made a will appointing Elbert H. English his executor, instructing him to sell one slave family "in a group for the best price that can be had so that they may remain together as a family," and to sell the slave woman Mariah and infant child to a friend for the ridiculously low price of $100, the obvious purpose being to secure her a good home and keep mother and child together rather than to derive income. Pulaski County Will Book "B", p. 10.

[11]Diary of Robert F. Kellam, January 4, March 28, 1860. The diary is in possession of a grandson, Mr. Charles Gee of Camden.

[12]*Southern Shield,* May 1, 1852.

person, who will treat them humanely, and not separate them."[13]

Slave children were always the property of the owner of the mother, which was another reason for encouragement of marriage between slaves in the same establishment. Special consideration was given to slave mothers before and after childbirth, with freedom from work "two weeks before—two weeks after" the general custom. And the owner who possessed a "special woman"—one who produced children often and over a long period of time—was even more careful of his very valuable property.[14] One such woman could soon be responsible for wealth far in excess of her own value.[15] A major reason for the common practice of owners giving slave girls to each member of their families at marriage or some other time was to furnish the nucleus of a new slave working force.[16]

But all slaves did not "jump the broomstick" or enter into "marriage" in other ways; many merely engaged in what would be considered "sexual immorality" by conventional standards. The level of sexual morality of Negro slaves should not be judged, however, by the same standards which applied to white people of the period. Marriage of slaves, as we have seen, did not legally exist, and so to begin with slaves were without what is probably the greatest curb to sexual promiscuity in the human social order. Certainly it would have required a high degree of social and moral consciousness for anyone—and especially an uneducated and

[13] *Arkansas Gazette*, April 15, 1829.

[14] Armstrong, *Old Massa's People*, pp. 165, 181.

[15] During the late 1850's the average value of slave women in Arkansas in the age-range most productive of children—from the late 'teens to the early thirties—was approximately $1100. In the same period a slave baby was worth at least $100 at birth, and by five or six years of age $500 or more. Information concerning the value of slaves was derived from a wide variety of sources found in both private and public collections in Arkansas and elsewhere: bills of sale, inventories of estates, deed records, will records, tax assessment lists, probate court records, county records of other types, diaries, plantation records, newspapers, and personal letters and papers of all types. Of especial value was a document entitled Appraisement of the Personal Property of the Estate of Junius W. Craig, as made on the 14th day of July, A. D., 1860 . . . . This document includes a detailed descriptive listing of the 211 slaves on Bellevue and Yellow Bayo Plantations in Chicot County. It is in possession of Mr. Robert Chotard, Lake Village, a descendant of the Craig family.

[16] Small slave boys were also given to children, but the practice of giving slave girls was more prevalent. See *Moody* v. *Walker*, 3 Ark. 147; *Hynson and Wife* v. *Terry*, 1 Ark. 38; *Carter et al* v. *Cantrell et al*, 16 Ark. 154; *Gaines as Ad.* v. *Briggs et al*, 9 Ark. 46; *Dodd* v. *McCraw*, 8 Ark. 84.

unsophisticated slave—to distinguish between "acceptable" sexual relations in an informal marriage and "unacceptable" relation where no such marriage existed. Particularly was this true when a slave might pass successively into the ownership of men with widely varying standards and requirements concerning the marital relationship of their slaves. The plain fact is that most, if not all, Arkansas slaves were sexually promiscuous by white standards at some time in their lives, partially because of the general lack of social restraint to such practices, and partially because in relation to other members of the slave class there was, legally speaking, no such thing as promiscuity. Another factor was the influence of an African background of universally polygamous marriage attaching no value to faithfulness to a single mate.

Despite widespread promiscuity, there are many instances of apparent faithfulness of slave married couples to each other. For example, "Uncle Charley" Nicholls of near Little Rock was married at an early age to Anna, his master's "house-gal," and the two lived faithfully together for many years, eventually producing, both before and after the abolition of slavery, twenty-four children, including several sets of twins.[17]

The slave social structure contained no such component as the "old maid" or spinster, since there was no real passage from the unmarried to the married state. Perhaps the nearest equivalent to this phenomenon present only in the more highly-regulated societies was the slave woman unable to bear children for physiological reasons, and of course even this was no deterrent to cohabitation. As a rule slave girls entered into unions at a very early age, and teen-aged mothers were commonplace.[18]

It is in the cloudy realm of sexual relations between members of the white race and Negro slaves that there has been the most interest and speculation in the past. Abolitionist literature of the slavery period made much of white-slave relations, loudly claiming that slave women were universally

[17]Armstrong, *Old Massa's People*, p. 165.

[18]Slave children were almost always listed in the various types of records immediately after their mothers. The various sources referred to above list many teen-age mothers, some with several small children.

made victims of the white man's lust, and intimating that this was one of the reasons for the South's persistence in maintaining slavery. Only one account from abolitionist literature referring to Arkansas need be cited here for purposes of illustration: all are very much of a type. This one was related by John Roles, who served as an overseer in the South for ten years and later published an abolitionist book.[19]

In telling of the past trials and tribulations of his slave cook while in the South, Roles described her as beautiful and intelligent, but decried the advantages to be achieved by such attributes, for, he wrote, ". . . the cruel and licentious abominations of slavery had destroyed her happiness from the day that she began to bloom into womanhood, and will continue to destroy it until the grave shall hide her from the oppressor, and her beautiful but welted and scarred body shall mix and moulder with its mother earth." The slave woman was born in Virginia of—as was fitting in such fierce anti-Southern propaganda—a slave mother and a white man, who, to add further fuel to the flame, was a Methodist preacher. As a young girl she was sold to a man in Fort Smith, Arkansas, who "made her the victim of his lust when she was very young, and threatened to sell her off to a cotton plantation if she let her mistress know what he was doing." The girl was too young to realize fully the wrong of what she was doing, but such a realization would have made no difference, "for her master was a stern man, and she would not have dared to resist."

The philandering master also carried on an affair with another house slave, and when jealously between the two girls arose, the second slave informed the mistress of the relationship between the master and the first. At an opportune time when the master was absent from home, the mistress, with the aid of the other slave, seized Roles' heroine, stripped her, tied her hands and feet, flogged her brutally, and then ordered the other slave to continue the whipping. The next stage of the punitive and vengeful treatment consisted of application of fire in a manner which, in keeping with the ideas of that Victorian day, Roles would

[19] John Roles, *Inside View of Slavery on Southern Plantations* (New York, 1864), pp. 29-30.

not even describe: "But I cannot give the revolting details of this cruel punishment. I have heard of jealous mistresses burning their slaves in a cruel manner, but propriety forbids me to describe the mode, for the same reason that I cannot give the vile slang used by slave-drivers towards their female slaves." Evidently Roles was hinting broadly at injury to the sexual organs. Just before the torture was to begin, the slave girl broke free and attempted to commit suicide by cutting her throat with a butcher knife, but was prevented from doing so.

A short time later the girl was sold again, this time to a merchant living on the Arkansas River. At her new home there was the same pattern of seduction, varied only by a vague promise that eventually she would be set free. But the hope never materialized, and in time she was traded off for dry goods. The new master also made glowing promises to win her sexual favors, but Roles' poor heroine never reached a status higher than that of house servant and concubine. And so went the tale.

John Roles' account doubtless contains elements of both truth and exaggeration, but it must be remembered that it, like similar literature, was written as propaganda, and thus naturally emphasized events which helped to prove the point of the writer. To believe that the experiences of Roles' slave girl was typical of the relationships between all female slaves and their masters in Arkansas would be like believing that *Uncle Tom's Cabin* gave a completely correct picture of slavery in all its aspects.

That many masters and their female slaves did engage in sexual relations there is no doubt, and there is considerable evidence, even though much of it indirect, to support the assertion. The generally furtive nature of such relationships prevents, however, any reasonable estimate of their prevalence. But there is irrefutable proof in the birth to slave women of children known to have been fathered by white men. It is impossible to ascertain the frequency of such births, because for every instance in which a white man admitted paternity certainly there were many more where no such admission was made. And of the cases in which white men were acknowledged fathers of slave children, probably only a small percentage were ever recorded in any form, and these usually only when some legal question, such as a grant of freedom or money to the slave, was involved.

It might appear that the proportion of slaves of mixed blood would give some indication of the frequency of births of white-fathered children, but even this can offer only insights, for when a slave, either black or of mixed blood, cohabited with another slave of mixed blood, obviously the children would also be of mixed blood, but the progeny of slaves. In addition, there was always some cohabitation between slaves and free Negroes, among whom there was a much higher percentage of mulattoes than among slaves, and this would tend, through the inevitable birth of mullatto children, to increase the number of mulattoes in the slave population, but not as a direct result of white-slave cohabitation. A final reason for the invalidity of the size of the mulatto slave population as a key to the frequency of births of white-fathered children is that some mulattoes eventually moved from the status of slaves to that of free Negroes as a result of having white fathers. But since the number of free Negroes in Arkansas was always small, this factor had little effect upon the proportion of mulattoes in the total slave population.[20]

Although it is evident, then, that the proportion of mulattoes in the slave population can offer no direct evidence as to the number of children born of interracial cohabitation, an examination of the available statistics is nevertheless of some interest. Prior to 1850 the federal censuses, chief source of such information, contain no data on the color or racial composition of slaves. The following table shows the percentage of mulattoes in the slave population of the more important slave states for 1850 and 1860:

[20]The number of Free Negroes in Arkansas was smaller at every federal census than in any other state, reaching a maximum of only 608 in 1850, and declining to 144 in 1860. These numbers were very small in comparison with the 47,100 slaves in the state in 1850, and the 111,115 in 1860. 66.94 per cent of the free Negroes were mulattoes in 1850, and 60.42 per cent in 1860. *Compendium of the Seventh Census,* 1850 (Washington, 1854), p. 83; *Census of* 1850 (*Population*), p. xiii.

Percentage of Mulattoes in Slave Population[21]

State	1850	1860	State	1850	1860
Alabama ...	6.73	7.89	Mississippi	6.80	8.39
Arkansas ...	15.61	12.64	Missouri	17.84	19.07
Florida	8.33	8.51	North Carolina .	6.19	6.94
Georgia	6.31	7.98	South Carolina .	3.36	5.26
Kentucky ...	16.40	19.19	Tennessee	9.29	13.63
Louisiana ...	8.22	9.83	Texas	15.27	13.68
Maryland ...	9.56	10.18	Virginia	10.34	14.24

An examination of the figures for 1850 reveals that the states with the lowest percentages of mulatto slaves were Alabama, Georgia, Mississippi, North Carolina, and South Carolina, all predominatly slave-*using* states of the older South. The states with the highest percentages of mulattoes fell into two groups: Arkansas and Texas, predominantly slave-*using* states of the newer South; and Kentucky, Virginia and Missouri, primarily slave-*selling* states. In 1860 the same group of states remained lowest in percentage of mulattoes, although all had shown increases. Of the high states in 1850, only two—Arkansas and Texas—had shown declines in percentages of mulattoes, while the group had been supplemented by Tennessee and Maryland, like the others primarily slave-exporting states.

The groupings and trends between 1850 and 1860 suggest these conclusions: (1) Slave-exporting states tended to have high and increasing percentages of mulattoes. Chiefly this was because black slaves sold more readily in the lower South, with mulattoes consequently being kept at home, where they formed an increasingly large percentage of the slave population.[22] (2) The slave-using states of the

[21]Compiled from statistics in *Compendium of the Seventh Census*, 1850, p. 83, and *Census of* 1860 (*Population*), p. xiii. The term "mulatto" was used in no sense in the censuses, but merely reflected the individual judgement of the census enumerators. A publication of the United States Bureau of the Census contains this statement: "At the census of 1850 and 1860 the terms 'black' and 'mulatto' appear not to have been defined. In 1850 enumerators were instructed simply in enumerating colored persons to write 'B' or 'M' in the space on the schedule, to indicate black or mulatto, leaving the space blank in the case of whites. In 1860 no instructions are known to have been given to the enumerators." U. S. Bureau of the Census, *Negro Population*, 1790-1915 (Washington, 1918), p. 207. Throughout this study "mulatto" has been used to mean a Negro of any degree of mixed blood.

[22]It was generally believed by white people that slaves of mixed blood were more intelligent and therefore less amenable to plantation regimentation. An additional fear was that a light-colored slave, especially if he were almost

older South had low percentages of mulattoes since they for many years had been purchasing mostly black slaves. But the percentage of mulattoes was increasing as these states in turn exported black slaves to the newer South. (3) The slave-importing states of the newer South (Arkansas and Texas) had high percentages of mulattoes at first because when settlers entered they took with them the slaves they already owned, including, presumably, a high proportion of house-servants, who were dominantly mulatto. The statistical importance of the mulattoes was also enhanced by the relatively small numbers of slaves in Arkansas and Texas in 1850.[23] But by 1860 the percentage of mulattoes had declined because slaves purchased to work on the rapidly-growing cotton plantations were mainly blacks rather than mulattoes. The fact that Arkansas and Texas had the largest percentages of increase in slave population in the 1850-1860 decade, and yet were the only states in which the percentages of mulattoes decreased tends to verify the latter conclusion.[24]

Most of the verifiable instances of slave women having children fathered by white men are found in the reports of cases which came before the Arkansas Supreme Court. The following are typical. When Duncan Campbell of Chicot County died in 1845, he acknowledged in his will that he was the father of Viney, small daughter of one of his slaves, granting her freedom and five thousand dollars when she reached the age of fifteen.[25] James H. Dunn, a merchant of Fulton, Hempstead County, readily and openly ad-

white, might be inclined to run away more readily than a black one, since detection and capture would be more difficult. Many light-skinned slaves in Arkansas did run away, some attempting to pass themselves for free white men. *Batesville News*, July 11, 1839; *Washington Telegraph*, August 12, 1846; *Arkansas Gazette*, April 19, 1836, June 28, 1836. James Sheppard, a large planter of near Pine Bluff, had difficulty in selling a slave woman because of her light color; the New Orleans agent with whom he had placed her for sale wrote him: "There is but little probability of finding a purchaser for this girl shortly at a fair price . . . A great objection to this girl is her color, but few persons are disposed to buy a servant that is so white—" Bradley, Wilson & Co. to James Sheppard, May 1, 1857, Sheppard Papers, in Manuscript Collection, Duke University Library, Durham, North Carolina.

[23]Since Arkansas and Texas had been the last two slave states to enter the Union, quite naturally they lagged behind most of the older states in number of slaves. But the rate of increase in both states was greater than that of any of the older states: from 1820 through 1850 Arkansas led in percentage of increase of slaves, and was second only to Texas in 1860. *Census of 1860 (Population)*, pp. 598-604.

[24]*Census of* 1860 *(Population)*, pp. 598-604.

[25]*Campbell et al v. Campbell*, 13 Ark. 513.

mitted that he was the father of a child born to his slave woman Mourning. Mourning was hired by Dunn from the estate of James Moss to serve as cook and housekeeper, and in time she gave birth to a girl named Eliza. "At divers times, and to divers persons," Dunn admitted that he was the father of Eliza, and he publicly recognized her as his daughter. He attempted to purchase Eliza from the Moss estate in order that he might free her, but died before he was able to do so.[26]

Allen T. Wilkins of Lafayette County was the acknowledged father of the slave boy John, son of his slave woman Sarah Jane, and also of another child which had died in infancy. A few months before Wilkins died in Lewisville, he engaged in a conversation with William H. Dillard which throws interesting light upon the frequency with which white men fathered children of slaves and then set them free, as Wilkins directed in his deathbed will. During the conversation Wilkins told Dillard that he was the father of the slave boy John, and Dillard advised him to set the boy free while he was still alive, since such manumissions were not always satisfactorily carried out after a man's death. Dillard cited "a number of cases in this county" to prove his point.[27]

In considering sexual relationships between white men and slave women, quite naturally this question arises: how willing were the women to enter into such relationships? This is another area within which there is little direct evidence, but common sense and a general knowledge of the operation of the slave system, along with the scanty evidence, help to provide an answer. There is no evidence to support the folk-belief that Negro women are by nature abnormally sensual and licentious, and that they therefore invited the attention of white men. But, as was pointed out earlier, there was a general lack of social and legal restraint to sexual promiscuity among slaves themselves, so certainly this attitude must have carried over to some extent into the relations of slave women with white men. Living under a social order which deprived them of virtually all means of gaining personal preferment except the granting of sexual favors, there is

[26] *Moss v. Sandefur*, Ex., 15 Ark. 381.
[27] *Abraham v. Wilkins*, 17 Ark. 292.

little doubt that many slave women submitted willingly to the advances of their masters, some of the family, or overseers, hoping thereby to receive favors in return. John Roles, who attempted to portray the slave girl in his account as an injured innocent, unwittingly alluded to this practice when he spoke of the jealousy between the two slave girls involved in sexual affairs with their Fort Smith master, and also of her later submission to various masters when promised freedom. And even if a slave woman had moral scruples against sexual relations with her white master, she had no effective means of restraining him, for she was a mere chattel with whom the master, short of actual physical injury, could do as he chose. Legally, there was no such thing as the rape of a slave woman by a white man.

A final matter for speculation in the realm of sexual relationship between whites and slaves is that of voluntary relationships between white women and male Negro slaves. This is by far the most obscure of all aspects of the matter. No verified incidents of this type in Arkansas were encountered, as in some other states,[28] although when the slave man Pleasant was being tried for the rape of a white woman, Sophia Fulmer, his defense counsel maintained that the woman, who had a reputation for sexual promiscuity, had not really been raped, but had submitted to Pleasant willingly. In commenting on this in the verdict of the Arkansas Supreme Court, before which the case was eventually taken, Chief Justice Elbert H. English expressed the generally-held white attitude toward relations between white women and slave men.

> But, surely, it may not be unsafe, or unjust to the prisoner, to say, that, in this State, where sexual intercourse between white women and negroes, is generally regarded with the utmost abhorrence, the presumption that a white woman yielded herself to the embraces of a negro, without force, arising from a want of chastity in her, would not be great, unless she had sunk to the lowest degree of prostitution.[29]

[28] Many accounts of voluntary sexual relationships between white women and slave men may be found in cases quoted in Helen Tunnicliff Catterall, *Judicial Cases Concerning American Slavery and the Negro* (5 vols., Washington, 1926-1937). See, for example, *Armstrong* v. *Hodges*, I, 357; *Re Puckett*, II, 12; *Horton* v. *Reavis*, II, 35; *Scroggins* v. *Scroggins*, II, 63; *Lamb* v. *Pigford*, II, 183; *Midgett* v. *McBride*, II, 192.

[29] *Pleasant* v. *The State*, 15 Ark. 624.

FEMALE SLAVES: SEX ROLES AND STATUS IN THE ANTEBELLUM PLANTATION SOUTH

Deborah G. White*

Abstract: This paper analyzes female slave life in the context of female slave interaction and familial roles. It looks at the bonded woman's work, her control of particular resources, her contribution to slave households, and her ability to cooperate with other women on a daily basis. It suggests that in relation to the slave family, too much emphasis has been placed on what men could not do rather than on what women could do and did. It finds that the bonded female made significant "economic" contributions to the slave family, that the slave's world was sex stratified so that the female slave world existed quite independently of the male slave world, and that slave families were matrifocal.

In his 1939 study of the black family in America, sociologist E. Franklin Frazier theorized that in slave family and marriage relations, women played the dominant role. Specifically, Frazier wrote that "the Negro woman as wife or mother was the mistress of her cabin, and, save for the interference of master and overseer, her wishes in regard to mating and family matters were paramount." He also insisted that slavery had schooled the black woman in self-reliance and self-sufficiency and that "neither economic necessity nor tradition had instilled in her the spirit of subordination to masculine authority" (1939:125). The Frazier thesis received support from other social scientists, including historians Kenneth Stampp (1956:344) and Stanley Elkins (1959:130), both of whom held that slave men had been emasculated and stripped of their paternity rights by slave masters who left control of slave households to slave women. In his infamous 1965 national report, Daniel Patrick Moynihan (1965: 31) lent further confirmation to the Frazier thesis when he alleged that the fundamental problem with the modern black family was the "often reversed roles of husband and wife," and then traced the origin of the "problem " back to slavery.

Partly in response to the criticism spawned by the Moynihan Report, historians reanalyzed antebellum source material, and the matriarchy thesis was debunked. For better or worse, said historians Robert Fogel and Stanley Engerman (1974:141), the "dominant" role in slave society was played by men. Men were dominant, they said, because men occupied all managerial and artisan slots, and because masters recognized the male head of the family group. From historian John Blassingame we learned that by building furnishings and providing extra food for their families, men found indirect ways of gaining status. If a garden plot was to be cultivated, the husband

*Deborah G. White is Assistant Professor of History at the University of Wisconsin, Milwaukee.

"led" his wife in the family undertaking (1972:92). After a very thoughtful appraisal of male slave activities, historian Eugene Genovese concluded that "slaves from their own experience had come to value a two-parent, male-centered household, no matter how much difficulty they had in realizing the ideal" (1974:491-492). Further tipping the scales toward partiarchal slave households, historian Herbert Gutman argued that the belief that matrifocal households prevailed among slaves was a misconception. He demonstrated that children were more likely to be named after their fathers than mothers, and that during the Civil War slave men acted like fathers and husbands by fighting for their freedom and by protecting their wives and children when they were threatened by Union troops or angry slaveholders (1976:188-191, 369-386).

With the reinterpretation of male roles came a revision of female roles. Once considered dominant, slave women were now characterized as subordinated and sometimes submissive. Fogel and Engerman found proof of their subordinated status in the fact that they were excluded from working in plow gangs and did all of the household chores (1974:141-142). Genovese maintained that slave women's "attitude toward housework, especially cooking, and toward their own femininity," belied the conventional wisdom "according to which women unwittingly helped ruin their men by asserting themselves in the home, protecting their children, and assuming other normally masculine responsibilities (1974:500). Gutman found one Sea Island slave community where the black church imposed a submissive role upon married slave women (1976:72).

In current interpretations of the contemporary black family the woman's role has not been "feminized" as much as it has been "deemphasized." The stress in studies like those done by Carol Stack (1974) and Theodore Kennedy (1980), is not on roles per se but on the black family's ability to survive in flexible kinship networks that are viable bulwarks against discrimination and racism. These interpretations also make the point that black kinship patterns are not based exclusively on consanguineous relationships but are also determined by social contacts that sometimes have their basis in economic support.

Clearly then, the pendulum has swung away from the idea that women ruled slave households, and that their dominance during the slave era formed the foundation of the modern day matriarchal black family. But how far should that pendulum swing? This paper suggests that we should tread the road that leads to the patriarchal slave household and the contemporary amorphous black family with great caution. It suggests that, at least in relation to the slave family, too much emphasis has been placed on what men could not do rather than on what women could do and did. What follows is not a comprehensive study of female slavery, but an attempt to reassess Frazier's claim that slave women were self-reliant and self-sufficient through an examination of some of their activities, specifically their work, their control of particular resources, their contribution to their households and their ability to cooperate with each other on a daily basis. Further, this paper will examine some of the implications of these activities, and their probable impact on the slave woman's status in slave society, and the black family.

At the outset a few points must be made about the subject matter and the source material used to research it. Obviously, a study that concentrates solely on females runs the risk of overstating woman's roles and their importance in society. One must therefore keep in mind that this is only one aspect, although a very critical one, of slave family and community life. In addition, what follows is a synthesis of the probable sex role of the average slave woman on plantations with at least twenty slaves.[1] In the process of constructing this synthesis I have taken into account such variables as plantation size, crop, region of the South, and the personal idosyncrasies of slave masters. Finally, in drawing conclusions about the sex role and status of slave women, I have detailed their activities and analyzed them in terms of what anthropologists know about women who do similar things in analogous settings. I took this approach for two reasons. First, information about female slaves cannot be garnered from sources left by slave women because they left few narratives, diaries or letters. The dearth of source material makes it impossible to draw conclusions about the slave woman's feelings. Second, even given the ex-slave interviews, a rich source material for this subject, it is almost impossible to draw conclusions about female slave status from an analysis of their individual personalities. Comments such as that made by the slave woman, Fannie, to her husband Bob, "I don't want no sorry nigger around me," perhaps says something about Fannie, but not about all slave women (Egypt et al., 1945:184). Similarly, for every mother who grieved over the sale of her children there was probably a father whose heart was also broken. Here, only the activities of the slave woman will be examined in an effort to discern her status in black society.

Turning first to the work done by slave women, it appears that they did a variety of heavy and dirty labor, work which was also done by men. In 1853, Frederick Olmsted saw South Carolina slaves of both sexes carting manure on their heads to the cotton field where they spread it with their hands between the ridges in which cotton was planted. In Fayetteville, North Carolina, he noticed that women not only hoed and shovelled but they also cut down trees and drew wood (Olmsted, 1971:67, 81). The use of women as lumberjacks occurred quite frequently, especially in the lower South and Southwest, areas which retained a frontier quality during the antebellum era. Solomon Northup, a kidnapped slave, knew women who wielded the ax so perfectly that the largest oak or sycamore fell before their well-directed blows. An Arkansas ex-slave remembered that her mother used to carry logs (Osofsky, 1969:308-309; Rawick, 1972, vol. 10, pt. 5:54). On Southwestern plantations women did all kinds of work. In the region of the Bayou Boeuf women were expected to "plough, drag, drive team, clear wild lands, work on the highway," and do any other type of work required of them (Osofsky, 1969:313). In short, full female hands frequently did the same kind of work as male hands.

It is difficult, however, to say how often they did the same kind of field work, and it would be mistake to say that there was no differentiation of field labor on Southern farms and plantations. The most common form of differentiation was that women hoed while men plowed. Yet, the exceptions to the rule were so numerous as to make a mockery of it. Many men hoed on a regular basis. Similarly, if a field had to be plowed and there were not enough male hands to do it, then it was not unusual for an overseer to command a strong woman to plow. This could happen

[1]The majority of the available source material seems to be from plantations or farms with more than one or two slave families. Relatively few ex-slave interviewees admit to being one of only three or four slaves. If Genovese is right and at least half of the slaves in the South lived on units of twenty slaves or more, this synthesis probably describes the life of a majority of slave women (Genovese, 1974:7).

on a plantation of twenty slaves or a farm of five.[2]

It is likely, however, that women were more often called to do the heavy labor usually assigned to men after their childbearing years. Pregnant women, and sometimes women breastfeeding infants, were usually given less physically demanding work.[3] If, as recent studies indicate (see Dunn, 1977:58; Gutman, 1976:50, 74, 124, 171; Trussell, 1978:504), slave women began childbearing when about twenty years of age and had children at approximately two and a half year intervals, at least until age thirty-five, slave women probably spent a considerable amount of time doing tasks which men did not do.[4] Pregnant and nursing women were classified as half-hands or three-quarter hands and such workers did only some of the work that was also done by full hands. For instance, it was not unusual for them to pick cotton or even hoe, work done on a regular basis by both sexes. But frequently, they were assigned to "light work" like raking stubble or pulling weeds, which was often given to children and the elderly.[5]

Slave women might have preferred to be exempt from such labor, but they might also have gained some intangibles from doing the same work as men. Anthropologists (Mullings, 1976:243-244; Sacks, 1974:213-222) have demonstrated that in societies where men and women are engaged in the production of the same kinds of goods and where widespread private property is not a factor, participation in production gives women freedom and independence. Since neither slave men nor women had access to, or control over, the products of their labor, parity in the field may have encouraged equalitarianism in the slave quarters. In Southern Togo, for instance, where women work alongside their husbands in the field because men do not alone produce goods which are highly valued, democracy prevails in relationships between men and women (Rocher et al., 1962:151-152).

But bondswomen did do a lot of traditional "female work" and one has to wonder whether this work, as well as the work done as a "half-hand" tallied on the side of female subordination. In the case of the female slave, domestic work was not always confined to the home, and often "woman's work" required skills that were highly valued and even coveted because of the place it could purchase in the higher social echelons of the slave world. For example, cooking was definitely "female work" but it was also a skilled occupation. Good cooks were highly respected by both blacks and whites, and their occupation was raised in status because the masses of slave women did not cook on a regular basis. Since field work occupied the time of most women, meals were often served communally. Female slaves therefore,

[2]For other examples of work done by female slaves and indications that they did the same work required of men, see Nairne, 1732:60; Kemble, 1961:65; Olmsted, 1971:67-81; Olmsted, 1907:81; Drew, 1969:92; Rawick, 1972, vol. 13, pt. 4:357; vol. 6:46, 151, 158, 270, 338.

[3]See Rawick, 1972, vol. 4, pt. 3:160; Hughes, 1897:22, 41; Rawick, 1972, vol. 10, pt. 7:255; Olmsted, 1856:430; SHC, Plantation Instructions; Olmsted, 1971:78, 175; Kemble, 1961:87, 179; Drew, 1969:128; Davis, 1943:127.

[4]Although Fogel and Engerman cite the slave woman's age at first birth as 22.5, other historians, including Gutman and Dunn, found that age to be substantially lower—Gutman a range from 17 to 19, and Dunn (average age at first birth on the Mount Airy, Virginia Plantation) 19.22 years. More recently, economists Trussell and Steckel have found the age to be 20.6 years (Fogel and Engerman, 1974:137-138; Dunn, 1977:58; Gutman, 1976:50, 75, 124, 171; Trussell and Steckel, 1978:504.

[5]For examples, see n. 3.

were, for the most part, relieved of this traditional chore, and the occupation of "cook" became specialized.[6]

Sewing too was often raised above the level of inferior "woman's work." All females at one time or another had to spin and weave. Occasionally each woman was given cloth and told to make her family's clothes, but this was unusual and more likely to happen on small farms than on plantations. During slack seasons women probably did more sewing than during planting and harvesting seasons, and pregnant women were often put to work spinning, weaving and sewing. Nevertheless, sewing could be raised to the level of a skilled art, especially if a woman sewed well enough to make the white family's clothes. Such women were sometimes hired out and allowed to keep a portion of the profit they brought their master and mistress (Rawick, 1972, vol. 17, 158; SHC, White Hill Plantation Books:13; Rawick, 1972, vol. 2, pt. 2:114).

Other occupations which were solidly anchored in the female domain, and which increased a woman's prestige, were midwifery and doctoring. The length of time and extent of training it took to become a midwife is indicated by the testimony of Clara Walker, a former slave interviewed in Arkansas, who remembered that she trained for five years under a doctor who became so lazy after she had mastered the job that he would sit down and let her do all the work. After her "apprenticeship" ended she delivered babies for both slave and free, black and white (Rawick, 1972, vol. 10, pt. 5:21).[7] Other midwives learned the trade from a female relative, often their mother, and they in turn passed the skill on to another female relative.

A midwife's duty often extended beyond delivering babies, and they sometimes became known as "doctor women." In this capacity they cared for men, women, and children. Old women, some with a history of midwifery and some without, also gained respect as "doctor women." They "knowed a heap about yarbs [herbs]," recalled a Georgia ex-slave (Rawick, 1972, vol. 2, pt. 2:112).[8] Old women had innumerable cures, especially for children's diseases, and since plantation "nurseries" were usually under their supervision, they had ample opportunity to practice their art. In sum, a good portion of the slave's medical care, particularly that of women and children, was supervised by slave women.

Of course, not all women were hired-out seamstresses, cooks, or midwives; a good deal of "female work" was laborious and mundane. An important aspect of this work, as well as of the field work done by women, was that is was frequently done in female groups. As previously noted, women often hoed while men plowed. In addition, when women sewed they usually did so with other women. Quilts were made by women at gatherings called, naturally enough, "quiltins." Such gatherings were attended only by women and many former slaves had vivid recollections of them. The "quiltin's and spinnin' frolics dat de women folks had" were the most outstanding remembrances of Hattie Anne Nettles, an Alabama ex-slave (Rawick, 1972, vol. 6:297, 360). Women also gathered, independent of male slaves,

[6]For an example of the privileges this occupation *could* involve, see Chesnut, 1905:24.

[7]For other examples of midwives see Rawick, vol. 6:256, 318; vol. 16:90-91; vol. 10, pt. 5:125. The job status of the midwife needs to be examined more closely than is possible here. Midwives were curers whose duty usually extended beyond delivering babies. Occasionally their cures spilled over into witchcraft or voodoo, and slaves who practiced these arts were often feared.

[8]See also Rawick, 1972, vol. 2, pt. 2:55; vol. 17:174; Olmsted, 1907:76.

on Saturday afternoons to do washing. Said one ex-slave, "they all had a regular picnic of it as they would work and spread the clothes on the bushes and low branches of the tree to dry. They would get to spend the day together" (Rawick, 1972, vol. 7:315).

In addition, when pregnant women did field work they sometimes did it together. On large plantations the group they worked in was sometimes known as the "trash gang." This gang, made up of pregnant women, women with nursing infants, children and old slaves, was primarily a female work gang.[9] Since it was the group that young girls worked with when just being initiated into the work world of the plantation, one must assume that it served some kind of socialization function. Most likely, many lessons about life were learned by twelve-year-old girls from this group of women who were either pregnant or breastfeeding, or who were grandmothers many times over.

It has been noted that women frequently depended on slave midwives to bring children into the world; their dependence on other slave women did not end with childbirth but continued through the early life of their children. Sometimes women with infants took their children to the fields with them. Some worked with their children wrapped to their backs, others laid them under a tree. Frequently, however, an elderly woman watched slave children during the day while their mothers worked in the field. Sometimes the cook supervised young children at the master's house.[10] Mothers who were absent from their children most of the day, indeed most of the week, depended on these surrogate mothers to assist them in child socialization. Many ex-slaves remember these women affectionately. Said one South Carolinian: "De old lady, she looked after every blessed thing for us all day long en cooked for us right along wid de mindin' " (Rawick, 1972, vol. 2, pt. 1:99).

Looking at the work done by female slaves in the antebellum South, therefore, we find that sex role differentiation in field labor was not absolute but that there was differentiation in other kinds of work. Domestic chores were usually done exclusively by women, and certain "professional" occupations were reserved for females. It would be a mistake to infer from this differentiation that it was the basis of male dominance. A less culturally biased conclusion would be that women's roles were different or complementary. For example, in her overview of African societies, Denise Paulme notes that in almost all African societies, women do most of the domestic chores, yet they lead lives that are quite independent of men. Indeed, according to Paulme, in Africa, "a wife's contribution to the needs of the household is direct and indispensable, and her husband is just as much in need of her as she of him" (1963:4). Other anthropologists have suggested that we should not evaluate women's roles in terms of men's roles because in a given society, women may not perceive the world in the same way that men do (Rogers, 1978:152-162). In other words, men and women may share a common culture but on different terms, and when this is the case, questions of dominance and subservience are irrelevant. The degree to which male and female ideologies are different is often suggested by the degree to which men and women are independently able to rank and order themselves and cooperate with members of their sex in the performance of

[9]Somtimes pregnant women were made to weave, spin, or sew, in which case they usually did it with other women. The term "trash gang" was probably used only on very large plantations, but units of pregnant women, girls, elderly females, as well as boys and elderly men, probably worked together on a farm with twenty slaves. See n. 2.

[10]See, for instance, Olmsted, 1856:423 and Phillips, 1909:I, 127.

their duties. In societies where women are not isolated from one another and placed under a man's authority, where women cooperate in the performance of household tasks, where women form groups or associations, women's roles are usually complementary to those of men, and the female world exists independently of the male world. Because women control what goes on in their world, they rank and order themselves vis à vis other women, not men, and they are able to influence decisions made by their society because they exert pressure as a group. Ethnographic studies of the Igbo women of Eastern Nigeria (Tanner, 1974:146-150), the Ga women of Central Accra in Ghana (Robertson, 1976:115-132), and the Patani of Southern Nigeria (Leis, 1974, 221-242) confirm these generalizations. Elements of female slave society—the chores done in and by groups, the intrasex cooperation and dependency in the areas of child care and medical care, the existence of high echelon female slave occupations—may be an indication, not that slave women were inferior to slave men, but that the roles were complementary and that the female slave world allowed women the opportunity to rank and order themselves and obtain a sense of self which was quite apart from the men of their race and even the men of the master class.

That bondswomen were able to rank and order themselves is further suggested by evidence indicating that in the community of the slave quarters certain women were looked to for leadership. Leadership was based on either one or a combination of factors, including occupation, association with the master class, age, or number of children. It was manifested in all aspects of female slave life. For instance, Louis Hughes, an escaped slave, noted that each plantation had a "forewoman who . . . had charge of the female slaves and also the boys and girls from twelve to sixteen years of age, and all the old people that were feeble" (Hughes, 1897:22). Bennett H. Barrow repeatedly lamented the fact that Big Lucy, one of his oldest slaves, had more control over his female slaves then he did: "Anica, Center, Cook Jane, the better you treat them the worse they are. Big Lucy, the Leader, corrupts every young negro in her power" (Davis, 1943:191).[11] When Elizabeth Botume went to the Sea Islands after the Civil War, she had a house servant a young woman named Amy who performed her tasks slowly and sullenly until Aunt Mary arrived from Beaufort. In Aunt Mary's presence the obstreperous Amy was "quiet, orderly, helpful and painstaking" (Botume, 1893:132).[12]

Another important feature of female life, bearing on the ability of women to rank and order themselves independently of men, was the control women exercised over each other by quarreling. In all kinds of sources there are indications that women were given to fighting and irritating each other. From Jesse Belflowers, the overseer of the Allston rice plantation in South Carolina, Adele Petigru Allston learned that "mostly mongst the Woman," there was "goodeal of quarling and disputing and telling lies" (Easterby, 1945:291). Harriet Ware, a northern missionary, writing from the Sea Islands in 1863 blamed the turmoil she found in black community life on the "tongues of the women" (Pearson,

[11]Big Lucy thwarted all of Barrow's instructions and her influence extended to the men also; see Davis, 1943:168, 173.

[12]On a given plantation there could be a number of slave women recognized by other slave women as leaders. For instance, when Frances Kemble first toured Butler Island she found that the cook's position went to the oldest wife in the settlement.

1906:210).[13] The evidence of excessive quarreling among women hints at the existence of a gossip network among female slaves. Anthropologists (Rosaldo, 1974:10-11, 38; Stack, 1974:109-115; Wolfe, 1974:162) have found gossip to be a principal strategy used by women to control other women as well as men. Significantly, the female gossip network, the means by which community members are praised, shamed, and coerced, is usually found in societies where women are highly dependent on each other and where women work in groups or form female associations.[14]

In summary, when the activities of female slaves are compared to those of women in other societies a clearer picture of the female slave sex role emerges. It seems that slave women were schooled in self-reliance and self-sufficiency but the "self" was more likely the female slave collective than the individual slave woman. On the other hand, if the female world was highly stratified and if women cooperated with each other to a great extent, odds are that the same can be said of men, in which case neither sex can be said to have been dominant or subordinate.

[13]Additional evidence that women quarreled can be found in a pamphlet stating the terms of an overseer's contract: "Fighting, particularly amongst the women . . . is to be always rigorously punished." Similarly, an ex-slave interviewed in Georgia noted that "sometimes de women uster git whuppins for fightin." See Bassett, 1925:32 and Rawick, 1972, vol. 12, pt. 2:57.

[14]Gossip is one of many means by which women influence political decisions and interpersonal relationships. In Taiwan, for instance, women gather in the village square and whisper to each other. In other places, such as among the Marina of Madagascar, women gather and shout loud insults at men or other women. In still other societies, such as the black ghetto area studied by Carol Stack, the gossip network takes the form of a grapevine. See Rosaldo 1974:10-11; Wolf, 1974:162; and Stack, 1974:109-115.

There are other aspects of the female slave's life that suggest that her world was independent of the male slave's and that slave women were rather self-reliant. It has long been recognized (Blassingame, 1972: 77-103) that slave women did not derive traditional benefits from the marriage relationship, that there was no property to share and essential needs like food, clothing, and shelter were not provided by slave men. Since in almost all societies where men consistently control women, that control is based on male ownership and distribution of property and/or control of certain culturally valued subsistence goods, these realities of slave life had to contribute to female slave self-sufficiency and independence from slave men. The practice of "marrying abroad," having a spouse on a different plantation, could only have reinforced this tendency, for as ethnographers (Noon, 1949:30-31; Rosaldo, 1974:36, 39) have found, when men live apart from women, they cannot control them.[15] We have yet to learn what kind of obligations brothers, uncles, and male cousins fulfilled for their female kin, but is it improbable that wives were controlled by husbands whom they saw only once or twice a week. Indeed, "abroad marriages" may have intensified female intradependency.

The fact that marriage did not yield traditional benefits for women, and that "abroad marriages" existed, does not mean that women did not depend on slave men for foodstuffs beyond the weekly rations, but since additional food was not guaranteed, it probably meant that women along with men had to take initiatives in supplementing slave diets. So much has been made of the activities of slave men in

[15]For instance, it is thought that Iroquois women obtained a high degree of political and economic power partly because of the prolonged absences of males due to trading and warfare (Noon, 1949:30-31).

this sphere (Blassingame, 1972:92; Genovese, 1974:486) that the role of slave women has been overlooked.[16] Female house slaves, in particular, were especially able to supplement their family's diet. Mary Chesnut's maid Molly, made no secret of the fact that she fed her offspring and other slave children in the Confederate politician's house. "Dey gets a little of all dat's going," she once told Chesnut (Chesnut, 1905:348). Frederick Douglass remembered that his grandmother was not only a good nurse but a "capitol hand at catching fish and making the nets she caught them in" (1855:27). Eliza Overton, an ex-slave, remembered how her mother stole, slaughtered, and cooked one of her master's hogs. Another ex-slave was not too bashful to admit that her mother "could hunt good ez any man." (Rawick, 1972, vol. 11:53, 267.)[17] Women, as well as men, were sometimes given the opportunity to earn money. Women often sold baskets they had woven, but they also earned money by burning charcoal for blacksmiths and cutting cordwood (Olmsted, 1971:26; Rawick, 1972, vol. 7; 23). Thus, procuring extra provisions for the family was sometimes a male and sometimes a female responsibility, one that probably fostered a self-reliant and independent spirit.

The high degree of female cooperation, the ability of slave women to rank and order themselves, the independence women derived from the absence of property considerations in the conjugal relationship, "abroad marriages," and the female slave's ability to provide supplementary foodstuffs are factors which should not be ignored in considerations of the character of the slave family. In fact, they conform to the criteria most anthropologists (Gonzalez, 1970:231-243; Smith, 1956:257-260, 1973:125; Tanner, 1974: 129-156) list for that most misunderstood concept—matrifocality. Matrifocality is a term used to convey the fact that women *in their role as mothers* are the focus of familial relationships. It does not mean that fathers are absent; indeed two-parent households can be matrifocal. Nor does it stress a power relationship where women rule men. When *mothers* become the focal point of family activity, they are just more central than are fathers to a family's continuity and survival as a unit. While there is no set model for matrifocality, Smith (1973:125) has noted that in societies as diverse as Java, Jamaica, and the Igbo of eastern Nigeria, societies recognized as matrifocal, certain elements are constant.[18] Among these elements are female solidarity, particularly in regard to their cooperation within the domestic sphere. Another factor is the economic activity of women which enables them to support their children independent of fathers *if they desire to do so or are forced to do so.* The most important factor is the supremacy of the mother-child bond over all other relationships (Smith, 1973:139-142).

Female solidarity and the "economic" contribution of bondswomen in the form of medical care, foodstuffs, and money has already been discussed; what can be said of the mother-child bond? We know from previous works on slavery (Bassett, 1925:

[16] Of male slaves who provided extra food, John Blassingame wrote: "The slave who did such things for his family gained not only the approbation of his wife, but he also gained status in the quarters." According to Genovese, "the slaves would have suffered much more than many in fact did from malnutrition and the hidden hungers of nutritional deficiencies if men had not taken the initiative to hunt and trap animals."

[17] For other examples of women who managed to provide extra food for their families see Rawick, 1972, vol. 16:16; Brent, 1816:9.

[18] See also Smith, 1956:257-260; Tanner, 1974:129-156.

31, 139, 141; Kemble, 1961:95, 127, 179; Phillips, 1909:I, 109, 312) that certain slaveholder practices encouraged the primacy of the mother-child relationship. These included the tendency to sell mothers and small children as family units, and to accord special treatment to pregnant and nursing women and women who were exceptionally prolific. We also know (Gutman, 1976:76) that a husband and wife secured themselves somewhat from sale and separation when they had children. Perhaps what has not been emphasized enough is the fact that it was the wife's childbearing and her ability to keep a child alive that were the crucial factors in the security achieved in this way. As such, the insurance against sale which husbands and wives received once women had borne and nurtured children heads the list of female contributions to slave households.

In addition to slaveowner encouragement of close mother-child bonds there are indications that slave women themselves considered this their most important relationship.[11] Much has been made of the fact that slave women were not ostracized by slave society when they had children out of "wedlock" (Genovese, 1974:465-466; Gutman, 1976:74, 117-118). Historians have usually explained this aspect of slave life in the context of slave sexual norms which allowed a good deal of freedom to young unmarried slave women. However, the slave attitude concerning "illegitimacy" might also reveal the importance that women, and slave society as a whole, placed on the mother role and the mother-child dyad. For instance, in the Alabama community studied by Charles S. Johnson (1934:29, 66-70) in the 1930s, most black women felt no guilt and suffered no loss of status when they bore children out of wedlock. This was also a community in which, according to Johnson, the role of the mother was "of much greater importance than in the more familiar American family group." Similarly, in his 1956 study of the black family in British Guyana, Smith (1956:109, 158, 250-251) found the mother-child bond to be the strongest in the whole matrix of social relationships, and it was manifested in a lack of condemnation of women who bore children out of legal marriage. If slave women were not ostracized for having children without husbands, it could mean that the mother-child relationship took precedence over the husband-wife relationships.

The mystique which shrouded conception and childbirth is perhaps another indication of the high value slave women placed on motherhood and childbirth. Many female slaves claimed that they were kept ignorant of the details of conception and childbirth. For instance, a female slave interviewed in Nashville, noted that at age twelve or thirteen, she and an older girl went around to parsley beds and hollow logs looking for newborn babies. "They didn't tell you a thing," she said (Egypt et al., 1945:10; Rawick, 1972, vol. 16:15). Another ex-slave testified that her mother told her that doctors brought babies, and another Virginia ex-slave remembered that "people was very particular in them days. They wouldn't let children know anything:" (Egypt et al.,

[11]Gutman suggests that the husband-wife and father-child dyad were as strong as the mother-child bond. I think not. It has been demonstrated that in most Western Hemisphere black societies as well as in Africa, the mother-child bond is the strongest and most enduring bond. This does not mean that fathers have no relationship with their children or that they are absent. The father-child relationship is of a more formal nature than the mother-child relationship. Moreover, the conjugal relationship appears, on the surface, to be similar to the Western norm in that two-parent households prevail, but, when competing with consanguineous relationships, conjugal affiliations usually lose. See Gutman, 1976:79; Smith, 1970:62-70; Smith, 1973:129; Stack, 1974:102-105.

1945:8; Rawick, 1972, vol. 16:25. See also Rawick, 1972, vol. 7:3-24 and vol. 2:51-52). This alleged naiveté can perhaps be understood if examined in the context of motherhood as a *rite de passage.* Sociologist Joyce Ladner (1971:177-263) found that many black girls growing up in a ghetto area of St. Louis in the late 1960s were equally ignorant of the facts concerning conception and childbirth. Their mothers had related only "old wives tales" about sex and childbirth even though the community was one where the mother-child bond took precedence over both the husband-wife bond and the father-child bond. In this St. Louis area, having a child was considered the most important turning point in a black girl's life, a more important *rite de passage* than marriage. Once a female had a child all sorts of privileges were bestowed upon her. That conception and childbirth were cloaked in mystery in antebellum slave society is perhaps an indication of the sacredness of motherhood. When considered in tandem with the slave attitude toward "illegitimacy," the mother-child relationship emerges as the most important familial relationship in the slave family.

Finally, any consideration of the slave's attitude about motherhood and the expectations which the slave community had of childbearing women must consider the slave's African heritage. In many West African tribes the mother-child relationship is and has always been the most important of all human relationships.[20] To cite one of many possible examples, while studying the role of women in Ibo society, Sylvia Leith-Ross (1939:127) asked an Ibo woman how many of ten husbands would love their wives and how many of ten sons would love their mothers. The answer she received demonstrated the precedence which the mother-child tie took: "Three husbands would love their wives but seven sons would love their mothers."

When E. Franklin Frazier (1939:125) wrote that slave women were self-reliant and that they were strangers to male slave authority he evoked an image of an overbearing, even brawny woman. In all probability visions of Sapphire danced in our heads as we learned from Frazier that the female slave played the dominant role in courtship, marriage and family relationships, and later from Elkins (1959: 130) that male slaves were reduced to childlike dependency on the slave master. Both the Frazier and Elkins theses have been overturned by historians who have found that male slaves were more than just visitors to their wive's cabins, and women something other than unwitting allies in the degradation of their men. Sambo and Sapphire may continue to find refuge in American folklore but they will never again be legitimized by social scientists.

However, beyond the image evoked by Frazier is the stark reality that slave women did not play the traditional female role as it was defined in nineteenth-century America, and regardless of how hard we try to cast her in a subordinate or submissive role in relation to slave men, we will have difficulty reconciling that role with the plantation realities. When we consider the work done by women in groups, the existence of upper echelon female slave jobs, the intradependence of women in childcare and medical care; if we presume that the quarreling or "fighting and disputing" among slave women is evidence of a gossip network and that certain women were elevated by their peers to positions of respect, then what we are confronted with are slave women who are able, within the limits set by slaveowners, to rank and order their female world, women who identified and co-

[20]See Paulme, 1963:14; Tanner, 1974:147; Fortes, 1939:127.

operated more with other slave women than with slave men. There is nothing abnormal about this. It is a feature of many societies around the world, especially where strict sex role differentiation is the rule.

Added to these elements of female interdependence and cooperation were the realities of chattel slavery that decreased the bondsman's leverage over the bondswoman, made female self-reliance a necessity, and encouraged the retention of the African tradition which made the mother-child bond more sacred than the husband-wife bond. To say that this amounted to a matrifocal family is not to say a bad word. It is not to say that it precluded male-female cooperation, or mutual respect, or traditional romance and courtship. It does, however, help to explain how African-American men and women survived chattel slavery.

BIBLIOGRAPHY

Bassett, John Spencer
1925 The Southern Plantation Overseer, As Revealed in his Letters. Northhampton, Massachusetts: Southworth Press.

Bibb, Henry
1969 Narrative of the Life and Adventures of Henry Bibb. In Gilbert Osofsky, ed., Puttin on Ole Massa, 51-171. New York: Harper and Row Publishers.

Blassingame, John W.
1972 The Slave Community: Plantation Life in the Antebellum South. New York: Oxford University Press.

Botume, Elizabeth Hyde
1893 First Days Amongst the Contrabands. Boston: Lee and Shepard Publishers.

Brent, Linda
1816 Incidents in the Life of a Slave Girl. Ed. Lydia Maria Child, Boston: by the author.

Brown, William Wells
1969 Narrative of William Wells Brown. In Osofsky, 1969: 173-223.

Chesnut, Mary Bokin
1905 A Diary From Dixie. Ed. Ben Ames Williams. New York: D. Appleton and Company.

Davis, Adwon Adams
1943 Plantation Life in the Florida Parishes of Louisiana 1836-1846 as Reflected in the Diary of Bennet H. Barrow. New York: Columbia University Press.

Drew Benjamin
1969 The Refugee: A North Side View of Slavery. Boston: Addison Wesley.

Dunn, Richard
1977 "The Tale of Two Plantations: Slave Life at Mesopotamia in Jamaica and Mount Airy in Virginia, 1799-1828." William and Mary Quarterly 34:32-65.

Easterby, J. E., ed.
1945 The South Carolina Rice Plantations as Revealed in the Papers of Robert W. Allston. Chicago: University of Chicago Press.

Egypt, Ophelia S., J. Masuoka and Charles S. Johnson, eds.
1945 Unwritten History of Slavery: Autobiographical Accounts of Negro Ex-slaves. Nashville: Fisk University Press.

Elkins, Stanley M.
1959 Slavery; A Problem in American Institutional and Intellectual Life. 2nd ed. Chicago: University of Chicago Press.

Fogel, Robert William and Stanley Engerman
1974 Time on the Cross: The Economics of American Negro Slavery. Boston: Little, Brown.

Fortes, Mayer
1939 "Kinship and Marriage among the Ashanti." In A. R. Radcliffe-Brown and Daryll Forde, eds. African Systems of Kinship and Marriage, 252-284. London: Routledge and Kegan Paul.

Frazier, E. Franklin
1939 The Negro Family in the United States. Chicago: University of Chicago Press.

Genovese, Eugene
1974 Roll, Jordan, Roll: The World the Slaves Made. New York: Vintage Books.

Gutman, Herbert
1976 The Black Family in Slavery and Freedom, 1750-1925. New York: Pantheon Books.

Gonzalez, Nancie
1970 "Toward a Definition of Matrifocality." In Norman E. Whitten, Jr. and John F. Szwed, eds. Afro-American Anthropology: Contemporary Perspectives, 231-243. New York: The Free Press.

Hakfin, Nancy J. and Edna G. Bay
1976 Women in Africa: Studies in Social and Economic Change. Stanford: Stanford University Press.

Hughes, Louis
1897 Thirty Years a Slave. Milwaukee: South Side Printing.

Johnson, Charles S.
1934 Shadow of the Plantation. Chicago: University of Chicago Press.

Kemble, Frances Anne
1961 Journal of a Residence on a Georgian Plantation. Ed. John A. Scott. New York: Alfred Knopf.

Kennedy, Theodore R.
1980 You Gotta Deal With It: Black Family Relations in a Southern Community. New York: Oxford University Press.

Ladner, Joyce
1971 Tomorrow's Tomorrow: The Black Woman. New York: Doubleday.

Leis, Nancy B.
1974 "Women in Groups: Ijaw Women's Associations." In Rosaldo and Lamphere, 1974:223-242.

Leith-Ross, Sylvia
1939 African Women: A Study of the Ibo of Nigeria. London: Routledge and Kegan Paul.

Moynihan, Daniel Patrick
1965 The Negro Family: The Case for National Action. Washington, D.C.: Government Printing Office.

Mullings, Leith
1976 "Women and Economic Change in Africa." In Hafkin, 1976:239-264.

Nairne, Thomas
1732 A Letter from South Carolina. London: J. Clark.

Noon, John A.
1949 Law and Government of the Grand River Iroquois. New York: Viking.

Northup, Solomon
1969 Twelve Years a Slave: Narrative of Solomon Northup. In Osofsky, 1969:225-406.

Olmsted, Frederick L.
1856 A Journey in the Seaboard Slave States. New York: Dix and Edwards.
1907 A Journey in the Back Country. New York: G. P. Putnam's Sons.
1971 The Cotton Kingdom. Ed. David Freeman Hawke. New York: Bobbs-Merrill.

Osofsky, Gilbert, ed.
1969 Puttin' on Ole Massa. New York: Harper and Row.

Paulme, Denise, ed.
1963 Women of Tropical Africa. Berkeley: University of California Press.

Pearson, Elizabeth Ware, ed.
1906 Letters from Port Royal Written at the Time of the Civil War. Boston: W. B. Clarke.

Phillips, Ulrich B.
1909 Plantation and Frontier Documents 1649-1863. 2 vols. Cleveland: Arthur H. Clarke.

Rawick, George, ed.
1972 The American Slave: A Composite Autobiography. 19 vols. Westport, Connecticut: Greenwood Press.

Robertson, Claire
1976 "Ga Women and Socioeconomic Change in Accra, Ghana." In Hafkin, 1976:111-134.

Rocher, Guy, R. Clignet, and F. N. N'sougan Agblemagon
1962 "Three Preliminary Studies: Canada, Ivory Coast, Togo." International Social Science Journal 14:130-156.

Rogers, Susan Carol
1978 "Woman's Place: A Critical Review of Anthropological Theory." Comparative Studies in Society and History. 20:123-162.

Rosaldo, Michelle
1974 "Woman, Culture and Society: A Theoretical Overview." In Rosaldo and Lamphere, 1974:17-42.

Rosaldo, Michelle and Louise Lamphere, eds.
1974 Woman, Culture and Society. Stanford: Stanford University Press.

Sacks, Karen
1974 "Engels Revisted: Women, the Organization of Production, and Private Property." In Rosaldo and Lamphere, 1974:207-222.

Smith, Raymond T.
1956 The Negro Family in British Guiana: Family Structure and Social Status in the Villages. London: Routledge and Kegan Paul.
1970 "The Nuclear Family in Afro-American Kinship." Journal of Comparative Family Studies 1:55-70.
1973 "The Matrifocal Family." In Jack Goody, ed., The Character of Kinship, 121-144. London: Cambridge University Press.

Southern Historical Collection [SHC]
Bayside Plantation Records (1846-1852)
Plantation Instructions (undated)
White Hill Plantation Books (1817-1860)

Stack, Carol
1974 All Our Kin: Strategies for Survival in a Black Community. New York: Harper and Row.

Stampp, Kenneth
1956 The Peculiar Institution: Slavery in the Ante-Bellum South. New York: Vintage Books.

Tanner, Nancy
1974 "Matrifocality in Indonesia and Africa and Among Black Americans." In Rosaldo and Lamphere, 1974:129-156.

Trussell, James and Richard Steckel
1978 "Age of Slaves at Menarche and Their First Birth." Journal of Interdisciplinary History 8:477-505.

Wolf, Margery
1974 "Chinese Women: Old Skill in a New Context." In Rosaldo and Lamphere, 1974: 157-172.

Journal of Sport History, Vol. 7, No. 2 (Summer, 1980)

The Play of Slave Children in the Plantation Communities of the Old South, 1820-1860

*David K. Wiggins**

Most of the earliest studies done on Southern plantation life portrayed slaves as people without a culture, without philosophical beliefs, and without educational instruments of their own.[1] Historians often viewed slaves as barbarians to be civilized; as perpetual children at best, and animals at worst. As such, it was assumed that slaves held no strong values or convictions and that they were without a coherent culture or social organization of their own. To suggest that slaves were capable of molding or fashioning their own particular life-style was inconceivable. The more current research, however, has altered our perceptions of what the "peculiar institution" was really like.[2] Many scholars now assert that slaves were capable of creating their own "unique cultural forms" largely free from the control of whites. However dehumanizing the plantation became for slaves, their struggle for survival never became so severe that it destroyed their creative instincts or prevented them from establishing their own personal way of life. The distinguishing elements of their culture—superstitions, religion, recreation, music, folktales, and language—allowed the slaves a degree of individual autonomy and self-respect. While slaves recognized the superior power which whites held as a group, they resisted the total assimilation of white culture.

The purpose of this study is to determine whether slaves living on Southern plantations developed a sense of community among themselves or generally identified with the interests and particular customs of their master.[3] More specifically, through an examination of the play of slave children between the years 1820 and 1860, this study attempts to determine whether slaves displayed an awareness of their uniqueness and separate identity as a group. Did members of the slave quarter fashion a society within a society or were they a culturally destitute group of individuals incapable of transcending such a con-

*Mr. Wiggins is an Assistant Professor in the Department of Health, Physical Education, Recreation, and Dance at Kansas State University, Manhattan, Kansas.

trolled institution? What is immediately apparent from this analysis is that play was essential to slave children because it was one means through which they learned the values and mores of their parents' world. Thus play became a means by which cultural traits were preserved from one generation to the next. Like all young people, slave children liquidated some of their problems and relieved themselves of worries and anxieties by talking about and dramatizing the things which disturbed them. Through play, slave children were also able to realize a much needed sense of community not only with other children of the plantation but with the adult slaves as well. Most importantly, it is apparent from this research that members of the slave quarter community generally viewed themselves as a familial group, with similar life-styles, similar concerns and problems, and a common need to stay together no matter the circumstances. Despite individual suspicions and hostilities, as a group, slaves recognized each other as a distinct society with a common historical experience and a common philosophical approach to the world. They were not a culturally rootless people but a vibrant group of individuals who created an energetic slave quarter community characterized by black solidarity not helpless dependency.

It should be stated at the outset that the evidence for this study is based largely on the first series of slave narratives edited by George P. Radwick.[4] This nineteen volume work, sixteen of which contain interviews prepared by the Federal Writers Project between 1936 and 1938, has some inherent problems in it. Since approximately two-thirds of the slaves were eighty or more years of age at the time they were interviewed, not only is there a concern about failing memories but also the question of whether longevity was the result of unusually good rather than typical treatment as slaves. Most of them were also recalling the experiences of their childhood, a period before the worst features of slavery were normally felt, and were likely, therefore, to give a more favorable picture of the institution. In addition, the biases, procedures, and methods employed by the predominately Southern white interviewers can be justly criticized. On the other hand, these narratives, as muddled and contradictory as they are, represent the voices of the inarticulate masses that scholars are always bemoaning. In spite of their imperfections, they are not much different from other types of historical sources. Historians simply have to use caution and discrimination when using the interviews. And naturally they should make use of all the skepticism their trade has taught them if they expect to come up with an honest interpretation. The narratives are certainly a most valuable piece of information on black history in America and should not be neglected. They contain evidence and answers for just about every kind of question that could be asked about life under slavery. For this particular study on the play of slave children they are the single best source available.

Slave children held a rather precarious position in the plantation community. For six days a week, while their parents were in the fields toiling under the hot sun or attending to chores in the "big house," slave children were generally left alone to raise one another. Exempted from routine labor until sometimes as late as fourteen or fifteen years old, a certain portion of the slave child's early life was spent in nurturing those younger than themselves and performing such chores as carrying water to the field hands, cleaning up the yards, fetching wood, tending the family garden, and feeding the livestock. The slave children's existence, however, was not all work and no play. On the contrary, when not engaged in their light tasks, they spent much of their time in the simple pleasures of eating, conversing, and playing with their companions.

Hardly anything was more enjoyable for the older slave children than roaming the fields and woods within the borders of their home plantation. Like all young people, slave children loved to explore the world around them. It helped them to discover their particular strengths and weaknesses and enabled them to cope with situations and events appropriate to their size and stamina. Acie Thomas spent much of his childhood roaming over the "broad acres" of his master's plantation with other slave children. "They waded in the streams, fished, chased rabbits and always knew where the choicest wild berries and nuts grew."[5] "On Sundays we'd strike out for the big woods and we'd gather our dresses full of hickory, walnuts, and berries," recalled Fannie Yarbrough from Texas. "I was jes' lying' here dreamin' 'bout how we use to go to the woods every spring and dig the maypop roots."[6]

The younger children did not have the privilege of wandering about the plantation. During the day parents expected their younger offspring to restrict their play activities to within the borders of the plantation nursery, slave quarters, or "big house."[7] Estrella Jones said the younger children on her master's Georgia plantation were allowed to play anytime "as long as they didn't wander away from the quarters."[8] It was much the same way on Ann Hawthorne's plantation in Texas. "We done our playing around that big house," recalled Hawthorne, "but that front gate we musn't go outside dat."[9]

The children frequently had the opportunity to visit their peer group on neighboring plantations. Parents usually did not mind if their children travelled to a nearby plantation, as long as they returned before nightfall. The slave children living on smaller plantations were especially anxious to make these excursions, since it was often the only chance they had to play with children of their own age group. "The patteroles never bothered the children any," remembered the Arkansas slave Allen Johnson. "And there wasn't any danger of them running off. It was all right for a child to go in the different quarters and play with one another during the daytime just so they got back before night."[10]

Older slave boys, and less frequently the girls, willingly contributed to the welfare of their family by hunting and fishing with their fathers during the evening hours. Exemption from field labor at night gave fathers and their children an opportunity to augment their diet by trapping small game and catching fish in nearby streams. They realized a much needed feeling of self-worth by adding delicacies to the family table. Often precluded by their masters from contributing to their families material welfare, slaves relished the chance to hunt and angle for food. Maybe most importantly, slave men found these two activities particularly satisfying because it allowed them the opportunity to teach their children the intricacies involved in hunting and fishing. There were not many activities in the plantation community where slave fathers and their children could share in the excitement of common pursuits. They both enjoyed the camaraderie and spirit that characterized these occasions. There was nothing quite like sitting around a blazing fire relating the tales of the phantom-like raccoon or the sixteen-foot catfish that got away. "My old daddy partly raised his chilluns on game," remembered Louise Adairs of North Carolina. "Mighty lot of fun when we could go with em."[11]

Like that of most young people, the play of slave children consisted of both traditional games passed down from the older to younger children and those improvised on the spot. Phyllis Petite of Texas said they used to play a game called "skeeting" when the lake would freeze over in the winter time. "No, I don't mean skating," recalled Petite. "That's when you got iron skates and we didn't have them things. We just get a running start and jump on the ice and skeet as far as we could go, and then run some more."[12] An ex-slave from Tennessee remembered playing a game they called "Smut." "We played it just like you would with cards only we would have grains of corn and call them hearts and spades, and so forth and go by the spots on the corn."[13] Charlie Davenport played a variety of the more traditional games on his Mississippi plantation. "Us played together in de street what run de length o' de quarters," remembered Davenport. "Us tho'owed horse shoes, jumped poles, walked on stilts, an' played marbles."[14] Chana Littlejohn played mumble peg, hop skotch, and "jumpin' de rope" when she was growing up on her small North Carolina plantation.[15]

The most popular group activities of the slave children, especially the girls, were "ring games" or "ring dances," accompanied by a variety of songs and riddles. There were infinite variations in these games, but the general procedure was to draw a ring on the ground, ranging from fifteen to thirty feet in diameter; depending on the number of children engaged in the dancing ring. The participants would congregate within the ring and dance to different rhythmic hand clappings.[16]

Often during their ring games the children would berate the whites in song:

My old mistress promised me,

Before she dies she would set me free.
Now she's dead and gone to hell
I hope the devil will burn her well.[17]

Or they would comment on their particular fears and anxieties:

Run nigger, run.
De patteroll git you!
Run nigger, run.
De patteroll come!
Watch nigger, watch.
De patteroll trick you!
Watch nigger, watch.
He got a big gun![18]

Many of the games played by children of the slave quarters had definite educational implications. Through the playing of games, slave children were often able to learn simple skills of literacy. "I learned some of the ABC's in playing ball with the white children," remembered Mattie Fannen of Arkansas.[19] Anna Parkes, who lived on a large plantation in Georgia, remembered nothing about special games except "Ole Hundred." "Us would choose one and that one would hide his face against a tree while he counted to a hundred. Then he would hunt for all the others. They would be hiding while he was counting. We learned to count a playing Ole Hundred."[20]

Much of the life of slave children consisted of role-playing and re-enacting those events which were most significant for them. Like all young people they wished to be grown-up and yearned to be wanted, needed, and a useful part of the grown-up world. It was natural for them to recreate that world using themselves as the leading characters. There were several distinguishing features about the imitative play of slave children. First, they did not necessarily re-enact those events found most enjoyable by the adult slaves. Second, they normally re-enacted events they had witnessed and heard of rather than experienced. Third, they usually imitated the social events of their own people and not those of the planters' family. Last and perhaps most important, the evidence strongly suggests that slave children attempted to relieve particular anxieties and fears through the medium of imitative play. By re-enacting certain events they attempted to master specific problems which they were not able to resolve realistically.

Slave children were not necessarily unique in their imitative play, but rather in the social events they chose to emulate. The frequency with which they conducted simulated church activities, funerals and auctions, subtly shows the importance that slaves attached to these three "cultural affairs." Benny Dillard, who lived on a Georgia plantation that contained over fifty slaves, remembered "the best game of all was to play like it was big meeting time . . . We would have make believe preachin' and baptism'. When we started playing like we were baptizing them we throwed all we could catch right in the creek, clothes and all, and ducked them."[21] Dinah Perry of Arkansas remembered how they made arrangements for a grand funeral. "We marched in a procession singing one of our folks funeral hymns," recalled Perry. "We stopped at the grave under the big magnolia tree by the gate, and my sister Nancy performed the ceremony."[22] Abe Livingston of Texas remembered playing the game of "Auction" on his "Massa's" plantation. One of the children would become the auctioneer and conduct a simulated slave sale.[23]

Two games which were played repeatedly by slave children were different variations of "Hiding the Switch" and "No Bogeyman Tonight." In the first activity the players hunted for a switch that had been concealed by one of the children. Whoever finds it runs after the others attempting to hit them. In the latter game one of the children assumes the role of an evil spirit and attempts to frighten the others. The girls found these games as popular as the boys. Julia Banks of Texas said they used to "get switches and whip one another. You know after you was hit several times it didn't hurt much."[24] Rachel Harris of Arkansas remembered playing "No Bogeyman Tonight" with the white children. "One would catch the others as they ran from behind big trees. Then whoever he caught would be the boogerman, till he caught somebody else."[25]

One historian of slavery feels these two particular games were means through which children assisted themselves in coping with their fear of "whippings" and evil spirits."[26] This is certainly a plausible explanation. Slave children who had witnessed the "floggings" of their parents or heard the frightening stories of ghost-like "spirits" could be expected to engage repeatedly in these games if it assisted them in lessening their fears. But this is only one of the possible interpretations. In these two games the children appeared to represent to themselves concretely those puzzling events they did not actually experience. The children may have been exploring their innermost feelings and emotions through a graphic representation. Or they may have been overtly "going over" two bewildering events in an attempt to confirm a vague memory. In other words, there was a need to physically re-enact "whippings" and "ghost stories" in order that their obscure features could be remembered more easily. Finally, slave children possibly participated in these two games simply for the excitement and sudden fear they wrought. Like most children they found a certain satisfaction in voluntarily exposing themselves to dangerous situations and inflicting what Roger Callois calls "a kind of voluptuous panic upon an otherwise lucid mind."[27]

Slave children played a variety of different ballgames. One of the distinctive features of these games was their simple organization; which was no doubt part of the reason why children of the slave quarters found them so popular.

Like their white counterparts, there were very few rules in their ballgames. Simplicity of this type was necessary because of the slave children's personal level of social maturity and their inability to continually acquire "sporting" accoutraments. "Shinny was de thing dat I like best," reminisced Hector Godbold of South Carolina, "just had stick wid crook in de end of it en see could I knock de ball wid dat."[28] Tom Johnson, also of South Carolina, "played lots of games, like rolly hole. There are two holes and you try to roll a ball in one hole."[29] Hanna Davidson of Kentucky remembered playing the game of "Anti-Over." Six of us would stay on one side of the house and six on the other side," recalled Davidson, "then we'd throw the ball over the roof. If you'd catch it you'd run around to the other side and hit somebody then start over."[30]

Older slave boys often mentioned playing "baseball." The available evidence does not specify the rules that were used or the number of players that made up a team. In all probability the games they usually played were the various modifications of "rounders" and "townball" engaged in by white Southerners.[31] The most popular game of these boys throughout the South was marbles. It was a game that required very little playing gear. A match could be arranged anytime two boys came together who were anxious to demonstrate their "shooting" abilities. The playing of marbles, furthermore, appeared to be one activity in which slave boys could experience a temporary feeling of "power." The collection of marbles was one instance in which they could acquire objects of material worth; no matter their monetary value. "Us boys played marbles," recalled James Southall of Tennesse. "I got to be a professional. I could beat em all."[32] Charles Coles of Maryland said that he "had many marbles and toys that poor children had then" and that his "favorite game was marbles."[33]

Slave boys, and less frequently the girls, challenged members of their peer group to impromptu contests that would test their physical prowess. They delighted in seeing who could run the fastest, jump the highest, throw the farthest, swim the longest, and lift the heaviest objects. "Athletic" accomplishments were a source of great pride for slave children. The ability to perform well in physical contests usually guaranteed them the respect of their impressionable young playmates. One of the fastest ways for them to attain a degree of status and the recognized leadership of their peer group was to be successful on the playing field. "Because of my unusual strength and spirit I would let none of them beat me at any game," remembered Robert Ellett of Virginia. "I was best of the young boys on the plantation."[34] Sam Stewart, who lived on a large plantation in North Carolina, recalled that the little boys "near my own age were playmates and companions and accepted me as their natural leader and chief. By the time I was eight years old, I could shoot, ride, fish, and swim with anyone."[35]

The more sportive slave boys enjoyed placing a wager or two in their game playing. They were especially fond of shooting craps and playing cards, but would place bets on just about any activity that was conducive to gaming. To elude the eyes of their virtuous parents as well as those of their concerned master they often had to resort to the woods or some other secluded spot. Not having much to gamble with their stakes consisted of any objects they attached special importance to. William Ballard and the other slave children used to play hide-the-switch, marbles, and several other games on their South Carolina plantation. But "later on some of de nigger boys started going to the woods to play cards and gamble."[36] "De only game I ever played wuz marbles," remembered John Smith of North Carolina. "I played fer watermelons. We didn't hab any money so we played fer watermelons."[37]

The play of slave girls differed in some respects from that of the boys. There were very few games the girls did not play or at least attempted to play during their childhood.[38] The activity they most frequently played was "jump rope."[39] A great deal of their time was spent playing with "dolls" and keeping "house."[40] Maybe most importantly, slave girls had a particular fondness for dances, parties, and other social entertainments. They repeatedly expressed, like other members of the slave quarters, a desire to be among their own people engaged in group activities. In examining the girls' various play activities, there comes through a sense of mutual affection and kinship-like spirit among all the slaves. Phoebe Anderson of Georgia remembered that she would "go fishin down on the creek and on Saturday night we'd have parties in the woods and play ring plays and dance."[41] Caroline Bevis of South Carolina said that when she was a little girl she "would play any over in the moonlight but enjoyed most the parties and dances on the plantation."[42]

Slave children spent very little of their leisure time in combative activities. There are occasional references to boxing and wrestling in the slave narratives, but the children generally preferred to engage in more gentle pursuits.[43] Physical abuse of one child by another was considered unjustifiable and a veritable threat to the general well-being of the group. Like their parents, slave children apparently viewed themselves as a distinct body with common concerns, problems, and life styles. They recognized the need to remain together as a familial group no matter the particular circumstances. The point here is not that slave children never fought each other, but rather that they understood that their mutual advantage required them to care for each other and to refrain as much as possible from foolish "skirmishes."[44] John Brown stated that he and his friends saw no wrong in cheating, lying, and fighting "so long as we were not acting against one another."[45] Susan Davis Rhodes, who lived as a slave in North Carolina said that "People in my day didn't know book learning but dey studied how to protect each other, and didn't believe in fightin' each other."[46]

One of the significant features about the play of slave children is the apparent absence of any games that required the elimination of players. Even the various dodge ball and tagging games played by the children contained designed stratagem within their rule structure that prevented the removal of any participants. Despite the personal animosities and jealousies that individual slave children might have had towards one another, there seemed to be a mutual affection between the mass of children that precluded the elimination of any players in their games. One of the fears in their daily life was that members of their family—father, mother, brothers, sisters, grandparents, uncles, aunts, nieces, nephews—could be indiscriminately sold or hired out at anytime. Possible separation from their loved ones was frequently a source of great uneasiness and apprehension for those slave children who were old enough to realize their social position in the plantation community.[47] Their "frivolous" play life was one area of their existence in which they could be assured that their companions would not be suddenly removed or excluded from participating. The lack of elimination in the slave children's games, moreover, can possibly be accounted for by some basic values generally held by members of the slave quarter community. A "survival of the fittest" or "natural selection" mentality did not normally characterize slave society. At the center of the slaves' social philosophy was a necessary belief in cooperation and community spirit. There was little room in the slaves' world for ruthless rivalry, unrestrained competition, and unprincipled domination. Personal conquest and individual success was certainly prevalent in their society but was considered much less important for survival than the belief in group solidarity and a sense of loyalty to fellow members of the slave quarter. Ma Eppes of Alabama remembered playing "Snail Away Rauley" all the time. "Us would hol' han's an' go 'roun' in a ring, gittin' faster an' faster an dem fell down was not outa de game but would have, tah ge' back in line."[48] Moses Davis of Arkansas recalled that in playing "Ant y Over" they "would get six on one side of de house and six on de other. When somebody got hit we would just start the game over again."[49]

Occasionally the slave children were permitted to continue their play at night. They longed for the close of day because it meant they could frolic with their parents and the other adult slaves—free from the continual surveillance of the planter and his family. The children loved to congregate outside of the cabins and listen to some "learned" old slave relate tales of Africa; gather around a blazing fire to dance and sing songs; accompany the more gamesome men on raccoon and possum hunts; travel with their family to a nearby plantation for a dance or corn-shucking' or simply stay around the slave quarters and "cut capers" with the other children. Pet Franks of Mississippi remembered playing "Hide-de switch" and "Goose and Gander" in the day time. "Den at nighttime when de moon was shinin' big an' yaller, us'd play ole molly bright. Dat was what us call de moon. Ud'd make up stories 'bout her."[50] Jane Simpson, who lived on a small plantation in Missouri, recalled that "de white folks didn't want to let de slaves have no time for der self, so de old folks used to let us children run and play at night, while de white folks sleep and dey watch de stars to tell about what time to call us in and put us to bed, 'fore de white folks know we was out."[51]

Slave children also eagerly looked forward to Saturday afternoons, Sundays, and various holidays because it was an opportunity for them to participate in family and community activities or merely play with their friends and relatives. These moments were prized by all members of the slave quarter not simply as periods free from labor but as times when slaves could be with one another. These were the most ideal times for children to become familiar with the structure, the style, and the leading personalities of their community. Through their mutual experiences they learned the ways in which their community operated, how it made common decisions, organized secretive events, provided for common recreational needs, and generally organized itself to be as independent as possible from the personal whims and strictures of their overseer or master. Unable to spend extended periods of time with the children because of a heavy work schedule, slave parents took advantage of these moments to play with and talk to their children. These interactions provided special meaning to the children because it was extremely important in determining their personality and their particular way in which they viewed the world. "One of de recreations us chil. had in dem days was candy pullings at Christmas times," reminisced Hemp Kennedy of Mississippi. "We all met at one house an' tol' ghost stories, sung plantation songs, as' danced de clog while de candy was cookin'."[52] "Christmastime was when slaves had their own fun," said the Georgia slave Jefferson Franklin Henry. "They frolicked, danced, run races, played games, and visited around, calling it a good time."[53]

Slave children not only played among themselves but frequently participated in the same games and played together in a relative degree of social equality with the white children of the plantation. Some planters did attempt to prevent their children from playing with the children of the slave quarters for fear that they would be "corrupted."[54] Their attempts to circumscribe the play of their children, however, usually proved futile. The white children of the plantation earnestly sought the friendship of the slave children their own age and thoroughly enjoyed the opportunity to frolic in the quarters. In fact, through the playing of games, slave and white children would often develop friendships that lasted a lifetime (although those relationships usually only existed between the white children and one or two blacks who became body servants or occupied some special station in the plantation community.) "I belonged to ole Massa Harry ebber sin' he was married," recalled an ex-slave from Virginia. "He an' me was jes' about of an age, n' tended him all his life. I allers 'tended to him when he was a boy, am' went out hunting, shooting, and trapping wid him all over the place."[55] "I hunted and fished with the slave children," responded Edward Pollard, the son of a Virginia slaveholder. "I have wrestled on the banks of the creek with him, and with him as my trusty lieutenant I have filibustered all over my old aunts dominion."[56]

Much of the leisure time of slave and white children was spent in getting into mischief and helping each other out of difficult situations. Hand in hand they would go about pilfering the plantation hen house and performing no small amount of reciprocal trading. There are also numerous examples of white children helping their slave playmates avoid punishments or assisting them in a variety of subtle ways. "Me and young master had the good times," recalled Jack Cauthern of Texas. "He was nigh my age and we'd steal chickens from old Miss and go down in the orchard and barbecue 'em."[57] Matilda Daniel said they sure did some "devilish" things on her Alabama plantation. "We hid red pepper in old Black Bob's chewin' bacca, an' you ought to seed de faces he made. Den we tuken a skunk dat us little white an' black debils katched an' turn him loose in de slave quarters."[58]

Notwithstanding those occasional friendships, a caste system frequently operated within the "play world" of the slave and white children just as it did in the everyday affairs of the plantation community. Older slave children in particular were often forced to assume a subservient position in their game playing. Many of the white children of advanced age were anxious to assume their position as "superiors." Candis Goodwin of Virginia remembered that when the war first started they would "play Yankee an' Federates, 'course de whites was always the 'Federates. They'd take us black boys prisoners an' make b'lieve dey was gonna cut our necks off; guess dey got dat idea f'om dere fathers."[59] Amelia Thompson Watts, who lived on a relative's Louisiana cotton plantation in the summer of 1832, described a scene that also illustrates the cast distinction between slave and white children:

> One of the negro boys had found a dead chicken and we arranged for a funeral. The boys made a wagon of fig branches, and four of them as horses. We tied a bow of black ribbon around the chicken's neck and covered him with a white rag and then marched in a procession singing one of the quaint negro hymns, all the white children next to the hearses marching two by two, and the colored children following in the same order.[60]

Many white children loved nothing better than to torment the slave children, and even adults, by simulating the role of an overseer or master of a large plantation in their imitative play. Soloman Northup, who labored on a number of Southern plantations, recalled the ten or twelve-year-old son of a despotic slaveholder who had no trouble in picking up all his father's habits. "Mounted on his pony," said Northup, "he often rides into the field with his whip, playing the overseer, greatly to his father's delight."[61] Frederick Law Olmstead, while traveling through Texas, observed the play of a planter's son which illustrates this point:

This gentleman had thiry or forty negroes and two legitimate sons. One was an idle young man. The other was already at eight years old a swearing tobacco chewing young bully and ruffian. We heard him whipping his puppy behind the house and swearing between the blows, his father and mother being at hand. His tone was an evident imitation of his fathers mode of dealing with his slaves. 'I've got an account to settle with you; I've let you go about long enough; I'll teach you who's your master; there; go now God damn you, but I haven't got through with you yet.[62]

Slave children were not always on the receiving end of such foolish mockings and harassments. Those children of the slave quarters who were clever enough to outwit the white children did not hesitate to return personal insults. Some planters even encouraged these rebukes, because they didn't always appreciate seeing their children become tyrants. A slave from Tennesse recalled how they "teased" the white children:

They didn't allow us to even look at the white chillen. I 'member we used to slip and play with 'em anyway. About a mile from the house there was a lane, and we would git all the chillen together and play with them down in that lane where our white folks couldn't see us' then we would make 'em skit home! We say 'ya'll gwan now, here come the white folks; he, he, he. We would drive 'em home and tell 'em ole master would whip them if they saw us with 'em . . . Next morning we would go and get 'em and play with 'em again. We would tell 'em we was better'n than they was, he, he, he.[63]

This feeling of confidence which shows through the account, was a theme throughout the slave narratives and the other black folklore. In fact, slave children normally thought of themselves not only as morally superior to white children but as superior on a physical level as well. Whereas most slave children thought of themselves as skillful "athletes," their white counterparts were generally felt to be less competent physically, unable to dance, run, jump, or throw! The white children were so inept they were hardly able to tie their own shoes or comb their own hair. "We was stronger and knowed how to play, and the white children didn't," recalled Felix Heywood of Texas.[64] Remembering life under slavery in South Carolina, Josephine Bauchus concluded that "white folks couldn' dance no more den dey can dance dese days like de colored people can."[65]

One of the most striking differences between the play of slave and white children was the type of equipment used in their game playing. In contrast to the planters' children who were normally able to purchase their own toys, the children of the slave quarters either made their own playthings, obtained various toys that their fathers handcrafted, or acquired "hand-me-downs" that the white children no longer found useable. Hanna Davidson of Kentucky said that "the kids nowadays can go right to the store and buy a ball to play with. We'd have to make a ball out of yarn and put a sock around it for cover."[66] Sam McAllum of Mississippi didn't "recollect any playthings" they had " 'cept a ball my young marster gimme."[67] Letita Burwell, the daughter of a Kentucky planter, remembered they "early learned that happiness consisted in dispensing it, and found no greater pleasure than saving our old dolls, toys, beads, bits of cake, or candy for the cabin children, whose delight at receiving them richly repaid us."[68]

The white children of the plantation engaged in many of the same activities as their slave counterparts. For example, Lanty Blackford, the son of a wealthy Virginia planter, played with his friends in a variety of activities that Brian Sutton-Smith refers to as central-person games.[69] These are games in which one child plays against the rest of the group. Some of the more popular ones among slave and white children were different variations of "Goosie, Goosie, Gander," "Pig in the Pin," "I Spy," "Base," "Hide-and-Seek," "Blind Man's Bluff," and "Fox and Hounds." In addition to these games the white children in Blackford's neighborhood also engaged in some organized activities as boating, swimming, fishing, hunting, and wrestling. The children, furthermore, often reenacted different situations from Southern life in their play. They were particularly fond of participating in mock "military drills," "court trials," and "political debates."[70] Interestingly enough, what was apparently lacking in the white children's play world were any games of chance. Assuredly, the admonitions they received from their parents quite possibly discouraged the children from playing these games or at least discussing them openly. Still, in comparison to the slave children they seemed to favor those games which principally required the skill and effort of the performers.[71] The emphasis on these particular kinds of games seems to reflect the particular cultural focus of the white Southerners more than anything else. The research on play has shown that games which emphasize physical prowess are usually found in those cultures which recognize that effort and individual initiative are the main determinants in achieving success.[72] The planters of the Old South certainly embraced these values. Consequently, through the playing of those games that required a degree of physical prowess the white children of the plantation were possibly learning that the outcome of particular endeavors was a result of the amount of effort that was expended and that other factors were basically superfluous. On the other hand, slave children could be expected to find gambling and other games of chance particularly enticing. Survival to the slave was not necessarily contingent upon the skill and effort one put forth, but rather on a variety of other uncontrollable factors—not the least of which was indiscriminate luck.[73]

The white children of the plantation not only placed a great deal of emphasis on the amount of effort expended in their games, but were also concerned about the specific manner in which they were played. In many instances they seemed more interested in the mode of play rather than in the outcome of the game itself. In contrast to the slave children, the limited goals of their games were often subordinated to the means by which they were to be achieved. In other words, white children were not simply concerned about the effort expended in their games, but found it necessary that they achieve their desired results in a deliberately stylized way.[74]

It is evident that slave children, like their parents, viewed themselves as a special kind of people and took pride in expressing their peculiar style in many of their play activities. It was often a way to assure themselves of their own self-worth, the medium through which they established life-long friendships, and the manner in which their individuality was asserted and maintained. Their play life consisted almost solely of informal and often times improvised games that could be arranged any time two children came together who were anxious to have some fun. Whether deliberate or not slave children often learned from each other how to play games. Generally left alone to raise each other, slave children typically had ultimate control as to what they did or did not play. Despite occasional attempts to restrict them from playing with their own children, Southern slaveholders did not normally concern themselves with the types of activities played by slave children. The majority of "proprietors" did allow their slaves a somewhat extended childhood in hopes they would attain the degree of health necessary to become "efficient" workers. However, this prolonged infancy did not include any formal program of games or exercise designed to improve the fitness of the slave children. In fact, the majority of planters generally did not pay much attention to the slave children's physical well being until they were old enough to join the regular plantation work force. In their way of thinking, freedom from strenuous labor was all that was needed to insure a "hearty" adult slave. Paradoxically, exeption from work and opportunities for play were probably more influential in providing the ground work for a potentially more self-reliant and spirited adult slave.

Like most young people, slave children realized a great deal of pleasure from participation in various play activities. It was often the medium through which they learned the values and mores of the adult world. By simulating those events characteristic of the grown-up world slave children were able to understand the complicated world about them and capable of perceiving the patent differences that normally existed between a master and his servants. The evidence also suggests that through various play activities slave children were able to relieve themselves of the fear and anxiety that normally characterized the lives of most of the children. By participating in certain "amusements" they apparently attempted to overcome particular problems which they were not able to resolve realistically.

A theme that frequently appeared in the narratives was the feeling of black supremacy exhibited by many slave children in their various play activities. Apparently, only at a certain point in their lives did slave children come to realize fully that they were "servants" and that their white companions held a more exalted position in the plantation community. Many did not recognize the difference until they were separated from their white playmates and sent out to the fields or up to the "big house" to begin their life of labor. On some plantations the slave children learned when one of their family members was suddenly sold or hired out; or when the planter or overseer precluded their parents authority in some way. Many slave children learned almost immediately because they might be forced to call a white baby "Young Massa" or "Young Misses." Still others immediately recognized the difference when they were forced to assume an obsequious position in their game playing or were excluded from participating altogether. Quite possibly then, prior to their realization that they occupied an inferior position in the plantation community, slave children were unaware of the usual decorum that normally existed between the races and therefore were probably more inclined not to comply with the desires of their white playmates. Of course, simply sharing in the excitement of various play activities probably did much to create temporary feelings of equality and fellowship between the children. It is when people are mutually involved in uninhibited merrymaking that intrinsic differences are most often disguised. The joy and pleasantry of the moment possibly helped erase some of the disparities that existed between the children. Furthermore, slave children could assume almost any attitude they wished considering there were very few adults around to keep watch over their every move. In any event, whatever the reasons for the slave children's feelings of superiority, they frequently thought of themselves as being more energetic dancers, better hunters, faster runners, and more imaginative in all their game playing. The white children were often portrayed simply as clumsy fools who were decidedly prosaical in their play activities.

Not only did slave children often exhibit a marked feeling of superiority but also realized a much needed sense of community with other slave members through various play activities. In fact, the joy they found in play seemed to be accounted for, more than anything else, by the group solidarity and fraternal spirit this activity brought forth. Their numerous play experiences were eagerly looked forward to by the slave children because it gave them opportunities to frolic and socialize with their peer group under conformable conditions. The fellowship attained during these occasions seems especially significant because it furnished individual slave children with a feeling of security they might not experience under any other circumstances. Moreover, the constant reinforcement, common language, and strong positive sanctions that normally characterized these events helped to succor the slave children in their struggle to discover their personal identities.

This did not mean that slave children ever felt any sense of community with the white children and their family. It is true that mutual enjoyment of various play activities did much to develop friendships among the children. But simply sharing in the excitement of popular pastimes was never influential enough to erase the intrinsic differences that existed between the children. To develop a true feeling of community requires at least a common life-style, common interests and problems, or a common philosophical approach to the world. It would be historically misleading to say that participating in several of the same play activities was responsible for developing these sentiments between the children—even for a brief period of time. This is not to argue that mutual participation in play activities did not temporarily eliminate the usual propriety between the races; only that play was incapable of developing a sense of community between two people whose view of this world was so alien.

Finally, the singular style of the slave children's various games cuts deep into the heart of one of the basic differences between slave and white society—specifically their differing notions about the concepts of work and play. Planters seemed to think of play primarily in contrast to work, whereas the dichtomy between these two activities was not quite as discernable in slave society. Relatively speaking, Southern slaveholders, like many people in today's world, frequently judged the worthiness of individuals by the amount of effort they expended in their work. They viewed labor as being both necessary for survival and as a virtue in its own right. This did not mean that the Protestant work ethic characterized the Southern planters' personal value scheme. On the contrary, they realized that hard work was inevitable to achieve success but not if it meant the indiscriminate acquisition of wealth, excessive abstinence, or an unrealistic devotion to "one's calling." The Southern slaveholders certainly did enjoy "living it up." Their reputation as a fun loving and frolicsome society is basically an accurate one. On the other hand, most planters considered play as generally trifling in the sense that it was immaterial to survival, should be engaged in by gentlemen only in the most organized and refined fashion, and ought to be exclusive in nature and devoid of any frivolous public displays.

Slaves seem to have had a much different view of work and play than their masters. They certainly did not place the same kind of emphasis or judge the personal worth of individuals by the successful completion of their regular plantation tasks. The slaves' sense of accomplishment was identified with the family unit and measured primarily by the successful maintenance of the familial order of the household. They realized the necessity of working long and difficult hours during planting and harvesting seasons, but expected to work considerably less during other seasons. They did not understand the incessant need for labor and resisted what they felt was senseless work. In other words, work was generally not the basis for evaluating one's personal integrity and character of his being. Conversely, play was one activity where slaves could realize a certain degree of dignity and could affirm and sustain their unique existence. They could withstand bondage much more easily when allowed to participate with fellow slaves in a variety of different play activities.

Notes

1. See for example: Stanley M. Elkins, *Slavery: A Problem in American Institutional and Intellectual Life* (Chicago: University of Chicago Press, 1959); Chase C. Mooney, *Slavery in Tennessee* (Westport, New York: Negro Universities Press, 1971); Ulrich B. Phillips, *American Negro Slavery* (New York: Appleton and Company, 1918); James B. Sellers, *Slavery in Alabama* (Birmingham: University of Alabama Press, 1964); Kenneth M. Stampp, *The Peculiar Institution: Slavery in the Antebellum South* (New York: Vintage Books, 1956); Charles S. Sydnor, *Slavery in Mississippi* (New York: D. Appleton-Century Company, 1933).

2. See for example: John W. Blassingame, *The Slave Community: Plantation Life in the Antebellum South* (New York: Oxford University Press, 1972); Eugene D. Genovese, *Roll, Jordan, Roll: The World the Slaves Made* (New York: Vintage Books, 1976); Herbert G. Gutman, *The Black Family in Slavery and Freedom, 1750-1925* (New York: Random House, 1976); Leslie H. Owens, *This Species of Property: Slave Life and Culture in the Old South* (New York: Oxford University Press, 1977); Thomas L. Webber, *Deep Like the Rivers: Education in the Slave Quarter Community* (New York: W. W. Norton and Co., 1978).

3. The term "community" is defined in this study as a group of people who shared a common set of values and attitudes, familal social structure, and displayed a unique identity as a group.

4. George P. Rawick, ed., *The American Slave: A Composite Autobiography*, 19 Vols., (Westport, Connecticut: Greenwood Publishing Company, 1972).

5. Rawick, ed., Vol. XVIII, *Florida Narratives*, p. 328.

6. Rawick, ed., Vol. V, No. 4, *Texas Narratives*, p. 226.

7. If the younger children did not have older siblings mature enough to take care of them, they were looked after either by older cousins; one or two slaves too old to work in the fields, or some younger woman who was appointed the job. See for example: Joseph Holt Ingraham, *The Southwest By a Yankee*, 2 Vols. (London: Fisher and Company, 1842), II, p. 28; Nancy B. De Saussure, *Old Plantation Days: Being Recollections of Southern Life Before the Civil War* (New York: Duffield and Company, 1909), pp. 38-39; Louis B. Hughes, *Thirty Years a Slave. From Bondage to Freedom, The Institution of Slavery as Seen on the Plantation and in the Home of the Planter* (Milwaukee, Wisconsin: M. E. Maferkorn, 1897), p. 44; Basil Hall, *Travels in North America in the years 1827 and 1828*, 3 Vols. (Edinburgh: Cadell and Co., 1829), III, p. 179; Frederick Law Olmstead, *A Journey in the Seaboard Slave States* (New York: G. P. Putnam's Sons, 1856) p. 424; *John Houston Bills Diary*, July 30, 1853; Ralph J. Jones and Tom Landess, ed., "Portraits of Georgia Slaves," *Georgia Review*, 22:1 (1968), 126; *Plantation Book of 1857-58* in the James H. Hammond Papers; William H. Russell, *My Diary North and South* (Boston: Burnham, 1863), pp. 274-275.

8. Rawick, ed., Vol. XII, No. 2, *Georgia Narratives*, p. 34.

9. Rawick, ed., Vol. IV, No. 2, *Texas Narratives*, p. 120.

10. Rawick, ed., Vol. IX, No. 4, *Arkansas Narratives*, p. 64.

11. Rawick, ed., Vol. XIV, No. 1, *North Carolina Narratives*, p. 245.

12. Rawick, ed., Vol. VII, No. 1, *Texas Narratives*, p. 239.

13. Fisk Collection, *Unwritten History of Slavery: Autobiographical Accounts of Negro Ex-Slaves* (Nashville: Social Science Institute, Fisk University, 1945), p. 15.

14. Rawick, ed., Vol. VII, No. 2, *Mississippi Narratives*, p. 36.

15. Rawick, ed., Vol. XV, No. 2, *North Carolina Narratives*, p. 58.

16. The narratives are replete with examples of slave children engaging in "ring" dances. See for example: Rawick, ed., Vol., IV, No. 2, *Texas Narratives*, p. 120; Vol. XIV, No.1, *North Carolina Narratives*, p. 95; Vol. X, No. 5, *Arkansas Narratives*, p. 162; Vol. IV, No. 2, *Georgia Narratives*, p. 136; Vol. VII, No. 1, *Oklahoma Narratives*, pp. 98-99; Vol. III, No. 4, *South Carolina Narratives*, p. 168; Charles L. Perdue, Jr., Thomas E. Barden, and Robert K. Phillips, eds., *Weevils in the Wheat: Interviews with Virginia Ex-Slaves* (Charlottsville: University Press of Virginia, 1976), p. 203.

17. Lyle Saxon, Edward Dreyer, and Robert Tallant, *Gumbo Ya Ya: A Collection of Louisiana Folk Tales* (Boston: Houghton Mifflin, 1945), p. 447.

18. Rawick, ed., Vol. VII, No. 1, *Oklahoma Narratives*, p. 65.

19. Rawick, ed., Vol. XIX, No. 2, *Arkansas Narratives*, p. 267.

20. Rawick, ed., Vol. XIII, No. 3, *Georgia Narratives*, p. 155.

21. Rawick, ed., Vol. XII, No. 1, *Georgia Narratives*, pp. 289-290.

22. Rawick, ed., Vol. X, No. 5, *Arkansas Narratives*, pp. 320-321.

23. Rawick, ed., Vol. V, No. 3, *Texas Narratives*, p. 24.

24. Rawick, ed., Vol. IV, No. 1, *Texas Narratives*, p. 97.

25. Rawick, ed., Vol. IX, No. 3, *Arkansas Narratives*, p. 181.

26. See Thomas L. Webber, *Deep Like the Rivers: Education in the Slave Quarter Community*, p. 184.

27. Caillois uses the term "ilinx" to describe these types of games. Interestingly, he suggests that as civilizations mature, these games, "lose their traditional dominance, are pushed to the periphery of public life, reduced to roles that become more and more modern and intermittent, if not clandestine and guilty, or are regulated to the limited and regulated domain of games." See Roger Caillois, *Man, Play, and Games* (New York: The Free Press, 1961), p. 97.

28. Rawick, ed., Vol. II, No. 2, *South Carolina Narratives*, p. 146.

29. Rawick, ed., Vol. III, No. 3, *South Carolina Narratives*, p. 62.

30. Rawick, ed., Vol. XVI, No. 5, *Kentucky Narratives*, p. 29.

31. For an excellent discussion and analysis of the evolution of baseball, see Robert K. Henderson, *Ball, Bat, and Bishop: The Origin of Ballgames* (New York: Rockport Press Inc., 1947), pp. 132-195.

32. Rawick, ed., Vol. VII, No. 1, *Tennessee Narratives*, p. 308.

33. Rawick, ed., Vol. XVI, No. 3, *Maryland Narratives*, p. 2.

34. Charles L. Perdue, Jr., Thomas E. Barden, and Robert K. Phillips, eds., *Weevils in the Wheat: Interviews with Virginia Ex-Slaves*, p. 84.

35. Rawick, ed., Vol. XV, No. 2, *North Carolina Narratives*, p. 322.

36. Rawick, ed., Vol. II, No. 1, *South Carolina Narratives*, p. 28.

37. Rawick, ed., Vol. XV, No. 2, *North Carolina Narratives*, p. 273.

38. See for example: Rawick, ed., Vol. IV, No. 2, *Texas Narrative*, p. 120; Vol. VI, No. 1, *Alabama Narratives*, p. 211.

39. See for example: Rawick, ed., Vol. XV, No. 2, *North Carolina Narratives*, p. 68; Vol. III, No. 4, *South Carolina Narratives*, p. 168; Vol. VIII, No. 2, *Arkansas Narratives*, p. 248.

40. See for example: Rawick, ed., Vol. V, No. 4, *Texas Narratives*, p. 147; Vol. IV, No. 2, *Texas Narratives*, p. 223; Vol. VIII, No. 1, *Arkansas Narratives*, p. 11.

41. Rawick, ed., Vol. IV, No. 2, *Georgia Narratives*, p. 136.

42. Rawick, ed., Vol. II, No. 1, *South Carolina Narratives*, p. 55.

43. See for example: Charles L. Perdue, Jr., Thomas E. Barden, and Robert K. Phillips, eds., *Weevils in the Wheat: Interview with Virginia Ex-Slaves*; p. 84; John W. Blassingame, ed., *Slave Testimony: Two Centuries of Letters, Speeches, Interviews, and Autobiographies*, p. 641.

44. See for example: Israel Campbell, *Bond and Free: Or Yearnings for Freedom, From My Green Briar House, Being the Story of My Life in Bondage and My Life in Freedom* (Philadelphia: By the author, 1861), p. 38; James Williams, *Narrative of James Williams, An American Slave, Who was for Several Years a Driver of a Cotton Plantation in Alabama* (Boston: American Anti-Slavery Society, 1838), p. 66; Orland Kay Armstrong, *Old Massa's People: The Old Slaves Tell Their Story* (Indianapolis: Bobbs-Merrill, 1831), pp. 160-163.

45. John Brown, *Slave Life in Georgia: A Narrative of the Life: Sufferings and Escape of John Brown, A Fugitive Slave Now in England* (London: W. M. Watts, 1855), p. 83.

46. Rawick, ed., Vol. XI, *Missouri Narratives*, p. 284.

47. See for example: Henry Box Brown, *Narrative of Henry Box Brown* (Boston: Brown and Stearns, 1849), p. 15; Benjamin Drew, Ed., *A North-Slide View of Slavery, The Refugee: Or the Narratives of Fugitive Slaves in Canada* (Boston: John P. Jewett, 1856), p. 30; Charles Ball, *Slavery in the United States: A Narrative of the Life and Adventures of Charles Ball* (Lewiston, Pa.: 1836), pp. 15-22; Shippee, Lester B., ed., *Bishop Whipple's Southern Diary, 1843-1844* (New York: DaCapo Press, 1968), pp. 69, 88-89; Elkanah Watson, *Men and Times of the Revolution* (New York: Charles Scribners, 1857), p. 69.

48. Rawick, ed., Vol. XI, No. 1, *Alabama Narratives*, p. 120.

49. Rawick, ed., Vol. IX, No. 3, *Arkansas Narratives*, p. 167.

50. Rawick, ed., Vol. VII, No. 1, *Mississippi Narratives*, p. 57.

51. Rawick, ed., Vol. II, No. 7, *Missouri Narratives*, p. 313.

52. Rawick, ed., Vol. VII, No. 2, *Missippi Narratives*, p. 85.

53. Rawick, ed., Vol. XII, No. 2, *Georgia Narratives*, p. 187.

54. Rawick, ed., Vol. VI, No. 1, *Alabama Narratives*, p. 103; Vol. VII, No. 2, *Mississippi Narratives*, p. 26;

Richard Parkinson, *A Tour in American in 1798, 1799, and 1800* 2 Vols. (London: J. Harding, 1805), I, p. 436.

55 Catherine C. Hopley, *Life in the South: From the Commencement of the War. By a Blockaded British Subject*, 2 Vols. (London: Chapman and Hall, 1863, I, p. 54.

56. H. H. Farmer, *Virginia Before and During the War* (Henderson, Kentucky: By the Author, 1892), p. 63.

57. Rawick, ed., Vol. IV, No. 1, *Texas Narratives*, p. 212.

58. Rawick, ed., Vol. VI, No. 6, *Alabama Narratives*, p. 103.

59. Charles L. Perdue, Jr., Thomas E. Barden and Robert K. Phillips, eds., *Weevils in the Wheat: Interviews with Virginia Ex-Slaves*, p. 109.

60. Amelia Thompson Watts, "A Summer on a Louisiana Cotton Plantation in 1832," in *Louise Taylor Pharr Book*.

61. Soloman Northup, *Twelve Years a Slave. Narrative of Soloman Northup, A Citizen of New York, Kidnapped in Washington City in 1841 and Rescued in January 1853, From a Cotton Plantation Near Red River in Louisiana* (Buffalo: Derby, Orton, and Mulligan, 1857), p. 261.

62. Frederick Law Olmsted, *A Journey Through Texas: Or a Saddle Trip on the Southwestern Frontier: With a Statistical Appendix* (New York: Dix, Edwards, and Company, 1857), pp. 116-117.

63. Fisk Collection, *Unwritten History of Slavery: Autobiographical Accounts of Negro Ex-Slaves*, pp. 21-22.

64. Rawick, ed., Vol. IV, No. 2, *Texas Narratives*, p. 134.

65. Rawick, ed., Vol. II, No. 1, *South Carolina Narratives*, p. 22.

66. Rawick, Vol. XVI, No. 5, *Kentucky Narratives*, p. 29.

67. Rawick, Vol. VII, No. 2, *Missippi Narratives*, p. 101.

68. Letita M. Burwell, *Plantation Reminiscences* (Kentucky, 1878), p. 4.

69. Launcelot Minor Blackford Diary, Southern Historical Collection, University of North Carolina, Chapel Hill.

70. Ibid.

71. Ibid

72. John M. Roberts, Malcolm J. Arth, and Robert B. Bush, "Games in Culture," *American Anthropologist*, 61 (1959), 597-605; Stephen N. Miller, "The Playful, the Crazy, and the Nature of Pretense," in *The Anthropological Study of Human Play*, ed., Edward Norbeck (Houston: Rice University Studios, 60, No. 4, Summer 1974), 36; Roger Caillois, *Man, Play, and Games*, p.27.

73. For examples consult any volume of George P. Rawick's, *The American Slave: A Composite Autobiography*.

74. See for example: Letita M. Burwell, *Plantation Reminiscences*, p. 2; James B. Avirett, *The Old Plantation: How we Lived in Great House and Cabin Before the War* (New York: F. Tennyson), p. 91; Nancy B. DeSaussure, *Old Plantation Days: Being Recollections of Southern Life Before the Civil War* (New York: Duffield and Company, 1909), pp. 38-39; Edward A. Pollard, *Black Diamonds Gathered in the Darkey Homes of the South* (New York: Pudney and Russell, 1859), p. 50; John J. Wise, *The End of an Era* (New York: Houghton, Mifflin and Co., 1902), pp. 153-154.

The Historical Journal, 30, 3 (1987), pp. 603–622
Printed in Great Britain

SOME ASPECTS OF FEMALE RESISTANCE TO CHATTEL SLAVERY IN LOW COUNTRY GEORGIA, 1763–1815*

BETTY WOOD
Girton College, Cambridge

Although often differing dramatically in their methodologies and conclusions, most studies of the slave societies of the American South either draw to a close by the middle years of the eighteenth century or begin their story only in the 1820s and 1830s. Moreover, whilst some scholars have differentiated between particular patterns of black behaviour, as for example between African- and country-born slaves, field hands and domestic slaves, until quite recently comparatively little interest has been shown in delineating the ways in which black women perceived and responded to their status and condition.[1]

Barbara Bush has commented of West Indian slave women that 'Popular stereotypes...have portrayed them as passive and downtrodden work-horses who did little to advance the struggle for freedom. The "peculiar burdens" of their sex allegedly precluded any positive contribution to slave resistance.'[2] Such 'stereotypes' are as untrue of the Georgia Low Country between 1763 and 1815 as they are of the sugar islands between 1790 and 1838.

The story of the Low Country's slave society before 1815 may be broken down into three, not altogether distinct, phases. The years down to the mid-1770s saw the creation of a slave-based plantation economy; the War for Independence severely disrupted that economy and the black workforce upon

* An earlier version of this article was read to the Eighth Annual Meeting of the Society for Historians of the Early American Republic, held in Knoxville, Tennessee, in July, 1986. The author is indebted to Verene Shepherd, Professors Jean Friedman, Catherine Clinton, Ann Boucher, and Robert Hall for their most helpful comments and to Professors Sylvia Frey and Clarence Mohr for permission to cite material from the papers which they presented to the Annual Meeting of the American Historical Association, held in New York City in December, 1985. Particular thanks are also due to Frederick, Charlotte, and Betsy Burin for their most generous hospitality during part of the time that this article was being prepared for publication.

[1] Although attention has been paid to various aspects of the life and labour of black women in the American South there has been a dearth of detailed studies which address the slavery experience from their perspective. For two studies which go a long way towards remedying this deficiency see Deborah Gray White, *Ar'n't I a woman? Female slaves in the plantation South* (New York, 1985) and Jacqueline Jones, *Labor of love, labor of sorrow. Black women, work, and the family from slavery to the present* (New York, 1985). Unfortunately, neither of these authors has much to say about black women in the eighteenth-century South.

[2] Barbara Bush, 'Towards emancipation: slave women and resistance to coercive labour regimes in the British West Indian colonies, 1790–1838', in David Richardson, ed., *Abolition and its aftermath. The historical context, 1790–1916* (London, 1985), pp. 27–54.

which it depended; and, finally, the post-war years witnessed the rebuilding of that economy and workforce.

Two things did not change dramatically during these years; the modes of resistance which theoretically, if not always in practice, were open to black men and women and, secondly, certain white assumptions about the institution of slavery. Few whites doubted that the Low Country's prosperity stemmed from the employment of slaves or that the ownership of land and slaves comprised the main route to economic, social, and political pre-eminence. These assumptions emerged virtually unscathed from the challenge posed by the ideas and events of the American revolution. Insofar as the white Georgians of the Revolutionary and early National periods were 'worried' about slavery then it was only in the albeit critically important sense of determining how they might ensure that the economic benefits of that institution were secured at a minimal cost to the white community.

Despite the bitter debate that had preceded the introduction of slavery into Georgia in 1751 there were, by the 1760s and 1770s, few dissenters.[3] Black dissidents, male or female, young or old, could expect little sympathy, let alone positive assistance, from any white Georgian.

I

Between 1751, when the restrictions imposed by the Trustees on land, labour and credit were finally lifted, and the mid-1770s the Georgia Low Country experienced sustained demographic and economic growth. The white population grew from less than 3,000 to roughly 18,000 whilst the black element soared from under 350 to approximately 16,000.[4] The Georgia settlers, as one of the Trustees' supporters had put it back in 1746, were 'stark Mad after Negroes'.[5]

As the Low Country became embroiled in the War for Independence this growth came to a fairly dramatic halt. Loyalist departures and wartime casualties took their toll of the white population, and possibly as many as 90 per cent of the region's slaves were removed by their Loyalist owners or the British, stolen, or managed to escape.[6] However, the vast majority of black men and women ended the war as they had begun it; as chattel slaves.

As during the colonial period so after 1783 Low Country rice planters

[3] For a recent discussion of the debate which preceded the introduction of slavery into Georgia, see Betty Wood, *Slavery in colonial Georgia, 1730–1775* (Athens, 1984), pp. 1–87.

[4] The demographic and economic growth of Georgia during the years of Royal government is dealt with by Wood, *Slavery in colonial Georgia*, pp. 89–98, 104–9 and Julia Floyd Smith *Slavery and rice culture in Low country Georgia, 1750–1860* (Knoxville, 1985), pp. 15–29, 93–100.

[5] John Dobell to the Trustees, Savannah, 11 June 1746, in Allen D. Candler and Lucian L. Knight, eds., *The Colonial records of the state of Georgia*, 26 vols. (Atlanta, 1904–16), XXIV, 72 (hereafter *Col. Recs.*).

[6] Sylvia Frey, '"Bitter fruit from the sweet stem of liberty": Georgia slavery and the American revolution' (paper presented to the Annual Meeting of the American Historical Association held in New York City, Dec., 1985), p. 13.

clamoured for slaves, now to replenish wartime losses. By 1790 Georgia's black population totalled 29,264 but, as Sylvia Frey has pointed out, 'whereas in 1775 two-thirds of Georgia's slaves lived within twenty miles of the coast, by 1790 over half of all Georgia's slaves lived in the backcountry'.[7] This infilling was to have important consequences for black resistance.

Both before and immediately after the war rice planters depended upon the African and domestic slave trades, rather than on natural increase, for the bulk of their black workers and, demographically, there were to be important similarities in the composition and structure of the pre- and post-war black populations of the Low Country.

Between 1752 and 1765 upwards of 3,000 blacks, most of whom appear to have been African-born, were brought by their owners, or shipped, to a labour-hungry Georgia from elsewhere in British America. In 1766 blacks began to be imported directly from West Africa.[8] After 1783 what Sylvia Frey has termed the 'pent-up demand' for slaves was also largely satisfied by recourse to the African slave trade.[9]

The Low Country's black population throughout this period was predominantly African-born, male, young, and unskilled. The main requirement was for workers who could undertake the arduous physical labour involved in rice and indigo cultivation and, by the 1760s, planters had a clear idea as to precisely which Africans fitted that bill. As in South Carolina, certain modes of black behaviour were associated with particular tribes and regions of West Africa.[10] But as, if not more, important was the African's age and state of health upon arrival in America. The constant plea of planters and merchants involved in the slave trade to Georgia was for 'prime Men & Women, with a few Boys & Girls, the Men and Women not exceeding twenty five years of age'.[11]

Unfortunately there is no detailed record of the sex ratios and age structure of the slave cargoes landed in Georgia during these years. However, such

[7] Ibid. p. 15.

[8] As Robert S. Glenn Jr. has observed, Georgia 'approximated the pattern of the other southern colonies in that it did not develop a direct slave trade with Africa until its economy was advanced enough to absorb cargoes of 150 to 200 slaves at a time'. Glenn, 'Slavery in Georgia, 1733–1793' (Senior thesis, Princeton University, 1972), pp. 63–4. Between 1766 and 1771, the only pre-war years for which there is detailed evidence, 2487 Africans were landed in Georgia and an unknown number of 'New Negroes' purchased by Georgia planters and merchants in the South Carolina slave markets. For discussions of the slave trade to Georgia in the eighteenth century see Wood, *Slavery in colonial Georgia*, pp. 98–104; Smith, *Slavery and rice culture*, pp. 93–8; and Darold D. Wax, '"New negroes are always in demand": the slave trade in eighteenth-century Georgia', *Georgia Historical Quarterly*, LXVIII (1984).

[9] Frey, '"Bitter fruit"', p. 14.

[10] Wood, *Slavery in colonial Georgia*, pp. 103–4; Elizabeth Donnan, 'The slave trade into South Carolina before the Revolution', *American Historical Review*, XXXIII (1928), 816–17; Daniel C. Littlefield, *Rice and slaves: ethnicity and the slave trade in colonial south Carolina* (Baton Rouge, 1981).

[11] Telfair, Cowper and Telfair to Robert Macmillan, Savannah, 2 Sept. 1773; to Thomas Wallace, Savannah, 2 Sept. 1773. Telfair papers, Item 43, Cover 2, Letterbook, 11 Aug. 1773 to 11 May 1776. Georgia Historical Society, Savannah.

evidence as there is confirms four crucial points. First, the great majority of black men and women had a knowledge, and often a recent knowledge, of freedom in Africa. In this context, the sheer novelty of Georgia's slave system as of the mid-late eighteenth century cannot be overemphasized.[12] Second, and vitally important in shaping various aspects of black life, the slave population conformed closely to the age structure specified by planters and merchants. Only 2 per cent of the 3,042 adult slaves listed on 235 colonial inventories of estates (records which, it must be said, seldom indicated the exact or even approximate ages of slaves) were said to be 'old'. The same was true of just under 5 per cent of the 1,563 men and women listed on ninety-eight inventories from Chatham County covering the years between 1776 and 1796.[13]

The last two points concern the size and sex ratios of slave-holdings in the Low Country. In neither respect was there a dramatic change between the 1760s and the end of the eighteenth century. Within a decade or so of the introduction of slavery into Georgia the Low Country already contained 'a pyramid shaped distribution of landholders with a handful of large slave-owning rice planters at the apex and small family farms with one or no slaves at the bottom', a social structure which endured down to the Civil War.[14]

At the top of this 'pyramid' 5 per cent of masters owned more than fifty slaves whilst at the other end of the spectrum 11 per cent before, and 6 per cent after, the war held just one slave. The average size of holdings increased from fifteen between 1755 and 1777 to around twenty by the turn of the century. But throughout this period as many as 70 per cent of Low Country slaves lived on estates containing more than twenty (but seldom more than fifty) slaves.[15]

In the black population as a whole, men outnumbered women. Before the war the sex ratio on the 235 estates surveyed was in the order of 148 men to every 100 women; on those drawn from Chatham County during the 1780s and 1790s it was 145 to 100. But there were significant variations. Men outnumbered women in the countryside, but the reverse appears to have been true in Savannah, as indeed it was in Charleston also.[16] In the

[12] Clarence L. Mohr, 'Slavery and Georgia's second War of Independence' (paper presented to the Annual Meeting of the American Historical Association held in New York City, Dec., 1985), p. 5.

[13] The colonial inventories are taken from Inventory Book F (1754–1771) and FF (1771–1778), Georgia Department of Archives and History, Atlanta and from the Telamon Cuyler Collection, Box 7 (special heading Georgia. Colonial. Estate Papers) and Boxes 38A and 38B (special heading Georgia. Governor. Wright, James, 1760–1776) held in the Manuscript Room, University of Georgia Library. The Chatham County inventories were consulted at the Chatham County Courthouse, Savannah.

[14] Ralph Gray and Betty Wood, 'The transition from indentured to involuntary servitude in colonial Georgia', *Explorations in Economic History*, XIII (1976), 363.

[15] Based on an analysis of the inventories cited in note 13 (above).

[16] In Savannah women outnumbered men by around 115 to 100. For a rare contemporary account of the sex ratio of Savannah's slave population see the census of 'all the people of color above the age of Fifteen in the City of Savannah' (dated 28 May 1798) in the Negro History Files, File 2: 1773–1800 folder, Georgia Department of Archives and History, Atlanta. For the sex ratio

countryside, the larger the slave-holding the larger the imbalance between the sexes.[17]

Twelve per cent of pre-war, and 5 per cent of post-war Chatham County estates contained only male slaves; those consisting only of women fell from 9 per cent before the war to around 5 per cent during the 1780s and 1790s. Men outnumbered women on 48 per cent of colonial, and 54 per cent of post-war, estates. The reverse was true of 10 and 17 per cent of holdings, respectively.

Both before and after the war numbers were equal on 17 per cent of estates. On the remaining holdings the slaves' sex was not mentioned by those compiling the inventory. Obviously these local, as well as Low Country-wide, sex ratios were to be of enormous significance in shaping patterns of black family life and, moreover, resistance.

Although the distinction between rural and urban slavery was not always clearcut, the vast majority of Low Country slaves lived and worked in the countryside on a permanent basis. Sometimes, especially on smaller estates, they might perform more than one type of work but no more than about 10–15 per cent of rural slaves were allowed, or required, to acquire skills. However, there was a crucial distinction between male and female slaves; insofar as it is possible to talk of an occupational elite, then that elite was predominantly male.

On large plantations as many as one-quarter of adult male slaves worked as artisans or as domestic servants of one sort or another. Certain skills and functions were effectively limited to men; plantation records do not reveal any women who worked as drivers, coopers, carpenters, brickmakers, and so on. Some, but by no means all, household jobs were reserved for women. On large estates upwards of 10 per cent of women were employed as cooks, maids, washerwomen, nurses, midwives, and seamstresses.[18] But even so, there was a very real sense in which black women were tied to the rice and indigo fields. Most had no specialized occupational skills such as might help them to secure

---

of Charleston's slaves see Philip D. Morgan, 'Black life in eighteenth-century Charleston', *Perspectives in American History*, new series, I, (1984), 188–9.

[17] On estates with more than twenty adult slaves the ratio of men to women was in the order of 161 to 100; on those with fewer than ten slaves it dropped to roughly 127 to 100. Based on an analysis of the inventories cited in note 13 (above). Thomas R. Statom Jr. has estimated that between 1755 and 1764 the sex ratio on all estates was 160:100 and between 1764 and 1776 134:100. His analysis is based on Inventory Books F and FF. Statom, 'Negro slavery in eighteenth-century Georgia' (unpublished Ph.D. dissertation, University of Alabama, 1982), pp. 180–1.

[18] For the occupational structure of one of colonial Georgia's largest holdings see *The Georgia Gazette*, 13 Feb. 1781, which lists the posessions of John Graham, Lieutenant-Governor of the colony. 18·5 per cent of his male slaves filled skilled or semi-skilled positions and another 7 per cent were 'Usually employed and kept around the House'. Of the women owned by Graham 23·5 per cent worked as seamstresses, washerwomen, cooks, midwives, and 'house wenches'. For the occupational structure of one of Chatham County's larger post-war holdings see the inventory of James Mackay's estate, drawn up on 1 January 1787. Seventeen, or 51·5 per cent, of Mackay's male slaves were skilled or semi-skilled. Only three, or 9 per cent, of his slave women worked as cooks (one), nurses (one), and maids (one).

an albeit precarious independence should they decide to take flight or, for that matter, take them legitimately off the plantation.

Although both the pre- and post-war demand for black women under the age of twenty five could be interpreted as an explicit interest in securing women of child-bearing age, there is no evidence that this was the case. Women were regarded primarily as workers rather than as potential mothers. Planters were certainly aware of the economic value of slave children but did not allude, at least not in print, to the reproductive capacity of black women, to their value as 'breeders'.[19]

Not least because of the continuing availability of 'surplus' slaves from the Upper South, Low Country planters, who were agitating for labour, very occasionally complaining about the low rate of natural increase of their slaves and, after the 1760s, coming under heavy external pressure to close the African slave trade, do not appear to have seriously contemplated the possibility that their labour needs might be largely, and more cheaply, satisfied were they to emulate Jamaican sugar planters and positively encourage black women to have more children.[20] Neither did they suggest that deliberate abortion or infanticide might be partially responsible for the low rate of natural increase of their slaves.

But although not making a substantial contribution to the overall growth rate of the black population natural increase, or more specifically the black partnerships and parenthood it signified, played a key role in shaping both the character and the incidence of black resistance. An essential, continuing, and often successful aspect of the struggle waged by black men and women was that of trying to ensure the integrity of their family life.

Whilst not self-consciously encouraging their slave women to 'breed', Low Country planters did take an interest in the sexual and family lives of their slaves. Many, and probably the majority, refused to grant, or impose upon, their slaves a Christian wedding ceremony but were by no means averse to the formation of monogomous relationships. They appreciated that 'such relationships [and] especially the sexual order and stability they conferred on the slave quarters, were very much to [their] advantage'.[21] They recognized, moreover, the extent to which the enforced separation of black couples, and parents from their children, comprised a powerful motive for running away. But death, indebtedness, or the prospect of profit could and did result in partnerships being broken and families torn asunder. The only small crumb of comfort

[19] None of the advertisements placed in *The Georgia Gazette* between 1763 and 1795 for the sale or hire of a slave woman, or the return of a runaway, mentioned the woman's value as a 'breeder'.

[20] For a rare contemporary comment about the rate of increase of Low Country slaves see James Habersham to William Knox, Savannah, 24 July 1772. *Collections of the Georgia Historical Society*, VI, 193–4. For late eighteenth-century Jamaican attempts to boost the rate of natural increase of the island's slave population, and the inducements offered to black women to produce more children, see Betty Wood and Roy Clayton, 'Slave birth, death and disease on Golden Grove Plantation, Jamaica, 1765–1810', *Slavery and Abolition*, VI (1985), 99–121.

[21] Wood, *Slavery in colonial Georgia*, p. 155.

offered to black mothers was that in all probability they would not be separated from their children before the latter reached the age of seven or eight.[22]

How much choice black men and women had in their selection of a marriage partner is debatable. Masters were not keen on their slaves leaving the plantation for any reason, including visits to a spouse, and it is probable that, sex ratios and age structure permitting, wedlock usually involved slaves who lived on the same estate.[23] Inventories give no indication of how, when, and why particular partnerships were formed, but they do offer some revealing insights into the incidence of slave marriage, black parenthood, and the separation of couples.

Of the 738 women listed on those colonial inventories which recorded marital and familial relationships, 196 were married and living with their husbands – 18 per cent of the men on those estates. 112, or 57 per cent, of these couples had at least one child who lived with them. The remainder either had no children or had been separated from them: it is impossible to tell which. Women known to have given birth to at least one child totalled 272, but 59 per cent of these mothers appear not to have had a husband, or the father of their children, living with them at the time the inventory was taken. There is no way of knowing whether the men in question were dead, living on a neighbouring estate, or had been sold away. Only 7 men (less than 1 per cent of those on the estates surveyed) lived 'alone' with their child or children.

A similar pattern characterized Chatham County in the 1780s and 1790s. Almost exactly one-third of the women on those estates where marital and familial relationships were recorded were married; their husbands accounted for 24 per cent of the men on these holdings. Two-thirds of the 188 couples listed had at least one child living with them. Fractionally under 42 per cent of women are known to have given birth at least once, and 47 per cent of these mothers (a drop of 12 per cent on the pre-war figure) lived 'alone' with their offspring. The same was true of 2 per cent of men.

The salient points to be drawn from this data would seem to be these; somewhere between one-quarter and one-third of Low Country slaves had no reason to take flight in search of their spouse. But roughly half the women known to have been mothers appear to have been living apart from their husbands. For both partners separation, however close or distant, provided a compelling reason to run away. But for mothers, especially of young children, even if they knew where their husband was living, and how to reach him, running away could prove problematical. Some mothers elected to take their

[22] Klaus G. Loewald, Beverly Starika, and Paul S. Taylor, trans. and eds., 'Johann Martin Bolzius answers a questionnaire on Carolina and Georgia', *William and Mary Quarterly*, 3rd ser., XIV (1958), 236, 256. An analysis of newspaper advertisements, wills, and miscellaneous bonds (which recorded the transfer of slaves by deed of gift and sale) strongly suggests that this practice continued throughout the period under consideration here.

[23] Wood, *Slavery in colonial Georgia*, p. 156.

21-2

children with them; virtually none were prepared to abandon them in the hope of thereby facilitating their own escape.[24]

Slave mothers did not lack the will to run away in search of their husbands, or permanent freedom, but were often obliged, or felt themselves obliged, to express their discontent by malingering and feigning illness rather than by absconding. The torment of separation was no less severe for slave husbands and fathers, but the circumstances of that separation often meant that when contemplating whether or not to take flight in search of their loved ones they were not confronted by the same logistical problems faced by the mothers of their children.

Many factors shaped the character and frequency of slave resistance in the Georgia Low Country between the early 1760s and 1815 but, in the final analysis, the decision as to whether, when, and how to resist rested with the individual slave. Unfortunately, a dearth of first-hand black evidence means that to some degree motives and the process of decision-making must remain matters for speculation. However, the one thing which made absolutely no difference whatsoever in determining the will to resist was the slave's sex. Women, just as much as men, could hope to run away, fire a gun, and destroy property. But did they so decide in the same numbers as men? If not, why not?

II

Between 1755 and 1770 the Georgia Assembly enacted a series of increasingly repressive laws designed to regulate the institution of slavery.[25] These laws, like those of the other Southern colonies, were predicated not on the belief that Africans were docile, submissive creatures but, on the contrary, that each and every one of them was a potential rebel. There was no suggestion in the slave codes that black women might behave differently from, or present a lesser threat than, black men. Neither was any provision made for the lighter punishment of female offenders.

Georgia's slave laws enumerated the kinds of black misconduct serious enough to warrant public attention. Capital crimes included insurrection and attempted insurrection, murder, assault, the destruction of certain types of property and, after 1770, the rape, or attempted rape, of a white woman. Capital courts were instructed to select 'such manner of Death' as would be

[24] Between 1763 and 1775 six of the female runaways advertised in *The Georgia Gazette* took at least one of their children with them. The same was true of eight women who ran away between 1783 and 1795. Another six women, who absconded with men who might or might not have been their husbands, also took children with them. The only advertised runaway between 1763 and 1795 said to have abandoned one of her children was Hannah, who ran away in 1786. Hannah's owner, Martha M. Melven, commented that although she had taken her daughter Lydia, 'about five years old', she had 'inhumanly' left 'a child at her breast'. Hannah had 'extensive acquaintances...in and around Savannah', and her mistress believed that she was being 'harboured by some ill-intentioned person'. *The Georgia Gazette*, 20 Apr. 1786.

[25] For a discussion of the framing and content of Georgia's slave laws see Wood, *Slavery in colonial Georgia*, pp. 110–30.

'most Effectual to deter others', and most opted for death by hanging or burning. Non-capital crimes, for which convicted slaves could expect to be whipped, included such offences as petty theft, being absent without a ticket, and working without a badge.[26]

The punishment of those misdeeds which comprised 'day to day resistance' was left to the discretion of individual owners. But the slave codes offered some guidelines. The castration, cutting out the tongue, putting out an eye, scalding, or burning a slave was deemed to be excessive 'Cruelty'; acceptable punishments included 'whipping or beating with a Horse Whip Cow Skin Switch or Small Stick', 'Putting Irons on', and imprisonment.[27] Beginning in 1763 those owners who, for whatever the reason, did not wish to whip their slaves themselves could obtain this service for a modest fee at the Savannah Workhouse.[28]

The mode of resistance which white Georgians feared above all others, organized rebellion on a scale which threatened to topple their society, was that which by the 1760s and 1770s was least likely to occur.[29] The most serious outbreak of slave violence in the Low Country between 1763 and 1815 occurred in St Andrew Parish in 1774 when eleven 'New Negroes' and a country-born slave killed four whites. The group was soon taken up, and the two men deemed to be the ringleaders burned alive.[30] This 'revolt' had a significance out of all proportion to the numbers involved; it reminded white Georgians of the need for constant vigilance and black slaves of the gruesome fate which awaited unsuccessful rebels. But in the present context it is also significant that two of the participants were women. We know nothing about them, not even their names. Yet their involvement suggests that far from being placid 'workhorses' some black women were prepared to kill, and run the risk of being killed in the most brutal fashion, in order to secure their freedom.

The failure of Georgia's black men and women to mount a rebellion during this period, and especially during the War for Independence when, on the face of it, the Low Country's white society was peculiarly vulnerable, should not be taken to mean that they were so psychologically devastated by their experience of slavery that they had given up all hope of regaining the freedom which so many of them had known in Africa. But by the 1760s and 1770s there were already virtually insurmountable obstacles to the launching of such uprisings, obstacles that were not significantly diminished by the onset of war

[26] Ibid. 120–2, 124–7, 129.

[27] AN ACT For the better Ordering and Governing Negroes and other Slaves in this Province. March, 1755. *Col. Recs.*, XVIII, 131–5.

[28] AN ACT For Regulating a Work House, for the Custody and Punishment of Negroes. April, 1763, ibid. 558–66. The Act permitted owners to send their 'stubborn, obstinate or incorrigible Negroes' to the workhouse, where they would be 'kept to hard Labour or otherwise...corrected'. Owners would be charged 6*d*. per diem for their upkeep and an additional 'one Shilling and fourpence for each Chastisement'.

[29] For white fears of organized slave rebellions, and the difficulties confronting would-be black rebels, see Wood, *Slavery in colonial Georgia*, pp. 125–8, 188–98.

[30] The only contemporary account of the St Andrew Parish 'revolt' is in *The Georgia Gazette*, 7 Dec. 1774.

and which were added to by the rapid infilling of the Backcountry during the post-war years.[31]

During the War blacks saw the British, who elsewhere in the mainland had shown their willingness to arm male slaves belonging to Patriots, as offering them the best prospect of freedom. But, as Sylvia Frey has argued, the wholesale emancipation of Georgia's slaves was never regarded by the British as a viable, or even as a wholly desirable, possibility.[32] On the Patriot side, the Laurens Plan, which envisaged freeing a maximum of 4,000 male slaves in South Carolina and Georgia, was a virtual non-starter in both states.[33]

An unknown number of black men and women took advantage of wartime dislocations not to rebel but to run away – if not to the British then to the Backcountry or into the coastal and river swamps. For most, that freedom was to prove both tenuous and temporary. Yet at least one of the runaway communities established in the river swamps not too distant from Savannah managed to survive until the mid-1780s, supporting itself partly by growing its own foodstuffs and partly by raiding outlying plantations. As white Georgians appreciated, such a community, if allowed to persist, would attract other slaves and possibly come to comprise the nucleus of the large scale rebellion which they so feared.

This community, which contained 'a number of women', was organized along strict military lines under the leadership of Lewis and Sharper, the latter referring to himself as 'Captain Cudjoe'. In this community the women 'planted rice' and 'stayed in Camp'. When the settlement was attacked by whites in 1787 'all' the women, by their own account, were 'ordered...in the Canes' by their menfolk and took no part in the fighting which resulted in the death of 'Captain Cudjoe' and the capture of Lewis. How many managed to remain at large is uncertain. Two of those who were taken up testified at Lewis's trial, whether voluntarily or under duress is debatable.[34]

In effect, the war years witnessed and facilitated not organized rebellion but the amplification of what was undoubtedly the most common expression of black rage and black despair; running away. Although by no means indicative of the total number of runaways, newspaper advertisements provide the best source of information about this mode of black behaviour.

During the thirteen years before the War for Independence advertisements

[31] Frey, '"Bitter Fruit"', pp. 14–15.

[32] Ibid. passim.

[33] For a discussion of the Laurens Plan and its reception in South Carolina and Georgia see Donald Robinson, *Slavery in the structure of American politics, 1765–1820* (New York, 1979), pp. 118–20.

[34] There had been runaway communities in the colonial period which greatly alarmed white Georgians. For the 'depradations' committed by the members of these communities, and white attempts to root them out, see *Col. Recs.*, XIV, 292–3. For a description of the post-war community headed by Lewis and 'Captain Cudjoe' see 'Trial of Negroe Man Slave Named Lewis the Property of Oliver Bowen for the Murder of John Casper Hersman, Robbing Philip Ulsmer, John Lowerman of Ga. & Col. Borquin of South Carolina, 1787', in Slave File, Telamon Cuyler Collection, Manuscript Room, University of Georgia Library. Lewis was sentenced to death.

Table 1. *The destinations of slave runaways, 1763–75*

Destination	Men	Women	Country-born	African-born	New Negro	Unknown	Total
In, near, or heading for Savannah	31	5	13	3	3	17	36
To family, friends, former residence	11	1	5	—	1	6	12
Harboured/hiding out in countryside	3	2	—	—	—	5	5
Master uncertain, assumes in Georgia	24	2	3	10	5	8	26
Will try to pass as free	10	—	3	1	—	6	10
Will try to escape by sea; heading for coast (other than ports)	16	4	1	2	10	7	20
To Backcountry; Indian Nation; going 'upriver'	15	1	2	—	—	14	16
To coast *or* Backcountry	3	3	—	—	6	—	6
To join other runaways	5	2	—	—	6	1	7
Other							
'Southerly'	1	—	—	—	—	1	1
Savannah *or* Carolina	1	—	—	—	—	1	1
Killed slave	1	—	—	—	—	1	1
Killed overseer	1	—	—	—	—	1	1
'Northward'	3	1	—	—	—	4	4
South Carolina	1	—	1	—	—	—	1
Harboured/stolen by white person	—	1	—	—	—	1	1
Total	126	22	28	16	31	73	148

for 453 runaways were placed in Georgia's only newspaper, *The Georgia Gazette*. Between 1783 and 1795 the same newspaper contained advertisements for 528 adult fugitives. The imbalance between the numbers of male and female runaways is immediately apparent. In the pre-war period only 61, or 13 per cent, were women; a proportion which increased to fractionally over 24 per cent between 1783 and 1795. These proportions did not reflect a similar sex ratio in the black population as a whole. Peter Wood has suggested that women were 'more likely than men to visit...and return of their own accord

Table 2. *The destinations of slave runaways, 1783–1795*

Destination	Men	Women	Country-born	African-born	New Negro	Unknown	Total
In, near, or heading for Savannah	35	20	13	1	—	41	55
To family, friends, former residence	33	8	8	2	—	31	41
Harboured/hiding out in countryside	53	19	9	6	3	54	72
Will try to pass as free	14	—	8	—	—	6	14
Will try to escape by sea; heading for coast (other than ports)	7	—	—	2	1	4	7
To Backcountry; Indian Nation; going 'upriver'	15	5	1	5	—	14	20
To join other runaways	7	—	2	1	2	2	7
Florida	7	1	1	2	—	5	8
Indian Nation *or* Florida	5	—	—	1	—	4	5
South Carolina	9	1	3	1	—	6	10
Other							
Skidaway	2	—	—	—	—	2	2
Ebenezer	1	—	—	—	—	1	1
Waynesborough	1	—	—	—	—	1	1
Tybee	1	—	—	—	1	—	1
'Southward'	1	—	—	—	—	1	1
South Carolina *or* Backcountry	1	—	—	—	—	1	1
Countryside *or* Florida	—	1	—	—	—	1	1
Carolina *or* Savannah	—	1	—	—	—	1	1
Total	192	56	45	21	7	175	248

in a pattern less likely to prompt public advertising',[35] and it is probable that, not least because of the constraints imposed by motherhood and occupation, this was indeed the case.

Less readily explained is the virtual doubling of advertisements for female runaways between 1783 and 1795. The available evidence offers no neat

[35] Peter H. Wood, *Black majority: negroes in colonial south Carolina from 1670 through the Stono rebellion* (New York, 1974), p. 241.

explanation. However, two possibilities lend themselves to consideration. First, it is conceivable that, mainly because of wartime dislocations and separations, more women were actually running away. Second, owners might have been more willing to advertise for the return of their female slaves, especially during the immediate post-war years when they were particularly hard-pressed for workers.

Broadly speaking, slaves ran away in order to be reunited with their family and friends; to join up with bands of fugitive slaves; to escape to the Backcountry, possibly in the hope of being harboured by Indians; or headed for, or remained in, Savannah, either with a view to blending into the black 'urban crowd' or making their escape by sea (see Tables 1 and 2). Men might have predominated among the advertised runaways but, with one or two exceptions, the proportions of men and women making for each of these destinations did not differ dramatically.

The destinations and motives of 305 (or 67 per cent) of colonial runaways were not mentioned by those placing the advertisement. Of the remainder (126 men and 22 women), fractionally under 25 per cent of men, and just over 22 per cent of women, were said to be in, near, or heading for Savannah (see Table 1). Another 41 slaves were said to be 'well known' in that town and its environs. Eight per cent of male runaways, and just 1 woman, were believed to be making their way to a member of their family (usually their spouse), a friend or friends, or back to a previous owner. The same proportion of men, but no women, were thought to be trying to pass as free blacks. This might involve eking out a precarious living in Savannah or attempting to escape by sea from the port of Savannah. Four women (18 per cent of those whose destination was mentioned) and 13 per cent of men were said quite specifically by their owners or overseers to be trying to do the latter. Another 12 per cent of men, and one woman, were thought to be making for the Backcountry, presumably also with a view to securing their permanent freedom from bondage.[34]

The destinations of runaways did not change dramatically after the War for Independence (see Table 2). In 53 per cent of cases owners and overseers did not mention the likely destination of their slaves. In the remaining cases (192 men and 56 women) 18 per cent of men, and 35 per cent of women, were thought to be in, or making for, Savannah. According to their owners, another 41 male, and 18 female, runaways were 'well known' in the town. One-third of the female fugitives whose destination was mentioned, and just over 27 per cent of men, were thought to be 'harboured', or hiding out, in the countryside. Roughly the same proportion of men (17 per cent) and women (14 per cent) were believed to be trying to reach a relation, friend, or former owner. The Backcountry still attracted some runaways; 7 per cent of men, and 8 per cent of women, were said to be making for the 'Upcountry' or the 'Indian Nation'. Fourteen, or 7 per cent, of male fugitives, but no women, were thought to be

[34] For a detailed discussion of black runaways in colonial Georgia see Wood, *Slavery in colonial Georgia*, pp. 169–87.

trying to pass as free blacks. As during the colonial period, other destinations, usually in Georgia and South Carolina, continued to attract smaller numbers of runaways.

A slave's sex, marital status, occupational experience, and place of residence all helped to define the options that were open to would-be runaways. But as important throughout this period was the slave's birthplace and, if African-born, the length of time spent in America.

During these years the Low Country's slave population remained predominantly African-born but, just as significant, contained a high proportion of 'New Negroes'. All the available evidence suggests that the behaviour of this population both before and immediately after the War for Independence conformed closely to that predicated by Mullin for eighteenth-century Virginia.[37]

'New Negroes', male and female, whether 'out of a sense of shock and bewilderment...or a more aggressive intent to escape' tried to 'put as many miles as they could between themselves and their owners and...to avoid contact with whites'.[38] Newly imported Africans, who often absconded in groups which shared a common African origin, spoke little or no English and at best had only a hazy knowledge of the Georgia landscape. Although at least one party, including a woman, set off in the hope of finding their way back to Africa,[39] most must have taken flight with little idea of their ultimate destination or even of what awaited outside the immediate confines of their owner's estate.

Their linguistic ability, and greater knowledge of the white world, opened up possibilities for country-born and acculturated blacks which were effectively closed to 'New Negroes'. For example, an awareness of the existence of Savannah or Charleston offered the prospect of some degree of personal autonomy as well as the possibility of escape by sea. The ability to speak English, and the realization that there was an albeit minute free black community in Georgia,[40] meant that there was some chance of passing as free and, if apprehended, of talking one's way out of trouble.

But even for those country-born and acculturated women who were not, or who did not feel themselves to be, constrained by maternal responsibilities there could be additional constraints imposed by their sex and occupational experience. For example, even if a woman, unhindered by small children, made her way to Savannah, without some help from family or friends it could prove immensely difficult for her to survive. Despite the regulations governing

[37] Gerald W. Mullin, *Flight and rebellion: slave resistance in eighteenth-century Virginia* (New York, 1972), passim.

[38] Wood, *Slavery in colonial Georgia*, p. 180.

[39] The fate of this group is unknown, but their overseer thought it 'probable' that those concerned would 'keep along shore and be taken up either to the southward or northward of Savannah'. *The Georgia Gazette*, 25 Jan. 1775.

[40] In 1790 there were 398 free blacks in the 'District of Georgia', of whom 180 lived in Wilkes County and 112 in Chatham County. 'Census of the District of Georgia', *The Augusta Chronicle*, 5 Nov. 1791.

the hire of slaves, unskilled men could hope to find casual employment as porters and carters without too many questions being asked of them.[41] Similarly, some whites would employ skilled male slaves even if they knew, or suspected, that they were fugitives. At best, all that unskilled women could hope for was occasional work as washerwomen and domestics. But even then, it was most unlikely that an 'unknown' slave would be taken into a white household, at least on a permanent basis, without some recommendation from a previous employer.

Black women, be they from the town or countryside, might have had sufficient English to try and pass as free but, unlike men, they could not easily use Savannah as a springboard for escape by sea. Male slaves, who could often quite legitimately claim 'a knowledge of the sea', might be taken on as crew by ships' captains who were not too fussy about those they employed as sailors. This did not mean that escape by sea was totally impossible for women. But what it did mean was that women like Flora, said by her owner to be 'harboured under the Bluff by Sailors', had to devise different stratagems if they were to make good their escape.[42]

The published advertisements for runaways give some indication of the courage, resourcefulness, and determination displayed by black men and women alike. Fugitives adopted different names and, whenever possible, changed their clothing in the hope of thereby avoiding detection. If challenged, they might try to pass as a free black. Even when identified as a runaway, some women refused to give up without a struggle. They may not have had the physical strength to overpower their captors but, if the opportunity presented itself, they seized the opportunity to escape. Sometimes this meant taking flight again in leg irons or handcuffs.[43] On at least one occasion some female runaways joined with male slaves in breaking out of Savannah Gaol.[44]

If organized rebellion was the most feared, and running away the most common, mode of resistance what about the other offences itemized in the slave codes? What was the incidence of such capital crimes as murder, assault, and arson and ostensibly less serious, but for whites often extremely worrying, offences such as theft, drunkenness, and being absent without a ticket?

The scanty evidence that has survived from the colonial period suggests that no more than about a dozen white Georgians met their deaths at the hands of slaves and that between 1766 and 1774 a minimum of seventeen slaves were

[41] For legislation regulating the hiring out and casual employment of slaves see Wood, *Slavery in colonial Georgia*, pp. 131–2, 142–5.

[42] *The Georgia Gazette*, 13 July 1774, 24 May 1775.

[43] See for example ibid. 4 Apr. 1764.

[44] The break-out in question occurred on 7 Oct. 1789 and involved five men and two women. Both women, Satira, who belonged to Levi Sheftall, and Eve, who was owned by Dr Beecroft, were said to be 'well known in and about Savannah', and no further description was given. One of the men, Tom, who belonged to Matthew McCallister, had 'a large iron on one leg' and another, a boy named Charles, was said to have 'lost one leg'. It is not clear from the published account precisely how they managed to engineer their escape or how long they remained at large. *The Georgia Gazette*, 8 Oct. 1789.

executed for crimes which included murder, attempted murder, arson, robbery, and attempted insurrection. The lists of payments made to owners of executed slaves do not always indicate the slave's sex. However, it appears that at least one black woman, 'a household Negress', was burned alive after having been convicted of attempting to poison her owner, Pastor Rabenhorst, and his wife.[45] There is no evidence that the pastor interceded on her behalf by, for example, petitioning the Royal Governor to commute her death sentence to deportation.

The colonial evidence concerning non-capital crimes is even thinner. No court records have survived (assuming that written records were kept) and contemporary accounts and complaints about such offences as theft seldom referred to the perpetrators' sex. Arguably the most complete evidence concerning the incidence of both capital and non-capital crimes in the post-war period comes in the form of the Savannah Gaol Book, a volume which lists the name, owner, place of residence, and alleged offence of every slave lodged in the gaol between April 1809 and May 1815. It also indicates the length of time each slave spent in prison, the number who escaped, and those who died.[46]

Obviously it would be foolish to extrapolate from the Gaol Book, which lists just under 3,800 offences, a pattern of black behaviour which characterized the years between 1763 (or even 1783) and 1815 or, for that matter, the Low Country as a whole. The black inmates of Savannah Gaol during these six years came from many different parts of Georgia and South Carolina, but around 84 per cent of male offences, and 92 per cent of female offences, were committed by slaves who were, or had owners who were, resident in Savannah. But even so, the Gaol Book offers unique insights into the range of offences committed by black men and women as well as into the role assigned to prisons in the attempt to maintain racial discipline.

Three features of the material contained in the Gaol Book are particularly noteworthy; the total number of slaves who were taken, or sent, to prison; the imbalance between the number of male and female inmates; and, finally, what appears to have been a relatively low incidence of capital crimes. (Low, that is, in the context of the anxieties expressed by white Georgians.)

As far as can be ascertained, at least 3,048 different slaves (2,366 men and 682 women) were taken to Savannah Gaol at least once during this six-year period.[47] For men and women alike, the two most common reasons for imprisonment were running away and 'safe-keeping'; together they accounted for around 86 per cent of all the offences recorded in the Gaol Book.

[45] Theodore G. Tappert and John W. Doberstein, trans. and eds., *The journals of Henry Melchior Muhlenberg*, 2 vols. (Philadelphia, 1942, 1958), II, 575, 576.

[46] The Gaol Book (which is unpaginated) is in the possession of the Georgia Historical Society, Savannah.

[47] There is no sure way of knowing how many of these slaves might have changed hands between 1809 and 1815. Also, on some larger holdings it was not unusual to find more than one slave with the same name.

Table 3. *The length of time spent by black slaves in Savannah Gaol, April 1809 to May 1815 (all offences)*

	Men		Women		All slaves	
Time in gaol	*n*	%	*n*	%	*n*	%
Released on same day	861	29·35	245	29·55	1,106	29·39
One night	364	11·79	108	13·02	472	12·54
2–6 nights	693	23·62	190	22·91	883	23·47
7–13 nights	282	9·61	91	10·97	373	9·91
14–20 nights	169	5·76	44	5·30	213	5·66
21–27 nights	114	3·88	25	3·01	139	3·69
28 or more nights	325	11·08	93	11·21	418	11·11
Not mentioned/unknown	125	4·26	33	3·98	158	4·19
Total	2,933	—	829	—	3,762	—

'Safe-keeping' was cited as the reason for the imprisonment of 59 per cent of men and 60 per cent of women. Slaves could be committed to gaol by their owners (which was the case with 47 per cent of the men and 51 per cent of the women imprisoned for 'safe-keeping') for three main reasons; for corporal punishment, prior to sale, or because adequate supervision could not be provided for them. Unfortunately the Gaol Book does not distinguish clearly between them.

Obviously, imprisonment, for whatever reason, meant the loss of often valuable workers, and most owners were reluctant to keep their slaves in gaol for longer than was absolutely necessary. Thus 17 per cent of the men, and 20 per cent of the women, sent to prison for 'safe-keeping' by their owners were released on the same day; 43 per cent of men, and 40 per cent of women, spent less than one week in gaol. Only 11 per cent of men, and 4 per cent of women, were kept in prison for more than a month by their owners.

A quarter of all the offences (male and female) listed in the Gaol Book related to slaves who had been picked up by the Savannah Watch or one of the rural slave patrols and taken to prison for 'safe-keeping'. In the majority of cases (60 per cent of men and 59 per cent of women) the slave was released on the same day, apparently without having been either charged or punished.

The rest of the slaves who were sent, or taken, to prison for 'safe-keeping' were committed either by individuals other than their owners or as the result of various legal orders. Although, in each category of 'safe-keeping', men outnumbered women, there was little difference in the length of time that they spent in gaol. Much the same was true of the other offences mentioned in the Gaol Book (see Table 3).

Ever since 1763 Savannah's Workhouse and Gaol had played a central role in the processing of black runaways. Fugitives who could not be identified, or who refused to identify themselves, were interned, advertised and, if not reclaimed, sold at public auction to recoup the cost of their imprisonment.[48]

Between 1809 and 1815 runaways accounted for around one-quarter of all the offences (male and female) listed in the Gaol Book. It is of note, however, that apprehended runaways were distributed fairly evenly over this six-year period. Although, as Clarence Mohr has argued, Low Country blacks made their way to the British forces during the War of 1812 in the hope of securing their freedom, this was not reflected in a dramatic upsurge in the number of fugitives taken to Savannah Gaol during the months when the British were operating off the Georgia coast.[49]

Clearly, the length of time that runaways spent in prison depended upon how long it took their owners to reclaim them. But the gaol served a second function in respect of runaways; slaves who had taken flight and been recaptured might be sent there by their owners in the hope that a harsh prison regime might persuade them of the error of their ways. At least 56 slaves (47 men and 9 women) were gaoled by their owners. Most spent less than a week in prison (which suggests corporal punishment) and only four men spent more than a month there.

The extent to which imprisonment, and the corporal punishment which it might have entailed, deterred slaves from running away again, or committing other offences, is difficult to determine. All that can be said with certainty is that at least 450 slaves (361 men and 89 women) who between them had committed, or who were believed to have committed, 1,164 offences (928 by men and 236 by women) were sent, or taken, to Savannah Gaol at least twice between 1809 and 1815.

It seems that no slave was taken to prison more often than Nancy, a woman who belonged to a Mr Gotong. She found herself in gaol on no less than eleven occasions during this six-year period; for running away (eight times) and for 'safe-keeping' (imprisoned once by her owner and twice by the Savannah Watch). Altogether she spent six weeks in gaol. Another woman, Nanny, who ran away eight times was in prison for a total of two months.[50] Sally, who was owned by a Mr Driscoll, was committed to gaol seven times between July, 1809 and December, 1814; for running away (twice), for 'safe-keeping' (four times) and for working without a badge (once). As far as can be ascertained, only one man, Adam, who was owned by a Mr Hulet, was taken to gaol eight times and none appear to have surpassed Nancy's record.

As mentioned above, roughly 86 per cent of the offences cited in the Gaol Book had to do either with running away or with 'safe-keeping'. Of the remainder, 3·6 per cent reflected on offence (usually indebtedness) on the part of the owner rather than the slave. At least 137 slaves (96 men and 41 women) were imprisoned through no fault of their own. These slaves, together with

[48] See note 28 (above). Virtually every issue of *The Georgia Gazette* between 1763 and 1795 carried an advertisement for runaways whose owners could not be identified.

[49] Mohr, 'Slavery and Georgia's Second War of Independence', pp. 5–6.

[50] Nanny was owned by Mary Barnet.

Table 4. *The length of time spent by black slaves in Savannah Gaol for running away and the indebtedness of their owners*

Time in gaol	Men *n*	Men %	Women *n*	Women %	All slaves *n*	All slaves %	All offences (%)
(A) Running away (excluding those runaways committed to gaol by their owners)							
Released on same day	109	14·78	31	14·76	140	14·78	29·39
1 night	78	10·58	29	13·80	107	11·29	12·54
2–6 nights	199	27·00	57	27·14	256	27·03	23·47
7–13 nights	98	13·29	36	17·14	134	14·14	9·91
14–20 nights	74	10·04	18	8·57	92	9·71	5·66
21–27 nights	35	4·74	7	3·33	42	4·43	3·69
28 or more nights	110	14·92	19	9·04	129	13·62	11·11
Not mentioned/unknown	34	4·61	13	6·19	47	4·96	4·19
Total	737	—	210	—	947	—	—
(B) Indebtedness							
Released on same day	3	3·12	1	2·43	4	2·91	29·39
1 night	4	4·16	5	12·19	9	6·56	12·54
2–6 nights	15	15·62	2	4·87	17	12·40	23·47
7–13 nights	5	5·20	3	7·31	8	5·83	9·91
14–21 nights	3	3·12	—	—	3	2·18	5·66
21–27 nights	16	16·66	3	7·31	19	13·86	3·69
28 or more nights	43	44·79	24	58·53	67	48·90	11·11
Not mentioned/unknown	7	7·29	3	7·31	10	7·29	4·19
Total	96	—	41	—	137	—	

those runaways whose owners could not be readily identified, were liable to spend the longest time in gaol (see Tables 3 and 4).

With one or two exceptions, the remaining non-capital offences involved fewer than ten slaves each. They ranged from 'drunkenness' (one man), 'impertinance' and 'abuse' (three women), and 'fighting' (two men) to harbouring runaways (two men and two women) and working without a badge (eighteen men and eighteen women). Virtually none of these offences could be described as exclusively, or typically, 'male' or 'female' in character.

Less than 1 per cent of the offences mentioned in the Gaol Book were capital crimes. There were 5 men awaiting trial or execution for murder, 2 for attempted murder, and 3 for arson; 9 were suspected, or had been found guilty of, assault and 125 of theft, offences which, under certain circumstances, might have been capital crimes. In most instances, however, release dates were given indicating non-capital, as opposed to capital, offences. No women were in prison on charges of murder or attempted murder; one was accused of assault and another of arson. Twenty-two were thought to have committed theft.

What on the face of it appears to have been a relatively low incidence of violent crimes, especially by women, should not be construed as evidence of black, or female, docility. All slaves, men and women, knew full well the penalty for such offences; to commit them, and to be caught, was 'tantamount to committing suicide and, understandably, this was a path which few chose to follow'.[51] But, as Eugene Genovese has argued, it was the fact, rather than the actual number, of violent crimes against white persons and their property which was so significant.[52] The murder or attempted murder of just one white person, the burning down of just one house 'served to reinforce white fears and to remind [whites] of the arbitrary and often unpredictable violence that might be indulged in by any of their slaves'.[53]

Largely through an often difficult process of trial and error, black men and women in the Georgia Low Country learned how they might assert themselves and their individuality in ways which did not invite barbaric retribution. To some degree, the options open to women, who did not lack the will and determination to resist, were restricted if not by their sex *per se* then by motherhood and occupational experience. But overt resistance was not the sole preserve of black men. Black women, albeit in smaller numbers, also rebelled, rioted, and ran away. There were those like Nancy, Nanny and Sally who, regardless of the floggings, irons, and imprisonment which was their lot, refused to submit, refused to be broken, but continued to offer resistance of the most stubborn and uncompromising kind.

[51] Wood, *Slavery in colonial Georgia*, p. 198.
[52] Eugene D. Genovese, *Roll, Jordan Roll: The world the slaves made* (London, 1975), pp. 616–17.
[53] Wood, *Slavery in colonial Georgia*, p. 197.

Acknowledgments

Dorothy Burnham, "Children of the Slave Community in the United States," *Freedomways* 19 (1979): 75–81. Reprinted by permission of *Freedomways*.

Catherine Clinton, "Caught in the Web of the Big House: Women and Slavery," in Walter J. Raser, Jr., R. Frank Saunders, Jr., and Lon L. Wakelyn, *The Web of Southern Social Relations: Women, Family & Education* (1985) 19–34. Reprinted by permission of the University of Georgia Press.

Catherine Clinton, "Fanny Kemble's Journal: A Woman Confronts Slavery on a Georgia Plantation," *Frontiers* 9 (1987): 74–79. Reprinted by permission of *Frontiers*.

Maria Diedrich, "'My Love is Black as Yours is Fair': Premarital Love and Sexuality in the Antebellum Slave Narrative," *Phylon* 47 (Fall 1987): 238–247. Reprinted by permission of *Phylon*.

E. Franklin Frazier, "The Negro Slave Family," *Journal of Negro History* 15, No. 1 (1930): 198–259. Reprinted by permission of the *Journal of Negro History*.

Robert W. Fogel and Stanley L. Engerman, "Recent Findings in the Study of Slave Demography and Family Structure," *Sociology and Social Research* 63 (1979): 566–589. Reprinted by permission of *Sociology and Social Research*.

Joan Rezner Gundersen, "The Double Bonds of Race and Sex: Black and White Women in a Colonial Virginia Parish," *Journal of Southern History* 52 (August 1986): 351–372. Reprinted by permission of the *Journal of Southern History*.

Herbert G. Gutman, "Slave Culture and Slave Family and Kin Network: The Importance of Time," *South Atlantic Urban Studies* 2 (1978): 73–88. Reprinted by permission of *South Atlantic Urban Studies*.

Michael P. Johnson, "Smothered Slave Infants: Were Slave Mothers at Fault?" *Journal of Southern History* 47 (November 1981): 493–520. Reprinted by permission of the *Journal of Southern History*.

Jacqueline Jones, "'My Mother Was Much of a Woman': Black Women, Work, and the Family Under Slavery," *Feminist Studies* 8, No. 2 (1982): 235–269. Reprinted by permission of the publisher *Feminist Studies*, Inc., c/o Women's Studies Program, University of Maryland, College Park, MD 20742.

Charles W. Joyner, "The Creolization of Slave Folklife: All Saints Parish, South Carolina, As A Test Case," *Historical Reflections/Réflexions Historiques* 6, No. 2, (Winter 1979): 435–453. Reprinted by permission of *Historical Reflections/Re'flexions Historiques.*

Allan Kulikoff, "The Beginnings of the Afro-American Family in Maryland," in Aubrey Land, ed., *Law, Society and Politics in Early Maryland* (Baltimore: Johns Hopkins, 1977): 171–196. Reprinted by permission.

Suzanne Lebsock, "Free Black Women and the Question of Matriarchy: Petersburg, Virginia, 1784–1820." *Feminist Studies* 8 (1982): 271–292. Reprinted by permission of the publisher *Feminist Studies*, Inc., c/o Women's Studies Program, University of Maryland, College Park, MD 20742.

Ronald L. Lewis, "Slave Families at Early Chesapeake Ironworks" *Virginia Magazine of History and Biography* 86 (1978): 169–179. Reprinted by permission of *Virginia Magazine of History and Biography.*

Ann Patton Malone, "Searching for the Family and Household Structure of Rural Louisiana Slaves, 1810–1864." *Louisiana History* 28 (Fall 1987): 357–379. Reprinted by permission of *Louisiana History.*

Todd L. Savitt, "Smothering and Overlaying of Virginia Slave Children: A Suggested Explanation," *Bulletin of the History of Medicine* 49, No. (1975): 400–404.

Judith K. Schafer, "'Open and Notorious Concubinage': The Emancipation of Slave Mistresses by Will and the Supreme Court in Antebellum Louisiana," *Louisiana History* 28 (Spring 1987): 165–182. Reprinted by permission of *Louisiana History.*

Loren Schweninger, "A Slave Family in the Ante Bellum South," *Journal of Negro History* 60, No. 1 (1975): 29–44. Reprinted by permission of the *Journal of Negro History.*

Orville W. Taylor, "'Jumping the Broomstick': Slave Marriage and Morality in Arkansas," *Arkansas Historical Quarterly* 17 (1958) 217–231. Reprinted by permission of the *Arkansas Historical Quarterly.*

Deborah G. White, "Female Slaves: Sex Roles and Status in the Antebellum Plantation South," *Journal of Family History* 8 (Fall 1983): 248–261. Reprinted by permission of the *Journal of Family History.*

David K. Wiggins, "The Play of Slave Children in the Plantation Communities of the Old South, 1820–1860," *Journal of Sport History* 7, No. 2

(Summer 1980): 21–39. Reprinted by permission of the *Journal of Sport History*.

Betty Wood, "Some Aspects of Female Resistance to Chattel Slavery in Low Country Georgia, 1763–1815," *Historical Journal* 30, No. 3 (1987): 603–622. Reprinted with the permission of Cambridge University Press.